The History

The History

Herodotus

TRANSLATED BY

David Grene

The University of Chicago Press

Chicago & London

The University of Chicago Press, Chicago 60637
The University of Chicago Press, Ltd., London

© 1987 by The University of Chicago
All rights reserved. Published 1987
Printed in the United States of America
96 95 94 93 92 91 90 89 88 87   5 4 3 2 1

Library of Congress Cataloging-in-Publication Data
Herodotus.
The history.
Includes index.
✓1. History, Ancient. 2. Greece—History.
✓I. Grene, David. II. Title.
D58.H4713 1987   930   86-13635
ISBN 0-226-32770-1 HBA
ISBN 0-226-32772-8 (pbk.)

DAVID GRENE is a professor in the Committee
on Social Thought of the University of Chicago.
He is the author of *Greek Political Thought: The
Image of Man in Thucydides and Plato* and *Reality
and the Heroic Pattern: Last Plays of Ibsen,
Shakespeare, and Sophocles*, both published by
the University of Chicago Press. With
Richmond Lattimore he edited *The Complete
Greek Tragedies*, also published by Chicago, and
translated five of the plays.

To Wendy

Contents

List of Maps

Acknowledgments

I have given a great many classes and tutorials on Herodotus' *History* over the years. Indeed, he has been a lifelong interest of mine. But since I undertook this translation, four years ago, I have read him more constantly with students than ever before. I therefore very gratefully acknowledge what I owe to the graduates of the Committee on Social Thought who took part in those discussions of the text, from 1980 on, at the University of Chicago.

I wish also to express my gratitude for the opportunity to express my views at Northwestern University's Wallace A. Bacon Conference on Interpretation in 1981, where I gave the inaugural lecture, entitled "Herodotus: The *History* and Its Presentation," and I am very grateful, too, to Virginia Hastings Floyd, who generously furnished funds for its subsequent publication.

During two of the past four years in which I have been engaged in the work of translating Herodotus I have received valuable financial help from the Earhart Foundation, for which I am extremely grateful. I am glad to recognize especially the kind interest of Richard Ware and Anthony Sullivan, who at different times were responsible for granting me these funds.

My friend Arthur Adkins tirelessly advised me on the nuances of Greek idiom when I consulted him, and, besides this, he and my friend and former student Tony Yu read large portions of the completed manuscript and helped me with criticism and praise.

My indebtedness to the fine two-volume *Commentary on Herodotus* by W. W. How and J. Wells (first published in 1912 by Oxford's Clarendon Press and reprinted many times since) will be evident to the reader in the footnotes to my translation. I am grateful, also, to Harvard University Press for permission to reprint the maps that appear in the Loeb Library edition of Herodotus and for permission to use an abridged version of the Index that appears in the Loeb edition.

Finally, and most importantly, I acknowledge with delight all that the participation of Wendy O'Flaherty in this book has meant to me; in the four years of preparing this English Herodotus I owe far more to her than anyone or anything else. It was not only that she made perfect typescripts of my messy drafts. That in itself was a tremendous labor, of a value not easy to assess, for a clean copy stimulates one to see clearly where the style and the vocabulary are headed. But that big job is the least of what she has done. She has again and again seen where the English faltered or was obscure. Her sense of the spoken word has helped immensely in a text that originally was intended largely for reading before its contemporary Greek audience. Last and most important, she has grown to love Herodotus' *History* and the writer it reveals, and her feeling for him has illuminated and deepened my own. I have dedicated this book to her as a token of some part of all that she has given me.

Introduction

Herodotus' only slightly younger contemporary, Thucydides, rejects the historical account of remote events in very telling terms; he does so at about the date of Herodotus' probable death. Thucydides says that even such a careful (and barely sketched) account as he is forced to give of an earlier Greece, as background for his own times, is only moderately satisfactory. "For," he says, "most of the events of the past, through lapse of time, have fought their way, past credence, into the country of myth" (perhaps the Greek *epi to muthōdes eknenikēkota* in Thucydides 1.21.8 is fairly translated as this). Thucydides conceived of acts and even words and thoughts as existent at a given moment and ideally recapturable in that form. They will, if allowed to do so by the lapse of time, become transfigured and so be useless to history. The word *eknikan*—"fight its way through completely"—implies that there is a natural tendency in the event so to do, and the perfect participle looks at the finished product: "they have got to the country of myth and there they stay."

Thucydides' preference for contemporary history as the only likely true history is to be followed, with few exceptions, for centuries by Western historians, as is also his conception that only military and political events constitute true history. In both respects, Herodotus runs against the current. Herodotus certainly also thought that acts and words fought their way through into the country of myth if you left them enough time. Indeed, he thought that the country of myth for acts and words was just around the corner from them the moment they were done or uttered. But he was very far from thinking that this rendered them valueless for history. He had chosen for his subject the enmity of the Greeks and the barbarians— by "barbarians" meaning the peoples of Asia Minor—which culminated in the great battles of Herodotus' childhood, Salamis and Artemisium and Plataea, in 480 and 479 B.C. But the beginning of the story, the origins of the enmity, as he saw it, stretched all the way back, almost to what was known as the beginning of the civilized world. To this vast area of the past Herodotus had no key, or almost none, other than oral tradition; for there were few written records and, for such as existed, he almost certainly lacked the necessary languages to understand them. Probably most of his informants as to myths and folklore were either Greeks settled in Asia or native inhabitants, probably a considerable number, who spoke Greek. This oral tradition constituted for him the imaginative record of the past as it mattered to the present.

Herodotus is the writer of Greek history who comes between Homer the epic poet, some four hundred years before him (as he himself thought), and Thucydides, the till now almost "modern" historian, who died perhaps twenty-five years after Herodotus. Herodotus, no less than Thucydides, thought of his *History* as a thing different from epic poetry—as much more bound by the necessity of covering the actual great events truly. For instance, he says that he believes (with some good evidence) that Homer knew that Helen had gone to Egypt and had in fact been there all through the Trojan War (2.116).[1] But, says Herodotus, because Homer found the other version of the story (Helen's stay in Troy) more suitable for his poetry, he chose it. Herodotus certainly sees his *History* as something not so malleable as this. Thucydides certainly knew Herodotus' *History* and regarded him as a very loose kind of historian. When in recommending his own work as "a possession for ever" he couples this with the remark that "it has not been composed for the pleasure of the hearers of the moment" (Thucydides 1.22.4), it is not difficult to identify the rival historian and his audience of listeners, especially when Thucydides follows his remark by criticizing two so-called "errors" in Herodotus' *History*.

Of course, there are facts given him by his informants that Herodotus rejects almost in the Thucydidean way. He corrects what he regards as false geographical statements by some of his predecessors (2.42). He expresses total disbelief in the existence of goat-footed men to the north of Scythia while accepting (one supposes

1. Here, and throughout, numbers in parentheses without further identification refer to books and chapters of Herodotus' *History*.

correctly) the other physical oddity, snub-nosed bald-headed men (4.24). He stakes his reputation on his account of the course of the Nile, telling us how far he had checked this personally (2.29). He denies the possibility of the sacrifice of Heracles on the grounds that the Egyptians never practiced human sacrifice (2.45).

But all these rejections are criticisms of single facts. It is when Herodotus is giving us folklore and myths that his opponents say he is uncritical. He does, in fact, never criticize the skeletons of his mythical stories. He accepts a story based on some historical act but conforming to a widely known psychological pattern, which is certainly not singular. It does not strike him that he ought to ask: Did this happen on this occasion, or is it the *kind of thing* that people describe on many such occasions? It is exactly because he does *not* ask that question that he is interesting and important as the unique kind of historian he is. I want to discuss in detail two such stories. The first concerns the birth of Cyrus, perhaps the greatest of the Great Kings of Persia and the founder of the Persian Empire.

Cyrus' birth was heralded by a prophecy that he would displace his grandfather, Astyages, King of Media, from the throne of Media (1.107 ff.). Astyages promptly married his daughter to a nobleman of the then socially inferior race of the Persians in the hope that this would render such a succession improbable. Moreover, when the child was born, he ordered it to be exposed, to become a prey to wild beasts. Through a breakdown in the chain of command, this order failed, and Cyrus survived through the kindness of a herdsman, who had been told to destroy him, and through the love and care of the herdsman's wife.

Herodotus very probably accepted the imaginative core of this story as something *real* when describing the survival of the royal child—a child, moreover, with a great destiny inside the setting of the court of the Great King, who was, in the minds of his subjects, a being unique and set apart. The herdsman's wife, "as God would somehow have it so, . . . gave birth when her husband had gone to the city" (1.111), and her child was born dead. This stillborn child is to be the necessary link in the survival of Cyrus, and, in the phrase "as God would somehow have it so," Herodotus indicates that he in some sense accepts the Persian story at face value. At least he certainly does not see the tale of Cyrus' survival, *de haut en bas*, as a trick practiced on a superstitious population. By contrast, that is exactly how he describes the pageant of the political agents who brought back Pisistratus, the tyrant of Athens, from exile (1.60). The tyrant was reintroduced to his state by a huge woman dressed up to look like Athena, and Herodotus comments on the silliness of this stratagem and its most unlikely success, which it all the same achieved. For these were Greeks, to whom a belief in the sanctity of rulers was entirely alien, and therefore the deception was all the more remarkable. The story of Cyrus lived among the Persians. Herodotus knows that the deepest sentiment of sacredness on the part of a people can actually alter the relationship of king and subjects on both sides. Herodotus bears testimony to this for the Great King throughout his *History*. He cannot be born like other people (Cyrus); he cannot die without portents and elaborate coincidences (Cambyses) (3.64). Most striking of all, when the royal family becomes extinct and, in defect of hereditary claim, a new Great King must be *chosen*, the elevation of Darius is preceded by a unique debate among the nobles of Persia on the merits of monarchy, aristocracy, and democracy. Herodotus tells us that the Greeks do not believe this debate took place but that he knows it did (3.80). The authenticity of this great moment is vouched for by him personally. I think that for Herodotus the Persian monarchy in its typical form, the essential antagonist of Greece in his story, has the very quality of Fate in it. Its individual kings are strangely protected or deluded by the gods. But there is human choice in the matter of the monarchy, too; for it is guided to a majestic and terrible end, as when, much later than this, the dream of Xerxes, on the eve of his invasion of Greece, drives him on to the tragic conclusion of that expedition (7.12–18). As I read it, this earlier scene of the choosing of Darius is of a similar kind. The Persian nobles, delivered from the hereditary claims on their religious sentiment by murders and deaths within the royal family, deliberately choose autocracy and absolutism under Darius after a prolonged debate as to the merits of the other systems, aristocracy and democracy. Of course, we do not know what special evidence Herodotus may have had for the existence of the debate. But it is certainly of the order of events he believed in, which necessarily included the significant shape of history in tragic terms, the powers (whatever they are) outside of man, the choices men themselves make, and the conjunction and interaction of all these as an uneasy blend in the making of destiny.

In the story of Cyrus' birth and survival Herodotus is playing with our sense of wonder or potential miracle, now almost guaranteeing our right to credulity, now drawing us back. He is also flavoring our sense of the meaningful with his sense of the meaningful by supplying realistic detail of his own invention for the tremendousness of the archaic myth.

The herdsman had been summoned unexpectedly to the palace. His wife was heavy with child and near her time. They were both much in each other's thoughts, the man thinking of the forthcoming birth, the woman of the reason for the surprise summons of her husband to the palace. Herodotus describes the scene when the herdsman returns. He had gone to the palace and been amazed to receive orders to expose a child, which he found all decked out in gold and embroidered clothes. To his terror, he learned from the palace servants that the child was royal, the son of Mandane, daughter of his own lord, Astyages, king of Media. He received his orders, of course, through an intermediary, Harpagus, a great noble of the court. The herdsman comes home, much troubled in his mind, with the future Cyrus in a box, dressed in all his glory.

> When his wife saw the child so big and beautiful, she burst into tears, and taking her man by the knees she besought him by no means to expose it. He said he could not do otherwise. . . . [Then the woman said:] "I too have given birth, and the baby I bore was dead. Take then the dead boy and expose it, and let us bring up as our own this child of Astyages' daughter. So you will not be detected in cheating our masters. . . . The dead child will have a royal burial, and the survivor will not lose his life." . . . [So the herdsman took up] his own child that was dead and placed [him] in the box wherein he had brought the other. He put on the dead body all the ornaments of that other child and bore it off to the loneliest part of the hills and left it there. [1.112–13]

Of course, the details, so skillfully, so evocatively, inserted, come from Herodotus the artist. They have no place in the History if, by history, we mean verifiable facts. They are there as additions to the myth pattern, made by Herodotus as he feels himself inside its reality and leads us to the moment of belief.

But in this story Herodotus appears also as the omniscient and seemingly common-sense intermediary between us and his informants and explains *away* another aspect of the traditional account, apparently one commonly given. Herodotus says (1.122) that the true parents of the child, the royal parents, in order for their own ends to make the birth seem even more miraculous, set afoot the rumor that the child, when exposed, had been suckled by a bitch and so had survived. This, he thinks, was suggested to them by the name of the herdsman's wife, the foster mother, to whom the boy repeatedly referred. Her name was Cyno, which is vaguely like the Greek word for dog (*kuōn*).

It is customary to regard such aspects of Herodotus' treatment as his "rationalizing tendency." This misses the point. For Herodotus, the basic elements of the myth attract to themselves other explanations, other aspects of the ordinary or the marvelous; one overlies the other. It is his job to report them all so that the nature of the belief and rejection that attend the myth comes before us in all its fullness. This, I think, is why he so often disowns responsibility for the truth or accuracy of a statement. It is its being thought or voiced that counts in the end, as it comes down from the past to us. The original facts, whatever they were, have taken to themselves a supervening shape—universal, cultural, or, in the deepest sense, religious. It is then that Herodotus thinks they have assumed their closest relation to reality, which is not for him coterminous with what happened in the physical world but rather what was released by the act into the world of thought and feeling and continued thereafter.

I doubt if Herodotus made an effective distinction—except about particular, singular facts, such as the course of the Nile or the sacrifice of Heracles—between the reality of verifiable truth and imaginative reality. He is a man who probably lived easily with myths. He certainly lived easily with the rationalized trappings that his age found conventional as the clothing of myth, much as Elizabethans and Jacobeans found Renaissance costumes natural for the representation of classical heroes and indeed for the kings and noblemen of any age or time. But I see no evidence that such rationalizing is designed by him to diminish the intrinsically incredible quality of the myth and make it into something nearer credibility. The credibility comes from something shared by him and his informants, the depth of meaning in the myth. The sheer unlikelihood—in many cases the sheer impossibility—of stories like that of Cyrus' exposure and survival is in no sense disarmed by the excision of the seemingly supernatural element. The degree of magic or the want of it, the direct intervention of the divine or its aloofness from the particular event, renders the story modish or the reverse for his informants, for himself, and for the audience who listened to his readings. It is the myth itself that reaches down through the impossible stretching of probability and guarantees its own truth. This and some of the other stories belong to the *dreams* of mankind, impossible, delightful, or in other cases fantastic and horrible. In their rationalized form (to borrow the nomenclature), they are being represented in their special costume of a given moment in history, as belonging to it, as part of what it finds "natural."

My second story comes from Herodotus 1.8, which deals with Candaules, the last member of the family of the Mermnadae, which lost the Lydian throne to Gyges, who was the ancestor of Croesus. Croesus is a very important monarch in Herodotus, for he is the man who (according to Herodotus) first began unjust actions against the Greeks (1.5). His ancestor, Gyges, is a very important man in Herodotus, for he is the one whose guilt in stealing his master's, the king's, wife and murdering the king, Candaules, was finally punished in the fourth generation—that of Croesus. Croesus pays for the sin of his ancestor and himself and is displaced by Cyrus. So it is Cyrus and the Persians who finally take the lead of the "barbarians" (Asiatics) against the Greeks when they come to invade Europe. Croesus therefore stands at the very front of the theme in Herodotus: he is the first man to molest the Greeks, the decisive figure whose displacement brought the Persians to Greece, and the first and great example of the downfall of a king through the action of fate based on past offenses. The way Herodotus tells of the primal sin is as follows:

> This Candaules fell in love with his own wife; and because he was so in love, he thought he had in her far the most beautiful of women. So he thought. Now, he had a bodyguard named Gyges,

the son of Dascylus, who was his chief favorite among them. Candaules used to confide all his most serious concerns to this Gyges, and of course he was forever overpraising the beauty of his wife's body to him. Some time thereafter—for it was fated that Candaules should end ill—he spoke to Gyges thus: "Gyges, I do not think that you credit me when I tell you about the beauty of my wife; for indeed men's ears are duller agents of belief than their eyes. Contrive, then, that you see her naked." [1.8]

The bodyguard protested, and Herodotus includes his evidence of how shameful it is among the barbarians for even a man, much less a woman, to be seen naked. But despite Gyges' objections, Candaules arranges that he should be hidden behind the open door of the bedroom when the queen undressed. Inevitably the lady spotted him when, departing, he slipped from behind the door; but despite her outrage she kept silent until the next day, when she offered Gyges the unpleasant alternative of killing the king and winning the queen or being killed himself. "So," says Herodotus, "he chose his own survival" (1.11). Hence the destruction of the dynasty of the Mermnadae, who were the descendants of Heracles, and the fulfillment of the oracle declared at Delphi, that retribution would come for this offense upon the Lydian king Croesus in the fourth generation after Gyges.

We know another version of this myth in Plato, and it is instructive to compare the two. In Plato, Gyges is a shepherd who one day, straying in the hills, comes upon a cave with a dead man in it and, on the dead man's hand, a ring. Gyges steals this. Later, accidentally turning it on his finger, he discovers that it renders him invisible. By this power he contrives to lie with the queen and afterwards to murder the king and take both queen and throne. In the *Republic*, where the story occurs, it is cited by the interlocutors of Socrates, who request him to take Gyges as the extreme case for justice that they want to make. Assuming that the just man had the ring of Gyges and his invisibility, would he persist in justice, as the true health of the soul, and ignore the potentiality of scatheless villainy? (Plato, *Republic* 359D).

There can be no doubt that these are two versions of the same story. The significant common mythic element would seem to be the relation of invisibility to guilt or guiltiness. This has shrunk in Herodotus from the magical ring to spying from behind the door and accepting the connivance of the husband. There is also, in both, the fantastic crime-stained rise to supreme power by someone who has no claim to it. There is, as bedrock in Herodotus' version, the murder of the king-father and the incest with the mother in a wholly paternalistic eastern monarchy. There is also in Herodotus the certainty that the crime will later be paid for as a crime, though not in the person of the criminal who committed it. I suggest that these are indeed the deep mythical elements, and, again in this instance, the absence of the magical ring does not affect the appeal of the fantasy in which it is rooted, nor does it diminish significantly the area of improbability or unreasonableness of the story. What we may guess is that the difference between the two stories lies in the disinclination of Herodotus' informants for overt magic. The magic is dropped out exactly in order to admit the entry of fantasy, which at that time balked at the vocabulary of magic. We are made to see the princes and kings of the distant days of the East as people like ourselves, in their most private human moments, in their most denationalized, declassed reality. But it is not as our ordinary selves that we see them; we see them, rather, the way we see David against Goliath, or Cinderella in the Cinderella story. What is being rejected for Herodotus' contemporaries is not only the remoteness and impersonality of the potentates but also their assimilation into a fairy-story world like that of the enchantresses of the *Odyssey*, Circe and Calypso. Admittedly, it is sometimes hard to see why Herodotus rejects a specifically magical form—for instance, of animal intervention—in one case and not in another. For Arion is rescued by a dolphin, who carries him home on its back (1.23). True, this is classified as a "wonder," the greatest that befell Periander during his reign. Herodotus is, of course, also recollecting the representation of the scene on a coin. But "wonder" though it is, Herodotus does not support disbelief in this instance as he does in that of the suckling bitch. The key is certainly in what his informants felt to be the proper dress of the myth. But perhaps we can go further. Plato's tyrant, as he arises in the democratic state, is someone who transfers into the daylight his dream fantasies (Plato, *Republic* 371A–375A). But scarcely literally. He did not go around sleeping with his mother or having sexual relations with beasts and gods. Perhaps the current

form of the myth, as in the Herodotean Gyges story, is a bridge between an earlier form, nearer to the literal expression of the fantasy,
and the daylight implementation, as Herodotus' informants and
contemporaries saw it.

For this particular myth also presents in its mythical elements a
funny and undignified reality that may, paradoxically, coincide (in
its origin, at least—in the psychology of the action) with something
that once happened. Today we are no longer completely convinced,
like the more solemn academic historians of the nineteenth century,
that history is invariably made by strategy and economics. It is conceivable that crowns have been lost by something as frivolous as
Candaules' peculiar voyeurism. Totally improbable though it is, this
tale may strike as deep in presenting a general human truth as does
the tragedy of another destroyed king Herodotus tells us of, one who
knew that the greatest suffering was too great for tears—that tears
belonged to the next-lowest grade of sorrow (3.14–15). For in the
story of Candaules, as in only a few of the myths, the very tone of
the myth strikes home. This one convinces and illuminates as much
by the humorousness of its suggestions *as to cause* as it does in stating
the causes themselves.

There are two very terrible stories in book 1 of men being made to
eat, unknowingly, human flesh—in one instance, the flesh of the
man's own child. They are then confronted with the truth. One of
these "feasts" was the revenge taken on King Cyaxares of Media by
some nomad Scythians he had hired as huntsmen and who, after a
dispute with him, kidnapped one of his pages, killed and cooked
him, and served him up to Cyaxares (1.73). The other (1.119) involved the revenge that Astyages (the king who tried to expose the
infant Cyrus in the story I have recounted) took on his servant, the
nobleman Harpagus, who was indirectly responsible for Cyrus' survival. Herodotus reports each of these instances in detail.

Let us again recall Plato, who affords us a generalized psychological insight into these horrors. He says, in his account of the tyrant
in the corrupt states, that the tyrant is one who enacts in daytime
with delighted license the fantasies that alternately tempt and terrify
ordinary men in sleep, when the rational part of them is not in
control (*Republic* 574E–575A). One part of this dreamworld, according to Plato, is "abstaining from *no* sort of food." This license

goes on the list along with incest and miscegenation. Apparently, the temptation to cannibalism had this fantastic bent in the Greek mind of the time, for we also know, from Aeschylus and others, of Thyestes' feast, where again a father in ignorance is made to eat the flesh of his children. Clearly, this fantasy had currency enough to figure in great plays written for public exhibition in fifth-century Greece.

Herodotus' informants reported both instances of cannibalism in book 1 as events that actually happened. Herodotus is probably indifferent to the Thucydidean question "But *did* they happen?" because, like Plato, he knew very well that men's fantasies and deeds live terribly close to each other and often move interchangeably. Besides, for Herodotus it is what the Greeks and barbarians *believed* had happened that counts, rather than anything so unique as to depend on Herodotus' personal verification.

All of this explains the preponderance of myth patterns in the first four books of the *History*, where the mental background of the Asiatics is being covered. For this background is one half of the *why* of the enmity between Greeks and barbarians, and that is one reason why Herodotus tells us at such length of the political climate of the court of the great Asiatic despots, the implicit obedience of their subjects, and the submerged but ever-threatening hatred of possible rivals for power.

Clearly, one big question mark is how right Herodotus is to transfer the fantasies current among fifth-century Greeks to Asiatics living two and three centuries earlier. To answer that, one can say only that Herodotus certainly believed in the universal characteristics of the human imagination and hence in the inevitability of certain patterns in human dreams and fantasies. Strong as he is on the side of the importance of local customs, and interested as he is in the eccentricities of men's beliefs and practices, he is sure of a certain common core where men think and feel alike. For instance, he says that all men "in my opinion" know equally about the gods (2.3). (Their differences of belief affect only the applicability of this knowledge to names and places and customs.) It is this attitude of his that would constitute his defense (if he thought of making one) for using, as authentic evidence for Asiatic folklore, what his Greek-speaking informants tell him. Nor would he be without additional support for this defense in *our* terms, such as the fact that most of the peoples from whom the folktales are derived are Indo-Europeans, so that what is drawn on may well be a common Indo-European mythology. Moreover, these peoples lived in a relatively small area of the earth's surface and had been in constant cultural contact for a long, long time. But, in the end, whether we think Herodotus is a significant historian or not depends on our acceptance or rejection of his thesis that in logic or illogic the mental and passionate structure of the human mind is the same, though separated and superficially diversified in time or place.

It is overwhelmingly evident that Herodotus makes no effective discrimination in his *History* between the skeletal act—for instance, the murder of Candaules by Gyges, which is "historical"—and the imaginative reality toward which the story reaches. His *History* is that of a storyteller who is never quite out of the frame of the narrative and never quite within it. The broad lines of the *History* are shaped like those of a Greek tragedy. But it is never an acknowledged artistic fiction; it is never an artistic fiction, completely, at all. It has another dimension, this creation of his. It lies in a threefold relation to reality: reality as ordinarily perceived, reality as coming to a special meaningful pattern in myth, and reality as expressed in the original creation of a tragic writer. For the author who builds the story of the Persian attack on Greece under the shadow of the text "It is always the greatest houses and the tallest trees that the god hurls his [lightning] bolts upon" (7.10) is a Greek tragic writer. It is a new art form, a kind of history. We dare say that, now that military and political history is no longer looked on as the sole lifeline by which to connect ourselves to great events of the past. But it is a history that nearly always suggests the observer within the framework. No doubt Herodotus actually checked the course of the Nile as he says he did. He certainly took notice of and recorded the customs of the Lydians and the Egyptians and all the peoples he visited. Such matters as these are the givens on which he rests the superstructure. This superstructure is the creation of his own dramatic imagination and partly consists of materials that are *imaginatively* dramatic in man's *remembrance*, man's myths and folklore, where the understanding is deepest and most explosive and least committed to the singular fact. These myths were certainly there for him in the mouths of his informants. Think, for example, of the miraculous birth and survival of the baby Cyrus and the vengeance taken by the cowgod upon the impious Cambyses, who mortally wounded her with his dagger but then himself perished through an injury in the selfsame part of the body where he had struck the god he sneered at as mortal (3.64).

The older editors, such as Sayce, respond to what they constantly refer to as the charm of Herodotus' stories, but they are far from seeing in what the charm consists. They regard the myths and folklore in the *History* as something removed from the very nature of reality, as the food of the child's mind before he grasps the conditions of the mature world. They understand nothing of the compelling pattern of the imagination to which the child and the adult alike respond. So they fail to grasp the magnitude of Herodotus' achievement. He has written a history of the greater part of the then known world, and backwards and forwards in man's then known span of civilization, with guidelines set by the archetypes of joy and sorrow, truth and falsehood, strength and feebleness as these live in *narrative form*, in the great primary stories. He supports this structure by scenes he himself has witnessed and by accounts of customs and places that are undeniably personally observed. There is thus a continuum from the palpable and checkable to the familiarity of the fantastic—familiar because it is the fantasy of all of us revisited. The *History* of Herodotus in its use of the human imagination is perhaps the solidest historical structure ever written. But the solidity is not that of reconstructed and verifiable fact but of the interaction between experience and dreams—between the uncommitted personal eyewitness and the generalized committedness of the patterns of fantasy and dreaming.

This is his famous introductory statement of purpose in book 1:

> I, Herodotus of Halicarnassus, am here setting forth my history, that time may not draw the color from what man has brought into being, nor those great and wonderful deeds, manifested by both Greeks and barbarians, fail of their report, and, together with all this, the reason why they fought one another. [1.1]

Two points in this statement should be noted. The first is that Herodotus sets himself against the power of time. Time is the destroyer,

Herodotus is the preserver, of what man has created. This involves "saving," to some extent, monuments and moments of entire civilizations ("What has come into being through men"). It shows us a Herodotus keenly aware of the huge remnants of a civilization, such as the Babylonian, among which he has to potter in the hope of finding the key to its significance and power. As a subject of the Persian Empire and a great traveler, at a time when records and archeological research were almost nonexistent, he sees nakedly the possibility of obliteration of whole systems of life and their accompanying buildings, customs, languages. Second, what he is bent on presenting in his fight with time, as it concerns the hostility between the Greeks and barbarians, is the *kleos*, what men say and hear about the subject. In Homer, *kleos* means the glory that the hero's great deeds have attracted to themselves, and it remains for his descendants to enjoy as the quintessence of their ancestor. However, in the history of the Greek language, the word has a broader application than "glory" as we understand it. It is nearer "report," which is the way I have translated it here. It is connected with words that mean to "call out" and "to be heard." It is a misconception, I think, to render, as some translators do, "that such deeds may not fail of their meed of glory"; for what is involved is not only the glory (in our sense) of the story of the Greek-Asiatic hostilities and the gallantry shown on both sides in the battles but what men tell and hear about the typical acts (or what they regard as typical acts) of both sides— and this is very often *not* what we see as glory, particularly when it deals with deeds of the enemy. King Xerxes, having been entertained by the richest of his subjects, tells the man he can ask for any boon and he will grant it (7.29–39). The man asks for his eldest son to be left behind when the Persian army marches to Greece. Xerxes complies by cutting the boy's body in two and marching his army away between the two parts. This deed belongs to the report of the Persians as the Greeks received it. It is the monstrousness of the act that counted, the arbitrariness and savagery of the Eastern despot and the submissiveness of his subjects. This is a most important aspect of the way the Greeks saw the conflict between the two political systems, if one can call them that, and certainly between the two "nations," the Greeks and the barbarians, where our nomenclature is on much safer ground.

Probably no Greek writer makes so strong an impression of talking directly to us as Herodotus. Certainly, no Greek historian does. Undoubtedly, this is related to the known fact that most of his "publishing" was done by public readings from his text. It is intensely exciting to hear the echoes of his voice still and the conscious appeal to us as we listen. In speaking of his book on Egypt, he distinguishes among several kinds of materials. "So far it is my eyes, my judgment, and my searching that speak these words to you; from this on it is the accounts of the Egyptians that I will tell to you as I heard them" (2.99). The Greek for "my eyes etc. that are speaking" is as strong and grammatically unusual as the English makes it appear direct and almost colloquial. Nor is the personality addressing us a matter even principally of style. There is the extreme boldness of many of the defining sentences themselves. He tells us about the people of Heliopolis, who "are the greatest chroniclers among the Egyptians." "Now, the part of their account that deals with the divine, and to which I listened, I am not anxious to set forth, save only the matter of the gods' names; for I think that all men know equally about the gods. When I do mention the gods, it will be because my history forces me to do so" (2.3).

Perhaps the most startling of all his statements on how his *History* is constructed runs as follows (he has been commenting on the various stories of the Persians and Phoenicians about the traditional hostility between Greeks and barbarians):

> For my part I am not going to say about these matters that they happened thus or thus, but I will set my mark upon that man that I myself know began unjust acts against the Greeks, and, having so marked him, I will go forward in my account, covering alike the small and great cities of mankind. For of those that were great in earlier times most have now become small, and those that were great in my time were small in the time before. Since, then, I know that man's good fortune never abides in the same place, I will make mention of both alike. [1.5]

These sentences correspond exactly to the manner of a very brilliant speaker, whose aphorism sticks in one's mind and forces one to wonder whether one has grasped all the implications of what one has heard. These are not the forms in which an expositor declares the nature of his argument or makes clear the grounding of his evidence. They sometimes look like this, but they are not. What they build is an illusion of a discussion between a storytelling friend and his listeners. The "I" who thinks divine stories uninteresting or dangerous in comparison with the human is accepted as a person like ourselves, only a little more surprising in attitude, more paradoxical in expression. (Is he saying all men know "equally much" or "equally little" about the gods?) As he stood before his audience, he comes before us on the page, invisibly watching us, presenting himself as clever, whimsical, at times naive and impulsive, at times reflective and tragic in emphasis. This history is designed to give the feeling of a personal appearance on the scene, to mediate between the great events and the audience. Sometimes the personal appearance is indeed personal; sometimes it is highly formalized. Herodotus is sometimes rather like the reader in Thornton Wilder's *Our Town* or the actor-commentator in Tennessee Williams' *Glass Menagerie*. He is introducing us to his great theme—the achievements in war of Greeks and Persians at one another's expense and the cause of their quarrel, together with all the more general features of the civilizations of the world of his day—as a thing which, with all its hugeness, can be seen as a unity and expressed as the vision of one man who, as a child, was a contemporary of the last of the great acts in this universal drama. Here is the man in front of us, seizing the myths, the folklore of the countries involved, the relevant bits of his own (the chronicler's) history, weaving them all together and constantly even appearing himself, to explain that he has checked this but not that. Paradoxically but very naturally, he does not account for his knowledge of such things as the conversation between Croesus and Cyrus when Croesus is upon the pyre and, at the last minute, the words he utters induce Cyrus to take him down and spare his life, nor does he tell us how he came to know the thoughts in the mind of the shepherd's wife, who exchanged her own dead child for the royal baby Cyrus. What one has here is the writer, akin to Homer, who exists throughout the work, acknowledged, but with no formal attribution.

This personality, then, formalized as speaker, commentator, intermediary, is integrated into the *kleos*, the report that attends on all the events and through which they live for future times. Some of the *kleos* that goes to create the artistic effect are the echoes of the human voice, the undress of personal interest, the glory of rhetoric, the joking comment.

The *kleos* itself is multifarious, as the different people who contribute to it bring in their different hopes and antagonisms, all of which are utilized for the total effect. This past carries with it the multiple hopes and thoughts men have invested in it. Moreover, Herodotus himself has a ranging mind and an incorrigible sense of distant relevancies, which further extend the relation of everything to everything else and can only very hardly be controlled within any crabbed confines of immediate applicability. He has often enough been taken to task for this by serious critics, of which he himself is the first. "This history of mine," he says somewhat ruefully, "has from the beginning sought out the supplementary to the main argument" (4.30).

But the extraordinary farrago of motifs, stories, geographical excursus, and reported observations of artistic objects, strange customs, and miraculous events has a deeper and, it seems to me, more serious reason for being what it is than comes out in any of the explanations I have given so far. Herodotus is in a very strong degree an uncommitted observer even as he creates his *kleos* of the past, and he is so for reasons that are startling and perhaps, in the end, convincing. Here is an illuminating comment on the theories of the Egyptians on various religious practices and also on the transmigration of souls (2.123): "As for the stories told by the Egyptians, let whoever finds them credible use them. Throughout the entire history it is my underlying principle that it is what people have said to me, and what I have heard, that I must write down." It is impossible to be sure what he means by "use" here. Because it is linked to what is persuasive, I should think it must mean something like "adopt as true for him." What is certain is that Herodotus is divorcing himself from the capacity or will to declare that one thing is true and another false, as beliefs go. One overlies another for the *use* of the different observers. This is exactly what is implied in his remark about the gorge in Thessaly: it is the result of an earthquake or the work of Poseidon—if you think that earthquakes are the work of Poseidon (7.129). It is the job of the historian, in Herodotus' terms, to identify objects, events, and thoughts in various ways, offending as few people as possible by strictness in psychological dogmatism. But there is always some fundamental matter that is thus being variously identified, and one cannot tell which system of nomenclature is most useful or especially will be so in the days to come. The passage on the transmigration of souls (2.123) is not in the narrative as a probing of the nature of man's soul and its pilgrimage. Herodotus wants us to realize that in it we have one more important addition to the way man saw his cosmos. How this belief affected the Egyptians in dealing with the Great King he does not say and perhaps does not know. In short, it is beliefs and traditions and practices in their totality that characterize each national unit in his story. This belief about the soul is clearly relevant, probably important, and so in it goes.

I am convinced that this is what underlies the oddest statement of this kind in the whole lot—the one in 1.5 that I have already quoted on the principle of all-inclusiveness in his treatment of cities, without concern for stricter differences of importance.

For Herodotus there is a real truth, that is, a line of true causation, involving many causes. Because the threads of this true causation lie in the hands of some supernatural power or some nonhuman order of the world that embraces all its multiplicity, Herodotus thinks it cannot be understood by men in its altogetherness. But there is at least a sequence of events that constitutes a unity (that may be a unity even within the gods' range of meaning), an episode framed of events that match one another in some system of counterpoise. At some point a significant conclusion can be drawn about success or the reverse, about happiness or the reverse, as far as man is concerned. (It is remarkable how much of Herodotus' presentation of history openly deals with its illustrative or even pedagogic value for human happiness or its failure.) But the verdict of importance on what actually *has happened,* made at too early a moment, is very fallible. The great towns of Herodotus' own day had many of them come to greatness from an earlier era of insignificance. Many of those now insignificant will one day be great. In that day the story he is now telling will not only look different but *be* different. The backward glance from the place of vantage the intervening years have given affords more evidence of what was taking place that made the previously great cities unimportant and vice versa. The principle on which all this operates is that it is impossible for human *well-being* to remain, established in one environment. The historian must then watch for its shifting, and how it shifts, and try to survey the conceivable factors, and conceivable possibilities, barely understood at an earlier moment, that were the potential major occasions for change. Herodotus' *kleos*, to be any good, must contain as many as possible of the seeds of the importance and *real* meaning of events—that is, their final consummation in time. For the present, it tries to show us a reasonable estimate of such a truth. But, as to the future, Herodotus is always hedging his bets. With Sardis and Susa, Babylon and Athens, and Sparta, the great centers of power, to the fore, he tries to retain in the picture some of the little towns: the rejection of emigration by the Ionians, the migrations to Italy. Some day, he implies, these may prove to have been the definitive places and the definitive events of the *History*. In the same willful jettisoning of simpler and more sharply defined standards of importance, he includes in his account of Periander of Corinth "the greatest wonder in all his life," the dolphin's rescue of Arion, the minstrel, by carrying him home, over the sea, on its back (1.23). A "wonder" means for Herodotus a disturbance of the psychic atmosphere. Who knows what this portends? Or even what it *does* to the world? Really to meet Herodotus is to realize how expansible the connections between events and thoughts can be when these connections are surveyed by the mind of a genius.

The famous meeting of Solon and Croesus (which, historically, probably never took place) has a crucial meaning for the *History*, occurring right at its beginning. It is at this meeting that Croesus learned from Solon, the Greek statesman and poet, to look on death, the last event of man's life, as the one necessarily overwhelming piece of evidence for the success or failure of that life. Because, says Solon, man's life, set at seventy years, contains so many months, days, etc., and because no day ever brings anything like any of its fellows, man is altogether what happens to him (*sumphorē*) (1.32). Death, since it stops the process, allows one to look on the life as an intelligible unit or at least as one that can be reckoned up. The life of a man or a city or a nation is composed of strips of reality (6.27). Each has its *telos*, which does not here mean, as it does in Aristotle, a perfection or crowning point but the end from which the unit as a whole makes sense. What Herodotus was doubtful of and sought for constantly and widely was this definition of the *telos* or end of the unit that was larger than the single unit—namely, the city or nation. In the service of this, he is surveying the interaction of the cities or nations in the history of the world. He looks at the past and builds a formidable list of contributions to his sense of the total reality of man in his world. Thus in his huge narrative he glances, in the past, at the oldest language spoken (2.2), the beginning of Greek religion (2.53), the oldest people (2.2), the youngest people (4.5), the potentially most powerful nation (5.3), the cleverest people (2.121), the stupidest people (4.46—those in the lands by the Euxine Pontus, except for the Scythians), the truest way of life in a community (3.21—the Ethiopians), and so on. All of these conditions, fully realized only in man's hopes or thoughts, lie on a continuum of existence, and that existence endlessly accommodates itself to the total span of reality. Hence the ambiguity of the importance of big cities as opposed to small ones, which will one day be big, and vice versa. Hence the inclusion of particolored elements in wonders and miracles and what men believe and the stories they tell of their wonders and beliefs. In the end, these elements of the total scene, which a narrower mind would neglect or subordinate, may have a bearing on the result out of all proportion to what the common sense of Herodotus' contemporaries would afford them. So Herodotus has a duty to these antiquities and to his own intuition in discovering them. The reality that the stories and the myths reveal, both those in the early accounts of Asia Minor and later, in the account of the invasion itself, is hardly, finally, the regular series of victories and defeats and the rise and fall of thrones. These indeed constitute the set of actions through which Herodotus works, dealing with our sense of wonder and its arousal of excitement and joy. What the *History* is really about lies behind this: man, giant-sized, seen against the background of the entire world, universalized in his conflict with destiny, the gods, and the cosmic order. The medium that is most fertile in showing the true nature of reality is the human mind, remembering, reflective, and fertile most of all when its memory and reflection are put at the service of its dreaming and fantastic side.

When Herodotus examined man in a historical setting, he apparently thought of human nature as possessed of a number of logical choices that are differently exploited. What determined the choice that was made was sometimes a series of unsought challenges that explored these potentialities; for instance, the Scythians developed a peculiar but effective way of protecting themselves as a result of their climate and their empty, new country and because of the course of their rivers (4.46–47). More often, however, one course of action supersedes or is preferred over another by the decision of one man or by the voluntary choice of a people referred to as "they." Cyrus, as a result of Croesus' advice, once Croesus was his captive, changed the entire way of life of the Lydians; they became pliable victims of their conquerors (1.155–57). At 5.3 we learn that "the nation of the Thracians is the biggest of all mankind, except for the Indians. If they were under a single ruler or could be of a single mind, none could fight them down, and they would, in my judgment, be far the mightiest of all the people on earth. But such agreement is quite impossible for them; no means can bring it about, and this is the respect in which their weakness lies."

His is a kind of universal history; that is, it is the record of all the logical possibilities, political and human, that coexist in the human world. The *kleos* is the tale that makes one understand and admire this; that obtrudes itself between one's bewilderment at the diversity of experience and one's inner single moral certainty of man's nature; that harmonizes what one knows is true of man, because he is oneself writ large, and the excitement of the vision of men and events greater than anyone, without Herodotus' aid, could easily conceive of. The moral stories are another form of this aid; for example, the king who wept for sorrows suitable for tears but was silent before those that were too great for weeping (3.14); the enormity of the army of Xerxes, drinking rivers dry on its march to Greece (7.43); Xerxes who wept at the review of his huge army when he reflected that in a hundred years not a one of them would be alive (7.45); and the story of the crafty Artemisia at Salamis (8.87).

The great innovative rulers also come before us in the *kleos*. There are Cyrus and Darius, founders of dynasties, with whom, on the whole, all goes well, who are decisive and will also listen to advice at the right moments, and whom, all the same, destruction finally overtakes when they disregard good advice, Cyrus in facing the Massagetae, Darius the Scythians. And Cambyses and Xerxes, who are their sons and their exact opposites. And, to set the whole in

perspective, we have the king of Ethiopia, who rejected and banished the spies of Cambyses with a denunciation of the clothes,
money, and imperialism of his contemporary world as decisively as
did the king of Brobdingnag in dealing with Gulliver; he stands for
an entirely different and elementary way of life. And in ways of life,
the bottom of the scale is held by the cannibals: "The Man-Eaters
have the most savage manner of life of all men; they believe in no
justice nor use any law" (4.106).

We have here, within the scope of Herodotus' history, the entire
gamut of human possibilities, in social, political, and, in a way,
moral terms. When I say this, I do not want to do away with the
difference between Herodotus and Homer, between the historian
and the poet. Herodotus did not invent the peoples; they and the
personalities were actually there or nearly always there, in his historical scene, to bear the weight he assigns them. But he did assign
them this weight. And the range and the significance are matters of
obvious selection, so that the *History* becomes a pattern, itself a
kind of myth. Inside, of course, there are massive passages of detail
that are the result of eyewitness work and of the careful balancing of
one aspect of probability against another. Yet these are built into a
framework that is poetic. Man lives on a continuum of intellectual
and moral possibilities. The king of Ethiopia may be right, may indeed be righter than Cambyses' spies or the contemporary powerful
Persian and Greek politicians. It is always within the power of any
ruler, or perhaps within that of any community, to opt out of moder-
nity and choose a different road. It is possible, and may be desirable,
to choose a different moral scheme for oneself and one's country.
This is as different a view of history as possible from that expressed
by the Corinthians, at the Lacedaemonian Congress before the beginning of the Peloponnesian War, in the pages of Thucydides
(1.71.3). They lecture the Spartans on the grounds that their institutions are "old-fashioned" (*archaiotropa*). They say that advances in
technology have their corollary in general human political institutions; the more advanced phases overcome the older. But in Herodotus the king of Ethiopia is the political equivalent of Solon
when the latter lectures Croesus on the superiority of the life of the
private man to that of the Eastern despot. One may choose a national (and international) position that willingly disregards power
politics, increase in money, technical development. Indeed, one of

the main emphases borne by the Persians in Herodotus' narrative is the disastrous disappearance of the private sphere within the distorted unity of their community.

So the *kleos*, the tale of glory, to be true to its *natural* function in man's report of past events, and to be true to Herodotus' artistic handling of it, must show all the facts and aspirations of human life that are present on this great continuum, stretching from King Cambyses to the cannibals, and this involves also individuals such as Cyrus and Darius along with Prexaspes.

Of course, Herodotus has his preferences in forms of life and political organization. Bias of Priene was *right* to advise as he did when he urged the Ionians to move away and form in Sardinia an empire of their own (1.170). Herodotus himself does not want to live like the Scythians. But he has an overwhelming sense of the diversity of man, of his fertile gift for innovations, at times his reseeking of elementary patterns in resistance to the trend of a time, or the supersession of one form of political theory by another that is temporarily superior.

Thucydides, in the passages of his *History* where he is clearly criticizing his predecessor, speaks, as I noted near the start of this introduction, of the contrast between his own work, which he intended to be "a possession for ever," and the other (by implication, Herodotus') as aimed at the delight of the immediate hearer. In the main, I think Thucydides is right about the immediate delight of the ear. Herodotus can be felt as a living voice fairly often. Listen to the end of the story of Adrastus, the man who killed his brother; whom Croesus then purified of bloodguilt; and who was assigned as bodyguard to Croesus' son, whom he then accidentally killed:

> So Croesus buried his son as was right. But Adrastus, the son of Gordias, the son of Midas, he who was the slayer of his own brother and had become the slayer of his purifier, who was, moreover, aware within himself that he was of all men he had ever known the heaviest-stricken by calamity, when there was a silence about the tomb and none was there, cut his throat over the grave. [1.45]

This is indeed as though we saw the figure before us on the stage, and we would do well to remember the bitterness of Thucydides' phrase—"I have not composed my work as a competition piece for the delight of the moment"—where "competition piece" (*agōnisma*) is certainly a reference to the theater or to the rhapsodes' or actors' competitions. But we would do well also to remember the line in the *Odyssey* where Odysseus is praising the minstrel at the court of Alcinous and speaks of the supreme power of the singer in rendering a subject "as though you were there yourself" (*Odyssey* 8.491). It is *as though*—not as a real onlooker. The *artifice* of Herodotus' *kleos* is very important. Its purpose is to give artistic substance to a moment or an event; thus there is an object that draws men's *natural* pleasure in the great moment or great deed to a single concentration of delight and meaning. The *kleos* will then, in the process of time and recollection, become part of the future of that moment or event. As the *kleos* deals with the natural possibilities of man's memory in their most significant form, the natural enemy is time and forgetfulness. And the most potent opponent of time and forgetfulness is the creation of the things that, in Helen's phrase, are "subjects of song for men of future days" (*Iliad* 6.348–57).

The listening audience is certainly the target of much of Herodotus' shaping of the narrative. In the later books, one thinks of the presentation of Xerxes' dream and the intervention of Artabanus and the obviously readable and actable conversation between the evil spirit of the dream and Artabanus. And of the ringing eloquence of the Athenian answer to the timid address of the Spartans when King Alexander of Macedon, in the name of the Great King, tried to tempt the Athenians to desert the Greek alliance: "There is our common Greekness: we are one in blood and one in language; those shrines of the gods belong to us all in common, and the sacrifices in common, and there are our habits, bred of a common upbringing" (8.144). The element of the theatrical, Thucydides' *agōnisma*, is plain in many places throughout the history. Often the parts are intricately fitted together but designed for a series of dramatic climaxes. There is the naturally supreme moment when Xerxes in his agony weeps at the thought that of all his magnificent army none would be alive in a hundred years (7.46), but the listing of the peoples and the description of their colorful uniforms are meticulously shaped to draw the historical detail into the moment of Xerxes' agony.

There are two worlds of meaning that are constantly in Herodotus' head. The one is that of human calculation, reason, cleverness, passion, happiness. There one knows what is happening and, more or less, who is the agent of cause. The other is the will of Gods, or fate, or the intervention of daimons. Herodotus did not, I think, have very clear notions of theology, at least as Christianity came to understand it. He does not feel sure of the identity of particular Gods, as intervening at particular moments, except on the rarest occasions. He gives us a glimpse of an Apollo who wished to save Croesus and couldn't (1.91), of a difference between the will of *one* God and Fate. Indeed, the oracle (or the priests) at Delphi document this by saying that even a God cannot cheat the Fates, who are personalized for this occasion. This is indeed the same dilemma we see in the *Iliad* when Zeus fails to save Sarpedon and, later, Hector, "long since condemned by fate" (*Iliad* 16.435 and 22.209–13). But in Herodotus, generally, any special God, or the Gods, or Fate, or (very commonly) The Divine (*to theion* or *to daimonion*) are all one. They all mean the power that controls the world of man. And this power's relation to man is bound up with a maddening relation between man's reason and understanding and such "signs" as the Divine has allowed us to have of its future or past intervention. Herodotus is quite definite on two points: that the Divinity is altogether "jealous" and prone to trouble us and that "there is, somehow, some warning given in advance [*prosēmainein*] when great evils are about to fall on either city-state or nation [*ethnos*]" (6.27). He also affirms his belief in oracles in general, although, like a sensible man, he can detect many occasions when one has a right to distrust a particular oracle (8.77).

A very great deal of the *History* is necessarily concerned with men's attempts to read these signs. The Egyptians, we are told, have the most complete set of records on wonders and their outcome (2.82), and, except for oracles, this is the only system that can lead to results (8.77). But, from first to last, man is dogged by the mysterious nature of the Divine purpose (if purpose it should be called) and its relation to his human understanding. For the outcome of a "sign" may accord in name and in some peculiar symmetry of form or meaning but, in the value and significance of the event, be quite altered. The Magi at the court of King Astyages had predicted that from his daughter he would have a grandchild who would take the crown from him. After the usual ineffectual effort to destroy the child by exposing it (an episode I have discussed above, in another context), the boy—Cyrus—reappears. He tells a story of how in the village, where his shepherd foster father lived, some children had in play chosen him king. Astyages now wanted to know from the Magi whether this fulfilled the oracle or whether further harm was to be feared for himself and his crown. The answer was as follows: "If indeed the boy survives and has become king with no connivance, be of good cheer and good heart: he will not come to rule a second time. Some, even of our prophecies, issue in very small matters, and in all that pertains to dreams the fulfillment is often in something trifling" (1.120). This story is all the more significant because, after all, the event proved that the Magi had been right the *first* time. The "real" meaning can be established only by hindsight. But this "real" meaning is what counts for human beings, and men have no indication whether the Divine recognizes any distinction between it and other outcomes that in some fashion bear the same name or the same shape.

At times the jealousy of the Gods, to which Herodotus refers, makes it look as though the *intention* of the God or Gods had been to deceive and maliciously to mock. It is hard to acquit of malice the utterance of Apollo given to Croesus ("if he made war on the Persians he would destroy a mighty empire," 1.53). Yet it does look as though the Delphic priests, in Herodotus' report at any rate, thought they had saved the God's reputation; for Croesus should, he was told, have asked "*what* empire" (as he now agrees), and the priests cite Apollo's undoubted aid to him when he was on the burning pyre (the deliverance through the rainstorm) and the benefit they claimed the God rendered in extending his period of success (1.91). On the whole, I think that Herodotus believes that the Divine is altogether jealous and prone to trouble us because it controls a world in terms that we cannot understand and that distort the outcome we would want; but it is not necessary that we believe that the Gods have personal vindictiveness against those who are destroyed. What is decisive is the impersonal hinge of fate. Particular Gods may at times be represented as the unwilling assistants as the hinge of fate turns. But fate in its compulsive patterns depends on the potency of single events or blocks of events. Croesus, we are told, was expiating the fault of his ancestor, Gyges (1.91). Also involved, though not always, is some personal act or attitude on the part of the person who suffers punishment. Croesus, we learn, suffered, "one may guess . . . because he thought he was of all mankind the most blessed" (1.34). And in the case of Apries, "since it was fated that he should end ill, something now caused it to happen, which I will [later] tell at greater length" (2.161). Yet such apparent causes or even superficial occasions are mainly *signs* to the human world; they do not correspond to the effective power of causation. This seems entirely due to a matching of acts from past to future. In such matching acts, however, moral wrongs seem to have a place. For instance, Herodotus speaks out as to his own conviction on the question of the cause of the Trojan War: "The reason of this, if I may declare my opinion, was that the Divine was laying his plans that, as the Trojans perished in utter destruction, they might make this thing manifest to all the world: that for great wrongdoings, great also are the punishments from the gods" (2.120). Again, about the Queen Pheretime: "But neither did Pheretime end her life well. For straightway after her vengeance on the Barcans she went back home to Egypt and there died very foully. For when yet living she bred of herself a mass of worms, so that mankind may see that violent vengeance earns the gods' grudges" (4.205). Yet it sometimes seems that it is the act that calls for the appropriate response, and only incidentally and occasionally the actor. Mycerinus, for example, was severely punished by the shortening of his life and reign because he did not understand that he was the third in a necessary sequence of three *bad* kings (2.132); his regrettable lapse into virtue necessitated his removal. And Xerxes, who clearly would have preferred to follow Artabanus' advice *not* to invade Greece, was forced on his evil course by a dream (7.18). Of course, we do not know what the antecedent events were, in the case of either Mycerinus or Xerxes, that constituted the impersonal pattern of Divine planning. Some such, we may conjecture, there must have been, given the evidence of the Divine urging. In such a system the choice of the individual man himself, his preference for virtue or vice, is valid only as it harmonizes with fate. Indeed, the individual man, saint or sinner, is hardly more important than the individual animal. For example, "There is a divine providence, with a kind of wisdom to it, as one might guess, according to which whatever is cowardly of spirit and edible should be prolific in progeny so that, with all the eating of them, they should not fail to exist; while things that are savage and inflict pain are infertile" (3.108). This certainly pictures a world of design, as far as Divine providence is concerned, since the fertility and infertility of the animals turn on the balance between eaters and eaten. But if one puts this together with the exclusive emphasis elsewhere on the sin and not the sinner, one comes out, I believe, with the conviction that great sins are punished because some order of the universe is maintained by divine punishment. But this simply does not reach down to the moral choice of the individual man any more than the general laws about fertility and infertility in the animal kingdom concern the fate of the individual rabbit or elephant.

Piety there is in Herodotus, but, interestingly enough, it concerns mostly not what you feel about the Gods but what you feel about your fellow men's feelings about the Gods or what the Gods feel about you. King Cambyses was crazy, said Herodotus, or he would never have outraged the feeling of the Egyptians by injuring their sacred cow (3.29). Illustrating this is the story of the wise Darius, the story of *nomos*. Darius asked his Greek and his Indian subjects about their burial customs and jokingly inquired of each what they would take to break with their ancestral customs, the one by eating, the other by burning, their ancestors. He is greeted with horror by both (3.38). From Herodotus' point of view, Darius is not only the wise but the pious ruler. Herodotus on the same model has tried to write as a pious and sensible historian, offending no one's religious susceptibilities and recording all religious accounts. There are, it is true, certain attitudes or acts that seem to directly provoke the Gods' wrath on human beings. God does not suffer anyone to "think high" but himself, says Herodotus (7.10). But such high thoughts nearly always appear only as the *apparent* cause (*prophasis*); the offense of Apries is an example. The weight of causation seems to lie solidly on an antecedent series of events. In a famous passage of Aeschylus' Agamemnon, the chorus says that theirs is a special and unusual belief, that they think that punishment does not come from the gods simply on the high and mighty in itself but on sin (Aeschylus, Agamemnon 757). It is quite possible that Herodotus would agree with the poet. But for him it would not be the sin of the individual, or at least not necessarily so, but a sin that, for some special reason (unknown), constitutes for the Divine the beginning of a significant sequence.

Piety also figures in Herodotus' book—in terms of a direct relation to the Gods—in his cautious avoidance of denying the existence of any daimon or God who can conceivably have done the things that people say he has done. Thus Herodotus severely questions the divinity of the Thracian daimon Salmoxis, but, when he passes to another subject, he has hardly denied the divinity explicitly (4.96). And when he tells us that the Egyptians do not believe in heroes at all (2.50) and is concerned to disprove the Greek stories about Heracles in Egypt, he concludes with this hope (2.45): "May both gods and heroes view me kindly!"

In speaking of animals in Egypt and their relation to religious practices, he says the following: "But if I were to say why it is that the animals are dedicated as sacred, my argument would drive me into talking of matters divine, and the declaration of these is what I would particularly shun. To the degree that I have spoken of them, it was with but a touch, and under the stress of necessity, that I have spoken" (2.65). Yet of course, since the gods or fate or the divine or the daimonic control the world, one is forced, even in history, to mention them, even with "but a touch."

Since all men know equally about the divine (2.3), it is only the names of gods, the customs of their worship, and the accounts and rituals that differentiate our notions of religion. It may be, and sometimes is, the historian's work to concern himself with these but only very rarely with the basic religious concepts underlying them all. It is the differences between peoples on which, to adapt Yeats's phrase in another context, history keeps house. That the Divinity is always jealous and prone to trouble us, as Solon tells Croesus (1.32), is perhaps a universal religious perception; that God allows no one but himself to think high is another (7.10). What these sentences mean is that two important aspects of the divine are caught by statements that are, strictly speaking, analogical. God can be understood *as if* he were a jealous and troublesome despot; he permits no one to be haughty but himself. This is one way of *speaking* about the inner knowledge that all men have of the Divine. It is the way of speaking when what is drawn on is the aspect of God that appears to man personal. God alone is free of danger or vulnerability. He therefore alone can "think high." Man never can and should never dare to. On the other side are the many references to an impersonal balance of fate, which is often shown as being independent of God's control and *a fortiori* of man's control or even his reasoned comprehension. The balance of fate can sometimes be traced to past events. Otherwise one can only hazard guesses, sometimes assisted by the Gods, sometimes by the semiscientific examination of similar cases and their outcomes. The basic religious "truths" thus analogically expressed underlie all the historical narrative, perhaps even give it its characteristic flavor and very form. But they are really not in need of comment; they are too basic and too general. But that the Persians approach their God not in human form but as the natural elements and therefore worship on the tops of mountains (1.131); that the Egyptians see Apis as a calf (3.28); that Homer and Hesiod had furnished the Greeks with an appropriate gallery of deities, with forms and honors assigned them (2.53); that the Indians' sense of the sacred commits them to eating their dead parents (3.38)—these are all of concern to the historian because, in their multiplicity, they extend the range of our understanding of man's condition in the world, the world that is ultimately entirely controlled by a power not his own. The human notion of fate as an evening-out of the balance—upset by some monstrous sin, such as Pheretime's punishment of the people of Barca—is a human metaphor for an observed religious truth that cannot be otherwise communicated. But granted the evening-out, the human observer is often at a loss to find the first and the last of the series of responsive events. Unlike the varying customs and rituals, the truth implied in the metaphor of balance is commonplace and universal, but its application to particulars is difficult and unsatisfactory. It is therefore sometimes communicated by Herodotus or commented on, but comparatively rarely.

This is a mystery, this relation between the two worlds, that of divine control and that of the human beings on the receiving end. And, I think, Herodotus would avoid, as far as he can, the world of divine control, not only because of the risk to himself as observer and recorder. There is in him a deep admiration and delight in the human, and this, in his terms, implies a certain neglect of the divine and a wish to leave it, if possible, out of consideration. "That time

may not draw the color from what man has brought into being"
(1.1): time is the destroying agent against which you erect the *kleos*.
Against the Gods there is nothing to be done. The world of human-
ity, controlled by finally incomprehensible powers, is a tragic world.
At best, the Divine meaning mocks the other. If one is to be great
and glorious as man or nation or city, one is the more likely to fall
into the traps of the supernatural. The most sensible course is to
choose the private life; but the purpose of Herodotus' *History* is to
chronicle the great men, great cities, and great deeds. So as a writer
he is almost committed to a world of tragedy, where good or great
intentions have but little to do with what happens. Still, the *kleos*
remains, not, I think, as a moral warning nor yet as a national eu-
logy. Perhaps Herodotus saw himself as securing for the great deeds
of the Persian War the only permanence in this world of relative values, the permanence of memory.

*   *   *

The English in which Herodotus comes before us should be direct,
powerful, and clear but also, I think, a little odd. His Ionic is a literary dialect; it links him with Homer, the main share of whose language is Ionic. This bond with Homer was intended to be very sug-
gestive. Herodotus' *History* is to be the story of another great war,
that of the Persians against the Greeks, as Homer's was that of the
Greeks against the Trojans. But it was to be something new—prose
history, not poetry, and history that would concern itself not only
with the glories of the great deeds in battle but with reasons why the
war and its great deeds had come about. It is this combination of
tradition and innovation that is at the heart of Herodotus' work.
The English in which he now speaks to us must have a flavor, at
least, that is as traditional and literary and a little archaic as Homer
sounded for the fifth-century Greek.

Of course, it is quite possible, and some would consider it desirable, to disregard any special quality of the original Greek style.
Rather concentrate, these critics might say, on a forceful English
version without bothering to render the peculiar character of the
Greek by some sought-out quirk in the English. But though this
seems a bold and telling attitude, it misrepresents the Greek that

faces the translator. It is indeed what makes de Selincourt's version in the Penguin edition much less satisfactory than it otherwise might be. His English is racy, it reads well, and it is sharp and to the point, but it entirely fails to convey any part of the conscious mask of Herodotus: his use of an inherited way of talking (from Homer) while treating of something new. The Penguin Herodotus sounds exactly as though new-minted by a twentieth-century journalist. There are keen strokes and very little nuance, which is quite false to the Greek style and to the strange man who is himself so preeminently the style. Herodotus must sound somewhat literary and whimsical. Still, he must, even more importantly, be powerful and direct, because the history is largely designed for public reading. Very many of his greatest stories are folklore that must have come straight from the mouths of local inhabitants and were to find their artistic form of publication in the mouth of the public reader and for an audience. If there is one feature an English Herodotus must pass on to us, it is an air of straightforward impact, especially in the conversations and speeches. But, paradoxically, it is exactly at those places that the literary background of Homer is most heavily laid under contribution. In reminiscences, interventions, and personal notes, the contribution of the writer must again appear direct, almost involuntarily so. One of the chief objections to the other current Herodotean translation, the older version of Rawlinson, is that it is dull and prolix. No one could read it, or listen to it, with surprise or enjoyment.

What I was looking for, then, was an English Herodotus who speaks not altogether with his own tongue but with echoes of the tongues of older writers; a powerful eccentric who has made even the traditional his own, so that we feel that no man but himself could have originated the phrase, the sentence, the cadence, which is so often a blend of Homer and himself. That is the ideal; how near this English Herodotus comes to it the reader will judge for himself.

Chicago
January, 1985

Book One

1. I, Herodotus of Halicarnassus, am here setting forth my history, that time may not draw the color from what man has brought into being, nor those great and wonderful deeds, manifested by both Greeks and barbarians, fail of their report, and, together with all this, the reason why they fought one another.

The chroniclers among the Persians say that it was the Phoenicians who were the cause of the falling-out; for they came from what is called the Red Sea[1] to our sea, and, having settled in the country in which they now live, they at once set about long voyages; and carrying Egyptian and Assyrian freights, they put into other lands, and among them Argos. At this time Argos excelled all others of what is now called Hellas. To Argos, then, came the Phoenicians, and there they put their cargo on display. On the fifth or sixth day after their arrival, when almost all their goods had been sold off, there came down to the sea, with many other women, the king's daughter; her name—it is the same in both the Greek and Persian accounts—was Io, and she was the daughter of Inachus. The women all stood by the stern of the ship and were buying from among the wares whatever they had most set their hearts on; as they did so, the Phoenicians let out a great shout and made for them. The most of the women, they say, escaped, but Io and some others were carried off. The Phoenicians loaded them into their ships and sailed away to Egypt.

2. That is how, the Persians say, Io came to Egypt (though that is not how the Greeks tell it), and that was the beginning of the wrongdoing. After that, say the Persians, certain Greeks, whose name they cannot declare, put into Tyre in Phoenician country and carried off the king's daughter, Europa. These must have been Cre-

1. Herodotus' Red (Erythraean) Sea is not our Red Sea (the long strip of water between Egypt and the Arabian Peninsula). It is, instead, our Indian Ocean, together with its several gulfs.

tans. So far, say the Persians, it was tit for tat, but after that the Greeks were guilty of the second piece of injustice; for they sailed with a long ship to Aea in Colchis and the river Phasis,[2] and from there, when they had done the business on which they came, they carried off the king's daughter, Medea. The king of the Colchians sent a herald to Greece to ask for satisfaction for the carrying-off of his daughter and to demand her return. But the Greeks answered (this is still the Persian story) that the Persians, on their side, had not given satisfaction for the carrying-off of Argive Io, and so they themselves would give none to the Colchians.

3. It was in the next generation after this, as the story goes, that Alexander,[3] the son of Priam, having heard of these deeds, wanted for himself, too, a wife from Greece by rape and robbery; for he was certain that he would not have to give satisfaction for it, inasmuch as the Greeks had not. So he carried off Helen. The Greeks first resolved to demand her back, as well as satisfaction for her carrying-off. But when they did so, the Persians brought against *them* the rape of Medea, saying that the Greeks had given no satisfaction for that nor had surrendered her when asked. Did they now want satisfaction from others?

4. Up to this point it was only rape on both sides, one from the other; but from here on, say the Persians, the Greeks were greatly to blame. For the Greeks, say they, invaded Asia before ever the Persians invaded Europe: "It is the work of unjust men, we think, to carry off women at all; but once they have been carried off, to take seriously the avenging of them is the part of fools, as it is the part of sensible men to pay no heed to the matter: clearly, the women would not have been carried off had they no mind to be." The Persians say that they, for their part, made no account of the women carried off from Asia but that the Greeks, because of a Lacedaemonian woman, gathered a great army, came straight to Asia, and destroyed the power of Priam, and from that time forth the Persians regarded the Greek people as their foes. For the Persians claim, as their own, Asia and all the barbarian[4] people who live in it, but Europe and the Greek people they regard as entirely separate.

2. This is the story of Jason, the Argonauts, and the Golden Fleece.
3. Alexander is the name by which Paris is usually known in Greek literature.
4. Herotodus uses the word "barbarians" in its Greek sense, which is simply those who by origin and speech are "foreigners," i.e., non-Greek-speaking.

5. That is how the Persians say it happened, and it is in the capture of Troy that they discover the beginning of their enmity toward the Greeks. But about Io herself the Phoenicians disagree with the Persians. For they say they brought her to Egypt, but not against her will; she lay, they say, with the ship's captain in Argos, and, when she found she was pregnant, in shame for her parents she sailed with the Phoenicians voluntarily, that she might not be discovered.

These are the stories of the Persians and the Phoenicians. For my part I am not going to say about these matters that they happened thus or thus, but I will set my mark upon that man that I myself know began unjust acts against the Greeks, and, having so marked him, I will go forward in my account, covering alike the small and great cities of mankind. For of those that were great in earlier times most have now become small, and those that were great in my time were small in the time before. Since, then, I know that man's good fortune never abides in the same place, I will make mention of both alike.

6. Croesus was a Lydian by birth, the son of Alyattes, and ruler of all the peoples west of the Halys, a river that flows from the south, between Syria and Paphlagonia, and northward goes out into the sea called Euxine.[5] This Croesus was the first of the barbarians of whom we know who subdued some of the Greeks to the payment of tribute and made friends of others. He subdued the Ionians, Aeolians, and Dorians who were in Asia, and he made the Lacedaemonians his friends. But before Croesus' rule all the Greeks were free. For the invasion of Ionia by the Cimmerians, which was elder than Croesus'

"Bar-bar-bar" is presumably the Greek impression of how such unfortunates expressed themselves instead of with the proper sounds of Greek.

It has been questioned whether the word "barbarian" belongs in the Greek text at this point. If one includes it, as I have (and as the main MS tradition seems to require), it would seem to mean that the Great King of Persia differentiated between his Greek and non-Greek subjects. However, both Greeks and non-Greeks were ruled by the Persian kings in Herodotus' History and, before them, by Croesus of Lydia. Possibly the text is restricting this distinction, in Persian thinking, to the Greeks of Europe as distinct from those living in Asia Minor. It is worth noticing that Herodotus quotes the Persians as considering Priam an Asiatic. As far as modern scholarship goes, he was not, but a Greek, and the war between Greeks and Trojans was a war between two peoples of Greek origin.

5. The Euxine Sea (also called Pontus) is the Black Sea.

day, was no subjugation of the cities but a matter of raid and plunder.

7. The sovereignty of Lydia belonged to the Heraclidae[6] but had devolved upon the family of Croesus, who were called Mermnadae; and this is how it happened. There was one Candaules, whom the Greeks call Myrsilus, the ruler of Sardis and descended from Alcaeus, the son of Heracles. For Agron, the son of Ninus, the son of Belus, the son of Alcaeus, was the first of the Heraclidae to be king of Sardis, and Candaules, the son of Myrsus, was the last. Those who had been kings of this country before Agron were descendants of Lydus, the son of Atys, from whom this whole Lydian region takes its name; for earlier it was called the land of the Meii. It was by the Meii that the sons of Heracles were entrusted with the rule in accordance with an oracle; the Heraclidae were born of a slave girl, belonging to Iardanus, and Heracles. They held sway for two and twenty generations of men, or five hundred and five years, son succeeding father in the rule, until Candaules, son of Myrsus.

8. This Candaules fell in love with his own wife; and because he was so in love, he thought he had in her far the most beautiful of women. So he thought. Now, he had a bodyguard named Gyges, the son of Dascylus, who was his chief favorite among them. Candaules used to confide all his most serious concerns to this Gyges, and of course he was forever overpraising the beauty of his wife's body to him. Some time thereafter—for it was fated that Candaules should end ill—he spoke to Gyges thus: "Gyges, I do not think that you credit me when I tell you about the beauty of my wife; for indeed men's ears are duller agents of belief than their eyes. Contrive, then, that you see her naked." The other made outcry against him and said, "Master, what a sick word is this you have spoken, in bidding me look upon my mistress naked! With the laying-aside of her clothes, a woman lays aside the respect that is hers! Many are the fine things discovered by men of old, and among them this one, that each should look upon his own, only. Indeed I believe that your wife is the most beautiful of all women, and I beg of you not to demand of me what is unlawful."

9. With these words he would have fought him off, being in dread lest some evil should come to himself out of these things; but

6. The ending -idae means "sons of," here "sons of Heracles."

the other answered him and said: "Be of good heart, Gyges, and fear neither myself, lest I might suggest this as a trial of you, nor yet my wife, that some hurt might befall you from her. For my own part I will contrive it entirely that she will not know she has been seen by you. For I will place you in the room where we sleep, behind the open door. After my coming-in, my wife too will come to her bed. There is a chair that stands near the entrance. On this she will lay her clothes, one by one, as she takes them off and so will give you full leisure to view her. But when she goes from the chair to the bed and you are behind her, let you heed then that she does not see you as you go through the door."

10. Inasmuch, then, as Gyges was unable to avoid it, he was ready. Candaules, when he judged the hour to retire had come, led Gyges into his bedroom; and afterwards his wife, too, came in at once; and, as she came in and laid her clothes aside, Gyges viewed her. When she went to the bed and Gyges was behind her, he slipped out—but the woman saw him as he was going through the door. She understood then what had been done by her husband; and though she was so shamed, she raised no outcry nor let on to have understood, having in mind to take punishment on Candaules. For among the Lydians and indeed among the generality of the barbarians, for even a man to be seen naked is an occasion of great shame.

11. So for that time she showed nothing but held her peace. But when the day dawned, she made ready such of her household servants as she saw were most loyal to her and sent for Gyges. He gave never a thought to her knowing anything of what had happened and came on her summons, since he had been wont before this, also, to come in attendance whenever the queen should call him. As Gyges appeared, the woman said to him: "Gyges, there are two roads before you, and I give you your choice which you will travel. Either you kill Candaules and take me and the kingship of the Lydians, or you must yourself die straightway, as you are, that you may not, in days to come, obey Candaules in everything and look on what you ought not. For either he that contrived this must die or you, who have viewed me naked and done what is not lawful." For a while Gyges was in amazement at her words; but then he besought her not to bind him in the necessity of such a choice. But he did not persuade her—only saw that necessity truly lay before him: either to

kill his master or himself be killed by others. So he chose his own survival. Then he spoke to her and asked her further: "Since you force me to kill my master, all unwilling, let me hear from you in what way we shall attack him." She answered and said: "The attack on him shall be made from the self-same place whence he showed me to you naked, and it is when he is sleeping that you shall attack him."

12. So they prepared their plot, and, as night came on—for there was no going back for Gyges, nor any riddance of the matter but that either himself or Candaules must die—he followed the woman into the bedroom. She gave him a dagger and hid him behind the very door. And after that, as Candaules was taking his rest, Gyges slipped out and killed him, and so it was that he, Gyges, had the wife and the kingship of Lydia. Archilochus of Paros, who lived at the same time, made mention of him in a poem of iambic trimeters.

13. He had, indeed, the kingship, and it was strengthened by an oracle from Delphi. For when the Lydians made a great to-do about what had happened to Candaules and were in arms about it, the conspirators who were with Gyges came to an agreement with the rest of the Lydians that if the oracle should proclaim him king of Lydia, he should indeed be king; if it should not, he should hand back the power to the Heraclids. The oracle gave its answer, and so Gyges gained his kingship. But this much the Pythia said: that the Heraclids should yet have vengeance on a descendant of Gyges in the fifth generation. But of this word neither the Lydians nor their kings made any account until it was fulfilled.

14. Thus it was that the Mermnadae gained the sovereignty and despoiled the Heraclids, and Gyges, when he became king, sent off dedicatory offerings to Delphi, and not a few at that. For of all the dedications of silver, the most of them in Delphi are his; and apart from the silver he dedicated a vast deal of gold, including what is most worth remembering, six golden bowls. These stand in the treasure house of the Corinthians and weigh thirty talents.[7] Though, truly spoken, it is not the treasure house of the commonalty of the Corinthians but that of Cypselus, the son of Eëtion. This Gyges was

7. For a discussion of Greek weights and measures, see the end notes at the back of the book.

the first of the barbarians of whom we know who dedicated objects at Delphi—the first, that is, after Midas, the son of Gordias, king of Phrygia. For Midas, too, dedicated his royal throne on which he sat and gave judgment, and this indeed is a marvel to see. The throne stands where Gyges' bowls stand. This gold and the silver that Gyges dedicated have been given the name Gygian by the Delphians, after him that dedicated them.

15. When Gyges became king, he, like others, invaded the country of Miletus and Smyrna, and he captured the city of Colophon. However, no other great deed was done by him, although he reigned thirty-eight years, and so we will pass him by with just such mention as we have made.[8] But I will speak of Ardys, his son, who became king after him. This man captured Priene and invaded the country of Miletus, and it was when he held power over Sardis that the Cimmerians, who had been driven out of their usual haunts by the nomad Scythians, came into Asia and took all of Sardis except the citadel.

16. When Ardys had reigned forty-nine years, his son Sadyattes succeeded him and reigned twelve, and then Alyattes, Sadyattes' son. It was Alyattes who made war upon Cyaxares, the descendant of Deioces, and the Medes, and he who chased the Cimmerians out of Asia and who took Smyrna, which had been colonized from Colophon, and who invaded Clazomenae. But from these last people he came back not at all as he would have chosen, for he suffered a great disaster there. Of all the other deeds in his reign, these that I will now tell you are the most worth recording.

17. He made war on the Milesians, having inherited this war from his father. He invaded and attacked Miletus in this way: as soon as the corn was ripe, he invaded the country; he would march in to the music of pipes and harps and flutes, treble and bass, and as often as he came into Milesian territory he would cast down no houses in the countryside, nor would he burn any or wrench the doors off, but let all stand in its place; but the trees and the crops of the land he would destroy and so home with him again. For the people of Miletus were in possession of the sea, and so there was no blockading them with his army. But the Lydian did not destroy the houses—and why was this? So that the people of Miletus might

8. Gyges ruled from 678 to 652 B.C.

have somewhere as a base from which to sow their land and work it
and he might have something of their working to destroy when he
invaded.

18. In this manner he made war for eleven years, and in that
time there happened to the people of Miletus two great reverses, one
when they fought in their own country, at Limeneion, and one in
the plain of the Maeander. For six of the eleven years of this war it
was Sadyattes, the son of Ardys, who was king of Lydia, and it was
he who invaded the country of Miletus. For it was Sadyattes who
had begun the war. But for the five years that followed the six, it was
Alyattes, the son of Sadyattes, who made the war, having, as I said
before, inherited it. For having had it from his father, he carried it
on very fiercely, and none of the Ionians, save only the Chians,
lightened the burdens of the war by sharing it with the Milesians.
By helping, the Chians were repaying like for like, for in former
days the Milesians had helped them in their fight against the
Erythraeans.

19. In the twelfth year, when the corn crop was being fired by his
army, the following thing happened: as soon as the corn caught fire,
the fire, driven hard by the wind, caught the temple of Athena
called Athena of Assesos, and the temple, when it caught fire,
burned to the ground. At the time no account was taken of it, but
afterwards, when the army came back to Sardis, Alyattes fell sick.
As his sickness lasted somewhat long, Alyattes sent a delegation to
Delphi, either through someone's counseling or because of some
thought of his own, to inquire of the god about his illness. And
when the messengers came to Delphi, the Pythia declared that
she would give no oracle to them until they rebuilt the temple
of Athena, which they had burned in that country of Miletus at
Assesos.

20. So much I know, for I heard from the Delphians that this was
how it was. But the Milesians add this besides, that Periander, the
son of Cypselus, sent a messenger to Thrasybulus, who was then
prince of Miletus[9] and his very close friend, telling him of the oracle
that he had heard had been given to Alyattes, so that with fore-

9. The Greek here reads "tyrant of Miletus." For Herodotus, "tyrant" means
simply a ruler, sometimes despotic and dictatorial, sometimes exerting power inside an existing constitutional system but having no traditional, and rarely any

knowledge of it Thrasybulus might lay his plans with respect to whatever faced him.

21. That, then, is how the Milesians say it happened. Now Alyattes, as soon as he got his reply from Delphi, straightway sent a herald to Miletus, being wishful to make a truce with Thrasybulus and the people of Miletus for whatever length of time it would take to rebuild the temple. His envoy went his way to Miletus. But Thrasybulus knew exactly the whole story in advance and knew what Alyattes was going to do. So he contrived as follows: he collected into the marketplace all the corn there was in the city, both his own and that of private persons, and gave an order to the Milesians that at a sign from himself they should all drink and be merry in revelry one with another.

22. Thrasybulus did this and gave these orders with a purpose: that the herald from Sardis, seeing a great store of corn heaped up and all the people enjoying themselves, should so report of the matter to Alyattes; and this indeed was what happened. When the herald had seen, and had given Thrasybulus the message his Lydian master had bidden him give, he went back to Sardis; and, as I learn, it was because of this matter, and nothing else, that the reconciliation between Thrasybulus and Alyattes took place. For Alyattes had believed that the scantiness of corn was severe in Miletus and that the people were forced to the extremity of distress; but when the herald returned from Miletus, he heard a story the very opposite of what he had looked for. Therefore, the reconciliation was made on terms: that the two princes should be guest-friends and allies, one with the other; and Alyattes built not one but two temples to Athena of Assesos, and he himself recovered from his sickness. So this is the story of Alyattes' war against Thrasybulus and the people of Miletus.

23. The Periander who gave Thrasybulus notice of the oracle was

---

hereditary, claim on it. He is a figure very similar to the present-day rulers of some South American states. But "tyrant" does not necessarily mean to Herodotus, and perhaps not to most of his contemporaries, a ruler who was harsh or cruel, although later in the fifth century that sense is almost invariably implied. Under these circumstances I have usually translated the Greek word *tyrannos* by the neutral and vague word "prince," as it might occur in Machiavelli. Occasionally it becomes necessary to substitute for it the rendering "despot."

the son of Cypselus and was himself prince of Corinth. It was to him, say the Corinthians (with the agreement of the people of Lesbos), that the greatest wonder in all his life happened—I mean, the safe carriage of Arion of Methymna on a dolphin's back to Taenarum. Arion was second to none of all the lyre-players of his time and was also the first man we know of to compose and name the dithyramb[10] and produce it in Corinth.

24. Arion, they say, who was spending the greater part of his time at the court of Periander, was seized with a longing to sail to Italy and Sicily; but when he had made a great deal of money there, he wanted to come home to Corinth. So he set sail from Tarentum, and, as he trusted no people more than Corinthians, he hired a boat of men of Corinth. But when they were out to sea, those Corinthians plotted to throw Arion overboard and take his money. When he understood what they would be at, he begged for his life at the sacrifice of the money. However, he could not prevail on them, and they, who were his ferrymen, bade him either kill himself—that he might have a grave when he was landed—or straightway jump into the sea. So, penned in helplessness, Arion besought them, since they were so determined, to stand by and watch him while he sang, standing with all his gear on him[11] on the poop deck of the ship; he promised, once he had sung, to make away with himself. They for their part thought what a pleasure it would be for them to hear the greatest singer in the world, and so they retreated from the stern of the boat to amidships. He put on all his gear, took his lyre in his hand, and taking his stance on the poop went through the High Shrill Song,[12] and, when it was finished, cast himself into the sea,

10. The dithyramb was a performance in which a chorus danced and sang to the accompaniment of a lyre. The term here rendered "produce" is literally "teach," because the poet (in this case, anyway) "taught" the chorus how to render his verses and the dances that accompanied them. The same word "teach" is used of Athenian tragedies when they were "produced" for the great festivals.

11. Apparently singers, or perhaps festival performers other than regular actors (who had their own kind of costumes and masks), wore very formal robes and possibly some sort of garland on the head. The point of this in the story would seem to be the encumbrance with which Arion loaded himself for his leap into the sea and also the consequent effectiveness of his appearance before the pirates in their later encounter.

12. A special and well-known song in honor of Apollo.

just as he was, with all his gear. Away they sailed to Corinth; but, says the tale, a dolphin picked Arion up on his back and brought him back to Taenarum. He disembarked from the dolphin and went to Corinth (with all his gear) and, on his coming, told all that had happened him. Periander—for he didn't believe him—held Arion under guard, suffering him to go nowhere else at all, and kept vigilant watch for his ferrymen. When they came, they were summoned to his presence and asked if they had any news of Arion. Yes, they said, he must be safe somewhere in Italy, since they had left him prospering in Tarentum. At that moment Arion appeared before them just as he was when he had leaped into the sea; whereupon they, in their utter confusion, were unable to deny what was brought home to them. This is what the Corinthians and Lesbians say, and there is at Taenerum a small dedicatory offering of Arion, made of bronze and figuring a man riding upon a dolphin.

25. So Alyattes the Lydian had carried on his war against the people of Miletus, and thereafter he died, having reigned fifty-seven years. The time he escaped from his sickness, he made a dedication at Delphi, being the second of his house to do so; this one was a large silver mixing bowl with a stand beneath it of welded iron—a thing well worth the seeing even among all the dedicatory gifts at Delphi; it was the work of Glaucus of Chios, who was the only man in the world by whom the welding of iron was discovered.

26. On Alyattes' death, Croesus, the son of Alyattes, succeeded to the kingdom,[13] being then thirty-five years old; and the first of the Greeks he attacked were the people of Ephesus. Then the Ephesians, being besieged by him, dedicated their city to Artemis by fastening a rope from her temple to their city wall. The distance between the old city, which is what was then being besieged, and the temple was seven stades.[14] The Ephesians were the first whom Croesus attacked, but afterwards he set upon each of the Ionian and Aeolian cities in turn, bringing different charges against them. When he was able to find greater grounds of complaint, he brought forward these, but against some of the cities, just the same, he advanced other offenses, though they were indeed very slight.

27. When, then, the Greeks in Asia had been subdued to the

13. Croesus' reign began in 560 B.C.
14. Nearly a mile.

payment of tribute, Croesus thereafter designed to build ships for himself and attack the people of the islands; but when everything was ready for the shipbuilding, something happened; some say it was Bias of Priene who came to Sardis, others that it was Pittacus of Mitylene; but of one of these, on his coming to Sardis, Croesus made inquiry—"What news in Greece?"—and it was what this man said that stopped the shipbuilding. "Sir," he answered, "the islanders are buying up ten thousand horses, as they have in mind to make a campaign on Sardis and yourself." Croesus imagined that he spoke seriously and said, "Would that the gods would put this idea into their heads: that islanders should come against the sons of the Lydians with horses!" Whereat the other answered him, "Sir, you seem to me to pray very earnestly that you might catch the islanders riding horses on the mainland, and your hope in this matter is very reasonable. But do you believe that the islanders, since they have heard that you are to build ships against them, have any other matter for prayer than that they will catch the Lydians at sea and so take vengeance on yourself, in requital for the Greeks that live on the mainland, whom you have made slaves of and hold as such?" Croesus was extraordinarily pleased with the turn of the answer, and since he thought that the man spoke aptly, he hearkened to him and gave over his shipbuilding; and so Croesus made a guest-friendship with the Ionians who live on the islands.

28. As time wore on, almost all were subdued who lived west of the river Halys; for except for the Cilicians and Lycians, Croesus subdued and held all the rest in his power. These were: Lydians, Phrygians, Mysians, Mariandynians, Chalybes, Paphlagonians, Thynians and Bithynians (these two are Thracians), Carians, Ionians, Dorians, Aeolians, and Pamphylians. All these were subjugated, and Croesus annexed them to his own Lydians. So Sardis was at the height of its wealth.

29. To Sardis, then, all the teachers of learning[15] who lived at that time came from all over Greece; they came to Sardis on their

15. The Greek word here, *sophistai*, was later to win a derogatory sense, when a "sophist" was one who taught for hire and was given to fallacious argument. Here it has only its earlier meaning, "one who seeks for *sophia* [wisdom]"—a kind of self-chosen seeker, from whom one might perhaps, as a favor, learn some of the fruits of that wisdom.

several occasions; and, of course, there came also Solon of Athens. At the bidding of the Athenians he had made laws for them, and then he went abroad for ten years, saying, indeed, that he traveled for sight-seeing but really that he might not be forced to abrogate any of the laws he had laid down; of themselves, the Athenians could not do so, since they had bound themselves by great oaths that for ten years they would live under whatever laws Solon would enact.[16]

30. This, then, was the reason—though of course there was also the sight-seeing—that brought Solon to Egypt to the court of Prince Amasis and eventually to Sardis to Croesus. When he came there, he was entertained by Croesus in his palace, and on the third or fourth day after his arrival the servants, on Croesus' orders, took Solon round the stores of treasures and showed them to him in all their greatness and richness. When he had seen them all and considered them, Croesus, as the opportunity came, put this question to Solon: "My friend from Athens, great talk of you has come to my ears, of your wisdom and your traveling; they say you have traveled over much of the world, for the sake of what you can see in it, in your pursuit of knowledge. So now, a longing overcomes me to ask you whether, of all men, there is one you have seen as the most blessed of all." He put this question never doubting but that he himself was the most blessed. But Solon flattered not a whit but in his answer followed the very truth. He said, "Sir, Tellus the Athenian." Croesus was bewildered at this but pursued his question with insistence. "And in virtue of what is it that you judge Tellus to be most blessed?" Solon said: "In the first place, Tellus' city was in good state when he had sons—good and beautiful they were—and he saw children in turn born to all of them, and all surviving. Secondly, when he himself had come prosperously to a moment of his life—that is, prosperously as it counts with us—he had, besides, an ending for it that was most glorious: in a battle between the Athenians and their neighbors in Eleusis he made a sally, routed the enemy, and died splendidly, and the Athenians gave him a public funeral where he fell and so honored him greatly."

31. Solon led on Croesus by what he said of Tellus when he

16. Solon's reforms date from his archonship at Athens in 594–593.

spoke of his many blessings, so Croesus went further in his questioning and wanted to know whom Solon had seen as second most blessed after the first, for he certainly thought that he himself would win the second prize at least. But Solon answered him and said: "Cleobis and Biton. They were men of Argive race and had a sufficiency of livelihood and, besides, a strength of body such as I shall show; they were both of them prize-winning athletes, and the following story is told of them as well. There was a feast of Hera at hand for the Argives, and their mother needs must ride to the temple; but the oxen did not come from the fields at the right moment. The young men, being pressed by lack of time, harnessed themselves beneath the yoke and pulled the wagon with their mother riding on it; forty-five stades they completed on their journey and arrived at the temple. When they had done that and had been seen by all the assembly, there came upon them the best end of a life, and in them the god showed thoroughly how much better it is for a man to be dead than to be alive.[17] For the Argive men came and stood around the young men, congratulating them on their strength, and the women congratulated the mother on the fine sons she had; and the mother, in her great joy at what was said and done, stood right in front of the statue and there prayed for Cleobis and Biton, her own sons, who had honored her so signally, that the goddess should give them whatsoever is best for a man to win. After that prayer the young men sacrificed and banqueted and laid them down to sleep in the temple where they were; they never rose more, but that was the end in which they were held. The Argives made statues of them and dedicated them at Delphi, as of two men who were the best of all."

32. So Solon assigned his second prize in happiness to these men; but Croesus was sharply provoked and said: "My Athenian

17. I have translated the two verbs (perfect and present infinitives) as I have (and *not* as "It is better to die than to live") because for Herodotus death is not a condition. A Christian might say that our condition after death is better than in this life, but what Solon is after is that, if you are dead, at least the risks of trouble are over. Hence to have the last settlement when you are lavishly winning, with all the assets of youth, beauty, and strength in the moment of triumph on your side, is the supreme gift, while to go on living is to go on being continually at risk.

friend, is the happiness that is mine so entirely set at naught by you that you do not make me the equal of even private men?" Solon answered: "Croesus, you asked me, who know that the Divine is altogether jealous and prone to trouble us, and you asked me about human matters. In the whole length of time there is much to see that one would rather not see—and much to suffer likewise. I put the boundary of human life at seventy years. These seventy years have twenty-five thousand two hundred days, not counting the intercalary month;[18] but if every other year be lengthened by a month so that the seasons come out right, these intercalary months in seventy years will be thirty-five, and the days for these months ten hundred and fifty. So that all the days of a man's life are twenty-six thousand two hundred and fifty; of all those days not one brings to him anything exactly the same as another. So, Croesus, man is entirely what befalls him. To me it is clear that you are very rich, and clear that you are the king of many men; but the thing that you asked me I cannot say of you yet, until I hear that you have brought your life to an end well. For he that is greatly rich is not more blessed than he that has enough for the day unless fortune so attend upon him that he ends his life well, having all those fine things still with him. Moreover, many very rich men are unblessed, and many who have a moderate competence are fortunate. Now he that is greatly rich but is unblessed has an advantage over the lucky man in two respects only; but the latter has an advantage over the rich and unblessed in many. The rich and unblessed man is better able to accomplish his every desire and to support such great visitation of evil as shall befall him. But the moderately rich and lucky man wins over the other in these ways: true, he is not equally able to support both the visitation of evil and and his own desire, but his good fortune turns these aside from him; he is uncrippled and healthy, without evils to afflict him, and with good children and good looks. If, in addition to all this, he shall end his life well, he is the man you seek, the one who is worthy to be called blessed; but wait till he is dead to call him so, and till then call him not blessed but lucky.[19]

18. The intercalary month was the Greek substitute for our leap year.

19. For the subtle nuances of meaning that Herodotus brings to this discussion of "blessedness" or "happiness" (nuances embedded in the Greek terms he employs), see the end note to this passage.

"Of course, it is impossible for one who is human to have all the good things together, just as there is no one country that is sufficient of itself to provide all good things for itself; but it has one thing and not another, and the country that has the most is best. So no single person is self-sufficient; he has one thing and lacks another. But whoso possesses most of them, continuously, and then ends his life gracefully, he, my lord, may justly win this name you seek—at least in my judgment. But one must look always at the end of everything—how it will come out finally. For to many the god has shown a glimpse of blessedness only to extirpate them in the end."

33. That was what Solon said, and he did not please Croesus at all; so the prince sent him away, making no further account of him, thinking him assuredly a stupid man who would let by present goods and bid him look to the end of every matter.

34. After Solon was gone, a great visitation of evil from the god laid hold of Croesus, and one may guess that it was because he thought he was of all mankind the most blessed. Lo, as he lay sleeping, a dream stood over him and declared to him the very truth of the evils that were to befall his son. Croesus had two sons, the one of them quite undone, inasmuch as he was deaf and dumb; but the other was far the first young man of his age; his name was Atys. It was concerning this Atys that the dream communicated with Croesus, namely, that he should have him stricken by an iron spearpoint. When Croesus woke up and considered with himself the dream's message, he was in terror of it and married his son to a wife, and besides, although the young man had been wont to captain the Lydians, he now would send him nowhere on any such business. And as for the javelins and spears and all such things as men use in war, he conveyed all these out of the men's halls and piled them in the chambers lest any of them,· as they hung on the walls, might chance to fall on his son.

35. Now when Croesus had in hand the marriage of his son, there came to Sardis a man in the grip of calamity, his hands full of impurity. He was a Phrygian by race and of the royal family. This man came forward into the house of Croesus and begged to win purification of Croesus after the customs of that country. So Croesus purified him. (The manner of purification is the same for the Lydians and the Greeks.) After he had performed the due rites, Croesus

asked him where he came from and who he was, in these words: "Sir, who are you? And from where in Phrygia have you come, that you have become a suppliant at my hearth? What man or woman have you killed?" He answered him: "King, I am the son of Gordias, the son of Midas, and men call me Adrastus; and it is my brother I have killed, and I did it unwittingly. I come before you having been driven out by my father and having had my all taken from me." Croesus answered him and said: "Friends are they from whom you spring, and it is to friends also that you have come. While you remain in my house, you will lack for nothing. As for your calamity, that you must bear as lightly as you may, for so it will be best for you."

36. So he had his daily living in Croesus' house. In that same time, on the Mysian Olympus, there appeared a boar, a great brute indeed. He made his headquarters in that mountain and would issue from it and ravage the tilled fields of the Mysians. Time and again the Mysians went against him but failed to do him hurt; rather, indeed, the suffering was on their side. So, at last, messengers of the Mysians came to Croesus and said: "King, the greatest brute of a wild boar has appeared in our country, and he is destroying our fields. We have sought to kill him, but we cannot. Now, therefore, we beg of you to send with us your son and bands of chosen young men and hounds, that we may drive the boar out of the land." That was what they asked. But Croesus, being mindful of the dream, spoke to them thus: "As to my son, speak of him no more. I will not send him with you. He is but newly married, and that is all his present care. But for the chosen Lydians and all the hunt establishment, that I will send with you and straitly order those who go to show the utmost zeal in helping you drive the beast out of the land."

37. Those were his words, and the Mysians were content with them. But just then there came in the son of Croesus, having heard what the Mysians requested. When Croesus refused to send the boy with them, he said to him: "Father, before this, the fairest and noblest achievements of our family were going to wars and to hunts and finding renown there. Now you have debarred me from both, though I am sure you cannot detect in me either cowardice or want of spirit. With what eyes can I show myself, going to and from the marketplace? What kind of man will I appear to be to my fellow

countrymen? What to my newly married wife? What sort of man will she think she is living with? Either let me go to the hunt, or let your words convince me that this action of yours is for the best."

38. Croesus answered him: "My son, it is not cowardice or anything ugly that I have spied in you that makes me do this but because of a dream vision, which stood by me and declared to me that you would be short-lived. You will die, it said, by an iron spear. So because of this vision I hastened your marriage and will not send you on this present business, guarding how I may possibly steal you through, for my lifetime at least. For you are the only son I have; as to the other, since his hearing is utterly destroyed, I count him as being no son to me."

39. The young man answered and said: "Father, you are not at all to blame for guarding me, since you have seen such a vision. But it is just that I should tell you what you do not understand and how the dream has escaped you. You say the dream declares I shall die by an iron spearpoint. What hands has a boar? Where is there the iron spearpoint you fear? Now, if the dream had said I should die by a tooth or anything else that fits this beast, you might well do what you are doing. But no, it was a spearpoint. Since, then, our fight is not with men, let me go."

40. Croesus answered: "My son, somehow you overcome my judgment in your reading of the dream, and being so overcome I yield to you and will change my resolve. I will send you on this hunt."

41. Having said that, Croesus summoned to him the Phrygian, Adrastus; and when he came, he said to him: "Adrastus, I purified you when you were smitten by an ugly calamity; but I am not taunting you with that. I took you into my house and have supported you altogether. Now then, since you owe me something—I mean the returning of good for my good to you—I would like to send you as my son's guardian when he goes to this hunt, lest on the way some villains of robbers set upon you both, to your hurt. Besides, you yourself ought to go to where brave deeds will cover you with the brightness of glory. That is what comes to you from your own father, and, besides, you are yourself a strong young man."

42. Adrastus answered: "King, were it not that you asked me, I would not go to any such sport. It is not fit that someone loaded with

such a calamity as mine should go among his fellows who are fortunate. Nor have I any such wish myself, and on many grounds I would have refused. But since you are eager for it, and I should surely gratify you—for indeed I owe you good for good—I am ready to do this. As for your son, whom you so urgently would have me guard, you may look to see him come back scatheless as far as this guardian is concerned."

43. Those were the words with which he answered Croesus. Thereafter they went their way, equipped with the chosen bands of young men and the hounds. Coming to the mountain of Olympus, they searched for the beast, and, having found him, they ringed him round and shot javelins at him. Then the guest-friend, he that had been purified of his bloodguilt, that was called Adrastus, cast his spear at the boar and missed him, but struck the son of Croesus. So the son died, struck by the point of the spear, fulfilling the declaration of the dream. And one ran to Croesus to tell him what had happened. This man came to Sardis and told him of the fight and the fate of his son.

44. Croesus was in agony for his son's death and made the more of it because he that had killed him was the one whom he himself had purified of bloodguilt. In his great sorrow for what had befallen, he cried upon Zeus the Purifier, calling him to witness what he had suffered at the hands of his guest-friend.[20] He called also on Zeus of the Hearth and Zeus of Comradeship (it was the same god he named

20. The Greeks felt very strongly about the relationship between *xenoi*, or "guest-friends." This was a relationship entered into with a person of another country (*xenos* means "stranger" or "foreigner" as well as "guest-friend"), usually after an encounter as guest or host. Ideally, the two divided a bone, and each kept his part. The original pair of friends or their descendants matched these tokens (*symbola*, "things united") to verify the truth and meaning of the experience they shared. The alienness of the guest-friend was overcome by emotion or by the feeling of obligation. To betray a *xenos*—for example, to surrender him to enemies or pursuers—was a vile act. Indeed, the *xenos* stood under the protection of Zeus Xenios, god of hospitality and protector of strangers and suppliants.

Guest-friendship could also bind two countries. Such is the situation in chapter 22, above, where Alyattes and Thrasybulus become *xenoi* as heads of state rather than as individuals, and in chapter 27, where Croesus enters into guest-friendship with the Ionian islanders.

Finally, in foreign countries a national of another country usually had the protection of a *proxenos*, which means "one who stands in the stead of a *xenos*."

as all of these): of the Hearth, because he had received this friend into his house and so had unknowingly given food to his son's slayer, and as god of Comradeship because, having sent him to be the boy's guard, he had found him his worst enemy.

45. After that, there came the Lydians, carrying the dead body, and behind the body followed the slayer. He came and stood in front of the body and surrendered himself to Croesus, stretching out his hands and bidding him cut his throat over the corpse. He spoke of his own former calamity and of how, on top of that, he had destroyed his purifier and should surely live no more. Now Croesus, when he heard this, took pity on Adrastus, although he was in such calamity of his own, and said to him: "Sir, from you I have all justice, since you render sentence of death upon yourself. But you are not the cause of my misfortune, save insofar as you unwittingly did the deed. Some god is the cause, who long ago predicted to me what should be." So Croesus buried his son as was right. But Adrastus, the son of Gordias, the son of Midas, he who was the slayer of his own brother and had become the slayer of his purifier, who was, moreover, aware within himself that he was of all men he had ever known the heaviest-stricken by calamity, when there was a silence about the tomb and none was there, cut his throat over the grave.

46. For two years, then, Croesus sat in deep mourning for his son. But after that it was the loss of sovereignty by Astyages, son of Cyaxares, at the hands of Cyrus, son of Cambyses, that put him from his grief—that and the growth of the power of the Persians; and he began to reflect how, if he could at all, he might forestall this increase in power before the Persians had grown really great. After he had framed this thought, he at once made trial of oracles, both those in Greece and those in Libya, sending various messengers, these to Delphi, those to Abae in Phocis, and others still to Dodona. There were some, too, sent to Amphiaraus and Trophonius and some to Branchidae, in the country of Miletus. Such were the Greek oracles that Croesus sent to consult; but to Libya also he sent messengers, to inquire of Ammon. His several sendings were to find out what it was the oracles knew, so that, if they should be found to know the truth of what he asked them, he might then send to them a second time and inquire whether he should make war upon the Persians.

47. His instructions to his Lydian messengers were these: they should reckon the days from the one on which they left Sardis, and on the hundredth day they should consult the oracle and ask what it was at that moment that Croesus, king of Lydia, son of Alyattes, was doing. What each of the oracles gave as its prophetic answer they were to write down and bring it back to him. Now there is no report by anyone of the answers given by the rest of the oracles, but the moment the Lydians entered the great hall at Delphi to make their consultation of the god, and asked their question as they had been instructed, the Pythia spoke as follows, in hexameter verse:

Number of sand grains I know, and also the measures of
    ocean;
I understand him that is dumb and can hearken to the
    voiceless.
A smell steals over my senses, the smell of a hard-shelled
    tortoise,
seethed in bronze with the meat of lambs, mingled together;
bronze is the base beneath, and bronze the vestment upon it.

48. This is what the Pythia gave as her answer, and the messengers, having written it down, departed and got them gone to Sardis. Then, as the various messengers who were sent round came in, bearing their oracles, Croesus unfolded each message and looked over what had been written down. Not one of them satisfied him. But the moment he heard the one that came from Delphi, he straightway did obeisance and acknowledged it with a prayer; he was convinced that only the oracle at Delphi *was* an oracle, because it had found out what he had been doing. For when he had sent his messengers to the oracles, he carefully kept track of the due day and contrived the following (setting his wits on something that was impossible to discover or to guess): he chopped up a tortoise and some lamb's meat and boiled them together in a bronze cauldron and put a bronze lid on it.

49. That, then, was the oracle that Delphi gave to Croesus. What answer the oracle of Amphiaraus gave to the Lydians when they performed the customary rites at his shrine, I cannot say, for there is no record of it—only that here, too, Croesus held that he had had a true oracle.

50. After that, Croesus set about propitiating the god at Delphi with great sacrifices; in all, of sacrificial animals he offered up three thousand of each kind, and couches overlaid with gold and silver, and golden goblets and purple cloaks and chitons—he made a great heap of all these and burned them, expecting that thereby he would be likelier to win the favor of the god; besides this, he bade all the Lydians sacrifice to the god whatever each could. When the sacrifice was over, he melted down a vast deal of gold and made out of it ingots, on the long side six palms' length, on the short side three, and in height one palm.[21] The number of these ingots was one hundred seventeen, of which four were of refined gold, each weighing two and a half talents; the rest were of white gold,[22] and each weighed two talents. He had made for him also an image of a lion, of refined gold, which weighed ten talents. This lion, when the temple at Delphi burned down, fell from the ingots on which it stood and now lies in the treasure house of the Corinthians; it now weighs only six and a half talents, for three and a half talents melted off it.

51. When Croesus had completed all these things, he sent them off to Delphi and other things with them: two immensely great mixing bowls, of gold and of silver, whereof the golden one stood to the right as you enter the temple, the silver one to the left. These also were moved about the time of the temple's burning. The gold one now rests in the treasure house of the people of Clazomenae, and it weighs eight and a half talents and twelve minae. The silver one is in the corner of the forecourt of the temple; it can hold six hundred amphorae and is used as a mixing bowl by the Delphians at the Theophania.[23] The Delphians say that it is the work of Theodorus of Samos, and I think it is; certainly it is not an everyday work of art. Croesus also sent four silver jars, which stand in the treasure house

21. A "palm" is four fingers' breadth, and the commentators say that it was taken as some four inches, exactly as "hand" is used in measuring horses today, for the "hand" is also four inches.

22. I.e., of gold alloyed with silver.

23. An amphora was a ceramic jar for storing liquids—here, wine. The Greeks did not drink their wine straight; hence the mixing bowl (kratēr), in which water and wine were blended. Since the amphora as a term of liquid measure is nine gallons, the bowl that Croesus sent to Delphi was indeed "immensely great." The Theophania was the festival at Delphi, held in the spring, to celebrate the reappearance of the sun god, Apollo.

of the Corinthians, and he dedicated as well two sprinkling bowls, one of gold and one of silver. On the gold one is an inscription where the Lacedaemonians say that it is their dedicatory offering. But they lie; this, too, is the offering of Croesus, and it was one of the Delphians who put that inscription on it because he wanted to win the favor of the Lacedaemonians; I know his name but will not mention it. However, there is a statue of a boy, the water running through his hand, which is a gift of the Lacedaemonians, but neither of the sprinklers is. There were many other unsigned gifts that Croesus sent with these, including certain circular silver castings. There was also the image of a woman three cubits high, made of gold; the Delphians say it is the likeness of her that was Croesus' baker. And, in addition to all these, Croesus dedicated the necklaces from his wife's neck, and her girdles.

52. These are what Croesus sent to Delphi; but to Amphiaraus, because he knew his virtue and what happened him, he made a dedication of a shield altogether of gold, and a spear of solid gold, the shaft and point alike made of gold. And till my day these were both still deposited at Thebes, in the Theban temple of Ismenian Apollo.

53. On those of the Lydians who were to bring these gifts to the shrines Croesus laid command that they should ask the oracles: "Shall Croesus make war on the Persians, and shall he take to himself any allied force?" When the Lydians came to where they were sent and dedicated the offerings, they consulted the oracles, saying: "Croesus, king of the Lydians and of other nations, inasmuch as he has come to think that these are the only oracles among mankind, has sent to you gifts worthy of your discoveries; so now it is you he asks if he should make war upon the Persians and if he should take to himself any allied force." That was their question; and the judgment of both oracles came out the same, declaring to Croesus that if he made war on the Persians he would destroy a mighty empire; and they advised him to find out which were the most powerful of the Greek peoples and make them his friends.

54. When Croesus heard the answers that were returned to him from the god, he was exceedingly pleased at the oracles, expecting of a certainty that he would destroy the kingdom of Cyrus; and he sent to Delphi and paid a fee to the Delphians at two gold staters a man (having found out their number by inquiry). The Delphians in re-

turn gave Croesus and the Lydians the right of primacy of consultation of the oracle, remission of all charges, and the best seats at the
festivals; and, moreover, anyone of the Lydians who chose to might
become a Delphic citizen for all time to come.

55. So Croesus, having paid this fee to the Delphians, consulted
them a third time; for since he had found very truth in the oracle, he
was for using it to the fullest. His consultation was now the question:
Would his monarchy last long? Whereupon the Pythia gave the following answer:

> Whenever a mule shall become sovereign king of the
>   Medians,
> then, Lydian Delicate-Foot, flee by the stone-strewn Hermus,
> flee, and think not to stand fast, nor shame to be chicken-
>   hearted.

56. When these words came to Croesus, he was most delighted
of all; for he thought that a mule would surely never become king of
the Medians instead of a man, and so neither he himself nor his issue
would ever be deprived of the power. After that he took thought and
inquired who were the most powerful of the Greeks that he should
win, besides, to be his friends. And in his inquiry he found out that
the Lacedaemonians and the Athenians were preeminent, the
Lacedaemonians of the Doric race, the Athenians of the Ionic. For
these had been the outstanding races from the olden time, the one
Pelasgian and the other Hellenic. The Pelasgian has never yet
moved out of its land, but the Hellenic has wandered exceedingly.
For in the time of King Deucalion the Hellenes inhabited the land of
Phthia, and in that of King Dorus, son of Hellen, they lived beneath
Ossa and Olympus in what was then called Histiaean country; they
were driven from there by the Cadmeans and then lived in Pindus,
in the land called Macednus. Then again they resettled to Dryopis,
and from Dryopis, you see, they came to the Peloponnesus and were
called Dorians.

57. But what language the Pelasgians spoke I cannot say exactly.
However, if I should speak on the evidence of those who are still
Pelasgians and live in the city of Creston above the Etruscans, and
who were once boundary neighbors of those now called Dorians but
who at that time still lived in what is now called Thessaliotis, and

from the evidence of the Pelasgians who once inhabited Placia and
Scylace on the Hellespont, who were fellow dwellers[24] with the
Athenians, and from the evidence of the other small Pelasgian
towns that later changed their names: I say that—if I should speak
on the evidence of all this—the Pelasgians originally spoke a non-
Greek language.[25] If all this stock was truly Pelasgian, the Attic race,
being itself Pelasgian, must also have changed its language when it
became one with the Greeks [Hellenes].[26] For the people of Creston
do not have a common language with any of their neighbors, nor do
the people of Placia either; yet these two peoples share a language. It
is clear, therefore, that they are retaining a fashion of speech that
they brought with them when they moved into these parts.

58. But the Greek stock, since ever it was, has always used the
Greek language, in my judgment. But though it was weak when it
split off from the Pelasgians, it has grown from something small to be
a multitude of peoples by the accretion chiefly of the Pelasgians but
of many other barbarian peoples as well. But before that, it seems to
me, the Pelasgian people, so long as it spoke a language other than
Greek, never grew great anywhere.[27]

59. Of these two peoples, then, the Attic, as Croesus learned,
was being held subject and split up by Pisistratus, the son of Hippocrates, this Pisistratus being now sovereign lord of Athens. For when
his father, Hippocrates, was but a private person and watched the

24. A term for a people who voluntarily or otherwise joined with another
people in settling a region or city. What Herodotus means here is that, in the
earliest times, there were Pelasgians along with Athenians in Attica.
25. "Non-Greek" translates barbaros, as in chapter 4, above.
26. This is all rather confusing. Clearly Herodotus is saying something arresting and, I think, not very palatable to his hearers. He apparently accepts a
common belief that the earliest stock (perhaps in all Greece) were "Pelasgians."
(They are referred to in Homer [Iliad 10.429; Odyssey 19.177] as "divine Pelasgians.") Herodotus then claims they were synoecs ("fellow dwellers," as in
note 24) with the Athenians, since they were there originally. What is curious,
however, is that he now says that the Attic race was Pelasgian, whereas a few
lines earlier he had said that the Pelasgians were only part of the Athenian community—the prehistoric part.
27. Herodotus uses the same word here—barbaros—for both the people and
the language—i.e., other-than-Greek language. He is quite explicit that it is
not any ethnicity that made for the significant difference in the growth and success but the use of Greek.

Olympic games, a great wonder befell him. When he had sacrificed and the jars were standing there, full of meat and water, they bubbled of themselves, without fire, and overflowed. Chilon the Lacedaemonian, who chanced to be there and who saw the wonder, gave counsel to Hippocrates: "First and best," said he, "take no wife to your house who can bear children; or, if you have one, as second best, send her away; and if you have a son by her, disown him." This was Chilon's advice to Hippocrates, but Hippocrates would have none of it. After that, Pisistratus was born to him. There was then among the Athenians a civil war between the faction of the Men of the Coast and those of the Plain. Megacles, son of Alcmaeon, was leader of the Coast, and, of those of the Plain, Lycurgus, son of Aristolaïdes. Now Pisistratus, laying his plans for the sovereignty, gathered yet a third faction. He assembled factionaries, in name as champion of the Hill folk, and played the following trick. He wounded himself and his team of mules and drove his carriage into the marketplace as though he had just escaped his enemies, who indeed (he said) would have made away with him as he drove into the country; so he besought the commonalty for a guard, he having formerly won high repute when he was their general against the Megarians and captured Nisaea and achieved many other great deeds as well. The people of Athens were deceived and chose some of the citizens and gave them to Pisistratus; yet these men did not become spear-bearers of Pisistratus, but club-bearers, for they attended on him carrying wooden maces. These, joining Pisistratus in a revolution, seized the Acropolis. So Pisistratus took over the power in Athens;[28] yet he in no way deranged the existing magistracies or the ordinances but governed the city well and truly according to the laws that were established.

60. But a short time after this, those who were factionaries of Megacles and those of Lycurgus made common cause and drove Pisistratus out. That was how Pisistratus took possession of Athens the *first* time and established his sovereignty there but had not

28. Pisistratus' first coup occurred in 560, and he apparently remained in power for only a year. The dates of the two exiles are controversial. According to How and Wells, his second coup occurred in 550, his second exile began in 549, and his third period of rule lasted from 539 until his death in 527. Others give 556–546 as the dates of the second exile.

rooted it firmly and so lost it. Now those who had, together, expelled him fell out anew among themselves, and Megacles, being hard put to it by the strife of the factions, sent a proposition to Pisistratus: would he be inclined to have Megacles' daughter in marriage in return for the sovereignty? Pisistratus accepted his offer and agreed on the terms, and then, in order to bring about the restoration, they contrived between them by far the most simple-minded thing, in my judgment, that has ever been; for the Greek stock from the most ancient times has been distinguished from the barbarians for its cleverness and for being free from such silly simple-mindedness, and, of the Greeks, the Athenians were reputed to be the very first in intelligence; yet these men perpetrated the following trick on the Athenians. There was in the deme of Paeania a woman called Phya, and in stature she was but three fingers short of four cubits, and beautiful besides.[29] They fitted her with full armor, put her on a chariot, arranged her pose so that she would appear at her most striking, and drove her into the city. They had sent heralds to run ahead of them, and these, when they arrived, spoke as they had been ordered: "Men of Athens, receive with good will Pisistratus, whom Athena herself, having honored him above all mankind, is bringing back from exile to her own Acropolis." So the heralds went about, saying these things, and the word immediately spread through the demes that Athena was bringing Pisistratus back. The people in the city believed that this woman was the goddess herself and offered prayers to her, for all that she was only human, and they welcomed Pisistratus.

61. In the way described, Pisistratus recovered his sovereignty, and, according to the compact he had made with Megacles, he married his daughter. But inasmuch as he already had children who were young men, and because the Alcmaeonidae were under a curse,[30] he did not want to have children by his newly wedded wife; and so he lay with her, but not after the customary manner. The wife concealed this at first, but then, perhaps under questioning, perhaps not, she told her mother, and the mother told her husband. Mega-

29. A deme is, in a general sense, a "district" in Attica. Phya was roughly five feet, ten inches, tall.

30. Megacles came from the family of the Alcmaeonidae, who were under a curse for having murdered suppliants within a temple.

cles was exceedingly angry and made up his quarrel with the other factionaries. Pisistratus, learning of what was doing against himself, got out of the country at once, and, coming to Eretria, he took counsel with his children. The judgment of Hippias prevailed, that they should win back the sovereignty, and they thereupon gathered donations from whatever cities owed them any obligation. Though there were many who furnished large sums, the Thebans exceeded all in their giving of money. Afterwards, not to make a long story of it, there was an interval, and they made everything ready for the restoration. For Argive mercenaries came from the Peloponnesus, and a man from Naxos, whose name was Lygdamis, came as a volunteer and displayed the greatest zeal in collecting money and men.

62. They made Eretria their base and, after ten years, came home from there, and the first place in Attica they took and held was Marathon. There they camped; and there came to them factionaries from the city,[31] and there was an influx, too, from the country villages, of people to whom the rule of one man was more welcome than freedom. These then assembled there; but the Athenians in the city paid no heed as long as Pisistratus was gathering money or even afterwards, when he had seized Marathon. But when they learned that he was marching from Marathon on the city, then and only then they sallied out against him and advanced with all their forces to confront the party of the restoration. Pisistratus' army set out from Marathon and came toward the city and made contact with the enemy at the temple of Pallenian Athena. There they encamped over against them. Then one Amphilytus, the Acarnanian—who was a soothsayer—was by god's guidance thereby. This man approached Pisistratus and delivered the following oracle in hexameter verse:

The cast has been thrown indeed, and the net has been truly
    outstretched;
swoop, swoop will the tunny-fish through the moon-lighted
    night.

63. So he spoke, being inspired, and Pisistratus received the oracle and said, "I welcome it," and led his army on. The Athenians of the city had at the moment gone to their breakfast, and after breakfast some of them went to play dice and others to sleep. The

31. Athens. (The "factionaries" here are the partisans of Pisistratus.)

followers of Pisistratus charged the Athenians and routed them. As they fled, Pisistratus employed an exceedingly clever device so that the Athenians should not rally again but remain scattered. He mounted his sons on horses and sent them on ahead, and to those of the fugitives they overtook they told what Pisistratus told them to tell, which was that each one of them should go to his own home and be of good cheer.

64. The Athenians obeyed them and so, for the *third* time, Pisistratus took Athens; and this time he rooted his power securely, with many mercenaries and revenues, drawn both from the people on the spot and from the districts about the river Strymon. Of the Athenians who had stood firm and had not fled immediately, he took their children as hostages and established them in Naxos. (Pisistratus had also captured this place and entrusted it to Lygdamis.) Besides, as a result of some oracles, he purified the island of Delos, and the manner of his purification was the following: as far as the view from the temple extended, from all that place he dug up the dead bodies and transferred them to another part of Delos. So Pisistratus became sovereign of Athens; and, of the Athenians, some had fallen in the fight, and some fled from their native land, along with the Alcmaeonidae themselves.

65. Such, then, was the condition of Athens as Croesus heard of it; but of the Lacedaemonians something else: that they had escaped out of great troubles and that, at this moment, they had proved themselves masters of the people of Tegea in a war.[32] For when Leon and Hegesicles were kings at Sparta, the Lacedaemonians, for all that they were successful in other wars, whenever they encountered the people of Tegea would always fail. Moreover, before this the Spartans had been, in respect of the laws, the very worst of all the Greeks, one might say, and in their dealings with others, and also among themselves, the least free in communication. But then they changed over toward good laws, and this is how it happened. There was one Lycurgus, a Spartiate and a notable man, who went to Delphi to the oracle; and as soon as he entered the temple hall, the Pythia immediately spoke as follows:

> Is it you, Lycurgus, that comes to my rich temple? Lycurgus,
> dear to Zeus and to all that hold the halls of Olympus?

32. The dates of Sparta's war with Tegea are 560–550.

> I ask myself whether, in prophecy, as a god or a man I shall
>   hail you.
> Nay, but 'tis rather a god that I see in you, Lycurgus.

There are some, too, who declare that, in addition, the Pythia dictated to him the present constitution of Sparta; but what the Lacedaemonians themselves say is that Lycurgus brought this constitution from Crete when his nephew, Leobotes, was king at Sparta and Lycurgus became his guardian. For as soon as he took over the guardianship, he changed all the laws and took care that the new rules should not be transgressed. And afterwards it was Lycurgus who made all the institutions about war, the sworn companies, the regiments of thirty, and the communal meals, and, besides these, the ephors and the council of elders.

66. So they changed, and toward good laws, and when Lycurgus died, they erected a statue to him and now do him great reverence. And inasmuch as theirs was a good country and a populous, they soon grew and flourished, and it was no longer enough for them to keep at peace; they had come to despise the Arcadians, as being themselves the stronger, and so they were for consulting Delphi as to winning all of Arcadia. Whereupon the Pythia prophesied to them thus:

> You ask Arcadia of me; 'tis a great thing; I'll not give it.
> Many there are in Arcadia, many men, eaters of acorns,
> who will prevent you. Still, it is not I that begrudge you.
> Tegea will I give you, to beat with your feet in dancing,
> and with a rope to measure, to your fill, her beautiful
>   plainland.

When the Lacedaemonians heard this answer, they kept their hands off the rest of the Arcadians but made their assault on Tegea, carrying fetters along with them, trusting in that false-coin oracle that they would enslave Tegea. But they were worsted in their attack; and those of them who were taken prisoner worked the plain of Tegea wearing the fetters they had brought with them and measuring the land with a rope. And those fetters wherewith they were bound were still in my day preserved in Tegea and hung round the shrine of Athena Alea.

67. So in all that former war the Lacedaemonians had steadily wrestled in vain against the people of Tegea; but in the time of

thought to what the man had said, compared it with the oracle and judged that this must be Orestes; for in his comparison he discovered that the bellows of the smith before his eyes must be the two blasts of wind, and the anvil and the hammer were the blow and counterblow, and the iron being welded on iron was the evil laid upon evil, the image being that it was to man's mischief that iron was invented. So he compared it, and he went away to Sparta and told the whole business to the Lacedaemonians. They made a pretense of bringing a charge against him and banishing him. So he came to Tegea and spoke of his personal misfortune to the smith and tried to rent the courtyard of him, but the smith would not; at last, however, the smith was overpersuaded, and Lichas settled in to live there, and he dug up the grave and collected the bones, and away he went, bringing them with him to Sparta. And from that time, whenever the two peoples made trial of one another in war, the Lacedaemonians had much the better of it, and indeed, by now, the most of the Peloponnesus was subject to them.

69. All of this, then, Croesus learned, and he sent messengers to Sparta with gifts, to ask for an alliance; and he himself instructed them what to say. The messengers came and said, "Croesus, king of the Lydians and other nations, sent us. What he says is: 'Men of Lacedaemon, the god gave me his oracle that I should win to myself, as a friend, the Greek; now as I understand that you are the chief power in Greece, I invite you, according to the oracle; and I wish to be your friend and ally, without fraud or deceit.'" This was the invitation that Croesus delivered through his messengers. The Lacedaemonians, who had already heard of the oracle that had been given to Croesus, were very glad at the coming of the Lydians, and they made a sworn compact with him for guest-friendship and alliance. Indeed, certain kindnesses done them before this by Croesus bound them to him already. For the Lacedaemonians had sent to Sardis to buy gold there, intending to use it for the statue of Apollo that has now been set up in Thornax in Laconia; but when they offered to buy the gold, Croesus gave it to them as a free gift.

70. Because of that, and because he had given them precedence, in his choice for friendship, over all the rest of the Greeks, the Lacedaemonians accepted the alliance. So when he made the offer, they were ready; and, moreover, they made a bronze mixing bowl,

filling it on the outside, around the rim, with little figures (the mixing bowl itself was of a capacity of three hundred amphorae) and sent it on its way to Croesus, wishing to match Croesus' gift to them with one of their own to him. But this mixing bowl never did reach Sardis, for which two reasons are given. The Lacedaemonians say that when, in its transport toward Sardis, it came near Samos, the Samians found out about it, sailed out with their long ships, and captured it; but the Samians themselves say that the Lacedaemonians who were bringing it came too late, heard that Sardis and Croesus had been captured, and sold the mixing bowl in Samos, and that some private persons bought it and dedicated it in the temple of Hera. And probably also those who sold it, when they arrived in Sparta, *would* say that it had been taken from them by the Samians. That, then, is the story of the bowl.

71. Croesus missed the meaning of the oracle and so made the campaign into Cappadocia, being convinced that he would destroy Cyrus and the power of the Persians. While he was making his preparations, one of the Lydians gave him some advice. This man had before been thought wise, but from this present counsel of his he won a great name among the Lydians. He was called Sandanis, and what he said was this: "My lord, you are making ready to campaign against men of a sort that wear leather—leather breeches and the rest of their clothing, too, made of leather—and who eat not what they want but what they have, for the country they live in is full of rocks. Besides, they use no wine, but are water-drinkers, have no figs to nibble on, nor any other good thing. Now, sir, if you conquer, what will you take from them—since they have nothing? But if you are the one who is conquered, note how many good things you will lose. For once they have tasted of *our* good things, they will cling to them and will not be cast off. For my part, I give my thanks to the gods, who have not put it into the Persians' heads to make war upon Lydia." This is what he said, but he did not convince Croesus; indeed, the Persians before they conquered the Lydians had nothing of delicate luxury nor any good thing at all.

72. The Cappadocians are called Syrians by the Greeks. These Syrians were, before they were ruled by Persians, the subjects of the Medes and were at this time the subjects of Cyrus. For the dividing boundary of the Median and Lydian empires was the river Halys,

which flows from the Armenian mountains through Cilicia and afterwards flows with the Matieni on the right and Phrygians on the left. When it has passed their territories, it flows north and divides the Syrian Cappadocians on the right from the Paphlagonians on the left. So the Halys cuts off almost the whole of the lower part of Asia, from the Mediterranean opposite Cyprus to the Euxine. This is the neck of all this land, and it is, in length of journeying, five days of travel for an active man.[33]

73. So Croesus advanced into Cappadocia, for these reasons: because he longed for additional territory to that which was his portion but, mostly, because he trusted in the oracle and because he wanted to take vengeance on Cyrus, son of Cambyses, on behalf of Astyages, son of Cyaxares, who was his, Croesus', brother-in-law and king of Media and had been subjugated by Cyrus. Croesus had become brother-in-law to Astyages in the following way. A troop of nomad Scythians, having split off from the rest, stole away into Media. At that time the ruler of Media was Cyaxares, son of Phraortes, son of Deioces. These Scythians King Cyaxares at first treated well, as being his suppliants—so well, indeed, that he entrusted to them some boys, to learn their language and their mastery of the bow. As time went on, the Scythians went constantly to the hunt for the king and constantly brought something home. But one day it so fell out that they took nothing. When they returned empty-handed, Cyaxares, who, as he proved herein, was extreme in his temper, treated them very harshly—and shamefully as well. In so suffering from Cyaxares the Scythians thought they had suffered something that was a personal degradation, and they formed a plot, which was to chop up one of the boys who were their pupils and, having dressed him as they were wont to do their wild game, to bring it to Cyaxares as though it were indeed such and, after that, to betake themselves

33. The distance is 280 miles, seemingly a great deal too much for any man, active or otherwise. The Greek word that I have translated as "active" means "well-zoned" or "well-belted," and some editors suggest that it means "without encumbrance." The difficulty of the distance remains. There is a suggestion that there may be a mistake in the letters of the alphabet involved (the Greeks used letters for numbers, in rather complicated combinations), and a plausible emendation of the text would yield fifteen days instead of five. (The Euxine is the Black Sea.)

with all speed to the court of Alyattes, the son of Sadyattes, at Sardis. This is exactly what happened. Cyaxares and those who were dining with him tasted of this meat, and the Scythians, having done as they planned, became suppliants of Alyattes.

74. After this, inasmuch as Alyattes refused to give up the Scythians to Cyaxares when he demanded them, war broke out between the Lydians and the Medes and lasted for five years, and during this period sometimes the Medes won and sometimes the Lydians; there was also one night battle. As the war was proving to be a draw between the two peoples, in the sixth year it happened that during a fight, when the combatants were already closely engaged, suddenly day became night. The occurrence of this eclipse of daylight had already been predicted to the Ionians by Thales of Miletus, and he had set as his limiting date the year in which the eclipse actually took place.[34] But the Lydians and the Medes, when they saw night instead of day before their eyes, gave over the fight, and both were more eager on their own behalf to make peace. Those who brought the two sides together were Syennesis the Cilician and Labynetus of Babylon. It was these who exerted themselves to bring about a sworn pact and an exchange of marriages; for their decision was that Alyattes should give his daughter, Aryenis, to Astyages, son of Cyaxares; without such strong ties, they said, agreements are not wont to be strong and to persist. These peoples make their sworn agreements as the Greeks do; and besides, when they cut the skin of their arms, they lick one another's blood.

75. This was the Astyages whom Cyrus had subjugated, and, although he was Cyrus' own grandfather on his mother's side, Cyrus held him in captivity on a charge that I shall declare later in my history. Croesus had this ground for blame against Cyrus when he consulted the oracle as to whether he should attack the Persians, and when that false-coin answer came his way, Croesus, supposing that it was truly in his favor, invaded Persian territory. When he came to the river Halys, he brought his army across—over existing bridges, in my opinion, though the general report of the Greeks is different. They say that Thales of Miletus brought the army across for him, and their story is this: Croesus was in perplexity as to how

34. This eclipse occurred on May 28, 585 B.C.

his army should cross the river, for (they *will* have it so) the bridges had *not* yet been built, and Thales was in Croesus' camp, and it was he who contrived that the river, which flowed on the left hand of the army, should flow on the right hand also. This (they say) is how he did it: he began by digging a deep ditch above the camp, and, making it moon-shaped, he led the stream away from its old course so that it would flow into the trench behind the army and, passing the camp, again issue into its old channel; as soon as it was split, the river would become fordable at both places. There are, indeed, still others who say that the old stream was entirely dried up. I personally do not accept this; for how, then, on their homeward course, did they cross it again?

76. Croesus, when he had crossed with his army, came in Cappadocian territory to what is called Pteria. Pteria is the strongest part of all that country and lies on a line with the city of Sinope, on the Euxine Sea.[35] There he encamped, destroying the farms of the Syrians, and he captured the city of the Pterians and made slaves of the people, and he captured all the neighboring towns; moreover, he drove the Syrians from their homes, though they had done him no manner of harm. Cyrus, on his side, gathered his own army and took on, as well, all the peoples who lived between him and Croesus, and he then confronted Croesus. (Before he set out to march at all, he sent heralds to the Ionians and tried to make them desert Croesus. But the Ionians would not listen to him.) So when Cyrus came and encamped over against Croesus, then and there in that land of Pteria they fought against one another with might and main. The battle was fierce, and many fell on both sides. At last they broke off, at the onset of night, without either having the victory; so hard did the two armies fight.

77. Now Croesus blamed the size of his army—and indeed, the army that had fought for him was far smaller than that of Cyrus—and, because it was the numbers he blamed, on the day following the battle, when Cyrus made no further attack, Croesus moved away to Sardis, intending to summon the Egyptians to help him in accordance with the sworn treaty he had made with Amasis, king of Egypt—a treaty he had made even before the one with the Lace-

---

35. "On a line with" is a rough approximation of our "longitude."

daemonians. He also sent for the Babylonians, since with them, too, he had made an alliance (the king of the Babylonians at the time being Labynetus), and he sent messages to the Lacedaemonians that they should be with him by a fixed date. His plan was that, when he had assembled all these and collected his own army, he would wait the winter out and, at the very beginning of spring, invade Persia. Such were his thoughts when he came to Sardis; and he sent off heralds, forewarning all that, in accordance with their alliance, they should assemble in Sardis by the fifth month from then. As for the army that he had on foot, which had fought the Persians, he dispersed the mercenary part altogether; for he never expected that Cyrus, after so equal an engagement as they had fought, would drive on to Sardis.

78. As Croesus thus reflected, lo! the whole of the outer part of his city was filled with snakes. When these appeared, the horses gave over their grazing on their pastures and came and ate up the snakes. To Croesus, seeing this, it seemed a portent—as indeed it was—and he sent straightway to the Telmessian diviners. The embassy arrived and learned from the Telmessians what the portent meant to signify, but matters did not so fall out that they could bring the message back to Croesus. For before they could sail back to Sardis, Croesus was captured. But this was the judgment that the Telmessians passed: that Croesus might look for a host, of alien speech, coming upon his land and that, when it came, it would overcome those who were native there; for, they said, "The serpent is a child of the land, and the horse an enemy and a newcomer." This was the answer given by the Telmessians to Croesus when he was already a prisoner, though when they gave it they had no knowledge of what had befallen Sardis or Croesus himself.

79. Now the moment Croesus moved away after the battle of Pteria, Cyrus, understanding very well that Croesus, once he had gone away, would disband his army, took counsel. What he found was that it would surely be to his advantage to march on Sardis as quickly as he might, before the power of the Lydians was rallied a second time. As he resolved the matter, so he put it into execution quickly; for he drove with his army into Lydia and came himself to Croesus as his own messenger. Croesus was in sore straits, as things had turned out so differently from what he had looked for; yet he led

his Lydians out to battle. There was at this time no people in all Asia who were braver or more valiant soldiers than the Lydians. Their fighting was from horseback, where they carried great lances, and they were themselves excellent horsemen.

80. So the two sides met in the plain, the great treeless plain in front of Sardis. Through it there are rivers flowing, among others the Hyllus, and these break together into the biggest of all, called the Hermus, which, flowing from the mountain sacred to Mother Din-dymene, issues into the sea at the city of Phocaea. Now when Cyrus saw the Lydians forming here for battle, because he was afraid of their cavalry he took the following measures on the suggestion of a man, Harpagus, who was a Mede. Cyrus had a number of camels that followed his army to transport the grain and the gear. All these he assembled, stripped them of their loads, and mounted men on them with gear appropriate to cavalrymen; and having so equipped them, he bade them charge Croesus' cavalry, in advance of the rest of the army. He ordered his infantry to follow the camels, and be-hind the infantry he stationed all his own cavalry. When they had all formed their ranks, he ordered his men to spare no Lydian and kill all before them, save only Croesus. Him they should not kill, even if he fought against them to resist capture. These were his in-structions; and he arranged his camels opposite the horse for this reason: the horse fears the camel and cannot abide the sight or the smell of it. Cyrus' stratagem was designed to render the cavalry useless to Croesus, and it was the cavalry by which the Lydian hoped to win glory. Indeed, as soon as the battle was joined, the very mo-ment the horses smelled the camels and saw them, they bolted back; and down went all the hopes for Croesus. Not that, for the rest, the Lydians proved cowards; for as soon as they saw how it was, they jumped down from their horses and joined battle with the Persians on foot. But at last, when very many had fallen on both sides, the Lydians were routed; and being penned within the city walls, they were beleaguered by the Persians.

81. So, then, the siege had set in. Croesus, thinking that it would last a long time, sent from his fortress other messengers to his allies. The former messengers had gone about to warn them to gather in Sardis after five months' space, but these went to request them to come with all possible speed to the help of Croesus, for he was already beleaguered.

82. Among the other allies, he sent, of course, to Lacedaemon. Now it happened that at this very time the Spartans themselves were engaged in a quarrel with the Argives about a place called Thyreae; Thyreae was a part of Argive territory that the Lacedaemonians had cut off and occupied. (At this time the land to the west, as far as Malea, both the mainland and Cythera and the rest of the islands, all belonged to the Argives.) The Argives came against the Spartans, in defense of their own territory as it was being cut off; but then the two sides came to an agreement that three hundred of each should fight and, whichever prevailed, theirs the country should be, the mass of each army to go away to their own land and not remain to watch as the champions fought, for fear that the armies, if present, and seeing their own side being defeated, might rally to their help. They made the agreement and went away, and the chosen champions on each side, being left behind, engaged. So they fought and, as they were so equally matched, there were left out of the six hundred only three—two on the Argive side, Alcenor and Chromios, and, of the Lacedaemonians, Othryades. These were the survivors at nightfall. The two Argives, assuming that they were the victors, made off to Argos; but the Lacedaemonian, Othryades, having despoiled the Argive dead and carried their arms into his own army's camp, stood at his station. Next day both sides came to find out the news. For a while each of the two parties claimed the victory, the one because more of their men had survived, the other claiming that their oppoents had left the field while their man had stood his ground and spoiled the enemy dead. Finally, from disputing, they fell to and fought. Though the losses on both sides were heavy, the Lacedaemonians won. (It is from this time that the Argives, who had formerly, of fixed custom, worn their hair long, now shaved their heads close and made a rule of it, with a curse to back it, that no Argive man should grow his hair long, and no woman among them wear gold, until they should recover Thyreae. The Lacedaemonians introduced a rule that was the contrary; for they, before this, had never worn their hair long, but after this they did so.) The story goes that the single survivor of the three hundred, Othryades, put to shame that he alone should come back to Sparta when all his comrades-at-arms had perished, made away with himself right there in Thyreae.

83. Such was the condition of the Spartans when the envoy from

Sardis arrived to beg them to send help to the beleaguered Croesus. Despite their own difficulties, the Spartans, on hearing the herald, were minded to help. But hardly were their preparations made and their ships ready when there came another message, that the Lydian fortress had fallen and that Croesus himself was made prisoner. So the Spartans, though they were very sorry for it, gave over their aid.

84. This is how Sardis was captured. When the fourteenth day came upon the beleaguered Croesus, Cyrus sent horsemen throughout his army and proclaimed the gifts he would give to the first man who should mount the wall of the fortress. After this the army made trial of it but had no success. When all the rest had given over the attempt, a Mardian named Hyroeades tried the approach at that part of the citadel where no guard had been set; for there was no fear that the citadel would be taken at this point, as the approach was sheer and impossible of attack. This was the only place where the former king of Sardis, Meles, had not carried round the lion cub that his concubine had borne him. The Telmessians had given their judgment that, once the lion cub had been carried round the walls, Sardis would be impregnable. Meles carried the beast around the rest of the fortress, where it was assailable, but he neglected this place, as being too sheer and impossible of attack. This is the side of the city that faces Mount Tmolus. Now this Mardian, Hyroeades, on the day before had seen one of the Lydian soldiers come down this part of the acropolis after his helmet, which had rolled down from above, and he retrieved it. The Mardian noticed that and reflected on it. Then, at the same spot, he climbed up, and other Persians with him; and as more and more of them joined the others, Sardis was captured, like that, and the whole town sacked.

85. But as for Croesus himself, this is what happened. He had a son, of whom I have spoken before, who was in other respects a handsome lad but was dumb. In the days of his former well-being, Croesus had taken all measures on the boy's behalf and, besides his other care for him, he had sent to consult the oracle at Delphi concerning him. The Pythia answered as follows:

> Lydian by breed, king of many, still are you a great fool,
>   Croesus:
> Wish not to hear, in your halls, the voice so much prayed
>   for, the voice

Of your son as he speaks. Nay, for you, far better it were to
   go wanting;
For the first day he speaks it shall be a day of luckless
   destruction.

Now, when the fortress was being taken, there came upon Croesus, to kill him, one of the Persians who did not know him. Croesus
saw the man coming at him, but in his misfortune he was past car-
ing; it was all one to him that he should be stricken and die. But the
son who was dumb, when he saw the Persian approaching, his voice
broke from him through his fear and the disaster, and he called out,
"Sir, it is Croesus; do not kill him." This is the first time the boy
spoke, and directly after that he spoke all the rest of his life.

   86. So the Persians held Sardis and made Croesus their prisoner.
Fourteen years he had reigned[36] and fourteen days been besieged,
and he had indeed fulfilled the oracle, in that he had destroyed a
mighty empire—his own. The Persians took him and brought him
to Cyrus. Cyrus heaped a huge pyre and set Croesus on the top of it,
fettered in chains, with fourteen of the children of the Lydians along
with him. He had in his mind either to offer these firstfruits to some
god or other, or perhaps he wished to fulfill some vow he had made,
or perhaps even, since he had heard that Croesus was a god-fearing
man, he set him on the pyre to know whether some one of Those-
that-are-Divine[37] would rescue him from being burned alive. This,
anyway, they say, is what he did. Now as Croesus stood upon the
pyre, there came into his head, for all that he was in such calamity,
that word of Solon: "No one of them that are living is blessed." How
that word had been uttered with god to back it! As this came to him,
he heaved a great sigh and broke into lamentation. He had till then
held his peace a great while, but now three times he called out the
name "Solon!" Cyrus heard him and told his interpreters to ask

   36. 560–546 B.C.
   37. The Greek word *daimōn* is Herodotus' most general term for divine
power. It covers therefore both the single god (*theos*) and the impersonal force of
fate. The latter sense is usually expressed by the neuter plural of the adjective
daimonios, meaning "those things that are out of man's control." In Homer
daimōn is often used by a speaker to refer to some divine presence that he cannot
identify more certainly. Thus Herodotus in this chapter is saying that Cyrus
wanted to see whether one of the divine beings (who knew which one!) would
rescue Croesus.

Croesus whom it was he called on. They approached Croesus and asked. For a while Croesus was silent, but they forced him to answer, and he said, "One whom I would have every ruler meet; more than a fortune I would have it so." His answer was so obscure that they asked him again what it was he said. And, as they were instant and bore hard on him, he told the story: of how at the beginning there had come to him this Solon, the Athenian, and how he had surveyed all the blessings that he, Croesus, had and had made little of them all ("Thus and thus it was," he said), and how it had all befallen himself as the man had said. "But it concerns me," said Croesus, "no more than every man in the world, and especially those who are in their own eyes blessed." So Croesus told his story, and, as he did so, the fire had been lit and the edges of it were burning. Cyrus listened to the interpreters telling him what Croesus said, and his mind was changed; he recognized that he too was a man and that it was another man, no whit less in great fortune than himself, whom he was giving alive to the fire; besides, he was afraid of what he must pay in retribution and thought again how nothing of all that is in the world of men could be secure. He bade them quench the fire, even as it burned, with all the speed they could, and bring Croesus down and those that were with him. The men tried to do so but could gain no mastery of the fire.

87. Then, as the Lydians tell the story, Croesus became aware of Cyrus' change of heart, and when he saw every man striving to quench the fire and no longer able to do so, he called in a loud voice to Apollo, bidding him, if ever he had received any gift of his that was pleasing, to come to his rescue and deliver him out of his present evil. With tears he called upon the god, and suddenly, out of a clear sky, with no wind in it, there gathered clouds, and a storm burst and a violent rain with it; and the fire was quenched. So Cyrus knew for certain that Croesus was loved of god and a good man, and he had him down from the pyre and asked him, "Croesus, who of all mankind persuaded you to make war upon my land and to be my enemy rather than my friend?" The other answered, "My lord, I myself did— to your good fortune and to my ill fortune; but the cause of it was the god of the Greeks, who incited me to fight. For no one is, of himself, so foolish as to prefer war to peace; in the one, children bury their fathers; in the other, fathers their children. I suppose, however, it was the will of the gods that this should have happened so."

88. These were his words, and Cyrus freed him of his chains and set him beside himself and took much thought for him; as he gazed, he admired him, and so did all the courtiers. But Croesus was in the grip of his own thoughts and was silent. After a while he turned and, as he saw the Persians ravaging the city of the Lydians, he said: "My lord, shall I tell you a thought I have just had, or should I, for now, hold my peace?" Cyrus bade him say cheerfully whatever he liked. At which Croesus asked this question: "What is this great concourse of people doing with such eagerness?" "Plundering and sacking your city and your possessions," said Cyrus. But Croesus answered, "It is no city of mine, and there is no property of mine for them to ravage. I have no share at all any more in any of these things. What they are sacking and pillaging is yours."

89. What Croesus said made an impression on Cyrus, and bidding the rest of the people about him to be gone, he asked Croesus what it was that was so particular that he saw being done there. Said Croesus: "Since the gods have given me to you as your slave, I think it right that, if I see somewhat further into any matter than the others, I should signify it to you. The Persians are by nature arrogant—and they are poor. If now you stand by and watch these men plunder and capture so much property, this is what you must look for from them: the one who wins most of the plunder you may expect next to see as a rebel against yourself. If what I say finds favor with you, do this: from among your own bodyguards take sentries and place them at all the gates. These shall take the stuff from all the men that are carrying it out, telling them that the property must be tithed—that one tenth of it must be dedicated to Zeus. Thus you will not be hated by them for taking away their property violently; they will confess that what you do is done justly and so give you willingly what you ask."

90. Cyrus was delighted at these words, for he thought it was good advice. After praising Croesus warmly and instructing his bodyguards to do what Croesus had suggested, he said to Croesus, "Croesus, since as man and king you are prepared to do so well, both in word and deed, ask of me whatever gift you please, to be yours at once." Croesus said, "Master mine, you will give me most pleasure if you suffer me to send these chains to that god of the Greeks whom I especially honored and to ask of him whether it is a rule with him to cheat those that do him good." Cyrus asked him what complaint

against the god lay behind the request, and Croesus repeated the story to him, of all his own intentions, and of the answers of the oracles, and chiefly of the dedicatory gifts, and how it was that, incited by the oracle, he had made war on Persia. As he told the tale, he came back again to his request that he might be given the chance to insult the god in this matter. At this Cyrus laughed and said, "Croesus, this you shall obtain of me, and anything else that at any time you shall need." When Croesus heard that, he sent some of his Lydians to Delphi and ordered them to set the fetters on the threshold of the temple there and ask the god if he were not ashamed of having incited Croesus by his oracles to make war on Persia with the story that he would destroy Cyrus' power. "Here," they should say, "are the firstfruits of that conquest," and at that should show the chains. That was to be their question of the god and, besides this, another: whether it was the rule for the Greek gods to be ungrateful.

91. It is said that when the Lydians came and said what they had been instructed, the Pythia answered as follows: "Fate that is decreed, no one can escape, not even a god. Croesus has paid for the offense of his ancestor in the fifth generation, who, being a bodyguard of the Heraclidae, following the lead of a treacherous woman, slew his master and took his honor, which in no way befit himself. Loxias[38] was eager that the destruction of Sardis should fall in the time of Croesus' children rather than in his own, but he proved unable to turn aside the Fates. Yet what little they allowed him, he accomplished and did Croesus service; for he postponed the capture of Sardis by three years. So let Croesus know that his fall is three years later than the destined moment. Secondly, the god came to his rescue when he was burning. As for the oracle that was given, Croesus does not rightly find fault. For the prophecy given by Loxias ran: if Croesus made war upon Persia, he would destroy a mighty empire. Now, in the face of that, if he was going to be well advised, he should have sent and inquired again, whether it was his own empire or that of Cyrus that was spoken of. But Croesus did not understand what was said, nor did he make question again, and so he has no one to blame but himself. Furthermore, when he put his last question to the god, and Loxias spoke of the mule, not even that did

38. Loxias is Apollo's title at Delphi.

Croesus comprehend. Truly, Cyrus was that mule. He was born of
two parents of different races, whereof his mother was of the higher,
his father of the lower, breed. For the mother was a Mede and Astyages' daughter, who was king of Media; but the father was a Persian
and a subject of the Medes, and, being in every way beneath her, he
cohabited with her that was his sovereign mistress." Such was the
answer that the Pythia gave to the Lydians, and they brought it back
to Sardis and told it to Croesus. When he heard it, he acknowledged
that the fault had been none of the god's but his own. Such is the
story of Croesus' empire and of the first conquest of Ionia.

92. There are many other dedications of Croesus throughout
Greece besides those of which I have spoken. In Thebes, in Boeotia,
there is a golden tripod, which he dedicated to Ismenian Apollo,
and in Ephesus there are cows, all of gold, and many of the pillars
there; and in the temple of Athena Pronaia at Delphi there is a great
shield of gold. These were still surviving till my time, but others
of the dedications had disappeared. There are also dedications of
Croesus at Branchidae in Miletus that are, as I learn, equal in weight
and alike to those at Delphi. Those at Delphi and those that he
dedicated at the temple of Amphiaraus were of his own estate and
firstfruits of what he received from his father's wealth. But the rest of
the dedications came from the property of one who was an enemy
and had led a faction against Croesus before he was yet a king, a
conspirator indeed, in the interest of Pantaleon, that this Pantaleon
might become king of Lydia instead of Croesus. Now Pantaleon was
the son of Alyattes, and Croesus was therefore his brother, though
not of the same mother; for Croesus was born to Alyattes of a Carian
woman, but Pantaleon of an Ionian. When his father gave Croesus
the rule and he had become master, Croesus killed the man who had
conspired against him by drawing him across a carding comb. As for
his estate, Croesus had already declared it sacred to the god, and
afterwards he dedicated it as I have said and in the places I have
said. That, then, is enough of Croesus' dedications.

93. Lydia does not have many marvelous things to write about in
comparison with other countries, except for the gold dust that is carried down from Mount Tmolus. But it has the greatest building there
is, except for those of Egypt and Babylon, and this is the tomb of
Croesus' father, Alyattes. The base of this is made of great stones,

but all the rest of the tomb is a mound of earth. And they that made it were the men of the marketplace and the handcraftsmen and the working whores. There were five marking stones, surviving till my time, on top of the tomb, and there, engraved on them, letters setting forth what each class had wrought; and when the calculations were made, it was clear that the greatest share of the work was done by the whores. All the daughters of the common people of Lydia practice as whores to collect dowries for themselves until, by doing so, they set up house with their man. So they give themselves in marriage with a dowry. The circumference of the tomb is six stades and two plethra, and the breadth is about thirteen plethra. Near the tomb there is a great lake, the waters of which, say the Lydians, are everlasting. It is called the Gygaean lake. This, then, is what this tomb is.

94. The Lydians have much the same usages as the Greeks, save for the prostitution of their daughters, but they are first of the men of whom we know to cut and use a currency of gold and of silver. They were also the first to become shopkeepers. The Lydians themselves say that the games now in practice among themselves and the Greeks were their special invention. They were invented among them, they say, at the time they also colonized Etruria—and this is how it was. In the time of King Atys, the son of Manes, there was a severe famine throughout all Lydia. The Lydians bore it at first with patience, but thereafter, when it did not cease, they sought for remedies; one man would devise this and another that. And it was thus, they say, and at this time, that the games of dice, and the bones, and the ball, and the varieties of all the other games were invented, save only for draughts; on the invention of draughts the Lydians make no claim. They made the discovery of games against the famine, say they. For they would play the whole of every other day that they might not seek for food in it, and then, the next day, they would give over their games and eat. So, according to the story, they managed to live for eighteen years. But when their troubles grew no less but became ever more violent, the king at last divided all the people of Lydia into two halves and cast lots, for the one half that should remain in the homeland and the other to emigrate. For the part that should draw the lot to remain, he appointed himself to be king; but for the one that should leave the country, he appointed

his son, whose name was Tyrrhenus. Now the part that was chosen by lot to leave the country came down to Smyrna and contrived boats for themselves, and into them they threw everything useful that would go aboard ship, and they sailed away in quest of a country and a livelihood. They passed many nations by, in their progress, and came to the Umbrians. There they established cities, and there they live till this day. From being called Lydians they changed their name: in honor of that son of their king who led them out, they called themselves, after him, Tyrrhenians.[39]

But as for the Lydians themselves, they, as I said, were enslaved by the Persians.

95. Our story must now go on to inquire who this Cyrus was who took the empire from Croesus and how it came about that the Persians became the leaders of all Asia. I will write my account according to the evidence of those Persians whose desire is not to make solemn miracles of all that concerns Cyrus but to tell the very truth. But I know three other ways to tell the story of Cyrus.

When the Assyrians had held sway over upper Asia for five hundred and twenty years,[40] the first to begin the revolt against them were the Medes: these, in fighting the Assyrians, proved themselves right good men, cast their slavery from them, and were free again. After them, other of the nations did the same as the Medes.

96. Now all of them on the mainland were free, but they relapsed into one-man rule, as I shall show. There was a man among the Medes, a clever man, whose name was Deioces, and he was the son of Phraortes. This Deioces had fallen in love with royal power, and this is what he did. At this time, the Medes lived in villages, and in the particular village of Deioces he had always been a man of note, and now he set himself to practice justice ever more and more keenly. There was at the time great lawlessness throughout Media, and Deioces did what he did because he knew that injustice is the great enemy of justice. The Medes in his own village, seeing the manner of the man's life, chose him to be a judge among them. And he, since it was power that he was courting, was always straight and just and, for being so, won no small praise from his fellow citizens—

39. I.e., Etruscans.
40. From 1229 to 709 B.C.

so much so, indeed, that the people in other villages learned that Deioces was the one man for judging according to the rule of right; these people had before met with unjust sentences, and when they heard the good news about Deioces they flocked to him to have their own cases decided by him; and at last they would entrust their suits to none but him.

97. As those who had recourse to him grew ever more in number (for they all heard that the cases he tried came out according to the truth of the facts), Deioces came to realize that now everything hung upon himself. Whereupon he refused to sit as judge any more and said that he would serve no longer. It did not profit him at all, he said, to decide cases for his neighbors all day long to the manifest neglect of his own affairs. So robbery and lawlessness grew even more in the villages than before. The Medes all came to a meeting place and conferred with one another on what they should do now. I suppose that those who spoke most were Deioces' friends. What they said was, "If we go on as we are going now, we will not be able to live in this country at all. Let us therefore set up a king over us. The country will then be well governed, and we shall betake ourselves to our own business and shall not be undone by lawlessness." These were the arguments with which they persuaded one another to be ruled by a king.

98. Then at once the question was proposed as to whom to make king. Deioces was so much in everyone's mouth, people both putting him forward and praising him, that all ended by agreeing that he should be their king. For his part, he bade them build him houses worthy of royalty and to strengthen him with a bodyguard. The Medes did all this. They built him great secure houses wheresoever in the country he indicated, and they gave him the privilege of selecting bodyguards for himself from all the people of Media. When he got the power, then, he compelled the Medes to make one fortress and, attending to this, to neglect the rest. Again, the Medes did as he told them; he had built for him those great strong walls that are now called Ecbatana, one circle of them inside the other. The building was so contrived that each circle of walls is higher than the next by the battlements only. The fact that the place chosen was itself a hill helps the design, but it was also much strengthened by contrivance. The circles of walls were, in all, seven, and within the

final circle are the royal palace and the treasuries. The longest wall is about the length of the wall that surrounds the city of Athens. The battlements of the first circle are white, the second black, the third scarlet, the fourth blue, the fifth orange. Thus the battlements of these five circles are painted with colors; but of the last two circles, the one had its battlements coated with silver, the other with gold.

99. These walls, then, Deioces built for himself and about his own palace, but the rest of the people he ordered to build houses outside the walls. When all was built, Deioces was the first who established this ceremony: that no one whatsoever should have admittance to the king, but that all should be transacted through messengers and that the king should be seen by none; moreover, to laugh or to spit in the royal presence was shameful for all alike. These solemnities he contrived about his own person so that those who were his equals and of the same age, brought up with him, and of descent as good, and as brave as he, might not, seeing him, be vexed and take to plotting against him but would judge him to be someone grown quite different—and all because they did not see him.

100. When he had ordered these matters and had strengthened himself in the royal power, he was very exact in his observance of justice. Men would write down their suits and send them in to him, and he would judge what was brought in and send the decisions out. Such were his arrangements with the lawsuits; but he had other matters of discipline in hand, too. As often as he heard of someone as a man of insolent violence, he would have him apprehended and do justice on him according to the merit of each offense; and his spies and eavesdroppers were everywhere throughout the land.

101. Deioces, then, united the Median nation, but this one only, and this he ruled.[41] The Median tribes are as follows: Busae, Parataceni, Struchates, Arizanti, Budii, Magi. That is all there is of them.

41. By this remark Herodotus is differentiating Deioces not only from his immediate successors but from the rest of the Eastern despots: Astyages, who extended the power of Media to conquer Persia but then fell victim to his Persian grandson, Cyrus; Cyrus, who, after a successful career of conquest, died trying to annex the Massagetae; Darius, in the same position with respect to the Scythians; and finally Xerxes, in the expedition to Greece. All exemplify the pattern of the monarch who cannot refrain from pushing his domains beyond

102. The son of Deioces was Phraortes, who took over the rule on Deioces' death, which happened after he had ruled for fifty-three years.[42] When Phraortes succeeded, it did not content him to rule the Medes only. He attacked the Persians. These were the first he set upon, and they were the first people whom he made subject to the Medes. Once he had these two peoples—and both of them strong— he began to subdue all Asia, going from people to people, until, in his campaigning, he came against the Assyrians, and especially those of the Assyrians who held Nineveh. These Assyrians had formerly ruled all of Asia but were now quite isolated, all their allies having dropped away from them. But in themselves they were as strong as ever, and when Phraortes fought them, he himself was killed, after a reign of twenty-two years, and also much of his army.

103. On the death of Phraortes, Cyaxares, the son of Phraortes, the son of Deioces, succeeded. He is said to have been a far better military man than his forebears. He was the first to organize the Asian army into regiments and the first to establish separately each unit of arms—as spear-bearers, archers, and cavalry. Before this they were all mixed up, pell-mell, together. It was Cyaxares who fought the Lydians when day turned into night upon their fighting, and it was Cyaxares who drew together under his own rule all Asia beyond the river Halys. Then, collecting all his subject peoples, he attacked Nineveh, and in vengeance for his father's defeat he wanted to destroy the city utterly. He had defeated the Assyrians in battle; but then, when he was beleaguering Nineveh, there came upon him a great host of Scythians, whose leader was their king, Madyes, the son of Protothyes. They had first expelled the Cimmerians from Europe, and it was in pursuit of the fleeing Cimmerians that the Scythians came into Median territory.

104. From the Maeotic lake[43] to the river Phasis and the territory

---

their natural or inherited boundaries and finally, in his last and usually most frivolous annexation, meets disaster. Many of these cases are marked by Herodotus by a conversation between the monarch and a "wise adviser" who points up, especially, the irrationality of the last deadly moment of expansion of the monarch's empire.

42. Deioces' reign, 704–647; Phraortes, 647–625; Cyaxares, 625–585; Astyages, 585–529.

43. The modern Sea of Azov.

of the Colchians is a thirty days' journey for an active traveler. From Colchis it is no great distance to cross over into Media; in between there is only one nation, the Saspires; pass them, and you are in Media. But the Scythians did not invade by this way but turned off onto the upper road, which is far longer, keeping the Caucasus Mountains on their right. There the Medes met the Scythians and were worsted in the battle and deprived of their rule, and the Scythians took possession of all Asia.

105. From there the Scythians marched on Egypt; and when they got to Syrian Palestine, the king of Egypt, Psammetichus, met them and with entreaties and bribes turned aside their forward march. They then retreated; and when in their retreat they came in Syria to the city of Ascalon, the majority of the Scythians marched by, doing no harm to anyone, but a few, left behind, plundered the temple of Aphrodite Urania. This temple, as I learned from my inquiries, was the oldest of all those belonging to this goddess; for the shrine in Cyprus was founded from it, according to the Cyprians themselves, and the one on Cythera was founded by Phoenicians who came from this land of Syria. Now, on these Syrians who plundered the temple at Ascalon and on their descendants forever the goddess has sent the "female sickness." As to this, the Scythians say that this is why these people have fallen sick; and they also say that those who come to their country of Scythia can see the condition of those whom the Scythians call "Enareis."

106. For twenty-eight years, then, the Scythians were masters of Asia, and all was wasted by their violence and pride; for apart from their exacting of tribute, which they laid upon each man, apart from the tribute they rode around and plundered whatsoever it was that anyone possessed. Cyaxares and his Medes massacred most of these Scythians after first entertaining them and making them drunk, and so the Medes recovered their empire and were again lords of those they ruled before; and the Medes also took Nineveh (but how they took it I will show in another part of my book), and they made the Assyrians their subjects, except for the province of Babylon.

107. After all this, Cyaxares died, having been king for forty years (if you include those years when the Scythians held sway), and Astyages, his son, succeeded him.

Now Astyages had a daughter whose name was Mandane, and

Astyages saw her in a dream making water so greatly that she filled all his city and flooded, besides, all of Asia. He confided this dream to those of the Magi who were dream interpreters, and, when he learned the particulars of their exposition, he feared greatly. When Mandane was ripe for a man, Astyages, since he dreaded his dream, gave her to no one of the Medes who were worthy to marry into his house but to a Persian called Cambyses, whom he found to be a man of good house and peaceable temper; and he thought this Persian was much below a Mede of even middle class.

108. When Mandane was living with her husband in their first year, Astyages saw another vision; it seemed to him that out of his daughter's privy parts there grew a vine, and the vine shaded all Asia. This, then, he saw; and again he entrusted the matter to the dream interpreters and sent to recall his daughter from where she lived among the Persians, she then being big with child. When she came, he kept her under ward, because he wished to destroy whatever should be born of her. For from his vision the interpreters among the Magi had read the signs to mean that the child of his daughter would become king in his place. It was against this that Astyages guarded, and so when Cyrus was born he summoned Harpagus, his kinsman, the faithfullest of the Medes and the steward of all that he had. "Harpagus," he said, "here is a matter I am entrusting to you; by no means mishandle it, nor yet deceive me and choose others: should you do so, you shall thereafter bring upon yourself a fall into ruin. Take this child that Mandane bore and bring it to your own house and kill it, and afterwards bury it in whatever way you please." Harpagus answered, "My lord, never yet have you seen even a hint of what is untoward in me, and I shall give heed that in the time to come, too, I shall not offend against you. If it is your pleasure that this be so, then it shall be mine to serve you duly."

109. So Harpagus answered him. When the baby was given him, all decked out for his death, Harpagus went weeping to his house, and on coming there he told his wife all the story that Astyages had told him. "And now what is in your mind to do?" she asked. "Certainly not what Astyages has ordered me," was his answer; "not though he shall be even more frantic and mad than now he is will I fall in with his judgment and be his servant in such a murder. There are many reasons why I will not murder the child: because he is akin

to me and because Astyages is an old man and childless in male issue. If it should happen that after his death the crown should devolve upon his daughter, whose son Astyages has killed by my hands, what is left for me, from then on, but the greatest peril? Yet for my own safety the child must die; but it must be one of Astyages' folk that will be its murderer and none of mine."

110. So he said and at once sent a messenger to that one of Astyages' herdsmen whom he knew to graze his flocks in the pastures most suitable for his purpose and in mountains where wild beasts were most common. The man's name was Mitradates, and he lived with a woman who was a slave like himself and was called in Greek Cyno[44] and in Median Spako; for the Medians call a bitch Spako. The foothills where this herdsman grazed his cattle were to the north of Ecbatana and toward the Euxine Sea; for at this point the country of the Medes, toward the Saspires, is hilly, high, and with dense thickets, but all the rest of Media is a flat plain. When the herdsman arrived in great haste at his summons, Harpagus said: "It is Astyages' command to you that you take this child and expose it on the loneliest part of the hills, that it may the soonest perish; and he has ordered me to tell you that if you do not kill it, but in any way bear a hand in its survival, he will cause you yourself to die the most terrible of deaths. I myself have instructions to supervise the child's exposure."

111. When the herdsman heard this, he took up the baby and went the same road home until he came to his steading. Now his own wife was near her time all that day, and, as God would somehow have it so, she gave birth when her husband had gone to the city. They were much in one another's thoughts, these two; for the man was afraid for his wife in labor, and the woman for her man, whom Harpagus, in so unaccustomed a fashion, had summoned to his presence. Then he came back and stood before her, and the woman, as the sight of him was unexpected, was the first to ask him why Harpagus had been so instant in sending for him. The herdsman said: "Wife, I came to the city and saw and heard something I wish I had not seen nor that it should have happened to our masters. For the whole house of Harpagus was in a tumult of lamentation, and I went

44. The Greek word for "dog" is _kuōn_.

into it bewildered. When I came in, I saw a baby lying there, struggling and crying; he was decked out with gold ornaments, and his
clothes were finely embroidered. When Harpagus saw me, he bade
me take up the child speedily and go and expose it on the hills where
the beasts are thickest; he said it was Astyages who had laid these
commands on me, and he added many threats if I should disobey. I
took up the child and bore it here, thinking it must be from one of
the household, since I had no inkling where it should have come
from. But I marveled to see the gold and the raiment and the lamentation so manifest in Harpagus' house. As I came along the road, I
learned the whole story from one of the servants, who escorted me
out of the city and put the baby into my hands. He said it was the
child of Mandane, the daughter of Astyages and of Cambyses, son of
Cyrus, and that it was Astyages' command that it should be killed.
So now, here he is."

112. Even as he spoke, the herdsman took the covering from the
baby and showed it to her. When his wife saw the child so big and
beautiful, she burst into tears, and taking her man by the knees she
besought him by no means to expose it. He said he could not do
otherwise; for spies were to come from Harpagus to oversee the
matter, and the herdsman would die a cruel death if he disobeyed.
So when the woman could not persuade her man, she said next,
"Since I cannot persuade you not to expose it, you must do this—if
a child must necessarily be seen exposed. I, too, have given birth,
and the baby I bore was dead. Take then the dead boy and expose it,
and let us bring up, as our own, this child of Astyages' daughter. So
you will not be detected in cheating our masters, and we shall ourselves have arranged our business well enough. For the dead child
will have a royal burial, and the survivor will not lose his life."

113. The herdsman thought that his wife counseled very well in
his present trouble, and he immediately did as she said. The child he
had brought and of whom he should have been the deathsman he
confided to his wife; but his own child that was dead he took up and
placed in the box wherein he had brought the other. He put on the
dead body all the ornaments of that other child and bore it off to the
loneliest part of the hills and left it there. When the third day came
on the exposed child, the herdsman went to the city, leaving one of
his underlings to guard it, and came to the house of Harpagus and

said he was ready to show him the body. Harpagus sent some of the trustiest of his bodyguard, and through their agency saw and buried the body that was the herdsman's child. So that one was buried, and he that was afterwards called Cyrus was taken over by the herdsman's wife and brought up by her, though of course she put another name on him and not Cyrus.

114. When the child was ten years old, the following thing happened to him and revealed him. He was playing in the village where the herdsmen's houses were, playing in the road with other children of the same age. The children in their play chose him for their king—him who was called the cowherd's son. So he made his several orders for all of them—these to build houses and those to be bodyguards, and one of them, I suppose, to be the King's Eye.[45] And to another he assigned the privilege of carrying messages to him. To each of them he gave his special function. One of the children the boy played with was the son of Artembares, a man of distinction among the Medes. This boy refused to discharge an order of Cyrus, at which Cyrus bade the other children arrest him; and when they obeyed him, he treated the rebel very roughly and had him whipped. As soon as he was let go, the child became even angrier (for he felt that he had suffered in a way unbefitting his rank) and went back to the town and complained to his father of how he had been dealt with by Cyrus, though of course he did not call him "Cyrus" (since that was not yet his name) but "the son of Astyages' herdsman." Artembares was very angry indeed and went to Astyages, taking his son with him and declaring that what he had suffered was not to be borne. "My lord," he said, "it is at the hands of your slave, the cowherd's child, that we have endured such insults as this," and he pointed to his son's shoulders.

115. Astyages listened to him and saw what had been done and wished to avenge Artembares' son, because of Artembares' high position, and so he sent for the cowherd and his son. When they

45. The Greeks' name for the chief-of-staff of the Great King's personal servants. (He is mockingly so presented in Aristophanes' comedy the Acharnians, of about 427 B.C.) Of course the king in the present passage is not the Great King, or the King, as the Greeks titled him, who is the king of Persia; but Herodotus assumes that the customs of the Lydian and Median monarchies, which preceded that of Persia and were absorbed by it, are much the same.

both came before him, Astyages glanced at Cyrus and said, "You are the son of such a father as this, and did you dare to chastise so shamefully the son of one who is of the first honor with me?" The boy answered him: "Master, I did this to him, and with justice I did it. For the children of the village, of whom he was one, in their play made me their king; they judged that I was the most suited to the office. All the other boys did what I bade them do, but this one was deaf to my orders and would none of them, until finally he was punished for it. So if for this I deserve to suffer some ill, here am I to take it."

116. As the boy spoke, Astyages was visited by a kind of recognition; besides, the look on the boy's face seemed to him to resemble his own and his style of answering to be too free for what he appeared to be; also, the date of the exposure seemed to jibe with this boy's age. The king was thunderstruck by all this and for a time could say nothing. Hardly, at last, he rallied himself and—anxious to get rid of Artembares so that he could examine the cowherd privately—he said, "Artembares, I will so deal with this matter that neither you nor your son will have grounds of complaint." So he sent Artembares off; and the servants, at Astyages' command, took Cyrus inside. Then, when the king and the cowherd were quite alone, Astyages put his question to him: "Where did you get this child, and who gave him to you?" The man said that the child was his own and that his mother was still at home. Astyages said: "You are not well advised to want to bring yourself to the extremity of what you may suffer," and with these words he gave a sign to his bodyguards to seize the man. The cowherd in his desperation told the real story. He began at the beginning, followed the truth of it right through, and ended with entreaties, begging Astyages to pardon him.

117. When the cowherd revealed the truth, Astyages took less account of him then and there; but he was furious with Harpagus and bade the bodyguards summon him. When Harpagus came, Astyages asked him, "Harpagus, what sort of death did you use to destroy my daughter's child, whom I entrusted to you?" Now Harpagus saw the cowherd in the house, so he did not turn to the road of lies, in which he would surely be discovered and refuted, but said: "My lord, when I received the child, I debated with myself how I might do your pleasure and be clear of offense toward you but also

how I might not be a murderer in your daughter's sight and in your own. This is what I did. I summoned this cowherd here and gave him the child, saying that it was your command to kill it. And in so saying I told no lie; for you had indeed given that order. So I gave it to him with instructions in this sense, that he should expose it on a lonely mountain and stand by and watch it till it died; and I used a world of threats if he should not do all of this. He did my commands; the child died, and I sent the trustiest of my eunuchs; and by their means I saw him dead and buried him. This, my lord, is exactly how it was, and this is how the child died."

118. So Harpagus told the story straightly; but Astyages concealed the anger he felt at what had happened, and first of all he told over to Harpagus what he had heard from the herdsman in the matter, and afterwards, when it had all been told twice, he ended by saying that the child was alive and that the business was well enough. "For I suffered greatly," he went on to say, "at what was done to this child, and I took it as no light thing to be estranged from my daughter. So since the luck has turned out well, will you send your son here to join this newcomer among us and will you yourself come to dinner? For I propose to celebrate a ceremonial sacrifice to those gods to whom honor is due for this saving of my grandchild."

119. Harpagus, on hearing this, did obeisance; and regarding it as a great thing that his offense had come out so well, and appositely, and that he was invited to dinner on such a fortunate occasion, went to his house. As he came in, he met his only son, a boy of about thirteen years, and sent him off to Astyages, telling him to go there and do whatever the king ordered him. And in his delight he told his wife all that had happened. When Harpagus' son came to Astyages, the king cut his throat and chopped him limb from limb, and some of him he roasted and some he stewed and, having dressed all, held it in readiness. When it was the dining hour and the other guests had come, then for those other guests and for Astyages himself there were set tables full of mutton, but, before Harpagus, the flesh of his own son, all save for the head and the extremities of the hands and the feet; these were kept separate, covered up in a basket. When it seemed that Harpagus had had enough of his meal, Astyages asked him how he liked the feast. "Very much indeed,"

said Harpagus; and then those whose instruction it was brought in the head and the hands and the feet of his son, covered; these men stood before Harpagus and bade him uncover and take what he pleased from it. Harpagus did so and, uncovering, saw the remains of his son. But when he saw them, he gave no signs of disturbance and remained quite himself. Astyages asked him if he knew what wild thing it was whose flesh he had been eating. "Yes," he said, "I know; whatsoever my lord the king does is pleasing." So he answered and, taking up what was left of the flesh, went home, resolved, I suppose, to gather all together and bury it.

120. This was the penalty Astyages laid upon Harpagus; but when he came to think about Cyrus, he summoned those same Magi who had expounded his dream in their sense. When they came, Astyages asked them how it was that they had expounded the dream. They answered in the same terms as before, declaring that had the boy survived and not died first, he must needs have become king. At this he answered them: "The boy lives, he has survived; and when he was living out in the country, the children in the village made him their king. He did all the things that real kings do: he appointed bodyguards and sentries and messengers and made all the other arrangements, and so he ruled. Now I would know toward what you think all these things tend." The Magi said: "If indeed the boy survives and has become king with no connivance, be of good cheer and good heart: he will not come to rule a second time. Some, even of our prophecies, issue in very small matters, and in all that pertains to dreams the fulfillment is often in something trifling." Said Astyages: "I am myself strongly of your opinion, Magi—that since the child has been called king, the dream has come out, and so the boy will be no future threat to me. Yet I would have you counsel me carefully, with heedful concern for what will be safest for my house and for yourselves." The Magi answered, "My lord, that your rule should stand safely is of the utmost importance to ourselves. For otherwise the crown will fall into alien hands; it will devolve on this boy, who is Persian, and we, being Medes, will be enslaved by the Persians and become of no consequence with relation to them, since we will be foreigners in our own land. But so long as you are king, who are our countryman, we have our share in the rule and great honor from you. So we must certainly look out for you and for your

authority. If now we saw anything to be feared in this matter, we would have told you everything. As it is, the dream has issued in something trifling; we are ourselves quite confident and bid you be the same. So send the boy away from your sight to the Persians and his parents."

121. When Astyages heard this, he was very glad and summoned Cyrus and said to him, "My boy, I did you a wrong because of a vision I saw in a dream, a vision that found no fulfillment; but through your own destiny you have survived. Go then, and fare you well, to the Persians, and I will send an escort with you. When you get there, you will find a father and mother of different style from Mitradates, the cowherd, and his wife."

122. With these words Astyages sent Cyrus away. When the boy came to the house of Cambyses, his parents received him; and after they had received him, they heard all; their welcome was full of joy, for they had understood him to have died so long ago; and they questioned him as to how he had survived. He told them, saying that until now he had himself not known of it but was greatly astray, but that on the road he had learned all that had happened him; he had believed that he was the son of Astyages' cowherd, but as he had traveled thither he had heard the whole story from his escort. He had been raised by the cowherd's wife, he said, and, as he told it, he was continually praising her, and indeed, in the tale he told, everything was Cyno. His parents caught at the name, and, so as to make the Persians think that their son's survival was even more a thing of God's contriving, they spread the rumor that Cyrus, exposed, had been suckled by a bitch.

123. From this, then, that legend has grown. But when Cyrus had become a young man and, indeed, of all those of his age the bravest and the most loved, Harpagus courted him with gifts, for he was eager to take his own vengeance on Astyages. He saw no possibility of any punishment coming upon the king from one who was only a private person, but, as he observed Cyrus growing up, he tried to make an ally of him; for in the shape of Cyrus' sufferings he saw his own. He had already done the following by way of prelude. Astyages was a very hard ruler for the Medes; now Harpagus held private conferences with each of the chief noblemen among them and urged that they should set up Cyrus as their leader and depose

Astyages. Harpagus had done all this and made everything ready, and now he wanted to make his thoughts known to Cyrus, who was living among the Persians. Because the roads were guarded, he had no other means but the following contrivance. He artfully prepared a hare by slitting its belly without removing any of the fur, and he inserted into the hare, just as it was, a paper on which he wrote what he wanted. He then stitched up the belly of the hare and gave it to the trustiest of his servants, along with a hunting net, as though he were a huntsman; he sent off this fellow to the Persians to tell Cyrus, by word of mouth, to cut open the hare with his own hands and to have no one present when he did so.

124. This, then, was accomplished, and Cyrus got the hare and slit it open. He found the paper inside and read it. The writing said: "Son of Cambyses: the gods watch over you. Else you had never had such luck. Now take vengeance on Astyages, who is your murderer. For in his intention toward you, you are dead, and it is only thanks to the gods and to me that you are alive. I suppose you have long ago learned all the truth of this—about what was done with respect to you and what I endured from Astyages because I did not kill you but gave you to the herdsman instead. If you will now listen to me, you will be king of all the land that now Astyages rules. Persuade the Persians to revolt, and do you lead their army against the Medes. If I am appointed by Astyages as his general against you, everything will go your way; if some other of the Median noblemen, still it will be the same. For these noblemen will desert him and join you and try to depose him. Know, then, that this is all ready here; do as I tell you, and do it quickly."

125. Cyrus heard this and thought about what was the subtlest means of persuading the Persians to revolt. As he thought, he found the following most suitable and took it. He wrote what he would upon a paper, and called an assembly of the Persians. At this he unfolded the paper[46] and read it aloud to the effect that Astyages had appointed him general of the Persians. "Now, men of Persia," he said, "I would have all of you appear before me, each one with a scythe." There are many tribes of the Persians, and those that Cyrus

46. The Greek word here and in the previous chapter, which in both places I have rendered as "paper," is *byblion*, which means, strictly speaking, a papyrus roll.

assembled and persuaded to revolt were those on whom all the rest depended. These are the Pasargadae, the Maraphians, and the Maspians. Of these the Pasargadae are the noblest, and it is among them that the Achaemenidae are, which is the clan from which the kings of Persia come. The other Persians are the Panthialaei, the Derusiaei, and the Germanii. These are all tillers of the soil; but the rest are nomads: the Dai, the Mardi, the Dropici, and the Sagartii.

126. These all came with their scythes, and Cyrus told them of a piece of ground about eighteen or twenty stades on each side and a mass of thistles. This he bade them clear within a single day. When the Persians had done their appointed task, he ordered them, after that, to come the very next day, all bathed. Meanwhile, he gathered his father's flocks of sheep and goats and herds of cattle in one place and killed them in preparation for entertaining the entire Persian army. He furnished as well the wine and the foods that were most suitable. When the Persians came the next day, he had them recline in a meadow and entertained them sumptuously. After their meal Cyrus asked them which they preferred, yesterday's condition or today's. They said that there was a great difference: "Yesterday we had everything bad and today everything good." Cyrus caught at the phrase and laid bare his whole design. "Men of Persia," he said, "this is how things are with you. If you will listen to me, you shall have all these good things, and ten thousand more, and no slavish work at all. If you will not listen, you shall have sufferings like yesterday's, and that beyond counting. Listen to me, and become free men. I believe that I was born by God's providence to take this matter into my hands; as for you, I think you are no worse than the Medes, either in war or in anything else. Since this is so, I say: revolt from Astyages, and do it quickly!"

127. The Persians had their champion now and were glad to free themselves. They had long taken it hard to be ruled by the Medes. But as soon as Astyages learned what Cyrus would be at, he sent a messenger to summon him. But Cyrus bade the messenger report that he would come to the king sooner than the king wanted him. When Astyages heard that, he armed all the Medes, and so godbesotted was he that he appointed Harpagus to command them, forgetting what he had done to him. As soon as the Medes joined battle with the Persians, some of them fought indeed—that is, those

time, Cyrus and the Persians rose against the Medes and from this time out dominated Asia. As for Astyages himself, Cyrus did him no further harm but kept him with him until he died.

Thus was Cyrus born and bred up and came to be king and later, as I have already said, subjugated Croesus, who was the aggressor in injustice; and with this conquest of Croesus Cyrus dominated all of Asia.

131. The following are customs practiced by the Persians of which I have personal knowledge. They are not wont to establish images or temples or altars at all; indeed, they regard all who do so as fools, and this, in my opinion, is because they do not believe in gods of human form, as the Greeks do. They offer sacrifices to Zeus, going up into the highest mountains and calling the whole circle of the heaven Zeus. They sacrifice, too, to the sun, moon, and earth and to fire, water, and winds. These were the sole gods of their worship at the beginning, but they have learned besides to sacrifice to the Heavenly Aphrodite. Her worship has come to them from the Assyrians and Arabians. The Assyrians call Aphrodite Mylitta, the Arabians Alilat, and the Persians Mitra.

132. The Persians have established sacrifice to the above-mentioned gods in the following way. They make no altars nor burn fire when about to sacrifice, nor do they use libations, or the music of pipes, or fillets, or barley grains. But when a man is minded to sacrifice to any one of the gods, he brings into an open space his sacrificial beast and calls upon the god, wearing his cap the while, crowned, usually with myrtle. He may not pray for good things for himself alone, the sacrificer, but only that all shall be well with all the Persians and the king; for among all the Persians is himself also. When he has cut in pieces the sacrificial animal, he stews the meat and, spreading a layer of the softest grass (clover, chiefly), puts all of the meat on this layer. When he has done this, a Magian stands by and chants a hymn of the birth of the gods—for such, they say, is their incantation. Without a Magian they may not offer any sacrifice. After a short while the worshiper takes away his meat and does whatever he wants with it.

133. Of all their days there is none each man honors so much as his birthday. On it they think it right to set forth more dishes than on any other. The rich among them serve an ox or a horse or a camel

or an ass roasted whole in great ovens; the poor serve the smaller beasts. They have few main dishes but a great many that are supplementary, and these served severally, and not all together. So the Persians say that the Greeks leave off eating hungry, because the Greeks have, after the main dinner, little or nothing additional. If the Greeks were given side dishes, say the Persians, they would never stop eating. They are very addicted to wine, and it is forbidden to vomit or make water in the presence of anyone else. They keep very strictly to this practice, too: that they are wont to debate their most serious concerns when they are drunk. But whatsoever they decide on, drunk, this the master of the house where they are when debating proposes to them again on the next day, when they are sober. And if they like it, too, when sober, they act on it; but if they do not like it so, they let it be. And whatever they debate, in preliminary fashion, sober, they give to final decision drunk.

134. When they meet one another in the street, there is a sign by which one may know if those who encounter are equals, and the sign is this: instead of greeting, they kiss one another on the mouth. If one of the two is a little humbler, they kiss on the cheek. If one of them is very much inferior in birth, he falls down and does obeisance to the other. Most of all they hold in honor themselves, then those who dwell next to themselves, and then those next to *them*, and so on, so that there is a progression in honor in relation to the distance. They hold least in honor those whose habitation is furthest from their own. This is because they think themselves to be the best of mankind in everything and that others have a hold on virtue in proportion to their nearness; those that live furthest away are the most base. When the Medes were the sovereign people, the nations even ruled each other. The Medes themselves ruled over all and also ruled the nation next to them. But those next to the Medes ruled those on their own boundaries, and these in turn those next to them, and so on; just as the Persians administer their system of honor, so among the Medes each nation that ruled, and had supervision, possessed the rule and supervisorship by steps of advance.[48]

48. How and Wells, in their commentary on this passage, say that Herodotus is comparing the Median system of graduated rule to the Persian system of graduated respect, and they then remark that he "represents accurately the broad facts of the contrast between Persian and Median rule; under the Medes,

135. The Persians welcome foreign customs more than any other people. For instance, they decided that Median dress was more beautiful than their own, and so they wear it. They wear Egyptian breastplates for their wars. Wherever they learn of enjoyments of all sorts, they adopt them for their own practice. From the Greeks they have learned to lie with boys. Each of the Persians marries many lawful wives, and they take to themselves even more concubines.

136. After valor in fighting, the goodness of a man is most signified in this: that he can show a multitude of sons. To him who can show most, the King sends gifts every year. For multitude, they think, is strength. They train their sons from their fifth to their twentieth year in three things only: horsemanship, archery, and truth-telling. Before he is five years old, the boy does not come into his father's presence but has his living among the women. This is done so that, should he die during his rearing, he may cause his father no distress.

137. That is one of their customs that I praise; and here is another: no one, not even the Great King himself, may kill anyone on charge of a single crime, nor may anyone of the rest of the Persians do irremediable harm to any of his servants on occasion of a single act. Only if, on consideration, he finds the wrongdoings more in number and greater than the good deeds may he use his pleasure. The Persians declare that never yet has anyone killed his own father or mother. As often as this takes place, say they, it must on investigation necessarily appear that the one who did it was either adopted or a bastard; for, they say, it is against all seeming that one who is a true parent should die at the hands of his own son.

138. Whatsoever things it is not permitted to them to do, of these they must not even speak. Lying is considered among them the very basest thing and, second, indebtedness—for many other reasons and especially because, as they say, the debtor is bound to lie somewhat. Whoever of the citizenry has leprosy or the white sickness, he comes not into the city nor joins company with other Persians. Now they say that those that have these illnesses are so af-

---

the subject kingdoms paid tribute or sent gifts, while they still ruled their own dependents; under Persia, all districts alike were under the satraps, and in direct relation to the great king."

flicted from having sinned against the sun. Every foreigner who takes such a sickness they drive out of their country, as they also banish the white doves, on the same charge. They do not make water into rivers or spit in them or wash their hands in them, nor will they stand by and watch if another do so, for they revere rivers most of all things.

139. Here is another matter that is true of the Persians, and, though they have not noticed it themselves, I have. Their names, which express their bodily powers or their magnificence, all end in the same letter, the one the Dorians call "san" and the Ionians "sigma." On searching the matter out, you will find no exceptions to this among their names.

140. These things I know surely about them, for I speak from personal knowledge. But the following are described as secret and obscure and have to do with the dead. They say that the corpse of no Persian man is buried until it is dragged and torn by bird or dog. I know, surely, that this is true of the Magi, for indeed they are open about it. Once they have embalmed the corpse with wax, the Persians bury it in the ground. The Magi are very different from all other men and also from the priests of the Egyptians. For the latter scruple to kill any living thing, save such animals as they sacrifice. But the Magi with their own hands kill everything but dog and man, and they vie mightily with one another in so doing, killing alike ants and snakes and everything that creeps or flies. So, as far as this custom goes, let it be as it has ever been.[49] I go back to the former track of my story.

141. As soon as the Lydians were reduced by the Persians, the Ionians and Aeolians sent messages to Cyrus at Sardis, wishing to be subjects to him on the same terms as they had been to Croesus. When Cyrus heard what they offered, he told them a story. He said

49. This phrase, used several times in the course of the *History*, is dismissive, i.e., "Let us say no more about the matter." But it also implies that Herodotus is *unwilling* to discuss the matter further, in either its good or bad aspects. Literally it means "Let it be about this custom as it has been *customarily held* from the beginning." For Herodotus, custom is the particular costume for the belief in the sacred, and, as such, it should be respected by observers who belong to other nations or to other religious persuasions. Cf. 3.38. The phrase always carries with it the notion that there is something in the record, as Herodotus has presented it, that challenges us to extend the tolerance that is due to an old and venerated religious practice.

that there was once a flute-player who saw fishes in the sea and played the flute at them in the thought that they might come out on to the land. When his hopes were disappointed, he took a net and cast it round a great multitude of the fish and drew them out. When he saw them leaping about, he said to the fishes, "Stop your dancing now; for when I piped to you, you would not come shorewards to dance." Cyrus told this story to the Ionians and Aeolians because, before this, he had requested the Ionians, through messengers, to desert Croesus, but they would not; now that everything was over, they were ready to listen to Cyrus. He was very angry when he sent them the story of the flute-player and the fish, and the Ionians, when they heard the message brought to them in their cities, readied the fortified walls round them and gathered into the Panionium— all, that is, save the people of Miletus, for with them alone Cyrus had made a sworn agreement on the same terms as they had had with Croesus. So the rest of the Ionians resolved, by a common decision, to send messengers to Sparta to beg help for Ionia.

142. These Ionians who possess the Panionium have founded cities in the most beautiful setting of climate and season of all of mankind that I know. The country to the north of them is not the same in these respects, nor yet to the south or the east or the west, for some of it suffers from cold and wet, and some from heat and drought. These people do not all use the same speech; there are in fact four dialects. The southernmost of their cities is Miletus and, north of that, Myus and Priene; these are settlements in Caria, and they speak the same dialect with one another. But the following cities are in Lydia: Ephesus, Colophon, Lebedos, Teos, Clazomenae, and Phocaea, and these cities have no relationship to the speech of the aforementioned; they have, however, a common dialect of their own. There are, besides, three Ionian cities left; two are islands— Samos and Chios—and one, Erythrae, is on the mainland. The Chians and the Erythraeans speak the same dialect, but the Samians have one entirely their own. These are the four different dialects.

143. Of these Ionians,[50] the people of Miletus were safe enough from fear, for they had their agreement with Cyrus; and there was no danger for the islanders, for the Phoenicians were not yet subjects of

50. I.e., those who share in the Panionium (the "All-Ionian"), a meeting place, including a temple.

Persia, and the Persians themselves were no sailors. These Ionians of the Twelve Cities are distinguished from the rest of the Ionians for one reason only, and I shall tell it. At this time the whole Hellenic race was weak, and far the weakest of all its constituent nations, and of the least note, were the Ionians. Indeed, except for Athens, they had no city of consequence. The other Ionians, and the Athenians too, shunned the name, not wishing to be called Ionians. Even now, it seems to me, the most of them are ashamed of the name. These twelve cities, however, took pride in the name and set up a holy place of their own, to which they gave the title Panionium. They took a resolution not to share this with any of the other Ionians— though indeed none requested a share except the people of Smyrna.

144. Much the same is true of the Dorians of what is now called the Five-City Country, formerly the Six-City Country. These too refused to admit any of the neighboring Dorians into the Triopian Holy Place and indeed debarred from the association any of their own who had committed offenses against the Holy Place. Long before, in the festival of Triopian Apollo, the judges assigned bronze tripods to the winners; but those who got them must not carry them away from the Holy Place but dedicate them there to the god. A man of Halicarnassus, whose name was Agasicles, won and then set the rule at naught by bringing the tripod to his own home and nailing it up there. Because of this offense, five cities—Lindus, Ialysus, Camirus, Cos, and Cnidus—debarred from the association the sixth city, Halicarnassus. This was the penalty imposed on the latter city.

145. I think that the Ionians made their twelve cities and would admit no more because, when they lived in the Peloponnesus, there were twelve divisions of them. It is the same now with the Achaeans, who drove the Ionians out; there are twelve divisions of them, too: Pellene, nearest to Sicyon, and, after that, Aegira and Aegae, where there is the river Crathis (it is a river fed by eternal springs, and from it the river in Italy got its name); and Bura and Helice, to which the Ionians fled when they were defeated by the Achaeans in battle; and Aegion and Rhype and Patrae, Phareae, and Olenus, where there is the great river Pirus, and Dyme and Tritaeae, which alone among these is inland. These twelve divisions are now of the Achaeans as, in those earlier times, they had been of the Ionians.

146. These were the reasons the Ionians made twelve cities. For it is mere folly to claim that they did so because they are more Ionian

than the other Ionians or are of nobler birth. Not the least part of the Twelve are Abantes, who came from Euboea and are not even in name Ionians, and mingled with them are Minyans of Orchomenus, and Cadmeans, and Dryopians, and those Phocians who were a breakaway part of their nation, and Molossians, and Pelasgian Arcadians, and Dorians of Epidaurus; there are many other nations, too, mixed with them. As for those of them who came from the prytaneum of Athens[51] and think of themselves as the bluest blood of the Ionians, these did not bring wives with them to the colony but took Carian women, whose parents they had killed. (Because of this murder, these women have imposed a sworn rule upon themselves, and have handed it on to their daughters, that they will not eat with their husbands, nor will any one of them call her husband by his name, because the men had killed the women's fathers, husbands, and sons and, after so doing, had lived with the women themselves.)

147. This happened in Miletus. As kings some of them set up Lycians descended from Glaucus, the son of Hippolochus, others Caucones of Pylos, descendants of Codrus, son of Melanthus, and some both. However, the Twelve do, as I say, set more store by the name Ionian than all the other Ionians; and so let it be taken that they are pure-blooded Ionians. Of course, all *are* Ionians that are of Athenian descent and keep the feast of the Apaturia. All do keep this feast except for the men of Ephesus and Colophon. These are the only Ionians not celebrating the Apaturia, and these because of the allegation of a certain murder.

148. The Panionium is a sacred place in Mycale, facing toward the north and set apart, by common agreement of the Ionians, for Poseidon of Helicon. Mycale is the point of the mainland to the west, running down to the sea opposite to Samos. It is to this place that the Ionians from the Twelve Cities resorted when they celebrated the festival to which they gave the name Panionia. It is true not only of the Ionian festivals that they all end in the same letter, a, as the Persian names end in san; all Greek festivals end in the letter a.[52]

149. These are the Ionian cities, as I have told of them. The fol-

---

51. Literally, the town hall of Athens, the center of Athenian civic life.

52. Some editors have bracketed this sentence, thinking it an intrusive gloss by a copyist who connected Herodotus' observation on Persian names to his own on Greek festivals. This is not a very important matter.

lowing are the Aeolian: Cyme, called Phriconian; Lerisae, the "New Fort," Temnos, Cilla, Notium, Aegiroessa, Pitana, Aegaeae, Myrina, Grynea. These are the eleven ancient Aeolian cities. There too were originally twelve on the mainland, but one of them, Smyrna, was detached from them by the Ionians. These Aeolians settled a country that was more fertile than that of the Ionians, but the climate was not so good.

150. This is how the Aeolians lost Smyrna. They gave shelter to certain men of Colophon who had been beaten in a fight between political factions and were ousted from their native city. These fugitives from Colophon waited until the Smyrnaeans were celebrating a festival to Dionysus outside their own walls. They then closed the gates against them and took possession of the city. All the other Aeolians came to help their countrymen, and an agreement was reached that if the Ionians [53] would give back to the Aeolians [54] their movable goods, the Aeolians would leave them the city. The Smyrnaeans settled for that, and the other eleven cities divided them up among themselves and made them citizens of their own cities.

151. These are the mainland Aeolian cities, outside of those that are established about Mount Ida; for the latter are quite separate. Of Aeolian cities on the islands, there are, in Lesbos, five (there was a sixth on Lesbos, called Arisba, but the Methymnaeans enslaved it, although its people were kinsfolk of their own), and there is one city established in Tenedos and one more in what are called the Hundred Islands. The Lesbians and the people of Tenedos had nothing to fear, like those of the Ionians who inhabit the islands. But the rest of the Aeolians decided, in common, to follow the leadership of the Ionians. [55]

152. When the messengers of Ionians and Aeolians came to Sparta—for matters were indeed set about very speedily—they

53. I.e., the exiles from Colophon.
54. I.e., the Smyrnaeans.
55. Herodotus' intimate knowledge of all the political doings of the vast number of Greek city-states—and at a date not far from a hundred years before his time—is remarkable. Not less remarkable, to the nonclassical reader, are the multiplicity, individuality, and squabbling of these states themselves. Finally, one must notice how completely it is true of the Greeks that the only significant political unit is the *city*. There were five *independent* cities on the island of Lesbos.

chose one man to speak for all. He was a Phocaean, by name Pyther-
mus. He had a purple cloak, which he wrapped about him to attract
the greatest attention and win the greatest audience among the
Spartiates; and there he stood and earnestly begged them all to succor his people. But the Lacedaemonians were not minded to listen;
they took a contrary resolution, that they would give no help to the
Ionians. So away went the ambassadors. But the Lacedaemonians,
having rejected the messengers of the Ionians, nonetheless sent men
in a penteconter (in my opinion, they were intended to spy on what
Cyrus was doing and what was happening in Ionia), and when these
came to Phocaea they sent their most notable man, whose name was
Lacrines, up to Sardis to Cyrus, to declare to him the formal decision of the Lacedaemonians. "Do not," they said, "injure a single
Greek city; we, the Lacedaemonians, will not suffer you to do so."

153. As the herald made his proclamation, it is said that Cyrus
asked of those present who, among the Greeks, were these Lacedaemonians, and how many of them there were, that they should
make such a speech as this to him. When he found out the answers
to his questions, he spoke, they say, to the Spartan herald as follows:
"I never yet feared men who have a place set apart in the midst of
their cities where they gather to cheat one another and exchange
oaths, which they break. If I continue in my health, it will not be
the sufferings of the Ionians that they will have at their tongues'
ends, but something nearer home." This taunt of Cyrus was directed
against all of the Greeks, because they set up marketplaces in which
to buy and sell. The Persians themselves do not have such places,
nor is there any such marketing among them. After this, Cyrus entrusted Sardis to a Persian, Tabalus; but the gold of Croesus and the
rest of the Lydians he entrusted to Pactyes, a man who was a Lydian,
for safekeeping. He then marched away himself to Ecbatana, bringing Croesus with him. The Ionians, at first at least, he took no account of at all. For Babylon lay in his path, and the Bactrian people
and the Sacae and the Egyptians, against whom he designed to lead
an army himself; but against the Ionians he decided he would send
another general.[56]

56. In the listing of Cyrus' further strategic and imperialistic aims, the reader
can see the sequence of Herodotus' treatment in the following books, which
deal, in turn, with Egypt, Babylon, and Scythia. (The Sacae are Scythians.)

154. But when Cyrus marched away from Sardis, Pactyes induced the Lydians to revolt from Tabalus and Cyrus; he came down to the coast, and, inasmuch as he had all the gold from Sardis, he set about hiring mercenaries and persuaded the men of the coast to take his part in the revolution. He then marched on Sardis and besieged Tabalus, shut up in the citadel there.

155. When Cyrus heard the story on his journey, he said to Croesus: "Croesus, what end shall I find in these matters? The Lydians, it seems, will never cease causing me troubles and bringing troubles on themselves. I wonder if it would not be best to enslave them outright. For, as it is, I am, to my mind, like a man who has killed the father of a family of children and then spared the children. So you, who are far more than a father to the Lydians, I have taken and carried off, and I have handed the city over to the Lydians themselves. And then I wonder that the Lydians rebel against me!" So Cyrus declared to Croesus what was really in his thoughts; but Croesus was afraid that he would indeed destroy Sardis utterly, and he answered the king thus: "My lord, what you have said is indeed reasonable, but, all the same, do not yield entirely to your wrath, nor destroy an ancient city, which is guiltless both of former transgressions and now of these. For the former acts, it is I who have done them; I wipe the stain of sin on my own head and bear it; for what has now chanced, it is Pactyes who is the wrongdoer, and it is you yourself who turned Sardis over to him; let him be the man who pays the penalty. Pardon the Lydians, but lay upon them these edicts, that they may revolt no more nor be any danger to you: send them an injunction that they carry no more arms; bid them wear tunics under their cloaks and soft slippers on their feet; and give them orders that they themselves shall play the flute and the lyre and educate their children to be shopkeepers. Soon enough, my lord, you shall see them become women instead of men, so that they will be no further threat to you as rebels."

156. This was Croesus' advice because he found it better for the Lydians than to be made outright slaves and sold away. He knew that if he had no compelling argument to advance he would not persuade Cyrus to change his mind, and he dreaded that the Lydians, if they should outrun the present peril, would again rebel against the Persians and be entirely destroyed. Cyrus was pleased with Croesus'

advice, abated his anger, and declared that he agreed. Whereupon he summoned Mazares, a Mede, and instructed him to make a proclamation to the Lydians, as suggested by Croesus, and further to enslave outright all those who had marched, along with the Lydians, to the attack on Sardis. Pactyes himself, he said, must at all costs be brought alive to his royal presence.

157. So, having given these commands on the road, Cyrus marched away into Persian country. But Pactyes, hearing that an army was hard upon him and directed against him, took fright and fled to Cyme. Mazares the Mede, with whatever part of Cyrus' army he had, advanced on Sardis but found Pactyes' men no longer there. So first he forced the Lydians to do what Cyrus had commanded, and, as a result of these orders, the Lydians changed their entire way of life. Thereupon Mazares sent messengers to Cyme, commanding the surrender of Pactyes. But the men of Cyme decided to consult the god that is in Branchidae about what they should do. There was an oracle established there from of old, which all the Aeolians and Ionians were wont to consult. The place is in the territory of Miletus, above the harbor of Panormus.

158. So the men of Cyme sent messengers to Branchidae and asked what action of theirs in respect of Pactyes would be pleasing to the gods. In response to their question an oracle was given to surrender Pactyes to the Persians. When the men of Cyme heard this answer of the god, they were ready to give him up. But though this was the inclination of the people, one Aristodicus, son of Heraclides, a man of note among the citizenry, stopped them from doing so. He distrusted the oracle given and believed that those who had inquired of the god had not spoken truly; until at last other inquirers were sent, the second time, to inquire about Pactyes. Aristodicus was one of these.

159. When they came to Branchidae, Aristodicus was the choice of all to put the question. "Lord," he said, "there has come to us Pactyes the Lydian as a suppliant, fleeing from a violent death at the hands of the Persians. They have demanded his surrender, bidding us of Cyme to give him up. We are afraid of the power of Persia but, till this present, have not dared surrender one who is our suppliant till it is made altogether clear to us by you which of the two ways we should act." So the question was put; but the god declared his oracle

to the same effect: Pactyes should be given up to the Persians. In the face of this, Aristodicus, as he had planned, did as follows: he went around the temple and tore out all the sparrows and the families of other birds that nested there in the precinct. As he did so, the story goes, there came a voice from the shrine, directed to Aristodicus, saying: "Wickedest of men, what is this that you dare to do? Would you ravish my suppliants from the temple?" Aristodicus was not at a loss but said: "My lord, do you succor these suppliants of yours but bid the people of Cyme to surrender theirs?" Then the god answered him again: "Yes, I did so bid you, that you may the quicker sin and be destroyed and thus come no more to consult this oracle about the surrender of a suppliant."

160. When this oracle was brought back to them, the men of Cyme, not wishing either to surrender Pactyes and perish themselves nor yet to keep him with them and stand a siege of the Persians, sent him to Mytilene. The Mytilenaeans, on the sending of Mazares, bidding them give up Pactyes, agreed to surrender him for a certain sum. I cannot say exactly what it was, for the bargain was never completed. For when the Cymaeans learned what was being done by the Mytilenaeans, they sent a ship to Lesbos to convey Pactyes to Chios. There, however, he was torn from the shrine of the City-Guardian Athena and surrendered by the Chians. The price for which the Chians surrendered him was Atarneus, a place in Mysia opposite Lesbos. The Persians, when they got their hands on Pactyes, kept him under guard, wanting to show him to Cyrus. For a long time no Chian would make any offering of barley grains from Atarneus to any god, nor would they bake sacrificial cakes from the produce of this place, but all that came from there was kept away from all sacred rituals.

161. The Chians then *did* surrender Pactyes; and thereafter Mazares made war against those who had borne a hand in besieging Tabalus; he enslaved Priene and overran all the plain of the Maeander, giving it up to his army to ravage. He did the same to Magnesia. After which he suddenly took sick and died.

162. On his death, Harpagus came down to succeed him in the command. He was a Mede, too—the man whom Astyages, king of the Medes, had feasted at that unnatural banquet and who also had borne a share in securing the kingship for Cyrus. Being appointed

general by Cyrus at this time, and coming to Ionia, he took their cities by his earthworks. That is, as soon as he had forced the men inside their walls, he dug earth and brought mounds of it against the walls and by this means sacked the city. 163. The first place in Ionia he attacked was Phocaea. The Phocaeans had been the first of the Greeks to engage in long sea voyages, and it was they who opened up the Adriatic and Etruria and Iberia and Tartessus. They sailed to these places not in rounded boats but in penteconters. When they came to Tartessus, they became friends with the king of Tartessus, whose name was Arganthonius, and he had been sovereign of Tartessus for eighty years and himself lived, in all, one hundred and twenty. The Phocaeans became such close friends with this man that at first he bade them leave Ionia and settle wherever in his country they pleased; afterwards, when he did not persuade the Phocaeans but had word from them of the increase of power of the Medes, he gave them money to build a wall around their city. The money he gave he gave without stint; for the circuit of the walls is of many furlongs, and it is all made of great well-fitted stones.

164. Thus the wall of the Phocaeans had been made. But Harpagus brought his army against them and besieged them. His proposals were that he would be satisfied if the Phocaeans were willing to tear down one outwork of this wall only and consecrate a single house.[57] But the Phocaeans, in agony at the slavery of submission, said that they wished for a single day to deliberate; they would make their answer after that. While they were deliberating, they asked

57. The passage is obscure. Ordinarily, the consecration of even a single house to some god would put the city under the god's protection and therefore make it inviolable to enemy attack. Cf. 1.26, where a city connected part of its buildings by a rope to the temple of a god outside the city and so broke off the enemy's action. In this case, however, what Harpagus seems to be seeking is a symbolic surrender of the town. I suggest that the consecration of one house was designed to give the city an "open-city" status (like Rome in World War II) and that the demolition of a single outwork of the wall meant that, when the Phocaeans got their city again, it would have suffered minimal damage. There is no way of knowing why Harpagus was so anxious to be favorable to Phocaea. However, the demolition of even a part of the wall and the dedication of the single house are undeniably symbolic of surrender and therefore connected for the Phocaeans with the "slavery" that made them so miserable.

Harpagus to draw off his army from the wall. Harpagus said he knew well what they would do, but all the same he would allow them to deliberate. When Harpagus withdrew his army from the wall, the Phocaeans, dragging their penteconters down to the sea, put in their children, womenfolk, and all their portable goods, and, besides, the images from the temples and all the dedicatory offerings except for what was made of bronze or stone or consisted of pictures; having embarked everything, with these exceptions, they went aboard themselves and sailed away toward Chios. So the Persians took possession of Phocaea, but desolate of all its inhabitants.

165. The Phocaeans tried to buy what are called the Oenussian Islands from the Chians, but the Chians would not sell them, for they feared these islands might become a market and so their own island would be cut off from its trade. So then the Phocaeans prepared to sail away to Corsica. Here, twenty years before, at the command of an oracle, they had built a city called Alalia. By this time Arganthonius was already dead. As they were about to sail to Corsica, they first of all put into Phocaea and murdered the Persian guard, which had been given the duty of guarding the city by Harpagus, and, having done this, they pronounced a mighty curse on any of their own people who should linger behind the expedition to Corsica; besides this, they sank in the sea a bar of iron and swore never to come back to Phocaea until the bar should surface again. But as they were setting out for Corsica, more than half of the citizenry were seized with such homesickness and pity for their city and the places they knew that they proved false to their oath and sailed back to Phocaea. But those of them who kept their sworn agreement lifted anchor from the Oenussian Islands and sailed away.

166. When they came to Corsica, they lived in a common community for five years with those who had come there earlier, and they set up holy places there. But inasmuch as the united Phocaeans were constantly harrying and plundering the neighboring peoples, the Etruscans and the Carthaginians made common cause against them, each of these two peoples with sixty ships. The Phocaeans, on their side, manned ships, also to the number of sixty, and sailed out to confront their enemy in what is called the Sardinian Sea. They joined battle, and in that seafight the victory went to the Pho-

caeans; but it was a kind of Cadmean victory,[58] for forty of their ships were entirely destroyed, and the remaining twenty were rendered useless, as their rams were twisted awry. They sailed to Alalia and took on board their children, womenfolk, and the rest of what belonged to them, everything the ships could carry, and, leaving Corsica behind them, they sailed to Rhegium.

167. Now the Carthaginians and Etruscans cast lots for the crews of the ships that were destroyed, and, of the Etruscans, it was the people of Agylla who won far the greatest number. These they brought ashore and stoned them to death. After this, among these Agyllaeans, every living thing that passed the place where the Phocaeans were stoned and buried—every living thing, be it flocks and herds or beasts of burden or men—became alike twisted, crippled, or paralyzed. The people of Agylla sent to Delphi, wishful to heal their offense. The Pythia laid upon them the command that the Agyllaeans are still discharging to this day. For they have splendid religious celebrations for the dead Phocaeans and in their honor hold athletic contests and horse races. Such was the fate of these Phocaeans. But the rest of them, those who fled to Rhegium, made that their base and founded a city again in the land of Oenotria, which is now called Hyele. They founded this on the instructions of a man of Posidonia who convinced them that the oracle had meant them to found a hero, Cyrnus, rather than an island Cyrnus.[59]

168. This, then, is what happened the Phocaea that is in Ionia. Very similar were the actions of the Teians. For when Harpagus captured their town with his earthwork, they, too, all took to their

58. A Cadmean victory is one in which the formal victors lose at least as much as the conquered. It is so called because of the story in the Theban Cycle where the two sons of Oedipus, leading opposing armies, died, each by the other's hand.

59. Cyrnus is Corsica. There was also apparently a local hero Cyrnus, presumably somewhere near Rhegium. One could "found" (ktizein) a hero by establishing rituals in his honor, as one "founds" a city (also ktizein). Both proceedings demand, properly, some festival or dedicatory rite, in the one case proclaiming the hero as the city's hero, in the other, proclaiming the city as the mother of its inhabitants. It is somewhat the same as the not quite laicized "opening" of a building or launching of a ship in present-day Britain when the ceremony is performed by royalty.

boats and sailed off for the parts of Thrace and there founded the city of Abdera, which, indeed, had been founded, before this time, by Timesias of Clazomenae; but Timesias had got no good of his work but was driven out by the Thracians. However, he is now honored as a hero by the Teians of Abdera.

169. These were the only peoples among the Ionians who left their countries rather than endure slavery. All the rest, except the Milesians, fought it out against Harpagus, just as those did who left their countries, and indeed they proved themselves good men and true, each fighting for his own land. But when they were defeated and conquered, they remained each of them where they were and did what they were commanded to do. The Milesians, as I said before, had already made a sworn compact with Cyrus and therefore remained at peace. Thus, for the second time, Ionia was enslaved; and when Harpagus had subdued the Ionians on the mainland, the Ionians of the islands took sudden fright and surrendered themselves to Cyrus.[60]

170. For all that the Ionians had fallen on evil times, they nonetheless gathered at the Panionium, and it was then, as I understand, that Bias, a man of Priene, laid his very useful judgment before the Ionians, which, had they accepted it, would have allowed them to be the most fortunate of all the Greeks. Bias bade the Ionians set sail and go to Sardinia, in a common enterprise, and there establish one city of all the Ionians. Thus they would deliver themselves from slavery and be truly fortunate, possessing the largest island in the world and ruling over others; if they remained in Ionia, said Bias, he saw no hope of freedom for them in the future. Such was the judgment of Bias of Priene, rendered to the Ionians when they were already a ruined folk; but good, too, was the judgment of Thales of Miletus (a man of remote Phoenician descent), and that was given before the ruin was accomplished. He bade the Ionians set up a supreme deliberative council, to be established in Teos, as this was the middle point of Ionia, all the other cities there to be held in no greater regard than as demes.[61] These, then, were the judgments delivered by these two men.

60. The Persian conquest of Ionia was accomplished in 546–545 B.C.
61. "Demes" is the name for the local voting units scattered throughout Attica. What is meant here is that the other sovereign cities of Ionia, treating Teos

171. Harpagus, having subdued Ionia, marched against the Carians and Caunians and Lycians, bringing with him, in his own army, the Ionians and Aeolians. Now, among these, the Carians had come to the mainland from the islands; for in the old days these Carians were subjects of Minos and were called Leleges when they possessed the islands. They paid no tribute to Minos, according to the furthest back that I could reach from hearsay; but whenever Minos made demand of them, they used to man ships for him; and, inasmuch as Minos conquered a great deal of land and was very successful in war, the Carian race was the most regarded of all at that time—far the most so. They made three discoveries of which the Greeks made use. They are the people who began the practice of binding plumes on helmets and painting designs on shields, and they were the first who made grips for the shields themselves. Before this time those who were wont to use shields carried them without handholds, guiding them by leathern baldrics, which they hung around their necks and left shoulders. Then, a long time afterwards, the Dorians and Ionians drove the Carians from the islands, and that is how these latter came to the mainland. At any rate, that is the story the Cretans tell of the Carians, though it is not what the Carians themselves say. The Carians declare that they have always lived on the mainland and were always called by the same name as now. As evidence they point to the ancient temple of Carian Zeus in Mylasa, to which Lydians and Mysians are admitted as brothers of the Carians; for Lydus and Mys, say the Carians, were brothers of Car. These are indeed admitted, but others, even those who speak the same language as the Carians, are not admitted if they are of another national origin.

172. Personally, I believe that the Caunians have always lived in the same country,[62] though they themselves say that they came from

---

as their capital town, would have their position radically altered to make them of merely local significance. Some editors have pointed out that Teos was intentionally chosen not only because it was centrally located but because it was a small community of no previous importance; thus the jealousy of the rest would be diminished. The editors also remark on the somewhat similar choice of Washington, D.C., to head the federal experiment in early U.S. history.

62. The adjective that Herodotus uses of the Caunians is *autochthonoi*, "themselves and their earth," the Greek word for having always lived where you now are. The same word is used by the Carians of themselves in chapter 171.

Crete. As to speech, theirs has grown very like the Carian speech, or the Carians' to theirs (for I cannot exactly decide that), but in their customs they are entirely different from the Carians and, indeed, from the rest of mankind. The finest of things for them is to keep company together, men, women, and children, in groups according to age and friendship—for drinking. There were foreign rites established among them, but later they turned against them and resolved to follow none but their own gods; and so all the Caunians, putting on their armor—all, that is, of military age—advanced to the boundaries of their country, beating the air with their spears and saying that they were driving out the gods of the foreigners.

173. Those, then, are the customs they practice. The Lycians *did* come from Crete in ancient times (for all of Crete in those days was possessed by barbarians). There was a rivalry in Crete about the throne between Sarpedon and Minos, Europa's sons. Minos won out in the struggle; he drove out Sarpedon and his party, and, when these latter were expelled, they came to the land of Milyas in Asia. This was in those days Milyas, which now the Lycians live in; at that time the Milyans were called Solymi. While Sarpedon ruled them, they were called by the name they brought with them (and by which the Lycians are still called by their neighbors): Termilae. But when Lycus, son of Pandion, came to the Termilae from Athens to join Sarpedon, they became, in the course of time, Lycians, taking him for their namesake; for Lycus, too, had been driven out by *his* brother, Aegeus. Their customs are partly Cretan and partly Carian, but they have one particular custom that they share with no people at all: they take their names from their mothers, not from their fathers. When one of them asks his neighbor who he is, the man will list his ancestry on his mother's side and call over his mother's mothers. And indeed, if a woman of birth lives with a slave, her children are counted freeborn. But if a man that is a citizen, and even the first of them, has a foreign wife or concubine, the children are dishonored.

174. The Carians, then, were enslaved by Harpagus, having achieved no gallant deed at all; neither, indeed, did any of the Greeks that dwell in that country, including the Lacedaemonian colonists, the Cnidians. Theirs is a piece of land, called Triopium,

facing toward the sea. It begins from the Bubassian peninsula, and all of Cnidos, except a tiny bit, is sea-girt; to the north, the gulf of Ceramicus bounds it, and, to the south, the sea off Syme and Rhodes. This small neck of land, which is some five stades wide, the Cnidians tried to dig through while Harpagus was conquering Ionia. They wanted to make their country an island indeed. The whole of the country was being brought within the entrenchment, for the isthmus through which they were digging was the place where the land of Cnidos ends in the mainland. They worked hard, and many hands were busy in it; but more of the workmen than was reasonable seemed to get hurt from the splintering of the stone, in all parts of their bodies and especially the eyes, till it appeared miraculous. So the Cnidians sent an embassy to Delphi to ask what it was that was thwarting them. According to the story of the Cnidians themselves, the Pythia gave them this answer in trimeters:

No walls across the isthmus; do not dig it.
If he so willed, Zeus would have made it island.

When the Pythia gave that oracle to the Cnidians, they gave over their entrenchment and, without fighting at all, surrendered to Harpagus when he invaded them.

175. There were Pedasians who lived in the hinterland above Halicarnassus. Now, as often as anything untoward was about to happen to these people or their neighbors, the priestess of Athena would grow a great beard. This happened to them three times. Of those who live about Caria, these were the only men who held out for any time against Harpagus, and they caused him the most trouble, fortifying a hill called Lide.

176. At last the Pedasians, too, were reduced; but the Lycians, when Harpagus drove his army into the plain of Xanthus, came out against him and fought; they were few against many, but they performed great deeds of bravery. Still, they were defeated, and, being driven into the city, they gathered their wives, children, property, and servants into the citadel and then set fire to the entire citadel, to burn it all. Having done so, and sworn mighty oaths to one another, they issued forth and died in battle, all the men of Xanthus. Of the Xanthians who now claim to be Lycians, the most part, except for eighty families, are of foreign descent. These eighty families

chanced to be away from the town at the time of the attack and so survived. So Harpagus captured Xanthus, much as he had also captured Caunus; for the most part the Caunians imitated the Lycians.

177. Now, Harpagus had devastated lower Asia, and the upper part Cyrus himself destroyed, subduing every nation and leaving none untouched. Most of these I will pass over, mentioning only those that gave him most trouble and did deeds most worthy of mention.

178. When Cyrus had made subjects of all the peoples of the mainland, he attacked the Assyrians. In Assyria there are many great cities, but the most famous and strongest, and the one where the royal palace was established after the destruction of Nineveh, was Babylon. This is the kind of city it is. It lies in a great plain, and, each side being one hundred and twenty stades, it is a square.[63] So the circumference of the city of Babylon is some four hundred and eighty stades. Such is its bigness, and it is planned as no other city of which we know. First a ditch, broad and deep, full of water, runs around it and, after that, a wall that is in thickness fifty royal cubits and in height two hundred. The royal cubit is greater by three fingers' breadth than the ordinary cubit.[64]

179. I must explain also where the earth was used that was taken from the trench and how the wall was built. As they dug the trench, they made bricks of the mud that was carried out of the trench; and when they had made enough of the bricks, they baked them in ovens. Then, using hot asphalt for cement and stuffing in mats of reeds at every thirty courses of bricks, they built first the banks of the trench and then the wall itself in the same manner. On top of the wall, along the edges, they built houses of a single room facing one another. A space was left between these houses big enough for a four-horse chariot to drive through. There were a hundred gates set

63. How and Wells, which is still the main archeological and historical commentary on Herodotus, says, of his account of Babylon, that Herodotus "gives a striking impressionist picture of this great scheme of fortification, but . . . it is incorrect in details." Aristotle, a century later, says that when Babylon was captured it took two days before some parts of the city heard the bad news (*Politics* 3.5.1276a; cf. below, chap. 191).

64. The common cubit is 18¼ inches, the royal 20½. Hence the walls were 335 feet high and 85 feet thick. Most authorities believe that Herodotus had visited Babylon.

in the circuit of the wall, all of bronze, and of bronze likewise the posts and the lintels. There is another city, some eight days' journey from Babylon, called Is, where there is a small river, also called Is. It empties into the stream of the Euphrates. This river Is brings to the surface, with its waters, many lumps of asphalt, and it was from it that the asphalt was conveyed for the walls of Babylon.

180. Such, then, had been the building of the walls of Babylon. There are two divisions of the city, for the river called Euphrates divides it in the middle. It flows from Armenia—a great, deep, and swift stream—and it issues into the Red Sea.[65] Each wall of the city has its ends brought right down to the river, and from there they turn and, in the form of a dry wall of baked bricks, stretch along the banks of the river. The city itself is full of three- and four-storied houses, and the roads that cut through it are straight, including those that run crosswise to the river. As each road ends at the wall beside the river, small gates are set in it, one gate for each alley-way. These gates are also of bronze and also open on the river.

181. This wall is the breastplate, but there is another wall inside it, not much weaker, though narrower, that also encircles the city. In each of the two divisions of the city there is a great fortification in the middle. Within the one is the royal palace, encircled by a high strong wall; within the other, the bronze-gated temple of Zeus Belus, a square of two stades each way, which was still there in my time. In the midst of the temple square there was built a solid tower, in length and breadth one stade, and on this tower was mounted another, and another still on the top of that—eight of them in all. The ascent to these has been constructed circularly, on the outside, around all the towers. Halfway up the ascent there is a halting place and seats to rest on, where the climbers sit and rest. In the last tower there is a great temple, and in the temple there stands a great bed, well covered, and by it is set a golden table. But there is no image whatever in the temple, neither does any human being spend the night there, save one woman only, of the natives of the place, whom the god has chosen out of all, as declare the Chaldaean priests of this god.

182. These same Chaldaeans say—though I myself do not believe their story—that the god is wont to come to this temple and

65. Here, the Persian Gulf (cf. note 1, above).

rest on this couch, as also in Egyptian Thebes, according to the account of the Egyptians. For there, too, in that temple of Zeus of Thebes, a woman sleeps, and both of these women (she in Thebes and she in Babylon) have no intercourse with men. This is also the case of the prophetess of the god at Patara in Lycia, whenever there is such a one; for there is not always a place of divination there. But when there is a prophetess, she is shut up in the temple by night.

183. In the Babylonian temple there is another shrine below, where there is a great golden image of Zeus, seated, and a great gold table set beside, and of gold, too, are the chair and its platform. As the Chaldaeans tell it, some eight hundred talents of gold were used in this. Outside the temple there is a golden altar and another great altar as well, on which full-grown victims are sacrificed. (On the golden one there may be sacrificed only sucklings.) On the bigger one, too, the Chaldaeans burn a thousand talents' weight of frankincense a year, when they celebrate the festival of this god. There was in that sanctuary at that time[66] a statue of solid gold, fifteen feet high. I did not see this myself but give my account on the strength of what the Chaldaeans say. This statue Darius, son of Hystaspes, was set to take, but his courage failed him; but Xerxes his son took it and, besides, killed the priest who forbade him to move the statue. This is the adornment of the shrine; there are many private dedications besides.

184. There were many kings of this city of Babylon, of whom I shall make mention in my Assyrian account,[67] who further adorned the fortifications and temples; and among the sovereigns there were two women. The first ruled five generations before the second; her name was Semiramis, and she built those dikes on the plain that are so remarkable to see; before that, the river used to run all over the plain and flood it.

185. The second of these queens was called Nitocris, and she was a wiser woman than the first. She left as a memorial the works I shall shortly tell you of and, besides, took certain measures of precaution, as best she could, for what was to come; for she saw that the empire of the Medes was great and never at rest and that cities belonging to

66. I.e., when Cyrus conquered Babylon.
67. Herodotus does not seem to have done so. There is much controversy as to whether he really meant to develop some independent history of Assyria.

the Assyrians had already been destroyed by it, among them even Nineveh.[68] First, then, as to the Euphrates, which flows right through the middle of the city of Babylon. Formerly it was straight, but she made it so crooked, by digging canals above the city, that the river in its course comes three times to one of the Assyrian villages. The name of this village to which the Euphrates comes is Ardericca. So now those who travel from our sea to Babylon, as they sail down the Euphrates, come thrice to this same village, and on three several days. This is what she did, and she built an embankment along either shore of the river that is, in greatness and height, very wonderful in its dimensions. Far above Babylon she dug a basin for a lake, stretching it by the side of the river and a little away from it, and in depth she dug it always down to find water, and in breadth she made the circuit of the lake to be fifty-two and a half miles. The spoil of this basin she used up by heaping it up along the banks of the river. When it was all dug, she brought stones and formed them in a coping all along the basin. She did both of these things—the making the river crooked and turning the basin into a marsh—so that the river might be slower, as it was broken by the many bends, and that the courses into Babylon itself might be crooked, and that then, after this, should come the long circuit of the lake.[69] These works were built at precisely the point of her country where were the passes of entry and the shortcuts from the road out of Media, so that the Medes might not get into contact with her people and learn of her affairs.

186. With these defenses she surrounded her city, but she added another work that grew out of them. The city has two divisions, the river being in the middle, and, in the time of former monarchs, when anyone wished to cross from one division to the other, he must use a boat, which, I suppose, was vexatious. Against this, too, the queen took measures. For when she had dug the basin of the lake, she left this other memorial out of this same work. She had huge stones cut, and when the stones were ready and the basin had been

68. Nineveh fell in 612 B.C.
69. As How and Wells point out, Herodotus contradicts himself in speaking of the "basin" or reservoir as a marsh and yet as navigable. They think he did not understand that these great works were intended chiefly for irrigation, not national defense.

dug, she turned the entire stream of the river into the place that was dug. While it was filling, the old riverbed dried out; and she bricked with baked bricks, in fashion like to the walls, the banks of the river in the city and the descents from the gates leading down to the river; and as near as possible to the middle of the city she built a bridge with the stones she had dug, binding the stones together with iron and lead. On this bridge she stretched, each morning, square hewn planks on which the people of Babylon could cross. By night the planks were withdrawn, so that the inhabitants might not keep crossing at night and steal from one another. When the dug part had become a lake, filled by the river, and her arrangements about the bridge were complete, she turned the Euphrates into its old course, out of the lake, and so the dug part, it would seem, served her purpose in becoming a swamp—and there! The citizens had a bridge ready built for them.

187. This same queen contrived the following cheat: she had a tomb made for herself right above the gate of the city where there was the most traffic of people. She had writing graven on the tomb which read: "Of those that after me are kings of Babylon, should any lack money, let him open this tomb and take what he will. But if he does not truly lack, let him not open it; it were better not." This tomb was undisturbed until the reign of Darius. But Darius found it strange that he should never use this gate and that the money should lie there inviting him and he should not take it. He never used this gate because, then, a dead body would be above his head as he passed through. He had the tomb opened and found no money but a dead body and an inscription, which read: "If you were not insatiate of money, and set on gain, however base, you would not have opened the coffin of the dead." This is the sort of woman this queen is said to have been.

188. It was against this woman's son that Cyrus made war; he had both his father's name, Labynetus, and his rule over the Assyrians. Now the Great King goes on campaign well equipped with food from home and with flocks and herds; he brings with him, too, water from the Choaspes River, which flows by Susa; it is from this river and none other in the world that the Great King drinks. The Choaspes water is boiled, and very many four-wheeled wagons, drawn by mules, carry it along, stored in silver containers, as often as he journeys, wherever it may be.

189. Cyrus, then, traveled toward Babylon and came to the river Gyndes. The springs of the Gyndes are in the Matieni Mountains, and it flows through the Dardanean country and issues into another river, the Tigris, which in turn flows by the city of Opis and empties into the Red Sea. Now when Cyrus was trying to cross this river Gyndes, which at this point could be crossed by boats, one of his sacred white horses dashed into the stream, full of high spirits and eager to win to the other side. But the river overwhelmed it and carried it under and away. Cyrus was furious with the river for its insolence and threatened it: "I will make you so feeble that, for the rest of time, even women will easily cross you without wetting their knees." After this threat he gave over his campaign against Babylon and divided his army into two. He then drew lines, mapping out one hundred and eighty canals along each bank of the Gyndes and running in all directions, and he drew up his army along the lines, where he bade them dig. There was a great mass of men working, and the task went ahead; yet they spent all summer on it before they finished working right where they were.

190. When Cyrus had thus punished the Gyndes by dividing it into three hundred and sixty channels and the first signs of the second spring had dawned, he drove again against Babylon. The Babylonians came out against him and stood their ground. When his advance brought him near to the city, the Babylonians joined battle but were worsted and were driven back within the city. Now inasmuch as they had known Cyrus, from before this, as one never at rest, and as they saw him attacking every nation alike, they had stored up provisions ahead of time, enough for many years. So now they made no account of the siege, and Cyrus was at his wits' end, as the time grew longer and longer and his business was no whit advanced.

191. Whether it was on the advice of someone else in his difficulty or from his own understanding of what needed to be done, this is what he did. He stationed his main army on the river where it enters the town and some other troops behind the town, where the river issues forth; and he bade his men, when they saw the stream becoming fordable, to enter the city by the riverbed. Having made his dispositions thus, and having given his instruction in this sense, he drew off, himself, with the least useful part of his army. When he came to the lake, Cyrus dealt with it, and with the river, just as the

Babylonian queen had done: he directed the river by a canal into the lake, which had become a marsh, and so, when the river had sunk, its old stream became fordable. When this happened, the Persians, who for this very purpose were stationed along the stream, entered Babylon by the riverbed when the Euphrates had sunk till it reached but to the middle of a man's thigh. If the Babylonians had had any foreknowledge or understanding of what Cyrus was at, they would have allowed the Persians to come inside and then have utterly destroyed them; for if they had closed all the gates down to the river and themselves mounted on the top of the drywalls that stretched along the banks of the river, they would have caught the Persians as in a trap. As it was, the Persians were upon them when they were quite unaware. By reason of the size of the city, as some of the inhabitants say, when the outer parts were all already taken, those who lived in the center of Babylon did not know that they, the Babylonians, had been captured. They had a festival going on at the time, and they continued dancing and enjoying themselves until they learned the truth all too well.

192. Thus was Babylon captured for the first time.[70] Now there are many ways by which I can show the power of Babylon, how great it is, but this shall be the special indication. The whole land over which the Great King rules is divided up for providing the maintenance of himself and his army—this apart from the tribute it yields. Of the twelve months of the year, the country of Babylon feeds him for four, and all the rest of Asia for the remaining eight. So, in power, the land of Assyria counts as one third of all Asia. Rule over this country—which rule is called by the Persians a satrapy—is of all the satrapies far the greatest; for instance, when Tritantaechmes, the son of Artabazus, held this satrapy from the Great King, he received each day an artaba full of silver. (This artaba is a Persian measure and contains three Attic choenixes more than an Attic medimnus.)[71] He had horses, too, for his private use, apart from his military chargers: eight hundred breeding stallions and sixteen thousand mares, one stallion to each twenty mares. Of Indian dogs for hunting he kept such a number that four great villages on the plain were exempted from all other tribute save for the assessment that they

70. Babylon fell to Cyrus in 538 B.C.
71. A medimnus is equal to twelve gallons or five bushels.

must feed these dogs. Such were the revenues of the governor of Babylon.

193. Very little rain falls in the land of Assyria, and this little is what nourishes the root of the crop; but it is in its watering from the river that the corn crop[72] wins to its ripeness and the bread grain comes into being. It is not as in Egypt, where the river itself rises over the fields; in Babylon the watering is done by hand-operated swing beams.[73] For all the Babylonian country, as in the case of Egypt, is cut up with canals. The greatest of these can carry boats; it runs toward the southeast, from the Euphrates to the Tigris, on the banks of which was the city of Nineveh. Of all the lands that we know, this is far the most fertile for Demeter's crop.[74] Other plants it grows not at all—neither fig tree nor vine nor olive. But for Demeter's crop it is so fertile that it yields on the average two hundredfold[75] and, at its best, three hundredfold. The blades of wheat and barley are easily three inches wide; as for the millet and sesame, though I know very well the size of the plant there, I will not speak of it; for I am aware that, for those who have not gone to Babylon, even what I have said so far about the crops has encountered great disbelief. The people use no oil from the olive, but only from sesame. There are palm trees growing all over the plain, yielding fruit from which the people make bread, wine, and honey. They treat these trees like fig trees; in especial, they tie the fruit of those palm trees the Greeks call male to the date-bearing palm so that the fruit wasp, creeping into the dates, may cause them to ripen and the date may not fall to the ground. For the male plants do indeed carry in their fruit the fruit wasp, just as the wild fig trees do.[76]

72. I have rendered the Greek word *sitos* in the British way as "corn," meaning all the small grains: barley, wheat, millet, etc. It does not mean American "corn"—i.e., maize—which the Greeks did not know.

73. The device referred to is a long pole with a water scoop at one end and a counterweight at the other. This pivots on a base built next to the source of water. The worker dips the scoop into the water, then swings it out and empties it into an irrigation ditch. This device is still in use today in Egypt and the Middle East.

74. I.e., "corn," in the sense indicated in note 72.

75. This means two hundred times the weight of the grain used as seed.

76. Here Herodotus has apparently confused the impregnation of the dates, through the medium of the fruit flies and pollen, with some idea that this prevents the fruit from falling to the ground, withered.

194. The greatest wonder of all this region, after the city itself, I will now tell you: it is the boats that travel down the river to Babylon. They are circular in shape and made all of skins. They build them higher up, beyond Assyria, in Armenia, and they cut ribs of willow to make them. Then they stretch, over these, hides to cover them on the outside, like a kind of hull. They do not broaden the stern or narrow the prow but leave the boat round, like a shield. They fill the whole boat with straw, load it with freight, and launch it downstream, to travel with the current. What the boats carry down mostly are palmwood casks full of wine. They are steered by two paddles, with the two men standing upright in the boat; the one pulls his paddle toward him, the other thrusts his out. The boats are made, some in very large size, and some in small. The biggest of them are up to one hundred and twenty-five tons burden. In each boat there is a live donkey, and in the bigger boats more than one. When in their voyage they come to Babylon and dispose of their cargo, they auction off the ribs of willow from the boats and all the straw, and they pack up the skins on their donkeys and drive off to Armenia. For it is in no way possible to travel upstream, because of the quickness of the current; that is why, also, the boats are made of skins instead of wood. When they have come back to Armenia, driving their donkeys, they make other boats again in the same way.

195. That is what the boats are like. For clothes, the people wear a linen tunic reaching to their feet and, over that, another one of wool, and they wrap themselves up in a small white cloak; and they wear shoes of their country, very like Boeotian sandals. They let their hair grow long, and they wear a kind of peaked cap or turban. They saturate their whole body with myrrh. Each of them has his own seal and a carved staff. On the staff is the image of an apple, rose, or lily or of an eagle or something else. It is customary with them never to have a staff without some device.

196. Such is the equipment of the body. Among their established customs there is one that in my opinion is the very wisest. (I learn that the Eneti of Illyria also practice it.) In every village, once a year, the people did the following: as the girls in the village became ripe for marriage, they gathered and brought together all such to one place. There was a great throng of men surrounding it, and the auctioneer put the girls up, one by one, for sale. He would begin with

the best-looking, and, after she had been sold and brought a great price, he would auction off her whose looks were next best. They were all sold to live with their men.[77] All the rich men of Babylon who were disposed to marriage outbid one another in buying the beauties. But those of the lower classes who wanted to marry were not set on fairness of form but took the uglier girls, with money to boot. For when the auctioneer had gone through all the best-looking girls, he would put up the ugliest, or one that was crippled, and would sell her off: "Who will take least money to live with this one?" This money came from the sale of the good-looking girls, so those who were handsome portioned off the ill-favored and the cripples. But no man might give away his daughters to whom he pleased, nor might any man take any girl by buying her without a guarantor; he must produce his guarantor for a solemn promise to live with her in his home and only so be allowed to take her away. If the couple could not agree, the law was that the money must be returned. It was also possible for anyone who pleased to come from another village and buy. This was their finest custom, but it has not persisted till this day. Lately they have discovered something new.[78] Since the conquest of Babylon and the general ruin, everyone of the common sort who is destitute of a livelihood prostitutes his female children.

197. Here is another of their customs, one that is second in wisdom. They bring their sick into the marketplace, for they do not use doctors at all. In the marketplace the passers-by approach the sick and give them advice about their sickness, whenever someone has suffered the same sickness as the patient or has seen another with it. They approach and advise and comfort, telling by what means they themselves have recovered from the sickness or have seen another do so. One may not pass by a sick person in silence, without asking him what ails him.

77. The word used is *synoikein*, which means "to live in the same house with." It was often used of two slaves who lived together when the marriage of such may not have been legal. In the present case, the term implies that the buyer is committed to having the woman in his house as mate and partner; he cannot treat her as a whore or get rid of her after she has come into his possession.

78. What follows in the Greek is a phrase that is apparently corrupt and has made its way into the text: "to prevent the wronging of the women or bringing them to another city."

198. Their burials are made with the dead embalmed in honey, and their dirges are much the same as those of the Egyptians. And whenever a man of Babylon has lain with his own wife, he sits about a burnt offering of incense, and the woman on the other side sits too, and as dawn comes they both of them wash themselves. For they will touch no vessel until they wash. This is the same also among the Arabians.

199. The ugliest of the customs among the Babylonians is this: every woman who lives in that country must once in her lifetime go to the temple of Aphrodite and sit there and be lain with by a strange man. Many of the women who are too proud to mix with the others—such, for instance, as are uplifted by the wealth they have—ride to the temple in covered carriages drawn by teams and stay there then with a great mass of attendants following them. But most of the women do thus: they sit in the sacred precinct of Aphrodite with a garland round their heads made of string.[79] There is constant coming and going, and there are roped-off passages running through the crowds of women in every direction, through which the strangers walk and take their pick. When once a woman has taken her seat there, she may not go home again until one of the strangers throws a piece of silver into her lap and lies with her, outside the temple. As he throws a coin, the man says, "I summon you in the name of Mylitta." (The Assyrians call Aphrodite Mylitta.) The greatness of the coin may be what it may, for it is not lawful to reject it, since this money, once it is thrown, becomes sacred. The woman must follow the first man who throws the money into her lap and may reject none. Once she has lain with him, she has fulfilled her obligation to the goddess and gets gone to her home. From that time forth you cannot give her any sum large enough to get her. Those women who have attained to great beauty and height depart quickly enough, but those who are ugly abide there a great while, being unable to fulfill the law. Some, indeed, stay there as much as three or four years. In some parts of Cyprus, too, there is a custom like this.

200. These, then, are the customs of the Babylonians. There are among them three tribes that eat nothing but fish. These fish, when

79. How and Wells note that the string is "a symbol of their service due to the goddess."

caught, they dry in the sun and then throw them into a mortar, where they bray them with pestles and finally strain the result through muslin. Some of them who like it so make a kind of cake of this; others bake it like bread.

201. When Cyrus had conquered this nation too, he set his heart on subduing the Massagetae. This is a race, said to be great and warlike, which lives toward the east and the rising of the sun, beyond the river Araxes and opposite the Issedones. Some say, besides, that they are a Scythian people.

202. The river Araxes is said by some to be greater than the Ister;[80] by others, to be smaller. People say that there are many islands in it as big as Lesbos and, in these, men who eat roots of all kinds, which they dig up in summer; and they have discovered fruit from bushes which, when it is ripe, they store for food, and this they eat in the winter; other bushes, too, they have found out, which produce a special crop. This fruit the people throw into a fire, which they light and gather round in crowds, and there they sit and sniff it as it burns, where they have thrown it on the fire. With the smell they grow drunk, as the Greeks do with wine, and, as more and more of the fruit is thrown on the fire, the people get drunker and drunker, till they rise up to dance and sing. Such, it is said, is how they live their daily life. The river Araxes flows from the Matieni, from which the Gyndes also comes (the river that Cyrus divided into the three hundred and sixty channels), and it empties out through forty mouths, all of which, except one, issue into swamps and marshes. It is said that in these marshes live men who eat their fish raw and are accustomed to wear clothes made of sealskin. The one of the mouths of the Araxes that flows through a clear channel empties into the Caspian Sea.

203. The Caspian is a sea on its own, not mingling with the other; for the sea on which the Greeks sail, and the entire sea outside the Pillars of Heracles, which is called the Atlantic, and the Red Sea[81] are all one. But the Caspian is on its own and is in length, for rowing, a voyage of fifteen days and, in breadth, at its broadest, eight days. Along the western side of this sea stretch the Caucasus

80. The Ister is the Danube.
81. See note 1.

Mountains, having more and higher peaks than any other. Many and every sort of nation the Caucasus contains within itself, most of them living from the fruit of wild trees. Among them, they say, there are trees with leaves such that, when they crush them and mix them with water, they can paint on their clothes figures of animals. These figures of animals do not wash out but grow old with the wool, as though they were woven into it at the beginning. Here the men and women couple openly (they say), like animals in flocks.

204. So to the west of this sea called Caspian there is the barrier of the Caucasus, but to the east and the rising sun there succeeds a plain that stretches endlessly to the eye. A very great share of this huge plain the Massagetae have as their portion; it was against them that Cyrus was bent on making war. There were many great inducements to urge him on; first, his own birth, in respect to which he appeared to be something more than human, and, second, his good luck in his wars. For wherever Cyrus directed his attack, that people could in no way escape.

205. The king of the Massagetae was dead, and his wife had taken over the sovereignty; her name was Tomyris. To her Cyrus sent and would have wooed her—in word—to be his wife. But Tomyris, who understood that it was not herself that he was wooing but the kingship of the Massagetae, said no to his approaches. After this, Cyrus, since he had gained nothing by craft, drove as far as the Araxes and now openly made a campaign against the Massagetae, building bridges over the river for the passage of his army and building towers on the rafts that were to carry his men over.

206. As he labored over all this, Tomyris sent him a herald and said: "King of the Medes, cease to be so eager to do what you are doing; for you cannot know whether, when accomplished, it will stand you in good stead. Give it over and rule over your own people, and endure to look upon us governing ours. Still, you will not follow this advice of mine, but will do anything rather than remain at rest. So, if you are so mightily set upon making trial of the Massagetae, give over your work of building bridges over the river; we will retreat three days' journey from the river, and do you cross over into our land. Or, if you would rather welcome us into yours, do you withdraw for the three days' journey." When Cyrus heard this, he called a council of the chief men of the Persians and in the assembly put the proposition to them, taking advice of them as to which he

should do. Their judgments were all the same, that they should admit Tomyris and her army into their own country.

207. But Croesus the Lydian was there and found fault with this judgment, and declared another that was the opposite to what was accepted. His words were these: "My lord, I told you long ago that, since Zeus had given me to you, whatsoever I saw that could make your house fall, I would to the extent of my power prevent it. My own sufferings have been a harsh teacher for me. If it is immortal that you think yourself, and immortal the army that you govern, there would be no ground for me to give you advice. But if you know that you too are a man and that even such are those you rule, learn this first of all: that all human matters are a wheel, and, as it turns, it never suffers the same men to be happy forever. So it is that I now have a different judgment about the matter in hand than these others. If we shall admit the enemy onto our land, there is a danger in that, and it is this: if you are worsted, you will lose your whole empire along with the battle. For it is clear that if the Massagetae conquer they will never flee back but will drive through into all your realms. But if you win, you will not win as much as if you had crossed into the enemy's country and, conquering the Massagetae, were hot on the heels of a flying enemy. For I will balance the two positions equally; I will assume that, having conquered those who confront you here, you will drive into the heart of Queen Tomyris' empire. Apart from all that I have said so far, it is a shame, and not to be borne, that Cyrus, son of Cambyses, should yield and give ground to a woman. So in my opinion we ought to cross over and advance as far as the enemy will let us, and from then on take the following measures to get the better of them. As I understand it, the Massagetae are inexperienced in the good things of Persia and have never tasted of what is great and glorious. For these men, therefore, I would have you unsparingly slaughter many from your flocks and herds, and dress the meat and set it out in our camp for a banquet, and unsparingly set on bowls of wine unmixed with water and all sorts of viands. Having done so, I would leave behind the meanest part of our army and march away with the rest as far as the river. If I do not err in my judgment, the enemy, when they see these many good things, will fall to, to possess them; and, from then on, what is left to you is the display of valiant deeds."

208. These, then, were the opposing judgments. And Cyrus let

go his former choice and took the opinion of Croesus. He bade Tomyris retreat, for he himself would cross over into her country. So she withdrew, as she had promised at the first. Cyrus put Croesus into the hands of his son, Cambyses, to whom he was giving the kingdom, and he charged the boy to honor him and treat him well, if his own crossing against the Massagetae should go ill with him. So then he gave these orders to his son and sent him and Croesus away to the land of Persia, and he himself and his army crossed the river.

209. When he had crossed the Araxes, the night came on him and, as he slept in the land of the Massagetae, he saw a vision and it was this: it seemed to him in his dream that he saw the eldest of the sons of Hystaspes with wings on his shoulders, and with one of these wings he overshadowed Asia and, with the other, Europe. Now Hystaspes was the son of Arsames, an Achaemenid, and his eldest son, Darius, was a boy of about twenty who had been left behind in Persia; for he was not yet of age to serve in the army. When Cyrus waked up, he reflected within himself about the dream; and inasmuch as he thought it a great one, he summoned Hystaspes and, taking him aside, said to him, "Hystaspes, your son has been caught plotting against me and my empire. I will signify to you how I know this so exactly: the gods have care for me and show me in advance all that is coming upon me. So now in this past night, as I slept, I saw the eldest of your sons with wings on his shoulders, and with the one he overshadowed Asia and, with the other, Europe. So by this dream it cannot but be that he is plotting against me. Go back now, you, quickly to Persia, and take measures that when I come thither again, after conquering these people here, you may put your son before me to examine him."

210. That is what Cyrus said, because he thought that Darius was plotting against him. But to him the god was giving signs that he himself should die, right there where he was, and that his kingship should pass to Darius. Hystaspes answered: "My lord, let never Persian be born that shall plot against you, and, if he exist, let him die right quickly. You have made the Persians from being slaves into free men and, instead of being ruled, to be the rulers of all others. If this dream tells you that my son is plotting against you, I will turn him over to you to do whatsoever you will with him."

211. So Hystaspes answered him and then crossed the Araxes and betook himself to Persia, there to guard his son against the com-

ing of Cyrus. Cyrus advanced one day's journey from the Araxes and accomplished what Croesus had advised. After that, Cyrus and the sound part of his army marched back to the Araxes, leaving the useless part behind. Then one third of the army of the Massagetae made an onslaught on them and butchered those of Cyrus' army that had been left behind, despite their resistance. The Massagetae saw the feasts set out before them, once they had conquered their enemy, and, having filled themselves with food and wine, they lay down to sleep. But the Persians stole on them and killed many and took prisoner even more, and among these was the son of Tomyris, who was general of the army of the Massagetae; his name was Spargapises.

212. When his mother heard what had happened to her son and her army, she sent a herald to Cyrus with this message: "Cyrus, insatiate of blood, be not uplifted by this thing that has happened—that with this fruit of the vine, whereof you Persians fill yourselves even to madness, so that, as the wine descends into your body, ill words rise up in you to the top—be not uplifted, I say, because with such a powerful drug you have overmastered my son by trickery and not by strength and fighting. Now, therefore, take this proposal from me, for I advise you well. Give back my son to me now and get out of our country, paying no penalty, although you have done violence and insolence to one-third of the army of the Massagetae. If you do not so, I swear by the sun, the lord of the Massagetae, that, for all your insatiability of blood, I will give you your fill of it."

213. But Cyrus paid no heed to these words, which were reported to him. The son of Queen Tomyris, Spargapises, when the wine had died in him and he knew in what calamity he was, asked Cyrus to be relieved of his chains, and he gained his request; but as soon as he was freed and was master of his hands, he made away with himself.

214. That was the end of him. Tomyris, since Cyrus would not listen to her, gathered all her host together and fought him. Of all the battles that were fought among the barbarians, I judge this to have been the severest, and indeed my information is that this is so. First, they say, the two sides remained at a distance from one another and shot arrows, and afterwards, when all their missiles were spent, they fought hand to hand with spears and daggers. Long they remained fighting in close combat, and neither side would flee. But

finally the Massagetae got the upper hand. The most of the Persian army died on the spot and, among them, Cyrus himself, having ruled, in all, twenty-nine years. Tomyris sought out his corpse among the Persian dead, and, when she found it, she filled a skin with human blood and fixed his head in the skin, and, insulting over the dead, she said: "I am alive and conqueror, but you have destroyed me, all the same, by robbing me of my son by trickery. Now it is you and I; and I will give you your fill of blood, even as I threatened." There are many stories of the death of Cyrus, but this that I have told seems to me the most convincing.[82]

215. The Massagetae wear the same kind of clothes as the Scythians and live much the same. They are both cavalry and infantry— for they have some of both—and archers and spearmen; and they are used to carry battle-axes as well. They use gold and bronze for everything. For their spearpoints and arrowheads and battle-axes are all made of bronze, but on their headgear, belts, and girdles they use adornments of gold. In the same way, the breastplates of their horses are bronze, but the reins, bits, and cheekplates are of gold. Iron and silver they do not use at all, for indeed there is none in their country, but there is a great plenty of gold and bronze.

216. These are their customs: each of them marries a wife, but the wives they have in common. The Greeks say that it is the Scythians that do this, but it is not the Scythians that do so but the Massagetae. When a man of the Massagetae desires a woman, he hangs his quiver on the front of her wagon and lies with her, fearlessly. There is no definite limit to life other than this: when a man grows very old, all his relatives come together and kill him, and sheep and goats along with him, and stew all the meat together and have a banquet of it. That is regarded as the happiest lot; any man who dies of disease they do not eat but bury him in the ground, lamenting that he did not come to being eaten. They do not sow land at all but live off cattle and also fish, which they have in abundance from the river Araxes. They are drinkers of milk. Of the gods, they worship the sun only, to whom they sacrifice horses, and their argument for the sacrifice is this: to the swiftest of all gods they assign the swiftest of all mortal things.

82. Cyrus died in 529 B.C.

Book Two

1. When Cyrus was dead, Cambyses inherited the kingdom.[1] He was the son of Cyrus and Cassandane, the daughter of Pharnaspes, and Cassandane had died before Cyrus himself; Cyrus had mourned greatly for her and instructed all his subjects to do likewise. Cambyses, then, was a son of this woman and Cyrus; he regarded the Ionians and Aeolians as slaves who were his by inheritance from his father, and he made war against Egypt, taking along his various subjects, including those Greeks whom he ruled.

2. The Egyptians, before Psammetichus became their king,[2] thought that they were the oldest of mankind. But Psammetichus, when he became king, wanted to know truly which were the oldest, and from that time the Egyptians consider that the Phrygians are older than themselves but that they, the Egyptians, are older than anyone else. For Psammetichus, when he could not in any way discover by inquiry which were the first people, devised the following plan. He took two newborn children of just ordinary people and gave them to a shepherd to bring up among his flocks. The manner of their upbringing was to be this: the king charged that no one of those who came face to face with the children should utter a word and that the children should be kept in a lonely dwelling by themselves. At a suitable time the shepherd was to bring the goats to them, give them their fill of milk, and do all the necessary things. Psammetichus did this and gave these orders because he wished to hear from those children, as soon as they were done with meaningless noises, which language they would speak first. This, indeed, was what happened. For when two years had gone by, as the shepherd was performing his tasks, he opened the door and went in, and the children clasped his knees and reached out their hands, calling out "bekos." At first, when the shepherd heard this, he remained silent about it. But as he came constantly and gave careful heed to

1. 529 B.C.
2. About 660 B.C.

the matter, this word was constantly with them. So he signified this to his master and at his command brought the children to his presence. When Psammetichus himself had heard, he inquired which of mankind called something "bekos." On inquiry he found that the Phrygians called bread "bekos." So the Egyptians conceded and, making this their measure, judged that the Phrygians were older than themselves. I heard this story from the priests of Hephaestus[3] in Memphis. The Greeks tell, among many other foolish stories, one to the effect that Psammetichus had the tongues of certain women cut out and made the children live with these women.

3. That is what they said about the rearing of the children. But I heard other things, too, in Memphis, when I conversed with the priests of Hephaestus. Indeed, it was because of this that I went to Thebes and Heliopolis: I wanted to know whether the people there would tell me the same story as those in Memphis. For the Heliopolitans are said to be the greatest chroniclers among the Egyptians. Now, the part of their account that deals with the divine, and to which I listened, I am not anxious to set forth, save only the matter of the gods' names; for I think that all men know equally about the gods.[4] When I do mention the gods, it will be because my history forces me to do so.

4. But as far as human things go, this is what they said and were in agreement with one another: that the Egyptians were the first of mankind to invent the year and to make twelve divisions of the seasons for it. They said that this invention of the year was based on the stars. Their reckoning, in my opinion, is much cleverer than that of the Greeks; for the Greeks must insert one intercalary month (because of taking account of the seasons) every other year, but the Egyptians, by allotting thirty days apiece to each of the twelve months (and adding five days outside of the number in each year), make the cycle of the seasons come out to the same point as the calendar. These authorities also say that the Egyptians were the first to use the names of the twelve gods, and that the Greeks took these from them, and that the Egyptians were the first to assign altars and images and temples to the gods and to carve figures on stone. Most

3. I.e., Ptah.
4. For a discussion of this ambiguous statement, see the end note to this passage.

of these things they showed me by clear proof. They said that the first king of Egypt was Min—the first, that is, who was human.[5] In his time, except for the Thebaic province, all of Egypt was a marsh, and no part of the present country that is north of Lake Moeris was above the water; Lake Moeris is seven days' journey from the sea, upstream the river.

5. These people who so describe the country seem to me right. For it would be clear to anyone of sense who used his eyes, even if there were no such information, that the Egypt to which the Greeks sail is land that has been given to the Egyptians as an addition and as a gift of the river; and this is true also of the land for three days' journey above this lake of which we have spoken; for it is of the very same kind as the other part of the country, although the priests have not so described *this* piece. For the nature of the land of Egypt is this: as you approach it and are still within one day's run from the land, and you drop a sounding line, you will bring up mud, though you are in eleven fathoms' depth. This shows that the deposit of earth reaches even as far as this.

6. The length of Egypt itself, on the seacoast, is sixty schoeni[6]— that is, of Egypt as we judge it to be, from the Plinthinete Gulf to the Serbonian Marsh, which is under the Casian mountain. Between these two points there is a length of sixty schoeni. Men who are pinched for land measure by fathoms; those who are less pinched, by furlongs; those who have much, by parasangs; those who have plenty, by schoeni. The parasang is thirty furlongs, and the schoenus, which is the Egyptian measure, is sixty furlongs.

7. So there would be along the coast of Egypt three thousand six hundred furlongs. From there inland, as far as Heliopolis, Egypt is a wide country, all flat, water, and marshy. The road to Heliopolis going up from the sea is roughly the same journey in length as from

5. Min (Menes) is the first Egyptian ruler for whom we have historical records. He seems to have united the southern and northern kingdoms around 3400 B.C.

6. The Greek word *schoinos* means "rope." It is one of those terms drawn from practical means of application, like the English "chain," a measurement of length, and "stone," a weight of fourteen pounds. We do not know how long a schoenus actually was. Herodotus apparently makes one schoenus equal to sixty stades (seven and a half miles). This, according to How and Wells, makes the Egyptian coastline extend about 420 miles, or one-third too long.

Athens, from the altar of the Twelve Gods, to Pisa and the temple of Olympian Zeus. You will find a small difference if you calculate these two roads, so that the length is not exactly the same, but different by not more than fifteen furlongs. For to Pisa from Athens is about fifteen furlongs short of fifteen hundred, and to Heliopolis from the sea it is an even fifteen hundred.

8. But for one going further and above Heliopolis, Egypt is a narrow country. On the one side the mountains of Arabia stretch along it, bearing from north to south and ever stretching toward what is called the Red Sea. In it are the quarries that were cut out for the pyramids that are in Memphis. This way the mountains turn and end in those places of which I speak. Their greatest length from east to west is, I learn, a two months' journey, and the parts toward the east yield frankincense. That is this range of mountains. But, towards Libya, Egypt is bounded by another range of rocky mountains, wherein are the pyramids. These mountains are all covered in sand, and they run in the same direction as the Arabian hills, which run southward. Above Heliopolis there is not much land—not, that is, of land that is Egypt; for here Egypt is narrow for the distance of a fourteen days' journey upstream the river. Between these aforementioned mountain ranges the land is flat, and it seems to me that, at its narrowest, it is not more than two hundred furlongs from the Arabian mountains to those that are called Libyan. Beyond this Egypt is again a wide country. Such is the nature of this land.

9. From Heliopolis to Thebes is a journey of nine days upriver, and the distance is four thousand six hundred and eighty furlongs or eighty-one schoeni. If, then, one puts together all the furlongs in Egypt, there are three thousand six hundred along the seacoast, as I have already shown; how far it is inland from the sea to Thebes I am now going to tell you: it is six thousand one hundred and twenty furlongs. From Thebes to the city called Elephantine there are one thousand eight hundred furlongs.

10. Of this country of which I speak, then, the most, according to the priests' story and also according to what I myself believe to be true, is land that has come, through time, as an addition to the original Egypt. For all that lies between the hills I have mentioned as being above the city of Memphis seems to me to have been once a gulf of the sea, just as the lands around Ilium and Teuthrania and

Ephesus and the plain of the Maeander were—to compare these small things with big ones. For of the rivers that silted up these places, no one of them is worth comparing in size with even one mouth of the Nile—and the Nile has five mouths. There are other rivers, too, that in bigness are not on the scale of the Nile but have achieved great effects. Among others I could name, there is the Achelous, which flows through Acarnania and issues into the sea and in its course has already made half the Echinades islands into mainland.

11. There is in Arabia, not far from Egypt, a gulf of the sea entering in from the sea called Red;[7] its length and narrowness are as I shall show. For length, if one begins a voyage from its inner end, to sail right through into the broad sea is a matter of forty days for a boat that is rowed. In breadth, at its broadest, the gulf is only a half day's voyage. It has floodtide and ebb every day. I think that once on a time Egypt was just such another gulf; there was one gulf running from the northern sea[8] toward Ethiopia, the other, the Arabian, of which I shall speak, bearing from the south toward Syria; their ends bored into the land near to one another but left a small strip of ground in between. If the Nile should now turn its stream into the Arabian Gulf, what would hinder it from being silted up inside of twenty thousand years? For myself, I could well believe that it would do so within ten thousand. How, then, in the huge lapse of time before my birth, would a gulf[9] not be silted up—a gulf even much larger than this one—when the river concerned was so vast and so hard-working?

12. So I believe those who say these things about Egypt and am myself convinced that it is so; for I have seen that Egypt projects into the sea beyond the neighboring land, and that seashells show up on the mountains, and that brine-salt comes to the surface, so that even the pyramids are corroded with it, and that the only sand mountain in Egypt is above Memphis; and besides, in soil Egypt is

7. As noted before, Herodotus' "sea called Red [Erythraean]" is our Indian Ocean, while "the gulf entering in" from it is *our* Red Sea (Herodotus calls it the "Arabian Gulf").
8. The Mediterranean.
9. In other words, the original "gulf running from the northern sea toward Ethiopia" *has* been silted up, thus creating the land of Egypt.

not at all like those countries that march on its borders, neither like
Arabia nor like Libya nor yet Syria (for Syrians live along the seacoast of Arabia); Egypt is a land of black soil, crumbly, so that it
must be swampland and silt from Ethiopia, carried down here by the
river. We know that Libya is a redder earth, and a trifle sandy, and
Arabia and Syria lighter clay, with stones underneath.

13. The priests, moreover, gave me the following strong proof
about their country; they said that, in the reign of King Moeris,
when the river rose only twelve feet it used to flood the whole of
Egypt below Memphis. Moeris was dead less than nine hundred
years when I heard this from the priests. But now if the river does
not rise at least twenty-three and a half or twenty-four feet, it does
not flood the country. And as for those of the Egyptians who live
below Lake Moeris, especially in the part called the Delta, it seems
to me that if their country shall continue to rise in such proportion
and likewise increase in extent, and the Nile no longer floods it,
then, for all time to come, the Egyptians will suffer what they used
to say would be the lot of the Greeks. For when they heard that rain
falls over all the land of Greece and that the earth was not wetted by
rivers, as their own was, they said that one day the Greeks would be
deceived in their great hope and would all miserably die of hunger.
This saying of theirs meant that if God should not be willing to rain
upon them but subjected them to drought, the Greeks would all be
destroyed by famine; for (they said), "You have no other source of
water save from Zeus."

14. That is what the Egyptians say about the Greeks, and very
true it is. But now I would like to say how it stands with the Egyptians themselves. For if the land below Memphis shall increase in
height, as I said before, and in proportion with its increase in past
time—this country below Memphis is where the increase occurs—
what will be left for the Egyptians that live there but starvation?
That is, if no rain falls in their land at all, and if the river cannot rise
high enough to flood their fields? As things stand of course, these
people harvest a crop with less labor than any people in the world,
including the other Egyptians. They have no hard work, raising fur-
rows with the plough or hoeing or doing any other manner of work
such as is done by all the rest of mankind for a corn crop; on a moment, self-invited, the river comes upon the fields and waters them

and, having done so, recedes again; then each man sows his own field and releases into it his pigs; when he has trodden in the seed with the pigs, there remains only the harvesting after that; the threshing of the corn he does too with his pigs, and so garners his crop.

15. If we were to follow the judgment of the Ionians about Egypt, who declare that only the Delta is Egypt (defining the Delta as the seaboard, stretching from the so-called watchtower of Perseus to the salting factories of Pelusium, a distance of forty schoeni, and stretching inward from the sea to the city of Cercasorus, where the Nile divides and flows to Pelusium and Canobus, all the rest of Egypt being, according to their story, either Libya or Arabia), we would be able to show, if one followed this account, that there was originally no country for the Egyptians at all. For the Delta, according to the Egyptians themselves (and I certainly agree), is alluvial silt and, one might say, a contribution of the day before yesterday. If the Egyptians had no land of their own at all, why should they be troubled about whether they were the first of mankind or not? They would have had no need to make trial of those children and what language they would first speak. No, I believe that the Egyptians did not come into existence along with what the Ionians call the Delta, but that they have been ever since the race of man was and that, as the land grew in extent, many of them stayed where they were, but many, too, spread down over the new land. It is true that, of old, Thebes was called Egypt. Whereof the circuit is six thousand one hundred and twenty furlongs.

16. If, then, we judge rightly in this matter, the Ionians are not correct about Egypt. But if the judgment of the Ionians *is* right, I can show that the Greeks and the Ionians themselves cannot count when they say that the whole earth is in three divisions, Europe, Asia, and Libya. For then they should have counted in a fourth, the Delta in Egypt, since it is neither Asia nor Libya. For according to this account of theirs, it is the Nile that is the divider of Asia from Libya; but the Nile divides at the apex of the Delta and flows around it, and so the Delta must be between Asia and Libya.

17. Now I shall let alone the opinion of the Ionians, but I will tell you what I think myself: I believe that all of Egypt is this country which is lived in by the Egyptians, just as Cilicia is what is lived in by the Cilicians and Assyria by the Assyrians, and I know of no fron-

tier, truly considered, between Asia and Libya save the boundaries of the Egyptians. If I were to follow the thoughts of the Greeks, I should consider all of Egypt, beginning from the Katadoupoi[10] and the city of Elephantine, as divided into two and claiming both names, the one part belonging to Libya and the other to Asia. For the Nile, starting from the Katadoupoi, flows right through the middle of Egypt, cleaving it into two, to the sea. As far as the city of Cercasorus the Nile is one in its flow, but after that city it splits into three ways. The one goes eastward and is called the Pelusian Mouth; another goes westward and is called the Canobic Mouth. But the direct channel of the Nile is that which in its downward course reaches the sharp point of the Delta and after that cleaves the Delta in two and issues into the sea. This is where by no means the least share of its water flows, nor the least famous. It is called the Sebennytic Mouth. There are two other mouths that separate themselves from the Sebennytic Mouth and flow into the sea. Their names are the Saïtic and the Mendesian. The Bolbitine and Bucolic mouths are not genuine mouths but dug channels.

18. I have further evidence for my judgment that Egypt is as I have declared it to be in my *History*, and this is an oracle of Ammon. I heard of it only after I had formed my own opinion of Egypt. There were people from the cities of Marea and Apis who, living in the part of Egypt that borders Libya, thought themselves Libyans and not Egyptians; they were vexed by certain religious observances and, in particular, did not wish to abstain from cows' flesh. They sent to Ammon saying that they had nothing in common with the Egyptians; for they lived outside of the Delta and had no manner of agreement with these people; they wanted also to be able to eat everything. The god refused to allow them to do so and declared that Egypt is all the land that the Nile waters in its course and that they are Egyptians who, living lower than the city of Elephantine, drink from the water of the Nile. That is the oracle that was given them.

19. The Nile, when it floods, spreads over not only the Delta but parts of what are called Libya and Arabia for two days' journey in either direction, more or less. Neither from the priests nor from anyone else was I able to learn about the nature of this river, and I was

10. The First Cataract of the Nile—the one furthest to the north.

exceedingly anxious to learn why it is that the Nile comes down with a rising flood for one hundred days, beginning from the summer solstice, but, as it gets near to this number of days, it recedes again, its stream sinking, so that for the whole winter it continues small until the summer solstice again. I was not able to find out anything at all about this from the Egyptians, despite my inquiries of them, as to what peculiar property the Nile possesses that is the opposite of every other river in the world. This that I have mentioned was the subject of my persistent asking why, and also why it is that it is the only river that has no breezes blowing from it.

20. But some of the Greeks who want to be remarkable for their cleverness have advanced three explanations about the river. Two of them I do not consider worthy of commenting on, save for simply indicating the position they advance. One of these says that it is the Etesian winds[11] that cause the Nile's flooding by preventing the Nile from flowing to the sea. However, the Etesian winds often do not blow at all, and the Nile nonetheless floods. Besides, if the Etesian winds were the cause, other rivers that face these winds would surely be affected in the same way as the Nile and even more so, since, being smaller, they have feebler streams. There are many other rivers, both in Syria and in Libya, but not a one of them shows the same qualities as the Nile.

21. The second opinion, which has even less knowledge to it than the aforesaid but is certainly more wonderful in the telling, is the one that speaks of the Nile effecting this thing itself—because it flows from Ocean—and of Ocean as flowing round the whole world.

22. The third opinion is more reasonable-seeming than the others yet is the most deceived; for it too makes no sense at all. It declares that the Nile comes from the source of melting snow. But it flows from Libya and through the midst of Ethiopia and issues into Egypt. How then can it flow from the snow when its course lies from the hottest parts of earth to those that are for the most part cooler? For a man who can reason about these matters, the first and strongest proof that the Nile does not flow from the snow is furnished by the winds themselves, which blow hot out of Libya and Ethiopia. The second proof is that the country is always without rain and frost;

11. The northwest winds of summer, which blow from the Mediterranean.

but, once snow has fallen, there must needs be rain following the snow within five days. So that, if it snowed at all, there would be rain in these places. The third proof is that the people there are black from the heat. And kites and swallows stay there all year round, and cranes, to avoid the winter in Scythia, come to these places for winterage. If, then, it snowed the least bit in these countries through which the Nile flows and where it has its origin, none of these things would happen, as necessity proves.

23. The person who urged the theory about the Ocean has carried his story, which is indeed only a tale, back to where it vanishes and so cannot be disproved. For myself, I do not know that there is any river Ocean, but I think that Homer or one of the older poets found the name and introduced it into his poetry.

24. But if, having found fault with the opinions set forth, I must declare my own view in these matters, which are far from clear, I will say why I think it is that the Nile floods in summertime. During the winter season the sun is driven by storms out of its regular path and into the upper parts of Libya. To make the matter clear in the briefest summary, here it is: whatever country that god is nearest to, and over it, must specially need to be thirsty of water and have the native streams of its rivers wasted away.

25. But to speak at greater length, the matter is like this: in his passage through the upper parts of Libya, the sun, in his course through an air that is always clear and land that is warm and winds that are cool—the sun, I say, produces the same effect as he does in summer going through the midst of the sky. For he draws to himself the water and, having so drawn it up, pushes it away to the upper country, and the winds, taking it on and scattering it, dissolve it; and naturally those winds that blow from that country, the south and the southwest winds, are, of all the winds there are, the most rainy. But I think that even so the sun does not disperse all of each year's water, year by year, that he takes up from the Nile, but keeps some back with himself. Now, as the winter mildens, the sun goes back to the middle of the heaven, and from then on he draws equally from all rivers. Meanwhile, the other rivers, swollen with the much rainwater that has fallen into them (for their country is rainy and full of gullies), flow in spate; but in summer, as the rains fail them and as the sun draws the water out of them, they become very weak.

The Nile, unfed by rain, and also the only river at that time drawn on by the sun, naturally is much below its normal flow of summertime; for in summer it has the moisture drawn out of it equally with all the other rivers, but in winter it is the only one to feel the pinch of the sun.

26. So it is my settled thought that the sun is the cause of these matters. And, in my judgment, the sun is also the cause of the dryness of the air there, as he burns his own way straight through: that is why it is a constant summer that possesses upper Libya. But if the constitution of the seasons were changed, and where now stand the winter and the north wind there should stand the summer and the south wind, and the south wind should take the position of the north—I say, if these things were to be so, the sun, as he is driven from the center of the heavens by the winter and the north wind, would go into the upper reaches of Europe even as now he goes into Libya, and, as he went through the whole of Europe, he would have the same effect on the Ister[12] as now he has upon the Nile.

27. As to the matter of no wind blowing from the river, I am of the opinion that it is not natural for a breeze to come from exceedingly hot places; it is only from those that are cool that the wind is wont to come.

28. Let these things, then, be as they are and as they were at the beginning. As to the sources of the Nile, none of the Egyptians or Libyans or Greeks who have come to speech with me professed to know these sources except for one, the clerk of the holy things of Athena in the city of Saïs in Egypt; and to me, at least, this man seemed rather to jest when he declared that he knew them exactly. This is what he said: there are two mountains, their peaks sharply pointed, lying between the city of Syene, in the Thebaïd, and Elephantine. The names of these mountains are Crophi and Mophi. The clerk said that the springs of the Nile flow between the two mountains, and these springs are unfathomable; the half of the water flows toward Egypt and the north, the other half toward Ethiopia and the south. That the springs are unfathomable, the clerk said, had been tested and proved by King Psammetichus of Egypt; for the king had twisted a cable thousands of fathoms long and let it

12. The Ister is the Danube.

down there to the depths but could not find bottom. If, then, the clerk were speaking of these things as things actually happening, he showed, I believe, that there are certain strong eddies there and a countercurrent, and, as the water rushes against the mountains, the sounding line let down cannot reach bottom.

29. From no one else could I learn anything whatever. But this much I found out by the furthest inquiry I could make, having myself gone as far as the city of Elephantine and seen with my own eyes there and, after that, investigating through hearsay. From the city of Elephantine, going upcountry, the land is steep. There travelers must bind the boat on both sides, as one harnesses an ox, and so go on their way. If the rope were to break, the boat would be borne to its destruction by the strength of the current. This part of the country is four days' journey by boat, and the Nile here is as twisting as the Maeander; there is a length of twelve schoeni to pass through in this fashion. Then you come to a plain that is smooth, and in it there is an island surrounded by the Nile. Its name is Tachompso. In the parts of the country south of Elephantine the inhabitants are Ethiopians, and one half of the island is inhabited by Ethiopians, the other half by Egyptians. Near the island is a great lake, round which live nomad Ethiopians. Sail through the lake and you will come to the Nile, which empties into the lake. You will then disembark and travel along the bank for forty days, for there are sharp rocks in the Nile and many reefs through which you will be unable to sail. Having marched through this country in forty days, you will embark again in another boat and sail for twelve days, and then you will come to a great city, the name of which is Meroë. This city is said to be the mother city of all Ethiopia. Those who live in that part worship alone among gods Zeus and Dionysus,[13] but these they honor deeply; they have a place of divination for Zeus among them. They send out armies when the god bids them by oracles to do so, and, where he bids them go, they go.

30. From this city, making a voyage of the same length of sailing as you did from Elephantine to the mother city of the Ethiopians, you will come to the land of the Deserters. The name of these Deserters is Asmach, which in Greek means "those who stand on the left

13. I.e., the Egyptian gods Amon and Osiris.

hand of the king." These were two hundred and forty thousand Egyptians, fighter Egyptians, who revolted from the Egyptians and joined the Ethiopians, for the following reason. In the time of King Psammetichus there were guard stations, one in the city of Elephantine, against the Ethiopians, and another in Pelusiac Daphnae, against the Arabians and Assyrians, and another in Marea, toward Libya. Still in my time these guard posts were held by the Persians in the same way as they were held in the reign of Psammetichus; there are Persian guards at Elephantine and at Daphnae. Now these Egyptians had done their guard duty for three years, and no one released them from it. So they took counsel together, and by general decision they all deserted and made for Ethiopia. Psammetichus heard of it and pursued them. When he came up with them, he entreated them mightily; he would have them, he said, not desert their household gods and their wives and children. At this, it is said, one of their number showed him his prick and said, "Wherever I have this, I will have wives and children." So they took themselves off to the king of the Ethiopians and surrendered themselves to him, who gave them a gift in return. There were some Ethiopians who had been at variance with him, and he bade the Egyptians expel these and take over their land and live there. When these people had settled among the Ethiopians, the Ethiopians became more civilized, through learning the manners of the Egyptians.

31. For four months of travel space, then, sailing and road, beyond its course in Egypt, the Nile is a known country. If you add all together, you will find that it takes four months of journeying from Elephantine to these Deserters of whom I spoke; the river flows from the west and the setting sun. But from here on, no one can tell clearly, for the country itself is a desert because of the heat.

32. However, this is what I heard from men of Cyrene: they said that they went to the oracle at Ammon and there spoke with Etearchus, the king of the Ammonians, and from other discourse with him came to talk about the Nile—how no one knew the springs of it; and Etearchus, they said, declared that there were people who had come to his court who were Nasamonians. This is a Libyan people, which lives in the Syrtis and parts east of the Syrtis, though not far to the east. When these Nasamonians came to him, he questioned them as to whether they had any more to add to the knowl-

edge of the deserts of Libya. They said that there were among them certain men of princely lineage, haughty and violent, who when they were grown to manhood did many wild things, and, in especial, they cast lots among themselves to choose five of their number to go and spy out the deserts of Libya, to see if they would discover something more than those who had so far prospected furthest. Libya in its seacoast, on the north, beginning from Egypt and stretching as far as the promontory of Soloeis, which is the end of Libya, is inhabited all along by Libyans—and many tribes of them—except for such territory as the Greeks and Phoenicians hold. The part of Libya above the sea and the men who come right down to the sea, all this upper part of Libya is exceedingly full of wild beasts. Farther inland, beyond the wild-beast country, it is sandy and waterless and barren of everything. The story is that these young men, sent out by their comrades and well provided with water and food, went first through the inhabited part and came then through that to the wild-beast part, and from there through the desert, making their journey ever toward the west. Having traversed a great deal of sandy country, and many days later, they then saw, at times, trees growing on a plain; they approached these and tried to pluck the fruit that was on the trees; but as they did so, there came upon them small men, well under the usual stature, who captured them and led them away. The Nasamonians could not understand the speech of these people, nor could their captors understand that of the Nasamonians. They led them on through huge swamps and at last came through to a city where, say the Nasamonians, all the people were of the measure of stature of those who had taken them prisoner, and they were black in color. Beside the city flowed a great river, and it flowed, they said, from west to east, and they could see crocodiles in it.

33. That, then, is what I have to say about the story of Etearchus, king of the Ammonians—save that he declared that, according to the Cyrenians' report, the Nasamonians came back safe and that the people to whose country they had come were all sorcerers. It was Etearchus who guessed that the river that flowed by the city was the Nile; and indeed, reason is on his side. For the Nile flows out of Libya and cuts Libya in the middle,[14] and, as I conjecture, arguing from what is seen to what is not known, its distance from its begin-

14. Herodotus thought that, beginning at Syene, the Nile flowed west, across Africa. See the map on pp. 294−95.

nings must be of the same measure as the Ister. For the river Ister begins in Celtic country and the city of Pyrene and cleaves Europe in two. The Celts dwell beyond the Pillars of Heracles, and they have common borders with the Cynesii, who live furthest of all the people that inhabit Europe toward the west; and the Ister ends, flowing into the Euxine Sea, flowing clear across Europe, at Istria, settled by Milesian colonists.

34. The Ister, since it flows through an inhabited area, is known by many, but about the springs of the Nile there is no one who can speak; for Libya, through which it flows, has none that live in it and is indeed a desert. About the course of the river I have told you to the furthest extent that my inquiries could reach to find out anything. It issues into Egypt. Egypt lies about opposite to the mountainous part of Cilicia. From there to Sinope on the Black Sea is a straight journey of five days for a man who is a good traveler. Sinope is opposite to the Ister as it issues into the sea. So it is that I think that the Nile, which passes through all of Libya, is equal to the Ister.

35. I have said all that I am going to say about the Nile. But I am going to be much longer in my story of Egypt. And this is because it has more wonders in it than any country in the world and more works that are beyond description than anywhere else. That is why I will say more about it.

Just as the climate that the Egyptians have is entirely their own and different from anyone else's, and their river has a nature quite different from other rivers, so, in fact, the most of what they have made their habits and their customs are the exact opposite of other folks'. Among them the women run the market and shops, while the men, indoors, weave; and, in this weaving, while other people push the woof upward, the Egyptians push it down. The men carry burdens on their heads; the women carry theirs on their shoulders. The women piss standing upright, but the men do it squatting. The people ease nature's needs in the houses but eat outdoors in the streets; their explanation of this is that what is shameful but necessary should be done in secret, but what is not shameful should be done openly. No woman is dedicated to any god, male or female, but men to all gods and goddesses. There is no obligation on sons to maintain their parents if they are unwilling, but an absolute necessity lies on the daughters to do so, whether they will or not.

36. In the rest of the world, priests of the gods wear their hair

long, but in Egypt they shave close. Among other people it is the custom, in grief, for those to whom the grief comes especially close to shave their heads, but the Egyptians, under the shadow of death, let their hair and beards grow long, though at other times they shave. Other people keep the daily life of animals separate from their own, but the Egyptians live theirs close together with their animals. Others live on wheat and barley, but such a diet is the greatest of disgraces to an Egyptian; they make their bread from a coarse grain, which some of them call zeia, or spelt. They knead dough with their feet but mud with their hands, and they lift dung with their hands. Other men leave the genitals as they were at birth, save such as have learned from the Egyptians; but the Egyptians circumcise. Every man has two garments, but each woman one only. The rings of their sails and the sheets are elsewhere fastened outside the boats, but the Egyptians fasten them inside. The Greeks write and calculate moving their hands from left to right, but the Egyptians from right to left. That is what they *do,* but they *say* they are moving to the right and the Greeks to the left. They use two different kinds of writing, one of which is called sacred and the other common.

37. In their reverence for the gods, they are excessive, more than any others in the world. Witness the following customs: they drink out of bronze cups and scour these every day—not one man doing so and another not, but every Egyptian. They wear linen clothes that are always new-washed—they are especially careful about this. They circumcise, out of cleanliness, for they would rather be clean than fair-seeming. The priests shave all their bodies every other day, that no louse or any unclean thing be engendered in them that serve the gods. For raiment the priests wear only a linen garment and shoes of papyrus; no other cloth is allowed them, nor any other kind of shoes. They wash twice daily in cold water and twice every night, and other forms of superstitious tasks they accomplish almost (I might say) past numbering. But they do well from their priesthood, too; they do not wear out, or spend, anything of their own cost, but they have holy food cooked for them, and beef and goose flesh in quantities are provided for them every day. They are also served wine from the grape. Fish they may not touch, and beans the Egyptians do not sow in their country, and those that grow there they do not eat either raw or cooked. The priests cannot even endure the sight of

them, for they think that the bean is an unclean kind of pulse. There is not just one priest dedicated to each god but many. Of these, one is the high priest. When one of these dies, his son is consecrated in his stead.

38. They consider that all bulls are the property of Epaphus,[15] and for that reason they make an examination of them. If they find as much as one black hair on the bull, they deem him impure. The beast is examined, both upright and on his back, by a priest assigned to this task; the priest also draws out the animal's tongue to see if it is clear of certain prescribed marks, which I will tell of elsewhere.[16] He also looks upon the hairs of the tail, to see if they grow naturally. If the beast is pure in all these things, the priest marks him by twisting a papyrus rope around his horns, and, smearing it with sealing-clay, he stamps it with a signet ring; and so they lead the beast away. To sacrifice an unstamped animal carries with it the penalty of death. This is how the animal is examined, and the manner of its sacrifice is as follows.

39. They lead the marked beast to the altar where they are sacrificing and light a fire; after that they pour wine on the altar over the victim and call upon the god and cut the animal's throat. Having so cut it, they cut the head off. The body they flay, but, for the head, they call down many imprecations on it and carry it off. Where there is a marketplace and Greek traders in that community, they turn the head over to them, and the traders take it to the marketplace and sell it; where there are no such Greeks, they cast the head into the river. The form of the curse on the head is this: "Whatsoever evil there is to be for us who are sacrificing or for all the land of Egypt, let it fall upon this head." In respect of the heads of the sacrificed animals and the pouring-on of the wine, all Egyptians follow the same customs alike in all their sacrifices. It is in accordance with this custom that no Egyptian will taste of the head of any creature that had life.

40. Now for the disemboweling of the victims and the burning of

---

15. "I.e., Epaphus, the holy calf of Memphis, by which the god Ptah-Socharis-Osiris was represented on earth. . . . Under the Ptolemies, as Serapis, he was the chief god in Egypt. The Greeks identified him with Epaphus, son of Zeus and Io . . . but this is obviously mistaken" (How and Wells).

16. Book 3, chapter 28.

them, there is a different form of ritual for each; but I am going to tell you about Her whom they think the greatest of their gods and in whose honor they hold the greatest festival. When they have flayed the ox, they say their prayers and draw out the whole stomach; but they leave the entrails in the body and the fat, and they cut off the legs and the end of the loin, the shoulders, and the neck. Having done this, they fill the rest of the body with pure loaves of bread and with honey and raisins and figs and frankincense and myrrh and all the other spices; having filled it with these, they consecrate it,[17] pouring on an abundance of olive oil. They make the sacrifice after a forefast; but as the victims are burning, they all beat their breasts in lament, and, when this is over, they set out a feast of what remains of the victim.

41. Bulls that are rated pure for sacrifice and bull calves all Egyptians sacrifice. But cows they are not allowed to sacrifice; these are sacred to Isis. For the image of Isis is female in form but with a cow's horns, as the Greeks represent Io. Cows the Egyptians, all alike, hold in reverence more than any other form of herd animals. For this reason no Egyptian man or woman will kiss a Greek on the mouth or use the knife of a Greek, or spit or cauldron; nor will they taste of the flesh even of a bull that is pure if it has been cut up with a Greek knife. The cattle beasts that die, they bury, and in this manner: the cows they throw into the river; the bulls they bury, each people in its own suburbs, with one or both of the horns projecting aboveground for a marker. When all is rotted and the appointed time comes, there arrives at each city a barque from the island that is called Prosopitis. This island is in the Delta and is, in circumference, nine schoeni. In this island of Prosopitis there are various other cities, but the one from which the barques come to pick up the bones of the cattle is called Atarbechis. In it there is a sacred shrine of Aphrodite. From this city many go about to different cities, and when they have dug up the bones, they bring them away and bury them, all in one place. They have the same way of burying for other beasts, when they die, as they do for cattle. For such is the ordinance about this, since the other beasts, too, may not be killed.

42. Those who have established among themselves a temple of

17. I.e., they burn it.

Theban Zeus, or are of the Theban province, all of these sacrifice goats but hold off from sheep. For by no means all Egyptians worship the same gods alike, except for Isis and Osiris, the latter of whom they say is Dionysus. These, it is true, they all alike worship. But those who possess a shrine of Mendes or are of the province of Mendes, these sacrifice sheep but will have none of goats. The Thebans and those who will not sacrifice sheep, through the influence of the Thebans, declare that this custom has been established among them for this reason: they say that Heracles had most earnestly desired to see Zeus, but the god would not be seen by him. But in the end, because Heracles was so insistent, Zeus made a contrivance of flaying a ram, taking off the ram's head and using it as a mask, and entering the fleece of the sheep and so displaying himself to Heracles. It is from this act that the Egyptians make an image of Zeus with a ram's head, and from the Egyptians the Ammonians have learned it, who are indeed colonists of Egyptians and Ethiopians and speak a language that is a mixture of the two. In my judgment it was also from this that the Ammonians gained this name for themselves. For the Egyptians call Zeus Amon. It is because of this, too, that the Thebans will not sacrifice rams, but the animals are sacred for them. But on one day of the year, at the festival of Zeus, they chop up one ram and flay it and dress the image of Zeus in the hide, as in the story, and thereafter bring the other image, that of Heracles, close to that of Zeus. Having done that, they all make lament for the ram, round about the shrine, and afterwards bury it in a sacred coffin.

43. I heard the following story about Heracles, to the effect that he was one of the Twelve Gods; but I never could hear a word anywhere in Egypt about that other Heracles, the one the Greeks know of. Now, certainly the Egyptians did not get the name of Heracles from the Greeks, but rather the Greeks got it from the Egyptians. And indeed, it was the Greeks who got it or who put the name of Heracles upon the son of Amphitryon. I have many proofs of this, and the chief one is that both of these parents of Heracles, Amphitryon and Alcmene, stemmed distantly from Egypt;[18] furthermore, the Egyptians declare they do not know the names of Poseidon or

18. Heracles' parents were grandchildren of Perseus, who was descended from Aegyptus, brother of Danaus and son of the Egyptian King Belus. See below, 2.91.

the Dioscuri, nor are these assigned any place as gods among their other gods. But if the Egyptians had taken the name of any god from the Greeks, they would most surely have had memory of these if they, the Egyptians, were already making voyages and certain of the Greeks too were seafarers, as I think and as my judgment, too, confirms; so that surely the Egyptians would have known the names of these gods (Poseidon and the Dioscuri) rather than that of Heracles. There *is* certainly an ancient god, Heracles, among the Egyptians. They themselves say it was seventeen thousand years before the reign of King Amasis[19] when the Eight gods became Twelve, and they regard Heracles as one of the Twelve.

44. And because I wanted to find out something clear in the matter, as far as I was able, I sailed to Tyre in Phoenicia, having learned that there was there a specially holy shrine of Heracles; I saw it indeed, very richly decorated and with many dedicatory offerings, and there were, moreover, in it two pillars, one of refined gold and one of emerald, a huge pillar that shone by night. I talked with the priests of the god there and asked them how long was it since the shrine was established. But I found that they too disagreed with the Greeks; for they said that the shrine had been founded at the same time as Tyre was settled and that people had lived in Tyre for twenty-three hundred years. I saw in Tyre, also, another temple of Heracles, which is called after Heracles of Thasos; and so I went to Thasos, and in it I found a temple of Heracles that had been founded by the Phoenicians when they had sailed out in quest of Europe and settled Thasos; this too was at least five generations of men before the birth of Heracles, son of Amphitryon, in Greece. These researches of mine indicate quite clearly that Heracles is an ancient god. I think that, among the Greeks, their procedure is most correct who have established and cultivated two cults of Heracles; to one they sacrifice as to a god and by title Olympian, and to the other they offer worship as to a hero.

45. The Greeks tell many stories that show no manner of thought. In particular, there is the tale they tell of Heracles to the effect that he came to Egypt and that the Egyptians put garlands on his head and led him in procession, with intent to sacrifice him to Zeus; that

19. 570–526 B.C.

for a while he held quiet, but when they brought him near the altar itself and had started the first rites on him, he took himself to his valor and slaughtered them all. In my opinion, the Greeks who tell this story know absolutely nothing about the nature of the Egyptians and their customs. Here is a people for whom the sacrifice of beasts themselves is unholy, except for pigs, bulls, bull-calves—that is, such as are pure—and geese; how could they sacrifice human beings? And furthermore, since Heracles was still only one, and also only a human being, as they themselves say, how can it accord with nature that he should slaughter that many tens of thousands? That is what I have to say about the matter; as I do so, may both gods and heroes view me kindly!

46. This is why the aforementioned Egyptians do not sacrifice she-goats and he-goats: these people, the Mendesians, reckon Pan to be one of the Eight Gods, and the Eight, they say, were before the Twelve. Both in painting and in sculpture their painters and image-makers make the image of Pan as the Greeks do, with a goat face and a he-goat's legs; it is not that they think the god *is* so—nay, they think him like the other gods; but why he is so depicted it is not pleasant for me to say. The Mendesians regard as holy all goats, but the males more than the females, and the herdsmen that tend these he-goats have more honor than those that tend the others. Of the he-goats there is one in especial, and, when he dies, great mourning is instituted in all the Mendesian province. The he-goat and Pan are both called Mendes in the Egyptian language. In this province, in my time, a monstrosity took place: a he-goat coupled with a woman, plain, for all to see. This was done in the nature of a public exhibition.

47. The Egyptians think the pig an unclean animal. If any one of the Egyptians, but passing by, touch a pig, he goes to the river and dips himself therein, garments and all. Furthermore, such native-born Egyptians as are swineherds, alone of all people, durst not enter any Egyptian shrine; nor is anyone willing to give his daughter in marriage to one of a family of swineherds or to marry one himself from such a family, and so the swineherds marry and are given in marriage only among their own folk. The Egyptians do not think fit to sacrifice the pig to any god except the Moon and Dionysus, and to these they sacrifice at the same time, the very full moon; it is then they sacrifice pigs and taste of their flesh. Why it is that they utterly

reject the pig at other festivals and sacrifice it at this one—as to this, there is a story told about the matter by the Egyptians; I know it, but it is not quite suitable to be declared.[20] This is how they make the sacrifice of pigs to the Moon: when the sacrificer makes his sacrifice, he puts together the tip of the tail, the spleen, and the caul and covers them up with all the fat that is about the belly of the beast; he then consecrates it in the fire. The rest of the flesh they eat in the Day of the Full Moon, the day on which they sacrifice the victim, but on no other day will they taste it. The poor people among them, through their poverty, make up pigs of dough and bake these and sacrifice them.

48. On the eve of the festival of Dionysus, each one of them cuts the throat of his pig in front of the doorway and then gives it, to take away, to the swineherd who has sold it to him. For the rest of the festival in honor of Dionysus, except for the dance choruses, the Egyptians celebrate it almost in everything like the Greeks. But instead of phalluses they have another invention, which are eighteen-inch-high images, controlled by strings, which the women carry round the villages; these images have a penis that nods and in size is not much less than all the rest of the body. Ahead there goes a flute-player, and the women follow, singing in honor of Dionysus. Now why the penis is so much bigger and is the only thing movable in the body—about this there is a sacred story told.

49. It seems to me that Melampus, son of Amythaon, was not ignorant of this sacrifice; indeed, he seems to have been well versed in it. For it is Melampus who was for the Greeks the expositor of Dionysus—of his name, his sacrifice, and the phallic procession; strictly speaking, he did not put all together and manifest the whole story for them, for there were teachers afterwards who advanced it further. But it was Melampus who instituted the phallic procession to Dionysus, and it was from him that the Greeks learned to do what they do. It is my opinion that Melampus was a clever man who had formed for himself an art of divination, and, having learned from Egypt, he introduced much that was new to the Greeks, including the ritual of Dionysus—and he made very little change in it. I will never believe that the rites in Egypt and those in Greece can re-

---

20. For some remarks on Herodotus' unwillingness to discuss such matters, see the end note to this passage.

semble each other by coincidence; for in that case the Greek rites would have been in the Greek fashion, and they would not have been so recently instituted. Nor will I admit that the Egyptians could have taken these from the Greeks—either these or any other thing of customary usage. In my opinion, Melampus learned these Dionysiac rites for the most part from Cadmus, the man of Tyre, and from those Phoenicians who came with him to the country now called Boeotia.

50. The names of nearly all the gods came from Egypt to Greece.[21] That these gods came from the barbarians I found on inquiry to be true; personally, I believe they came from Egypt. For except for Poseidon and the Dioscuri, as I mentioned before, and also Hera, Hestia, Themis, and the Graces and Nereids, of all the other gods the names[22] have always existed in Egypt. I say what the Egyptians themselves say. In the case of gods of whom the Egyptians say they do not know the names, these, I think, were named by the Pelasgians, except for Poseidon. This god the Greeks learned of from the Libyans. No other people save the Libyans have had Poseidon's name established among them from the beginning, and they have always honored him. The Egyptians do not proffer ritual honors to heroes at all.

51. These things—and other things besides, which I shall show—the Greeks learned from the Egyptians; but the making of the Hermes statues with the phallus erect, *that* they did not learn from the Egyptians but from the Pelasgians, and it was the Athenians first of all the Greeks who took over this practice and, from the Athenians, all the rest. For the Pelasgians came to settle with the Athenians in their land when the Athenians themselves were already counted as Greeks.[23] Thereby the Pelasgians too came to be regarded

21. Herodotus does not mean by this the actual *names*, for he frequently remarks on the difference in the names, e.g., "The Egyptians call this god [Zeus] by an Egyptian name—Amon." What he does mean is the complex of personality referred to broadly as the god's "name." How and Wells, in their commentary, without committing themselves to Herodotus' theory of the Egyptian origins of Greek gods, agree in the main with his exceptions and with his general grouping of the attributes of the gods of both countries.

22. Here too the "name" embraces the personality.

23. The matter of the origins and speech of the Pelasgians is extremely difficult. It is here sufficient to say that Herodotus thought, as we can see from 1.56–57, that there were two original Greek stocks, Ionians and Dorians, and

as Greeks. Anyone who has been initiated into the rites of the Cabeiri, which the Samothracians celebrate, taking them from the Pelasgians, knows what I am talking of. For these Pelasgians, who came to live with the Athenians, once lived in Samothrace, and it was from them that the Samothracians took over the orgies. The Athenians, then, were the first of the Greeks to make the statues of Hermes with the penis erect, and it was from the Pelasgians they learned it. The Pelasgians tell a holy story about this—matters that are made clear in the Samothracian mysteries.

52. Formerly the Pelasgians made all their sacrifices with invocations to gods (I know of this from what I heard at Dodona) but put no special title or name on any one of them; for they had not yet heard of any such. [24] They gave them the title "gods" [theoi] from the circumstance that they had disposed [ti-thémi, root thé] everything in order [cosmos] and arranged all. But afterwards, after a great while, they learned the names that came from Egypt—those of the other gods, that is; for the name of Dionysus they learned long after that. And after a time they consulted the oracle at Dodona about the names. This oracle at Dodona was the most ancient oracular place of all among the Greeks, and at that time it was the only one. When the Pelasgians asked the oracle in Dodona whether they should take on the names that came from the barbarians, the oracle bade them use the names. And from that time on they sacrificed using the names of the gods, and afterwards the Greeks received the names from the Pelasgians.

53. But whence each of these gods came into existence, or whether they were for ever, and what kind of shape they had were

---

that the latter were the only true Greek (Hellenic) stock. For the Ionians were of the *original* inhabitants of Greece, who, according to Herodotus, were Pelasgians. They spoke a non-Greek tongue; later they learned Greek. Here Herodotus is speaking of a later influx of Pelasgians, at a time when "the Athenians themselves were already counted as Greeks"—i.e., when they, as Pelasgians, had assimilated themselves in speech to the Greeks (Hellenes).

24. Here is a further complication of the matter of the gods' names (cf. 2.50), for the first word here (*epōnumiēn*) is the patronymic, which expresses descent from ancestors. It is not clear whether it also comes to mean the god's local title or his special function. The Pelasgians knew no "names," strictly speaking, for the gods. They worshiped the sun, not Apollo. Cf. the How and Wells commentary on this passage.

not known until the day before yesterday, if I may use the expression; for I believe that Homer and Hesiod were four hundred years before my time—and no more than that. It is they who created for the Greeks their theogony; it is they who gave to the gods the special names for their descent from their ancestors and divided among them their honors, their arts, and their shapes.[25] Those who are spoken of as poets before Homer and Hesiod were, in my opinion, later born. The first part of this that I have said[26] is what the priestesses at Dodona say, but the latter, as concerns Homer and Hesiod, is my own statement.

54. Concerning the oracles, the one that is among the Greeks and the other in Libya, this is the story that the Egyptians tell. The priests of the Theban Zeus declared that two women, priestesses, were carried away from Thebes by Phoenicians and that they (the Theban priests) had learned that one of them was sold into Libya and the other to the Greeks. These women, they said, were the first to set up places of prophecy among these aforementioned peoples. When I asked them from what source they spoke with such exact knowledge, they said that there had been a great search by their own people after these women, but they could never be found, but that afterwards they had learned about them what they had now told me.

55. That is what I heard from the priests in Thebes, but the following is what the priestesses of Dodona had to say. There were, they said, two black doves that flew from Thebes in Egypt, and the one of them came to Libya and the other to themselves at Dodona, and the latter one settled upon an oak tree and with a human voice proclaimed that there should be there, in that place, an oracle of Zeus; they themselves then grasped that this proclamation to them was a thing divine, and because of it they made the place of the oracle. The dove that flew to Libya, they say, bade the Libyans also

25. "Theogony" means "the birth of the gods," and there is a poem by Hesiod called exactly this, the *Theogony*. The word for names expressing descent from ancestors is *epōnumiai*, as in note 24.

26. Herodotus is probably referring to chapter 52, which he wishes to distinguish from his own opinion in this chapter, where he deals with the whole question of Greek religion and its relation to Homer and Hesiod. In his view, their poems correspond, but with clearly tremendous differences, with what we would call sacred texts in the Greek tradition.

make the oracle of Ammon there, and again the Libyans did what it said. The latter is also an oracle of Zeus. These things were told me by the priestesses of Dodona, the eldest of whom is called Promeneia, the second-eldest, Timarete, and the youngest, Nicandra. The other people of Dodona who are concerned with the shrine agreed in the account of the priestesses.

56. My judgment of the matter is this: if the Phoenicians sold these women, one to Libya and one to Greece, it seems to me that the woman who was sold into what is now Greece but in those early days was called Pelasgia—the very same land—was sold into Thesprotia; that then, being a slave there, she set up a shrine in honor of Zeus, under an oak that grew there. It was natural that she should do so since she had been a handmaid in the temple of Zeus in Thebes, whence she came, and so she would have remembered that. After she had learned the Greek language, she founded a place of prophecy there. At this point she told the people of Dodona that her sister had been sold into Libya by the very same Phoenicians who had sold herself to them.

57. I believe that the women were called by the Dodonaeans "doves" because they were barbarians, and so they seemed to the people of Dodona to talk like birds. After a time they said, "The bird spoke with a human voice," as soon as the woman talked comprehensibly. As long as she talked her own barbarian language, she seemed to them to speak like a bird. How, after all, could a dove speak with a human voice? That they said that the dove was black indicates that the woman was an Egyptian.[27]

58. The methods of divination at Thebes in Egypt and at Dodona are very similar to one another. Furthermore, divination from sacrifices came from Egypt. Also, the Egyptians were the first people to

27. An interesting story. Herodotus is not saying that the Dodonaeans misconstrued the *event*, so that they thought that what were two women were in fact doves. He also (sharing what appears to me to be the Greeks' strong objections to magic) rejects utterly the notion of a dove with a human voice. He proceeds from what may have been a fact: that the priestess at Dodona was called "dove," just as Pindar records that the priestess at Delphi was sometimes called "bee" (*Pythians* 4.60; cf. Pausanias 7.21.2). He joins to this both the strongly asserted story of the foreign origins of the cult of Zeus at both Dodona and Libya and the "human voice" incident and tries to explain how the *name* "dove" came about. It is the name that caused the mistake that led to the story.

organize holy assemblies, processions, and services of the gods, and it was from them that the Greeks learned these things. My proof of this is that the Egyptian practices are clearly very ancient indeed, and the Greek ones only lately established.

59. The Egyptians hold their assemblies not once a year but very often. The chief of these and the most reverentially celebrated is in honor of Artemis, at the town of Bubastis. The second is at the city of Busiris and is in honor of Isis. In that city there is the greatest shrine of Isis, and the city was established at the center of the Egyptian Delta. Isis is in the Greek tongue Demeter. The third assembly is in the city of Saïs and is in honor of Athena; the fourth is in the city of Heliopolis in honor of Helios; the fifth is in honor of Leto in the city of Buto; and the sixth is in the city of Papremis in honor of Ares.

60. When they travel to Bubastis, this is what they do. They sail thither, men and women together, and a great number of each in each boat. Some of the women have rattles and rattle them, others play the flute through the entire trip, and the remainder of the women and men sing and clap their hands. As they travel on toward Bubastis and come near some other city, they edge the boat near the bank, and some of the women do as I have described. But others of them scream obscenities in derision of the women who live in that city, and others of them set to dancing, and others still, standing up, throw their clothes open to show their nakedness. This they do at every city along the riverbank. When they come to Bubastis, they celebrate the festival with great sacrifices, and more wine is drunk at that single festival than in all the rest of the year besides. There they throng together, man and woman (but no children), up to the number of seven hundred thousand, as the natives say.

61. That, then, is what is done there. How, at the city of Busiris, they celebrate the festival in honor of Isis I have already said. But in this festival, after the sacrifice, all the men and all the women, assuredly many tens of thousands of human beings, beat their breasts in lament; but whom it is they lament I may not declare; it would be unholy for me. But those of the Carians who are living in Egypt do even more than this, inasmuch as they cut their foreheads with knives, and thereby it is clear that they are foreigners and not Egyptians.

62. When the people gather to the city of Saïs, on the night of the sacrifice everyone burns many lamps, under the open sky, around their houses. The lamps are saucers full of oil and of salt and, on top, a wick, which burns all night long; and the name they call the festival is the Festival of the Lamps. Even those of the Egyptians who do not come to the festival itself keep the night of the festival heedfully, all of them, too, burning lamps; so the lamps burn not only in the city of Saïs but throughout all Egypt. Why it is that this night has won light and honor—as to that, there is a sacred story told.

63. Those who go to Heliopolis and Buto perform the sacrifice only. But in Papremis they perform the sacrifice and the holy rites as elsewhere, but also, when the sun is sinking, some few of the priests remain busied with the service of the image; but the most of them, with wooden clubs, stand at the entrance of the shrine. More than a thousand men, who are performing their vows and also carrying wooden clubs, stand all massed opposite to the first set. The image itself, in a small wooden gilt shrine, they have conveyed, the day before, to another holy chamber. Those few of the priests who have been left with the image drag a four-wheeled cart bearing the shrine and the image within the shrine; but the priests standing at the entrance will not suffer the cart to enter. But the votaries come to the rescue of the god and strike at those who would keep him out. There is a sharp battle, then, with the wooden clubs, and they break one another's heads; and, in my opinion, many die of their wounds, though the Egyptians tell me that no one *dies*. The natives explain this festival as follows. They say that Ares' mother dwelt in the temple; Ares himself was reared elsewhere, but, when he came to manhood, he returned and wished to couple with his mother. His mother's servants would not let him come in but kept him off—for they had never laid eyes on him before. But the god went and brought people from another city and handled the servants roughly, and so he came in to where his mother was. It is from this, they say, that, at the festival of Ares, blows are part of the ritual.

64. The Egyptians were the first of mankind to feel religious scruples in certain matters—notably, not to lie with women in holy places nor yet to go into the holy places after lying with a woman

without first washing oneself. For nearly all the rest of mankind, except for the Egyptians and the Greeks, have intercourse in holy places and rise from intercourse with a woman and go into a shrine without washing, for they think that men are much as other beasts; they see the other beasts and the tribes of birds riding one another in the temples and sacred precincts of the gods. If this were not pleasing to the god, the beasts would not do it. But this kind of reasoning that they bring forward is one that for me, especially, is distasteful. Still, certainly, the Egyptians, in this and in all other matters of the holy things, are excessively given to religious scruples.

65. Egypt, though it marches on the borders of Libya, is not very populous in wild animals. But those that there are, wild or tame, are all considered sacred, both those that have their living with mankind and those that do not. But if I were to say why it is that the animals are dedicated as sacred, my argument would drive me into talking of matters divine, and the declaration of these is what I would particularly shun. To the degree that I have spoken of them, it was with but a touch, and under stress of necessity, that I have spoken. There is a custom about the animals, and it is this. There are keepers appointed for the maintenance of the animals, for each kind separate, and men and women alike are keepers from among the Egyptians, child succeeding father in this office of honor. In the cities, each man, discharging his vows, does it thus: they pray to the god whose beast it is, and they shave off their children's hair, either all the head or a half or a third, and they weigh the hairs in a scale against silver. When the scale tips, this sum is given to the keeper of the beast, and she, up to the value of it, cuts up fish and gives it to the animal to eat. Such is their arrangement for the animals' maintenance. Whoever kills one of these animals, if the act was willed, death is his penalty; but, if involuntary, he must pay such fine as the priests shall determine. But a man who kills an ibis or a hawk, whether of intent or not, he must die.

66. There are indeed many animals that have their lives along with the people, but there would be still more if it were not for what happens to the cats. When the female cats give birth, they will no longer frequent the toms, and the latter, for all their desire to mate with them, cannot do so. So they contrive the following trick. They

steal and carry off the kittens from their mothers and kill them; but although they kill them, they do not eat them.[28] The females, deprived of their young and eager to have more, go then, and then only, to the toms; for cats are a breed with a great love of children. When there is a fire, something eerie happens to the cats. The Egyptians, neglecting altogether to quench the fires, stand in a line, with men at intervals, and heedfully try to save the cats. But the cats slip through the line and, jumping over the men, leap into the fire. This, when it happens, causes great grief to the Egyptians. In whoever's house a cat dies naturally, those who dwell in the house all shave their eyebrows, but only these; if the dead animal is a dog, they shave all their body and head.

67. The dead cats are carried away to sacred houses where they are buried, as soon as mummified, in the city of Bubastis.[29] Bitches each man buries in his own city in holy coffins. Ferrets are treated in the same way as dogs. Shrewmice and hawks they take to the city of Buto, ibises to the city of Hermes. Bears are very rare, and wolves are not much larger than foxes; these they bury wherever they find them lying.

68. The nature of the crocodile is of this kind: for the four winter months it eats nothing at all; it is a four-footed creature and is of both land and water; that is to say, it lays its eggs on land and hatches them out, and it spends most of the day on dry land but all the night in the water, for the water is warmer than the open air and the dew. Of all the mortal creatures we know, it grows greatest from smallest beginnings. For the eggs it lays are no larger than those of a goose, and the young thing that hatches is in proportion to the egg; but it is born and grows to a length of twenty-three feet or more. It has the eyes of a pig and great teeth and tusks in proportion to its greatness of body. Alone of animals it has no tongue; nor does it

28. This is a quite accurate piece of observation about cats, except that Herodotus has made his statement too general. Many tomcats will kill the kittens; most cats, along with most suckling animals, will not mate while suckling. Both rules have a fair number of exceptions, and Herodotus will almost never, in any of these observations on natural history, allow for exceptions. As for his point that the toms do not eat the dead kittens, in most instances I have seen them do so.

29. This account is apparently entirely correct, though again—according to How and Wells—more cities are involved than Bubastis.

move its lower jaw but alone of animals draws its upper jaw toward its lower. It has powerful nails and a scaly skin, which is unbreakable, on its back. It is blind in the water but has the sharpest of sights in the air. As it makes its livelihood in the water, it has a mouth that, inside, teems with leeches. Other birds and animals flee it, but the sandpiper has come to peace terms with it, for the crocodile owes him much. For when the crocodile comes out of the water onto the land, and thereafter opens its mouth, which it is wont to do for the most part toward the west wind, then the sandpiper crawls into its mouth and gulps down the leeches. This is of great benefit to the crocodile, who likes it and does the sandpiper no hurt.[30]

69. For some of the Egyptians the crocodile is sacred; but for some it is not—in fact, they treat it as an enemy. Those Egyptians who live about Thebes and the lake of Moeris regard them as especially sacred. At each of these places there is one crocodile, selected out of all, who has been trained and is tame, and the people put ornaments of glass and gold into his ears, and he wears bracelets on his front feet; they give him food specially set aside for him, and offerings, and in all treat him so that he has the best of lives. When the animals die, they mummify them and bury them in sacred coffins. But those people who live around Elephantine even eat crocodiles; they do not think them sacred at all. The Egyptians do not use the name "crocodile" for the animal, but "champsa." The Ionians called them crocodiles because they thought their forms like the lizards that in their own country live in the dry-stone walls.

70. There are many ways of hunting the crocodile, and of every sort. I will tell you about the one that seems most worthwhile relating. The hunter puts his bait, the back of a pig, on a hook and lets it go out into the middle of the stream; he himself stays on the riverbank, where he has a young pig, alive, and he hits the pig. As soon

30. Herodotus, for all the demand for marvels that one may reasonably assume in his audience and readers, is remarkably accurate in nearly all these descriptions of animals and the customs of the inhabitants with relation to them. (The holes bored for the pendants [mentioned in the following chapter] can still be seen in the skulls of the mummified crocodiles.) It is notable that Aristotle, in his *History of Animals* (5.33, 558a17–24) repeats Herodotus' description of the crocodile largely word for word. The only evidence that Herodotus owes this crocodile description to Hecataeus is taken from Porphyry, quoted by Eusebius in the third century A.D.

as the crocodile hears the squeal of the pig, he makes for the sound and meets the bait (the dead pig's back) and swallows it down. Then they draw him in. When he has been hauled to land, first of all the hunter smears his eyes with mud. After he has done that, he masters the animal, for the rest, right easily; but if this is not done, he does so only with trouble.

71. The hippopotamuses are sacred in the province of Papremis but not so among the rest of the Egyptians. This is the kind of form they have: four feet, cloven hooves like cattle, a snub nose, and with the mane of a horse; they show tusks, a horse's tail and voice, and are of the bigness of the greatest ox. Hippopotamus skin is so thick that, when it is dried, men make spearshafts out of it.

72. In the river there are also otters, which the people think are sacred. They also regard as sacred the fish they call the lepidotus and the eel; these, they say, are sacred to the Nile, as, among birds, is the fox-goose.

73. There is another sacred bird, the name of which is the phoenix. I never saw one myself, except in pictures; for indeed it comes but rarely—the people of Heliopolis say only every five hundred years. They say that he comes at the time his father dies. If he is indeed like his pictures, he would be of this kind and this size: he has gold on his wings, which are otherwise mostly red, and the outline and size of him are likest to an eagle. The people say that this bird manages the following contrivance, though for my part I do not believe it. He sets out from Arabia and conveys his father to the shrine of the Sun, and he carries his father emplastered in myrrh and buries him in the Sun's shrine. The manner of his conveyance is this: first he forms an egg of myrrh, of a weight that he is able to carry, and after that he tries carrying it; and when the trial of it is over, he hollows out the egg and stows his father into it, and with more myrrh he plasters over the place he had hollowed out and stowed his father within. When his father lies within it, the weight is then the same as at first; and so, having plastered it over, he carries his father to the shrine of the Sun in Egypt. This is what the bird does, they say.

74. There are also sacred serpents about Thebes that do no harm at all to man. They are small and have two horns growing on the top of their heads; and these, when they die, they bury in the shrine of Zeus, for, they say, they are sacred to that god.

75. There is a place in Arabia just about the city of Buto, and to this place I went to inquire about the winged serpents; and when I came there, I saw the bones and backbones of serpents past all telling for numbers; there were heaps of backbones, great heaps and lesser, and some even lesser than these; and truly many were the heaps. Now this place where the backbones are strewn about is where there is a pass, from narrow mountains into a great plain, and this plain neighbors the plain of Egypt. There is a story that with the coming of spring the winged serpents fly from Arabia into Egypt, and the ibis birds meet the serpents at this pass and will not suffer the snakes to come through, but kill them. It is for this deed that the Arabians say the Egyptians have held the bird in great honor. And the Egyptians themselves agree that they honor the ibis on these grounds.

76. The form of the ibis is like this: it is wonderfully black all over, has the legs of a crane, and a very hooked beak. In size it is about that of the corn crake. This is the form of the black ones, those that fight the serpents; but those that most frequent the society of men (there are two sorts of ibis) have heads and necks that are bare, and this bird is white-feathered, save for the head, the neck, and the tips of the wings and the tail, all of which are wonderfully black; and the legs and beak of the bird are like the other variety of them. The form of the snakes is that of the water snake, but their wings are not feathered but are pretty much like the wings of the bat. That is all I have to say about animals that are sacred.

77. Of the Egyptians themselves, those of them who live around the sown part of the country are great in cultivating the memory of mankind and are far the greatest record-keepers of any people with whom I have been in contact. Here is their manner of life: for three days in succession in each month they physic themselves, hunting health with emetics and purges, because they think that from the food that nourishes mankind come all their diseases. Indeed, in general the Egyptians are the healthiest of all men (after the Libyans), and it is because, I think, of their climate; for their seasons do not change much, one from the other. It is in changes that diseases grow most among men, and in no matter does change make such difference as in changes of seasons. They eat bread, which they make of barley grain and call "cyllestis." The wine they use is made of barley, for there are no vines in their country. Some of their fish they dry in

the sun and eat raw, but others they eat pickled in brine. Of birds they eat quails and ducks and small birds raw, having pickled them first. But other meats, which, among them, belong to the class of birds or fishes, except for such as are appointed them as sacred, they eat roasted or boiled.

78. In social gatherings of the wealthy among the Egyptians, when they are done with the dinner, there is a man who carries round the likeness of a dead man in a coffin, very exactly rendered, both in painting and wrought work, and made of wood; in size it is between eighteen inches and three feet. The man shows the figure to each of the diners and says: "Look upon him, drink and enjoy yourself; for even such you shall be when you are dead." That is what they do at banquets.

79. They follow their fathers' customs and take no others to themselves at all. Among other remarkable customs is their one chant, the Linus Song, which is sung also in Phoenicia and in Cyprus and elsewhere, with different names throughout the nations; but it is agreed that it is the same song that the Greeks, when they sing it, call the Linus Song. There are so many matters at which I marvel among the Egyptians, but certainly one is whence they got the name of the Linus Song. It is clear that they have sung it forever. Linus, in Egyptian, is called Maneros. The Egyptians said that he was the only son of the first king of Egypt and that, dying untimely, he was honored by the Egyptians with this funeral chant and that this was their first and only song.

80. There is this other custom, which the Egyptians have in common with the Lacedaemonians alone among the Greeks: young men, when they encounter their elders, yield the road to them and step out of the way; also, when the old men approach, the young stand up from their seats. But in this they are like none of the Greeks: instead of speaking a greeting to one another in the streets, they do obeisance, dropping the hand to the knee.

81. They wear linen tunics, with fringes about their legs, which they call "calasiris," and they wear white woolen mantles on top of these again. But they never bring into the temple anything of wool, nor may they be buried in such. That contravenes their religion. In this they agree with those rites that are called Orphic and Bacchic but are in fact Egyptian and Pythagorean. For in the case of these

rites, too, whoever has a share in them may not be buried in woolen garments. There is a holy tale about this.

82. Here are some other discoveries of the Egyptians. They find each month and each day belongs to a god, whichever he may be; and on whatever day a man was born depends what events he will encounter and how he will die and what manner of man he will be. Some of the Greeks who are in the way of poetry have used this.[31] The Egyptians have discovered more monstrous happenings than any other people in the world. When one such happens, they write it down and watch for the outcome, and, if anything like it happens again hereafter, they think that the same result will take place.

83. Their divination is as follows: to no man is the art assigned, and only to certain of the gods. For there is a place of divination of Heracles, and of Apollo, and Athena, and Artemis, and Ares, and Zeus, and the one they hold in the greatest honor of all, that of Leto in the city of Buto. However, the methods of divination are not the same in all these places, but they vary.

84. About medicine, they order it thus: each doctor is a doctor for one disease and no more. The whole land is full of doctors; there are some for the eyes, some for the head, and some for the teeth, and some for the belly, and there are some for the diseases that have no outward sign.

85. These are the ways they keen for and bury the dead: when a man that has repute is dead and his household has lost him, then all the womenkind from that house plaster their head and face with mud, and afterwards, having left the corpse in the house, they themselves wander through the city, beating their breasts; while so doing, they wear their clothes girt up and show their breasts, and with them are all their kindred women; on the other side, the men beat their breasts, and they too wear their clothes girt up. When they have done all this, they then carry the corpse to the embalming.

86. There are those who set themselves to this very trade and make it their special craft. When a corpse is brought them, they show to those who bring it models of dead men done in wood, imitations, and painted. The most perfect form of these, they say, belongs

31. A most peculiar phrase. "Those of the Greeks who are *in* poetry" (we would colloquially say "into poetry"), i.e., those Greeks who are writers or interested in what writers write about—in this case, astrology.

to One whose name I may not mention in connection with such a matter.[32] The second class they show is somewhat inferior to this and cheaper, and the third cheapest of all. Having so told them, they inquire of them according to what model they wish the dead man prepared. So the people who brought him agree on a price and then go away, and the others, left in their house, do their embalming. Here is the proceeding for the most perfect model: first they draw out the brains with a hooked iron tool through the nostrils, and in place of what they draw out they pour in drugs. Then, with a sharp Ethiopian stone knife, they make a cut in the flank and clean out the belly completely and rinse it with palm wine and chopped-up spices. Thereafter they fill it with pure ground myrrh, cassia, and other spices (except for frankincense) and stitch up the anus. Having done this, they embalm the body in saltpeter and hide it away for seventy days. More days than that one may not embalm it. When the seventy days are over, they wash the corpse and wrap up the whole body with bandages of fine linen cut into strips, smearing these with gum, which for the most part the Egyptians use instead of glue. Then the relatives take back the corpse and make a hollow wooden form, man-shaped, and, having so made it, they enclose the corpse within, and, having shut it up, they store it in a coffin chamber, placing it upright against a wall.

87. That is how they prepare the dead on the dearest plan; but those who preferred the middle form of burial, because they would shun the greatness of the expense, they prepare as follows: they fill their syringes with pure oil of cedar and fill up the belly of the corpse, neither making any incision nor taking out the guts but

32. This "One" is Osiris. It was thought that in order to reach the kingdom of Osiris in the other world the dead man must *be* an Osiris in counterfeit.

It is worth remarking how deep is Herodotus' sense of reverence when he speaks about the religious beliefs of people other than the Greeks. In no case is this truer than in his accounts of Egypt. We must remember that Herodotus thinks that many of the Greek gods came from Egypt. But I think the reverence is given everywhere in his *History*. It is relevant to think here of 2.3, in which he says that all men know "equally" about the gods. He avoids discussion of them, except in regard to their names (*onomata*), which, as we saw, are more than mere names, for they involve the entire personality of the god. But in some cases even the name in itself belongs to the forbiddenness of expression and discussion—and Herodotus acquiesces again.

pumping the drench in through the anus and sealing it up against flowing out again; then they embalm the body for the prescribed days, and on the last day they draw out of the belly the cedar oil they had put in. This has such power that it brings out with itself the guts and the intestines, all dissolved. The saltpeter eats away the flesh, and so what is left of the dead man is a skin only and the bones. When they are done with all this, they give back the body, having done nothing further to it.

88. The third method of embalmment, which is what prepares the poorer dead, is this: they rinse out the belly with a purge, embalm the body for the seventy days, and, after that, give it back to be carried away.

89. The wives of distinguished men, when they die, they do not give for embalmment right away, nor yet women who are especially beautiful and of great account. Only when they have been dead three or four days do they hand them over to the embalmers. This is done to prevent the embalmers from copulating with these women. For they say that one of them was caught copulating with a freshly dead woman and that a fellow workman told on him.

90. Whoever, either of the Egyptians themselves or a foreigner, has been carried off by a crocodile, or has clearly come by his death by the action of the river itself, at whatever city he comes to land must, with the greatest concern, be embalmed and treated as well as ever is possible and be buried in a holy coffin. No one may put a hand on him, either of his relatives or friends, but the burial must be conducted by the very priests of the Nile, inasmuch as they are handling a corpse that is something more than human.

91. The Egyptians avoid following Greek customs and, to speak in general, the customs of any people other than their own. All the other Egyptians keep to this zealously; but there is one great city, Chemmis, in the Theban province, near Neapolis, in which there is a square temple of Perseus, the son of Danaë, and round it grow palm trees. The gateway of this temple is of very great stones, and on this stand two very huge stone figures. Within this surrounding enclosure there is a shrine, and in it stands an image of Perseus. The people of Chemmis say that Perseus often appears in their country, here and there, and often within the temple, and that a sandal worn by him is discovered, three feet long in size, and that when this appears all

Egypt prospers. This is what they say, and they do certain Greek things in honor of Perseus: they hold a gymnastic contest, covering all forms of competition; for prizes they have cattle and clothing and skins. When I asked them why it was that Perseus appeared to them alone and why it was that they alone among the Egyptians set up a gymnastic festival, they said that Perseus came originally from their own city; for Danaus and Lynceus were men of Chemmis, and they sailed away to Greece, and, counting over the generations from them, they come at last to Perseus. He came to Egypt, they say, for the same reason that the Greeks give: to bring the Gorgon's head out of Libya. They said that he came to their country and recognized all his kinsfolk, and that he came to Egypt thoroughly knowing the name of the city of Chemmis because he had heard it from his mother. It was at his bidding, they say, that they celebrated the gymnastic contest.

92. All these are the customs of the Egyptians who live above the marsh country. Those who live in the marshes have much the same customs as the rest—there, too, each man lives with just one wife, as the Greeks do—but with respect to cheap food they have made certain innovations of their own. When the river is full and floods the plains, there grow in the water many lilies, which the Egyptians call lotus. They pick these and dry them in the sun and then crush the center part of the lotus, which is like a poppy, and make of it loaves, which they bake in the fire. The root of the lotus is also eatable and to some extent sweet; it is round and about the size of an apple. There are other lilies like roses; these grow in the river too, and from them there is a fruit, growing in a calyx, which comes from the root by a separate stem and which is in form most like a wasp's honeycomb. In this there are many seeds, about the size of an olive stone, and these are eaten both fresh and dried. The papyrus, which grows yearly there, they draw out of the marshes; the upper part of it they cut off and use for other purposes, but the lower part, to the length of some eighteen inches, they eat; they sell it, as well. Those who want to have papyrus at its best bake it in a redhot oven and eat it. Some of the people live altogether on fish; they catch these, gut them, and then dry them in the sun and eat them dried.

93. Fish that go in shoals are mostly not born in the rivers; they are born and reared in the lakes. For when the heat is on the fish to

conceive, they go in shoals to the sea, the males leading and shedding their seed and the females following and gulping it down and, from this, conceiving.[33] When the fish become pregnant in the ocean, they head back again to their native haunts, both males and females; but now they have not the same leaders, for the leadership has passed to the females. As these lead the shoal, they do as the males did before. They shed their eggs, like millet seeds, several at a time, and the males, which are following, eat them up. These seeds are fish. From the surviving seeds, the ones that are not gulped down, come the fish that are reared. Those of the fish that are caught as they swim toward the sea show bruises on the left of their heads; those on the return journey, on the right. This is because they swim to the sea keeping the land on their left, and, swimming back, on their right, grazing the bank and touching it, as often as they may, so that they do not lose the way through the stream. When the Nile begins to fill, the hollows of the ground and the pools along the river begin to fill first, as the water passes through to them from the river, and the moment these are full, all of them are full of small fish. I think I understand how these come into existence. For the year before, when the Nile receded, the fish laid their eggs in the mud, and then, with the last of the water, away went the fish. Then, as the season came around and the water came upon the mud again, these fish hatched at once from the eggs that were there.

94. That, then, is the story of the fish. Egyptians who live about the marshes use an oil that is made from the fruit of the castor bean, which the Egyptians call "kiki." This is how they do it. Along the banks of the rivers and the lakes they sow this castor bean, which in Greece grows of itself, wild. The sown variety in Egypt produces a heavy crop, but it has an unpleasant smell. When the people collect it, some of them chop it up and press it; others roast it and, after, boil it and collect the liquid that flows from it. This is thick and as serviceable for lamps as olive oil, only for the heavy smell.

95. The mosquitoes are very many there, and against them the people have made contrivance. Those of the inhabitants who live

---

33. Aristotle, in the *Generation of Animals* 3.5.755b6, comments on this statement: "A very simple-minded and popular story. . . . The passage from the mouth goes into the belly and not to the womb." Rather unkindly, he cites our author for that story under the title of "Herodotus the Mythmaker [Mythologus]."

above the marshes are helped by the towers; they can ascend these and get sleep, for the mosquitoes are prevented by the winds from flying high. The people who live around the marshes have, instead of towers, contrived something else again. Every man of them owns a net, which by day he uses to catch fish but at night uses otherwise. He drapes the net around the bed where he is sleeping and then creeps under it and sleeps. For the mosquitoes, if one wraps oneself in any kind of garment or in linen and tries to sleep, bite right through such clothes; but through the net they never even attempt to bite.

96. The boats with which they carry freight are made of the acacia tree, which is in form very like the lotus of Cyrene. Its sap is a kind of gum. From this acacia tree they cut planks about three feet long and lay them together like bricks, doing their shipbuilding in this fashion: they fasten these three-foot planks about long wedges, set close together, and they stretch the deck beams on top of these. They use no ribs but caulk the joinings on the inside with papyrus. They make one rudder stick, and that is bored through the keel. Their mast is also of acacia wood, and their sails of papyrus. These boats cannot sail upstream unless there is a clear wind blowing straight on them, but they are towed from the land. But downstream this is how they manage: they make a raft of tamarisk fastened with a mat of reeds, and they have a stone, of perhaps four hundredweight, pierced at the bottom. This raft is tied by a rope ahead of the boat and is let draw the boat along, and the stone is tied with another rope behind the boat. As the current hits the raft, she travels fast and tows the "baris"—that is the name they give to these boats of theirs—and the stone, being towed behind and in the depths of the water, straightens the course of the boat. There are very many of these boats, some of many thousand talents' burden.

97. When the Nile comes out upon the country, only the cities show above the watery surface, very much like islands in the Aegean Sea. The rest of Egypt is a sea, and only these cities float on the top of it. When this happens, the people ferry themselves about, no longer just in the streams of the river but right through the plain. If you are sailing from Naucratis to Memphis, you will sail right by the pyramids. This is not the usual course; that is by the point of the Delta and the city of Cercasorus. But *toward* Naucratis from the sea

and Canobus, when you sail through the plain, you will come by the city of Anthylla and the town called after Archandrus.

98. Of these, the city of Anthylla is a well-known one and is especially assigned to the wife of the reigning king of Egypt for the provision of her shoes (this is the case since Egypt has been under the rule of Persia). The other city has its name from Archandrus, son of Phthius, grandson of Achaeus, and son-in-law of Danaus; for it certainly is called after Archandrus. (There may, of course, have been another Archandrus; in any case, the name is not Egyptian.)

99. So far it is my eyes, my judgment, and my searching that speak these words to you; from this on, it is the accounts of the Egyptians that I will tell to you as I heard them, though there will be, as a supplement to them, what I have seen myself. The Egyptian priests say that Min, who was the first king of Egypt,[34] dammed off this place of Memphis from the Nile. For the whole river flowed close by the sandy mountain that is toward Libya, but Min, damming up the southern bend of it, about a hundred furlongs south of Memphis, dried up the ancient channel and channeled the river to flow through the middle of the mountains. Even to this day this bend of the Nile is most heedfully observed by the Persians, that it may flow in its confined course, and every year the barriers are built up again. For if the river should break out at this point, there would be a danger that all Memphis would go down in the flood. When Min, this first king, had made the cut-off part into dry land, he founded within it the city that is now called Memphis—for Memphis, too, lies in this narrow part of Egypt—and, outside it, he dug a lake away from the river to the north and west (for the Nile itself was the barrier toward the east), and he founded within the city the temple of Hephaestus, which is indeed a great one and exceedingly worth telling of.

100. After him, the priests, from their papyrus lists, told me the names of three hundred and thirty kings. Among so many generations of mankind there were eighteen Ethiopian kings and one woman, native to the country; all the rest were men and Egyptians. The name of the woman who became a sovereign was Nitocris—the same name as her of Babylon. They say that this queen had a brother

34. On Min, see note 5, above.

who was king of Egypt, whom the Egyptians killed when he was their king and they turned over the sovereignty to her, and she, to avenge him, contrived to destroy many of the Egyptians by craft. She had a long underground chamber made and said she would handsel it, but it was far other thoughts she had in her mind. She invited those of the Egyptians whom she had known as being most concerned in her brother's death, and when they were at their feasting she turned the river in upon them through a great secret channel. That is all the priests have to say about her, save that, so that her deed might not itself be revenged, she, after the deed was done, hurled herself into a cellar full of hot ashes.

101. Now, as for the rest of the kings, the priests had no great achievement to tell of them, nor any distinction, save only for the last of them, Moeris. He created as his memorial the propylaea[35] to the north of the temple of Hephaestus, and he dug a lake, and the number of furlongs in the circuit of it I will declare later; and he built pyramids in it, the greatness of which I will declare when I tell of the lake itself. These were his great deeds, but none of the rest did anything.

102. Passing them over, then, I will speak of the king who came after them, whose name was Sesostris.[36] Of him the priests say that he was the first that set out with his warships from the Arabian Gulf and subdued all that dwell along the Red Sea until, as he sailed forward, he came to a sea too shallow to be sailed on by his great ships. Then, after he had come back to Egypt, according to the report of the priests he gathered a great army and drove right through the mainland, conquering every people that lay in his way. Now, wherever he encountered men of bravery, who strove for their freedom, among such folk he set up pillars in their lands that declared his own name and country and how he had conquered them by his own power. But when he had taken over cities without a fight and easily,

35. A propylaea is a roofed gateway opening into the courtyards surrounding a temple. It is often a structure of monumental size and importance (it may include porticoes, colonnades, wing-buildings, etc.).

36. Identified by some as Ramses II, who ruled in the fourteenth century B.C. (How and Wells discuss other possibilities.) The "Arabian Gulf," mentioned below, is our Red Sea, and, as I have pointed out before, Herodotus' "Red Sea" is our Indian Ocean.

for them he also made records on the pillars in just such terms as he used for the men who were brave, but, you see, he also had a cunt drawn thereon, because he would make clear that they were cowards.

103. Such were his actions while he traversed the mainland, until he crossed from Asia into Europe and conquered the Scythians and the Thracians. This, I think, was the furthest the Egyptian army came. For in that country pillars were set up and are to be seen, but none further on. Then he turned back and went home. When he came as far as the river Phasis, either King Sesostris himself left a certain part of his army there to settle the country, or—for I cannot, from this on, speak with certainty—some of his soldiers, sick of his wanderings, remained of themselves about the river Phasis.

104. For the Colchians are clearly Egyptians; I thought that myself before I heard it from others. As soon as it came into my head, I asked both peoples questions, and the Colchians remembered more of the Egyptians than the Egyptians did of the Colchians. The Egyptians said that they thought the Colchians were part of the army of Sesostris. My own guess was based on the fact that they are dark-skinned and woolly-haired; this, however, means nothing, since there are other people such. But the following is more important: that alone of mankind the Colchians, the Egyptians, and the Ethiopians have circumcised from the first. The Phoenicians and the Palestinian Syrians [37] themselves agree that they learned this from the Egyptians; and the Syrians who live near the Thermodon and Parthenius rivers and the Macrones, who are their neighbors, say that they have learned circumcision from the Colchians—and lately. These are the only people who circumcise, and they clearly do it the same as the Egyptians. Of the Egyptians themselves and the Ethiopians, I cannot say which learned from the other, for it is clearly a very ancient practice. But that the others learned it from intercourse with Egypt, the following, to my mind, is great proof: such of the Phoenicians as have intercourse with Greece no longer imitate the Egyptians with respect to their genitals; they do not circumcise their children.

---

37. Under this heading Herodotus includes all the people who lived in Palestine, without distinguishing the Jews especially.

105. I would like to mention another matter in which the Colchians are similar to the Egyptians. These and the Egyptians are the only peoples to work linen and in the same way; indeed, their whole way of life and their language are similar to one another. The Colchian linen is called by the Greeks Sardonian, but that which comes from Egypt is called Egyptian.[38]

106. Of the pillars that King Sesostris of Egypt set up throughout the lands, most are no longer there to be seen. But I saw some of them myself in Palestinian Syria, with the inscriptions I speak of on them and the cunts. There are, besides, in Ionia two statues of this man carved in the rock, one where one goes from Ephesus to Phocaea, the other, from Sardis to Smyrna. In each there is sculpted a man of near seven feet with a spear in his right hand and a bow in his left, and the rest of his gear is similar—that is, it is both Egyptian and Ethiopian in its fashion. From one shoulder to the other, across the breast, runs an inscription in sacred Egyptian script saying: "I won this land with my shoulders." Who he is and where from, it does not show there, but it is shown elsewhere. Some of those who have seen it think that it is a statue of Memnon, but they are far from the truth.[39]

107. This Egyptian Sesostris returned and brought with him many men of the nations he had subjugated; thus say the priests, and they say that when, on his return journey, he came to Daphnae in

38. The Greek word meaning Sardonian ought to mean "from Sardinia." No one seems to think this can be relevant, for Herodotus is not talking about Sardinia in connection with Colchis and Egypt. This is something of an unsolved mystery. However, it *is* interesting that Herodotus apparently knows the trade terms for different kinds of cloth. Some editors conclude that this is one of the indications that he was some sort of trader or merchant himself.

39. The two statues were there, at least in the time of How and Wells and other archeologists in the twentieth century. It appears that they were probably Hittite rather than Egyptian, but Herodotus knew nothing of this ancient empire, which preceded that of Egypt. He thought it was a figure of Sesostris. It appears that the Memnon conjecture (the son of Dawn) was probably correct. The editors all solemnly refuse to believe in the obscene illustrations on the pillars. They are not there now, though they may quite well have faded; the letters of the inscriptions on the statues have also become indecipherable. But Diodorus and other Greek authorities record the obscene drawings, as well as Herodotus, though it is certainly possible that they were following his lead. How and Wells are in general very impressed with the correctness of Herodotus' observations.

Pelusium, his brother, to whom he had entrusted Egypt, invited him to a banquet, and with his children as well; but then the brother heaped the house on the outside with firewood and set fire to it. When Sesostris was aware of this, he at once consulted with his wife—for he had brought her, you see, along too. She advised him to take two of his sons (there were six in all) and stretch them over the fire to build a kind of bridge over it so the rest could escape, treading on them. This is what Sesostris did, and two of his children were burnt to death in this fashion; but the rest were saved, along with their father.

108. When Sesostris had come back to Egypt and had taken vengeance on his brother, he made the following use of the vast crowd of those he had brought from the conquered countries. It was under this king that those stones, of enormous size, were conveyed to the temple of Hephaestus. It was these captives that dragged them there, and it was they who digged, under compulsion, all those canals that are now in Egypt; and so it is they who, without intending it, made Egypt defective in horses and chariots that beforetime was all a land of horses and wagons. For, from this time on, all Egypt, although it is level enough, knows no horse nor any cart. The cause is the canals, which are so numerous and going in every direction. The king cut these canals for a purpose: those of the Egyptians who had cities that were not on the banks of the river, but inland, were short of water when the river withdrew from their land, and they had to drink brackish water, drawn from wells.

109. That was why Egypt was cut up by canals. The priests also say that it was this king who divided the land among all the Egyptians, giving to each man as an allotment a square, equal in size; from this the king derived his revenues, as he appointed the payment therefor of a yearly tax. If the river should carry off a portion of the allotment, the man would come to the king himself and signify what had happened, whereupon the king sent men to inspect and remeasure by how much the allotment had grown less, so that for the future it should pay proportionally less of the assigned tax. I think it was from this that geometry was discovered and came to Greece. For the sun-clock and the sundial and the twelve divisions of the day the Greeks learned from the Babylonians.

110. This was the only Egyptian king who also ruled Ethiopia.

He left as his memorials, in front of the temple of Hephaestus, two stone statues, forty-five feet high, of himself and his wife and, of his four children, statues thirty feet high. A long time afterwards, Darius the Persian would have set up a statue in front of them. The priest of Hephaestus would not have it so, saying, "You have not done such deeds as Sesostris the Egyptian; for Sesostris conquered as many nations as you, but he also conquered the Scythians; but you, Darius, could not conquer the Scythians. Therefore, it is not right that you should set up a statue in front of the dedications of the man whose deeds you could not surpass." Darius, they say, pardoned the priest on the strength of these words.

111. They say that, on the death of Sesostris, his son, Pheros,[40] succeeded to the throne. This man achieved no deed of war, and he became blind through the following event. The river came upon them, at that time, higher than it had ever done, to the extent of some twenty-seven feet; and when it flooded the fields, the wind blew upon it, and the waves made it stormy. They say that the king was so infatuated that he took his spear and threw it into the heart of the river's eddies. He was at once stricken with a disease of the eyes and became blind. For ten years, then, he was blind. But in the eleventh year there came to him an oracle from the city of Buto to the effect that the time of his punishment was drawing to an end and that he should see again if he washed his eyes with the piss of a woman who had known only her own husband and no other men at all. So he essayed first with his own wife, but he saw no better than before. Then he tried them all, one after another. When he *did* recover his sight, he gathered together all the women he had tried, save for her whose piss had cured his eyes, into one city, which is now called "The Red Sod." And having collected them all there, he set fire to them, city and all. And the woman in whose piss he had washed and seen again, her he took to be his wife. When he was cured of this disease of his eyes, he made dedications at all the famous temples, and, at the temple of the Sun, he dedicated his offering that is the most worthy of mention, being two stone obelisks, each made of a single block of stone. Each of them is one hundred and fifty feet high and twelve feet broad.

40. Apparently this is not a proper name but simply the title "Pharaoh."

112. They said that Pheros was succeeded in the kingship by a man of Memphis whose name, in Greek, was Proteus. The beautiful and well-equipped precinct in Memphis is his, lying to the south of the temple of Hephaestus. It is Phoenicians from Tyre who live around this precinct, and the whole place is called "The Tyrian Camp." In the precinct of Proteus there is a shrine called after "The Foreign Aphrodite." My guess is that this shrine is the shrine of Helen, daughter of Tyndareus; I think so because I have heard the story of how Helen stayed with Proteus and also because the shrine is called after "The Foreign Aphrodite." Of all the other temples of Aphrodite, not one is called after the goddess as "foreign."

113. When I asked of the priests, they told me that what had happened to Helen was this: Alexander carried off Helen from Sparta and set sail for his own country; when he got into the Aegean, wrecking winds forced him out of his course into the Egyptian sea; and after that, as the winds did not let up, he came to Egypt and, in Egypt, to what is now called the Canobic Mouth of the Nile and to the Saltpans. There was, on the shore (it is still there), a shrine of Heracles. If a servant takes refuge in that, be he whose servant he may, and has put upon himself certain sacred brand-marks, thereby surrendering himself to the god, no one may lay a hand on him. This is the law, which is the same from the beginning right up to this time of mine. Now the servants of Alexander, having learned of the law that pertained to the shrine, deserted their master and sat as suppliants of the god. They accused Alexander—because they wished to injure him—by telling the whole story of Helen and the wrong done to Menelaus. They pressed this accusation before the priests and him who was the warden of this Nile mouth, whose name was Thonis.

114. When Thonis heard this, he sent at once to Memphis, to Proteus, with the following message: "Here has come a foreigner, in race a Teucrian.[41] He has done in Greece an act of impiety; for he has cheated his host of his wife and then has come here, bringing her with him, as well as much property. The winds drove him ashore to this land. Are we to suffer him to sail away scatheless, or shall we take from him that wherewith he came?" To this message Proteus

41. I.e., Trojan.

made answer: "For this fellow, whoever he may be, who has done impious deeds against his very host, arrest him and bring him before me, that I may see what he will then have to say."

115. On hearing this, Thonis arrested Alexander and held his ships where they were and, after, brought Alexander himself to Memphis and, along with him, Helen and the property and the suppliants as well. When they were all brought before him, Proteus asked Alexander who he was and where he sailed from. Alexander told him his breeding and the name of his country and, furthermore, the voyage on which he had sailed. After that Proteus asked him where he got Helen from. When Alexander faltered in his story and failed to speak the truth, the suppliant servants bore witness against him, setting forth the whole story of the wrong done. Finally Proteus rendered his judgment: "If I did not think it of the first consequence not to kill any stranger who, under duress of the winds, has come to this land of mine, I would myself have taken vengeance on you on behalf of that Greek. Scoundrel, you had hospitality at his hands and then did the unholiest thing against him: you came at your host's wife. And, truly, this was not enough for you, but you turned her head so with passion that you succeeded in stealing her away with you. And *that* was not enough for you, but you must plunder your host's house before you came here. As matters stand, I make great scruple not to kill one that is my guest; but this woman and the property I will not let you take with you, but I will keep them myself for your Greek host till the day he comes here and wants to take them away. For yourself and those who share your voyage, I give you three days to quit your anchorage, out of my country; if you do not do so, you will be treated as enemies."

116. This is how Helen came to Proteus, according to what the priests say. And I think Homer knew the tale; but inasmuch as it was not so suitable for epic poetry as the other, he used the latter and consciously abandoned the one here told. But he has given proof that he knew the story, for in the *Iliad*—he has nowhere else retracted this—he spoke of Alexander's "wandering": how, in bringing Helen, he was "carried out of his course" and in his "wandering" came to "Sidon in Phoenicia, among other places." He makes mention of this in the Prowess of Diomedes.[42] The verses run like this:

42. *Iliad* 6.289–92. Before the division of the poem into the present twenty-

There were the robes subtly woven, subtly colored, the work
   of women
of Sidon; for once from Sidon Prince Alexander the godlike
brought them from there himself, as he sailed over the broad
   seas
on the voyage he carried home Helen, descendant of glorious
   fathers.

There is also a mention in the *Odyssey*, in these lines:[43]

Such were the drugs she possessed, the daughter of Zeus,
   drugs cunning,
drugs of good help, once given her by the wife of Thon,
   Polydamna,
a woman of Egypt, where fertile the earth yields drugs in
   great plenty;
many when mixed are good, and many more are destructive.

Here is another comment of Menelaus to Telemachus:[44]

For all I was eager for home, the gods held me fast in Egypt,
For I had failed to give them perfect victims in hundreds
   slain.

In these verses it is plain that Homer knew of Alexander's wandering
to Egypt; for Syria is the neighboring country to Egypt, and the
Phoenicians, to whom Sidon belongs, live in Syria.

117. These verses and this passage are the strongest proof that
the *Cypria* are not by Homer but by someone else. For in the *Cypria*,
true enough, the poet says that Alexander arrived in Ilium after a
two days' voyage from Sparta, that he brought Helen with him, and
that he had wind and sea to suit him on his journey. But in the *Iliad*
it says that he strayed from his course in the trip on which he
brought Helen.

118. That is enough about Homer and the *Cypria*. When I asked
the priests whether the story the Greeks told of the happenings at
Troy was false or true, they said on this point that in their researches
they knew the truth of the matter from Menelaus himself. After the

---

four books, titles such as "Prowess of Diomedes," or "Prowess of Agamemnon,"
or whatever title suited a particular block of narrative, were commonly used.

43. *Odyssey* 4.227–30.
44. *Odyssey* 4.351–52.

carrying-off of Helen, they said, there came a great host of Greeks to the Teucrian land, to help Menelaus; they disembarked and established a camp there. Then they sent messengers to Ilium and, among the messengers, Menelaus himself. These entered the walls of Ilium and demanded back Helen and the goods that Alexander stole when he took her away; and they also demanded satisfaction for the crimes committed. The Teucrians said exactly the same things then and thereafter, and with declaration under oath and without, that they did not have either Helen or the goods that were claimed but that all was in Egypt. "It would be very unjust," they said, "that we should be punished for what the Egyptian King Proteus possesses." The Greeks thought that they were being laughed at, and so they continued the siege until they took the town. But when they captured the walls—there was no Helen! Then the Greeks learned the very same story as before, but now they believed the Trojans' first word; and so they sent Menelaus himself to Proteus.

119. Menelaus came to Egypt and sailed up to Memphis, told the truth of what had happened, and received great hospitality and took back Helen, quite unhurt, and all his own possessions as well. But though this was his treatment, Menelaus proved an unjust man to the Egyptians. For when he was eager to sail home, contrary winds held him there; and to deal with this, he did something very wicked: he took two children of the natives and sacrificed them. When his deed was discovered, he was hated and pursued as he fled with his ships to Libya. Where he went from there the Egyptians cannot say. Part of these matters, the priests told me, they learned from their researches; but they said that what happened in their own country they knew for absolute fact.

120. This is the story the Egyptian priests told. I myself concur in what they have said of Helen. My reasoning is as follows: if Helen had been in Ilium, she would have been given back to the Greeks, whether Alexander wanted it so or not. For Priam was not so besotted, nor the rest of his kinsfolk, that they would be willing to risk their own bodies, children, and city so that Alexander should lie with Helen. If indeed that had been their sentiment at the first, surely when many of the rest of the Trojans had perished in their encounters with the Greeks, and when, in Priam's own case, two or three of his sons on every occasion of battle—if we are to speak on

the testimony of the epic poets—when all these matters of such consequence happened, I am confident that, if it had been Priam himself who was living with Helen, he would have given her back to the Greeks if thereby he could have been quit of the troubles that were upon him. It was not even as if the kingship was going to devolve upon Alexander, so that, Priam now being old, things were at Alexander's disposal; for it was Hector, older than Alexander and more of a man, who would have taken over the kingdom on Priam's death; and Hector it would certainly not have suited to comply with his erring brother—and that, too, one who had caused great disasters to him personally and to all the rest of the Trojans. No, the Trojans did not *have* Helen to give back, and, when they spoke the truth, the Greeks did not believe them; and the reason of this, if I may declare my opinion, was that the Divine was laying his plans that, as the Trojans perished in utter destruction, they might make this thing manifest to all the world: that for great wrongdoings, great also are the punishments from the gods. That is what I think, and that is what I am saying here.

121. The king who succeeded Proteus was Rhampsinitus, said the priests. He is the king who left as his memorial the western propylaea of the temple of Hephaestus, and facing the propylaea he set up two statues, being in greatness thirty-eight feet high; the Egyptians call the one to the north Summer, the one to the south Winter. Summer they do obeisance to and treat well, but that which is called Winter they treat in the contrary fashion. This king had great wealth of silver; none of those who came after him exceeded him in this or came near him. As the king wished to store his treasure in safety, he built himself a stone chamber whereof one of the walls abutted upon the outer wall of his house. His workman laid a plot and contrived as follows: he took heed that one of the stones should be such as to be easily removed by two men or even one. When the chamber was completed, the king stored his treasures in it. Now, as time went on, the builder was at his life's end and called his sons to him—he had two of them—and explained to them his forethought on their behalf: that they might want for nothing, he had made his contrivance while building the king's treasure house. He showed them clearly all about the withdrawal of the stone and gave them the measurements of it. "Keep but these," he said, "and

you shall be the stewards of the king's money." So he ended his life, and the boys were not long about it before they approached the royal palace by night, and, easily finding the stone in the chamber, shifted it and took out a great deal of the treasure. When the king chanced to open the chamber, he was amazed to see certain of the vessels short of their money, and no one could be found to blame for it, since all the seals were unbroken and the chamber shut tight. Twice and thrice more he opened the chamber, and each time the treasure always seemed to him to be less—for of course the thieves did not cease their raids. So this is what he did. He gave orders to have traps made and set them up around the vessels where the money was stored. The thieves came as they had done before; one of the two of them entered the chamber and, as he approached the treasure vessel, he was straightway caught in the trap. As soon as he realized in what case he stood, he called his brother and told him what had happened him. He bade him come in quickly and cut off his head so that he might not be seen and recognized and so destroy his brother as well. The brother thought he was right and was persuaded to do as he said; and having done so, he replaced the stone and went home, carrying his brother's head with him. At dawn the king came to the chamber, entered it, and was bewildered to see a headless thief caught in the trap but the chamber undisturbed, with no sign of entrance or exit. In his perplexity he did this: he hung the thief's body on the outer wall, set sentries over it, and gave them charge that whomever they saw mourning the dead or showing pity on him they should arrest and bring to the king.

So the corpse hung there; but his mother took it terribly to heart, and she had much to say to the surviving son and bade him, in whatever way he could, contrive to take down the hanging body of his brother and bring it home. If he neglected what she said, she threatened, she would herself go to the king and give information that her son had the money. So terribly did the mother rate the surviving son—and all he had to say to her went for nothing—that the boy made another contrivance. He got donkeys and filled some skins with wine and laded them on the donkeys and proceeded to drive them along. When they came to the spot where the corpse was hanging and where the sentinels were, he pulled down two or three of the corners of the wineskins, where the fastenings were, so as to loosen them. As the wine ran out, the young man started to beat his head and cry aloud, as though he did not know which of the donkeys to run to first. The guards, as soon as they saw the wine running freely, collected down to the road with buckets and began to scoop up the spilled wine, thinking themselves lucky fellows. The boy abused them all, pretending to be furious. The guards soothed him down, and at last he feigned to be pacified and to give over his anger, and at last he drove the donkeys off the road and tried to settle the loads on them. So they talked some more, and one of the soldiers mocked the boy with a joke and made him laugh (so the boy pretended), and so the boy ended by giving them one of the wine-skins. The guards sat down, just where they were, and decided to drink. They took the boy in and told him to stay and drink with them. So of course he was convinced—and stayed. As they grew fond of him in the charitableness of their drinking, he gave them another of the wineskins. The guards had now had a great deal to drink and became totally drunk. The wine won out completely, and they went to sleep just where they had had their party. But the boy, as soon as the night was far advanced, took down the body of his brother and, by way of derision of the guards, shaved the right cheek of each of them, loaded the corpse on the donkeys, and went off home. He had done what his mother ordered.

The king, as soon as he heard that the body of the thief had been stolen, was in a fury. He wanted more than anything in the world to find out who it was that had played the trick, and so he did something—though I myself do not believe it. He set his daughter in a room and ordered her to consort with all the men that came to her, alike. But before they enjoyed her, she must compel each to tell her what was the cleverest and wickedest thing he had ever done in his life. Whoever told her the story of the thief, she was to lay hold of and not let get away. His child did what her father ordered her, and the thief, knowing why all this was being done, wanted to surpass the king in resourcefulness, and so *he* did something. He cut off the arm of a freshly dead man at the shoulder, and he took this with him under his cloak when he went to the chamber. So he went in to the king's daughter and was asked what all the rest were asked, and he said, "The wickedest thing I did was to cut off the head of my brother who was caught in a trap in the king's treasury; the cleverest is when I made the guards drunk and took down the body of my brother, which was hanging there." When she heard that, she grabbed at him. But the thief, in the dark room, stretched out to her the hand of the corpse. She took hold of it and held it, thinking she was grasping the hand of the man himself. Then the thief left it to her and made his escape through the doors.

When this news, too, was brought to the king, he was astounded at the wit and daring of the man, and finally he sent round to all the cities making proclamation of immunity and promising a great reward if the thief would come into his sight. The thief trusted him and came. Rhampsinitus admired him greatly and gave him his daughter to wife, as being the man who understood more than anyone else in the world. "The Egyptians excel all others," he said, "and this man the rest of the Egyptians."

122. After that, said the priests, this king descended alive into what the Greeks are used to call Hades, and there he played at dice with Demeter; and sometimes he beat her, and sometimes was worsted by her, and he came back up again, having, as a gift from her, a golden napkin. From this descent of Rhampsinitus—from the moment when he returned, say the priests—the Egyptians have kept a festival; that festival I know they were still celebrating in my time, though I cannot say whether this was the true occasion of it. The priests, on the day of the festival itself, weave a robe and then bind the eyes of one of themselves with a headband; and they lead him out, with the robe in his hands, on the road that leads to the temple of Demeter, and there they themselves turn back home. The priest that is so blindfolded, they say, is conducted by two wolves to the temple of Demeter, which is three and a half miles from the city, and then the wolves lead him back again from the temple to the same place.

123. As for the stories told by the Egyptians, let whoever finds them credible use them.[45] Throughout the entire history it is my un-

45. This is a fascinating and ambiguous comment. How "use"? A little later in this chapter Herodotus refers to certain Greeks who "used" this story. Does he mean "framed their beliefs about life on the basis of these stories"? Clearly, the story of Rhampsinitus' return from the dead leads Herodotus to discuss the general theory of the transmigration of souls, which he declares is an Egyptian doctrine originally. Some authorities are doubtful that it is in fact Egyptian, on the

derlying principle that it is what people severally have said to me, and what I have heard, that I must write down. The Egyptians say that Demeter and Dionysus[46] are the lords of the underworld. The Egyptians are the first who have told this story also, that the soul of man is immortal and that, when the body dies, the soul creeps into some other living thing then coming to birth; and when it has gone through all things, of land and sea and the air, it creeps again into a human body at its birth. The cycle for the soul is, they say, three thousand years. There are some Greeks who have used this story, some earlier and some later, as though it were something of their own. I know their names but will not write them down.

124. Now, till the reign of King Rhampsinitus, what the priests had to tell of was of nothing but the rule of good laws and the great prosperity of Egypt; but, after him, Cheops became king over them, and he drove them into the extremity of misery. For first he shut up all the temples, to debar them from sacrificing in them, and thereafter he ordered all Egyptians to work for himself. To some was assigned the dragging of great stones from the stone quarries in the Arabian mountains as far as the Nile; to others he gave orders, when these stones had been taken across the river in boats, to drag them, again, as far as the Libyan hills. The people worked in gangs of one hundred thousand for each period of three months. The people were afflicted for ten years of time in building the road along which they dragged the stones—in my opinion a work as great as the pyramid itself. For the length of the road is more than half a mile, and its breadth is sixty feet, and its height, at its highest, is forty-eight feet. It is made of polished stone, and there are figures carved on it. Ten

---

grounds that the practice of mummification denies it implicitly. Others think it may have come to Egypt from India when both Egypt and parts of India were under the domination of Persia. Perhaps more important than the particular doctrine is what follows in this chapter: Herodotus' assertion (several times repeated) that it is the beliefs that people maintain, not their necessary truth, that concerns him. His History is as much about what people believe and think as it is about events that happen—and less about whether events did happen than that people thought they did. Because history, for him, is the total fabric of a moment and an era and a nation or civilization, where thought is as important as acts or events.

46. Isis and Osiris.

years went to this road and to the underground chambers on the hill on which the pyramids stand. These chambers King Cheops made as burial chambers for himself in a kind of island, bringing in a channel from the Nile. The pyramid itself took twenty years in the building. It is a square, each side of it eight hundred feet long, and the same in height, made of polished and most excellently fitted stones. No stone is less than thirty feet long.

125. This is how the pyramid was made: like a set of stairs, which some call battlements and some altar steps. When they had first made this base, they then lifted the remaining stones[47] with levers made of short timbers, lifting them from the ground to the first tier of steps, and, as soon as the stone was raised upon this, it was placed on another lever, which stood on the first tier, and from there it was dragged up to the second tier and on to another lever. As many as were the tiers, so many were the levers; or it may have been that they transferred the same lever, if it were easily handleable, to each tier in turn, once they had got the stone out of it. I have offered these two different stories of how they did it, for both ways were told me. The topmost parts of the pyramid were finished first, and after that they completed the next lowest, and then, finally, the last and lowest, which was at ground level. There is Egyptian writing on the pyramid telling the amounts spent on radishes, onions, and garlic for the workmen. As far as my memory serves me, the interpreter, reading the writing, said that sixteen hundred talents of silver had been spent. If this is so, how much more must have been spent on the iron with which they worked and on the workmen's food and clothing—considering the time that I have mentioned, during which they built the works, and the rest, as I see it, during which they cut the stone and brought it and worked at the underground chambers—altogether a huge period.

126. But to such a pitch of wickedness did Cheops come that, when in need of money, he sent his own daughter to take her place in a brothel, instructing her to charge a certain sum—the amount they did not mention. The girl did what her father told her, but she

---

47. How and Wells explain that these "remaining stones" were the ones that filled in the triangular gaps created by the "steps." For "the great pyramid when finished presented a smooth surface, though in the present day the stripping off of most of its stone covering has made it once more 'like steps.'"

also got the idea of leaving some memorial of her own; and so she asked each man that came at her to make her a present of one stone in the works, and from these stones, they say, a pyramid was built midmost of the three, in front of the great pyramid. Each side of it measures one hundred and fifty feet.

127. This Cheops, they said, reigned for fifty years, and on his death the kingship was taken over by his brother Chephren. He acted like Cheops in general and also made a pyramid, though not of the measure of his brother's. I have measured them. There are in this second no underground chambers; nor is there any channel from the Nile into this one, as into the other, where the river comes through a built passage and surrounds an island in which they say Cheops is buried. This man built the first course of his pyramid of colored Ethiopian stone; it is forty feet lower than his brother's pyramid but otherwise of the same greatness, and he built it close to the big one. They stand on the same hill, which is some hundred feet high. Chephren reigned, they say, for fifty-six years.

128. So they reckon one hundred and six years during which every evil fell upon the Egyptians, and for all that time their temples were shut against them and were never opened. Out of hatred, the Egyptians do not mention by name these rulers, but call the pyramids after the shepherd Philitis, who at this time grazed his cattle in these regions.[48]

129. After he had been king of Egypt, they say, there succeeded Mycerinus, the son of Cheops. His father's acts were not pleasing in his sight; he opened up the temples and let the people, who were worn down to the extremity of misery, go freely to their own work and their sacrifices. Of all their kings, too, he judged lawsuits most justly, and, in respect to this, he is praised by the Egyptians above all that were ever kings among them. Not only were his judgments just,

48. There is, according to the authorities, a good deal of suppression and disguise in any Egyptian account of this area of history, and Herodotus encountered it, without, of course, being able to notice, because of his want of the language. Egypt was for a period, of unknown length, dominated by invaders from the north, known as Hyksos, a name which, according to Manetho (third century B.C.), means "Shepherd Kings." It is this conquest that tied the tongues of Herodotus' informants and interpreters, and the silence is elsewhere attested. The pyramid-builders, it seems, are included in the dislike with which the northern conquerors were in retrospect viewed.

but if anyone was dissatisfied with the judgment rendered, he gave money from his own store to satisfy him. Kind he was to his fellow citizens, and such was his way of life; but the beginning of his misfortunes was the death of his daughter, the only child he had in his house. He took his grief very bitterly and wished to bury this daughter in a style that exceeded all other burials. So he made a hollow cow of wood and, after gilding it, buried her in it, her, his dead daughter.

130. Now this cow was not buried in the earth; it was still visible in my time in the city of Saïs, lying in an adorned chamber in the royal palace. They burn incense of all kinds beside it every day, and every night there is a lamp burning there all night long. Near the cow, in another chamber, stand the images of the concubines of Mycerinus, as the priests in the city of Saïs told me. They stand there, huge statues made of wood, to the number of twenty, made in the likeness of naked women. But who they are I cannot say, save to repeat what I have been told.

131. There are some who tell this story about the cow and the statues: that Mycerinus was in love with his own daughter and thereafter lay with her against her will; that the girl hanged herself out of grief, and he buried her in that cow; and that her mother cut off the hands of the servant girls who had betrayed her to her father; and so now (they say) the statues of these girls have suffered the same fate as the girls did in life. This is, in my opinion, nonsense, both the rest of the story and the part about the hands of the statues. For as to these, I myself saw that they had lost their hands through the force of time, and the hands were still in my day clearly visible there, lying at the foot of the statues.

132. The rest of the cow is covered in a scarlet robe, but the neck and the head are visible, plated with exceedingly thick gold. Between the horns there is the likeness of the circle of the sun, done in gold. The cow is not upright but on her knees, and her size is about that of a big cow in life. Every year she is brought out from the chamber when the Egyptians mourn for the god that I do not name in such a matter; and it is then that they bring the cow into the light. For, they say, the girl begged her father Mycerinus, when she was dying, that once each year she should see the sun.

133. After what had happened his daughter, something else be-

fell this king. There came to him from the city of Buto an oracle to the effect that he would live only six years more and die in the seventh. The king took this very ill and sent to the oracle, in return, a reproachful message to the god. His blame on the god, in return for his oracle, was that his father and grandfather had shut up the temples and regarded the gods not at all, and, furthermore, they had murdered men; yet they had lived a long, long time. He himself had been pious, and so now he was to die so quickly! From the oracle came a second message, that it was just because of this that his life was shortened. For he had not, said the message, done what was fated. Fate was that Egypt should be afflicted for one hundred and fifty years, and those two kings who were before him had understood that; but he himself had not. When Mycerinus heard this—that he was already condemned—he lighted many lanterns, whenever it was nighttime, and, having lighted them, he took himself to drinking and enjoying himself, ceasing neither night nor day, wandering into the marshes and groves and wherever he knew there were places most suitable for pleasure. He managed all this because he wished to prove the god a liar, that he might have twelve years instead of six, since nights became days.

134. This man left a pyramid, much smaller than that of his father. It is a square, and each side is two hundred and eighty feet and, up to one half of its height, made of Ethiopian stone. Some of the Greeks say that this pyramid was built by Rhodopis, a courtesan, but that is quite wrong. They appear to me not even to know who Rhodopis was. For they never would have attributed to her the building of such a pyramid, on which, as one might say, countless thousands of talents must have been spent. Besides, Rhodopis was in her heyday during the reign of King Amasis and not during this king's reign. For Rhodopis was born many years after the kings who left the pyramids behind them, and she was of Thracian origin and was a slave of Iadmon, the son of Hephaestopolis, a man of Samos, and a fellow slave of Aesop, the story-writer. He too belonged to Iadmon, as is clearly proved by the following: that when the Delphians constantly proclaimed (as an oracle bade them) that whoever wished to should claim the atonement money for the murder of Aesop, no one appeared to claim it save Iadmon—another of the same name, a grandson of the first. So it is proved that Aesop belonged to Iadmon.

135. Rhodopis came to Egypt by the conveyance of Xanthes of Samos and, when she came there, was freed to follow her professional work, the price paid for her freedom being great and paid by a man of Mytilene, one Charaxus, the son of Scamandronymus and brother of the poet Sappho. So Rhodopis was freed and remained in Egypt. In sexuality her gifts became so great that she gained a fortune—great indeed for a Rhodopis but not reaching to the construction of such a pyramid. For even to this day it is possible for anyone who wants to, to know the value of one-tenth of her money, so that one cannot attribute very great wealth to her. For Rhodopis was eager to leave a memorial of herself in Greece by having something made that no one else had discovered and dedicated in a temple, and then to dedicate this in Delphi as her memorial. So with one-tenth of her money she had roasting-spits made, big enough for a whole ox, many of them, wrought of iron, up to the limit of the one-tenth of the money, and sent them to Delphi. These are now piled up behind the altar that the Chians set up and in front of the temple itself. Somehow, the courtesans in Naucratis are specially gifted in sexuality. For here is this woman, of whom this story is told, and she became so famous that all Greeks knew her name—Rhodopis; and there was another, after her, whose name was Archidice, who became celebrated in poetry through all Greece, though she was less on men's lips than the other woman. Charaxus, when he had freed Rhodopis, returned home to Mytilene, and in one of her poems Sappho made bitter mockery of him.

136. I have done now, in what I have to say of Rhodopis. The priests declared that after Mycerinus there became king of Egypt Asuchis, who made the eastern propylaea of the temple of Hephaestus; this propylaea is the most beautiful and far the biggest of all. All of them have figures carved on them and an infinite amount of beautiful architecture to see; but this one has more than all the rest. They say that in the time of this king, inasmuch as there was a great constraint in the circulation of money, there was laid down a law for the Egyptians that a man might take out a loan by giving as security the corpse of his father. But there was a rider attached to the law to the effect that the lender had also a lien on the whole burying-place of the man who received the loan, and that, for the man who offered this form of security, there was this penalty attached: that, if

he would not repay the money, when he died he might not be buried either in his ancestral burying-place or anywhere else, and there was also an injunction against burying any of his kinsfolk. This king, because he wished to surpass his predecessor kings, left as his memorial a pyramid he made out of bricks. On it he had words cut in stone that declared: "Do not belittle me in contrast with the pyramids made of stone; for I excel them as much as Zeus the other gods. They struck a pole clear under the lake's surface, and whatever mud adhered to this pole, this they collected and made bricks of, and so they built me."[49]

137. This, then, was his achievement. After his reign there was a blind man from the city of Anysis, whose own name was Anysis. During his reign the Ethiopians and their king, Sabacos, invaded Egypt with a great army. At this, the blind man fled away to the marshes, and the Ethiopian ruled over Egypt for fifty years, during which he did certain notable things. Whenever any Egyptian offended in any respect, he would kill none of them but passed judgment on each in terms of the greatness of the offense, bidding the criminal raise an embankment in the city to which he belonged. And so the cities were continually becoming higher. For first, in the reign of King Sesostris, they were so mounded up by those who dug the canals, and then, secondly, during the reign of this Ethiopian, they became very high indeed. And though other of the Egyptian cities were indeed tall, it seems to me that it was Bubastis most that was built up with mounds. In it there is a temple of Bubastis that is exceedingly remarkable. There are greater temples, and temples on which more money has been spent, but none that is more of a pleasure to look upon. Bubastis in Greek is Artemis.

138. This is the nature of her temple. Save for the entrance, it is an island. For two channels from the Nile approach it, not mingling with one another, but each approaches it as far as the entrance, the one running round from one direction and the other from the opposite. Each is one hundred feet wide and shaded with trees. The propylaea is sixty feet high and decorated with striking figures, nine

49. It is not possible to say what, exactly, Herodotus means the king to claim. Possibly that the difficulty of extracting the mud and its transformation into bricks implies an artificial process and technique that surpassed the construction in stone. There are several pyramids made of brick.

feet high. The shrine stands in the middle of the city, and, inasmuch as the city has been raised high by the embankments and the shrine has not been stirred from the beginning, the shrine can be seen into from all sides. There runs round it a dry-wall, carved with figures, and within it a grove is planted round the great temple, with the hugest of trees, and in that temple there is an image. The temple is a square, a furlong each side. At the entrance there is a road made of laid stone, running for about three furlongs through the marketplace toward the east, and in breadth it is four hundred feet wide. On both sides of the road are trees towering to the sky, and the road leads to the temple of Hermes. Such is this shrine.

139. This is how they say Egypt was rid of the Ethiopian: he saw a vision in his sleep and fled from it, and the vision was this. It seemed to him that a man stood over him and counseled him to gather together all the priests in Egypt and saw them all apart in the middle. Having seen this vision, he said that he thought that the gods were showing him this as a pretext for themselves, that he might sin against what was holy and so receive his punishment from gods or men. He would not do so, he said; moreover, the time was now run out wherein it was foretold that he should hold his rule of Egypt and then depart. For in Ethiopia, when he was there, the oracles that the Ethiopians consult had proclaimed that he should rule Egypt as king for fifty years. Since, then, the time was expired, and the vision of the dream troubled him as well, Sabacos of his own will departed from Egypt.

140. When the Ethiopian had left, there ruled again the blind man, who came back from the marshes, where he had lived for fifty years, having built up an island of ashes and earth. For as often as Egyptians came to him, bringing him food, as they had been bidden to do, though the Ethiopian knew nothing of it, he bade them bring him ashes also, as a gift. This island none could discover before the time of Amyrtaeus; for more than seven hundred years, those who became kings before Amyrtaeus failed to find it. The name of the island is Elbo, and it is of ten stades' length in each direction.

141. After him, then, there became king the priest of Hephaestus, whose name was Sethos. This man held in contempt the warriors among the Egyptians and mistreated them, as having no further

need of them; in addition to dishonoring them in other ways, he took their land away from them. (Each man among them had, in the time of the former kings, been assigned twelve choice fields.) Thereafter there came against Egypt a great army, and its leader was Sennacherib, king of the Arabians and the Assyrians; but the warrior Egyptians would not fight him. The priest of Hephaestus was utterly at a loss and went into his great hall to the god's image there and bewailed what was to betide him. And as he made his lament, sleep came upon him, and in his vision there seemed to him that the god stood over him and bade him be of good heart: "You will suffer nothing untoward if you confront the Arabian host; for I will send you allies." He trusted in this dream, and, taking with him such of the Egyptians as would follow him, he pitched his camp in Pelusium, for that was where the enemy were to invade. There followed him not one of the warriors, but shopkeepers and handworkers and fellows from the marketplace. But when their enemies came, there spread out against them, at nightfall, field mice, which gnawed their quivers through, and through, too, the bows themselves and the handles of their shields, so that on the next day they fled, defenseless, and many of them fell. So nowadays this king stands there, in stone, in the temple of Hephaestus, and in his hand he holds a mouse, and he speaks these words through the inscription that is there: "Look on me, all of you, and be pious."

142. Up to this went the record of the Egyptians and their priests; and they counted, from the first king to this priest of Hephaestus as the last, three hundred and forty-one generations of men, and in these generations there had been, in each, a king and a high priest. Now three hundred generations of men added up to ten thousand years, for three generations of men are one hundred years. And the forty-one of the generations that remain make up thirteen hundred and forty years. So, in eleven thousand three hundred and forty years, said the priests, there had never been a god in man-shape; nor, moreover, neither beforetime nor thereafter, among the rest of those who became kings of Egypt, had any such thing happened. During this time, they said, there were four times when the sun rose out of his wonted place—twice rising where now he sets, and twice setting where now he rises—and, say the priests, nothing became

different among the Egyptians, for all these disturbances, neither products of the earth nor products of the river, nor yet in respect of diseases or death.

143. Once upon a time Hecataeus, the historian, was in Thebes[50] and was tracing his family tree and connecting his descent to a god in the sixteenth generation. The priests of Zeus there did for him what they did for me, too—though *I* was not tracing my family tree. They brought me into a great hall and showed me the huge wooden figures there, counting them up to the number they had already given. For each high priest, in his own lifetime, sets up in that place an image of himself. The priests counted up and showed me each son succeeding his father, from the image of the most recently dead, going right through all of them, until they had traced through all. Hecataeus had traced his family tree and connected himself with this god in the sixteenth generation; but the priests countered by constructing a family tree by their method of reckoning, because they would not take it from him that a man had been born from a god. As they established their rival family tree, they declared that each one of these huge figures was a "piromis" succeeding a "piromis," until they had gone through the entire line of three hundred and forty-five figures, and they failed to connect any one of these with either a god or a hero. A "piromis" is, in Greek, a "gentleman."[51]

144. So, those whose images were there the priests have shown to be all human and quite different from gods; but, they say, before these men there were gods who were rulers of Egypt, who lived not at the same time as these men; and, of these gods, one was always supreme ruler. The last of these divine beings to rule Egypt was Horus, the son of Osiris, whom the Greeks call Apollo. He, they say, deposed Typhon and became the last god to rule Egypt. Osiris, in the Greek language, is Dionysus.

145. Among the Greeks, Heracles and Dionysus and Pan are thought to be the youngest of the gods, but among the Egyptians Pan is the oldest and is one of the first gods, those who are called the Eight. Heracles is of the second group, those called the Twelve, and Dionysus is of the third, who were born of the Twelve. I have

50. In *Egyptian* Thebes.
51. The Greek here is actually "a good and handsome man," which is stock Greek for something like our "gentleman."

already made clear the number of years the Egyptians themselves say stretch between Heracles and King Amasis.[52] Pan is said to be still earlier; and, though the number of years between Dionysus and King Amasis is the smallest, even it is reckoned as being fifteen thousand. The Egyptians claim that they know these matters absolutely because they are continually making their calculations and continually writing down the number of the years. Now the Dionysus who was said to be the son of Semele, the daughter of Cadmus, was sixteen hundred years before my time, and Heracles, the son of Alcmene, nine hundred. And Pan the son of Penelope—for according to the Greeks, Pan was born of Penelope and Hermes—was after the time of the Trojan Wars and about eight hundred years before my time.

146. Of these two,[53] then, one may use whichever account seems most trustworthy; for my own part, I have stated my opinion. For if these (Dionysus, son of Semele, and Pan, son of Penelope) had openly appeared in Greece and grown old there, like Heracles, son of Amphitryon, one would have said that these also were men like others and had taken the names of gods who had gone before. As it is, however, the Greeks claim that Dionysus at the moment of his birth was stitched into his thigh by Zeus and carried by him to Nysa in Ethiopia, above Egypt; and about Pan the Greeks cannot say what happened him after his birth. To me, then, it seems clear that the Greeks learned the names of these after they had learned those of the other gods. They have attributed their birthdate to the moment when they learned of their existence.

147. So far, it is what the Egyptians themselves say that I have declared; now there remains to record what other men and the Egyptians say in agreement as having happened in this country. There will be additional support to the narrative from what I saw myself.

When the Egyptians were freed, after the kingship of the priest of Hephaestus, they could not live a day without a king; so they set up twelve of them and divided all Egypt into twelve provinces. These kings made marriages between their families and held their rule under a sworn agreement that forbade destroying one another or any one of them seeking to have more than another, but rather all

52. In 2.43, where Herodotus gives the number of years as seventeen thousand.
53. Pan and Dionysus.

should be staunch friends. The following was the reason for this arrangement (which they enforced strongly): it was prophesied to them at the beginning, when they initiated the kingships, that the one of them who poured libations in the temple of Hephaestus from a bronze vessel should be king of all Egypt. (They were used to assemble in all the temples.)

148. Furthermore, they resolved to leave a memorial of themselves in common, and in pursuance of this resolve they made a labyrinth, a little above Lake Moeris, and situated near what is called the City of Crocodiles. I saw it myself, and it is indeed a wonder past words; for if one were to collect together all the buildings of the Greeks and their most striking works of architecture, they would all clearly be shown to have cost less labor and money than this labyrinth. Yet the temple at Ephesus and that in Samos are surely remarkable. The pyramids, too, were greater than words could tell, and each of them is the equivalent of many of the great works of the Greeks; but the labyrinth surpasses the pyramids also. It has twelve roofed courts, with doors facing one another, six to the north and six to the south and in a continuous line. One wall on the outside encompasses them all. There are double sets of chambers in it, some underground and some above, and their number is three thousand; there are fifteen hundred of each. We ourselves saw the aboveground chambers, for we went through them and so can talk of them, but the underground chambers we can speak of only from hearsay. For the officials of the Egyptians entirely refused to show us these, saying that there were, in them, the coffins of the kings who had builded the labyrinth at the beginning and also those of the holy crocodiles. So we speak from hearsay of these underground places; but what we saw aboveground was certainly greater than all human works. The passages through the rooms and the winding goings-in and out through the courts, in their extreme complication, caused us countless marvelings as we went through, from the court into the rooms, and from the rooms into the pillared corridors, and then from these corridors into other rooms again, and from the rooms into other courts afterwards. The roof of the whole is stone, as the walls are, and the walls are full of engraved figures, and each court is set round with pillars of white stone, very exactly fitted. At the corner where the labyrinth ends there is, nearby, a pyramid two hundred and forty

feet high and engraved with great animals. The road to this is made underground.

149. Such was the labyrinth; but an even greater marvel is what is called the Lake of Moeris, beside which the labyrinth was built. The circuit of this lake is a distance of about four hundred and twenty miles, which is equal to the whole seaboard of Egypt. The length of the lake is north and south, and its depth at its deepest is fifty fathoms. That it is handmade and dug, it itself is the best evidence. For in about the middle of the lake stand two pyramids that top the water, each one by fifty fathoms, and each is built as much again underwater; and on top of each there is a huge stone figure of a man sitting on a throne. So these pyramids are one hundred fathoms high, and these one hundred fathoms are the equivalent of a six-hundred-foot furlong, the fathom measuring six feet, or four cubits (the cubit being six spans).[54] The water that is in the lake is not fed with natural springs, for the country here is terribly waterless, but it enters the lake from the Nile by a channel; and for six months it flows into the lake, and then, another six, it flows again into the Nile. During the six months that it flows out, it brings into the royal treasury each day a silver talent for the fish from it; and when the water flows in, it brings twenty minas a day.

150. The natives say that the lake itself pours out its waters underground, into the Libyan Syrtis, turning westward inland by the mountains above Memphis. When I saw no spoil anywhere from the digging of this lake—for I was concerned about that—I asked those who lived nearest the lake where was the spoil that was dug out. They told me where it had been carried, and they easily convinced me, for I had heard stories of something similar happening in Nineveh, the city of the Assyrians. For Sardanapalus, the king of Nineveh, had great wealth, and it was kept in a treasure-house underground, and some thieves were set to steal it. These thieves began from their own houses and measured and dug from there to the royal palace, and at night they took out the spoil they had dug out from their excavation and brought it to the river Tigris, which flowed by, until they had achieved the distance they wanted. This I heard had happened also in regard to the digging of the Egyptian lake, save

54. The pyramids are 600 feet tall—300 feet below water, 300 feet above.

that it was done not at night but in daylight. For the Egyptians dug the spoil out and cast it into the Nile, and this would naturally take it up and cast it out. That is how this lake is said to have been dug.

151. So these twelve kings lived in all justice. And on a time they were sacrificing in the temple of Hephaestus, on the last day of the festival, and they were about to pour the libation. The high priest brought them out golden vessels, with which they were used to pour the libations, but he missed his count and brought out only eleven for the kings, who were twelve. When, then, he who stood last among them, Psammetichus, had no vessel, he took off his helmet, which was bronze, and held it out and poured the libation with it. Now all the other kings also were wont to wear helmets and, at this time, were so doing; so Psammetichus held out his without any guile involved, and the other kings, grasping what Psammetichus had done and the prophecy—where it was prophesied that he among them that should have poured the libation with a vessel of bronze should be sole king of Egypt—as they recollected that oracle, they nonetheless did not think fit to kill Psammetichus when they found, on examination, that he had done what he did without any forethought in the matter; but they resolved to chase him away into the marshes, having stripped him of most of his power, and from these marshes he was never to issue forth or have to do with the rest of Egypt.

152. This Psammetichus had earlier been an exile, fleeing from the Ethiopian, Sabacos, who had killed his father, Necos. Psammetichus had gone into exile in Syria and was brought back from there by the Egyptians of the province of Saïs when the Ethiopian fled as the result of his dream vision. Now after he had, for the second time, become king, it befell him to be banished by the eleven kings, owing to the matter of the helmet, and to flee into the marshes. Psammetichus understood that there was indeed great insolence in the way he had been treated by the eleven, and he resolved to be avenged on them, his pursuers. He sent to the oracle of Leto in the city of Buto, where the Egyptians have an oracle that is, of all, the least given to lying, and there came an oracle in answer, to the effect that there would come revenge, on his side, in the shape of men of bronze emerging from the sea. A flood of doubt enfolded Psammetichus himself that bronze men would ever come to his rescue;

but, not long after, necessity constrained some Ionians and Carians, who were sailing about as pirates, to put into Egypt and come ashore. They came ashore all clad in bronze armor. Now one of the Egyptians who had never before seen men armed in bronze came to the marshes to Psammetichus and told him that bronze men were come from the sea and were ravaging the plain. Psammetichus understood that the oracle was being fulfilled and made friends with the Ionians and Carians and promised them great things and so persuaded them to be on his side. Having persuaded them, he then, with the help of those of the Egyptians who were of his party, and with these allies, put down the kings.

153. When Psammetichus became master of all Egypt, he built the propylaea in Memphis for Hephaestus—that is, the one to the south—and opposite it he built a court for Apis, in which Apis, whenever he appears, is fed and kept. It has an inner colonnade all round it, full of carvings. Instead of pillars there are, to support the roof, huge statues, eighteen feet high. (Now Apis is called, in Greek, Epaphus.)

154. To the Ionians and the Carians, who had taken his side, Psammetichus gave, to dwell in, lands that lie opposite to one another; their name is The Camps, and the Nile runs between the two peoples. These places he gave them and awarded them everything he had promised as well. Furthermore, he turned over to them Egyptian children, to learn the Greek language. It is from these who learned the language that the present interpreters in Egypt come. The Ionians and Carians lived long in these places, which lie near the sea, a little below the city of Bubastis on what is called the Pelusian Mouth of the Nile. Afterwards these Greeks were moved away by King Amasis and resettled in Memphis, as his personal guard against the Egyptians. It was because these men were settled in Egypt, and we Greeks were able to have contact with them, that we have such exact knowledge of all that happened in Egypt, beginning from the time of King Psammetichus.[55] For these were the first people of foreign speech to be settled in Egypt. In those places from

55. Psammetichus reigned from 663 to 609 B.C. He was a contemporary of Gyges, king of Lydia, who in fact helped him become king. See the How and Wells commentary on 2.152.

which they were moved by Amasis, the capstans of their boats and the ruins of their houses were still there in my time.

155. This, then, was how Psammetichus got Egypt. I have several times mentioned the oracle in Egypt, and I will now tell you about it, for it is worth the telling. This oracle is a shrine of Leto, and it is established in a great city at what is called the Sebennytic Mouth of the Nile, on the way up from the sea. The name of the city where the oracle is is Buto, as I called it earlier. There is in this city of Buto a temple of Apollo and Artemis as well as this shrine of Leto, in which the oracle is. It is itself of great size and has a propylaea sixty feet high. Of the things that were there, plain to see, I will tell you what amazed me most. It is a temple in this sanctuary of Leto, made of a single stone, each side equal in length, sixty feet long and sixty high. One more stone forms the surface of the roof, and its eaves are six feet wide.

156. This temple is the most wonderful thing of what is there to see in the shrine; the next most wonderful thing is the island they call Chemmis. It lies in a deep, broad lake by the temple at Buto, and it is said by the Egyptians to be a floating island. I myself never saw it float or move, and I was amazed to hear that it should truly be a floating island. In it is a great temple of Apollo and three altars, and there grow in it many palm trees and other trees, some yielding fruit and some not. The Egyptians add this story to their account of it as a floating island: they say that in the island, which used not to be floating, Leto, who was one of the first Eight Gods, lived, in the city of Buto, where this oracle is. She received Apollo into her charge from Isis, and hid him for safety's sake in what is only now known as the floating island, when Typho came searching everywhere for him, wishing to discover the child of Osiris. They say that Apollo and Artemis were children of Dionysus and Isis and that Leto became their nurse and savior. In the Egyptian language, Apollo is Horus, Demeter is Isis, and Artemis is Bubastis. It is from this story and nowhere else that Aeschylus, son of Euphorion, who in this differs from the poets who preceded him, stole the thing that I tell; for he created Artemis as the daughter of Demeter. This is the reason, say the Egyptians, that the island came to float. That is how they tell it.

157. Psammetichus was king of Egypt for fifty-four years. During

twenty-nine of these he beleaguered the great Syrian city of Azotus and conducted the siege until he captured it. This city of Azotus, of all the cities I have knowledge of, endured the longest time under siege.

158. The son of Psammetichus was Necos, and he too became king of Egypt,[56] and he was the first to attempt to dig a canal into the Red Sea; Darius the Persian was the second to dig it. The length of it is a journey of four days, and the breadth of it was dug so that two triremes can sail it abreast when rowed. The water comes into it from the Nile, and it comes into it from a little above Bubastis, past the Arabian town of Patumus, and enters the Red Sea. The parts of the Egyptian plain that are nearest to Arabia were the first dug. The mountains that stretch toward Memphis are nearest this plain and south of it. In these mountains are the stone quarries. The canal comes along the foothills of these mountains in a long line from west to east; it then stretches into a ravine, and then, passing out of the mountains, it goes south to the Arabian Gulf. Now the most direct and shortest passage from the northern sea (the Mediterranean) to the southern sea, which is called the Red Sea, is from the Casian hill, which is on the border between Egypt and Syria, to the Arabian Gulf; this is a distance of exactly one hundred and twenty-five miles. This is at its most direct; but the canal is far longer, in proportion as it is crookeder. In the digging of this canal, Necos lost one hundred and twenty thousand Egyptians. In the course of his digging Necos was stopped by the opposition of an oracle—to wit, that he was doing work for the barbarian who would come after him. The Egyptians call all those who do not speak their own language barbarians.[57]

159. So Necos then stopped his canal-building and turned to warfare; some of his triremes were built on the northern sea and others in the Arabian Gulf, near the Red Sea; the capstans are still visible. These ships he used as circumstances demanded. Necos also engaged the Syrians on land and won a victory at Magdolus, and after that battle he took the great city of Cadytis[58] in Syria. The gar-

56. Necos, 609–593 B.C.
57. Here, again, Herodotus is putting this Greek expression into the mouth of another people. Cf. 1.4 and the accompanying note.
58. Gaza.

ments he wore when he performed these deeds he sent to Apollo in Branchidae in Miletus, where he dedicated them. He afterwards died, having reigned, in all, sixteen years, and his rule he passed on to his son, Psammis.

160. To this Psammis, when he was king of Egypt, there came messengers of the Eleans, who boasted that in the Olympic games they had established the justest and fairest festival of all mankind, and they thought that in comparison with the Olympics not even the Egyptians, the wisest men in the world, would be able to improve on their invention. When the Eleans came to Egypt and said what they had come for, this King Psammis summoned those of the Egyptians who were said to be the wisest. The Egyptians assembled and inquired of the Eleans, who told them all that those who competed must do in the games. Having given this account, the Eleans said that they had come to find out if the Egyptians could invent anything fairer than this. The Egyptians took counsel and then asked the Eleans if their own citizens could compete in the games. The Eleans said yes; anyone who pleased, of their own citizens or any other Greek, was allowed to compete. Then the Egyptians said that in so arranging it they had entirely missed justice. For it could not be but that the Eleans would favor their own citizen if he were to compete, and so they would wrong a foreigner. If they wanted to establish the games justly, and that is why they had come to Egypt, they bade them make the games open only to foreigners, with permission to no Elean to compete. That was the suggestion the Egyptians made to the Eleans.

161. Psammis reigned only six years over Egypt; he made an expedition against Ethiopia, died immediately after, and was succeeded by his son, Apries.[59] He, after Psammetichus, his great-grandfather, was the most fortunate king of Egypt, more than all who had gone before him. He ruled twenty-five years, in which he invaded Sidon and fought a naval battle at Tyre. But since it was fated that he should end ill, something now caused it to happen, which I will tell at greater length in the Libyan history but at moderate length for the present. Apries sent his expedition against the people of Cyrene and met great disaster there. The Egyptians cast it

59. Psammis, 593–588 B.C.; Apries, 588–569 B.C.

up against him and revolted, holding that Apries had intentionally sent them into manifest ruin so that many of them should be killed and it would be safer for him to rule what was left of them. Greatly angered at this, those who came back safe joined in open revolt with the friends of the men who were killed.

162. When Apries heard of it, he sent to them, to stay them with talk, one Amasis. This man came to the Egyptians and pressed them hard not to do as they were doing; but, even as he spoke with them, one of the Egyptians, who stood behind Amasis, put a helmet on his head and said he was doing so as a sign of sovereignty. What was done was to Amasis' liking, as he showed. For when these rebel Egyptians made him king, he made ready to attack Apries. Apries heard of it and sent to Amasis one of the distinguished Egyptians he had with him, whose name was Patarbemis. He bade him bring Amasis to him alive. Patarbemis came to Amasis and summoned him to the king. Amasis was mounted at the time; he lifted himself up off his horse's back and farted and told Patarbemis to carry that back to the king. But Patarbemis kept on urging him to return. "It was," he said, "the *king* who summoned him." But the other answered that he had long been preparing to do this, and, as far as coming to the king, Apries would not fault him for that. He would come himself—and bring others with him. As a result of what he said, Patarbemis was in no doubt about what he meant to do; and seeing him make his preparations, he made all haste himself to go away to tell the king, as soon as he could, what was afoot. When he arrived in Apries' presence without Amasis, the king in his fury, without giving him a chance for any explanation, ordered his ears and nose cut off. The rest of the Egyptians, who till then had been on Apries' side, seeing their most distinguished man so shamefully and despitefully treated, did not wait any longer but joined the others in their revolt and gave themselves to Amasis.

163. Apries, having word of this too, armed his mercenaries and made for the Egyptians. He had with him Carians and Ionians, a bodyguard, to the number of thirty thousand. His palace was in the city of Saïs, and very great and marvelous it was. So those with Apries went against the Egyptians, and those with Amasis went against the foreigners on the other side. They both came to the city of Momemphis and were ready to make trial, one of the other.

164. There are in Egypt seven classes, which are called, respectively, priests, warriors, cowherds, swineherds, shopkeepers, interpreters, and pilots. These are the classes of the Egyptians, and their names are given them from their crafts. The warriors are called Calasiries and Hermotybies and are from the following provinces (for all Egypt is divided into provinces).

165. Of the Hermotybies, the provinces are these: Busiris, Saïs, Chemmis, Papremis, the island that is called Prosopitis, and half of Natho. From these provinces are the Hermotybies, and their number at its maximum was one hundred and sixty thousand. Of these no one has ever learned any mechanical trade but has been freed solely for soldiering.

166. These other provinces are those of the Calasiries: Thebes, Bubastis, Aphthis, Tanis, Mendes, Sebennys, Athribis, Pharbaïthis, Thmuis, Onuphis, Anytis, and Myecphoris (this province is in an island opposite Bubastis). These are the provinces of the Calasiries, whose number, at its maximum, was two hundred and fifty thousand men. They too may follow no other trade save only the practice of arms, son succeeding father.

167. Whether it was from the Egyptians that the Greeks learned this I cannot exactly say, for I see that also the Thracians, Scythians, Persians, Lydians, and nearly all the barbarians think those of their fellow citizens who learn trades (and their descendants as well) inferior and regard as noble those who keep themselves clear of any form of handwork and, in especial, those who are freed to engage in the art of war. All the Greeks have learned this, and especially the Lacedaemonians. The Corinthians have the least contempt, among Greeks, for handworkers.

168. For these warriors alone among the Egyptians, except for the priests, there were privileges set apart: for each man a chosen plot of twelve acres, free of tax. Their acre is one hundred cubits each way and is the equal of the Samian acre. These plots were set aside for them all, but they cropped them in rotation and never the same men each year. Every year, one thousand Calasiries and one thousand Hermotybies constituted the king's bodyguard; over and above their estates these men were given each day a measure of roast grain, five pounds of it, besides two pounds of beef and four cupfuls

of wine. These allowances were given to each of the bodyguards as they served.

169. So they joined battle and fought, Apries with his guards and Amasis with all the Egyptians, when they came to the city of Momemphis. The foreigners fought well, but their numbers were far less, and because of that they were beaten. It had, it is said, been Apries' opinion that no one, not even a god, could cast him from his throne, so firmly did he think he was established. So now he fought and was worsted and was taken prisoner and carried to the city of Saïs, to what had formerly been his own house but was now the palace of Amasis. There, then, they kept him in the palace for a while, and Amasis treated him well. But at last the Egyptians objected that Amasis did unjustly in so keeping one who was their bitterest foe— and his own. So he turned Apries over to the Egyptians, and the Egyptians strangled him and, after, buried him in his ancestral grave. This is in the temple of Athena, nearest the sanctuary, on the left-hand side as you go in. The people of Saïs buried all their kings that come from this province within the temple. The tomb of Amasis is farther from the sanctuary than that of Apries and his ancestors, but it too is within the court of the temple. It is a great stone colonnade, adorned with columns in the form of palm trees and every kind of rich ornament. In this colonnade there are two doors, and within the doors lies the coffin.

170. Also at Saïs is the burial place of the One[60] whom I regard it as not holy to name in such a connection; it is in the shrine of Athena, behind the temple, close to the entire wall. Also in the precinct there are great stone obelisks, and, near by, a lake with an ornamental stone coping, very well wrought in a circle; its size, in my opinion, is about that of what is in Delos called the Round Pond.

171. On this lake they hold, at night, an exhibition of the god's sufferings, a performance that the Egyptians call the Mysteries. I know more about each element of these, but let me hold my peace. And again, about the rites of Demeter that the Greeks call the Thesmophoria, let me hold my peace—save insofar as it is right for me to speak. It was the daughters of Danaus who brought this rite from

60. Osiris.

Egypt and taught it to the Pelasgian women. Afterwards, when the Peloponnesus had its population driven out by the Dorians, the rite perished, and it was the only people in the Peloponnesus who were not driven out but remained—namely, the Arcadians—who preserved it.

172. When Apries had been removed, as I said, Amasis became king,[61] being of the province of Saïs and from the city the name of which is Siuph. Now at first the Egyptians made little of Amasis and held him in no esteem, because he was formerly a man of the people and of no very distinguished house. But afterwards Amasis conciliated them by his cleverness and his want of stiff-neckedness. He had countless treasures, and among them a golden footbath, in which Amasis himself and his fellow guests washed their feet on each occasion of need. Amasis cut this up and made out of it an image of a god and set it up at the most suitable part of the city. The Egyptians, as they came constantly to the image, showed it great reverence. Amasis noticed what was done by the citizens, and he summoned them together and made them clear about the matter; he said that the image had been made out of a footbath in which formerly the Egyptians used to vomit and piss and wash their feet, and now they reverenced it mightily. So now, he said to them, he himself was just like that footbath. For if he had been formerly a man of the people, he was now and in the present their king, and so he bade them honor him and respect him.

173. That was how Amasis conciliated the Egyptians to the justice of their slavery to himself, and the following is how he ordered his way of life: in the early morning, until when the market was full, he would zealously do all matters that were brought to him; but from then on he drank and joked with those who drank with him and was indeed an easygoing and sportive companion. Certain of his friends were aggrieved at this and chid him, saying, "My lord, you do not take due care for yourself in bringing yourself so low. You ought rather to sit solemnly all day on a solemn throne and conduct business, and so the Egyptians would know they were governed by a great man and you would have a fairer fame. What you are doing now is not the least royal." He answered them: "Those who have

61. Amasis, 569–525 B.C. This king was allied with Croesus, king of Lydia.

bows string them when there is need. If they were strung all the time, they would break, and so their owners would not have them to use when they needed them. A man is just like that. If he will be serious always and never let any part of him trifle, he will, without knowing it, become crazy or idiotic. I know that, and so I give each part its due." That was how he answered those friends of his.

174. It is said that Amasis, even when he was a private person, was one who loved drink and jokes and was altogether not a serious man; and whenever, in his drinking and enjoying himself, the supplies ran out, he would go around stealing. The people who said, in spite of his denials, that he *had* taken their goods would hale him to the oracle, wherever there was one among them. Many times he was convicted by the oracles, and many times he got off. Now, as soon as he became king, he took no care at all of those shrines that had acquitted him of thievery, nor would he make any contribution to their decoration, nor would he go there and sacrifice; for he saw them as nothing worth but possessed of lying oracles. But those of them that had strictly convicted him of being a thief, those he took good care of, as being truly gods and possessed of oracles that knew not lying.

175. In the city of Saïs he made a marvelous propylaea for the temple of Athena, which in height and size, and in the greatness and splendor of the stones that made it, surpassed all those that others had built. And he also dedicated great images and man-headed sphinxes of immense size and conveyed hither for the repair of the temple other stones of unnatural bigness. Some of these he brought from the stone quarries that are at Memphis and others, tremendous ones, from the city of Elephantine, which is twenty days' voyage from the city of Saïs. But the following is the thing that of all amazed me most: he brought from the city of Elephantine a chamber made of a single stone. This took three years in the bringing, and two thousand men were assigned to the conveying of it, and they were all of them pilots. On the outside, the length of this chamber measures one and twenty cubits, in breadth, fourteen, and in height, eight. These are the measurements on the outside of the chamber made of a single stone; and inside it is, in length, eighteen cubits and four-fifths of one more, in breadth it is twelve, and, in height, five. This shrine lies by the entrance of the temple. But they

say they did not bring it into the temple itself for this reason: the
builder of it let out a groan as the chamber was being drawn in, by
reason of the length of time and the vexation of the work, and
Amasis took this to heart and would not have it drawn further. But
there are some that say that the man was killed by the shrine as they
were levering it in, and that was why it was not pulled in further.

176. Amasis also dedicated, in other distinguished temples,
works of a size well worth admiring; among them there is in Memphis
a huge statue, lying on its back right in front of the temple of
Hephaestus; the image is seventy-five feet long. On the same base
and made of the same stone there are two immense statues, each of
them twenty feet high, one on each side of the great image. There is
in Saïs just such another one, lying in the same fashion as that
in Memphis. It was also Amasis who built the temple to Isis in
Memphis, and very great and most remarkable it is.

177. It is said that under King Amasis Egypt was exceptionally
prosperous, both in respect of what the river did for the country and
what the country gave to the people, and that at that time there
grew to be in Egypt twenty thousand inhabited cities. It was also
Amasis who decreed this law, that every year each Egyptian should
make a declaration to the governor of his province of his means of
livelihood. If he failed to do so or failed to declare an honest way of
life, he should be corrected by the penalty of death. Solon the Athenian, taking this law from Egypt, imposed it upon the Athenians; it
is an excellent law—long may they use it!

178. Amasis was a great lover of the Greeks, which he showed in
various ways, including the grant of Naucratis, a city to live in,
to certain of the Greeks who came to Egypt. To those of them who
did not want to settle there but who made voyages to Egypt, he
gave lands where they might set up altars and sanctuaries to their
gods. The biggest of these sanctuaries and the most famous and the
most frequented is called the Hellenium. These are the cities that
combined to found it: of the Ionians, Chios, Teos, Phocaea, and
Clazomenae; of the Dorians, Rhodes, Cnidus, Halicarnassus, and
Phaselis; of the Aeolians, only the city of Mytilene. These cities
own this sanctuary, and it is they who furnish the superintendents of
the port. Other cities that claim a share in this claim what they have
no part in. Apart from this, the Aeginetans have set up on their own

a sanctuary of Zeus, and there is another one, in honor of Hera, built by the Samians, and another, to Apollo, by the people of Miletus.

179. In the old days Naucratis was the only port; there was no other in Egypt. If anyone sailed into any other of the mouths of the Nile, he must take an oath that he had come there unintentionally and, having so disavowed, on oath, he must then sail in the same ship to the Canobic Mouth; or if, thanks to contrary winds, he was unable so to sail, he must carry the freight in barges around the Delta until he came to Naucratis. Such preeminence in honor had Naucratis.

180. When the Amphictyons contracted for the finishing of what is now the temple at Delphi (the earlier temple burned down quite accidentally) for three hundred talents, it fell to the Delphians to furnish one-fourth of the contractor's fee. The Delphians wandered among the cities begging gifts, and in the course of this appeal they got by no means the least sum from Egypt. Amasis contributed a thousand talents of alum, and the Greeks who lived in Egypt gave twenty minas of silver.

181. With the people of Cyrene[62] Amasis concluded a treaty of friendship and alliance, and he thought fit, also, to connect himself by marriage with that place, either because he desired to have a Greek woman or because of his general friendship with the Cyrenaeans. This marriage, according to some, was with the daughter of Battus, but others say that of Arcesilaus, and others still the daughter of Critobulus, a man of distinction among the citizenry. Her name was Ladice. Now when he came to go to bed with her, he could not mate her, and was always using his other women. When this happened several times, Amasis spoke to the woman called Ladice: "Woman, you have surely bewitched me. There is no way but that you must die the most horrible of deaths of all womankind." Ladice denied it, but Amasis became no whit the easier; and so she prayed in her heart to Aphrodite that if in that very night Amasis should rightly mate her, the evil would have a cure and she, the woman, would send to the goddess in Cyrene an image. After the

62. Cyrene, a city on the Libyan coast, not far from Egypt, was settled by Greeks in the seventh century B.C.

vow, Amasis straightway mated her, and, for the future, whenever Amasis came to her, he mated her, and he loved her very dearly after that. Ladice fulfilled her vow to the goddess. She had an image made and sent it to Cyrene. And there it was safe and sound in my time, still facing outward from the city of Cyrene. This was the same Ladice whom, when Cambyses conquered Egypt and learned who she was, Cambyses sent unharmed to Cyrene.

182. Amasis dedicated offerings in Greece, too: a golden image of Athena, which he sent to Cyrene, and also a painted picture of himself; and to Athena of Lindus he sent two images of stone and a marvelous linen breastplate; and to Samos he sent, to Hera, two wooden statues of himself, which still stood in my time in the great temple, behind the doors. The gifts he sent to Samos were because of the guest-friendship between himself and Polycrates, son of Aeaces;[63] what he sent to Lindus was because of no guest-friendship but because it is said that the temple of Athena there was founded by the daughters of Danaus when they landed there, fleeing from the sons of Aegyptus. Such were the dedications of Amasis; he was also the first man to capture Cyprus and force it to pay tribute.

63. Polycrates' rule in Samos began about 532 B.C.

Book Three

1. Against this Amasis, then, Cambyses, the son of Cyrus, made war, bringing with him other subjects of his and, among the Greeks, the Ionians and Aeolians. The reason for his invasion was this: Cambyses had sent to Egypt a herald to demand the daughter of Amasis in marriage. He had asked for her on the advice of an Egyptian who had a grudge against Amasis because, out of all the doctors in Egypt, he had singled out himself, tearing him from his wife and children and shipping him off to Persia. (This was when King Cyrus had sent to Amasis and asked for the most skillful eye-doctor in Egypt.) This was the grudge the Egyptian entertained and was urgent in his advice to Cambyses to ask for Amasis' daughter, so that, indeed, Amasis might have to give up his daughter and be hurt at that, or refuse to give her and make Cambyses his enemy. Amasis was burdened sorely by the power of Persia, and he was so frightened of it that he did not know how to give up the girl nor yet to refuse the Persian king's demand. In truth he knew well that Cambyses was not going to have his daughter as a wife but as a concubine. He had these calculations in his head, and this is what he did. There was a daughter of the former king, Apries, there, a girl tall and beautiful, the only one left of her house. Her name was Nitetis. This girl Amasis decked out in fine clothes and gold and sent her off to Persia as his own daughter. After a while King Cambyses, in greeting her, called her by the name she had from her father, and at that the girl answered him: "My lord," she said, "you do not grasp how you have been put upon by King Amasis. He decked me out in all this apparel, as though I were his own daughter whom he was giving to you, but in truth I am the child of King Apries. This Apries was Amasis' own master; this Apries Amasis rose against and murdered with the help of the Egyptians." This was her word, and this was the occasion, created thus, that brought Cambyses against Egypt in mighty wrath.

2. This is how the Persians tell the story. The Egyptians, however, claim Cambyses for their own. They say he was the *son* of this same daughter of Apries and that it was Cyrus, and not Cambyses, who sent to Amasis to demand his daughter in marriage. Their story is not true. For they know well—there is no one who understands Persian customs better than the Egyptians—that in the first place it is impossible for a bastard son to succeed the king of Persia when there is alive a son of lawful wedlock, and they also know that Cambyses was the son of Cassandane, the daughter of Pharnaspes, an Achaemenid, and certainly not of any Egyptian woman. The Egyptians have twisted this story because they want to lay claim to be connected with the house of Cyrus as true kinsfolk.

3. That, then, is enough for that. But there is also a story—though personally I do not believe it—that one of the Persian women, coming to visit Cyrus' wives, saw Cassandane with her children standing by her, in all their size and beauty, and was extravagant in her admiration and praise of them. Then Cassandane, who was Cyrus' wife, said to her, "Yes, I am the mother of such children as these, but King Cyrus holds me in contempt and has replaced me in honor by this new acquisition out of Egypt." She said this because of her resentment of Nitetis; and then the elder of her sons, Cambyses, said, "Mother mine, when I am a man, I will make the bottom of Egypt the top and the top the bottom." As the story goes, he said these words when he was ten years old, and the women were in amazement at him. But when he became a man and king, he remembered them and so made the expedition against Egypt.

4. There was something else that happened that favored this expedition of Cambyses. There was a man among Amasis' bodyguards whose name was Phanes, by birth of Halicarnassus. He was someone very competent in his judgments and a stout soldier. He had some grudge against Amasis and ran away from Egypt in a boat because he wanted to come to speech with Cambyses. As he was someone of considerable account among the bodyguards and with the most accurate knowledge of matters Egyptian, Amasis was exceedingly anxious to capture him and sent in pursuit of him. The man he sent was the trustiest of his eunuchs, and he sent him in a trireme. This man overtook Phanes in Lycia, and, although he took him, he failed to bring him back to Egypt; for by his subtlety Phanes beguiled him. He

made the guards thoroughly drunk and slipped away to Persia. Now Cambyses was eager to start his campaign against Egypt, but he was at a loss as to the approach—as to how to cross the desert. Phanes came and told him all about Amasis and also instructed him about the desert. His advice was that he should send to the king of the Arabians and beg him to give Cambyses a safe passage through his country.

5. The only clear entry pass into Egypt is this: from Phoenicia as far as the boundary of Cadytis is the country of what are called Palestinian Syrians; from Cadytis, a city that in my judgment is not much smaller than Sardis, to the city of Ienysus the seaports are in the possession of the Arabians, but from Ienysus as far as the Serbonian marsh, along which the Casian mountain stretches to the sea, they are again owned by the Syrians. Beyond the Serbonian marsh— where, the story goes, Typho was hidden—it is already Egypt. But between Ienysus and the Casian mountain and the Serbonian marsh, which is a fairly large piece of territory—some three days' journeying—it is all terribly waterless.

6. I am going to tell what very few of those who voyage to Egypt have noticed. From all of Greece and from Phoenicia as well, earthen jars full of wine are imported twice each year; yet there is not one empty jar at all to be seen there. What, one might ask, happens to them all? I can tell you that, too. Each chief of a district must collect from his own city and bring to Memphis every single wine jar, and the people of Memphis fill them with water and convey them into those Syrian deserts. It is thus that the jars that go to Egypt and are emptied there find their way into Syria to join all the others that before them have come there.

7. As soon as the Persians had taken possession of Egypt, it was they who thus provided for this manner of entry into the country, loading up the jars with water; but at the time we are speaking of there was no water to be had, and so Cambyses, on the information of his friend from Halicarnassus, sent messengers to the Arabian king and begged safe conduct, giving pledges to him and receiving others in return.

8. The Arabians honor pledges as much as any people in the world, and this is how they make the pledge. Someone, a man other than the two parties to the compact, stands between the two and

with a sharp stone cuts the inside of the hands, near the thumbs, of those who would make the pledge. Then, taking from the cloak of each of the two contracting persons a piece of wool, he smears with the blood seven stones that are set in between. As he does so, he calls upon Dionysus and the Heavenly Aphrodite. When he has done that, he that has executed the security formally commends to his friends the stranger (or the citizen also, if it is a citizen that is a party to the contract). And these friends claim that they will honor the pledge. They think only Dionysus and the Heavenly Aphrodite are gods, and they shave the hair of their heads as, they say, Dionysus shaved the hair of his. That is, they cut their hair in circular shape and shave the temples. They call Dionysus Orotalt; the Heavenly Aphrodite, Alilat.

9. As soon, then, as the Arabian king had given these pledges to the messengers who came from Cambyses, he made his contrivance, which was as follows: he filled camel-skins with water and laded them upon all his live camels and then drove these into the desert and there waited the oncoming of Cambyses' army. That is the story told, which seems the more credible to me; but there is another less so—yet, since it *is* told, I must recount it. There is a great river in Arabia, the name of which is Corys, and it issues into what is called the Red Sea. It is said that from this river the king of the Arabians drew a long conduit into the desert, making this of ox-hide and other animal hides, and brought the water through these skins; and in the desert he dug great tanks to receive the water and keep it. It is twelve days' journey from this river to the desert. There were three conduits, they say, and through them he brought the water to three places.

10. In what is called the Pelusian Mouth of the Nile, Psammenitus, the son of Amasis, encamped, awaiting Cambyses. As for Amasis, when Cambyses made his invasion of Egypt he found Amasis no longer living. Amasis had died; he had ruled as king for forty-four years, and during all those years nothing terrible had befallen him. He died and was embalmed and buried in the burial-place in the temple that he had himself built. In the time of Psammenitus, son of Amasis, the greatest of wonders, surely, befell Egypt: rain fell in Egyptian Thebes, though rain had never fallen there before nor afterwards until my time, as the people of Thebes themselves say.

Rain does not fall at all in upper Egypt. But this shower did fall then in Thebes.

11. The Persians crossed through the desert and encamped near the Egyptians to prepare for the combat; and then the mercenaries of the king of Egypt, those Greeks and Carians, who bore ill will against Phanes for having brought a foreign army against Egypt, contrived this deed against him. Phanes' children had been left behind in Egypt. The Greek mercenaries brought them out to the camp and, in sight of their father, set up a great mixing bowl in between the two armies, and, bringing Phanes' children, one by one, cut their throats into the mixing bowl. When they had gone through all the children, they brought wine and water to the mixing bowl and poured it in, and all of the mercenaries drank of the blood before they fought. The battle was very fierce; many fell on both sides, and at last the Egyptians were defeated.

12. I saw a great wonder here, having learned of it from the natives. The bones of those who had fallen in that battle were all scattered about, the bones of the Persians separate on the one side, those of the Egyptians on the other, just as the two armies had been separated at the beginning. The skulls of the Persians are so brittle that, if you struck them with a pebble only, you would go right through them; but those of the Egyptians are so stout that you could scarcely break them with the stroke of a stone. The reason the natives give for this—and I was persuaded by them—was that the Egyptians, from childhood on, shave their heads, and the bone grows thicker through exposure to the sun. The same reason holds for the scarcity of baldness among them. For one sees fewer bald men in Egypt than anywhere else in the world. This, then, is the reason why their skulls are so thick, and it is the same reason why the Persians, on the other hand, have such brittle skulls. For from *their* childhood they shelter their heads by wearing woollen caps. That is the way this matter of the skulls was. I saw something similar in the case of those Persians who were killed, along with Achaemenes, son of Darius, by Inarus the Libyan at Papremis.

13. When the Egyptians were routed, they fled in disorder. They shut themselves up in Memphis, and Cambyses sent upriver to them a Mytilenaean ship with a Persian aboard, a herald, by whom Cambyses invited the Egyptians to an agreement. But when the Egyp-

tians saw the ship coming to Memphis they poured out of their fortress, destroyed the ship, cut the men to pieces like very butchers,
and dragged them within their walls. After that the Egyptians were
besieged and eventually reduced. Their neighbors, the Libyans, terrified by what had happened in Egypt, surrendered without a fight,
paid tribute, and sent gifts. The Cyrenaeans and Barcaeans took
fright like the Libyans and did the same as they. Cambyses accepted
the gifts that came from the Libyans graciously, but he was dis-
pleased with those from the Cyrenaeans—I think because they were
scanty. The Cyrenaeans had sent five hundred minas of silver. Cambyses seized the coins and with his own hands scattered them among
the army.

14. On the tenth day after Cambyses had captured the fort at
Memphis, he set King Psammenitus (who had reigned just six months)
in the outer part of the city to do him deliberate injury. He set him
there with the other Egyptians and made trial of the very soul of
him. He did it thus: he put Psammenitus' daughter into slave's rags
and sent her with a pitcher to draw water; he sent with her the
daughters of noblemen, whom he had chosen out of the rest, all
dressed like the princess herself. The girls passed by their fathers,
screaming and crying; the fathers screamed and cried in answer as
they saw their children so maltreated. Psammenitus looked fixedly at
them first, took it all in, and then he bowed himself to the ground.
When the water-carriers were past, Cambyses sent Psammenitus'
son, along with about two thousand Egyptians of the same age, with
ropes tied around their necks and bits in their mouths. They were
led along to pay for those Mytilenaeans who had been murdered
when they came to Memphis with their ship. (The royal judges had
rendered judgment that for each man lost on Cambyses' side ten of
the leading Egyptians should be killed.) Psammenitus saw these go
by, noticed his own son leading the death procession, and, though
all the other Egyptians around him lamented in terrible distress, he
did just the same as he had done in the case of his daughter. When
they were all gone by, it happened that a somewhat elderly man
passed Psammenitus, son of Amasis, and those other Egyptians who
were set in the outer part of the city. He had been one of the king's
drinking companions, had lost all his estate, had indeed nothing but
what a beggar might have, and he was begging from the army. When

Psammenitus saw *him,* he burst into tears and called his old comrade by name and beat his own head. There were guards around who reported his every action, as the different persons emerged, to King Cambyses. Cambyses was surprised at what he did in this and sent a messenger to question him: "Psammenitus, your master Cambyses demands of you why, when you saw your daughter in distress and your son led to death, you raised no outcry, shed no tears, but here is a beggar, who, we understand from others, is no kin to you, and you honor him thus." That was Cambyses' question, and this the reply: "Son of Cyrus, my own griefs were too great to cry out about, but the sorrow of this friend is worth tears; he had much, and much happiness, and has lost all and become a beggar when he is upon the threshold of old age." The Egyptians say that when this answer was reported, King Cambyses and his friends found it well said, and Croesus cried (he was there too, for he had followed Cambyses to Egypt), and the Persians present cried too. A kind of pity entered Cambyses himself. He ordered them at once to save the boy from the number of those to be destroyed and to bring Psammenitus himself from the city's outskirts to where he was.

15. Those who were sent after the boy did not find him alive. He had been the first cut down. But Psammenitus himself they brought before Cambyses, and henceforth he lived in Cambyses' household, suffering no further violence. Indeed, if he could have understood that he must not be overbusy, it might have been his lot to be regent of Egypt. For the Persians are used to honor kings' sons. In the case of those who have revolted, even in these they are used to give the rule back to their children. There are many other indications that this is the customary proceeding, especially the matter of Inarus' son, Thannyras, who was given back the power his father had lost, and Pausiris, the son of Amyrtaeus, for he, too, recovered the authority his father had held. Yet no one had done more harm to the Persians than Inarus and Amyrtaeus. As things stood, however, Psammenitus *did* plot trouble, and he got his reward. He was caught trying to make the Egyptians revolt, and, when he was discovered to Cambyses, he drank bull's blood on the spot. That was how he died.

16. Cambyses went from Memphis to the city of Saïs, wishing to do what he then did. When he entered the palace of Amasis, he ordered the dead body of Amasis to be brought out from its burying

place; and when this was done, he bade his men whip it and pull the hair out and stab it and in various other ways show it outrage. After the men had grown tired of these acts—for the corpse had been embalmed and offered resistance to their efforts and did not break up— Cambyses ordered them to burn it. Now, in this his orders were contrary to religion, for the Persians think that fire is a god. Indeed, burning corpses is not a proper practice for either Persians or Egyptians, the Persians for the reason I have given (since they say that it is wrong to assign to a god the dead body of a man) and the Egyptians because, among them, fire is regarded as a living beast. They say that this beast eats everything it seizes on, and, when it is sated with its food, it dies along with that on which it feeds. It is not at all their custom to give the dead to wild creatures, and that is why they embalm the corpse: that it may not lie around and be devoured by worms. So Cambyses ordered what was against the law for either race of his subjects. As the Egyptians tell the story, it was not Amasis who suffered this indignity but some other Egyptian, of about the same age as Amasis, and in insulting whom the Persians believed they were insulting Amasis. They say that Amasis learned from a prophecy what was going to befall him when he was dead and, to cure what was to come, had this dead man buried—the one who later suffered the flogging—right at the door within his own burying place. He ordered his son to bury him, himself, as far as possible over in the corner of the burying place. These, they say, were the commands of Amasis about his dead body and the other corpse. I do not believe they ever were given but rather that the Egyptians tell them out of a vain attempt to glorify Amasis.

17. After this, Cambyses laid his plans for three expeditions. One was against the Carthaginians, one against the Ammonians, and one against the long-lived Ethiopians, who live in that part of Libya toward the southern sea.[1] In his plans he resolved to send his fleet against the Carthaginians and a part of his land army against the people of Ammon. But against the Ethiopians he would first

1. Herodotus seems here to have combined two peoples, the "real" Ethiopians, who were indeed subjects of the Persian empire and were perhaps conquered at this time (3.97), and the fabulous Ethiopians, who live at the uttermost ends of the earth and are constantly taking up the attention of Poseidon in the Odyssey when he goes to enjoy their feasts.

send spies, to see whether the famous Table of the Sun actually existed among them, and, besides this, to spy out matters in general in that country. Their pretext was to be to bring gifts to the king of the Ethiopians.

18. This is what they say the Table of the Sun is. There is a meadow in the outskirts of the city, and it is full of the boiled meat of every four-footed thing. To this meadow, those of the citizens who on each occasion are in authority bring the meat by night; by day anyone who pleases may come and eat there. But the people of the place declare that the earth of itself continuously renews the food.

19. That, then, is the story of what is called the Table of the Sun. When Cambyses had made up his mind to send spies to the Ethiopians, he immediately summoned from the city of Elephantine certain of the Fish-Eaters who know the Ethiopian language. While they were being fetched, he ordered his navy to sail against Carthage. But the Phoenicians refused his orders; they were bound by solemn oaths, they said, and it would not be right for them to serve against those who were their own children. Since the Phoenicians would not go, the rest were of no account as soldiers. So the Carthaginians escaped being enslaved by the Persians. For Cambyses refused to use force on the Phoenicians, for they had voluntarily surrendered to Persia, and the whole navy depended on the Phoenicians. The Cyprians, also, of themselves had joined the Persians and served against Egypt.

20. When the Fish-Eaters came to Cambyses from Elephantine, he sent them to the Ethiopians, with instructions as to what they should say and carrying gifts, including a purple cloak and a twisted gold necklace and armlets and an alabaster box of myrrh and a jar of wine made from the fruit of the palm tree. These Ethiopians to whom Cambyses was sending the men are said to be the tallest and most beautiful men in the world. They have customs very different from everyone else, especially in regard to their monarchy. For whichever of their citizens they judge to be tallest, and with strength proportionate to his height, him they think fit to be their king.

21. When the Fish-Eaters came to these people, they gave the gifts to the king of the Ethiopians and said: "King Cambyses of the Persians, because he wishes to be your friend and guest-friend, has sent us and bidden us come to speech with you, and he sends you

such gifts as give peculiar pleasure to himself to use." But the Ethiopian king was well aware that they had come as spies, and he said to them: "Neither has the Persian king sent me these gifts because of his great concern to make a friend of me more than other men, nor do you speak the truth, for it is as spies of my kingdom you have come. Nor is that man, your king, just. Were he just, he would not have coveted other land besides his own, nor would he have led into slavery men who have never done him any harm. Here, now, give him this bow, and do you speak to him these words: 'The king of the Ethiopians counsels the king of the Persians that when you Persians can draw so easily, as I do now, bows as big as this one, then come against the long-lived Ethiopians—and come in overwhelming force. Till then, be grateful to the gods who have not put it into the heads of the sons of the Ethiopians to win land additional to their own.'"

22. Those were his words, and he unstrung the bow and handed it to the messengers. Then he took the purple cloak and asked them what it was and how it was made. On the Fish-Eaters' telling him the truth about the purple and the dyeing process, the king said, "You are treacherous, and so are your garments." Then he asked them about the twisted gold necklace and the bracelets; the Fish-Eaters explained about the way the gold was for decoration, but the king laughed, and thought that the objects were fetters, and said that in his own country they had stronger fetters than these. Thirdly he asked about the myrrh, and when they explained about how it was made and how smeared on the body, he said the same to them about it as about the dyed clothing. But when he came to the wine and inquired about its making, he was delighted with the draught and then questioned the men as to what their king ate and how long the longest-lived Persian lived. The messengers said that the king ate bread, and they explained how the grain was grown in the ground, and they said that the fullness of a life for a man at his oldest was about eighty years. At this the Ethiopian king said that it was no wonder that they lived so few years, since they ate dung for food, and "they would not be able to live even so long if they did not recuperate themselves with that drink," by which he signified to the Fish-Eaters the wine. "That," said he, "is the one thing in which the Persians are superior to us."

23. Now it was the turn of the Fish-Eaters to ask, and they inquired of the king about the life and life habits of the Ethiopians. The Ethiopians, said the king, lived mostly for one hundred and twenty years, but some of them lived longer than that, and they ate boiled meat and drank milk. When the spies expressed surprise about the length of years, the king led them to a spring; those who washed there, went the story, became smoother of skin, as though the water were olive oil. There was a smell from it, too, as it were of violets. The water was so light, they said, that nothing could float on it, neither wood nor anything lighter than wood, but all went directly to the bottom. (It may be, if this water is really as it is described, that people who used it for everything would thereby become long-lived.) Then, they said, they left the spring, and the king led them to a dungeon full of men, where everyone was bound with golden fetters. (There is nothing rarer among the Ethiopians than bronze, and nothing more valuable.) They saw this dungeon, then, and saw also the so-called Table of the Sun.

24. After this, and last, they saw the Ethiopian coffins, which are said to be made of crystal, as follows: they shrink the dead body, whether by the Egyptian process or some other; then they smear it all over with gypsum and paint it, likening the outside as much as possible to the man as he was when alive, and then they frame it in a hollow tube made out of crystal; the crystal, which they mine, is plentiful and easily wrought. In the middle of the tube is the dead man, clearly visible; he gives off no unpleasant smell or anything improper; everything is clear and obvious, as though the dead man were just himself. For one year the nearest relatives keep this tube in their houses, giving it a share of the firstfruits and offering it sacrifices. Thereafter they take these tubes out and set them up around the city.

25. When the spies had observed all these things, they went home again. But when they brought their message, Cambyses became furious and immediately started his expedition against the Ethiopians, sending for no relays of supplies of food for the way nor reflecting, in himself, that he was about to make a campaign to the uttermost ends of the earth. Indeed, he was insane and out of his wits as soon as he had had the story from the Fish-Eaters; and so he marched off, ordering those of the Greeks who were with him to stay where they were,

but bringing with him all his land army. When, in the course of his march, he came to Thebes, he divided off about fifty thousand of his army and ordered them to enslave the Ammonians and burn the oracle of Zeus in Ammon; but he himself, with the rest of his army, marched against the Ethiopians. Before the army had got through one-fifth of their journey, all that they had in the way of provisions entirely failed them; after that they ate the baggage animals, and then this supply also failed. If, even then, Cambyses had realized and given over the fight and led his army back, he might have been a wise man, even on top of the blunder he made at the beginning; but no, he made no account of all this and marched ever forward. While his soldiers could get anything from the land, they ate grass and managed to keep alive. But when they came to the desert, some of them did something dreadful. They cast lots and chose one out of every ten men among them and ate him. When Cambyses heard of this, he was afraid—of the cannibalism—and abandoned the expedition against the Ethiopians and marched back to Thebes. By the time he got there, he had lost many of his army. From Thebes he came down to Memphis and sent the Greeks to sail away.

26. That is what happened to the expedition against the Ethiopians. Those of the army of Cambyses who were sent against the Ammonians started out from Thebes and marched along, with guides. People saw them reach the city of Oasis, possessed by those of the Samians who are said to be of the Aeschrionian tribe. These people live some seven days' march from Thebes through the desert, and this place is called in Greek the Isle of the Blessed. To it, it is said, the army came; after that, no one is able to say anything at all about them except the Ammonians and such as have their information from them. They never came to the Ammonians, and they never came back again. What the Ammonians say about them is this: when they were on their road from Oasis to the Ammonian country through the desert and were indeed about midway between the Ammonian country and the Oasis, while they were taking breakfast there blew upon them suddenly a violent southern wind, bringing with it piles of sand, which buried them; thus it was that they utterly disappeared. That is what the Ammonians tell as the story of the destruction of that army.

27. When Cambyses came to Memphis, Apis appeared among

the Egyptians—Apis, whom the Greeks call Epaphus. On his appearance, the Egyptians immediately put on their best clothes and
engaged in festival. At the sight of the Egyptians doing this, Cambyses formed the suspicion that they were making merry at his misfortunes. He sent for the men who were in charge of Memphis and,
when they came before him, asked them how it was that when he,
Cambyses, was in Memphis before, the Egyptians had done nothing
of this sort, but only now, when he was there after having lost most
of his army. The Egyptians told him that their god was wont to appear only at very long intervals of time and that, whenever he did so
appear, all the Egyptians rejoiced and kept festival. Cambyses, when
he heard that, said that they were lying, and, as liars, he punished
them with death.

28. These, then, he killed and afterwards sent for the priests. But
these told the same story. Cambyses said: "What! Some sort of tame
god has come to the Egyptians, and I not to know of it!" and so he
bade the priests bring Apis to him. They went to fetch him. This
Apis-Epaphus is born in the form of a calf from a cow that no longer
is able to conceive. The Egyptians say that a lightning bolt from
heaven has struck the cow and so from it the calf-Apis is born. The
calf called Apis has the following marks: he is all black but has a
white triangle on his forehead and, on his back, the likeness of an
eagle; on his tail the hairs are double, and there is a knot under his
tongue.

29. When the priests brought Apis to him, Cambyses was nearly
lunatic. He drew his dagger and made to stab Apis in the belly but
struck the calf in the thigh. At this he burst into laughter and said to
the priests, "You miserable wretches, is that the kind of your gods,
things of blood and flesh and susceptible of iron? Surely this god is
worthy of the Egyptians; but, all the same, you will not lightly make
a mock of me." With these words he ordered those who did that sort
of thing to whip the priests and to kill any of the other Egyptians
they found festival-making. The festival among the Egyptians was
broken up, and the priests were punished, and Apis, wounded in the
thigh, died as he lay on the floor of the shrine. After he had died of
his wound, the priests buried him in secret from Cambyses.

30. It was directly as a result of this, say the Egyptians—this
deed of wrong—that Cambyses went mad, though indeed he was

not in true possession of his wits before. The first of the evil deeds he did was to do away with his brother Smerdis (who was his full brother), whom he had sent away from Egypt to Persia out of envy. This was because he was the only one among the Persians who was able to draw, even to two fingerbreadths, the bow the Fish-Eaters had brought from the Ethiopians. No other one of the Persians could draw it at all. When this Smerdis had gone to Persia, Cambyses saw a vision in his sleep. There seemed to come to him from Persia a messenger who told him that Smerdis sat on the royal throne and reached for heaven with his head. Cambyses was afraid for himself in interpreting this dream—that his brother would kill him and rule instead. So to Persia he sent Prexaspes, who was among the Persians the man he trusted most, to kill Smerdis. Prexaspes went up to Susa and killed Smerdis—some say taking him out hunting to do so, but others say that he took him out to the Red Sea[2] and drowned him there.

31. This was the first bad thing, they say, that Cambyses did. The second was the murder of his sister, who had followed him into Egypt and with whom he lived; she was, too, a full sister of his, and he came to marry her in the following way; for before his time the Persians never did live with their sisters. Cambyses fell in love with one of his sisters and afterwards wanted to marry her, but, because what he intended to do was against usage, he summoned and questioned the royal judges, and his question was this: Is there a law that orders any man who so wishes to live with his sister? The royal judges are a picked body of men among the Persians, who hold office till death or till some injustice is detected in them. This is the only limitation on their term of office. They judge suits among the Persians and are the interpreters of the ancestral statutes, and everything is referred to them. When Cambyses put his question to them, they gave him an answer that was both just and safe. They said they could find no law that ordered brothers to live with sisters; but they *had* found another law, which said that he who was king of Persia could do anything he wished. So they did not break the law through fear of Cambyses, but, so as not to destroy themselves while protecting the law, they discovered another law, which would serve to help

2. Here probably the Persian Gulf, an arm of the Indian Ocean.

one who desired to live with his sister. At that time Cambyses married the one he was in love with; but, some little time after, he had
another sister too. It was the younger of these two who followed him
into Egypt and whom he killed.

32. About her death there are two stories, as there were about
Smerdis. The Greeks say that Cambyses set to fight one another a
lion cub and a dog and that this woman also looked on. As the
puppy was losing the fight, another puppy, its brother, broke his
chain and came to the rescue, and the two of them beat the lion
cub. Cambyses was pleased at watching the fight, but the woman sat
by and cried. Cambyses noticed it and asked her why she cried, and
she said she cried because she saw the pup helping his brother and
remembered Smerdis and realized that he, Cambyses, had no one
now left to rescue him. The Greeks say that it was because of this
that Cambyses murdered her; but the Egyptians say that as they two,
Cambyses and his sister-wife, were sitting at table, the woman took a
lettuce and stripped it of its leaves and then asked her husband
whether the lettuce was prettier stripped or with its foliage, and,
when Cambyses said, "Prettier when it was thick," she said, "But
you stripped the leaves off the house of Cyrus and made it like this
bare lettuce!" At this he was enraged and jumped on her—she was
pregnant at the time—and she miscarried as a result of the wound
and died.

33. These were the crazy acts that Cambyses perpetrated against
those of his own house, either because of that affair of Apis or from
some other cause, as indeed there are so many ills that beset mankind. For instance, it is said that from birth Cambyses had a great
sickness that some call the Sacred Sickness.[3] It would indeed not be
unnatural for one whose body suffered a great sickness to have his
wits diseased also.

34. But he did other mad things against the rest of the Persians,
too. It is said that he spoke to Prexaspes as follows. (Prexaspes he
honored especially, and he had him to carry messages for him, and
his son was Cambyses' winecup-bearer, which was a very particular
distinction.) To Prexaspes he said: "Prexaspes, what sort of man do
the Persians think I am? What stories do they tell about me?" The

3. Epilepsy.

other answered, "Master, in all other respects they praise you highly, but they say you are overaddicted to the bottle." That is what he said about the Persians; but the king was furious and answered him, "Now the Persians say I am given to winebibbing and am thereby rendered crazy and senseless! Their former words about me were a lie too." For before this, when certain Persians were sitting along with Cambyses, and Croesus was with them, Cambyses asked them how they saw him in comparison with his father, Cyrus, as a man for achievement; and the company had answered that he was a better man than his father, for he had all the possessions of his father, Cyrus, and had added, besides, Egypt and the control of the sea. That is what the Persians had said, but Croesus, who was there and did not like the answer given, spoke to Cambyses: "I do not think, son of Cyrus, that you are your father's equal. For you have no son such as he left after him in you." Cambyses was hugely delighted at hearing this and praised Croesus' judgment.

35. It was this he remembered when he spoke to Prexaspes in his fury and said: "Now, you yourself mark whether the Persians are speaking the truth or whether they themselves are out of their wits when they say such things of me. Your son shall stand there in the doorway; if I shoot and hit him in the middle of the heart, the Persians are manifestly talking nonsense. If I miss him, you may say that the Persians are right and I am not in my senses." That was what he said. He drew the bow and hit the boy, and, as the boy fell, Cambyses ordered the attendants to slit him open and see the wound. When the arrow was found in his heart, he turned to the boy's father, burst into laughter, and said with delight, "Prexaspes, so I'm not mad and the Persians are! It is all perfectly clear. Now, you tell me what man in the world do you know who could make a hit like that?" Prexaspes saw that Cambyses was out of his mind and, terrified for himself, he answered, "Master, for my part I do not believe that even the god himself could have made so splendid a hit." That was what Cambyses did on that occasion. On another he took twelve Persians who were the equals of the very noblest and on no significant charge at all buried them alive up to their heads.

36. That is what he was doing when Croesus the Lydian thought fit to correct him with these words: "My lord, do not do everything according to the dictates of your youth and your humor. Put some

hold and restraint on yourself. It is a good thing to see ahead a little, and forethought is wise. You are killing men who are your own citizens, seizing them on no significant charge at all, and you are killing children. If you do many things like that, you had better take heed lest the Persians revolt against you. You see, your father Cyrus ordered me many times to take you to task and suggest to you what I find for your advantage." This was the counsel Croesus gave, and its good will was manifest. But Cambyses answered him: "Do you have the effrontery to advise me? You governed your own country brilliantly, I suppose, and gave my father the best of counsel too! You bade him cross the Araxes River and go into the territory of the Massagetae, though they were willing to cross into ours; you lost your own country through your ill management of it; you destroyed Cyrus by persuading him to listen to you; but you will not get away with it. I have long wanted an opportunity to catch you." At this he took up his bow with intent to shoot Croesus down, but Croesus jumped up and ran outside. When the king failed to shoot him, he ordered his attendants to catch and kill him. They knew their master's disposition and kept Croesus hidden; and their calculation was that, if Cambyses repented of what he had done and came looking for Croesus, they would bring him to light and get a reward for preserving him as a live prisoner; but if he did not so repent and look for Croesus, they could kill him then themselves. Cambyses *did* miss Croesus some time later, and the attendants, who heard of it, informed him that Croesus was still alive. Cambyses said he was glad of Croesus' survival, but those who had ensured the survival should nonetheless not go scot free but be killed. And that was what he did.

37. Many such deeds of madness he did against the Persians and the allies. He stayed in Memphis and opened the ancient coffins and peered at the dead bodies. In the same spirit he came into the temple of Hephaestus and made great mockery of the image there. There is an image of Hephaestus very like the Phoenician Pataici, which the Phoenicians carry round on the prows of their ships. I will describe this, for those who have not seen it, as the likeness of a dwarf. Cambyses also went into the shrine of the Cabiri, where it is unlawful for any but the priest to enter. These images he even burned, with much mockery. These are very like the images of Hephaestus and are said to be his children.

himself. Having got it, he made an agreement, a guest-friendship pledge, with Amasis, king of Egypt. He sent gifts to him and received others from him in turn. In a very short space indeed, Polycrates' fortunes rose so high that they were cried up throughout Ionia and the rest of Greece. Wherever he decided to strike in a campaign, everything went well for him. He got himself one hundred penteconters and a thousand archers, and he harried and plundered every state without distinction. He said that he would win more gratitude by giving back to a friend what he had taken than never having seized it in the first place. He captured a great number of the islands and many of the towns on the mainland. Among his conquests were the Lesbians. They had come in full force to the rescue of the Milesians, but he beat them in a sea battle, and it was they who in chains dug the whole of the trench around the fortification in Samos.

40. Now Polycrates' great good fortune was noticed by Amasis, but it troubled him. As Polycrates' success grew greater and greater, Amasis wrote Polycrates a dispatch and sent it to Samos: "Amasis to Polycrates says: It is sweet to hear of the good hap of one who is a friend and a guest-friend, but these, your great pieces of good fortune, do not altogether please me. For I know that divinity is a jealous power. So for myself and those I care for, I would wish some success and some failure in what happens and so to live life through with these variations rather than good hap in everything. For I have never yet heard in story of anyone whose good fortune was complete who did not end up in complete ruin. Please listen to me and take these measures in the face of your successes: think what it is that you find to be of the utmost worth to you—that which, when lost, would cost you most agony of soul—and cast it away where it shall never come to the world of men again. If, after that, there is still no variation in the events that befall you, try to cure it further by the means I have indicated."

41. Polycrates thought this over, and because he saw in his mind that Amasis' advice was good, he questioned himself as to what among his treasures would twist his soul most in agony if lost. His inquiries brought this result. He had a signet ring, which he wore continually. It was bound in gold, and its stone was an emerald, the

whole the work of Theodorus, son of Telecles the Samian. He resolved to throw away this ring and did it thus: he manned a pentecounter, went aboard himself, and ordered the boat to sea. When he was far from the island, he took off the ring in full sight of the onlookers and threw it into the sea. Having done so, he sailed back again, went to his house, and gave way to his grief at what he had done.

42. Five or six days afterwards, the following thing happened. A fisherman caught a large and beautiful fish and thought fit that he should give it as a gift to Polycrates. He went to the door of the palace and said that he wished to see the prince. When this was granted him, he gave the fish, saying, "My lord, I caught this fish but did not think I should go to market with it, though indeed I am a man who works with my hands for a living; for I thought that it was worthy of you and your great station. So, here, I bring and give it you." Polycrates was delighted at what the man said and answered, "That is extremely kind of you, and I feel a double gratitude, both for the gift and for your words; so please come to dinner." The fisherman was transported by the invitation and went off home; but the servants, when they cut up the fish, found in its belly Polycrates' signet ring. As soon as they saw it and took it out, they brought it in their joy to Polycrates, gave him the ring, and told him how it had been found. It came into the prince's mind that there was in this something of God's contrivance. So he wrote down in a dispatch all that he had done and what also had happened him, and sent the letter off to Egypt.

43. When Amasis read the letter from Polycrates, he realized that it was impossible for one man to deliver his fellow man from what is by fate to happen to him, and that Polycrates, despite his entire success, would not end well, since he had also found what he had cast away. He sent a herald to Samos and said he must dissolve the guest-friendship between himself and Polycrates. He did this so that, when something great and terrible befell Polycrates, he might not feel in his soul the pain that would be due for one that was his guest-friend.

44. It was against this Polycrates, then at his moment of universal success, that the Lacedaemonians made war, being summoned to

the island by those of the Samians who afterwards colonized Cydonia in Crete. Polycrates, in secret from the people of Samos, sent a message to Cambyses, who was at that time collecting an army against Egypt, asking him to send to himself in Samos and request help for the expedition. Cambyses, as soon as he heard this, sent to Samos with the request to Polycrates for the sending of a fleet against the Egyptians. Polycrates selected the citizens whom he most suspected of planning to rise against him and put them into forty triremes and sent them off. He sent word to Cambyses not to send them home again.

45. Some say that these Samians who were sent by Polycrates never did get to Egypt—that when they, in the course of their voyage thither, were at Carpathus, they began to talk among themselves and did not like the prospect of going further. Others say that they did get to Egypt and, being put under guard, contrived to run away; that when they returned to Samos, Polycrates met them with his fleet and fought them; that the exiles had the better of it but that, when they disembarked on to the island, they were worsted in the land battle and sailed off to Lacedaemon. There is another story—that the Samians who came from Egypt beat Polycrates on their own; but this story seems to me surely incorrect. For there would have been no need to summon in the Lacedaemonians if they, the Samian exiles, were themselves able to overcome Polycrates. Besides, it is unreasonable to suppose that the prince, who had hired mercenaries, along with archers of his own race in great numbers, would have been defeated by the exiles, who were few in number. As for his subjects at home, Polycrates conveyed their women and children into the dockyards, which he had ready, and shut them up there so that, if their menfolk should betray him to the returned exiles, he could burn them up, dockyards and all.

46. When the Samians who had been banished by Polycrates came to Sparta, they went to the authorities and made a long speech, in view of the greatness of their need. At the first meeting, the Spartans said in answer that they had forgotten the first words of the request and could not understand the last. After that, the Samians had another meeting with the Spartan government, and this time they said nothing but, carrying a sack, said simply, "The sack needs

grain." At this the Spartans answered, "You did not need to say 'sack.'"[6] But they resolved to help the exiled Samians.

47. After this, having made their preparations, the Lacedaemonians made their expedition against Samos. As the Samians tell the story, this was to repay the kindness done to the Lacedaemonians by the Samians when they helped them against Messenia. However, the Lacedaemonians say that this was not the reason for their assisting the Samians in their need; rather, they themselves wanted to take revenge for the theft of the bowl that the Samians stole from them when they were taking it up to Croesus, and also the theft of the breastplate that Amasis, king of Egypt, had sent to them, the Spartans, as a gift. The Samians[7] had stolen the breastplate the year before they took the bowl. The breastplate was of linen and with many figures woven into it, and decorated with gold and cotton embroidery. The greatest wonder of it is that each single fine thread of the fabric has in itself three hundred and sixty strands, and they all can be seen to be there. One exactly like it was dedicated by Amasis, in Lindus, to Athena.

48. The Corinthians, as well, took a hand, zealously, in bringing about the expedition against Samos. For they too had had an insult done to them by the Samians in the generation before this expedition, and about the time of the theft of the mixing bowl. There were three hundred of the sons of the chief men of Corcyra whom Periander, the son of Cypselus, was sending up to Sardis to King Alyattes for castration as eunuchs. The Corinthians who were bringing the boys thither put in at Samos. The Samians, learning of the occa-

6. This is, of course, a reference to the famous Spartan taciturnity and dislike of unnecessary eloquence. In this case, what is probably meant is that, if they brought the sack with them, it was not necessary to use the word "sack" in the sentence. One could just point at it and say, "Needs grain." The typical Spartan ephor, Sthenelaidas, as reported by Thucydides, in the conference at Sparta before the beginning of the Peloponnesian War opens his speech by saying, "I do not understand all this talking."

7. This passage is rather confusing. One must understand that the "Samians" whom the Spartans now helped were the exiles, who had appealed to them. The "Samians" on whom the Spartans wanted to take vengeance were the sailors or soldiers of the Samian government who, before this, had stolen the mixing bowl and the breastplate. The story of the mixing bowl and the doubtfulness of the thieves' identity is told by Herodotus in 1.70.

sion of the boys' being carried to Sardis, told the boys to lay hold, for sanctuary, on the temple of Artemis. This was the Samians' first move. Afterwards, they refused to allow the suppliants to be haled from the temple, and, when the Corinthians cut off the boys' access to food, the Samians made a festival (which they celebrate to the present day in the same way). At nightfall, all during the time the suppliants were in their suppliant position, the Samians held dances of young men and girls, and they made it the custom at these dances for those who danced to carry cakes of sesame and honey, so that the Corcyraeans might grab at the cakes and have something to eat. This continued until the guards of the Corinthians gave up and went away. Then the Samians took the boys back to Corcyra.

49. Now if, when Periander died, the Corinthians and the Corcyraeans had been on friendly terms, the Corinthians would never have taken a hand in this expedition against Samos on such grounds as these. As it was, however, from the moment of the colonization of Corcyra by Corinth, the two states had been at enmity with one another despite their kinship. And this is why the Corinthians bore a grudge against the people of Samos.

50. Periander himself had sent up these boys, the sons of the nobles of Corcyra, for castration—he had picked them out carefully—because he wanted vengeance. For the Corcyraeans had been the aggressors in doing something terrible to him. Periander had killed his own wife, Melissa, and, in addition to this calamity, there overtook him another as well. There were two sons of Melissa, one of seventeen years and one of eighteen. Their grandfather on the mother's side, Procles, who was prince of Epidaurus, sent for them and made much of them, as was natural enough, they being his daughter's sons. But when he sent them home again, his parting words were, "Do you know, children, who it was that killed your mother?" The elder of the two boys paid no heed to these words, but the younger, whose name was Lycophron, was in such agony at what he heard that when he came to Corinth he refused to greet his father, refused to talk when his father spoke to him—as being indeed his mother's murderer—and would not answer any of his questions. At last Periander was so furious with him that he drove him out of the house.

51. Having driven him out, he asked the elder of his sons what it

was that his grandfather had said to him. The boy answered that his grandfather had received them very kindly; but he never remembered the words that he had said at parting, because indeed he had taken no heed of them. Periander said that Procles must certainly have made some suggestion to them, and so he persisted in questioning the boy, who eventually recollected the matter and told this too. Periander, understanding it and resolving to show no soft spot, sent to the people with whom his banished son had found a living and told them by messenger not to receive him into their house. So he was driven out of this and went to another house, and was driven out of that too; for Periander sent threats to them all and ordered them to bar the doors against him. The boy was always driven out and came to yet another among his friends, and these, although they feared greatly, received him in, since he was, after all, a son of Periander.

52. Then Periander made a proclamation that anyone who received the boy into his house or even spoke to him must pay a fine devoted to Apollo, and he mentioned a certain sum. In the light of this proclamation no one would converse with him or take him into his house. Indeed, the boy did not think fit himself to try to defy the edict, but in the obstinacy of his heart roamed about in the stoas. Three days later Periander saw him, all unwashed and hungry as he had come to be, and took pity on him. His anger lessened, and he approached his son and said, "Son, which of these two conditions seems the better to you—your present state or the sovereignty and the good things I now enjoy, which you may take over from me if you will be subject to your father? You are my son and a prince of rich Corinth but have chosen the life of a beggar, in opposition to your father and with rage against one whom it least befitted you to treat so. If there was a calamity in all of these matters that leads you to suspect me, it is to me it happened, and I have the greater share in it, inasmuch as it was I who did the act. You have learned how much better it is to be envied than pitied and what it is to have indulged your anger against your father and your prince—so come home again." That is how Periander spoke to him. But the boy never answered his father a word but said only that he, Periander, owed a fine to the god for having spoken to him. Periander then, seeing how incurable and past help was the settled trouble of his son, fitted up a boat and sent him out of his sight to Corcyra—for he was also lord of

that island—and, after sending him there, Periander made war upon his father-in-law Procles, as being the chiefest cause of all his present difficulties. He captured Epidaurus and Procles himself and made him his prisoner.

53. As time went on, Periander aged and was aware in himself that he was no longer able to oversee and administer his affairs, and so he sent to Corcyra and summoned Lycophron home to take over his monarchy; he saw no prospects in the elder of the two boys, whom indeed he judged somewhat dull of mind. But Lycophron did not even think the bearer of the message worthy of an answer. Still, Periander was so set on having the young man that he sent again to him and, this time, sent the boy's sister, his own daughter, thinking he would most listen to her. She came to Corcyra and said, "Brother, do you want the sovereignty to fall into others' hands, and the house of our father to be torn apart rather than leave here and possess it yourself? Go off home; stop punishing yourself. Pride is a very poor sort of possession. Do not cure ill with ill. Many men set clemency above strict justice, and many, before this, have sought their mother's interest and so have lost their father's possessions. A throne is a treacherous thing; there are many who lust after it, and the old man is indeed old, his full strength gone from him. Do not give over the good things that are your own to other men." She had been taught a most attractive lesson for recitation by her father, and she told it all to her brother. But the boy merely answered that he would never come to Corinth so long as he heard his father was still alive. When the girl brought this message back, Periander sent a herald for the third time. He was willing, he said, to go to Corcyra himself and have the boy come to Corinth as his own successor in the monarchy. The boy consented to make the change on these terms, and so Periander made ready to set off for Corcyra and the boy for Corinth. But when the Corcyraeans learned of the whole matter, they did not want Periander to come to their country, and so they killed the young man. It was in requital for this that Periander punished the Corcyraeans.

54. The Lacedaemonians came with a great host and besieged Samos. They attacked the wall and climbed on to the tower that stood seaward, in the outer part of the city; but afterwards, when Polycrates himself with large forces came against them, they were driven out. At the upper tower, which stands on the ridge of

the mountain, the foreign mercenaries and many of the Samians themselves sallied out and, having withstood the Lacedaemonians for a short time, fled, and the Lacedaemonians pursued them and killed them.

55. If all of the Lacedaemonians who were present that day had been the equals of Archias and Lycopes, Samos would have been captured. For Archias and Lycopes had been the only Lacedaemonians who had joined the Samians as they fled into the fortress and, being shut off from their escape road, died there in the city of the Samians. I myself met with another Archias, son of Samius and grandson of the original Archias, who was killed in Samos. I met him in Pitane, for he belonged to that deme. He especially honored the Samians among all his foreign guest-friends and said that his father had been given the name of Samius because his grandfather, called Archias, had died in Samos, having fought like a hero there. He, Archias, honored the Samians so, he said, because they had honored his grandfather, the original Archias, with a public funeral.

56. The Lacedaemonians, having besieged the Samians for forty days and having advanced their cause not a jot, went away to the Peloponnesus. There is a silly story that Polycrates coined a lot of currency in lead and gilded it and gave it to them and that they took it and, on those terms, went away. This was the first expedition made into Asia by Lacedaemonian Dorians.

57. Those of the Samians who had made the expedition against Polycrates sailed off to Siphnos as soon as it was clear that the Lacedaemonians were going to abandon them. They were in need of money, and at this time the Siphnians were at the height of their prosperity and the richest of all the islanders. They had on the island gold and silver mines such that even from one-tenth of their revenues a treasury was created at Delphi that was the match of the very richest there. Each year, too, they made a distribution to the citizens from the revenue of the mines. When they were building the treasury, they inquired of the oracle whether the good things that were theirs would last for long. To this the Pythia gave the following answer:

When the town hall shall be white in Siphnos, and white-
   browed the market,

Then and truly you need a wise man to give you counsel,
What to avoid and whom—the ambush of wood, the red
  herald.

At this time the marketplace and the town hall in Siphnos were
decorated with Parian marble.

58. The Siphnians could make nothing of this oracle either then
or later, when the Samians came. For immediately the Samians
touched at Siphnos, they sent one of their ships, carrying ambassadors, into the city. In those old days all ships were painted vermilion; this was the meaning of the warning of the Pythia to the
Siphnians, telling them to avoid the wooden ambush and a red herald. The messengers, when they came, asked the Siphnians to lend
them ten talents. The Siphnians refused; whereupon the Samians
began ravaging their country. Being informed of this, the Siphnians
came out in force and encountered the invaders but were defeated.
Many of them were cut off from their town by the Samians, and the
Samians then exacted from them one hundred talents.

59. From the men of Hermione the Samians took, instead of
money, the island of Hydrea, which lies off the Peloponnesus; this
they gave to the Troezenians to guard for them. They themselves
settled in Cydonia in Crete, though their intent in sailing there had
not been this but to drive out the Zacynthians who were in the island. They stayed there for five years and grew so prosperous that all
those temples that are now in Cydonia were built by these Samians.
In the sixth year, however, the Aeginetans beat them in a sea fight,
with the help of the Cretans, and made them slaves; the wild boars,
which the Samians had as figureheads on their ships, they cut off and
dedicated in the temple of Athena in Aegina. This the Aeginetans
did because of a grudge they bore against the Samians. For formerly,
when Amphicrates was king in Samos, the Samians had attacked
Aegina and did much harm to the Aeginetans; they also suffered
much at the Aeginetans' hands. This was the cause of their enmity.

60. I have talked at such length about the Samians because, of
all the Greeks, they have made the three greatest works of construction. One is a double-mouthed channel driven underground through
a hill nine hundred feet high. The length of the channel is seven
furlongs, and it is eight feet high and eight feet wide. Through the

whole of its length there is dug another channel, thirty feet deep and three broad, through which water is piped and brought into the city from a great spring. The architect of this channel was a Megarian, one Eupalinus, the son of Naustrophus. This is one of the three great constructions. The second is a mole in the sea around the harbor, one hundred and twenty feet deep. The length of the mole is a quarter of a mile. The third work of the Samians is the greatest temple that I have ever seen. Its first builder was Rhoecus, the son of Philes, himself a Samian. These are the reasons I have spoken so much of the Samians.

61. So Cambyses,[8] the son of Cyrus, dallied in Egypt, crazed in his wits. There rose against him in conspiracy two Magi, brothers, one of whom Cambyses had left as the steward of his house. This man, as soon as he had learned that the death of Smerdis[9] had been kept secret—and how, indeed, there were few of the Persians who knew anything of it and that the most of them believed that he was still alive—laid his plots to win the throne. I have said he had a brother, who helped in the conspiracy. This man was exceedingly like Smerdis, the son of Cyrus, in his appearance, the very brother whom Cambyses had killed. Moreover, he had the same name, Smerdis. The Magian Patizeithes persuaded this man that he, Patizeithes, would manage the whole thing for him, and he took his brother in and put him upon the royal throne. When he had done

8. We go back to the direct narrative, interrupted at 3.38, where we left the fortunes of Cambyses and followed the stories of Polycrates, Amasis, and the Cypselids of Corinth—the dynasty of Periander and his sons. In the digression, the focus of interest shifts to Samos, Corinth, and Corcyra. The feuds and special interests of these very important Greek centers and their relations with Egypt are part of the web of events, for Cambyses subdued Egypt preparatory to the eventual Persian attack on Greece. As we learned in 3.17, after his conquest of Egypt, Cambyses had planned expeditions against the long-lived Ethiopians, the Ammonians, and the Carthaginians, but all these were canceled or were abandoned after a great measure of failure. When we now revert to the story of Cambyses, we are faced with the last phase of the first family of Persian despots (that of Cyrus and Cambyses) as they were destroyed by internal trouble. We then get to the transfer of the monarchy, by a measure of choice on the part of the Persian nobility, to Darius and his descendants, who directed the actual invasion of Greece and retained the throne for many hundreds of years—the Achaemenids.

9. Murdered by order of Cambyses (3.30).

that, he sent heralds around to various places, and especially one to Egypt, to declare to the army there that for the future they must obey the orders of Smerdis, the son of Cyrus, instead of Cambyses.

62. The other heralds did their work, and so did he that was sent to Egypt. He had found Cambyses and his army in Ecbatana—but the Ecbatana that is in Syria—and he stood there in public and made the proclamation with which the Magian had instructed him. Cambyses heard the herald's proclamation and was convinced that the man spoke truth and that he had been betrayed by Prexaspes; for he was sure that, although he had been sent to kill Smerdis, he had not done so. Fixing his eyes on Prexaspes, he said, "Prexaspes, is this how you dealt with the matter I entrusted to you?" Prexaspes answered: "Master, all this is not true: your brother Smerdis has not risen in rebellion against you, nor shall there be any quarrel from him that can affect you, either great or small. For I myself, when I had done all that you bade me, buried him with my own hands. If the dead rise again, you may look for Astyages the Mede, too, to rise against you in rebellion. But if all is in the world as before, nothing new to hurt you shall grow out of Smerdis. As it is, I would have you send for the herald and examine him, asking from whom he came when he proclaimed that we should obey King Smerdis."

63. These were Prexaspes' words, and, as he pleased Cambyses, the herald was sent for at once and came. Prexaspes asked him, "You, fellow, you say you come from Smerdis, the son of Cyrus, as a messenger. Now tell the truth and get out of here—you will be lucky to do so: was it Smerdis, in visible form before you, that gave you these instructions, or did you hear it from one of his servants?" He said: "For my own part, I have not seen Smerdis, the son of Cyrus, from the day King Cambyses marched into Egypt. It is the Magian whom Cambyses installed as steward of his household who gave me my instructions. It was he who told me that Smerdis, son of Cyrus, charged me to tell you what I have told." This was the answer of the man; he had no intent to lie about it. Cambyses said: "Prexaspes, you have done what a good man should and performed my bidding, and you are clear of all blame. But which of the Persians can it be that trades upon the name of Smerdis and rebels against me?" The other answered: "I believe I understand what has happened, my lord. It is the Magians who have risen against you—the one whom

you left behind as steward of your house, Patizeithes, and his brother, Smerdis."

64. When Cambyses heard the name of Smerdis, the truth of both word and dream struck home. In his dream it had seemed to him that someone brought him the news that Smerdis, sitting on the royal throne, reached to touch the sky with his head. He learned now that he had killed his brother all for nothing, and he wept for Smerdis. When his tears were over and the agony of the whole event laid hold of him, he jumped on to his horse. He had in mind to get to Susa as quickly as he might and make war upon the Magian. But as he leaped on the horse's back, the cap fell off the scabbard of his sword, and the naked blade pierced his thigh. He was wounded at just that point of his body at which he had struck the Egyptian god Apis. Cambyses felt that the wound was mortal and asked what was the name of this city. They told him "Ecbatana." Now, there had been given him an oracle from the city of Buto that he would end his life in Ecbatana. He, of course, thought that he would die an old man in the Median Ecbatana, where all his concerns were; but the oracle had meant, as it now showed, the Ecbatana in Syria. As he asked the question and heard the name, he was overwhelmed at once by what the Magian had done to him and also by his wound, and he came to his senses. He understood the prophecy and said, "Here is where Cambyses, son of Cyrus, is fated to die."

65. For this occasion, that was all; but some twenty days later he sent for the most notable of the Persians who were with him and spoke to them as follows: "You men of Persia, I am forced to tell you openly what of all matters I would have hidden from you. When I was in Egypt, I saw in my sleep a vision—I would I had never seen it. It seemed to me that a messenger came from home and told me that Smerdis sat upon the royal throne and reached for the heavens with his head. I was afraid that my brother would take the power from me, and I acted with more speed than wisdom. For it is surely not in the nature of man to be able to turn aside that which is fated to be. Vain fool that I was, I sent Prexaspes to Susa to kill Smerdis, and when that great evil deed was completed, I lived free of fear, giving no further thought that, with Smerdis removed, some other man might rise against me. So I missed utterly the meaning of what was to be. I have become a brother's murderer for no need, and I am

cast out from my kingdom nonetheless. Smerdis, you see, was the Magian whom the god wished to reveal to me in a dream as the rebel against me. But the deed *was* done by me; you must count Smerdis, son of Cyrus, as no longer among the living. It is the Magians, you will find, who are masters of the royal power, the one whom I left as steward of my house and his brother, Smerdis. I have been shamefully wronged by the Magians, and the one who, most of all, should have avenged me is dead, killed by his closest kinsman. He is no more; therefore, as the second choice possible for me, I lay upon you, men of Persia, my most urgent command for what I want to be done, as I now am dying. I lay this charge upon you, calling to witness the gods of my royal line and appealing to all of you, and particularly those of you here present who are Achaemenids, that you do not suffer the supremacy again to pass to the Medes. If they have won it by craft, you must take it away from them by craft; if they have made it theirs by some kind of violence, then with violence must you take it back again. If you do this, may the earth bear you its fruits, may your women and your flocks and herds be fruitful, and may you live for all time as free men! But if you do not recover the power to yourselves, nor make any effort to do so, I pray upon you the contrary of these good things and that, besides, the end of every man in Persia may be such as has now overtaken me." These were Cambyses' words, and he wept for all that had happened him.

66. When the Persians saw their king in tears, they rent their garments and lamented bitterly. Afterwards the bone gangrened and the thigh rotted, and this carried off Cambyses, son of Cyrus, who had reigned, in all, seven years and five months and was entirely childless, having neither female nor male issue. The Persians who were present were filled with disbelief that it was the Magians who had seized the power. They thought that Cambyses had said this about Smerdis' death out of malice, that all the stock of the Persians might be at war with him. They believed that Smerdis, son of Cyrus, had indeed been installed as king. For Prexaspes vehemently denied that he had ever killed Smerdis; it would not have been safe for him, now that Cambyses was dead, to say that he had killed a son of Cyrus with his own hand.

67. The Magian, then, on Cambyses' death, ruled with nothing further to fear, trading on the identity of his name and that of Cyrus'

son Smerdis, for the seven months that were left to fill out the eight
years of Cambyses' reign. During this time he did all his subjects
great kindnesses, so that, on his death, all those in Asia except the
Persians themselves missed him sorely. For this Magian sent to every
nation that he ruled and made a proclamation freeing them from
military service and taxation for three years.

68. This proclamation he made at the very beginning of his
reign, but in its eighth month he was discovered, and this is how it
happened. There was one Otanes, the son of Pharnaspes, the equal
of the very greatest of the Persians in birth and wealth. This Otanes
was the first to suspect the Magian to be the person he actually was
and not the son of Cyrus. He suspected it because the Magian never
came out of the citadel and never summoned to his presence any of
the Persian notables. With such suspicions, Otanes did as follows.
Cambyses had married Otanes' daughter—her name was Phaedyme.
The Magian now had this girl and lived with her, as he did with all
the other women who had been Cambyses' wives. Otanes sent to his
daughter and inquired of her who it was with whom she slept: was it
Smerdis, the son of Cyrus, or someone else? She answered and said
she did not know, since she had never seen Smerdis, the son of
Cyrus, nor did she know with whom she slept. Otanes sent to her a
second time, saying, "If you yourself do not know Smerdis, the son
of Cyrus, find out from Atossa with whom she and you are sleeping.
Certainly she knows her own brother."

69. His daughter sent him a message in answer: "I cannot get to
speak with Atossa or see any of the women who live in her household. As soon as this man, whoever he is, took over the kingdom,
he scattered us all, some here and some there." When Otanes heard
this, the matter became clearer and clearer. He sent a third time to
the girl, saying, "Daughter, you are of noble birth, and it is your duty
to venture on any risk your father orders you to undergo. If this is
not Smerdis, son of Cyrus, but the man I suspect he is, he should not
get off scot free with sleeping with you and ruling Persia; he must pay
for both crimes. Do this now: when he is sleeping with you and you
know he is deeply asleep, feel for his ears. If you find that he has
ears, you may be sure that you are sleeping with Smerdis, the son of
Cyrus. If not, you are with Smerdis the Magian." Phaedyme sent
him an answer that she would be in sore danger; for if it turned out

that he had no ears and she were discovered feeling for them, she was very sure he would kill her; all the same, she would do as her father bade her. So she undertook the task set her by him. (Cyrus, the son of Cambyses, had cut off the ears of the Magian Smerdis when he detected him in some grave offense.) The girl discharged the task she promised her father to do, for, when her turn came for going in to the Magian—among the Persians the wives go to their husbands in regular rotation—she came to him and slept with him, and, when the Magian was fast asleep, she felt for his ears. She found out without difficulty—indeed, very easily—that the man did not have any. And so at daybreak she reported to her father all that had happened.

70. Otanes took to himself Aspathines and Gobryas, who were chief among the Persians and his closest and most trusty friends, and he told them the whole business. They had themselves suspected that things were as they were, and so they readily accepted what Otanes said to them. They resolved that each of them would take as a comrade whichever among the Persians he trusted most. Otanes brought in Intaphrenes; Gobryas, Megabyzus; and Aspathines, Hydarnes. These, then, were six, when there came to Susa, from Persia, Darius, the son of Hystaspes. His father was vice-gerent of Persia. When he arrived, the six Persians resolved to coopt Darius to their number.

71. So the Seven came together and discussed matters and exchanged oaths of trust. When it came to Darius' turn to declare his judgment, he said, "I believed that I was the only one to know that it was the Magian who had become our king and that Smerdis, son of Cyrus, was dead. It was for that reason that I came here in haste to arrange death for the Magian. Since, however, it turns out that it is not only myself but you, too, who know this, it is my belief that we should act at once and not delay. It would be better not to delay." Otanes answered, "Son of Hystaspes, you are the son of a good man, and you look to me as though you are proving yourself to be no less good than your father. Still, do not be foolish about this plan, in hastening it unduly; follow your plan, but do so at a more prudent pace. It would be better to make the attempt when there are more of us in the plot." Darius said, "You men who are here: if you follow the way described by Otanes, you will find that you will die, and die

most horribly. For someone will give information to the Magian; this someone's aim will be personal gain. You would have done best to have run the risk on your own. Since you decided to enlarge the conspiracy and take me in, we must either act today or, I would have you know, if a single day goes by beyond this, no informer will outstrip me myself: I will go and tell the whole matter to the Magian."

72. When Otanes saw how angry Darius was, he said, "Since you compel us to hasten and will not let us postpone the attempt, come, tell us how we are to get into the palace and attack these men. You know yourself how the guards are set all around; if you have not seen them, you at least have heard of them. How shall we get past these guards?" Darius answered, "Otanes, there are many things which cannot be described in word and yet they may be done; again, there are many that are capable of being planned in word, and yet no great action has ever resulted. You know that it is no great matter to pass these guards that are set. None of the sentries will deny admittance to such as we are, partly out of respect for us and partly out of fear. Moreover, I have the finest excuse for passing in; I can say that I have just come from Persia and wish to convey a message from my father to the king. Where a lie must be told, let it be told. Those of us who lie and those of us who tell the truth are bent upon the same object. The liars lie when they would win profit by convincing others of their lies; the truth-tellers tell truth so that by their truth they may draw gain to themselves and be the more trusted. Our practices are different, but our aim is the same. If it were not for the hope of gain therefrom, the man who tells the truth might equally well lie, and the liar tell the truth. Whichever of these guards lets us in willingly, it will be better for him in the time to come. Whoever tries to stand against us, let him be declared there and then as our enemy, and let us at once push him aside and go in to deal with our work."

73. Gobryas said, "My friends, when will we have a fairer opportunity of winning back our power or, if we cannot do that, of dying? Seeing, that is, that we Persians are being ruled by a Mede, a Magian—and an earless fellow, at that. Those of you who were present at the death of Cambyses will surely remember the curses he laid upon the Persians at this, his life's end, if they did not attempt to recover the rule. We did not believe him at the time, for we thought that he spoke to spread hatred among us. But now I give my vote on

the side of Darius: no breaking-up this council without an immediate attack upon the Magian!" That is what Gobryas said, and the other five agreed with him.

74. While the conspirators were debating, the following chanced to happen. The Magians, in their planning, had resolved to woo Prexaspes to their side because of the vile thing Cambyses had done to him when he shot and killed his son with an arrow. They also wanted him because he alone knew of the death of Smerdis, son of Cyrus (since he had killed him with his own hand), and, besides all this, Prexaspes was a man in the greatest esteem among the Persians. So for these reasons they summoned him to join their party, with pledges and oaths that assuredly he would keep the secret to himself and unveil to no human being the deception they had put upon the Persians; and they promised to give him every treasure in the world. Prexaspes agreed to do all this; and, having so convinced him, the Magians made him a second proposition. They said that they were calling together all the Persians to the palace wall, and they ordered Prexaspes to go up on to a tower and make a speech to the effect that the kingship was in the hands of Smerdis, son of Cyrus, and no one else. They laid this charge upon him because he was certainly the man most likely to be believed by the Persians and because he had already many times declared his judgment that Smerdis, son of Cyrus, was alive; he had also disowned his own act in murdering him.

75. When Prexaspes said he was ready to do this also, the Magians summoned the Persians and put Prexaspes on the tower and bade him speak. But he chose to forget every word of what they requested of him, and, beginning from Achaemenes downward, he traced the family of Cyrus; and when at last he came to Cyrus himself, he described what benefits he had done the Persians, and, as he went through it all, he told the clear truth, saying that formerly he had concealed it, for it had not been safe to say what had actually happened, but that now he must tell it all. So, as he went on, he said how he himself had been compelled by Cambyses to murder Cyrus's son, Smerdis, and that it was the Magians who had the kingship. He called down many curses on the Persians if they should not win back the power and punish the Magians. Then he threw himself headlong down from the tower. Such was Prexaspes, a notable man all his life and in his death also.

76. The Seven, having resolved to attack the Magians at once

and not delay, said their prayers to the gods and, so far knowing nothing of what had happened about Prexaspes, were halfway on the road to their object before they *did* learn what had befallen in that matter. Then they went aside from the road and discussed with one another again. Those of Otanes' party were strongly for postponement; they were against an attack while the "boil was still swelling." But Darius' men were for going at once and putting their intentions into action without delay. While they were hotly disputing, there suddenly appeared seven pairs of hawks, pursuing and tearing and savaging two pairs of vultures. As the Seven watched, all of them agreed with the opinion of Darius and went on toward the palace, heartened by the birds.

77. When they approached the gates, everything happened as Darius had thought it would. The guards were full of respect for these, the chief men of the Persians, and never suspected that any such matter would come from them as was actually planned, and so they let them through. God was somehow on their side; no one even asked them a question. When they came into the inner court, they encountered the eunuchs who carry messages to the king. These men asked them what they had come there for, and, as they put the questions, they threatened the sentries for letting them through, and, when the Seven wished to go further, they stopped them. The Seven cried aloud to one another, drew their daggers, and stabbed those who would have held them up, right where they were, and themselves headed for the men's quarters at a run.

78. It happened that at this time the Magians, both of them, were inside and were consulting about what would come of the affair of Prexaspes. When they saw the eunuchs in confusion and yelling loudly, they both sprang to their feet; and when they saw what was afoot, they made to defend themselves. The one of them was quick to get his bow; the other seized his spear. Then the two parties, seven and two, joined battle. The Magian who had taken up the bow could do nothing with it, for his enemies were too near him and at close quarters. The other defended himself with his spear and struck Aspathines in the thigh and Intaphrenes in the eye. Intaphrenes lost the eye from the blow but did not die. So this one of the Magians wounded these two. The other Magian, finding his bow useless, took refuge in an apartment that opened into the men's

chamber and tried to shut the doors. But two of the Seven, Darius and Gobryas, rushed in with him. Then Gobryas was locked in a fight with the Magian, and Darius stood by, and, for it was dark, was at a loss to strike for fear he would hit Gobryas. Seeing Darius doing nothing, Gobryas asked him why he did not strike. "For fear of hitting you," said Darius. Gobryas answered: "Drive the sword through, even through the two of us." Darius obeyed, struck with his dagger, and by some chance reached the Magian only.

79. So they killed the Magians and cut off their heads; and they left their own wounded where they were, partly because of their inability to move and partly so that they could guard the citadel. The Five then, with the Magians' heads, ran with great shouts and clamor and called on all the other Persians to join them; they explained what had happened and showed the heads, and, at the same time, they killed every Magian that they met. The general body of the Persians, finding out from the Seven what had taken place and the deception put upon them by the Magians, thought fit to do like the Seven; they drew their daggers and killed, wherever they found a Magian. If night had not come on, they would have left not a single Magian alive. This day the Persians now celebrate publicly, more than any of their other holy days, and conduct a great festival on it. It is called by the Persians "The Slaughter of the Magians." On it no Magian dare appear in public, but they must keep strictly to their own houses.

80. When the confusion had settled, five days later, the conspirators against the Magians held a debate about the entire condition of affairs. Here speeches were made that some of the Greeks refuse to credit, but the speeches *were* made, for all that. Otanes proposed that power should be entrusted to the main body of the Persians: "It is my conviction that we should no longer have a monarch over us. It is neither pleasant nor good, the monarchy. You yourselves know how far Cambyses' outrages went, and you have had a taste of the outrageousness of the Magian. How can a monarchy be a suitable thing? The monarch may do what he pleases, with none to check him afterwards. Take the best man on earth and put him into a monarchy and you put him outside of the thoughts that have been wont to guide him. Outrageousness is bred in him by reason of the good things he has, and envy is basic in the nature of man. He has these

two qualities, then, and in them he has all evil. Out of his satiety his outrageousness grows, and he does many appalling things out of that; but he does many, too, out of envy. You would think that a man who was an absolute sovereign would be free of jealousy, for he has all good things at his disposal, but the contrary is true of him with respect to his fellow citizens. He is jealous that the best of them should continue alive; he is pleased that the worst of them should continue alive. He is a master at receiving slanders. He is the most difficult of all men to deal with: if your admiration of him is moderate, he is offended because the flattery is not abject; if the flattery is abject, he is offended with you as a toady. I have still my biggest charge to make against him: he turns upside down all ancestral observances, forces women, and kills men without trial. When the people is ruler, in the first place its title is the fairest of all—namely, equality before the law; secondly, it does none of those things I have objected against the monarch. The government holds office by decision of lot, and the power it holds is subject to the check of audit, and all its propositions it must put before the commonalty for judgment. I vote therefore that we abolish the monarchy and increase the power of the people; for in the Many lies All."

81. Such was the judgment contributed by Otanes. But Megabyzus would have them turn things over to an oligarchy, and his speech was as follows: "What Otanes has said about the abolition of the monarchy you may regard as being my opinion also. But when he proposes to turn over power to the Many, he has fallen short of the nicest judgment. There is nothing stupider, nothing more given to outrage, than a useless mob. Yet surely for men who are fleeing the outrage of the despot to fall into the clutches of the outrageous Many, on whom, too, there is no restraint, is in no way bearable. The despot, if he does something, does it of knowledge; but knowledge is what does not inhere in the Many. How can men know anything when they have never been taught what is fine, nor have they any innate sense of it? They rush into things and push them this way and that without intelligent purposes, like a river in winter spate. Let those who have ill will to the Persians press for a democracy; but let us choose a society of the Best Men and entrust the power to them. Among this number we shall be ourselves, and we may reasonably assume that, when the men are the Best, their counsels will be so too."

82. Such was the judgment of Megabyzus. Darius gave his judgment as third among them: "What Megabyzus has said about the Many seems to me truly said; not so his comments on oligarchy. Suppose, for the argument, that all three constitutions are of the very best—the best democracy, the best oligarchy, the best monarchy. I declare to you that, of these three at their best, monarchy is far superior. Nothing is manifestly better than the one best man. He will have judgment to match his excellence and will govern the Many blamelessly, and what measures he must devise against ill-doers will be wrapped in a similar well-judging silence. In an oligarchy, many try to practice virtue for the public good, but in doing so they engender bitter private enmities. Each of the oligarchs wants to be chief man and to win with his opinions, and so they come to great hatreds of one another, and from this comes faction, and from faction comes murder. From murder there is a relapse into despotism—and *there* is an indication again how much despotism is the best! When the Many are rulers, it cannot but be that, again, knavery is bred in the state; but now the knaves do not grow to hate one another—they become fast friends. For they combine together to maladminister the public concerns. This goes on until one man takes charge of affairs for the Many and puts a stop to the knaves. As a result of this, he wins the admiration of the Many, and, being so admired, lo! you have your despot again; in this case, too, it is clear that monarchy is the best of the systems. In one word: from what source did we gain our freedom, and who gave it us? The people, or the oligarchy, or the despot? I give my vote that, as we were freed by one man,[10] so we should keep this freedom *through* one man; apart from this, we should not abolish any of our ancestral laws that are sound. It would be better so."

83. These were the three opinions that were put forward. Four of the Seven gave their support to the last—that of Darius. So when Otanes was worsted in his proposition to establish among the Persians equality before the law, he made the following statement to all the conspirators: "My friends and partners: it is clear that one of us must become king, either by choice of lot, or by our turning over to

10. It is worth noticing that Darius' position is that Cyrus conferred freedom on the Persians because he delivered them from the rule of the Medes. This *freedom* was quite compatible with the internal rule of an absolute monarch—Cyrus himself.

the Persians the privilege of choosing whomever they please, or by some other method. For my own part, I abdicate from this contest with you; I will not rule or be ruled. But I withdraw from any chance of rule on one condition: that I shall not be ruled by any one of you, neither myself nor my descendants." That is what he said, and the six others accepted his proposition on these conditions. He, then, would not join the contest but withdrew, and till this day his house continues as the only free one in Persia and is under the rule of another only insofar as it itself chooses, providing it does not overstep the laws of Persia.

84. The remainder of the Seven debated as to how they might most justly choose a king. They resolved that if the kingship should devolve upon someone else among the Seven, other than Otanes, there should be given to him and all his descendants, every year, special privileges: a gift of Median dress and all the awards that are most honorable among the Persians. They resolved to give him these things because he had been the first to plan the conspiracy and had brought them all together. These, then, were to be Otanes' special privileges. But in regard to all the other conspirators, they made the following decisions: any one of the Seven that pleased might come into the palace without formal announcement unless the king was sleeping with a woman; the king should not be allowed to marry of any other stock than that of the Seven. As for the selection of a king, they resolved this: that all of them should mount their horses in the outskirts of the city and, as the sun rose, whichever horse neighed first, his rider should possess the throne.

85. Now, Darius had a groom whose name was Oebares, and he was a clever fellow. When the meeting broke up, Darius spoke to this man: "Oebares, we have resolved to deal with the kingship this way: when we are all on horseback, whichever of our horses neighs first, as the sun rises, makes his rider king. Now if you have any trick to deal with this, contrive that we win the prize and not someone else." Oebares answered him: "Master, if being king or not being king lies in this only, be confident and of good cheer as far as this goes, for no one will become king other than yourself; I have potent medicines for that." Darius said: "If you have any such contrivance, you had better put it into practice without delay, for our game is on for tomorrow." When Oebares heard this, he did the following: at

nightfall he led out that one of the mares that Darius' stallion loved most and tied her in the outskirts of the city. He then led out Darius' stallion and led him around a great while in the neighborhood of the mare, at times just suffering him to touch her; finally he let him go, to mount and breed her.

86. At the day's dawning, the Six, as they had agreed, came mounted; they rode through the city's outskirts, and when they came to the place where the mare had been tied up the night before, Darius' horse plunged forward and neighed. At the very moment this happened, there was a flash of lightning (though the sky was cloudless) and a rattle of thunder. These additional signs clinched the selection of Darius; they were additional to the trick, and what happened was, as it were, a collusion between it and something else. The other riders jumped down from their horses and did obeisance to Darius.

87. That is one story of how Oebares contrived the outcome. There is another—for the Persians tell the story both ways—that Oebares had rubbed his hand against the mare's loins and then hidden his hand in his breeches. As the sun rose and the Six were letting their horses go, Oebares, stretching out his hand, brought it close to the nostrils of the stallion, who, immediately he smelled it, neighed and whinnied.

88. So Darius, son of Hystaspes, became king,[11] and all the peoples in Asia became his subjects, having been conquered by Cyrus and, after him, by Cambyses. All, that is, but the Arabians. These were never reduced to slavish subjection to the Persians but were guest-friends, because they had let Cambyses through into Egypt. Without the good will of the Arabians, the Persians could not have invaded Egypt. The first two marriages Darius made were among the Persians. He married the two daughters of Cyrus, Atossa and Artystone. Atossa had previously been married to her brother Cambyses and also to the Magian; Artystone was still a maid. He also married the daughter of Smerdis, son of Cyrus, whose name was Parmys; also Otanes' daughter, who had discovered the Magian to the conspirators. Everything was full of the power of Darius. First of all he made and set up a monument of stone. On it was an engraving

11. In 521 B.C.

of a man on horseback, with an inscription: "Darius, son of Hystaspes, with the help of his horse's excellence" (he there mentioned the stallion's name) "and that of Oebares the groom, won the kingship of Persia."

89. Having done these things in Persia, he set up twenty provinces, which the Persians themselves call satrapies. He set up the satrapies and appointed governors to them and appointed the tribute they should pay, nation by nation. He assigned to each nation those that were nearest to it, but the farther peoples he assigned to one nation or another. The governments and the yearly taxation were as follows. Those who were paying in silver must use the Babylonian talent, those in gold the Euboic. The Babylonian is worth one and one-sixth of the Euboic. In the reigns of Cyrus and Cambyses there had been no regular fixed tax, only collection of gifts. Because of his tax assessment, and other things of the same kind, the Persians have a saying that Darius was a shopkeeper, Cambyses a master of slaves, and Cyrus a father. What they mean is that Darius kept petty accounts for everything, that Cambyses was hard and contemptuous, and that Cyrus was gentle and contrived everything for their good.

90.[12] From the Ionians, the Magnesians in Asia, and the Aeolians, Carians, Lycians, Milyans, and Pamphylians there came an aggregate of 400 talents of silver; this was the total tax assessed. This was the first tax province. From the Mysians, Lydians, Lasonians, Cabalians, and Hytennians came 500 talents; this was the second province. From the Hellespontines (as you go in on the right-hand side), Phrygians, Asiatic Thracians, Paphlagonians, Mariandynians, and Syrians there was a tribute of 360 talents; this was the third province. From the Cilicians came 360 horses, all white, one for each day of the year, and 500 talents of silver. Of these silver talents,

12. What follows is a systematic account of the provinces (satrapies) of the Persian empire under Darius. The information involved roughly coincides with what we know from the inscriptions of Darius that we possess. Herodotus is looking at the geographical organization of the territory as well as its assessment for tax purposes. We do not know where Herodotus got this document—or, rather, the information it contains—but the comparison with Darius' inscriptions seems to warrant us in rating highly Herodotus' accuracy, in the simplest sense of historical accuracy. After chapter 97 he is dealing with the far eastern boundary of the empire, and here he does not have the quality of information that marks the earlier part.

140 were spent on the cavalry that guarded Cilicia; the remaining 360 went to Darius. This was the fourth province.

91. From the city of Posideium—established by Amphilochus, the son of Amphiaraus, on the border between the Cilicians and Syrians—as far as Egypt (and always omitting the Arabians, who were not subject to tax), there was a tax assessment of 350 talents. In this province was all of Phoenicia, Palestinian Syria, and Cyprus. This was the fifth province. From Egypt and those parts of Libya that neighbor Egypt, and Cyrene and Barca (for these areas were all reckoned into this province of Egypt), there came a tribute of 700 talents, apart from the silver from Lake Moeris, which was from the fisheries. Apart from this silver and the grain that was measured out, there came, I say, 700 talents. As concerns the grain, this was 120,000 bushels, measured out to the Persians and their allies who were guarding the White Fort in Memphis. This was the sixth province. The Sattagydae, Gandarii, Dadicae, and Aparytae paid, all together, 170 talents. This was the seventh province. From Susa and the rest of the Cissian country came 300. This was the eighth province.

92. From Babylon and the rest of Assyria came 1,000 talents of silver and 500 boys, to be eunuchs. This was the ninth province. From Ecbatana and the rest of Media and from the Paricanians and the Orthocorybantians, 450 talents. This was the tenth province. The Caspii, Pausicae, Pantimathi, and Daritae paid jointly 200 talents. This was the eleventh province.

93. From the Bactrians, as far as the Aegli, came a tribute of 360 talents. This was the twelfth province. From the Pactyic country and Armenia and the neighboring parts, as far as the Euxine Sea, there came 400 talents. This was the thirteenth province. From the Sagartii, Sarangeis, Thamanaei, Utii, Myci, and those who live on the islands in the Red Sea, where the King establishes the men who are called "The Transplanted"—from all these came a tribute of 600 talents. This was the fourteenth province. The Sacae and the Caspii contributed 250 talents. This was the fifteenth province. The Parthians, Chorasmians, Sogdians, and Arians paid 300. This was the sixteenth province.

94. The Paricanii and Ethiopians in Asia contributed 400 talents. This was the seventeenth province. To the Matieni and Saspiri

and Alarodii was assigned a tax of 200 talents. This was the eighteenth province. To the Moschi, Tibareni, Macrones, Mossynoeci,
and Mares was assigned a tax of 300 talents. This was the nineteenth
province. The number of Indians is far greater than any other people
I know of, and they contributed more also than any others. Theirs
was a tax of 360 talents of gold dust. This was the twentieth province.

95. The Babylonian silver, reckoned in terms of the Euboic currency, comes to 9,880 Euboic talents. If one then counts the gold as
worth thirteen times the silver, the gold dust is worth 4,680 Euboic
talents. Putting all together, the yearly tribute to Darius amounts to
14,560 talents. In this total I disregard units of less than ten talents.

96. This tribute came to Darius from Asia and some few parts of
Libya. But as time went on, there was another field of taxation in
the islands[13] and again in Europe, as far as Thessaly. His tribute the
King stores as follows: he melts it down and pours it into earthen
vessels, and when he has filled the vessel, he breaks off the outer
layer of baked earth. When he needs money, he cuts off from the
ingot as much as he wants for the coinage.

97. These were the governments and the settings of the taxation. I have not recorded any taxation of Persia, which is the only
country not subject to tax. The Persians hold their land free of tax.
The following peoples are not ordered to pay any taxes, but they
contribute gifts. The Ethiopians who are neighbors to Egypt—that
is, those Ethiopians whom Cambyses subdued on his way to the
long-lived Ethiopians—and those who are settled about holy Nysa
and celebrate festivals to Dionysus—these two peoples together
bring their gifts every other year. (These Ethiopians and their neighbors are like the Callantian Indians in that they have black semen
instead of white; they live in underground dwellings.)[14] The gifts of
these peoples, which were still being given in my time, were two
choenixes of unrefined gold and two hundred ebony logs, five Ethiopian boys, and twenty great elephant tusks. The Colchians also contributed gifts, and so did their neighbors as far as the Caucasus
Mountains (for as far as these mountains the government is Persian,
but north of there no one regards the Persians); these people still

13. The Greek islands in the Aegean Sea.
14. See, for the same observation, chapter 101 of this book. Some editors
think that the passage was mistakenly transferred from there to here. The Callan-
tians are also referred to in 3.38, where they are called Callatians.

contributed gifts in my time and made the collection every four years. Their gifts were a hundred boys and a hundred girls. The Arabians contributed a thousand talents of frankincense every year. These, then, were the gifts that these peoples brought to the King, apart from the taxes.

98. The great abundance of gold, from which they bring to the King their gold dust, is won by the Indians as I shall show. All the eastern portion of India is sand. Indeed, of all the people whom we know and about whom there can be said anything with exactness, the Indians, of all the nations in Asia, live furthest to the east and the rising sun; and all the country of the Indians to the east is desert because of the sand. There are many peoples among the Indians, all speaking different languages, and some of them are nomads and some are not, and some of them live in swamps round rivers and eat raw fish, which they catch out of the reed boats from which they fish. Each boat is made of a single section of a great reed. These Indians also wear garments made of reeds. They mow and cut the reeds from the river and then weave them together, in the fashion of a mat, and put it on like a breastplate.

99. Others of the Indians, living to the east of these, are nomads and eaters of raw meat. They are called Padaei, and these are their customs: when one of their citizens falls sick, be it man or woman, those of closest association with him—men if he be a man—kill him, saying that, as he wastes away with disease, his flesh is being lost to them. If he denies that he is sick, they will still not grant him that but will kill and eat him anyhow. If it be a woman that is sick, it is again those that have had most to do with her that treat her just as the men treated the man. When a man comes to old age, they kill him and make a banquet of him; but not many of the people come to be of this kind because, before that, they fall sick and are, every one, killed.

100. There are other Indians, again, and another style of life. These will not kill any living thing, nor do they sow or possess houses; and what they eat is herbs. There is among them a grain about the size of millet within a husk, and this grain grows unsown out of the earth. The people collect it and boil and eat it, husk and all. When one of these falls sick, he wanders into the desert and lies down, and no one troubles about him, whether he is sick or dead.

101. Among the Indians I have spoken of, sexual intercourse is

quite public, as it is among the animals; their skin is as black as that of the Ethiopians. The seed that they ejaculate into their women is not, like the rest of mankind, white but black, as their skin is. The seed of the Ethiopians is likewise black. These Indians live furthest from the Persians, toward the south, and they were not subjects of King Darius.

102. There are others of the Indians who are neighbors of the city of Caspatyrus and the Pactyic country, north of the rest of India, and these live much like the Bactrians. They are the most warlike of the Indians, and it is they who go in quest of the gold; for in these parts all is desert because of the sand. In this desert, and sand, there are ants that are in bigness lesser than dogs but larger than foxes. Some of them have been hunted and captured and kept at the palace of the Persian king. These ants make their dwelling underground, digging out the sand in much the same fashion as ants do in Greece, and they are also very like them in form. The sand that they dig out has gold in it. The Indians start off into the desert to get at this sand. Each of these hunters harnesses together three camels, a male on either side, on a trace, and the female in the middle, on which the rider is mounted. He takes care that this mare camel should have offspring as young as possible, from which she has been taken away for the ride. Among these people, camels are every bit as quick as horses, apart from being far more capable of carrying burdens.

103. The Greeks know camels, so I will not write to describe their shape; but I will tell something that is not known. The camel in the hind legs has four thighs and four knees, and its genitals are turned toward the tail, between its hind legs.

104. Such is the gear of the Indians and such their method of harnessing when they go after the gold. They go expressly at that hour of day that will allow them to be in their hunt for gold when the heat is greatest; for by reason of the heat the ants will have vanished underground. In India the sun is hottest early in the morning—not, as among other people, at midday; in India it is hottest from sunrise till the breaking-up of the market. During this period it is far hotter than at midday in Greece, so that it is said the inhabitants at this time wet themselves over with water. The midday heat is in India about the same as it is among other men. But, as the afternoon comes on, the Indian sun becomes much as it is elsewhere in

the early morning, and from then it grows cooler and cooler, till at sunset it is indeed exceedingly cold.

105. The Indians then come to the place with bags, and after they have filled their bags with sand, they make off for home as fast as they can. For, as the Persians say, the ants become aware of them by smell and pursue them. There is nothing quicker than these ants, and so, if the Indians did not get well ahead of them while the ants were collecting, not one of the men would escape alive. The male camels, which are inferior to the females in quickness, begin to lag behind and are cut loose by the riders, one at a time. But the mare camels, as they think of their young, do not slack off at all. This is how, say the Persians, the most of the gold is won by the Indians. The rest of it, a smaller amount, is mined in their country.

106. Somehow the furthest parts of the world have the finest things in them; but, in the same way, Greece has much the best blend of seasons. So, as I have just said, there is India, furthest to the east. In it all living things, four-footed and winged, are far bigger than elsewhere, except for the horses. Indian horses are inferior to the Median horses that are called Nesaean. And there is this tremendous store of gold, some of it mined, some of it carried down by rivers, and some plundered from the ants, as I have shown. They have wild trees there that bear a fruit that is in beauty like wool and in excellence as good as that which comes from sheep. The Indians wear clothes made from these plants.[15]

107. Furthest to the south of all the world is Arabia, and this is the one country on earth for growing myrrh and cassia and cinnamon and gum-labdanum. All of these are won by the Arabians, but with difficulty, except for the myrrh. They collect frankincense by burning storax, which the Phoenicians export to Greece. This burning is a part of the harvesting of the frankincense. For the bushes that grow frankincense are guarded by tiny winged snakes, of dappled color, and there are great numbers of them around each bush; these are the snakes that attack Egypt.[16] There is nothing that can drive them from the bushes except the smoke of the storax.

108. The Arabians say that the whole land would be filled with

15. Cotton.
16. Cf. 2.75.

these snakes if something did not happen to them which I have known to happen to vipers. There is a divine providence, with a kind of wisdom to it, as one might guess, according to which whatever is cowardly of spirit and edible should be prolific in progeny, so that, with all the eating of them, they should not fail to exist; while things that are savage and inflict pain are infertile. For instance, the hare is hunted by every wild beast, bird, and man; but it is very prolific. It is the only one of all creatures that conceives on top of an existing pregnancy. Some of its children in the womb have fur already, while others are still bare; some are being shaped in the womb while others are being conceived. That is how the hare is. But the lioness, which is the strongest and most daring of animals, gives birth only once in her life and to but one cub. When she gives birth, she expels the womb with the cub. The reason is that, when the cub in the womb begins to stir, it has the sharpest nails of any creature and tears at the womb; as it grows bigger, the scratching grows worse, and, when the birth is near, there is hardly any of the womb left whole.

109. So it is also with the vipers and the winged snakes in Arabia: if these were to be born as nature is in them to do, there would be no living for man. But, as it is, when they are mating in couples and the male is in the very act of emitting his seed, the female, as he does so, seizes him by the neck and, hanging on, never lets him go till she has bitten the neck through. This is how the male dies; but the female pays a kind of recompense, too, to the male. For the children, while still in the womb, take vengeance for their male parent by eating through their mother's insides and so make their entry into the world after eating up her womb. Other snakes, which are not destructive of man, lay eggs and hatch out an infinity of children. Vipers are all over the earth; but these winged snakes are all concentrated in Arabia and nowhere else. That is why they seem so numerous, because they are all in this place only.

110. That is how the Arabians get their frankincense; and this is how they get the cassia: they bind ox-hides and other kinds of leather over all their body and their faces, except their eyes, when they go out to get cassia. This grows in shallow ponds, and round the pond and in it there live winged creatures, very like bats, with a dreadful squeak and very ready to fight. You must ward these off your eyes if you are to harvest the cassia.

111. Their method of collecting cinnamon is even more remarkable. Where it grows and what sort of land produces it they cannot say, except that they declare, with a show of reason, that it grows in the places where Dionysus was reared. They say that great birds carry these dry sticks, which we have learned from the Phoenicians to call cinnamon, and that the birds carry the sticks to their nests, which are plastered with mud and are placed on sheer crags where no man can climb up. The Arabians have found the following trick to deal with this. They cut out the limbs of dead oxen and asses, taking as much of the limbs as possible, and carry them to the part of the country where the nests are, and there they put them near the nests and themselves withdraw to a distance. The birds swoop down and carry off the limbs of the beasts to their nests, and the nests, being unable to bear the weight, break and fall down, and the Arabians approach and collect what they want. Thus is cinnamon gathered in these parts, and so from there it comes to other countries.

112. Gum-labdanum, which the Greeks call ledanum and the Arabians ladanum, is even more strangely produced. It is the most sweet-smelling of all things, and yet its birth is in the worst of stinks. For it is found growing in the beards of he-goats; it forms in them like tree gum. This is a substance useful for many perfumes, and the Arabians burn it chiefly as incense.

113. That, then, is enough about spices and perfumes. There is a most marvelous sweet smell from all this land of Arabia. There are there also two varieties of sheep that are worthy of wonder and occur nowhere else. The one of these has a long tail, not less than four and one-half feet. If this were suffered to trail after the sheep, it would be injured because of the rubbing of the tail on the ground. As it is, every shepherd knows enough of carpentry to make a small cart on which to fasten the tail, one for each sheep. The other variety of sheep has a thick tail that is one and one-half feet broad.

114. To the southwest of the world, Ethiopia is the furthest of all inhabited lands. It has much gold and abundant elephants, and all manner of wild trees and ebony, and the tallest, handsomest, and longest-lived men.

115. These, then, are the countries that are at the uttermost ends of the earth in Asia and Libya. But about the limits of the world toward the west, in Europe, I cannot speak with certainty. For my own part, I do not accept that there is a river, called Eridanus by

the barbarians, that issues into a sea toward the north, from which it is that amber comes; nor do I know of the actual existence of the Tin Islands, from which our tin comes. The very name Eridanus speaks against their story, for it is a Greek, not a barbarian, word, made up by some poet or other. Nor have I been able, for all my efforts that way, to hear from anyone who was an eyewitness that there *is* a sea beyond Europe. But certainly our tin and our amber come from the edges of the world.

116. It is clear that there is far the greatest supply of gold to the north of Europe, but how it is got is again something I cannot tell exactly; it is said that the Arimaspi—men with one eye—steal the gold from the griffins. I cannot be persuaded about this either—that there exist in nature men who are just like everyone else except that they have only one eye. Certainly, however, it seems likely that the ends of the earth, which enclose and entirely shut in all the rest, should have in themselves what we think most beautiful and rarest.

117. There is a plain in Asia shut in on every side by mountains, and there are five ravines that break through the mountains. This plain was once owned by the Chorasmians; it lies on the borders of the Chorasmians themselves and the territory of the Hyrcanians, Parthians, Sarangians, and Thamanaeans; afterwards, when the Persians conquered, the land became the property of the Great King. From the mountains that surround the plain flows a mighty river, the name of which is the Aces. Now this river in the old days divided into five and watered the territories of the five nations just mentioned, each one through its ravine; but when the Persians took over, this is what was done with the river and its openings: the King built and set up a gate at each ravine. As the water was cut off from getting out, the plain within the mountains became a huge lake; for the river flowed in but had nowhere egress. So those who were wont to use the water and now have none are greatly at a loss. For in winter there is rain there, as in all other countries, but in summer the inhabitants have constant need of water for the millet and sesame seed that they sow. So when no water is given them, they and their womenfolk come to the Persians and, standing at the gates of the royal palace, raise a great to-do, and the King gives orders to open the gates that lead to these people's country, for those who need it worst. When their land is satiated with drinking up the

water, these gates are closed off again and the King orders the other gates opened to the other peoples who are in need. From what I hear, the King levies great sums for the opening of the gates, apart from the other tribute he exacts.

118. So much for that. Of the Seven who had formed the conspiracy against the Magian, one—Intaphrenes—had already been overtaken by death; he had done a deed of violence and insolence shortly after the uprising, and he died. This is how it was. He wanted to enter the palace on some business with the King, and the law stood, as I have related, that the Seven had free entry to the palace without announcing themselves, except at such times as the King was in bed with a woman. Therefore, Intaphrenes thought fit that no one should announce him, but that, since he was one of the Seven, he might enter. Now, the gatekeeper and the messenger-bearer would not suffer it; for, they said, the King *was* in bed with a woman. Intaphrenes thought that the men lied; he drew his scimitar and cut off their ears and their noses, threaded them on his horse's bridle and tied this round the men's necks, and so let them go.

119. They showed themselves to the King and told him why they had so suffered. Darius was terrified that the Six might have done this by common agreement, and so he sent for them, one by one, and made test of their mind toward himself—as to whether what had been done was done to their common liking. When he found out that Intaphrenes had not acted with the consent of the rest of them, he had him arrested, together with his sons and all his household. For he had strong thoughts that the man was plotting a rising against him, together with his kinsfolk. So he arrested them and put them in prison, to await their death. The wife of Intaphrenes came constantly to the King's door and wailed and lamented. And this she did again and again—so much so that Darius was moved to pity her. So he sent his messenger to her and said, "Woman, King Darius grants you the release of whichever of your imprisoned household you will choose." She took thought and then said, "If the King gives me the life of one of them, I will, of all of them, choose that of my brother." Darius heard this and was astonished at what she said, and so he sent again: "The King asks you on what grounds you would abandon your husband and sons and choose your brother to survive. Surely he is more distant from you than your children and less dear

to you than your husband." She answered and said, "My lord, I can get a husband again, if it is God's pleasure, and other children if I lose these; but my father and mother being dead, in no way can I have another brother. This is why I have spoken as I did." Darius thought that the woman had spoken well, and so he released the brother she had asked for and also her eldest son, he was so pleased with her; but he killed all the others. So one of the Seven died immediately, and I have told how.

120. What I am now going to tell took place about the time Cambyses fell sick. There had been appointed as viceroy of Sardis, by Cyrus, Oroetes, a Persian. This Oroetes set himself to do something monstrously wicked. He had received no hurt from Polycrates, the ruler of Samos—he had never as much as seen him—but he longed to take and kill him. Most people agree that the reason was this: one day Oroetes and another Persian, by the name of Mitrobates, who was governor of the province at Dascyleium, were sitting at the King's door. They had been talking and then fell to abusing one another as they compared one another for their respective excellence. Then Mitrobates brought forward against Oroetes this business of Polycrates: "Why," said Mitrobates, "you, Oroetes, are hardly to be counted in the roll of men at all, seeing that you did not add to the possessions of the King the island of Samos. It lay next to your province and was so easy of conquest that one of the natives, with fifteen men-at-arms, rose and secured it and now rules it."[17] People say that Oroetes, when he heard this, was bitterly stung by the reproach and set his heart not so much on taking vengeance on the man who had uttered it as on the complete destruction of Polycrates, who was the occasion of his, Oroetes', ill reputation.

121. There are others, though less numerous, who say that Oroetes sent a herald to Samos, asking for something or other—what this was is not recorded—and that Polycrates happened to be lying there in the men's apartments and, with him, Anacreon of Teos.[18] What happened was either that Polycrates intentionally showed his contempt for Oroetes and his concerns, or that it was all pure chance. Anyway, as Oroetes' herald came forward and spoke to

17. See 3.39.
18. The lyric poet.

Polycrates, who happened to be lying with his face toward the wall, Polycrates neither turned round nor gave any answer.

122. These are the two reasons given for Polycrates' death; you may believe which you prefer. Oroetes established himself in Magnesia, above the river Maeander, and sent to Samos a Lydian, Myrsus, the son of Gyges, with a message; for he had learned of Polycrates' designs. Polycrates is the first of the Greeks we know to lay plans for mastery of the sea, except for Minos of Cnossus and any of those that before him were lords of the sea. But Polycrates is the first of the human race to do so, and he had high hopes of mastering Ionia and the islands. Oroetes, then, having found this out, sent a message: "These are the words of Oroetes to Polycrates: I learn that you are laying plans for great matters but that you have not money to match your plans. Do as I bid you, and you will save yourself and save me too. For King Cambyses is plotting my death—I have clear information on that. Take me away safely, me and my money too. Keep some of the money for yourself, and let me have the rest. As far as money goes, you will be ruler of all Greece. If you mistrust what I say about the money, send someone you trust most in the world, and I will show the money to him."

123. When he heard this, Polycrates was delighted and willing to do what Oroetes suggested. He was, you see, very fond of money, and he sent, to spy out the land, first Maeandrius, the son of Maeandrius, one of Polycrates' fellow citizens. This man was his secretary and the very person who, a little later, dedicated the fine things from the men's apartments in Polycrates' palace—and very extraordinary they were—in the Heraeum. When Oroetes learned that this spy was to be expected, he filled up eight chests with stones, except for a small space near the top of the chests, where he threw in gold on top of the stones, and he then roped the chests about and had them ready for inspection. So Maeandrius came and saw and told what he saw to Polycrates.

124. Polycrates then determined to make his voyage to Oroetes—this, though there were many oracles that were against it and much urging of his friends to the same purport. Besides, his daughter saw this vision in her sleep: there was her father, aloft in the air, being washed by Zeus and anointed by the sun! Having seen this vision, she stopped at nothing in begging Polycrates not to go to

Oroetes; and indeed, when he was already going on board the penteconter, she pursued him with words of bad omen. He in turn threatened her that, if he came back safe, it would be long indeed that she should remain a maid. She prayed that such might in truth be the case, for, she said, she would rather be long a maid than lose her father.

125. Polycrates made nothing of all counsel and sailed to Oroetes, bringing with him many friends, including Democedes, the son of Calliphon, a man of Croton. This was a doctor who practiced his profession more skillfully than any other of his time. So Polycrates came to Magnesia, and there he died in a way that dishonored himself and all his high ambitions; for, except for the tyrants of Sicily alone, there is not one of the rest of the Greek despots who is worthy to be compared with Polycrates for magnificence. Oroetes killed him in a way not fit to be told and then crucified him. Of Polycrates' followers, those who were Samians he let go, bidding them be grateful to himself for their freedom, but those who were foreigners, or were slaves of those who followed Polycrates, he made slaves of himself. So Polycrates hung there and fulfilled all the vision his daughter had had; for he was washed by Zeus when it rained, and he was anointed by the sun when he yielded to it the moisture of his body.

126. So the many successes of Polycrates ended in this, just as Amasis, king of Egypt, had prophesied to him. But no long time after, the powers of vengeance of Polycrates overtook Oroetes too. After the death of Cambyses, when the Magi had taken over the sovereignty, Oroetes remained in Sardis and did no service at all to the Persians at this time when they were robbed of their rule by the Medes. Indeed, at this moment of confusion, he murdered Mitrobates, the viceroy of Dascyleium (the man who had taunted him in the matter of Polycrates), and also Mitrobates' son Cranaspes, both of them men of repute among the Persians, and he did a variety of deeds of violence and insolence; included was the murder of the messenger whom Darius had sent to him, because his message was not to his liking. He killed this man on his way back, having hired assassins to waylay him; and, having killed him, he made away with his body and even his horse.

127. When Darius took over the rule, he was eager to punish

Oroetes for all his wrongdoings and especially on account of Mitrobates and his son. But he did not think that he should send an armed force against him directly, when violence swelled like an ulcer and when he had but lately taken over the government; moreover, he learned that Oroetes had great strength. A thousand Persians were his bodyguard, and he was viceroy of the provinces of Phrygia, Lydia, and Ionia. Against all this Darius contrived a stratagem. He summoned together the most distinguished men of the Persians and spoke to them: "Men of Persia, which of you will undertake for me a deed that must be done by cunning rather than by force or numbers? Where cunning is what is needed, the work to be done does not call for force. Which of you will bring to me Oroetes alive or else will kill him? This man has done no service to the Persians at all; indeed, he has injured us greatly. First, he has made away with two of us, Mitrobates and his son, and now he has killed those I have sent to summon him to my presence; this is open insolence that cannot be endured. Death must overtake him before he does the Persians any further mischief."

128. Such was the question Darius put to them, and thirty men gave him their undertaking, each one being willing to do what he asked. As they competed with one another, Darius stopped them by bidding them cast lots; and, out of all of them, the lot fell on Bagaeus, son of Artontes. This is what this man, so chosen out, did. He wrote many dispatches on many subjects and sealed them with Darius' seal, and away he went with them to Sardis. He came into the presence of Oroetes and, taking out the dispatches one by one from their cases, he gave each one of them by itself to the royal secretary to read aloud. (All the viceroys had these royal secretaries.) Bagaeus gave the dispatches to the secretary to try the bodyguards and see whether they were receptive to revolting against Oroetes. He saw that their reverence for the dispatches was great and their reverence for the words in them even greater, and so he gave the secretary yet another dispatch, with these words in it: "Men of Persia, King Darius forbids you to continue as bodyguards to Oroetes." When the men heard this, they dropped their spears. Bagaeus, seeing that they obeyed the dispatch in this, took heart and gave the secretary the last dispatch, in which was written, "King Darius hereby bids the Persians that are in Sardis to kill Oroetes." When

the bodyguards heard this, they drew their scimitars and killed him on the spot. It was thus that the avenging powers of Polycrates caught up with the Persian Oroetes.

129. When Oroetes' possessions had been packed up and brought to Susa, it happened some time later that King Darius, while out hunting, jumped down from his horse and twisted his ankle. It was a very severe twist; in fact, the bone was twisted from its socket. Before this, Darius had kept about him those of the Egyptians who were thought to be chief in the medical art, and now he used them. They manipulated the joint violently, but they only made the trouble worse. For seven days and nights Darius was in agony with the injury, so that he could not sleep. On the eighth day he was in very poor condition when someone who had heard in Sardis of Democedes' skill sent word to Darius. The King ordered the man brought before him at once. They found him quite neglected among Oroetes' slaves, and so they brought him before the King, loaded with chains and in rags.

130. As he stood there before him, Darius asked him whether he was a master of the medical art. He denied this, since he was afraid that, if he so revealed himself, he would lose Greece for ever. Darius saw clearly that he understood medicine, and so he ordered the men who had dragged Democedes before him to bring the whips and the goads for use on him. Democedes then made another declaration; he admitted knowing medicine not exactly as a true doctor but as one who had been associated *with* a doctor and had some slight knowledge of the art. Darius submitted to his care, and then Democedes, using Greek remedies and gentle rather than forcible means, after the latter had been tried by the others, succeeded in getting Darius his share of sleep and, in a while, healed him completely, though the King had never expected to have the proper use of his foot again. Darius then made him a present: two pairs of golden fetters. At which Democedes asked him whether the King had expressly doubled his punishment because he had healed him. Darius was delighted at the witticism and sent the doctor off to the royal wives. The eunuchs who conducted him told the wives, "Here is he who restored life to our King." Then each one of the wives, scooping with a bowl from a chest full of gold, rewarded Democedes so lavishly that the servant attending and following him, whose name was Sciton, gathered

himself a great fortune of gold from the staters that fell from the bowls.

131. Now it was for the following reason that this man Democedes had come from Croton to attend on Polycrates. In Croton he had had to deal with his father, who was very harsh-tempered, and Democedes, being unable to put up with him, left and went to Aegina. Having set up there, within the first year he surpassed all the other doctors, although he was quite unfurnished and lacking all the things that are, for a doctor, working equipment. In his second year the people of Aegina took him for public physician at a fee of one talent; in his third year the Athenians, for the same work, gave him a hundred minas; and in the fourth year Polycrates hired him for two talents. So he came to Samos, and it was because of this man not least that the Crotoniates gained their reputation as doctors. For this was the time when the Crotoniates first became spoken of as doctors throughout Greece; the second place was held by the Cyrenaeans. (At this same time, too, the Argives were reputed the first of the Greeks in music.)

132. Now that Democedes had cured Darius in Susa, he had a huge house and was a guest at the royal table. He had everything—except a return to Greece. When the Egyptian physicians who had formerly treated the King were about to be impaled, because they had been bested by a Greek doctor, he begged their lives of the King and saved them; then there was an Elean soothsayer who had followed Polycrates and was now neglected among the slaves; he rescued him, too. With the King, Democedes was all in all.

133. A little time after this, something else happened. Atossa, the daughter of Cyrus and wife of Darius, had a growth on her breast. It broke, but it spread further. For as long as it was small, she hid it and out of shame told no one. But afterwards she was in real trouble and sent for Democedes and showed it to him. He said that he could cure it but made her swear an oath that, in return, she would grant him what favor he asked—always providing he asked nothing dishonorable.

134. Atossa was cured, and then Atossa, under instruction of Democedes, approached Darius in bed and said, "My lord, you have very great power and yet you sit idle. You have not added any nation or power to the empire of Persia. It is but right for a man who is

young and is master of great wealth to achieve something for all to see, that the Persians may know that he who rules them is truly a man. Indeed there is a double benefit in such a course; the Persians will know that their leader is a man, and also they themselves will be worn down by the war and will not plot against you—as they might, were they at leisure. And it is *now* you should do this, while you are young. For as the body grows, so the mind grows with it; and as the body grows old, so does the wit grow old and is blunted toward all matters alike." So she spoke under her instruction, and Darius answered, "Wife, you have bidden me do the very thing I purposed. I plan to build a bridge from this continent to the other and make war upon the Scythians, and that will, indeed, be done within a very short time." Atossa said, "See you: for now, let the Scythians be; they will be there for you whenever you want them. But do you attack Greece. I have heard stories and would like to have servants from among the Greeks—Laconian, Argive, Attic, and Corinthian girls. And you have the most suitable of all men to instruct you and explain everything about Greece to you, the very man who cured your foot." Darius said, "Wife, since you think I should first try Greece, I think we had better, first of all, send some Persians with the man you speak of, to spy out everything. They will discover and see and tell us every detail. Afterwards, when I understand all this, I will invade Greece."

135. No sooner said than done. When day dawned, he summoned fifteen of the Persian notables and bade them to attend Democedes all along the seacoast of Greece, to see that Democedes did not run away from them, and at all costs to bring him back to Persia. That was what he charged the Persians with. Second, he called Democedes to himself and asked him to explain and show all Greece to these Persians—but surely to return to Persia. He bade Democedes take all his goods that were movable as presents for his father and his brothers, and he declared that he, the King, would give him others that would replace these many times. Besides, he said, to carry the gifts, he would send along a merchant ship and would fill it also with all manner of good things. In all of these offers, to my mind, Darius did not act with any crafty intent. Democedes, however, was afraid that the King was only trying him. He did not show eagerness to receive what was offered but said that he would leave

his own property where it was, that it might be there for him on his return. But the merchantman that Darius offered for the carriage of the gifts for his brothers he accepted. So Darius, having laid the same orders upon Democedes as he had upon the Persians who were to attend him, sent them all off to the sea.

136. They came down to Phoenicia and, in Phoenicia, to the city of Sidon, and there they put aboard crews on two warships and, with them, a great merchantman, loaded with every sort of good thing; and having made all these preparations, they sailed away to Greece. They put in at various places on the coast and surveyed them and made charts of them until they had observed their many notable features, and then they came to Tarentum in Italy. There the king of Tarentum, Aristophilides, out of his complaisance for Democedes, removed the steering gear from the Median ships and arrested the Persians themselves, on the pretext that they had come as spies. While the Persians were in this trouble, Democedes made off to Croton; and when he had arrived there—his own country— Aristophilides released the Persians and restored to them the steering gear he had taken off their boats.

137. From there the Persians sailed and, in pursuit of Democedes, came to Croton; they found him there in the marketplace, shopping, and laid hands on him. Some of the people of Croton were for handing him over to the Persians because they were afraid of the Persian power; but others resisted his arrest, beating off the Persians with their staves. The Persians objected: "Men of Croton, see what you are doing! This is a man who is a runaway slave of the King, and you are taking him from us. Do you imagine that King Darius will be content to be so insulted? How do you think that things will go well with you if you *do* take him from us? What city will we attack ahead of yours? What city will we enslave ahead of yours?" That is what these men said, but they did not persuade the Crotoniates; and so the Persian escort lost Democedes and the merchantman they had brought with them and sailed back to Asia without further investigating Greece, which they had come to discover—for they had now lost their guide. But this much charge Democedes laid upon them as they were putting to sea; he said they should tell Darius that Democedes was contracted to marry the daughter of Milon. (Milon was a wrestler who had great fame with

Darius. To my mind, Democedes was so eager for this marriage, for which he had paid a great sum, that he might seem to Darius a great man in his own country, too.)

138. The Persians put to sea from Croton but were shipwrecked off Iapygia. There they were enslaved; but Gillus, a man of Tarentum, who was himself an exile, redeemed them and brought them to King Darius. In return, Darius was willing to give him whatever he wanted. Gillus asked to be restored to Tarentum (he had first explained the misfortune of his exile). But he did not want to bring Greece into confusion and ruin if a great armament should sail to Italy to bring about his return. So he said that the Cnidians would be enough to bring him back from exile; he thought that it would be managed most easily so, since they were especial friends of the Tarentines. Darius did what he asked. He sent a messenger to Cnidus and told the people there to restore Gillus to Tarentum. The Cnidians obeyed Darius, but they failed to persuade the Tarentines and were not able to force them. That was how all this happened. These were the first Persians that came from Asia to Greece; and for the reason I have given they came as spies.

139. After that, King Darius got possession of Samos, the first of Greek and barbarian cities to become his, and this was the reason for the capture. When Cambyses, son of Cyrus, made war on Egypt, many Greeks came to that country, some, naturally, for trading, and some just to see the country. Of the latter, one was an exile from Samos: the son of Aeaces and brother of Polycrates. This Syloson had had a piece of good luck. He was wearing a red cloak when he was shopping in Memphis, and Darius saw him then. At this time Darius was a bodyguard of Cambyses and not yet a man of great account. He coveted the cloak very much and approached Syloson and sought to buy it of him. Syloson saw that Darius wanted the cloak very badly and in a moment of inspiration said to him, "I will not sell you the cloak for any price, but if you absolutely must have it, I will give it to you for nothing." Darius agreed to this and took the cloak.

140. Syloson thought that he had lost his cloak out of mere foolishness. However, as time went on, Cambyses died, the Seven rose against the Magian, and Syloson learned that the royal power had devolved upon the very man to whom in Egypt he had given his

cloak at his request. So Syloson went up to Susa and sat at the doorway of the King's palace and said that he "was a Benefactor of the King." [19] The doorman, when he heard this, announced Syloson in these terms to the King. Darius was very surprised and said, "Who can this Greek be, to whom I have some obligation, seeing that I have only just taken over the throne? Almost none of this nation has come up to Susa to us, and I cannot say that I owe any debt to a Greek. But bring the man in, that I may know what he means by such a statement." The doorman brought in Syloson and, in the presence of the King, the interpreters asked Syloson what he had done that he claimed to be the King's Benefactor. So Syloson told the whole story of the cloak and how he was the man who had given it to Darius. At this Darius answered, "You are the most generous of men; when I had as yet no power at all, you gave me something even if it was a small thing; my gratitude for it is as great as if now I should receive something immense. For it I will give you countless gold and silver, that you may never repent of having been the Benefactor of Darius, son of Hystaspes." Syloson said to him, "Give me no gold or silver, my lord, but for your gift give me back my fatherland, Samos. My brother Polycrates is now dead at the hands of Oroetes, and the country has become the property of our slave. Give me that back, without murders or enslavings."

141. When Darius heard this, he sent off an expedition with Otanes, one of the Seven, in command and ordered him to fulfill whatever Syloson requested. So Otanes came down to the coast and made his army ready.

142. Maeandrius, son of Maeandrius, at this time governed Samos, having received his power as deputy of Polycrates. Maeandrius was one who wished to be the justest of mankind, but in his wish he had not succeeded. For when the death of Polycrates was told him, he did the following: first he dedicated an altar to Zeus, God of Freedom, and set an enclosure about it that is still there, in the outskirts of the city. Second, having finished with the altar, he

19. At 8.85 Herodotus tells us of a class of men formally enrolled, in recognition of some service, as "Benefactors of the King." They would be roughly the equivalent of those who find their way into the New Year's Honours List in Britain. I take it that Syloson used this title, perhaps informally, but certainly to attract the attention of the guards and doormen at the palace.

called an assembly of the citizens and made them this speech: "This scepter and all the power of Polycrates, as you know as well as myself, has been entrusted to me; I can now be your ruler. But what I find fault with in others I will not do myself, if I can help it. I did not like it when Polycrates held absolute authority over men as good as himself, nor would I choose that another should hold this sort of authority. Polycrates has fulfilled his destiny; so now I wish to open his power to all of you, and I proclaim equality before the law for the commonalty entire. This much I demand as a privilege for myself: six talents taken from the property of Polycrates and, in addition, the priesthood of Zeus, God of Freedom, for myself and for my descendants forever. It is I who have founded this shrine in his honor and I who now offer you this freedom." Such was his proclamation to the Samians. One of them rose up and said, "No, you are not worthy to be our ruler, lowborn as you are and a scoundrel besides. Rather than that, see to it that you give an account of the moneys you have laid your hands on."

143. So spoke among the citizens a man of distinction, called Telesarchus. Maeandrius understood that, if he gave up the power, someone else would become despot in his stead; and so he resolved not to let it go. He retreated to the citadel and sent for each of the citizens severally, on the pretext of giving an account of the money; he then arrested them and put them in prison. While they were in prison, Maeandrius fell sick. His brother, whose name was Lycaretus, thought he was going to die, and, so that he himself might find it easier to take over the power in Samos, he killed all the prisoners. They had, it seems, no will to be free.

144. So when the Persians got to Samos, in their project of restoring Syloson, not a man in Samos lifted a hand against them. Maeandrius himself, and those of his party, proclaimed that they were ready to evacuate the island under truce. Otanes agreed to their terms and made the treaty, and the most distinguished of the Persians sat down on seats opposite the citadel.

145. Maeandrius the despot had a half-crazed brother called Charilaus. This man had committed some offense or other and had been lodged in a dungeon in chains. He heard what was going on and, peering through a hole in his dungeon, saw the Persians sitting there peacefully. At this he roared for Maeandrius to come and talk

to him. When Maeandrius heard this, he told his people to take the chains off Charilaus and bring him to himself. When Charilaus was brought before him, he abused and insulted Maeandrius and tried to persuade him to attack the Persians: "You are the worst of villains; here am I, your brother, and for no reason at all you have thought fit to load me with chains and put me in a dungeon! But you look on at the Persians, who have driven you out of your home, and dare not take vengeance on them, though, as you see, they are easy enough to overcome. If you are in such dread of them yourself, give me your mercenaries and I will punish them for their coming hither. For yourself, I am willing to ship you out of the island."

146. Such were the words of Charilaus. Maeandrius took his proposal, not, in my opinion, because he was such a fool as to imagine that such force as he possessed would overcome that of the Great King, but because he grudged Syloson the taking-over the city unharmed, with so little trouble. He wanted to provoke the Persians and render Samos as weak as possible when it was handed over to the Persians, knowing well that the Persians, if they suffered in the process of obtaining the island, would be further embittered against the Samians. He knew that he himself would have a safe escape from the island whenever he wished. For he had had constructed a hidden passageway leading from the citadel to the sea. So Maeandrius himself sailed away from Samos. Charilaus, having armed all the mercenaries and thrown the gates open, led his men against the Persians, who never expected anything like this, since they believed that an agreement had been concluded. The mercenaries fell upon those of the Persians who were people of the greatest account and were riding about in their carriages and killed them. That the mercenaries did; but the rest of the Persian army came against them, and so the mercenaries, being hard pressed, were driven back into the citadel.

147. Otanes, the general, seeing that the Persians had suffered a great loss, forgot all about the commands of Darius, which till now he had remembered. For Darius had ordered him, as he sent him away, not to kill or enslave anyone in Samos and to give back the island to Syloson undamaged. Otanes now gave word to his army that whomsoever they should lay hands on, man or child, they should kill. So, while some of the Persians besieged the citadel, the

others killed everyone that came in their way, in sacred places or outside of them.

148. Maeandrius, then, ran away from Samos and sailed to Lacedaemon. When he got there and had gathered up all he came possessed of, he did the following thing. Whenever he got out his gold and silver drinking cups, and his servants were scouring them, at that time Maeandrius would be in conference with Cleomenes, king of Sparta, and would bring him to his house. When Cleomenes saw the cups, he was all admiration and astonishment, at which Maeandrius would tell him to take away as many of them as he pleased. Maeandrius said this two or three times, but Cleomenes was a just man through and through. He refused to take the gifts himself; but because he knew that Maeandrius, if he offered them to others, would find people to help him in Sparta, he went to the ephors and said that it would be better for Sparta that this guest of theirs from Samos should quit the Peloponnese before he convinced either himself, Cleomenes, or someone else of the Spartiates to turn traitor. The ephors agreed with him and proclaimed the banishment of Maeandrius.

149. Samos the Persians "swept with the net" and turned it over to Syloson entirely empty of people.[20] But afterwards the general, Otanes, helped to resettle it. He did so as the result of a vision he saw in a dream and also in response to a disease of the genitals that had seized him.

150. When the fleet had gone to Samos, the Babylonians revolted, having laid their preparations very carefully. For during the rule of the Magian and after the insurrection of the Seven—for all this time, when everything was in confusion—they prepared for a siege and, for some reason or other, were able to do so unnoticed. After their revolt came into the open, they took the following action: they sent away the mothers, and then each man chose, out of his own household, one woman, whichever he pleased; all the rest they gathered into one place and strangled. The one that each chose he chose for a breadmaker, and the others were strangled that they might not use up the supply of bread.

20. "Swept with the net": in 6.31 this procedure is described as a hand-to-hand linkage of an army sweeping the population of a place before it and so literally leaving it desolate.

151. Darius, learning of this and collecting his whole power, made war upon the Babylonians and drove as far as Babylon itself and laid siege to it; but those who lived in it made nothing of his siege. They would go up into the bastions of the wall and dance and chant in mockery of Darius and his army. One of them once said, "Why do you sit around here, Persians? Why don't you take yourselves off? You will capture us when mules bear foals." That is what that Babylonian said, never dreaming that a mule would have a foal.

152. Seven months and a year passed by, and Darius chafed there; and his whole army was unable to capture Babylon, though Darius had devised every sort of stratagem and machine against it. Even so he failed. Among his clever attacks he tried the one by which Cyrus had captured it before.[21] But the Babylonians were strictly on the watch, and Darius could not take them at all.

153. Then, in the twentieth month, a marvel happened. It happened to Zopyrus, the son of Megabyzus, who had been one of the Seven who killed the Magian. One of his pack mules, used for carrying the bread, had a foal. When Zopyrus heard, he did not believe it and went himself to see the foal. He told those who had seen it not to tell of it to anyone—and then he considered. "When mules bear foals," the Babylonian had said at the beginning of the siege, "then the fortress of Babylon will be captured." That was the saying, and now, in the light of it, Zopyrus thought that Babylon was capturable. For surely the man's word had been spoken with God in it, and it was with God also that his own mule should have a foal.

154. So since, as he saw it, now, at last, it was fated that Babylon should fall, he approached Darius and asked him if he was truly set on capturing the city. Zopyrus was told that certainly the King was set upon it. So now Zopyrus considered something else, which was how he himself might be the agent of the capture and the deed be his. For among the Persians the system of Good Deeds advances a man mightily in honor.[22] He could not conceive of any other way of taking the city except to mutilate himself and then desert to the Babylonians. He counted it a slight matter to mutilate himself past cure, and he did it; he cut off his nose and ears and shaved his hair to

21. Cyrus lowered the river by diverting it into the great marsh, upstream. His soldiers were then able to storm the walled city via the riverbed (1.191).

22. See 3.140 (the case of Syloson). See also 3.160, 6.30, and 8.85.

disfigure himself, and laid lashes on himself—and so he came before Darius.

155. Darius took it very ill when he saw a man of such great note so disfigured, and leaping from his throne he shouted at Zopyrus, demanding who it was that had so disfigured him and what he had done to deserve it. Zopyrus said, "There is no man save yourself that has the power to reduce me to this condition. Nor is there any other hand, my lord, that has done this to me save my own, out of grief that Assyrians should have the laugh at Persians." Darius answered, "Most reckless of men, you have put the fairest of names on the foulest of deeds when you say that you have done yourself this irreparable injury because of these people here, besieged by us. Why, you fool, will our enemies be reduced by our siege one moment sooner for your mutilation? You must surely be quite out of your wits to have destroyed yourself so." The other said, "If I had confided in you what I intended to do, you would not have suffered me to do it. As it is, I have taken the gamble on myself and have done it. See now, if you do not fail in your part, we shall take Babylon. In the shape I have made for myself I will desert to the fortress of the Babylonians and will tell him that it was you who did this to me. And I think that, once I have convinced them that this is so, I will get an army from them. From the day I get inside that fortress, you must count up ten days and then take some thousand men from that part of your army whose loss would be least serious for you. Station these thousand at the Gate of Semiramis. After these ten days, let an interval of a week elapse and station another two thousand, this time at the gate called the Gate of the People of Nineveh. After this week, leave another twenty days and lead out a contingent of four thousand and station them at the gate called Chaldaean. None of these three bodies of troops should have any weapons except daggers; daggers they may have. After the twentieth day, immediately order the rest of your army to attack the entire circuit of the fortress, but station the Persians at the gate called the Gate of Belus and the gate called Cissian. As I think, once I shall have done such great exploits for them, the Babylonians will entrust me with everything and, among everything, the keys to these gates. From there on, it will be up to me and the Persians to do what needs doing."

156. With these instructions, he went off to the gates of the for-

tress, turning round constantly to look back, as though he were really a deserter. The sentries who were stationed on the towers saw him and ran down and, opening one of the gates a crack, asked him who he was and what he wanted. He told them he was Zopyrus and was deserting to their side. The gatekeepers brought him in when they heard that and took him to the assembly of the Babylonians. Zopyrus stood before the assembly and pitied himself. He said that Darius had done to him what he had done to himself and that this had been his punishment for advising the King to break off the siege, since indeed there was no apparent hope of the capture of the town. "Now," he went on to say, "I have come to you, men of Babylon, as the greatest of blessings and the greatest of ills to Darius, his army, and the Persians. He shall not, I tell you, get off unpunished after doing such outrage on me. I know all the ins and outs of his plans." That was what he said.

157. The Babylonians saw the most notable man in Persia with his nose and ears cut off and streaming with blood from the effects of the whip and were entirely sure that he was speaking the truth and had come to be their ally; and so they were ready to entrust to him what he asked. What he asked for was an army. When he got that from them, he did what he had agreed with Darius to do. On the tenth day he led out his Babylonian army and encircled the thousand—those first soldiers he had told Darius to station there—and killed them all. The Babylonians thus learned that he had deeds to match his words; they were altogether delighted and were ready to serve him in everything. After the interval of the agreed number of days, Zopyrus again picked out his Babylonian troops and killed the soldiers of Darius—two thousand this time. When the Babylonians saw this, the praise of Zopyrus was in every one of their mouths. Again he let the agreed days pass and led the Babylonians to the agreed place and encircled, and killed, the soldiers of Darius—the four thousand. After that action, Zopyrus was all-in-all to the people of Babylon, and he was appointed their commander-in-chief and warden of the fortress.

158. When Darius made his assault on the fortress, all round the whole of it, Zopyrus' treachery came to light. For the Babylonians, ascending to the walls, fought off Darius' army, which was attacking them, but Zopyrus threw open the Cissian and Belian gates and let

the Persians into the fortress. Some of the Babylonians saw what was done, and these fled to the temple of Belus; others did not see it and stood, each firm in his position, until they too realized that they had been betrayed.

159. So was Babylon captured for the second time. When Darius became its master, he pulled down the walls and wrenched the gates from their hinges. Neither of these things had been done by Cyrus when he made the first capture of the town. Darius also impaled three thousand of the chief men but turned over the town to the rest of the Babylonians. Also, that the Babylonians might have women to carry on the race—as I said earlier, the Babylonians had strangled their own women in their forethought for the food supply—Darius in his forethoughtfulness ordered the surrounding peoples to provide women and to bring them to Babylon, appointing such and such a number to each people so that the sum total of women supplied came to fifty thousand. It is from these women that the present Babylonians spring.

160. No man has ever surpassed Zopyrus in the ranks of the Doers of Good Deeds for Persia. So, at least, judged Darius: neither among men of former times or afterwards—save only Cyrus himself; for with Cyrus no Persian would think of comparing himself. It is said that often Darius would say that he would rather have Zopyrus unblemished of his foul mutilation than twenty more Babylons added to the existing one. He honored him very much. Every year he gave him the gifts that the Persians think most honorable, and he gave him Babylon to rule, free of all taxes, for the term of his natural life, and much else he gave him. Megabyzus was the son of this Zopyrus, the Megabyzus who in Egypt was the general commanding against Athens and her allies; and it was yet another Zopyrus, the son of this Megabyzus, who deserted from the Persians to the Athenians.

Book Four

1. After the capture of Babylon, Darius made his invasion of Scythia. Asia was now at its flower, in numbers of people and greatness of revenues, and Darius wanted to punish the Scythians because in former times they had taken it upon themselves to invade Media; they beat those who opposed them, and they had been the aggressor in this injustice between the peoples. As I have said earlier,[1] these Scythians ruled upper Asia for twenty-eight years. They had followed the Cimmerians in pursuit and so invaded Asia and had put down the Medes from their empire. (The Medes had ruled Asia before the Scythians invaded.) But after their twenty-eight years in Asia they went home again, and, when they came to their own country after so long, they found waiting them a trouble no whit less than the war against the Medes, which they had finished: they found a great army of opposition in their own land, for the Scythian women, when their menfolk had been away such a time, had lived with their slaves.

2. Now all the slaves in Scythia are blinded by the Scythians, and this custom is because of the milk—for the Scythians are milk-drinkers. This is how they do the milking: they take a kind of bellows, with pipes made of bone (very like a flute); this they insert into the vulva of their mares and blow into the bellows-pipes by mouth; some of the people blow, while others milk the mare. They say that the blowing makes the mare's veins swell and makes her udder come down. When they have drawn the milk, the pour it into hollow containers of wood. They range their blind slaves about the buckets and get them to shake the milk. The top part of the milk they draw off and think the most valuable; that which sinks to the bottom, less so. This, then, is why they blind all their prisoners of war. The Scythians are, you see, not cultivators at all, but nomads.[2]

1. See 1.15–16 and 103.
2. This is, if a minor difficulty of interpretation as far as importance goes, one of the most insoluble. Clearly, Herodotus is making a connection between

3. A race of children then grew up from the slaves and the women. When they had learned the facts of their own breeding, they fought against the Scythians when they came back from among the Medes. First of all they cut off the country where they were by digging a broad trench, stretching from the Tauric Mountains to the Maeetian lake[3] where it is at its biggest. Then, when the Scythians tried to invade, they took up fixed positions against them and fought. The fight took place again and again, and the Scythians were unable to get the better of them in battle. At this one of the Scythians said: "What a thing we are doing, fellow countrymen! We are fighting with our own slaves. We get killed ourselves, and we are that much fewer. We kill them, and we have that many fewer subjects to rule. I think we should leave by our spears and bows. Let each one of us take up a horsewhip and go for them with that. As long as they are used to seeing us with arms, they think that they are our equals and that their fathers are likewise our equals. Let them see us with whips instead of arms, and they will learn that they are our slaves; and, once they have realized that, they will not stand their ground against us."

4. When the Scythians heard this, they carried it out. The slaves were bewildered by what happened and forgot their fighting spirit and fled. This, then, is the story of how the Scythians came to rule Asia, how they were driven out by the Medes, and how they came back again to their own land. And this is why Darius wanted to punish them and gathered an army against them.

5. The Scythians themselves say that their nation is the youngest of all the nations and that it came into existence in this way: the first man to be in this country of theirs, which then was desolate, was

---

the Scythians' total dependence on their horses for not only transport but milk ("kumiss," as it is called in Tolstoy, who applied the term to mare's milk of this very region). Their slaves do not need to work the fields, ploughing, etc. They are used for producing dairy products. (I take it that the curious stimulation of the mares' udders is to be the work of the Scythians themselves, who would need to be very far from blind for this work.) I suppose that, to keep the slaves at the dull job of incessantly "churning" the milk, it would be useful to have them deprived of sight—to hinder their moving about like ordinary mortals. This, however, is only a guess. No editor has any definitive answer to the difficulties.

3. The modern Sea of Azov.

one Targitaus by name. They say—they *do* say so, though for my part I do not believe it—that the parents of this Targitaus were Zeus and a daughter of the river Borysthenes.[4] From this breeding came Targitaus, and he had three sons—Lipoxaïs, Arpoxaïs, and the youngest, Colaxaïs. At the time that these ruled the land, there fell from heaven certain golden objects: a plough, a yoke, a sword, and a flask. They fell, that is, into the Scythian country. The first of the sons to see them was the eldest, and he drew near, intending to pick them up; but at his approach the gold caught fire. When he withdrew, the second approached, but the gold did the same for him. When the burning gold had driven away these two, the third and youngest came up, the fire was quenched when he came, and he took the gold home. So the elder brothers, in the face of these signs, were convinced and turned over the whole sovereignty to the youngest.

6. From Lipoxaïs were born those of the Scythians who are called the breed of the Auchatae; from the middle one, Arpoxaïs, those called Catiari and Traspians; and from the youngest of them, who was the king, came those called Paralatae. The name of all of them is Skoloti, so called after the king.[5] The Greeks call them Scythians.

7. This is how their nation came into being, say the Scythians; and the total of the years, they say, from their first king, Targitaus, to the crossing of Darius into Scythia was, in all, one thousand years— no more, but just so many. This sacred gold the kings guard with the utmost care, and every year they approach it with great sacrifices to propitiate it. Whoever has the sacred gold with him at the festival and falls asleep in the open air, he, say the Scythians, will not live the year out. Because of this he is given as much land as he can ride around in a day.[6] As the territory is very large, Colaxaïs established three kingships for his sons, but that in which the gold is under

4. The Dnieper.
5. Apparently "Skoloti" is some approximation of, or a pet name for, Colaxaïs.
6. Tolstoy builds a story around just such a custom among the Baskirs, who may have lived in the territory described by Herodotus; but in his story the man must *walk* to gain his land, for the space of a day. The story is called "How Much Land Does a Man Need?"

guard is far the largest. The country of those that neighbor Scythia to the northward and above them—beyond this, none can see or penetrate, they say, by reason of the showers of feathers; the earth and the air are full of feathers, and these shut off the view.[7]

8. This, then, is the account the Scythians give of their own land and that north of them. But the Greeks who live in Pontus tell the story thus: Heracles, driving the oxen of Geryon, came into this country, which now the Scythians inhabit but was then desolate. Geryon, they say, lived west of the Pontus[8] in what the Greeks call the Red Island near Gadira, outside the Pillars of Heracles, and on the shore of Ocean. They declare that Ocean flows from the east all round the world, but they cannot show that this is so in fact.[9] From there, so they say, Heracles came to what is now called Scythian country, and the winter and the frost overtook him, so that he drew his lion's skin all over himself before he went to sleep; and his mares, which were grazing under the yoke, at that time were spirited away by some divine intervention.

9. When Heracles woke up, he looked for them and, searching every part of the country, at last he came to the land called Woodland; and there he found, in a cave, a monster, half-woman, half-snake; from the haunches up she was woman and, below, snake. He saw and marveled at her and asked her whether she had anywhere seen his mares straying about. She had them herself, she said, and would not give them back to him until he had lain with her. This was her price, and on these terms Heracles lay with her. But she kept postponing the return of the mares because she wanted to stay with Heracles as long as she could, and she knew that, once he had the horses back, he would be off again. At last she did give them back and said: "These horses of yours that came here I saved for you—and you paid me a fee for saving them; for I have three sons from you. Now tell me, when they are grown up, what I should do with them. Shall I settle them here—I have the lordship of this land—or send

7. Herodotus explains the feathers in chapter 31.

8. Quite a bit west! From somewhere near southwest Russia to Spain; for the Pontus is the Black Sea, the Pillars of Heracles are the Straits of Gibraltar, and Gadira is Cadiz.

9. At 3.115 Herodotus also denies that he can find evidence for "a sea beyond Europe."

them to you?" That was what she asked, and he answered her, "When you see these boys grown to manhood, do as I shall tell you and you will make no mistake. That one of them that you see stringing this bow, thus, and girdling himself with this belt, thus, him make to be a dweller in this country. But whichever of them fails in these tasks I have set, send him out of the land. If you do this, you will be glad of it yourself, and you will carry out my commands."

10. At that Heracles drew one of his bows (for until then, they say, he always bore two) and showed her the belt and gave her the bow and the belt. The belt had at the point of its buckle a golden flask. Having given her these, away went Heracles. But she, when the boys had grown to manhood, gave them their names—Agathyrsus to the one, Gelonus to the second, Scythes to the third. And mindful of her charge, she carried out all she had been bidden. The two of the boys, Agathyrsus and Gelonus, were not able to reach the extent of their required task, and so they were expelled by their mother and went out of the country. But the youngest, Scythes, was successful and stayed where he was. And so, say the Greeks, all kings of the Scythians are descended from Scythes, the son of Heracles, and it is because of the flask on the belt that to this day Scythians carry flasks attached to their belts. This, alone, the mother of Scythes did for him. That is the story that those Greeks who live in Pontus tell of this.

11. There is another story, which is strongly urged, and it is this one to which I myself incline. It is this: the nomad Scythians living in Asia were hard pressed in war by the Massagetae and crossed the river Araxes into Cimmerian country. You see, what is now the country inhabited by the Scythians was in the old days said to be that of the Cimmerians. These Cimmerians, then, when the Scythians were invading them, debated what to do, since those who invaded them were so great a host. The opinions among them, of course, differed. Both of the chief ones were strongly held, but the better one was that of the princes. The judgment of the commonalty tended to running away, as being in their interest, rather than in standing firm and risking all for what was only dust, said they; but the judgment of the princes was that they should fight the invaders to the death for the country that was theirs. The commonalty refused to follow the princes' judgment, and the princes, similarly,

that of the commonalty. The commonalty resolved to leave the country without a fight and surrender it to those who would take it over. But the princes resolved to lie in their own land when they were dead and not join in the flight of the commons. They reflected on all the many good things they had had from their fatherland and the many ills that were to be looked for to overtake them if they fled from her. As this was their resolve, they—the princes—split into two groups and, being of about equal numbers, fought against one another. They all died at one another's hands, and the commonalty of the Cimmerians buried them by the river Tyras—you can see their graves there still—and, having so buried them, they made their march out of the country, and the Scythians came in and took over an empty land.

12. Even today in this Scythian country there are Cimmerian walls, a Cimmerian ferry, a part of the country called Cimmeria, and what is called the Cimmerian Bosporus. It is also clear that, as the Cimmerians fled before the Scythians into Asia, they founded a colony in the peninsula where now the Greeks have established the city of Sinope. It is also clear that the Scythians pursued the Cimmerians and invaded the country of the Medes and that they did the latter thing because they mistook their road. For the Cimmerians fled constantly along the seacoast, but the Scythians, in pursuit, kept the Caucasus on their right hand until they entered the land of Media, where they turned inland from their road. This, then, is the other account of the Scythians, which is told by Greeks and barbarians alike.

13. A man of Proconnesus, one Aristeas, son of Caÿstrobius, came to the Issedones and, being inspired by Apollo, wrote a poem in which he declared that above the Issedones there lived a tribe of Arimaspians, being men with one eye, and, above these, the griffins that guard the gold, and, above these, the Hyperboreans, whose land reaches to the sea. All of these peoples, beginning with the Arimaspians and excepting only the Hyperboreans, continually make war upon their neighbors. The Issedones, says Aristeas, were thrust out of their lands by the Arimaspians, the Scythians by the Issedones; and the Cimmerians, living by the southern sea, being hard pressed by the Scythians, also left their country. So this story of Aristeas also does not agree with the Scythians about this country.

14. I have told you where Aristeas came from, who said all this. But I will tell you a story about him that I heard in Proconnesus and Cyzicus. The story goes that Aristeas, who was, in family, second to none in Proconnesus, went into a fuller's shop in the town and died there. The fuller closed up his shop and went off to tell the relatives of the dead man the news. The news spread through the town that Aristeas was dead; but, to contradict it, there came a man who was a citizen of Cyzicus but had come to Proconnesus from the town of Artaca, and he said that he had met with Aristeas, who was on *his* way to Cyzicus, and that he had spoken with him. This man, then, sharply disputed the death; but the relatives of the dead man came to the fuller's shop with all the equipment appropriate to taking up the corpse. When they opened up the house, there was no Aristeas to be seen, dead or alive. In the seventh year after this he appeared in Proconnesus and wrote the poem that is now called by the Greeks the *Arimaspeia*; after having produced this poem, he vanished for the second time.

15. That is the story told in these towns. But I know something that happened to the Metapontines, in Italy, two hundred and forty years after the second disappearance of Aristeas, as I have calculated from what I know of what happened in Proconnesus and Metapontum. The Metapontines say that Aristeas appeared in their country and bade them establish an altar to Apollo and set beside it a statue of Aristeas of Proconnesus, so denominated. For Aristeas said to them that they were the only Greeks living in Italy to whose country Apollo had come and that he himself—who was now Aristeas—had followed him; but then, at the time he had followed the god, he was a crow. After he had told them this, he vanished, and the Metapontines said that they sent to Delphi to ask the god what this phantom of a man might be. The Pythia said that they should hearken to the phantom and, if they did so, it would be the better for them. So they received this oracle and did what it said. So now there stands there a statue that bears the name of Aristeas, next to the image of Apollo, and round about it are bay trees. The statue is set in the market-place. Let that be enough for me to have said about Aristeas.

16. North of this land (which this part of my *History* has started to discuss) no one knows what there is. For I could not learn from anyone who claimed to be an eyewitness. Not even Aristeas himself,

whom I have just now mentioned, said, even in those very poems, that he had gone anywhere beyond the Issedones. What he said about the parts beyond he spoke by hearsay, declaring that it was the Issedones who were his informants. I shall, however, tell everything as exactly as I can, depending on the furthest researches to which my hearsay evidence goes.

17. From the port of the Borysthenites, which is the midmost point of the coastline of Scythia, the first tribe are the Callippidae, who are Greek Scythians; beyond these there is a tribe called the Alazones. These and the Callippidae in other matters have much the same practices as the Scythians, but they sow and eat grain and onions, garlic, lentils, and millet. Beyond the Alazones live the Scythians who are tillers of the ground but who sow corn for sale and not for their personal food.[10] Beyond these live the Neuri; but north of the Neuri the whole country is uninhabited, as far as we know.

18. These are the tribes along the river Hypanis, to the west of the Borysthenes.[11] If you cross the river, Hylaea, the Woodlands, is the first country nearest the sea; as you go north of this, there dwell Scythian farmers whom the Greeks who live by the Hypanis river call Borysthenites. (These Greeks call themselves "the people of Olbiopolis.")[12] These farmer Scythians inhabit the land to the east for a distance of three days' journey as far as the river called Panticapes and, northward, a journey of eleven days by boat up the Borysthenes. North of this the land is empty of men for a long way. After this uninhabited land are the Man-Eaters, a tribe that is entirely peculiar and not Scythians at all. Beyond that is truly desert, and not a tribe of mankind lives in it, as far as we know.

19. East of these farmers, if you cross the river Panticapes, is the territory of the nomad Scythians, who neither sow nor plough. The

10. This refers to the Ukraine, which then, as for so long later, was the great source of the grain that was imported by Greece and by Europe generally. It is clear that Herodotus is far more used to the idea of people who grow grain for their bread and would market only such *surplus* as they had—i.e., a subsistence system of grain-farming. Such were the Callippidae, Alazones, etc.; but when one gets to the big open country of the Ukraine, the grain fields as the source of export and mass marketing take over.

11. The Hypanis river is the Bug; the Borysthenes is the Dnieper.

12. The Greek word here means "dwellers in the Blessed City," i.e., the big grain port of Olbia.

whole country is bare of trees except for Hylaea. These nomads occupy the country to the east for a journey of fourteen days, as far as
the river Gerrhus.

20. Across the river Gerrhus are the territories called Royal, and
here live the best, and the most, of the Scythians, who regard the
other Scythians as their slaves. The land of these people stretches to
the south as far as the Tauric country and, to the east, to the trench
that was dug by the children of the blind slaves and, on the Maeetian lake, to the trade station called Cremnoi.[13] Part of their country, too, stretches to the river Tanais.[14] Above this country of the
Royal Scythians, to the north, live the Black Cloaks, another tribe,
which is not Scythian at all. Above the Black Cloaks is marshland,
and this is desolate of men, as far as we know.

21. If you cross the Tanais, you are no longer in Scythian country, but here, in the first of the divisions, are the Sauromatians, who
begin from the corner of the Maeetian lake and have territory to the
north to the extent of fifteen days' journey, it being all bare land and
treeless in respect both of wild and cultivated trees.[15] Above these
live the Budini, in the second division, and all their land is thick
with every sort of tree.

22. Above the Budini to the north is, first of all, a desert of
seven days' journey and, after the desert, if one turns a little toward
the east, there are the Thyssagetae, a large tribe, quite peculiar to
themselves. They live by hunting. Near them, in the same stretch of
country, dwell the people called Iyrcae; these also live by hunting,
and the manner of their hunting is this: a man of this tribe climbs a
tree and lies in wait—trees are plentiful through all this land—and
has his horse trained to crouch on its belly, to lie low on the ground,
and be ready, as is also his dog. When from his lookout post in the
tree the man spots a quarry, he shoots at it with his bow and mounts
his horse and makes after it, the dog following him close behind.
Above these folk, a little to the east, live other Scythians, who revolted from the Royal Scythians and so came to this country.

23. As far as the country of these Scythians, all the land I have

13. The name Cremnoi can be translated as The Cliffs.
14. The Don.
15. Herodotus means that there are neither native forests nor cultivated
olive groves.

spoken of is flat and has deep soil, but from here on it is stony and rough. When you have passed through the rough country, there are people living in what are foothills of high mountains. These people are all bald from birth, men and women alike. They have snub noses and great beards, and they speak a language of their own; but they wear Scythian-style clothing, and their food comes from trees. The name of the tree that gives them their livelihood is "ponticum," and in greatness it is about the size of a fig tree. The fruit it bears is the size of a bean and has a stone in it. When this fruit is ripe, they strain it through cloths, and what they get is a flow of thick black liquid. The name of this juice is *aschy*.[16] This they lick up and also drink it mixed with milk, and the thickest of the lees of it they compound into cakes, and these they eat. They have few of the smaller livestock,[17] for the pastures there are poor. Each man lives under a tree, and in winter he covers the tree with a covering of white felt; but in summer he dispenses with the felt. No one does any injury to these people, for they are accounted sacred and own no weapons of war. These are men who settle disputes among their neighbors, and, if anyone who is a fugitive takes refuge with them, no one does him wrong. Their name is the Argippaei.

24. As far as these Baldies[18] there is much that is clear about the country, as also there is about those people I have mentioned before them. For some of the Scythians come as far as these, from whom it is not difficult to make inquiries; also from the Greeks of the trade port on the Borysthenes and the other ports on the Pontus. Those of the Scythians who come to these people transact their business through seven interpreters and in seven languages.

25. As far as the country of these people, then, there is something we know. But north of the Baldies, no one can say that he knows anything exactly, for high, impassable mountains bar the way, and no one has scaled them. The Baldies themselves declare— though I personally do not believe it—that these mountains are the dwelling of goat-footed men, and beyond these, they say, there are

16. The editors connect this with a Cossack drink called *atschi*. The tree is a variety of cherry.

17. The general Greek word for sheep and goats.

18. The bald people of the earlier chapter have now acquired Baldies as a national name.

people who sleep through six months of the year. This I cannot accept at all. But to the east of the Baldies there is country that is defi-
nitely inhabited by the Issedones; however, of what is to the north,
both of the Baldies and of the Issedones, there is no knowledge to be
gained except on their say-so.

26. Here are some of the customs that are said to obtain among
the Issedones. When a man's father dies, the relatives all bring sheep
and goats, and, having killed these, they chop up the flesh and cut
up too the flesh of their host's father and, mixing all together, serve
up a feast. The dead man's head they lay bare, and clean out, and
gild and afterwards use it as a sacred image, offering great yearly sacrifices in its honor. Each son does so by his father, just as the Greeks
celebrate anniversary feasts of the dead. Otherwise these people,
too, are said to observe rules of justice strictly, and among them men
and women have equal power.

27. In this case again we have actual knowledge; but from here
onward it is the Issedones who say that there are men with one eye
and griffins that guard gold. The Scythians have got these stories
from the Issedones, and we have taken them from the Scythians and
believed them and called the one-eyed people Arimaspians, as the
Scythians do. For the Scythians call "one" *arima* and an "eye" *spou*.

28. The whole of this aforementioned country is so gripped by
winter that for eight months of the year there is truly unbearable
frost such that, in those months, when you spill water, you do not
make mud, but if you light a fire you will. The sea freezes over and
also the entire Cimmerian Bosporus, and the Scythians who live this
side of the trench move in campaign over the ice and drive their
wagons across into the land of the Sindi. So it is winter all the time
during the eight months, and in the remaining four there is still cold
there. This is a winter different, in its fashion, from the winter in
any other country; for, in the natural season for rain, [winter,] there
falls none to speak of, but in summer it rains incessantly. When
there are thunderstorms in other lands, here they do not occur, but
in summer they are plenty. If there is a thunderstorm in winter in
Scythia, it is thought to be a marvel and a portent. So also an earthquake, when it happens, be it summer or winter, in Scythia is
thought to be a portent. Horses can endure this winter of theirs, but
neither mules nor asses can tolerate it at all; but in the rest of the

world, horses standing on ice get their limbs frostbitten, but mules and asses can endure it.

29. It seems to me that this is the reason why the hornless breed of cattle in Scythia fails to grow horns. On my side is the testimony of Homer, who has a verse in the *Odyssey* which says, "Libya, the land where the very lambs come to their birth with horns." This verse is correct, for in hot places horns grow quickly; but in intense cold cattle either do not grow horns at all or, if they do grow them, barely so.

30. In Scythia, then, this happens because of the cold. But I wonder all the same—for this *History* of mine has from the beginning sought out the supplementary to the main argument—that in all the country of Elis no mule can be bred, though it is not a cold land, nor is there any other manifest cause why this should be so. The Eleans themselves say that it is some curse that lies on them that no mules may be bred among them; but when the time for their mares to come in season approaches, they drive them into the neighboring territory and, in that neighboring territory, put the jackasses on the mares until such time as they conceive. After that, they drive them home again.

31. Now concerning the feathers of which the Scythians say the air in the country beyond them is full and that that is why they are unable to get through it or even see it: here is what I think about that. North of that Scythian country the snow is continuous, though less in summer than in winter, as is natural. Anyone who has seen heavy snow falling from near at hand knows what I mean about my judgment of the "feathers." For the snow *is* like feathers; and it is because of the winter, which is such as this, that the northern parts of this continent are uninhabited. I think that the Scythians and their neighbors speak of the snow as feathers in a kind of image. That is, then, what I have to say about the most distant parts.

32. Considering the Hyperboreans, then, the Scythians have nothing to tell, nor do any of the other peoples who live in those parts, except, perhaps, for the Issedones. In my opinion, even these have nothing to tell; for, if they had, the Scythians would have told it, too, as they did in the case of the one-eyed people. But Hesiod *does* talk about the Hyperboreans, and so does Homer in the *Epigoni*—if, indeed, that poem is truly by Homer.

33. But far the most that is told about these people comes from the Delians. These say that holy offerings come wrapped in wheat straw from the Hyperboreans into Scythia, and, after the Scythians, each of their neighbors successively forwards these offerings to the point furthest west, at the Adriatic, and, as they are then conveyed to the south, the people of Dodona are the first Greeks to receive them, and from there they come down to the Melian Gulf and are carried across into Euboea and, again from city to city, as far as Carystus; after that, Andros is omitted from the chain, because the people of Carystus carry them to Tenos, and the Tenians carry them to Delos. That is how, they say, the offerings get to Delos. They say too that on the first journey the Hyperboreans sent, to bring the offerings, two girls, whom the Delians call Hyperoche and Laodice. With these, for safety's sake, the Hyperboreans sent along with them five men as escort, citizens of their own, those who are now called Peripherees and have great honor in Delos. But when those whom the Hyperboreans had sent out did not come home again, the Hyperboreans made a great outcry that it should always be their lot to send out men who never came back; and so they have the offerings borne, wrapped in wheaten straw, to their borders and bid their neighbors convey them from their own land to the next. And so, they say, by this form of constant escort the offerings come to Delos. I myself know of something like this done with offerings; for the Thracian and Paeonian women, when they sacrifice to Queen Artemis, have their offerings packed in wheat straw.

34. This, too, I know that they do: girls and boys at Delos cut their hair in honor of the Hyperborean girls who died at Delos. The girls before marriage cut off a tress of their hair and, winding it about a spindle, lay it on the tomb. The tomb is on the left-hand side as you go into the temple of Artemis, and an olive tree grows over it. The Delian boys, too, twine some of their locks of hair around a green stalk, and they likewise put this on the tomb.

35. These, then, have this honor from the inhabitants of Delos. But these same inhabitants of Delos say that Arge and Opis, being maids, came to Delos from the Hyperboreans and traveled through the same peoples on the way, and that this was before Hyperoche and Laodice. The two latter, indeed, came bringing the tribute that they were assessed to pay, for ease of childbirth, to Eileithyia; but

Arge and Opis, say the Delians, came with the gods themselves,[19] and other honors were granted them by the people of Delos. The Delian women, they say, collected gifts for them, giving them names in the hymn that Olen, a Lycian, made for them. It was from Delos that the islanders and Ionians learned to sing in honor of Opis and Arge, calling them by these names and collecting gifts for them. (This Olen made other of the old hymns that are sung in Delos, when he came there out of Lycia.) It is said, too, that when the thigh bones are burnt on the altar, the ashes are used up by casting them on the grave of Opis and Arge. This grave of the two girls is behind the temple of Artemis, to the east, and nearest to the refectory of the Ceans.

36. That is now enough said about the Hyperboreans; for I will not tell that tale of the man called Abaris the Hyperborean—that he carried an arrow round the whole earth without eating anything at all. But if there are Hyperboreans, then there are others, Hypernotians.[20] I am amused to see those many who have drawn maps of the world and not a one of them making a reasonable appearance of it. They draw Ocean flowing round an earth that is as circular as though traced by compasses, and they make Asia of the same size as Europe. In some few words I will myself make plain the greatness of each of these divisions and what shape each should have for the map.

37. Where the Persians live stretches all the way to the southern sea, called the Red Sea; above them to the north are the Medes, and above the Medes the Saspires, and above the Saspires the Colchians, who reach to the northern sea,[21] into which the river Phasis issues. These are the four nations that live between one sea and the other.

38. From the region bounded by these two seas, westward there stretch out two peninsulas (which I will now describe) to the sea.[22]

19. Apollo and Artemis, twin children of Leto, were born on the island of Delos, which was sacred to Apollo and one of the most important centers of his worship. Eileithyia is the goddess of childbirth.

20. Hyperboreans means "people living beyond the north wind," and Hypernotians, "people beyond the south wind."

21. Here the southern (Red) sea is the Indian Ocean, and the northern one is the Black Sea.

22. The Mediterranean.

On the north side, one of these peninsulas, starting from the Phasis, stretches seaward along the Pontus and the Hellespont as far as Sigeum in the Troad. To the south, this same peninsula stretches along the seacoast from the Myriandic Gulf in Phoenicia as far as the Triopian Cape.[23] In this peninsula there are thirty nations.

39. This, then, is the one of the two peninsulas. The other stretches from the territory of the Persians to the Red Sea; this comprises Persian land and, after that, Assyria and, after that, Arabia. This ends, though ends only by a kind of convention, at the Gulf of Arabia,[24] into which Darius drew the channel from the Nile. From Persian territory, as far as Phoenicia, there is a great flat expanse of land. But from Phoenicia this peninsula runs beside *our* sea, by Palestinian Syria and Egypt, in which it ends. There are, in this peninsula, only three nations.

40. That is what there is to say of the parts of Asia west of Persia. As to what is beyond Persia, Media, the Saspires, and the Colchians: to the east, the Red Sea is the boundary, and, to the north, the Caspian and the river Araxes, which flows eastward. Asia is inhabited as far as India. After that, it is, to the east, desert, and no one can say what kind of land is there.

41. Such and so great is Asia; but Libya is in this second peninsula, for after Egypt comes Libya. Where the peninsula joins Egypt, it is narrow, for from *our* sea to the Red Sea is a distance of 100,000 fathoms—that is, 1,000 furlongs. But after this narrow bit the peninsula called Libya is very broad.

42. I am surprised, then, at those who have drawn the boundaries and made the divisions of Libya, Asia, and Europe. For the differences between them are great. In length Europe stretches parallel to *both* of them,[25] and in breadth it seems to me incomparably broader. For Libya is clearly surrounded by the sea except for its boundary with Asia; it was King Necos of Egypt who, first of the

23. According to How and Wells, the Triopian Cape is the southwest corner of Asia Minor, near the island of Cnidus.

24. *Our* Red Sea. The peninsula ends only "conventionally" because Libya (Africa) is really a continuation of it.

25. As How and Wells point out, Herodotus is regarding all of northern Asia as part of Europe. ("Length" here is lateral, running from west to east, and "breadth" is vertical—the opposite of our map conventions.)

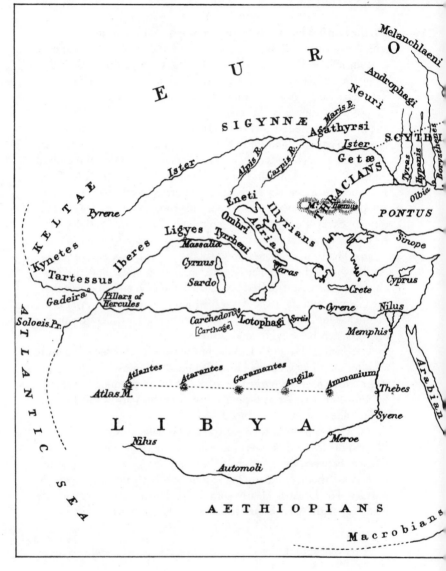

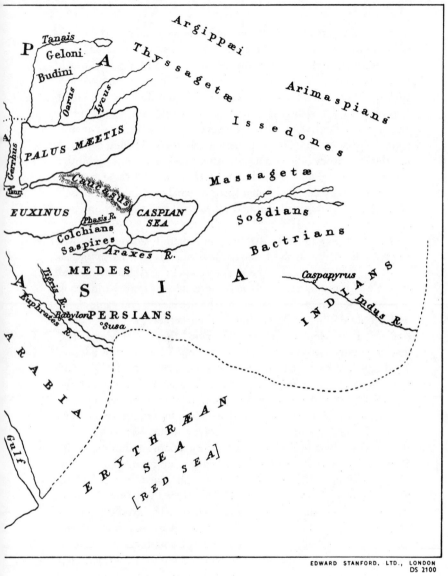

men we know, proved this. When he had stopped digging the channel from the Nile into the Arabian Gulf, he sent off Phoenicians in
merchantmen, bidding them, on their return journey, sail through
the Pillars of Heracles till they came to the northern sea and so come
back to Egypt. The Phoenicians set out from the Red Sea and sailed
the southern sea. When it came to be autumn, they would put in
and sow the land wherever they happened to be in Libya in the
course of their sailing and wait the harvest there. Having gathered
in their crop, they sailed on again. After two years of sailing, in the
third year they rounded the Pillars of Heracles and came back to
Egypt. And they declared (what some may believe, though I myself
do not) that as they sailed round Libya they had the sun on their
right.[26]

43. That was how, at the first, information about Libya was
gained. After this it is the Carthaginians who say that Libya has sea
all around it. For Sataspes, the son of Teaspes the Achaemenid, did
not sail right around Libya, though expressly sent to do so; he took
fear at the length of the voyage and the desolation and came back,
and did not discharge the task his mother had set upon him. For he
had raped the virgin daughter of Zopyrus, the son of Megabyzus,
and, being then about to be impaled by King Xerxes for this offense,
was begged off by his mother, who was the sister of Darius; she said
that she would impose upon him a penalty greater than the one the
King had set; for she would force him to sail around Libya until, in
his voyage round, he should come back again into the Arabian Gulf.
When Xerxes agreed to spare him on these terms, Sataspes went to
Egypt, took a boat and a crew from the Egyptians, and sailed to the
Pillars of Heracles. He sailed through them and rounded the promontory of Libya that is called Solois, and sailed south. Having
crossed so much sea in so many months—since there was ever more
still to cross—he turned right round and came back to Egypt. From
Egypt he came to the presence of King Xerxes and said that, having
sailed to the farthest he could, he sailed by a country of dwarfs, who
wore raiment made of palm leaves; and as often as the voyagers put

26. This is one of the very striking pieces of information left us by Herodotus. There is now little doubt that these Phoenicians, sent by Necos, circum-
navigated Africa, rounding the Cape of Good Hope. See, further, the end note
to this passage.

in there, these dwarfs fled to the hills, leaving their cities. The Persians claimed that they never did any harm to these people but took from them only what they needed for food. As to his failure to sail around Libya completely, said Sataspes, this was the reason: his boat would sail forward no more but was stayed where it was. But Xerxes, being sure that he was not speaking the truth, and because he had not discharged the task assigned him, impaled him on the old charge he had preferred against him. A eunuch of this Sataspes ran away to Samos as soon as he learned of his master's death; this man had great possessions, which a certain Samian acquired; I know his name, but of my own will have forgotten it.

44. Most of Asia was discovered by Darius, who wished to know at what point the Indus River enters the sea. (This river is the second river in the world for the number of its crocodiles.) Darius sent boats with crews whom he trusted to tell him the truth, and among these men was Scylax of Caryanda. These set out from Caspatyrus and the Pactyic country and sailed down the river eastward to the sea and, through the sea, west; and in the thirtieth month they arrived at the place from which the king of Egypt had sent out the Phoenicians (of whom I spoke before) to sail around Libya. After these *had* sailed round, Darius subdued the Indians and made use of this sea. So it was found out that Asia, except for the parts of it to the east, is in other respects like Libya.

45. Of Europe—whether *it* is surrounded by water on the east or the north—there is no knowledge clearly possessed by anyone at all. But its length—that it stretches the full length of the other two [Asia and Libya] *is* known. I cannot guess why, since the earth is all one, there should be three names set on it, all indicating descent from women, or why, for boundaries, the Egyptian Nile is given as one and the Colchian river Phasis as another—though there are those who speak for the Maeetian river Tanaïs and the Cimmerian Ferries. Nor can I find out the names of those who established these boundaries or whence they got these names of descent. For instance, Libya is said by many Greeks to have that name from Libya, a woman native to the land, and Asia has *its* name by attribution to Prometheus' wife. (Yet the Lydians claim a share in the name Asia too, in that they say Asia was so called from Asies, the son of Cotys, the son of Manes, from whom the tribe of Asiads in Sardis is called;

and so, according to them, the name is not from Prometheus' wife at all.) But about Europe, no one knows whether it is surrounded by water, nor is it known whence came its name or who it was that put the name on it, unless we say that the country got its name from Tyrian Europa, being till then without a name, like the other countries. But this woman was clearly from Asia and did *not* come to this land that is now called by the Greeks Europe, but only from Phoenicia to Crete and, from Crete, to Lycia. What I have said so far should be enough. We will, of course, use the customary names for these lands.

46. The Euxine Pontus, against which Darius made his campaign, contains—except for the Scythians—the stupidest nations in the world. For within this country of Pontus we cannot put forward any nation for its cleverness, nor do we know from there of any learned man; the exceptions are, among nations, the Scythians, and, of men, Anacharsis.[27] For the Scythian nation has made the most clever discovery among all the people we know, and of the one thing that is greatest in human affairs—though for the rest I do not admire them much. This greatest thing that they have discovered is how no invader who comes against them can ever escape and how none can catch them if they do not wish to be caught. For this people has no cities or settled forts; they carry their houses with them and shoot with bows from horseback; they live off herds of cattle, not from tillage, and their dwellings are on their wagons. How then can they fail to be invincible and inaccessible for others?

47. They have made this discovery in a country that is very suitable for it, and their rivers are also their allies; for the land is level, grows clover, and is well watered, and the rivers that flow through it are in number not much less than the canals in Egypt. Those of them that are famous and are navigable from the sea I will name. There is the Ister, with its five mouths, and after that the Tyras, and Hypanis, and Borysthenes, and Panticapes, and Hypacyris, and Gerrhus, and Tanaïs.[28] These flow in the directions I will show.

48. The Ister, which is the largest of any river we know of, flows with always the same volume, summer or winter. It is the furthest to

27. For Anacharsis, see chapter 76 of this book.
28. Ister = Danube; Hypanis = Bug; Borysthenes = Dnieper; Tanaïs = Don.

the west of any of the Scythian rivers, and the reason for its greatness is this. Many are the rivers that flow into it, and, among them, those that make it great are the five that flow through Scythian country: the river called by the Scythians Porata and by the Greeks Pyretus, the Tiarantus, the Ararus, the Naparis, and the Ordessus. The first one I have mentioned is a great stream and flows eastward and shares its waters with the Ister; the second, the Tiarantus, is more to the west and is lesser in volume; and then the Ararus and the Naparis and Ordessus, all of which flow between the other two and pour their water into the Ister.

49. These are the true-born Scythian rivers that increase the waters of the Ister, and from the Agathyrsi the Maris flows to join it; and three other great rivers that pour into it, the Atlas, Auras, and Tibisis, flow northward from the heights of Haemus. Through Thrace and the Thracian Crobyzi flow the Athrys and Noes and Artanes and empty into the Ister. From the Paeonians and Mount Rhodope the river Cius cuts through the middle of Haemus and empties into the Ister. From Illyria there flows to the north the river Angrus, which empties into the Triballic plain and then into the river Brongus, and then the Brongus into the Ister; so both these rivers, in themselves great, are received by the Ister. And from the land north of the Ombrici the Carpis and another river, called Alpis, flow north and issue into the Ister. Indeed, the Ister flows clean through all Europe, beginning from the Celts, who, except for the Cynetes, live furthest to the west of those in Europe; and flowing thus through all Europe it issues forth along the borders of Scythia.

50. Because these and many others contribute their waters to it, the Ister is the greatest of rivers. Stream for stream, the Nile surpasses it in volume, for into it no stream nor spring enters to swell its bulk. The reason, in my opinion, why the Ister has its water the same, winter and summer, is this: in winter it has its natural size or very little more, for the land there in winter has little rain but snow everywhere. In summer the snow, which fell in abundance in winter, melts everywhere and enters the Ister. This snow, as it enters the stream, increases the volume of water, and there are, besides, many violent showers; for in summer it rains a great deal. Now the sun draws to itself more water in the summertime—more, that is, than it does in the winter—but so do the mingled waters of the Ister grow

many times more in summer than in winter; as these are matched against one another, there is a balance, so that the water always appears the same.

51. This, then, is one of the rivers of the Scythians—the Ister. And then there is the Tyras,[29] which comes from the north and flows first from the great lake that is the border between the Scythian and Neurian countries. At the mouth of it live those Greeks who are called Tyritae.[30]

52. The third is the river Hypanis, which rises in Scythian country and flows from a great lake round which wild white horses graze. The lake is called—rightly so—the mother of the Hypanis. Rising from here, then, the Hypanis flows shallow and sweet for five days' journey, but from there on to the sea, a matter of four days' voyage, it is terribly briny; for there issues into it a salt spring so exceedingly briny that, though it is small in volume, it renders brackish the river Hypanis, which is as big as few rivers are. This spring is on the border between the land of the farmer Scyths and the Alazones. The name of the spring and the country from which it comes is called in Scythian language Exampaeus and, in the Greek tongue, the Sacred Roads. The Tyras and the Hypanis draw close together in the territory of the Alazones, but from there on each turns aside from the other and broadens the space in between.

53. The fourth river is the Borysthenes, which is the biggest after the Ister and, in my judgment, the most productive, not only of Scythian rivers but of all others except for the Egyptian Nile. One cannot compare any other river to the Nile; but, of the rest, the Borysthenes is the most productive, inasmuch as it affords the fairest and most nourishing pastures for cattle, and the fish are the very finest and most plentiful, and its waters are the pleasantest to drink, being clear where others are muddy, and along its banks are excellent ploughland and deep clover where the land is not sown for grain. There are great crusts of salt that form of themselves at the mouth of it, in great amounts, and there are huge spineless fish, called sturgeons, which may be pickled, and many other marvelous

29. Apparently the Dniester.
30. Few of these rivers can be identified certainly. The territory to which Herodotus refers as the locale of these rivers is mostly in the Balkans.

things besides. It flows from the north, and we know it as far as the country of the Gherri, a matter of forty days' voyage upstream. Beyond that no one can say through whose territory it flows. But it seems to flow through the uninhabited country to the land of the farmer Scyths. For these Scyths work the land along its banks for a distance of ten days' voyage. Only of this river and the Nile can I not tell the springs, where they rise; I think no other Greek can, either. Near the sea, the Borysthenes and the Hypanis mingle, flowing into the same marsh. The country between the two rivers, which projects like a ship's beak, is called the Cape of Hippolaus, and there is built there a temple of Demeter. Beyond the temple, on the river Hypanis, is the settlement of the Borysthenites.

54. This, then, is what we know, as far as these rivers can tell us. After the four we have mentioned there is a fifth river, the name of which is Panticapes. It also flows from the north and from a lake, and the land between it and the Borysthenes is the country of the farmer Scyths; and it issues into the Hylaea—the Woodland—and, once it has passed this, it joins with the Borysthenes.

55. The sixth is the river Hypacyris, which comes from a lake and, flowing through the middle of the country of the nomad Scyths, issues out near the city of Carcinitis, skirting, on the right, the Hylaea and what is called the Racecourse of Achilles.

56. The seventh is the river Gerrhus, which is divided from the Borysthenes at about that part of the country that is the limit of what is known of the Borysthenes. At this place it divides off, and it has the name of the place itself, Gerrhus; and, as it flows into the sea, it is the border between the land of the nomads and the Royal Scythians and issues into the Hypacyris.

57. The eighth is the river Tanaïs, which in its upper course comes from a great lake and issues into an even greater called the Maeetian; the lake is the border between the Royal Scythians and the Sauromatae. And into this river, Tanaïs, there issues another river, the name of which is the Hyrgis.

58. With these famous rivers the Scythians are provided. But for cattle, the clover which grows in Scythia produces more bile than any other clover we know of. It is possible to make this judgment by opening up the cattle after death.

59. These are the biggest things that are freely at their disposal.

What remains for me to do is to describe the customs among these Scythians. Here are the only gods they worship: Hestia, in especial, and then Zeus and Earth. Earth they regard as Zeus's wife. After these, they worship Apollo, the Heavenly Aphrodite, Heracles, and Ares. All of the Scythians have belief in these as gods, but those who are called the Royal Scythians sacrifice also to Poseidon. In the Scythian language, Hestia is called Tabiti, Zeus is called (in my judgment very rightly) Papaeus,[31] Earth is called Api, Apollo Goetosyrus, Heavenly Aphrodite Argimpasa, Poseidon Thagimasadas. Images, altars, and shrines they do not make customarily, except to Ares. In his case only, they do so.

60. In all their sacred rites they all conduct the sacrifice in the same way. The victim stands there, his front feet entangled in a rope. The sacrificer stands behind the animal and pulls the end of the rope to bring him to the ground. While the victim is falling, the worshiper invokes whatever god may be involved in his sacrifice. He then throws a noose about the animal's neck, inserts a small stick to tighten the rope, twists it round, and so throttles the victim. He lights no fire, nor offers firstfruits, nor pours libations. When he has choked the animal and flayed it, he turns to cook it.

61. Since the land of Scythia is terribly starved of wood, the people have invented this means of cooking meat: having flayed the victim, they lay bare the meat from the bones and then throw it into cauldrons of their country (if they have them), which are most like to Lesbian cauldrons, save that they are much larger. When they put the meat into these, they set fire to the bones under the cauldron and cook the meat. If they have no cauldron, they put all the meat into the stomachs of the victim, after mixing water with the meat, and again they make a fire beneath, of the bones. The bones blaze right merrily, and the stomachs contain easily the meat, once it is laid bare of the bones; and so the ox cooks itself, and all the other victims do likewise, each cooking itself. When the meat is cooked, the sacrificer takes the firstfruits of meat and entrails and casts them in front of him. They use animals of the flocks, like sheep and goats, for sacrifice, but especially horses.

62. That is how they sacrifice to the other gods, and such are the

31. Great Father.

beasts sacrificed. But to Ares they do it thus: in each of the districts of the governmental divisions there is a shrine established to Ares. Bundles of faggots are heaped up for three furlongs in width and length but less in height. On this is built a square, quite level, with three of its sides sheer and one that can be ascended. Each year they pile one hundred and fifty wagons' worth of firewood upon this, for each year some of it gradually wastes away, from the winter seasons. On this pile is set an ancient iron sword for each of the peoples sacrificing, and this is the image of Ares. To this sword they bring yearly sacrifices of smaller cattle and of horses; indeed, they offer to these images more victims than to the other gods. Of such of their enemies as they take alive they sacrifice one out of every hundred, not in the fashion in which they handle the beasts, but differently. They pour wine on the men's heads and cut their throats into a bucket. This they then carry up on to the pile of firewood and pour the blood on the sword. The carrying-aloft is the work of some of the sacrificers, while others, below, cut off the right arms of all the slaughtered men and, hands and all, throw them into the air.[32] Afterwards they finish the sacrifice of the rest of the victims and then go away. The arm lies where it has fallen, and the rest of the dead body apart from it.

63. These are their sacrifices. They make no offerings of pigs, nor will they keep them at all in their country.

64. As concerns war, this is how it is among them. When a Scythian kills his first man, he drinks his blood; of all those he kills in battle he carries the heads to the king. When he has brought in a head, he takes a share of whatever loot they have obtained, but without bringing a head he has none. The warrior scalps the head thus: he cuts it in a circle round the ears and, taking the head in his hands, shakes it loose. Then he cleans out the flesh with the rib of an ox and kneads the skin with his hands. When he has softened it all, he has got himself, as it were, a napkin. He hangs the napkin from the bridle of the horse he rides himself and takes great pride in it. The man who has most skins as napkins is judged the greatest man among these people. Many of them also make garments, to

32. "The victim is robbed of his right arm to render his spirit after death helpless" (How and Wells).

wear, out of the scalps, stitching them together like the usual coats of skin. Many Scythians also take the right hands of their enemies, when dead, and stripping the skin off, nails and all, make of them coverings for their arrow quivers. The skin of man, it would seem, is thick and bright—indeed, in point of whiteness, the brightest of all skins. Many of them, too, flay whole men and, stretching the skins upon a frame, carry them round on their horses.

65. Such are the customs among them. But for the heads themselves—though not of all, but of a man's deadliest enemies—each man saws off all the part beneath the eyebrows and cleans the rest. Then, if the man who does this is poor, he simply stretches a strip of raw oxhide over the outside and so uses it. But if he is rich, he gilds it on the inside and uses it in this form for a drinking cup. They do this, too, in the case of kinsmen with whom they have had differences and whom they have finally conquered in combat in the king's presence. And when strangers of consequence come to visit, their host brings round these heads and tells, over each one, how they were his kinsfolk but waged war upon him, and how he himself conquered them; and they speak of this as the act of a hero.

66. Once a year the governor, each in his own district, brews a bowl of wine from which the Scythians drink who have killed their enemies. If they have killed none such, they may not drink of the wine but sit aside, dishonored. This is indeed the greatest disgrace among them. Those of them who have killed many men, each have two cups and drink of them both.

67. There are many soothsayers among the Scythians who prophesy by means of many willow rods. This is how they do it. They bring in great bundles of these rods and lay them on the ground and unfasten them. Over each rod as they set it on the ground they make their prophecy. But as they make the prophecy, they are picking up the rods, making them again into one bundle. This is their ancestral form of prophecy. But the Enarees, who are androgynes, say that their prophesying is given them by Aphrodite. They practice divination with the bark of the lime tree. When they split the bark in three, the prophet makes his prophecy, braiding and unbraiding the bark with his fingers.

68. When the king of Scythia falls sick, he sends for the three most reputed prophets, who prophesy in the form I have told you.

As a rule, they say something like this: "Someone, so-and-so, has sworn by the Royal Hearth and perjured himself." They mention the name of some citizen, whoever he may be. (It is the custom of the Scythians to swear by the Royal Hearth when they wish to take their greatest oaths.) The man whom they describe as having forsworn himself is then seized and brought in. The prophets accuse the man brought in, alleging that he has manifestly—their prophetic gift has so manifested it—sworn falsely by the Royal Hearth and therefore the king is sick. He denies it—denies that he has perjured himself— and makes a great to-do. On his denial, the king sends for twice as many prophets. If these, on looking into their prophetic art, confirm the man's perjury, his head is at once stricken off, and the first party of prophets divides his goods among them. But if the new prophets acquit him, yet other prophets are sent for and again others. If the majority acquit the man, it is decided that the first prophets themselves shall be killed.

69. They then kill them in this way: they fill a wagon with firewood and yoke oxen to it. They tie the prophets' feet and their hands behind them and gag them. They then shut them into the middle of the firewood, set fire to it, and, terrifying the oxen, drive them off. Many of the oxen are burned up with the prophets, and many escape, only singed, when the pole of the wagon is burnt through. In this way they burn prophets on other charges, too, calling them "liar prophets." When the king kills someone, he does not leave his children alive but kills all the males; the females, however, he does not injure.

70. This is how the Scythians make sworn agreements with whomsoever they make them: into a big earthenware bowl they pour wine and with it mingle the blood of the contracting parties. They extract the blood by striking the body with an awl or making a small cut in it with a knife. Then they dip into the bowl a sword, arrows, an axe, and a javelin. Having done that, they pray a great deal and thereafter drink off the bowl, both those who contract on both sides and the most important of their followers.

71. The burial places of their kings are in the country of the Gerrhi, the place up to which the Borysthenes is navigable. At this place, when their king dies, they dig a great four-cornered pit, and, having made it ready, they take up the dead man—having coated

his body with wax and cut open his belly and cleaned it and filled it with chopped marsh plants and incense and parsley seed and anise, and sewn it together again—and put him on a wagon, in which they carry him to another nation. These in their turn receive the corpse when it is brought them and do what the Royal Scythians do: they cut off a piece of ear, shave their hair, cut their forearms, tear forehead and nose, and drive arrows through their left hand. Then they convey the corpse of the king on the wagon to another nation of those they rule. Those to whom they have already come follow along. When they have conveyed the corpse around to all the subject nations, they are in the country of the Gerrhi, who live furthest of all whom they rule, and at the place of burial. Afterwards, when they put the dead man in his grave on a bed, they fix spears on either side of the corpse and stretch above them planks of wood and roof these in with plaited rushes; and in the open space that is left in the burial place they bury one of his concubines, after strangling her, and his wine-bearer, cook, groom, valet, and message-bearer. Also his horses, and the firstfruits of everything else, and his golden cups (the Scythians use neither silver nor bronze). Having done this, they rear a huge barrow of earth, showing the greatest zeal and rivalry with one another to make it as big as possible.

72. When the year has come round in its course, they do something else. Of the king's remaining servants they take those most suitable for their purposes (and these are native-born Scythians, for the servants of the king are those he bids to serve him; he has no purchased slaves), and they strangle fifty of them and fifty of his most beautiful horses; and they remove their bellies, and clean them out, and fill them with chaff, and stitch them up. Then the half of a wheel is fixed, upside down, on two pieces of wood, and the other half of the wheel on two other posts, and they fix many more in this fashion. They then drive long stakes lengthwise through the horses' bodies, up to the necks, and mount the horses upon the half-wheels. The half-wheels in front support the horses' shoulders; those behind, the belly, by the hindquarters. The legs on both sides hang loose. They put bits and reins in the horses' mouths and stretch these to the front and fasten them from pegs. Each one of the fifty young men who were strangled they mount on a horse. They contrive the mounting of the horsemen by driving an upright stake along the

spine, up to the neck; but a part of the stake projects below, so that they can fit it into a hole they make in the stake that goes through the horse lengthwise. They set these, horses and riders, in a circle around the tomb, and, having done so, they ride off themselves.

73. That is how they bury their kings. But as to the rest of the Scythians, when they die, their nearest relatives carry them around among their friends on wagons. Each friend receives and entertains those who follow the procession and offers a share of all the food to the dead man, the same as to everyone else. For forty days all these people who are not kings are carried round in this way, and then they are buried. When they have buried the dead, the relatives purify themselves as follows: they anoint and wash their heads; as to their bodies, they set up three sticks, leaning them against one another, and stretch, over these, woollen mats; and, having barricaded off this place as best they can, they make a pit in the center of the sticks and the mats and into it throw red-hot stones.

74. Now, they have hemp growing in that country that is very like flax, except that it is thicker and taller.[33] This plant grows both wild and under cultivation, and from it the Thracians make garments very like linen. Unless someone is very expert, he could not tell the garment made of linen from the hempen one. Someone who has never yet seen hemp would certainly judge the garment to be linen.

75. The Scythians take the seed of this hemp and, creeping under the mats,[34] throw the seed onto the stones as they glow with heat. The seed so cast on the stone gives off smoke and a vapor; no Greek steam bath could be stronger. The Scythians in their delight at the steam bath howl loudly. This indeed serves them instead of a bath, as they never let water near their bodies at all. But their women pound to bits cypress and cedar and frankincense wood on a rough rock and mix water with it. When they have made of the wood and the water a thick paste, they smear it all over their bodies and faces. A wonderful scent pervades them from this; a day later they take off the plaster, and they have become shining clean.

33. The Greek word I have translated is *kannabis*. It is apparently identical with the modern plant so called.

34. Herodotus is referring back to chapter 73 and the tent-like structure enclosed with mats and having the red-hot stones in a pit in the center.

76. These people dreadfully avoid the use of foreign customs, and especially those of the Greeks, as the case first of Anacharsis and, later, that of Scyles prove. First of all, Anacharsis. He traveled over much of the world, sight-seeing, and showed that he had gained great wisdom in the course of his travels; and then he came back to Scythia. On his homeward journey he put in at Cyzicus after sailing through the Hellespont. He found there the people of Cyzicus celebrating a festival to the Mother of the Gods,[35] with great pomp. And so Anacharsis prayed to the Mother that, if he came back to his own land safe and sound, he would sacrifice as he saw the Cyzicenes doing and would establish an all-night festival there. When he came back to Scythia, he stole away to the district called Hylaea (this is near the Racecourse of Achilles, and the whole district is heavily wooded). Slipping into this place secretly, Anacharsis celebrated the whole festival to the Goddess, carrying the drum and wearing the images tied to himself. One of the Scythians noticed him doing all this and informed the king, Saulius, who came and, when he himself saw Anacharsis at his celebrating, shot him dead with his bow. Now when anyone mentions Anacharsis, the Scythians say they do not know any such person—and that is because he went traveling to Greece and adopted foreign customs. As I heard from Tymnes, the deputy for Ariapithes, Anacharsis was uncle of Idanthyrsus, king of Scythia, and the son of Gnurus, son of Lycus, son of Spargapithes. So if Anacharsis was of this descent, he should know that he was killed by his own brother! For Idanthyrsus was the son of Saulius, and it was Saulius who killed Anacharsis.

77. Indeed, I *have* heard another story, which is told by the Peloponnesians. According to this, Anacharsis was sent by the Scythian king to become a student of Greece, and, when he came back, he told him who sent him that all Greeks were overrestless for any kind of learning, save only the Lacedaemonians. With them alone it was possible sensibly to urge arguments and listen to them in turn. This must be a silly story fabricated by the Greeks themselves; in any case, the man was killed, as I have said before.

78. That is how Anacharsis fared as a result of his foreign customs and his association with the Greeks. And, a great many years

35. Cybele.

after, it was much the same with Scyles, son of Ariapithes. Ariapithes, the king of Scythia, had among other sons, Scyles. But he
was born of a woman of Istria, not a native-born Scythian at all. His
mother taught him Greek speech and letters. Later, Ariapithes died
through the treachery of Spargapithes, king of the Agathyrsi, and
Scyles took over the throne of the Scythians and also his father's
wife, whose name was Opoea. This Opoea was a native Scythian,
and Ariapithes had had by her a son, Oricus. Though Scyles became
king of Scythia, he was not pleased with the Scythian manner of life
but was far more given to Greek ways, from the training he had had.
So this is what he did: as often as he led the army of the Scythians to
the city of the Borysthenites—these Borysthenites declare that they
are Milesians—he would leave his army in the suburbs but himself
go within the walls and shut up the gates. Then he would take off his
Scythian clothes and take on Greek clothes and in that shape would
go and walk about the marketplace, with no bodyguards or indeed
anyone else. They guarded the gates that no Scythian might see him
wearing Greek dress. He followed a Greek way of life, and, in especial, he made offerings to the gods in the Greek fashion. When he
had spent a month or more like this, he would put on his Scythian
clothes and go back. He did this very often, and built himself a
house in Borysthenes, and married a wife from these parts and
brought her to the house.

79. Now he was destined to end ill, and this ill overtook him in
the following instance.[36] He was eager to be initiated in the rites of
the Bacchic Dionysus, and when he had this project in hand, a very
great portent occurred, for all to see. He had (as I said a little time
ago) this great rich house in the city of the Borysthenites, and all
about it stood sphinxes and griffins made of white stone. Upon this
the god hurled his thunderbolt. Though it burned down entirely,
Scyles nonetheless completed his initiation. Now the Scythians

36. This is a sentence that occurs several times in Herodotus. By it he means
to distinguish a deeply underlying impersonal sequence of cause and effect (a
chain of matching events and consequences reaching into the distant past and
involving a balance of evil and evil) from the events that precipitate the final
destruction of the individual person. The Greek word *prophasis* sometimes, but
certainly not always, means "excuse." It does not mean that here but may fairly
be rendered by something as neutral as "this instance."

taunt the Greeks about the Bacchic rites; they say that the Greeks, against all reason, discover a god who sets men on to madness. So when Scyles was initiated into the Bacchic mystery, one of the Borysthenites made a joke of the matter to the Scythians: "You are always laughing at us, Scythians, because we worship Bacchus and the god takes possession of us. Now it is your own king that the god has seized upon, and he is mad under his inspiration. If you doubt me, come, and I will show him to you." The leading men among the Scythians did indeed come; the Borysthenite man, who had so talked, brought them there secretly and stowed them in a tower to watch. When Scyles appeared with his band of devotees and the Scythians saw him in Bacchic frenzy, they were furious at it and went and told the whole army what they had seen.

80. When, after that, Scyles went back to his own country, the Scythians rebelled against him and set up in his stead his brother, Octamasades, who was the son of the daughter of Teres. Scyles, perceiving what was growing against him and from what it derived, took refuge in Thrace. Octamasades, when he learned of this, led an expedition into Thrace. When he came to the Ister, the Thracians met him there. As they were about to join battle, Sitalces [37] sent to Octamasades and said: "Why should we make trial of one another? You are my sister's son. You have my brother with you. You give him back to me, and I will give you Scyles. But neither I nor you need bring danger on our armies." This was the message that Sitalces sent by his heralds. (There *was* under the protection of Octamasades a brother of Sitalces who had fled from Sitalces to him.) Octamasades agreed to the terms and gave up his own uncle to Sitalces and took back his brother, Scyles. Sitalces, when he got *his* brother, took him away; but Octamasades beheaded Scyles on the spot. So careful are the Scythians to guard their own customs, and such are the penalties that they impose on those who take to foreign customs over and above their own.

81. The numbers of the Scythians I was not able to learn with accuracy. I heard, indeed, different accounts of how many they are, some saying they are very many and some few—few, that is, as far as

37. The king of the Odrysians, a well-known personage. His father was Teres. He was thus the uncle of Octomasades.

they are true Scythians. But they showed me something that I could actually see in this matter. There is between the river Borysthenes and the river Hypanis a place, Exampaeus. I mentioned it a little while ago when I said that there was a brackish spring there and that the water flowing from it renders the river Hypanis undrinkable. In this place is set a bronze bowl that in size is some six times larger than the bowl at the mouth of the Pontus that Pausanias, son of Cleombrotus, dedicated. For anyone who has not yet seen Pausanias' bowl, I will show the size of the other this way: the Scythian bowl contains easily 5,400 gallons and in thickness is about four inches. This vessel, the natives say, was made out of arrowheads. For, they say, their king, Ariantas, wanted to know the number of the Scythians, and he bade them all bring, each one, an arrowhead. He threatened with death whoever failed to bring the arrowheads. Thus was collected a huge mass of arrowheads, and then he resolved to make and leave after him a memorial made of them. So he made this bowl from the arrowheads and dedicated it in this place, Exampaeus. So much have I heard of the number of the Scythians.

82. The country does not have great marvels except for the rivers, which are the greatest and most numerous in the world. But the thing, apart from the rivers and the size of the open country, that is most notable I will tell you. They showed me the footprint of Heracles, on rock; it is like a man's footprint but is three feet long, and it is by the river Tyras. That is enough about that. I will now go back to the story I began to relate.[38]

83. When Darius was making his preparations against the Scythians and had sent out messengers, commanding some of his subjects to furnish a land army and others ships and others, still, to bridge the Thracian Bosporus, Artabanus, son of Hystaspes and thus a brother of Darius, begged him by no means to make a campaign against the Scythians. The Scythians, he said, were impossible to deal with. But, for all his good advice, he failed to persuade Darius. So Artabanus gave over his urging, and Darius, when all was prepared, marched his army off from Susa.

84. Then Oeobazus, a Persian, begged Darius to leave behind one of his sons; he had three, and all were with the army. The king

38. The story of Darius' invasion of Scythia, begun in chapter 1 of this book.

said, as to one who was his friend and indeed had made a moderate request, that he would leave them all. Oeobazus was delighted, believing that his sons were released from their military service. But the king ordered those who were responsible for such things to kill the sons of Oeobazus, all three.

85. So these three were indeed left where they were, with their throats cut. Darius, marching from Susa, came, in the country of Chalcedon, to where the Bosporus was bridged, and from there, taking ship, he sailed to the so-called Dark Rocks, which earlier the Greeks called the Wandering Rocks. He sat upon a headland there and looked at the Pontus, which is indeed a sight worth looking at. For it is the most marvelous of all seas. The length of it is eleven thousand one hundred furlongs and the breadth, at its broadest, three thousand. The channel at the entrance of this sea is four furlongs broad. The neck of the channel, which is called Bosporus, where the bridge was built, is in length one hundred and twenty furlongs. The Bosporus stretches into the Propontis, and the Propontis is in breadth five hundred furlongs and in length fourteen hundred. It issues into the Hellespont, which is no wider than seven furlongs and in length is nearly four hundred. The Hellespont issues into a gulf of the sea that we call the Aegean.[39]

86. This is how these measurements were taken. In a long day's journey a ship will mostly accomplish about 70,000 fathoms and, in a night, 60,000. From the mouth of the Pontus to the Phasis river— that is, the greatest length of the sea—is a journey of nine days and eight nights. That is, 1,110,000 fathoms, or 11,100 furlongs. From Sindice to Themiscyra on the river Thermodon (the broadest part of the Pontus) is a journey of three days and two nights. That represents 330,000 fathoms, or 3,300 furlongs.[40] This is how I have mea-

39. According to this, the "channel at the entrance" is a half-mile wide; the Bosporus is about 15 miles long; the Propontis (Sea of Marmora) is about 60 miles wide and 170 miles long; and the Hellespont is a little short of a mile wide and is 50 miles long. For the inaccuracy of some of these figures, see How and Wells.

40. This means an approximate length and breadth of 1,380 and 400 miles. Modern authorities find that Herodotus miscalculated to the extent of making the Black Sea twice as long as it actually is at this particular point. His way of measuring the length, i.e., by multiples of the average day's voyage of a ship, is

sured the Pontus, Bosporus, and Hellespont, and they are, in measurement, as I have said they are. There is, as well, a lake that issues
into the Pontus and is not much smaller than the sea itself. It is
called the Maeetian lake and also is known as "The Mother of the
Pontus."[41]

87. When Darius had viewed the Pontus, he sailed back to the
bridge, of which Mandrocles the Samian was the builder; and when
he had viewed the Bosporus also, he set up at it two pillars of white
stone and engraved on them letters, on the one Assyrian, on the
other Greek, listing all the nations he had led thither; those he led
were indeed drawn from all his subjects. They were counted to the
number of seven hundred thousand, including the cavalry but ex-
cluding the fleet, and ships to the number of six hundred. Now these
same pillars, later, the Byzantines brought into their city and used
for the altar of the Orthosian Artemis—all except for one stone.
This was left beside the temple of Dionysus in Byzantium, filled with
the Assyrian letters. The place on the Bosporus at which King
Darius bridged it—at least as far as I can conjecture—is midway between Byzantium and the temple at the entrance of the sea.

88. After that, Darius was so delighted with his bridge of boats[42]
that he gave Mandrocles every sort of reward. This man took the
firstfruits of his honors and had a picture made with figures depicting
the whole bridging of the Bosporus and of King Darius sitting high
over it and the army crossing; he dedicated it in the temple of Hera
and made this inscription:

This is the bridge of boats over the fish-haunted Bosporus;
Mandrocles built it, and Hera received it as her memorial;
A crown for himself its builder made it, a glory to Samos;
All that he wrought he accomplished by the will of the King,
    Darius.

---

interesting and is expanded by what he says in 7.183. What seems indisputable is
that single ships, given favorable weather, were capable of doing more than a
hundred miles in twenty-four hours. Fleets naturally were much slower, since
their pace was geared to the slowest members of the whole contingent.

41. The Maeetian lake is the modern Sea of Azov.

42. The word I have translated as "bridge of boats" means literally a "raft,"
which seems to indicate that the "bridge" over the Bosporus was constructed of a
combination of boats or rafts tied together.

89. This was the memorial of the man who built the bridge of boats. But Darius, having made his awards to Mandrocles, crossed over into Europe and sent word to the Ionians to sail into the Pontus as far as the river Ister; when they came to the Ister, they were to wait for him there, bridging the river meanwhile. (You see, the Ionians, Aeolians, and Hellespontines led the navy.) The navy, having sailed through the Dark Rocks, sailed straight for the Ister, and having sailed up the river a two days' journey from the sea, bridged the neck of the river, where the mouths of the Ister split. As soon as Darius had crossed the Bosporus over his bridge of boats, he marched through Thrace; and when he came to the springs of the river Tearus, he encamped there for three days.

90. The Tearus is said by the neighboring people to be the best of all rivers for healing, with especial regard to the cure of the itch among both men and horses. It has some thirty-eight springs, and they issue from the same rock; and some of them are cold and some hot. The road to them is the same length both from the city of Heraeum, by way of Perinthus, and that from Apollonia on the Euxine;[43] in both cases it is a journey of two days. This river, the Tearus, empties into the river Contadesdus, and the Contadesdus into the Agrianes, and the Agrianes into the Hebrus, and the Hebrus into the sea, by the city of Aenus.

91. Darius came to this river and camped there, and being delighted with the river he set up, here too, a pillar on which he had an inscription written, saying: "The headsprings of the Tearus give water that is the best and most beautiful of all rivers. And to these headsprings, in his invasion of Scythia, came the best and most beautiful of all men, Darius, the son of Hystaspes, King of the Persians and of all the mainland." That was what he had written there.

92. Setting off from there, Darius came to another river, the name of which is Artescus, which flows through the country of the Odrysians. Having got to this river he did the following: he appointed a special place for the army, and he bade them, as each man passed by this place, every single one, to place a stone on it. The army did as he ordered, and so, when he marched away, he left these great heaps of stones there.

43. Another name for the Black Sea.

93. Before he came to the Ister, Darius subjugated the Getae, who believe they are immortal. The Thracians of Salmydessus and those who live above the towns of Apollonia and Mesambria, who are called the Cyrmianae and Nipsaei, surrendered to Darius without a fight. But the Getae turned obstinate; however, they were enslaved right away. They are the bravest and most law-abiding of the Thracians.

94. This is the nature of their belief in immortality: they do not think that any one of them dies but that the one who perishes goes to the daimon Salmoxis. There are some among them who call him Gebeleïzis. Once in every five years they send off one of their number, who is chosen by lot, as a messenger to go to Salmoxis. They give him instructions in what they need on each of these occasions, and this is how they send him. Certain of them, who are appointed for it, hold three spears. Others seize the man who is to be sent by his arms and feet, and they throw him aloft so that he falls on the spear points. If he is pierced through and dies, the god, they think, is favorable to them. If he does not die, they blame the messenger, saying that he is a bad man; and once they have laid the blame upon him, they send off another messenger. The instructions they give are given to the man while he is still alive. These are the very Thracians who also threaten the god, shooting their arrows into the sky at a moment of thunder and lightning. They do not think that there is any god except their own.

95. As I learn from those Greeks who live on the Hellespont and the Pontus, this Salmoxis, when he was a man, was a slave in Samos, being a slave to Pythagoras, son of Mnesarchus; thereafter he became free and made a great deal of money, and, after the money-getting, he went back to his own country. The Thracians live hard and are rather stupid; and Salmoxis, who had come to know the Ionian way of life and characters, which are deeper than the Thracians'—for he had been living with Greeks and with not the weakest sophist among them, namely Pythagoras—got himself a hall. There he would receive all the best people among his countrymen and would give them hospitality. Meanwhile he taught them that neither he nor those who drank with him nor their descendants in each generation would die but would come to a place where, surviving forever, they would have all manner of good things. While he

was doing the things I have said and teaching like this, he was constructing an underground dwelling for himself. As soon as it was completed, he vanished from the presence of the Thracians, descended into his underground place, and lived there for three years. His followers missed him and mourned for him as dead. In the fourth year he reappeared to the Thracians, and so what Salmoxis had told them became credible. That is what they say he did.

96. About him and his underground dwelling I neither disbelieve nor do I believe overmuch; but I do think that Salmoxis lived many years before Pythagoras. But whether there was a *man* Salmoxis or this is some local daimon among the Getae—well, let that be enough about him.

97. This was, then, how these people lived; and they were subdued by the Persians and followed the rest of Darius' army. When Darius and, with him, the land army came to the Ister and all had crossed, he bade the Ionians break up the bridge of rafts and follow him by the mainland, along with the men of the fleet. The Ionians were on the point of breaking the bridge, as they had been told, when Cöes, the son of Erxander, who was general of the people of Mytilene, made a speech to Darius (he had first made inquiry whether it was agreeable to the King to take opinions from anyone who was willing to put them forward): "My lord, you are about to march into a land where you will find no trace of ploughed ground or inhabited city. Do you let this bridge stand where it is, leaving as guards of it those who built it. If we find the Scythians and fare as we hope we will, there is a way for us to go home; if we cannot find the enemy, there is still a safe way home for us. For I have never been afraid that we will be beaten by the Scythians in battle but rather that we may come to some mischance as we wander about, being unable to find them. Perhaps someone may say that I speak so on my own behalf—that I may remain here. But what I am urging is for the common good, and I myself will follow you and will not remain behind." Darius was delighted with this judgment and answered him: "My friend from Lesbos, when I come back safe to my own home, do you, by all means, appear in my presence, that for your good advice I may give you a requital of good deeds."

98. With that he took a strap and tied some sixty knots in it and summoned to him the princes of the Ionians and said to them: "Men of Ionia: I abandon my former resolve with respect to the bridge.

Here is this strap, and this is what you must do. As soon as you see me marching away into Scythia, from that moment undo one of these knots every single day. If I do not come within the time—if you find the days have outpaced the number of knots—sail away to your own country. But till that time—inasmuch as I have changed my plan about the bridge—guard it and show all diligence for its safety and guarding. So doing, you will render me a great service." That was what Darius said, and he hastened on his forward march.

99. The land of Thrace runs further into the sea than that of Scythia. Where there is a bay in Thrace, there Scythia begins, and the Ister empties its waters into the sea in that country, its mouth facing to the southeast. Starting from the Ister, I am going to tell you of the seacoast of Scythia proper, for the measuring of the land. For it is from the Ister that the ancient Scythia begins, facing the south and the south wind, as far as the city that is called Carcinitis. From this city on, the land that fronts the sea is hilly and lies out into the Pontus, and the Tauric nation lives there as far as what is called the Rough Peninsula (this stretches to the sea that lies to the northeast).[44] Two of the boundaries of Scythia, that to the south and that to the east, thus reach to a sea. This is just like Attica. The Tauri live, too, in this part of Scythia: it is as though some other race, and not the Athenians, lived in the heights of Sunium, from Thoricus to the deme of Anaphlystus—though Sunium would have to project further into the sea for the comparison. (Of course, I am comparing small things with big.) That is what the Tauric country is like. If my reader is someone who has not sailed along the coast of Attica, I will make the matter clear otherwise: it would be as if in Iapygia some people other than the Iapygians should be cut off, and dwell in, the promontory, from the harbor of Brentesium to Taras. I mention only these two places, though there are many more that Tauris resembles.[45]

100. Beyond the Tauric country, north of it and beside the east-

---

44. The "sea to the northeast" is the Maeetian lake (Sea of Azov).

45. This is an interesting example of how Herodotus tries to convey geographical information for readers who would not have maps at their disposal. It is also worth noticing that in comparing Tauris with Attica and the heel of Italy (where Brundisium and Tarentum are located) he throws in, along with the geographical information, the fact that the Taurians are not true Scythians but that the people of Attica and those who live in southern Italy are of the same stock as their neighbors.

ern sea, the Scythians live, and also west of the Cimmerian Bosporus and the Maeetian lake as far as the river Tanais, which empties
into a corner of that lake. Starting from the Ister, in the parts that
are northward and bear inland, Scythia is bounded first by the
Agathyrsi, secondly by the Neuri, then by the Man-Eaters, and finally by the Black Cloaks.

101. Scythia, then, is four-sided, with two parts reaching to the
sea; and the frontiers that run inland and those that run to the sea
are exactly equal. For from the Ister to the Borysthenes is a journey
of ten days, and from the Borysthenes to the Maeetian lake is ten
days again; and from the seacoast inland as far as the Black Cloaks,
who live above the Scythians, is a twenty days' journey. The day's
journey I have figured out to be two hundred stades.[46] So the cross-
measurement of Scythia would be four thousand stades, and, up to
the inland, it would be just the same: four thousand. That is the
greatness of that land.

102. The Scythians reasoned that they were not able to resist
Darius' army in a straight fight on their own, and so they sent messengers to their neighbors. Those who were kings of these neighboring states had already come together and were taking counsel, in the
face of the great host that was about to attack them. The kings who
assembled were the kings of the Taurians, the Agathyrsi, the Neuri,
the Man-Eaters, the Black Cloaks, the Geloni, the Budini, and the
Sauromatians.

103. Of these peoples, the Taurians have the following customs.
They sacrifice to the Maiden[47] such shipwrecked folk and those of
the Greeks whom they have taken in their pirate raids. They make
the preliminary rites of the sacrifice, and then they smash the victim's head with a club. Some say that then they push the body down
from a crag—for the holy place is established on a crag—and mount
the head on a pole. Other informants agree about what is done with
the head, but they disagree about the body, which they say is not
launched from a crag but buried in the ground. The spirit to whom
the Taurians make the sacrifice they themselves say is Iphigenia,
the daughter of Agamemnon. In the case of such enemy warriors as

---

46. About 25 miles.
47. Probably she whom the Greeks call Artemis Orthia. Cf. chapter 87.

they capture they do as follows: each man cuts off his enemy's head and takes it home, where he sets it on top of a great pole, which projects far above the roof of his house—for the most part, above the chimney. They say that these heads hang aloft there as sentinels over the house. These people live from plunder and war.

104. The Agathyrsi are the ones who live most delicately of these peoples; they wear gold jewelry a lot. They enjoy all their women in common, so that they may all be brothers and so, being all kinsfolk of one another, have neither envy nor hatred against one another. In their other usages they are very close to the Thracians.

105. The Neuri follow Scythian customs. One generation before the invasion of Darius it befell them to be banished from their own land by snakes. For their country brought forth many of the snakes, and, besides, others attacked them from the deserts to the north of them, until in their suffering the Neuri left their own land and settled in with the Budini. It may be that these people are wizards. For it is said by both the Scythians and the Greeks who live in Scythia that once every year every one of the Neuri becomes a wolf for some days and again turns back into his own shape. I personally do not believe this story, but they assert it all the same and swear to its truth.

106. The Man-Eaters have the most savage manner of life of all men; they believe in no justice nor use any law. They are nomads, wear clothing like that of the Scythians, but have a language all their own. They are the only one of these people who eat human flesh.

107. The Black Cloaks all wear black garments, from which they have their name, and their customs are those of the Scythians.

108. The Budini are a great and numerous nation, with very blue eyes and red hair. They have a city among them, built of wood, and it is called Gelonus. Each side of the wall of it is thirty stades, and the wall is high and made of wood, and of wood, too, are the houses and the holy places. For there are holy places there belonging to the Greek gods and furnished out in Greek fashion, with images and shrines and altars made of wood; and they celebrate a festival to Dionysus every third year and perform the revels. For the Geloni are anciently Greeks who moved away from their trading posts and settled among the Budini, and the language that they speak is partly

Scythian and partly Greek. The Budini and Geloni do not speak the same language at all, nor is their way of life the same.

109. The Budini are the true natives of the country and are nomads; they are the only people in that region who eat lice. The Geloni work the soil, eat grain, and cultivate gardens; neither in shape nor in coloring are they like the Budini. It is true that by the Greeks the Budini are called Geloni, but they are wrongly so called. The whole country is full of dense thickets of every kind of tree. In the greatest thicket there is a great, large lake, and a marsh with reeds round about it. In this they capture otters and beavers and certain other square-faced animals, whose skins are used for the fringes of mantles, and the testicles of them are useful for the cure of troubles of the womb.

110. There is this story told about the Sauromatians. The tale goes that when the Greeks fought with the Amazons and conquered them at the battle of Thermodon, they sailed away with three ships loaded with all the Amazons they could capture alive, but these women, when they were out to sea, set upon the men and cut them down. (The Scythians call the Amazons Oiorpata, which in Greek would signify "man-slayers," for the Scythians use *oior* for "man" and *pata* for "kill.") But they did not know anything about boats or how to use rudders, sails, or oars; so, once they had cut down the men, they drifted with wind and wave and came at last to The Cliffs, which are at the Maeetian lake. The Cliffs were in the possession of the free Scythians. There the Amazons disembarked from their ships and made it on foot to the inhabited country. The first herd of horses they fell in with they seized, and, mounted on these, they ravaged the Scythian country.

111. The Scythians could not make sense of the business. They had no knowledge of the speech or the clothes or the nation of the Amazons but were in great wonder as to where they came from. They thought that they were men of the same age and fought against them. After the battle, the Scythians took possession of some of the dead and so came to know that they were women. So they held a debate and decided that by no means should they kill any more of the Amazons but should send the youngest of their men to them, in numbers guessing as close as they could to the number of Amazons, and these young men were told to camp near the Amazons and do as

they did. If the Amazons should pursue them, they should not fight but run away; and when the pursuit was over, they should again approach and camp near the Amazons. The Scythians determined to do this because they wanted to breed children from these women. The young men who were sent off did what they were ordered.

112. When the Amazons saw that those who came had not done so to injure them, they let them be, and the two camps grew, every day, nearer to each other. The young men, like the Amazons, had nothing except for their arms and their horses, and they lived the same kind of life as the women, by hunting and plundering.

113. Toward noonday the Amazons used to act thus: they would scatter in ones and twos, separating out from the others to relieve themselves. The Scythians noticed this and did likewise. One of the young men approached one of the women who had separated off, and the Amazon did not reject him but let him do what he would with her. She could not speak to him—for they could not understand each other—but with her hand she indicated that he should come next day to the same place and bring another man with him; she signed to him that there should be two and that she would bring another woman. The young man went away and told his comrades. So on the next day he came to the place himself and brought another along with him, and he found another Amazon there to meet him. So the other young men, when they heard this, came themselves and enjoyed all the rest of the Amazons.

114. After that the camps were combined, and the people lived there in common, each man having the woman with whom he had lain at the first. The men could not learn the women's language, but the women learned the speech of the men. When they came to understand one another, the men said to the Amazons, "We have parents and we have possessions. Now let us live no longer like this but go back and join the multitude of our people. But as wives we will have you and no others." But the women said, "We cannot live with your women. For we and they have not the same customs. We shoot the bow and the javelin and ride horses, but, for 'women's tasks,' we know them not. Your women do none of these things we have spoken of. They stay in their wagons and do 'women's work' and never go hunting or anywhere else. We cannot get on with women like these. If you want to have us as your women and want to

be thought to be honorable men, go to your parents, take the al-
lotted share of your property, and then come and let us live together
on our own." The young men agreed and did this.

115. When they had divided up the property and taken what fell
to their share, they came back to the Amazons, and the women said
to them, "We are afraid and in dread to live with you in this place;
we have robbed you of your parents, and we have done great damage
to your countryside. Since you have thought fit to have us for your
women, let us together move out of this land and cross the river
Tanaïs and live there."

116. The young men agreed to this too, and they crossed the
Tanaïs and journeyed toward the rising sun a distance of three
days from the crossing of the Tanaïs and then three again from the
Maeetian lake northwards. So they came to the country in which
now they live and settled it. And from then on the women of the
Sauromatians follow their old way of life; they go on horseback,
hunting with their men and without them, and they go to the war,
too, and wear the same dress as the men do.

117. The Sauromatians use the language of the Scythians, but
their usage of it is not correct and deviates from the old language
because the Amazons never learned it properly. Their arrangements
about marriage are these: no maiden may marry until she has killed a
man of the enemy; some of them die old women before they marry,
because they cannot fulfill their law.

118. So the kings who were rulers over these aforesaid nations
came together, and the messengers of the Scythians arrived and informed them that the Persian, having subdued all of the other continent to himself, had now built a bridge at the neck of the Bosporus
and had crossed over into this continent; and having so crossed and
conquered the Thracians, he was now bridging the river Ister, since
he wanted everything on this side of the world, too, to belong
to him: "Do not, then, sit apart and look on at us being destroyed;
let us come to a common resolve and face the invader together.
Won't you agree to do this? If you do not, we shall, under pressure,
either quit the country or remain and come to an agreement with
the Persian. For what is going to happen us, if you do not help us? In
your case, too, nothing will be easier once this occasion is over. For
the Persian is coming against you every whit as much as against us.

Nor will he be content, once he has subjugated us, to keep his hands off you. We have strong evidence of what we are urging. For if it were against us only that the Persian was campaigning—because he wanted to punish us for the slavery we inflicted on his people before—he would surely have avoided injuring all the other peoples and advanced solely against our territory. He would have thus proved to everybody that the Scythians and no one else were the object of his invasion. As it is, the moment he crossed to this continent, he reduced every people that lay in his road. Not only does he hold the Thracians in his power; he also holds your neighbors, the Getae."

119. Such was the message of the Scythians. The kings who had come from the nations debated the matter, and their opinions were divided. The kings of the Geloni, Budini, and Sauromatians all agreed that they would undertake to help the Scythians. But the kings of the Agathyrsi, Neuri, Man-Eaters, Black Cloaks, and Taurians made the following answer to the Scythians: "If you had not been the aggressors in wronging the Persians and starting the war and had then come before us with the requests you now make, you would have been, in our view, perfectly right, and we would have hearkened to you and made an agreement. But as it is, you invaded *their* land, without us, and became masters of the Persians for as long a time as God gave you so to do, and they, on their side, now that the same God stirs them up, will give you as good as they got. We have never wronged these men, and we will not now be the first to do them wrong. If the Persian comes to our land, too, and begins the injustice, we will surely not put up with that. But until we see that moment, we shall remain in our own country; for we ourselves do not believe that the Persians have come against us but against those who have been guilty of the wrong done."

120. This is the answer that the Scythians received; so they determined that they could not wage an open stand-up fight, seeing that their allies would not join them, but that they would withdraw and, withdrawing, fill in the wells and springs as they passed and destroy the grass from the land, dividing their own army into two to do this. The one of these parts (of which Scopasis was king) had the addition of the Sauromatians. These troops the king was to withdraw if the Persian turned in their direction, flying straight for the river Tanaïs along the Maeetian lake. However, if the Persian moved

away, they were to follow him and attack. This was the one division of the royal forces, and this was the road they were told to take; but the two other parts of the royal armies, the big one, under the leadership of Idanthyrsus, and the third, under King Taxakis, were to unite and, with the addition of the Geloni and Budini, should withdraw also, but just one day's march ahead of the approaching Persians, and, as they withdrew, carry out the plans that had been laid. They were to withdraw, first, straight into the territories of those people who had refused to make an alliance with them, so that they would force these people, too, into the war. If they would not enter the war against the Persians voluntarily, said the Scythians, let them do so against their will. After this maneuver, they were to turn back into their country and attack if, on deliberation, this seemed to be a good plan.

121. Having laid these plans, the Scythians went out to face Darius' army, and they sent out the best of their cavalry as advance units. All their wagons, in which their women and children lived, and all of their flocks, except such as they needed for their own food, of these they kept none back but sent them off with the wagons, telling the people to drive always northward.

122. So the wagons and the gear went off first. The advance guard of cavalry discovered the Persians some three days' journey from the Ister, and, having found them, they kept camping just a day's march ahead, cleaning the land of every plant that grew on it. The Persians, as soon as they saw the Scythian cavalry appearing before them, advanced along the track as the Scythians continuously retreated. Then the Persians directed their assault on one of the Scythian divisions and pursued it to the east and straight for the river Tanaïs. When their opponents crossed the Tanaïs, the Persians crossed after them and pursued them on, until they went clean through the country of the Sauromatians and came into that of the Budini.

123. All the time the Persians went through the Scythian and Sauromatian country, they were unable to damage anything, for the land was all dry and barren. But when they came into the land of the Budini, they came upon the wooden fortified town, which the Budini had left and which was totally empty of everything. This they burned. Having done so, on they went, ever forward along the

track, until in their course they came to the desert. Now, this desert is quite without inhabitants. It lies above the country of the Budini and is about seven days' journey in length. Above this desert is where the Thyssagetae live, and there are four great rivers that flow from their country through the country of the Maeetians and empty into what is called the Maeetian lake. The names of the four rivers are Lycus, Oarus, Tanaïs, and Syrgis.

124. When Darius came to the desert, he stopped the advance and established his army on the river Oarus. Having done so, he set about building eight great forts, separated from one another by a distance of about sixty furlongs. The ruins of them were still there in my time. While he was busy at this the Scythians whom he was pursuing wheeled northward and turned back into Scythia. Indeed, they entirely vanished; and when Darius could find no trace of them, he gave over the forts, half built, and himself wheeled to the west, under the belief that these were all the Scythians there were and that they had fled westward.

125. But when, with all the speed his army could make, he got into Scythia, he met with both divisions of the Scythians and pursued them; but again they kept just one day's march ahead of him. Darius would not give over the pursuit, and the Scythians, according to their plan, retreated into the territory of those who had refused them their alliance—and first into the country of the Black Cloaks. As both armies, both the Scythians and the Persians, invaded these peoples, they disturbed the inhabitants very much; and then the Scythians led the way into the land of the Man-Eaters. And when these, too, were disturbed, the Scythians still withdrew into the country of the Neuri, and, having caused the same disturbance there, they withdrew further, to the country of the Agathyrsi. The Agathyrsi, seeing their neighbors all fleeing before the Scythians and in utter confusion, sent a herald to the Scythians, before they came into their country, and forbade them to set foot in it, saying that, if they tried to invade, they must first fight to a finish with the Agathyrsi themselves. The Agathyrsi, having sent off this message, went out to their frontiers, intending to bar any invaders from crossing. But the Black Cloaks and the Man-Eaters and the Neuri, when both the Scythians and the Persians got into their land, put up no fight at all, and, quite forgetting their threats, they in their con-

fusion fled ever to the north and the desert. The Scythians made no further attempt to invade the Agathyrsi, once these people had warned them off, but led the Persians from the land of the Neuri into their own country.

126. As this was proving a long and endless matter, Darius sent a horseman to the Scythian king, Idanthyrsus, and said: "You are a strange fellow. Why do you keep on flying from me when you might make a choice of courses? If you think yourself strong enough to oppose my power, stop this wandering to and fro and stand and fight. If your mind tells you that you are the weaker, then, likewise, stop running away, give gifts—namely earth and water—to one who is your master, and come to words with me."

127. To this the Scythian king, Idanthyrsus, answered: "Persian, matters are thus with me. I have never fled from a man in fear in days past nor now. I am not fleeing from you. What I am doing now is no different from what I am wont to do in peacetime. I will also tell you why I do not instantly fight you. We have neither cities nor sown land among us for which we might fear—that they be captured or destroyed—and so might be quicker to join in battle against you to save them. But if you needs must come to a fight with us quickly, there *are* our fathers' graves. Find them and try to ruin them, and you will discover whether we will fight you or not—for the graves. Before that, we will not fight, unless some argument of our own takes possession of us. That is all I have to say to you about a fight. But for my *masters*, I count them to be Zeus, who is my ancestor, and Hestia, queen of the Scythians. These only. To you, instead of gifts of earth and water, I will send such gifts as are fit to come your way. In answer to your claim to be my master, you will be sorry you said it." That is the speech Darius got from the Scythians.

128. So the herald went away to tell Darius this. But the Scythian kings, when they heard the very name of slavery, were filled with fury. They sent the division that was stationed with the Sauromatians, the one commanded by Scopasis, to the Ionians, bidding them come to have conference with them. (These were the Ionians who had built the bridge over the Ister and were guarding it.) The rest of the Scythians decided no longer to lead the Persians round and about but to attack them when they were gathering provisions. So they waited till Darius' men were out gathering provisions and

then carried their plans into effect. The Scythian cavalry always routed the Persian cavalry, and the Persians would then fly for refuge to the infantry, and the infantry would help them. The Scythians, having driven the enemy cavalry back into the foot, wheeled round in retreat; for they were afraid of the foot. This kind of attack the Scythians made, by night as well as day.

129. There was one thing that helped the Persians and hindered the Scythians when the Scythians attacked Darius' army. This is a wonderful thing I will tell you; it was just the voice of the asses and the appearance of the mules. For the land of Scythia produces neither ass nor mule, as I have said before; there is not in the whole country of Scythia an ass or a mule at all, because of the cold. So the asses, when they brayed, drove the Scythian horses wild. And often, in the midst of their charge against the Persians, when they came within earshot of the asses' bray, the Scythian horses wheeled round in confusion, their ears pricked upright in bewilderment, for they had never before heard that noise or seen the form of the animals.

130. This was one small gain that the Persians made in the fighting. But the Scythians, once they saw that the Persians were thoroughly frightened, laid the following plan, so that their enemies might stay on for longer in Scythia and, so staying, be in sheer distress by lack of everything needful. They would, from time to time, leave behind some of their own flocks, along with their shepherds, while they themselves went off somewhere else. The Persians would come upon these and take the flocks and be very elated by the success that they had.

131. As this sort of thing happened very often, Darius was finally in cruel straits, and the Scythian kings, understanding that, sent him a herald with gifts for Darius: a bird and a mouse and a frog and five arrows. The Persians asked the bearer what was the meaning of these gifts. But the man said that he had no instructions given him save to give his gifts and get back home again with all good speed; the Persians, he said, if they were clever, would know the meaning of the gifts.

132. When the Persians heard that, they debated with one another. It was the opinion of Darius that the Scythians were in fact surrendering to him—themselves and the earth and water. He formed his conjecture this way: that the mouse is a creature of the

earth and eats the same fruit of the earth as man; that the frog lives in water; that the bird is the likest to a horse; and that the surrender of the arrows was the surrender of the people's own valor. Such was the opinion delivered by Darius. But a rival to it was the opinion of Gobryas, who was one of the Seven who had killed the Magi, and his interpretation of the gifts was as follows: "If you do not become birds and fly away into the sky or become mice and burrow into the earth or become frogs and leap into the lakes, there will be no home-coming for you, for we will shoot you down with our arrows."

133. Such were the guesses of the Persians about the gifts. The single detachment of Scythians—which had formerly been told to keep guard along the Maeetian lake but now to advance to the Ister and speak with the Ionians—when they came to the bridge said: "You men of Ionia: we come bringing you freedom if you will give ear to us. We understand that Darius instructed you to wait sixty days only in your guarding of this bridge. If he failed to arrive within that time, you should take yourselves off home again. If now you do as follows, you will be out of blame from him and out of our blame, too. Stay here for the prescribed days and thereafter get you gone." The Ionians undertook to do this, and the Scythians hastily departed.

134. After the gifts had gone to Darius, the Scythians who were left behind those who had gone to talk to the Ionians ranged them-selves, horse and foot, to attack the Persians. As the Scythians stood there in their ranks, a hare ran between the two sides, and every Scythian who saw it pursued the hare. As the Scythians were wildly excited and shouting, Darius asked the meaning of this tumult among his enemies. When he learned that they were pursuing a hare, he spoke with his usual confidants and said: "These people de-spise us utterly. I think now that Gobryas' judgment of what the gifts meant was right. Since I too now see the matter thus, we will need a very good plan to get safely back home out of this place." Gobryas said to him: "My lord, from what I had heard, I had a fair knowledge of how difficult these people would be to deal with; but since I have come here, I have completed my education in them, when I see them making such a mockery of us as this. My judgment is that at nightfall we should light our watchfires, as we do at other times, and deceive and leave in the lurch all of our soldiers who are least able to bear fatigue; we should also picket all our asses here, when we go

away, before the Scythians make for the Ister to break our bridge down or before the Ionians decide on some measure that will be able to destroy us."

135. Such was the counsel of Gobryas. Afterwards, night fell and Darius followed his adviser's judgment. Those of his men who were worn out with toil and whose loss would matter least he left there in the camp. He left the asses, too, and the weakest of the soldiers, for the following reasons: the asses in order that they might bray, and the men because of their want of strength. The pretext he gave the latter was that, with the sound part of his army, he was going to set upon the Scythians, while those he left would protect his camp at the same time. Such was the message Darius left to those he abandoned, and he lit his fires and made off with all haste to the Ister. The asses, because they were deserted by the bulk of the army, brayed a great deal more than usual. The Scythians heard the noise and assumed that the Persians were in their usual encampment.

136. When day dawned, those who were left behind realized that they had been betrayed by Darius. So they reached out their hands to the Scythians in surrender and told them their circumstances. When their enemies heard, they quickly gathered their army into one mass, the two divisions of the Scythians and the one that had with it the Sauromatians, the Budini, and the Geloni, and pursued the Persians straight for the Ister. Now inasmuch as the Persians were for the most part on foot and, moreover, did not know the roads, because they were not regularly cut roads, while the Scythians were on horseback and knew every short way, the two armies missed each other, and the Scythians got to the bridge long before the Persians. When they realized that the Persians had not yet got there, the Scythians spoke to the Ionians, who were in the ships: "You men of Ionia: your days have gone through the required number and beyond, and you do wrong to remain here. You stayed here before out of fear; now break up this bridge and get you gone with speed, free and glad to be so, with gratitude in your hearts to both the gods and the Scythians. As to him who was formerly your master, we will soon put him in such a position that he will not lead his host against anyone else, ever."

137. In the face of this, the Ionians debated what they should do. Miltiades was an Athenian general and prince of the people of

the Hellespontine Chersonese. It was his judgment that they should do as the Scythians bade them and free Ionia. But Histiaeus of Miletus held just the opposite view. As it was, he said, every one of these princes held power, each one over his city, thanks to Darius. If the power of Darius were destroyed, he himself would not be able to control Miletus, nor would any of the rest of them hold his city. Each of these cities would prefer to be governed democratically than by a prince. Such was the judgment declared by Histiaeus, and at once all the others turned toward him, though before they had chosen Miltiades' side.

138. That, then, is how they voted, these men who were of account with the King. They were, among the Hellespontine princes, Daphnis of Abydos, and Hippoclus of Lampsacus, and Herophantus of Parium, and Metrodorus of Proconnesus, and Aristagoras of Cyzicus, and Ariston of Byzantium. These six were from the Hellespont; and from Ionia itself were Strattis of Chios, and Aeaces of Samos, and Laodamas of Phocaea, and Histiaeus of Miletus, whose judgment was propounded as the opposite of that of Miltiades. Among the Aeolians, the only one of account was Aristagoras of Cyme.

139. These, then, chose the judgment of Histiaeus, and they resolved, in addition to the vote, to put both words and deeds to it— that is, to break the bridge on the Scythian side for so far as an arrow would reach, so that they might seem to be doing something when they were doing nothing and so that the Scythians would not try to force the passage in their wish to cross the Ister over the bridge of boats. The Ionians would tell them, while they were breaking the bridge on the Scythian side, that they would, of course, do everything the Scythians wanted. This is what they added to the plan for which they voted; and afterwards Histiaeus, on behalf of them all, said: "Men of Scythia, what you brought us when you came was good, and you have made haste to a favorable end. You have built a road for us very well indeed; and, on our side, we will serve you very suitably. As you see, we are breaking the bridge and will show all diligence in our longing for freedom. But while we are breaking the bridge, it is your opportunity to look for these Persians and, once you have found them, to take such vengeance on them as fits them to receive, both on our behalf and your own."

140. So, for the second time, the Scythians trusted that the Ionians spoke the truth and turned away to look for the Persians and

missed entirely the way they had traveled through the land. The cause of this was the Scythians themselves, for they had destroyed the horses' grazing grounds in that area and filled in the waterholes. If they had not done so, they could, if they liked, have easily found the Persians. As it was, this, which had seemed so well planned by them, proved their undoing. For the Scythians went through that part of their own country where there was forage for the horses and water and looked for their enemy there, thinking that they too would run away through districts so provided. But the Persians went along sticking closely to the track they had been on before, and so with difficulty they found the passage over the river. It was night when they came; they met with a bridge broken down and were in utter terror that the Ionians had deserted them.

141. There was among Darius' people an Egyptian who had the loudest voice in the world. Darius bade this man stand on the bank of the river and call aloud on Histiaeus of Miletus. The man did this, and Histiaeus, hearing him at the first shout, brought forward all the ships to carry the troops over, and united the bridge again.

142. So it was that the Persians escaped. The Scythians, when they looked for them, missed them a second time. So they judged the Ionians in two ways: as free men, said the Scythians, they were the basest and most unmanly of anyone; but if one spoke of them as slaves, they were the most subservient and staunchest in their loyalty. These were the taunts that the Scythians bestowed on the Ionians.

143. Darius then marched through Thrace and came to Sestos in the Chersonese. From there he crossed, himself along with his ships, into Asia and left as his general in Europe Megabazus, a Persian. To him Darius had once granted honor, saying the following thing about Megabazus when among the Persians. Darius was eager to eat some pomegranates, and when he opened the first of them, his brother, Artabanus, asked him what, if he had his choice, he would choose to have in such number as the seeds in a pomegranate. Darius said that if he could have as many Megabazuses, he would prefer that to having Greece as his subject. That is what he said and so honored the man when he was among the Persians. On this occasion he left him as commander-in-chief of his own army, composed of eighty thousand men.

144. This Megabazus left an immortal memorial of himself among

the Hellespontines by an expression he used. When he was in Byzantium, he learned that the Chalcedonians had founded their city seventeen years before the Byzantines had founded theirs. "The Chalcedonians must have been blind at the time," he said, "for they certainly would not have chosen a worse site than a better when they had the option—unless they were blind." This, then, was the Megabazus who was left as general in the country of the Hellespontines, and he subjugated all those people who did not take to the Persian cause.[48]

145. That is what Megabazus did. But at the same time there occurred, but now against Libya, another great launching of an armament, on grounds which I shall set forth soon.[49] I must first preface it with this: the descendants of those who were aboard the ship Argo[50] were driven out of their country by those Pelasgians who had carried off the Athenian women from Brauron. These were, I say, driven out of Lemnos, and they sailed off from Lemnos to Lacedaemon and encamped on Mount Taygetus and lit a fire. The Lacedaemonians saw and sent a messenger to them to ask who they were and where they

48. Literally, "those who did not Medize." "Medizing" was the technical slogan word for choosing the Persian side against the Greeks, since the Medes and Persians were regarded as two aspects of the same national entity. Actually, as readers of Herodotus know, the Medes had been conquered by the Persians, and there was still considerable friction between the two nations. See also, in the King James version of the Bible, the Old Testament phrase, "the laws of the Medes and Persians, that alter not."

49. Herodotus now promises to continue the main flow of the narrative with an account of the Persians' expedition against Libya, but in fact he does not do so until chapter 200. What intervenes is a very long and self-conscious digression about the history and geography of Libya. It seems likely—since he has been describing both Asia and Europe from the point of view of Darius' conquests, and since he has accepted what was in his day the conventional division of the world into three continents, Asia, Europe, and Libya—that Herodotus is now going to give Libya its turn on the stage, though he is nowhere explicit about this, merely saying, at the beginning of this chapter, that there is something he has to tell us *first*, before his account of the campaign against Libya. For other evidence that Herodotus had this tripartite plan for the early books of his *History*, see footnotes 60 and 77, below.

50. On their way to Colchis to capture the Golden Fleece, Jason and the Argonauts stopped at Lemnos for supplies. Finding the island inhabited by women only (they had slain their husbands), the Argonauts stayed long enough to father a new population.

came from. In response to the messenger's inquiries they said that they were Minyae and that they were children of the heroes who had sailed on the Argo, for these latter had put into Lemnos and begotten them. The Lacedaemonians, listening to this story of the descent of the Minyae, sent a second time to these people and asked what they wanted that they had come to their country and why they had lighted the fire. They said that they had been expelled by Pelasgians and so came to their fathers. This act of theirs was truly just, said they; for their purpose was to live with their kinsfolk and have a share in their honors and an allotment of their land. The Lacedaemonians were contented to receive the Minyae on the Minyan terms, urged principally to do so because, indeed, the Tyndaridae had been shipmates with them in the Argo. So, having received the Minyae, they shared portions of the land out to them and divided the people themselves among the tribes. The Minyae made marriages at once among the Lacedaemonians and gave in marriage to others those women they had brought from Lemnos.

146. But after some short time the Minyae suddenly turned insolent; they laid claim to a share in the kingship and committed other extravagances. So the Lacedaemonians resolved to kill them; they arrested them and put them in jail. Now the Lacedaemonians never kill those they execute by day but only by night. When the Lacedaemonians were about to make away with them, the wives of the Minyae persuaded the authorities to let them into the jail to talk, each one with her own man; they were, after all, citizens and daughters of the very chief of the Spartans. So the authorities let them in, assuming that there could be no stratagem that could be devised against them by these women. But when the women got in, they gave their men all the raiment they were wearing and took in return that of the men, and the Minyae in women's clothing walked out of the jail as though they were really women, and so they escaped. And again they established themselves on Taygetus.

147. At about this time there was a colony being launched from Lacedaemon. It was led by Theras, the son of Autesion, the son of Tisamenus, the son of Thersander, the son of Polynices. This Theras was by descent a Cadmean, being the maternal uncle of Aristodemus' children, Eurysthenes and Procles. While these boys were minors, Theras held the royal power in Sparta as regent. When his

nephews grew up and assumed the kingship, Theras took it very hard
to be ruled by others, having tasted power over others himself. So
he declared that he would not stay in Lacedaemon but sail away to
join his kinsfolk. There were in the island that is now called Thera,
but in those former times was called Calliste,[51] descendants of Membliarus, the son of Poeciles, a Phoenician. For Cadmus, son of
Agenor, searching for Europa, had put in at the island now called
Thera; and when he put in there, the place pleased him so much (or
he may have had some other personal reason) that he left in it,
along with other Phoenicians, one of his own kinsfolk, Membliarus.
These occupied this island, Calliste, for eight generations before
ever Theras came there from Lacedaemon.

148. It was to these kinsfolk, then, that Theras directed his expedition, taking along with him a host of people from the tribes in
Lacedaemon, because he wished to settle among those who lived in
Calliste and in no way to drive them out but truly claim them to be
his people. After the Minyae had run away from the jail and settled
on Taygetus and the Lacedaemonians wanted to kill them, Theras
begged for their lives, that there might be no murder. He promised
the Lacedaemonians that he himself would take them out of the
country. The Lacedaemonians conceded his request, and he sailed
off with three ships of thirty oars to those descendants of Membliarus. He did not, however, take all the Minyae but only a few
of them. For the most of them made off to the Paroreatae and
Caucones. They drove these peoples out of their own country and,
dividing themselves into six divisions, founded, in the country they
had won, the cities of Lepreum, Macistus, Phrixae, Pyrgus, Epium,
and Nudium.[52] Most of these towns were in my time sacked by the
Eleans. But the island to which Theras sailed was called, in honor of
its colonist, Thera.

149. His son, however, said he would not sail with his father,
and so Theras said he would leave him there, "a lamb among wolves."
Because of this witticism the young man's name became Oeolycus—
"Lamb-among-Wolves"—and somehow the title won out over his

51. Calliste = "The Most Beautiful."
52. These were six towns in the northwestern part of the Peloponnese. The
"other" Minyae, therefore, left Lacedaemon and dispossessed the inhabitants of
the land at a considerable distance from Lacedaemon itself.

other name. Of this Oeolycus there was a son Aegeus, after whom a great tribe in Sparta, the Aegidae, were called. In the case of the men of this tribe, it was found that their children never survived, and so, in accordance with an oracle, they established a temple of the avenging spirits of Laius and Oedipus.[53] After that, the children survived. The very same thing happened with the descendants of these men in Thera.

150. So far, the Lacedaemonians tell the same story as the Theraeans, but after this it is only the Theraeans who say what happened. Grinnus, the son of Aesanius, who was a decendant of this Theras and was king over Thera, came to Delphi, bringing with him a hecatomb from his city. There followed him, among other citizens, one Battus, the son of Polymnestus, who was by lineage a descendant of Euphemus, of the race of the Minyae. When Grinnus, king of Thera, consulted the oracle about other things, the Pythia declared, "You shall found a city in Libya."[54] The king answered, "My Lord, I am too old and too heavy to be moved about. Do you lay these commands of yours upon some one of the younger people." As he said this, he pointed at Battus. That was as far as it went. But when they went away, they took no heed of the oracle; they did not know where on earth Libya was, nor did they dare to send off a colony to some destination unknown.

151. After this there fell no rain in Thera for seven years. Every

53. The avenging spirits are the embodiments of a father's or mother's wrath. Hence Orestes fears the Erinyes of his mother, justly, but is driven to murder her because Apollo threatens him, if he does not follow his orders, with the Erinyes of his father, whom the mother had slain. In the case cited, the Erinyes of Oedipus were directed at his sons, Polynices and Eteocles, who, he claimed, had cast him out of Thebes.

54. Here begins the story of the Greek colonization of the north coast of Africa, and what follows, from here through chapter 159, is a specimen story of a colonization undertaken in the seventh century B.C. Apparently there is a solid skeleton of fact in what Herodotus has to say about the process, and the whole is an extremely significant narrative of what the Greeks regarded as the regular sequence of events in the launching of a colony. It is often marked by trouble in the homeland (here, drought; sometimes it is political strife, and the dissidents leave); a leader, usually a man of talent (like Theras in chapters 147–48); the authority of Apollo (speaking through his oracle at Delphi) in regard to the location of the colony; and the equivocal relation of the natives to the settlers, which almost always seems to start well but eventually becomes hostile.

tree in the island, save one, perished of the drought. The Theraeans consulted the oracle, and the Pythia told them: "Colonize Libya." As there was no cure for the trouble they were in, they sent messengers to Crete to ask whether there was any Cretan, or any alien who had come to live among them, who had ever gone to Libya. These messengers wandered about the island and came to the city of Itanus, where they met with a man who was a murex fisherman,[55] named Corobius, who said, yes, he had once come to Libya when he had been driven out of his way by winds, and in Libya he had come to the island of Platea. They hired this man and brought him to Thera, and from Thera they sailed off, though at first as only a few men, to spy out the land; and under the guidance of Corobius they came to that very island of Platea. They left Corobius there with provisions for so-and-so-many months and themselves sailed with all speed to tell the Theraeans about the island.

152. They were away longer than the appointed time, and Corobius ran out of all provisions. After that a vessel of Samos, whose captain was Colaeus, was sailing to Egypt and was driven out of her course to Platea. The Samians heard from Corobius the whole story, and they left him enough food for a year. They themselves put out to sea from the island and, aiming for Egypt, sailed on but were driven astray by an easterly wind. The wind would not leave them be but forced them through the Pillars of Heracles, and they came, by God's guidance, to Tartessus. This port was at this stage quite unspoiled,[56] and so these men came home having made greater profits from their venture than any Greeks of whom we have exact information—except for Sostratus the Aeginetan, the son of Laodamas; no one can, of course, compare with him.[57] Six talents are what the Samians took out, as 10 percent of their profit, and made a bronze vessel like an Argolic mixing-bowl. There were heads of griffins all round the

55. The murex was a shellfish from which the Greeks and other Mediterranean peoples extracted a purple-red dye.

56. This seems to mean that as yet it had not become part of the regular trade route of Greek merchants, which naturally, after a time, would reduce the rate of profit. Tartessus was a port on what is now the Spanish coast.

57. It is tantalizing not to know anything at all about Sostratus. This and other passages showing Herodotus' interest in trade and its profits have made some commentators believe that Herodotus may have been a trader himself and done some of his traveling as such.

rim, projecting outward. They dedicated it in the temple of Hera and set under the bowl three gigantic bronze figures, seven feet high, which supported it on their knees. It was from this deed that there began a strong friendship between the Cyrenaeans and Theraeans on the one side and the Samians on the other.

153. The Theraeans, having left Corobius on the island, arrived in Thera and told the people there that there was indeed an island off Libya and that they had colonized it. The Theraeans decided to send men from all their seven regions, taking one from a pair of brothers in every case, by selection of lot, and, as leader and king of them, Battus. Thus it was that they sent two penteconters to Platea.

154. That is what, for their part, the Theraeans say, and in the rest of the story they and the people of Cyrene are agreed. For, in the earlier part, the Cyrenaeans do *not* tell the same story as the Theraeans do about Battus. Rather, this is how they tell it. There is a city in Crete called Oaxus in which Etearchus was king. This man had a motherless daughter (whose name was Phronime), and he went and married another woman to be her stepmother. The newcomer proved herself a very stepmother in truth to Phronime, for she did her great harm and contrived in every way against her; finally she charged her with lechery and convinced her own husband that she was telling the truth. So he, being overpersuaded by his wife, did something outrageous in respect to his daughter. There was one Themison, a Theraean trader, in Oaxus. This man the king took as his guest-friend in solemn compact and laid an oath upon him that in very truth he would do him whatever service he required of him. Then, having done this, he brought out and gave him his own daughter and bade him take her away and drown her at sea. Themison was furious at how he had been tricked in the matter of the oath. He broke off the guest-friendship and took his own measures against it, like this. He sailed away with the girl, but when he was in the open sea he absolved himself of his oath to Etearchus by tying ropes round her and lowering her into the sea; but he drew her up again and came to Thera.

155. After that, Polymnestus, who was a man of note among the Theraeans, took Phronime as his concubine, and after some time she had a son whose speech was halting and who had a stammer. The name given him was Battus—"Stammerer"—say both the The-

raeans and Cyrenaeans, though I personally believe it must have been something else, which he changed, when he came to Libya, as a result of the oracle that was given him in Delphi and from the honor that he made out of this name he had taken on. You see, the Libyans call a king *battus*, and this is why, I believe, the Pythia in her oracle called him Battus. She was calling him so in Libyan language because she knew that he was going to be a king in Libya. For when he grew to manhood, he went to Delphi to consult it in the matter of this voice of his, and, when he put the question, the Pythia answered him:

> Battus, you come for a voice, but our king, Phoebus Apollo,
> Sends you to Libya, sheep country, to found a colony in her.

This is as if you were to say to him in Greek, "King [i.e., Battus], you come for a voice." But he answered the oracle, "My Lord, I came to consult you about my voice, but you give me oracles about all sorts of impossible things, bidding me colonize Libya. What power have I? What strength of hand have I?" That is what he said; but he did not persuade the oracle to give him any other direction than it had already done. As the oracle continued to chant just what it did before, Battus left in the middle and went home to Thera.

156. Afterwards, things went badly for both the Theraeans and Battus. The Theraeans, who did not know what was wrong, sent to Delphi about the difficulties in which they found themselves. The Pythia said that, if they helped Battus colonize Cyrene in Libya, things would go better for them. So the Theraeans sent off Battus with two penteconters. These sailed to Libya; but since they did not know how to do anything beyond that, they sailed home again to Thera. The Theraeans shot at them when they were putting in and would not let them land but bade them sail right back again. So back they sailed under compulsion, and they colonized an island that lay *off* Libya, the name of which, as I said before, was Platea. The island is said to be as big as what is now the city of Cyrene.

157. They lived there two years, but nothing good came of it; and so they left one of their number there, and the rest sailed away to Delphi. When they came there, they went to the oracle and consulted it, saying that they had colonized Libya and were dwelling

there and were none the better for so doing. To this the Pythia made answer:

So you know, better than I, Libya, land of sheepfolds!
You haven't gone there; *I* have. I wonder indeed at your
    knowledge.

When they heard that, the followers of Battus sailed back there again. The god, you see, would not let them off the project of the colony until they should come to Libya itself. So they came to the island and picked up the man they had left there and settled a place in Libya itself that is right across from the island. Its name is Aziris. There are beautiful valleys that shut it in on both sides, and a river flows by one side of it.

158. In this place they lived for six years; but in the seventh the Libyans, declaring that they would bring them to a better place, persuaded them to leave where they were. They led them westward from there, and, so that the Greeks, in passing through, should not see the fairest place, they measured carefully the stretch of the daylight and brought them past it at night. The name of this fairest place was Irasa. When they had brought them to what is called Apollo's Spring, they said, "Here, you men of Greece, is a suitable place for you to live. For here heaven has a hole pierced through it."[58]

159. In the lifetime of the Battus who founded the colony,[59] who ruled for forty years, and that of his son Arcesilaus, who ruled for sixteen, the Cyrenaeans who lived there were about as numerous as they were when they were first sent there as a colony. But in the reign of the third ruler, called Battus the Fortunate, the Pythia, by her oracles, urged all Greeks to cross the sea and join the Cyrenaeans in colonizing Libya. The people of Cyrene promised a distribution of land, and the Pythia said this prophecy:

58. I.e., there would be plenty of rain.
59. Battus, according to various authorities, was some sort of ceremonial name. How and Wells suggest that, like Augustus, it later became the name of an individual sovereign. It occurs in the latter form in Thucydides 4.43. There seems to be an alternation between the names Battus and Arcesilaus.

Whoever comes late into Libya, the land delightful, and
  misses
Too late the division of land, in very truth he will rue it.

An immense collection of people came into Cyrene. Now, the
Libyans who lived about there, and their king, whose name was
Adicran, saw themselves being curtailed of a great part of their land
and, indeed, robbed and insulted by the Cyrenaeans. So they sent to
Egypt and surrendered themselves to the protection of Apries, king
of Egypt. He gathered a large army of Egyptians and sent it against
Cyrene. But the Cyrenaeans, advancing as far as Irasa and the spring
called Thestes, fought the Egyptians and beat them in the battle.
Indeed, as the Egyptians had, prior to this, no experience of the
Greeks and despised them, they were destroyed in such numbers
that only a few came back to Egypt. The Egyptians were so angry at
this result that they turned against Apries and revolted from him.[60]

160. This Battus had a son Arcesilaus, who, as soon as he became king, was at feud with his brothers until they quit the country
and went off to another region of Libya and, venturing on their own
hand, established a city that even then was called Barca, as it still
is. At the same time as they established this city, they drew off to
themselves some of the Libyans, whom they made to revolt against
Cyrene. After that, Arcesilaus led an army against these Libyans
who had received his brothers and revolted against himself. The
Libyans, who were afraid of him, ran away to the eastern Libyans.
But Arcesilaus followed their flight until, in his pursuit of them, he
came to Leucon in Libya, and there the Libyans determined to attack him. They fought and beat the Cyrenaeans so heartily that
seven thousand of the Cyrenaean men-at-arms fell there. After that

---

60. The main issues of this are covered in 2.161, where Herodotus discusses
the episode in his history of the Egyptian kings. Now it is seen from the stand-
point of the development of Libya, which suggests to me that he is, in fact, looking at the history of the world in its third component—Libya—as distinct from
Europe and Asia, and all within the broad circumference of Darius' aggressive
imperialist designs. It is worth noting that in 2.161 he said that he would deal
with this action further on, in the "Libyan story," and that there, in the Egyptian part, he would handle it at such moderate length as would suffice for the
moment. Clearly, there is a very well-conceived and detailed plan for the *History*
when such interconnections are indicated.

defeat, Arcesilaus, who was sick and had taken a drug against the sickness, was strangled by his own brother, Haliarchus. Arcesilaus' wife, by the name of Eryxo, then murdered Haliarchus by stratagem.

161. Arcesilaus' successor in the kingship was his son, Battus, who was lame and halted in his gait. In the face of the calamity that had befallen them, the Cyrenaeans sent to Delphi to ask what order of government they should set up that they might live to the best advantage. The Pythia instructed them to bring in from Mantinea, in Arcadia, a commissioner for reform. The Cyrenaeans made their request, and the Mantineans gave them the most renowned of their citizens, whose name was Demonax. This man came to Cyrene, and, having learned all the details, divided the people into three tribes. The arrangement was as follows: one section was made from the Theraeans and the original Libyan inhabitants, their neighbors; one from the Peloponnesians and Cretans; and a third from all the islanders. In another change, he set aside certain domains and certain priesthoods for King Battus, but all the rest of the original possessions of the kings he assigned as public property.[61]

162. During the reign of this King Battus, everything remained in this form; but in that of his son, Arcesilaus, there was considerable disturbance about the king's privileges. For this Arcesilaus, the son of the lame Battus and of Pheretime, said he would not put up with the arrangements of Demonax the Mantinean. He demanded back all the rights of his ancestors. He founded his opposition on this; but he was worsted and fled to Samos, and his mother fled to Salamis in Cyprus. At this time the ruler of Salamis was Euelthon. (This is the man who dedicated the remarkable censer in Delphi, which is placed in the treasury of the Corinthians.) Pheretime came to Euelthon and begged him for an army to bring her son and herself back again to Cyrene. Euelthon was ready to give her anything but an army. So she took whatever he gave her and said, yes, this too was very fine, but the other thing was even better—that he should

61. What is described is a typical shift, in the constitutional development in Greece, from a monarchy to some form of democracy. The king becomes, in fact, only the formal head of the state religion, and the former tribes, which tended to be based on associations of blood brotherhoods, are replaced by associations of geographical origin. This is exactly what was done in Athens by Cleisthenes in the last years of the sixth century.

give her the army she demanded. She said this in regard to every-thing he gave her, and so, finally, Euelthon sent her a present of a spindle made of gold, and a distaff, and wool besides. When Phere-time made her usual comment on this, Euelthon said that these were the proper presents for a woman, but not an army.

163. During this time Arcesilaus was in Samos, gathering every-body with an offer of land distribution. As a huge force of people collected, Arcesilaus went off to Delphi to consult the oracle about bringing him back home. The Pythia gave her oracle in the follow-ing terms: "For the time of four Battuses and four Arcesilauses, eight generations of men, Loxias gives you the kingship of Cyrene. For more than that time, he bids you not even to attempt anything. Go back to your native land and remain quiet. If you find an oven full of pots, do not bake the pots but let them go downstream. If you heat the oven, yet enter not the land encompassed with water; if you dis-obey, you shall surely die yourself, together with the bull in all his beauty." That was the prophecy of the Pythia to Arcesilaus.[62]

164. Arcesilaus, with his men from Samos, returned to Cyrene and gained control of the government. But he forgot the oracle and claimed vengeance on those people of the opposition for his banish-ment. Some of these escaped out of the country altogether, but others Arcesilaus laid his hands on and shipped them off to Cyprus to be made away with. But these were carried out of their course by the weather to Cnidus, and the Cnidians rescued them and sent them to Thera. Others of the Cyrenaeans fled to a great tower that was the private property of Aglomachus, and Arcesilaus piled up wood against it and burned them all. When he had done so, he saw that this was surely the oracle—that the Pythia would not have him, if he found the pots in the oven, to bake them; and so he intentionally kept away from the city of Cyrene, fearing the predic-tion of his death; for he thought that Cyrene was the sea-girt land mentioned. His wife was kin to himself, being the daughter of the king of Barca, whose name was Alazir. Arcesilaus came for help to this king of Barca; but the people of Barca and some of the exiles

62. It is interesting that this is one of the few cases in which Herodotus cites a Delphic oracle neither in hexameters nor simply as a prose report; for this is in prose, but the fragments of the hexameters are there to see, or certainly the phrases out of which the hexameters are to be formed.

from Cyrene found out that he was walking around the marketplace in the city and killed him, and they killed, too, his father-in-law, Alazir.[63] So Arcesilaus, either willfully or accidentally, missed the meaning of the oracle and so fulfilled his destiny.

165. While Arcesilaus was yet living in Barca, having taken the action that was his undoing, his mother, Pheretime, had her son's prerogatives in Cyrene, doing all the business there, including sitting in the council. When she learned that her son was dead in Barca, she went away and fled to Egypt. For Arcesilaus had done deeds of service to Cambyses, the son of Cyrus; for it was this Arcesilaus who gave Cyrene to Cambyses and agreed to pay tribute. When she got to Egypt, Pheretime sat as suppliant to Aryandes and urged him to avenge her, on the grounds that her son had been killed because he had taken the Persian side.[64]

166. This Aryandes was viceroy of Egypt, appointed to the post by Cambyses; he later lost his life for trying to make himself the equal of Darius. For he learned (and had seen) that Darius was eager to leave a memorial of himself such as no other king had made. Aryandes imitated him—till he got his reward for it. Darius, you see, had refined gold to the finest possible purity and so coined it, and Aryandes, when he was ruler of Egypt, did the same thing with silver, and now the Aryandic is the purest silver coinage obtainable. Darius found out what he was doing and had him killed, though the charge against him was not this but the suspicion of rebellion.

167. At this time, then, Aryandes took pity on Pheretime and gave her, for an army, all the land and sea forces of Egypt; as general of the army he appointed Amasis, a Maraphian, and, of the navy, as admiral, Badres, who was of the tribe of the Pasargadae. But before he sent off the expedition, Aryandes sent a herald to Barca to inquire who it was who had killed Arcesilaus. All the Barcaeans claimed the deed for their own, for, they said, they had received much ill at his hands. When he heard that, Aryandes sent off the expedition, along with Pheretime. This charge was the excuse for the expedition, but to my mind it was sent to conquer Libya. For the races in

63. Apparently Alazir is the bull referred to in the oracle, but it is impossible to say why. Possibly his name has something to do with it.
64. Again the word is "Medism."

Libya are many and of all kinds, and very few of them were subjects
of the King. Most of them cared nothing about Darius.

168. This is how Libya is inhabited. Starting from Egypt, the first
of the Libyans that dwell there are the Adyrmachidae, who have for
the most part customs like those of the Egyptians, but their garments
are like those of the rest of the Libyans. Their women wear a bronze
ring around each of their legs. They wear their hair long. When they
catch lice, each one of them her own, they bite them and throw
them away. They are the only ones among the Libyans so to do.
These are also the only people among the Libyans who display their
maidens to the king when they are about to marry; whichever girl
finds most favor in the sight of the king, he gets her maidenhead.
These Adyrmachidae are settled all the way from Egypt as far as the
harbor that is called Plynus.

169. Next to them are the Giligamae, who hold the country to
the west as far as the island Aphrodisias. But, before this is reached,
the island of Platea lies off the coast. This is the island that the
Cyrenaeans colonized. On the mainland is the harbor called Menelaus, and also Aziris, which the Cyrenaeans colonized. From this
place begins the country that produces the silphium plant; it extends
from the island of Platea as far as the mouth of the Syrtis. The customs of this people are much like the others.

170. Next to the Giligamae, to the west, are the Asbystae. They
dwell above Cyrene; their territory does not come down to the seacoast, for the Cyrenaeans live along the sea. The Asbystae, more
than any others of the Libyans, are drivers of four-horse teams to the
chariot, and in most of their customs they imitate the Cyrenaeans.

171. Next to the Asbystae, to the west, are the Auschisae. They
live above Barca and come down to the seacoast at Euesperides. In
the middle of the land of the Auschisae live the Bacales, a very small
population, which comes down to the seacoast at the city of Tau-
chira, a city in Barcaean territory. Their customs are the same as
those of the people who live above Cyrene.

172. Next to these Auschisae, to the west, are the Nasamones, a
very numerous people, who in summer leave their flocks by the sea
and themselves go up to the country of Augila to gather the dates
there from palm trees, which are particularly many, and all are the
fruit-bearing kind. They hunt locusts, dry them in the sun, grind
them to powder, and, sprinkling the powder on milk, drink it off. It

is their custom for each man to have many wives, but their enjoyment of them is in common, just as it is among the Massagetae.
Among the Nasamones, when a man sets up a staff in front of his
dwelling, he is lying with a woman. When a Nasamon first marries,
on that first night the bride goes through all those that dine at the
house and is had by them all. As each man has her, he gives her a
gift, which he has brought from his own house. In the matter of
oaths and of prophecies they do the following: they swear by those
men who are said to be, among them, the justest and the best; that is
to say, they lay their hands on the tombs of these men and so swear.
For prophecy, they go to the graves of their ancestors, utter a prayer,
and then, after, go to sleep; whatever dream a man sees in that
sleep, he uses as prophetic. In matters of pledge, this is what they
do: they give another to drink from their hand and themselves drink
from the hand of the other; if they have no liquid, they take of the
dust of the earth and lick that.

173. The nearest neighbors of the Nasamones are the Psylli, who
were destroyed in the following way. There was a south wind that
blew upon them and dried up all their water tanks, and the whole
country within the region of the Syrtis was waterless. They took
common counsel and marched southward (the story I am telling is
that of the Libyans), and when they got to the sandy part, the south
wind blew a storm upon them and buried them. When they met
their end thus, the Nasamones took over their country.

174. Southward and inland of these are the Garamantes, who
live in a beast-haunted country. These people avoid everyone and
the company of anyone. They have no warlike arms at all, nor do
they know how to defend themselves.

175. These live inland of the Nasamones. But along the seacoast, to the west, the neighbors of the Nasamones are the Macae,
who shave their heads but let the middle of their hair grow, shaving
it off on either side of the divide. Going to war, they carry the skins
of ostriches for bucklers. Through their territory flows the river
Cinyps from the hill that is called the Hill of the Graces, and it empties into the sea. This Hill of the Graces is thick with woods, though
all the parts of Libya I have previously described are quite bare. The
distance from the sea to this mountainous part is two hundred
furlongs.

176. Next to the Macae are the Gindanes. Their women wear

leather rings on their ankles; according to the story, every woman puts on an anklet for each man she has lain with, and she that has the most anklets is considered the best of them all, because she has been loved by the most men.

177. There is a cape that projects into the sea from the land of the Gindanes, and there dwell the Lotophagi, who live solely from the enjoyment of the lotus fruit. The fruit of the lotus is about as big as a mastic berry and in sweetness is like the fruit of the palm tree. The Lotophagi also make wine of this fruit.

178. Next to the Lotophagi, along the coast, are the Machlyes, who also use the lotus, but less than the aforementioned people, and their territory reaches to a great river, the name of which is Triton. This issues into the great Tritonian lake, and in this there is an island called Phla. This island, it is said, the Lacedaemonians were urged by an oracle to colonize.

179. There is also the following story. Jason, when the Argo was built below Mount Pelion, put into the boat a hecatomb and a bronze tripod as well and so sailed round the Peloponnesus, making for Delphi. As, in his sailing, he came about Cape Malea, a north wind overtook him and drove him astray to Libya. Before he saw land, he was in the shallows of Lake Triton. He could not find a way out; but the story goes that in his difficulty Triton appeared to Jason and bade him give up the tripod, saying that he would then show them the channel and send the sailors through unharmed. Jason agreed, and so Triton showed them the way through the shallows, and he also placed the tripod in his own shrine. But he first prophesied, over the tripod, and indicated the entire tale to Jason's comrades: that when one of their descendants—that is, of those who sailed on the Argo—should carry off the tripod, then must needs a hundred Greek cities be established round the Tritonian lake. When they heard that, the Libyan natives hid the tripod.

180. Next to the Machlyes are the Auseans. These and the Machlyes live around the Tritonian lake, but the river Triton divides them as a boundary between the two. The Machlyes grow their hair long at the back of their heads, the Auseans in front. There is a yearly festival of Athena among them, where their young girls, dividing into two parties, fight one another with stones and sticks, and so, they say, they discharge their ancestral duties to their native god,

which is her we call Athena. Those who die as a result of their
wounds they call "false virgins." Before they set the girls to fighting,
they do the following thing, as a public function: the girl that is the
fairest among them they deck out with a Corinthian helmet and a
complete armor, in Hellenic style, and put her on a chariot and
drive her right round the lake. What they used to dress up these girls
in *before* the Greeks came to live beside them, I have no means of
knowing, but I imagine that they were dressed up in Egyptian arms.
For my belief is that from Egypt the helmet and the shield came to
the Greeks. They declare that Athena is a daughter of Poseidon and
the Tritonian lake and that, having fallen out with her father for
some cause or other, she put herself under the protection of Zeus,
and Zeus made her his own daughter. That is what they say. These
people enjoy their women in common. They do not live in couples
at all but fuck in the mass, like cattle. When a woman's child is
rather older, in three months' space the men come together, and
whichever of the men the child most resembles, his the child is regarded as being.

181. These, then, are the seacoast Libyan nomads of whom I
have been speaking. Further inland there is a part of Libya that is
given over to wild beasts, and beyond this wild-beast-haunted place
there is a ridge of sand that stretches all the way from Thebes in
Egypt to the Pillars of Heracles.[65] Along this ridge, at intervals of
about ten days' journey, there are huge lumps of salt in great heaps,
and on the top of each heap there springs up, from the middle of the
salt, water that is cold and sweet. Around it live the people who are
furthest toward the desert and inland from the place of the wild
beasts. The first of them on the way up from Thebes, and that at ten
days' journey, are the Ammonians, who have a temple there derived
from the Zeus of Thebes; for in Thebes, too, as I said before, there is
an image of Zeus depicted with a ram's face. There is also another
spring of water there. Toward dawn it is warm; about the time of the

65. What Herodotus is describing here, with some correctness along with
great inaccuracies, is the caravan route from Egypt to northwest Africa. In this
route the oases are of prime importance. Apparently Herodotus makes the occurrence of the oases far too regular, in both direction and frequency. One wonders how much of his account is derived from personal observation and how
much from secondhand information. Probably a combination of both.

crowding of the marketplace it becomes cool; and at noon it is downright cold, and that is when they use it to water their gardens. As the day wanes, the chill relaxes from the water until the sun sinks, and then the water grows warm.[66] It increases in warmth as it draws near to midnight, and then it bubbles and boils. Once midnight is past, the chill sets in again till dawn. They call this spring the spring of the sun.

182. After the Ammonians, and going still through the ridge of sand for another ten days' journey, there is a hill of salt like that of the Ammonians and again a spring and again men living around it. The name of this place is Augila. It is to this place that the Nasamones come when they are picking the fruit of the palm trees.

183. From the Augilae there is another journey of ten days' space, another hill of salt, another spring, and many other date-bearing palm trees, as in the other instances. Men live here, too, and are called the Garamantes, a very great tribe, who put earth on the top of the salt and then sow it. This is the shortest cut into the land of the Lotophagi; the distance between the two is a matter of thirty days. Among these people there are the backward-grazing oxen. The reason for their backward-grazing is this: they have horns that are curved forward, and therefore they go backward when they graze, for they cannot go forward because their horns project into the ground ahead of them. Otherwise they are no different from other oxen, except that their skins excel for thickness and feel. The Garamantes hunt the cave-dwelling Ethiopians with four-horse teams. For the cave-dwelling Ethiopians are the swiftest of mankind on their feet, swiftest of all those of whom stories are brought to us. The cave-dwellers eat snakes and lizards and that sort of reptiles. They speak a language not like any other, for it is like the squeaking of bats.

184. From the Garamantes, and again ten days' journey, there is yet another hill of salt and a spring, and there are men living round it too, whose name is the Atarantes, and they are the only ones of mankind of whom we know that have no names; that is, they have a

---

66. Herodotus concentrates on the paradox of coldness and warmth at unexpected times of the day. It is apparently explained by the fact that the water, naturally warm as a volcanic spring, feels cooler by day by contrast with the air.

name belonging to them all together, which is Atarantes, but no name for each man among them. These people curse the sun when it is uncommonly hot and, besides, use all kinds of foul reproaches, saying that it oppresses them by burning themselves, the people in it, and their land. And, after them, there is again a ten days' journey and a hill of salt and a spring and men that live round it. Near this salt there is a mountain the name of which is Atlas. It is very narrow and a complete circle. It is said to be so high that one cannot see the peaks of it, for, summer and winter, the clouds never quit it. This, the natives say, is the pillar of the sky. From this mountain these people take their name, for they are called Atlantes. They are said to eat no living creature and to see no dreams.

185. As far as the Atlantes I can tell the names of those peoples who live along the ridge, but from there on I no longer can. Yet the ridge goes right through to the Pillars of Heracles and beyond. There is on it a salt mine, at every ten days' journey, and people living there. Their houses are all built of blocks of salt. These parts of Libya are quite without rain, for the houses, being of salt, could not persist if it rained. The salt that is dug here in the mines is both white and purple. Beyond the ridge, to the south and inland, there is a part of Libya that is barren and waterless; it has neither beasts nor rain nor trees; there is no moisture in the whole country.

186. So from Egypt as far as the Tritonian lake there are nomads who are flesh-eating and milk-drinking, not eating the flesh of cows, however, for the same reason as the Egyptians do not, nor do they keep pigs at all. The women of the Cyrenaeans also do not think it right to eat cow meat because of Isis in Egypt; they celebrate, in her honor, fasts and festivals. And the Barcaean women do not eat pigs either, in addition to refusing cows.

187. So much for that. To the west of the Tritonian lake the Libyans are no longer nomads, nor do they have the same customs as the nomads are accustomed to have, especially not in the matter of their children. For the nomad Libyans—I will not say all of them, but certainly very many—do the following: when their own children are four years old, they burn with sheeps' grease the veins in their scalps, and some of them the veins in their temples, so that, for all time, the phlegm running down from the head may do them no damage. That is why, they say, they are so healthy. Truly, the Liby-

ans are the most healthy people we know of; but whether this is *why* they are the healthiest, I do not exactly know. Certainly they are very healthy indeed. If, as they are burning their children, a convulsion occurs, they have a cure for that too; for by pouring goat's piss on the wound, they save the patient. I tell you what the Libyans themselves say.

188. Here are the customs of sacrifice among the nomads. When they begin the sacrifice with the ear of the animal, they throw it over the house and, having done so, bend back the victim's neck. They sacrifice to the sun and moon and these only. All the Libyans sacrifice to these; but those about the Tritonian lake pay especial respect to Athena and, after her, to Triton and Poseidon.

189. The robe and the aegis of the statues of Athena the Greeks copied, I think, from the Libyan women. For except that the dress of the Libyan women is made of leather and that the tassels they have for their "aegises" are not snakes but made of leather, their dress is exactly the same. Indeed, the name suggests that the raiment of the Palladia[67] came from Libya. For over their other clothing the Libyan women wear tasseled goatskins, stripped of hair and steeped in madder, and it is from these "goatskins" that the Greeks have borrowed and transformed the word into "aigides."[68] I personally also believe that the *ololugē*[69] first occurred at sacrifices in Libya. Certainly the Libyan women chant it very prettily. The Greeks also learned from the Libyans the practice of harnessing four horses together.

190. The nomads bury their dead much as the Greeks do, except for the Nasamones. *They* bury the dead in a sitting position, being very careful, when his life is deserting him, that they have the man seated and do not let him die on his back. Their houses are compacted of asphodel stalks wrapped around rushes, and the houses are movable. These are some of the customs of this people.

67. Wooden statues of the Greek Pallas Athena.
68. *Aiges* means "goats" in Greek. This whole explanation depends on the word *aix*, plural *aiges*, being a Libyan word. It has, apparently, no such kinship. The Greek aegis is a kind of buckler worn by Athena in statues and in poetic descriptions (but, incidentally, worn by several other of the principal Greek gods as well). Whether the Libyan dress is in any sense a model for the Palladia cannot be determined. The Greeks and Libyans certainly had a great deal to do with one another, but I do not think anyone knows whether the costume of Pallas Athena originated particularly in Libya.
69. The Greek version of some cry like "Hallelujah!"

191. To the west of the river Triton and next to the Aseans are the cultivator Libyans, who also own houses; and their name is the Maxyes. They wear their hair long on the right side of their heads and shaven on the left, and they smear their bodies with vermilion. They say they are descended from men who came from Troy. This country of theirs and the rest of Libya to the west are far more populated by wild beasts and heavier-forested than the country of the nomads. For the east part of Libya, which the nomads live in, is low and sandy as far as the Triton river, but from there on, to the west, the country of the cultivators is hilly, forested, and full of wild beasts. There are monstrously large snakes and lions in those parts, and elephants [70] and bears and asps, and asses that are horned, [71] besides dog-faced beasts [72] and headless ones that have eyes in their chests—at least that is how the Libyans describe them—and wild men and women [73] and many other wild creatures the existence of which cannot be denied. [74]

192. In the nomads' country there are none of these creatures but others, such as white-rumped antelopes and gazelles and hartebeests and asses—not the horned kind but others that never drink—they really never drink—and oryxes, the horns of which are made into the sides of a lyre (the beast itself is about as big as an ox), and foxes, hyenas, and porcupines, and wild sheep, and dictyes, jackals, and panthers, and boryes, and land crocodiles three cubits long, very like lizards, and ostriches, and little serpents, each one with a horn. These are the wild things in that country, in addition to others that occur elsewhere, except for deer and the wild boar—there are none of these in Libya. There are three varieties of mice in that country, one called "two-footed mice," [75] others called "zegeries"—that is the Libyan name for them, and in Greek the word

70. Herodotus, according to How and Wells, is the first literary author to use the word "elephant."

71. Possibly a gnu, which is a kind of antelope but with a body very much resembling an ass or horse, a face that is reminiscent of neither horse nor deer, and horns on the head.

72. Possibly dog-faced baboons.

73. Quite possibly gorillas.

74. Herodotus is clearly not backing *all* the marvels retailed by his native informants. Yet actually only the "headless ones" are probably fictitious.

75. Presumably jerboas.

means "hills"—and still others, called "spiny-haired." There are
weasels there among the silphium plants, very like the Tartessian variety. These are the wild things in the land of the Libyan nomads, as
far as by the furthest inquiry I was able to learn of them.

193. Next to the Maxyes of Libya are the Zaueces, whose women
act as their drivers when they take their chariots into war.

194. Next to these are the Gyzantes, a people where their bees
produce a great deal of honey, but, it is said, craftsmen make much
more.[76] All these people smear themselves with vermilion, and they
eat monkeys, which are especially plentiful in their hills.

195. Off their coast there is an island (say the Carthaginians) the
name of which is Cyrauis, in length two hundred furlongs but very
narrow, and you can cross to it from the mainland. It is full of olives
and vines. There is a lake in it from which the girls of that country
draw up gold dust out of the mud with bird feathers smeared with
pitch. I do not know if this is exactly true; I write down just what I
am told. Still, anything *may* happen, seeing how also I myself have
seen pitch brought out of the waters of the lake in Zacynthus. There
are many pools there, the biggest of them being seventy feet, both in
length and breadth, and in depth two fathoms. They let down into
this lake a pole and tie to the tip of it myrtle, and then they bring up
pitch on the myrtle. The pitch there smells like asphalt and is otherwise superior to Pierian pitch. They pour it into a pit that they have
dug near to the lake, and when they have collected a lot of it, they
pour it out of the pit into jars. Whatever falls into that lake travels
underground and reappears in the sea, which is only four furlongs
distant from the lake. So the story that comes from the island that
lies off Libya seems likely to be the truth.

196. The Carthaginians also say that there is a place in Libya,
and people living in it, beyond the Pillars of Heracles. When they,
the Carthaginians, come there and disembark their cargo, they
range it along the seashore and go back again to their boats and light
a smoke signal. The natives, as soon as they see the smoke, come
down to the shore and then deposit gold to pay for the merchandise
and retreat again, away from the goods. The Carthaginians disem-

76. At 7.31 Herodotus repeats this piece about "craftsmen" making artificial
honey. Apparently what is involved is some sweetened substance made of tamarisk
juice and wheat.

bark and look; if they think that the price deposited is fair for the merchandise, they take it up and go home again. If not, they go back to their boats and sit there. The natives approach and bring more gold in addition to what they have put there already, until such time as the Carthaginians are persuaded to accept what is offered. They say that thus neither party is ill-used; for the Carthaginians do not take the gold until they have the worth of their merchandise, nor do the natives touch the merchandise until the Carthaginians have taken the gold.

197. These are those of the Libyans that I can put a name to, and, of their kings, most neither now nor in the past cared anything for the King of the Persians. I can further say this about this country: that four peoples inhabit it and no more. Two of these races are indigenous and two not. The Libyans and the Ethiopians are indigenous, the Libyans in the north and the Ethiopians in the south of the land; the Phoenicians and the Greeks are the foreigners.

198. Libya does not seem to me, for the quality of its ground, to be seriously compared with Asia and Europe,[77] except only for the region called Cinyps. (This land is called by the same name as the river Cinyps.) This particular part is the equal of the best countries for the production of Demeter's crop;[78] but it is not at all like the rest of Libya. For Cinyps is black-earth country and watered by springs; it has no reason to care for drought, nor does it suffer from over-draughts of rain; for indeed these parts of Libya *have* rainfall. The output of crop is about the equal of that of the land of Babylon. The part of the country that the Euesperides live in is also good. It yields up to one hundredfold at its best, but the Cinyps country up to three hundredfold.[79]

199. The country of Cyrene, which is the highest of the part

77. It is here obvious that the three parts of the world—Asia, Europe, and Libya—have successively been brought before us in detailed accounts of their geography, inhabitants, economics, customs, etc., since they were each subject to exploration and conquest by the Great King. We now stand on the threshold of the actual events, in the late sixth and early fifth century, that are the prelude to the King's invasion of Europe and, specifically, Greece.

78. This is the most general and picturesque name for corn, comprising wheat, barley, and rye.

79. This is a common way of describing yields of grain right up to the eighteenth century in English. The production of corn is reckoned in terms of the multiple of the original seed put into the ground to grow it.

of Libya that the nomads inhabit, has within it three marvelous growing seasons. For first the crops by the sea grow ripe for harvesting and picking. When these crops have been garnered, the middle areas, which are above the seacoast and called the Hills, are ready; and when this middle harvest has been gathered, the crop on the highest ground is ripe and ready, so that the first crop has been eaten and drunk up when the last is just ready and ripe. So the harvest lasts for the Cyrenaeans for eight months. That, then, is enough about that.[80]

200. Those Persians who had come to the help of Pheretime, sent by Aryandes from Egypt, when they came to Barca beleaguered the city, demanding that the inhabitants surrender whoever had been guilty of the murder of Arcesilaus. The people of Barca, whose entire commonalty claimed joint guilt in the matter, refused the proposition of the Persians. Then the Persians besieged Barca for nine months; they dug underground passages against the wall and made their attacks very strongly. But a blacksmith on the Barcaean side managed to discover their passages by means of a bronze shield, and he did it this way: he carried round the shield inside the wall and struck it against the ground of the city. What he struck the shield against gave forth a dull sound except for the places that were being dug. There the bronze of the shield rang out, and there the Barcaeans dug down and killed the Persians who were building the tunnels. So the method of the besiegers was found out, and the Barcaeans beat off the attacks.

201. For a long time, then, both sides were sorely in stress, and many fell—again on both sides, and not least on that of the Persians—when Amasis, the commander of the land army, contrived the following. He understood that the Barcaeans could not be conquered by force, but by stratagem they might be. And this is what he did: he dug, by night, a broad trench, and stretched weak planks on the top of it, and above the timber he carried out the spoil of the digging and spread the earth on the top, so that all was even with the rest of the ground. At daybreak he invited the Barcaeans to a parley. They were pleased to listen to him to the point at which they were satisfied to make a treaty. They made their treaty in such terms as these: as they swore the oaths over the covered trench, they said,

80. We now rejoin the narrative abandoned in chapter 167.

"As long as this earth abides, so long may the oath, too, abide." The Barcaeans said that they would pay an indemnity to the King; the Persians, that they would make no changes in their dealings with the Barcaeans. After the oath, the Barcaeans, trusting the Persians, came out of the city themselves and admitted any of their enemy who wanted to come within their wall, for they opened all the gates. Whereupon the Persians broke down the hidden bridge over the trench and ran into the city. They broke the bridge they had made that they might preserve intact the oath they had sworn to the Barcaeans: that the oath should remain intact as long as earth remained beneath them. They broke the bridge, and so the oath no longer remained intact.

202. Those of the Barcaeans who were most guilty were handed over to Pheretime by the Persians, and she had them impaled all around the walls. In the case of their women, she had their breasts cut off and set these too on the wall around. For the rest of the Barcaeans, she bade the Persians make booty of them, save for the Battiadae and those who had had no share in the murder; and Pheretime turned over the city to these latter people.

203. The Persians then made slaves of the rest of the Barcaeans and went away. When they appeared before the city of Cyrene, the Cyrenaeans let them through their town, making a religious scruple of some oracle in the matter. When the army went through, Badres, who was commander of the fleet, urged that they should take the city, but Amasis, the general of the army, would not have it so. He had been sent against Barca, he said, and only against Barca, of all Greek cities. When they had come through and taken up their position on the hill of Lycaean Zeus, they were sorry that they had not taken Cyrene and tried a second time to go into it, but the Cyrenaeans would not suffer them. Then some panic fell upon the Persians, though no one attacked them, and they ran away for a matter of sixty furlongs and camped. And when their camp was pitched, there came a messenger from Aryandes, recalling them. The Persians asked the Cyrenaeans for provisions for their journey and, when they got them, marched back toward Egypt. But, then, those of them that the Libyans succeeded in catching—those left behind as stragglers—they killed for the sake of their clothing and gear. This happened all the way until they reached Egypt.

204. The furthest part of Libya to which this Persian army ad-

Book Five

1. Those of the Persians who had been left behind in Europe by Darius, commanded by Megabazus, subjugated first among the Hellespontine peoples the Perinthians, for they found them unwilling to submit to be subjects of King Darius. These people had already, in the past, been harshly treated by the Paeonians. For the Paeonians from the Strymon had been told by an oracle that they should make a campaign against the Perinthians. If, the oracle said, the Perinthians, being encamped against them, should call upon them by name, then they should make their attack upon them, but, if they did not so call, they should not. Now the Perinthians were encamped in the foreparts of the Paeonians' city, and, after a herald's challenge, a set of three duels took place: man against man, horse against horse, and dog against dog.[1] When the Perinthians won two of the three bouts, they cried out "Paean" in their exultation for the victory. At once the Paeonians understood that this was their oracle[2] and probably said to one another, "*There* must be the fulfillment of the oracle for us, and here and now is work for us to do." So the Paeonians attacked the Perinthians (who had only shouted their triumph cry) and won a great victory over them and left very few of them alive.

2. That is what had been done to the Perinthians, in days gone by, by the Paeonians. But now the Perinthians proved themselves good men in their fight for freedom, and it was only through force of numbers that the Persians and Megabazus mastered them. When Perinthus was overcome, Megabazus and his army drove right through Thrace, subduing to the King every city and every nation that lived

1. The Paeonians were famous for both their horses and their dogs.
2. The sound "Paean," which was an ordinary Greek cry of triumph—actually a greeting of Apollo by his title of "healer" (Paian)—is punningly construed as the name of the Paeonians, who were hill tribes from Illyria; but perhaps they may themselves have had their name from some association with Apollo.

there. For that was the charge that Darius had given him: to bring all Thrace into subjection.

3. This nation of the Thracians is the biggest of all mankind, except for the Indians. If they were under a single ruler or could be of a single mind, none could fight them down, and they would, in my judgment, be far the mightiest of all the people on earth. But such agreement is quite impossible for them; no means can bring it about, and this is the respect in which their weakness lies. They have many names, each in his own territory, but they all use much the same customs in everything—all, that is, except the Getae, the Trausi, and those who live above the Crestonaeans.

4. I have already spoken of what the "immortalizing" Getae do.[3] The Trausi do other matters very much like the rest of the Thracians, but they have special practices in regard to birth and death. The kinsfolk surround the newly born and lament for him, for all the ill he must endure, once he has now been born, and they set forth all the sufferings of men. But the dead they hide in the grave with joy and delight and say over him what evils he is now quit of and how he is now in perfect happiness.

5. Those of the Thracians who live above the Crestonaeans do the following: each man of them has many wives, and when a man among them dies, there is a great judging of the wives, and much earnestness among his friends in this respect: as to which he had loved the most. She that is so adjudged to be best loved, and is so honored, is greatly praised by men and women and then slaughtered at his tomb by her closest kinsfolk, and, being so slaughtered she is buried with her man. The other wives feel this as a great calamity, for it is for them the greatest of reproaches.

6. There is this custom among the other Thracians: they sell their children for export. As far as young maidens are concerned, they keep no watch over them but let them couple with whom they will. But they watch their wives very diligently indeed and buy them from their parents at large prices. Being tattooed is among them a mark of high birth, and being free of such marks is for the lower-born. Idleness is most noble and being a worker of land most dishonorable. Noblest of all is living from war and plunder.

3. In 4.94.

7. These are the most notable of their customs. Of gods they worship only these: Ares, Dionysus, and Artemis. Their kings, as apart from the rest of the citizenry, worship Hermes chiefly among the gods, and they swear by him alone and declare that they themselves are sprung of his lineage.

8. The practices of burial among the wealthy are these: for three days they lay out their dead and, having cut the throats of all sorts of victims, they feast; before this they have made their lamentation. Afterwards they conduct the funeral, either by burning or just by hiding the body in the earth; and when they have built the mounded earth over him, they set up a games festival, consisting of all sorts of contests, in which greatest prizes are offered for single combat. That is how the Thracians hold their funerals.

9. Who are the inhabitants to the north of this country, no one can exactly say, but beyond the river Ister the country seems desolate and limitless. The only people I could hear of as living beyond the Ister are people called Sigynnae, who wear Median dress. They have horses that are shaggy all over their bodies, and the hair is to a depth of five fingers; they are small and snub-nosed and useless for carrying men on their backs, but harnessed under the cart they are very quick; so the inhabitants are great drivers of carts. It is said that the borders of these people come down near those of the Eneti[4] on the Adriatic. They say of themselves that they are a colony of the Medes. How they have come to be a colony of the Medes I surely cannot explain, but, in a vast length of time, anything *may* happen! The Ligyes who live above Massalia[5] call shopkeepers "sigynnae," and the Cyprians use the same word of spears.

10. According to the Thracians, bees possess the entire country the other side of the Ister, and it is because of the bees that none can travel further than this. Their explanation does not seem to me likely, for these creatures are very sensitive to cold. Indeed, I think it is the cold that renders the countries to the north uninhabited. That is what I have to say about this country. It is the parts of it that lie along the sea that were subjugated by Megabazus.

11. As soon as Darius had crossed the Hellespont and come to

4. I.e., Veneti, who lived around Padua, in Italy.
5. Massalia = Marseilles. Ligyes = Ligurians.

Sardis, he remembered the good service of Histiaeus of Miletus and the advice of Cöes of Mytilene.[6] He sent for them both to Sardis and gave them a choice of whatever they wanted. Histiaeus, being already prince of Miletus, wanted no more extension of his sovereign power, but he asked for Myrcinus in the Edonian country, since he wished to establish a city there. That, then, was his choice; but Cöes, who was no prince but an ordinary citizen, begged to become ruler of Mytilene.

12. So, for both, their wishes were accomplished, and they turned to the roads they had chosen. But it befell that Darius saw something that made him desire to lay his commands on Megabazus to conquer the Paeonians and take them right out of Europe and into Asia. There were two Paeonians, Pigres and Mantyes, who themselves wished to hold rule over the Paeonians. As soon as Darius had crossed into Asia, these men came to Sardis and brought with them their sister, who was tall and beautiful. They waited until Darius had established himself in the outskirts of the Lydian city, and this is what they did: they dressed up their sister as well as ever they could and sent her out to bring water, with a vessel on her head, leading a horse behind her with a bridle on her arm, and spinning flax. As she passed the King, Darius noticed her; for what was done by this woman was not done like the women of the Persians, Lydians, or any of the people of Asia. So the King noticed it. Whereupon he sent certain of his bodyguard, bidding them watch what the woman would do with the horse. The soldiers followed her, and when she came to the river, she watered the horse; and after watering him she filled the vessel with water and went back the way she had come, bearing the water on her head and drawing the horse after her with a bridle on her arm, while she constantly turned the spindle.

13. Darius marveled at what he heard from the scouts and what he had seen himself and bade the men bring the woman before him. When she was brought, her brothers came with her; for indeed they

6. Histiaeus had deceived the Scythians into believing that the Greek guarding force was ready to break the raft-bridge, which was Darius' lifeline to home. Cöes was the man who had advised Darius to maintain the raft-bridge when he invaded Scythian country at a moment when Darius himself had been in favor of destroying this safeguard. (See 4.97.)

had been watching from somewhere close by. On Darius' inquiring
of what nation she was, the young men said that they were Paeonians
and that this was their own sister. The King answered, "Who are the
Paeonians, and where on earth do they live, and what do you want,
that you have come to Sardis?" The men said that they had come to
surrender to him, the King, and that the land of Paeonia was full of
cities established on the Strymon, and that the Strymon was a river
not far from the Hellespont, and its people were sent out as colonists
from the Teucrians in Troy. When they had answered each detail, he
asked them if all the women in that country were as diligent workers
as this girl. To which they readily answered, "Yes"—for indeed, this
was exactly why they had done the whole thing.

14. Then Darius wrote out a dispatch to Megabazus, whom he
had left as his general in Thrace, bidding him move the Paeonians
out of their accustomed country and bring them to himself—them
and their children and womenfolk. The horseman, bearing the message, set off with all speed for the Hellespont, and, crossing there,
gave it to the general, who read it over and, taking guides from the
Thracian country, marched upon Paeonia.

15. The Paeonians, learning that the Persians were coming
against them, gathered themselves together and marched out in the
direction of the sea, because they thought that it was on this side
that the Persians would attack them. They were ready to repel the
onset of the army of Megabazus; but the Persians, as soon as they
found out that the Paeonians had concentrated their forces and were
guarding the approach on the seaside, got guides and turned to the
upland road and, unknown to the Paeonians, fell upon their cities,
which were destitute of men. Indeed, since these cities that they
were attacking were almost empty, they got possession of them
easily. When the Paeonians learned that their cities were in enemy
hands, they broke up, each into their several units, and surrendered
to the Persians. So it was that, of the Paeonians, the Siriopaeonians
and the Paeoplae and those people who live as far as the Prasiad lake
were driven out of their native land and brought to Asia.

16. But the people who live around Mount Pangaeum and the
country of the Doberes and the Agrianes and the Odomanti and
the Prasiad lake itself—these were not conquered by Megabazus at
all, though he did try to conquer the lake-dwelling peoples, too.

The fashion in which these people live is as follows: a platform, set on high stakes, is placed in the middle of the lake. This has a narrow exit to the mainland, through a single bridge. The stakes that support the platform were in olden times put in place by all the citizenry as a common venture. But later, following their custom, they have arranged the matter so: they bring the wood from the mountain Orbelus, and for each woman a man marries he puts in three stakes. Everyone marries a number of wives. The manner of their living together is that each man on the platform is master of the hut in which he lives and of a trapdoor, which leads down through the platform into the lake. They tie their infant children with a cord by the foot, fearing lest they roll down into the water. The fodder they give to their horses and transport animals is fish. For they have such a plenty of fish that when a man opens his trapdoor and lets down into the lake an empty basket by a cord, in no time he can draw it up full. They have two breeds of fish, which they call "paprakes" and "tilones."

17. So those of the Paeonians who were conquered were brought away into Asia. After this victory over the Paeonians, Megabazus sent messengers to Macedonia; the messengers he sent were the seven Persians in his camp who were of the most distinction after himself, and they were sent to Amyntas to ask for earth and water for King Darius. There is a very short cut from the Prasiad lake into Macedonia. First of all, there is the mine, which is next the lake itself. (This is the mine from which, after this time, Alexander used to obtain a talent of silver a day.) Once you have passed the mine, you then cross the mountain called Dysorum and you are in Macedonia.

18. These Persians who were sent came to Amyntas and into his presence, and there they asked for earth and water for King Darius. Amyntas gave them what they asked and, besides, invited them to partake of his hospitality. He put on a magnificent banquet and received the Persians lavishly. After the banquet the Persians stayed drinking and finally said to Amyntas: "Our Macedonian host, we Persians have a custom; when we put on a great feast like this one, we bring in our wives and our mistresses to sit with us. You have received us with such cordiality, you have entertained us so lavishly, you have given King Darius earth and water—now comply with this

custom of ours." Amyntas answered: "Persians, this custom of yours is not ours; with us the men and women are separated. But since you are our masters and request this of us, this privilege too shall be yours." With these words, Amyntas sent for the women, and they came at his bidding and sat down opposite the Persians. Then the Persians, seeing these handsome women, said to Amyntas, "This that you have done is not a clever thing. It were better that the women should never have come at all than to come and not sit alongside of us. To seat them opposite is but a torment to the eyes." So Amyntas, being pressed to it, bade the women sit alongside of the men; and when they complied, the Persians, who were fairly drunk by now, began to touch their breasts, and here and there one of the Persians would try to kiss the women.

19. Amyntas endured this in silence, though he was very discontent, because he was exceedingly afraid of the Persians. But his son Alexander, who was there and saw it all and was, moreover, a young man to whom nothing bad had ever yet happened, could no longer contain himself, so that in his fury he spoke to Amyntas: "Father, you are an old man; yield to it and go and take a rest, and do not persist with the drinking. I will remain here and give our guests everything they should have." From what he said, Amyntas knew well that Alexander was plotting something, and he said, "My son, you are on fire with anger, and I pretty well understand that your words are meant to send me away that you may commit some violence. I must beg of you not to let the violence touch these men, lest you destroy us ourselves. Look on at what is being done and have patience. Still, about my going away, I will do as you want."

20. This was the request that Amyntas made to his son, and, having done so, he went away. Then Alexander spoke to the Persians: "As for the women, sirs, you may be quite easy, whether you would lie with all of them or however many you choose. You may make your own determination of that. However, the hour for your going to bed draws near, and I see that you are far gone in liquor; and so, if you please, send the women off to bathe, and, after they have bathed, you may welcome them back again." That was what he said, and, as the Persians too were pleased, Alexander, when the women went out, sent them off to the women's quarters. But he himself dressed up young men who had no beards, to the number equal to

that of the women, and gave each of them a dagger and brought them in to the company again. As he brought them back, he said, "You men of Persia: I think you have had to perfection the fullness of your feast. We have given you all that we have, and you have, besides, everything that lay at our disposal to find for you; so now, greatest of all, we would crown the profusion we give you with the persons of our mothers and our sisters, that you may know completely how honored you are by us in all the matters wherein you are worthy of honor and that, besides, you may tell the king who sent you how well that Greek who is his viceroy over Macedonia received you, with table and bed." With these words Alexander put alongside each Persian man one who seemed in truth a woman, and when the Persians tried to feel them, the young men struck them dead.

21. Such was the death they died, both themselves and their servants. For there had come with them their carriages, and men to tend them, and their whole gear. And all these were made away with, utterly, along with the men themselves—all of them. Some time afterwards there was a great search made by the Persians after the men. But Alexander checked it by his cleverness. He gave a great deal of money and his own sister, called Gygaea, to one Bubares, a Persian who was the general in charge of the search for the dead men. And this stopped the whole business.

22. So the death of these Persians was suppressed and passed into silence. But that the descendants of Perdiccas are, in fact, Greeks (as they themselves say) I happen to know; and I will, moreover, prove that they are Greeks in the latter part of my history. Besides, those marshals of the games, who arrange the Olympics, have given the same in judgment. For when Alexander chose to compete and entered the arena for the purpose, certain of the Greeks who were his competitors would have debarred him, on the grounds that this was no contest for foreign contestants but for Greeks only. Alexander then proved that he was an Argive and was therefore adjudged to be a Greek and took his part in the footrace, where he ran a dead heat with the winner.[7]

7. The Greek-ness or otherwise of the Macedonian kings was a very disputed point. Herodotus here, and again in 8.137–39, shows himself on the side of their Greek ancestry. Demosthenes in the fourth century, a staunch opponent of Philip of Macedon, not surprisingly declared the exact opposite (*Philippics* 3.31).

23. That, then, is how this all fell out. Megabazus with his Paeonians came to the Hellespont and then crossed it and came to Sardis. Now at this time Histiaeus of Miletus was busy fortifying Myrcinus on the river Strymon, the place that he had asked of Darius in return for his safekeeping of the raft-bridge. Megabazus heard of what Histiaeus was doing, and when he came to Sardis with the Paeonians, he spoke to Darius and said, "My lord, what a thing you have done! You have given to this Greek, as cunning and clever as he is, a city to fortify in Thrace, where there is abundant wood for ship-building and the making of many oars and also the silver mines and a big population, both Greek and barbarian. Once these people find their champion, they will work night and day at executing what he tells them to do. Stop this man from his work or you will find yourself in the grip of a war on your own doorstep. But send him some pleasant message, when you do the stopping. Then, when you get him into your hands, see to it that he never again goes to Greece."

24. That is what Megabazus said, and he easily convinced Darius that what he foresaw of the future was correct. So Darius sent to Myrcinus, and his message said: "Histiaeus, here is what King Darius says to you. I have thought and can find no one who is so truly loyal to me and my concerns as yourself. I know this on the proof not of words but of deeds. Now I have in mind the achievement of something very big; will you come to me, at all costs, so that I may confide it to you?" Histiaeus trusted in the message. He thought it a great thing to be the adviser of the King, and so he came to Sardis; and, on his coming, Darius said to him, "Histiaeus, the reason why I have sent for you is this: as soon as I came home again from Scythia and I saw you no more, there was nothing else I so sought, in so short a time, as to see you again and to talk with you. I have come to know that of all possessions there is none so valuable as a friend, intelligent and loyal; and, as to both your intelligence and your loyalty to my interests, I can speak my testimony. Now, since you have been so kind as to come to me here, what I suggest to you is this: that you leave alone Miletus and this new construction of a city in Thrace and instead follow me to Susa, where all that I have is yours and where you will be the sharer of my table and my counsels."

25. Such were the words of Darius. He appointed Artaphrenes

(who was his brother by the same father) to be viceroy of Sardis, and away he went to Susa, bringing with him Histiaeus. But first he appointed Otanes to be general of the peoples who lived by the sea. The father of this man had been Sisamnes and one of the royal justices; but King Cambyses, for an unjust judgment Sisamnes was bribed to render, had had his throat cut and flayed off all his skin. He made strips of this skin into straps and stretched them on the chair in which Sisamnes had sat to give judgment. Having done so, the King appointed the son of this very Sisamnes (whom he had killed and flayed) to be a justice in place of his father, Sisamnes, bidding him to remember which seat it was on which he sat to render justice.

26. This, then, was the Otanes (and this the seat on which he sat) who now succeeded Megabazus as general. He captured Byzantium and Chalcedon and Antandrus in the Troad, and Lamponium. He also got some ships from the Lesbians, and with these he took Lemnos and Imbros, both of which islands were at this time still inhabited by Pelasgians.

27. The Lemnians fought right well in their own defense but at last were worsted. Over those of them who survived, the Persians set as governor Lycaretus, the brother of Maeandrius, who had been king of Samos. This Lycaretus met his death while he was governor in Lemnos, and the reason is that he enslaved and bullied everybody, charging some with refusal to serve against the Scythians, others of acts of hostility against Darius' army on its way back from Scythia.

28. Such were, then, the achievements of Otanes, once he had become general. But then, after there had been a short letup in the troubles, evils began again; and now it was from Naxos and Miletus that they befell the Ionians. Naxos was, in prosperity, way ahead of the rest of the islands, and Miletus was then at its strongest and was in the forefront of all Ionia. It had, for two generations before this, been torn by faction, until the Parians brought the factions together. It was the Milesians, indeed, who had chosen the Parians out of all the Greeks to be their reconcilers.

29. This is how the Parians did the reconciling. When the best of them came to Miletus and saw the people of Miletus with their households utterly destroyed, they declared that they wished to go through the entire country. This they did and passed through all the

territory of Miletus; and wherever in that country, with its desolate and ruined households, they saw a well-worked farm, they wrote down the name of the owner of the farm. They drove through all the country and found few such; and as soon as they came back to the city, they called an assembly and declared that these owners, whose fields they had found well worked, should administer the city; for, they said, in their opinion these men would look after the public interests as they did their own. The rest of the people of Miletus, who had been engaged in the factions, should, they ordered, obey these others.

30. That was how the Parians reconciled the people of Miletus. But it was from these cities of Naxos and Miletus that the troubles of Ionia began again, and it was in this fashion. There were certain rich men who had been banished from Naxos by the party of the democrats, and they came to Miletus as exiles. At that time Miletus was being administered by Aristagoras, the son of Molpagoras and the son-in-law and cousin of Histiaeus, the son of Lysagoras—the Histiaeus whom Darius held in Susa. For Histiaeus was prince of Miletus and was in Susa when the Naxians came, they having been formerly his guest-friends. When the Naxians came to Miletus, they requested Aristagoras to give them some power, that they might return to their homeland. Aristagoras reflected that, if it was through his means that they made their return home, he would rule Naxos; so he made a pretext of the guest-friendship they had with Histiaeus and urged on them the following argument: "I am myself unable to furnish you with a power adequate to bring you back from exile against the will of those Naxians who hold the city—I understand that they dispose of eight thousand soldiers and many warships. But I will take all the pains I can and contrive this for you. The way I see it is this: Artaphrenes is my friend, and Artaphrenes, I would have you know, is son of Hystaspes and brother of King Darius, and he rules all the people of Asia who are on the coast. He has a great army and many ships. He is the man who, I am sure, will do whatever we want." When the Naxians heard this, they left it to Aristagoras to do his best in the matter and bade him promise gifts and the maintenance of the army—an expense which, they said, they would discharge themselves. They had great hope that, as soon as they should appear in Naxos, the Naxians would do all that they ordered them,

and so, they thought, would the rest of the islanders. For at this time not one of the Cyclades was under Darius.

31. Aristagoras arrived in Sardis and told Artaphrenes that Naxos was an island, not very big but beautiful, fertile, and near Ionia, and that in it there was much property and many slaves: "Do you make a campaign against this island, bringing back to it these exiles. Once you have done that, I have much money at your disposal, apart from all the expenses incurred by your army. It is only just that we who bring you there should furnish these. Furthermore, you will win, for the King, Naxos itself and those islands that depend upon it: Paros, Andros, and the rest of what are called the Cyclades.[8] If you start out from there, you will easily be able to attack Euboea, which is a big, rich island, not less than Cyprus and very easy to take. One hundred ships would be enough to make all these conquests." Artaphrenes answered, "Your suggestions are good for the King's house. In all of this, what you advise is good—save for the number of the ships. Instead of one hundred ships you shall have two hundred, come spring. But the King himself must also give his consent to all of this."

32. Aristagoras, when he heard this, returned to Miletus in great delight. When Artaphrenes sent word to Susa and passed on what Aristagoras had suggested to him, Darius himself also gave his consent; and so Artaphrenes prepared two hundred triremes and a large army, composed of both Persians and their allies, and appointed as commander Megabates, a Persian, one of the Achaemenids and a cousin of himself and Darius. (Later on, if the story is true, King Pausanias of Lacedaemon, the son of Cleombrotus, contracted for this man's daughter as his wife; for he, Pausanias, had a passion to become the prince of Greece.) Artaphrenes, having appointed Megabates as general, sent off the army to Aristagoras.[9]

33. So Megabates took Aristagoras with him from Miletus, and an army of Ionians, and the Naxians and sailed, avowedly to the Hellespont; but when he came to Chios, he stopped his ships at Caucasa so that, with the north wind to aid him, he might cross

8. The name Cyclades means "The Encircling Islands." Probably the name was given because they "encircle" the island of Delos, which was an important religious center.

9. This and the events of the next few chapters took place in 499 B.C.

from there to Naxos. But Naxos ws not fated to be destroyed by *this* expedition. This is what happened: as Megabates went his rounds of the guards of the ships, there was a ship of Myndus where no one was on guard. Megabates was very angry and ordered his personal escort to find out the captain of this ship—his name was Scylax—and to bind him and put him through an oar-hole of the ship in such a fashion that his body was on the inside and his head on the outside. When Scylax was so bound, someone informed Aristagoras that Megabates had painfully and insultingly tied up Aristagoras' friend from Myndus. Aristagoras came and entreated the Persian for Scylax but failed to get anything he asked for, and so he went himself and released the man. Megabates was told of this and was furious and attacked Aristagoras about it. To which the latter replied, "You—what have you to do with all this? Didn't Artaphrenes send you to take my orders and sail where I bid you? Why are you so meddlesome?" Megabates was so angry that at nightfall he sent men in a boat to Naxos to inform the Naxians of all that was going to happen them.

34. The Naxians had not the least expectation that the expedition was directed against them; but when they heard the news, they immediately conveyed everything from the fields inside of their fortifications; they prepared food and drink for a siege and strengthened their walls. They made all their preparations on the assumption that the war was upon them; and so, when their enemy crossed over with their ships from Chios to Naxos, it was a barricaded city they found to attack—and they besieged it for four months. When, then, the Persians had spent all the money they had come with, and all the large expenses provided by Aristagoras were also gone, and the siege demanded still more, they built a fort for the Naxian exiles and went back to the mainland, in poor condition.

35. Aristagoras was unable to fulfill his promise to Artaphrenes; and, along with that, the expenses of the campaign that were demanded of him were causing him distress, and he was afraid because of the ill success of the army and his quarrel with Megabates, and he thought the kingship over Miletus would be taken from him. Because every one of these matters was a terror to him, he meditated revolt. At that same moment there came to him from Susa a fellow from Histiaeus, with his head tattooed, urging Aristagoras to desert

from the King. For Histiaeus wanted to urge Aristagoras to revolt but had no other safe way of communicating with him (for all the roads were watched); so he took the most trustworthy of all his slaves and shaved his head and then tattooed a message on it and waited until the hair grew in again. He sent the man off to Miletus with no instructions save that, when he came to Miletus, he should bid Aristagoras to shave his hair off and examine his head. The tattooed marks did, as I said before, urge Aristagoras to revolt. Histiaeus acted this way because he found it dreadful to be held in Susa so long. If there were a revolt, he had great hopes that he would be sent down to the coast; but if there were no revolution in Miletus, he reckoned that he would never go home again.

36. This was what Histiaeus was thinking of when he sent off his messenger, and all these matters befell Aristagoras at the same time, in combination. So he took counsel with those of his party, declaring to them his own opinion and also what news had come to him from Histiaeus. All the others declared their opinions to the same purport—that they should revolt; but Hecataeus, the chronicler, was first and foremost against undertaking any war against the King of Persia, listing all the nations that Darius ruled and the greatness of his power. However, when he failed to convince the others, he urged, as second best, that they should act so as to be masters of the sea. There is no other possibility of this, he said—for he knew well that the power of Miletus was small—save by seizing the treasures deposited in the shrine at Branchidae, which Croesus the Lydian had dedicated there. In that case he had great hope that they would be masters of the sea, since they would have at their disposition much wealth, and their enemy would not be able to plunder it for himself. (The treasure was indeed great, as I showed in the early part of this *History*.) [10] This opinion of Hecataeus did not win out, but those concerned nonetheless resolved to revolt. They also decided that one of their number should sail to Myus, to the force that had left Naxos and was at Myus, and try to arrest the generals who were aboard the ships.

37. Iatragoras was sent for this purpose, and he contrived by craft

10. In 1.92.

to arrest Oliatus of Mylasa, son of Ibanollis, and Histiaeus, son of Tymnes of Termera, and Cöes, son of Erxander, to whom Darius had given Mytilene, and Aristagoras of Cyme, the son of Heraclides, and many more. Now Aristagoras' revolt was in the open, all his acts being directed against Darius. First of all, in word he laid by his princedom and introduced in Miletus a constitution of equality before the law, so that the Milesians might voluntarily join his revolt, and afterwards he did the same for all the rest of Ionia. Some of the princes he drove out; but those he had arrested from the ships that had sailed to Naxos he handed over to their cities, because he would be friends with these cities; he gave each prince to the city from which he came.

38. The Mytilenaeans, once they had their hands on Cöes, led him out and stoned him to death; but the people of Cyme let their man go—as, indeed, did most of the others. So there was made an end of the princes throughout the cities; and Aristagoras of Miletus, once he had put down the princes, ordered each of the peoples in each city to set up military governors. Then he himself set off for Lacedaemon in a trireme, for he needs must discover some very great alliance to help him.

39. Anaxandrides, son of Leon, the Spartan king, was no longer in life but was dead, and Cleomenes, son of Anaxandrides, had the throne, coming to possession of it not through personal quality but through descent. For Anaxandrides had to wife his sister's daughter, but, though she was dear to his heart, they had no children. Since this was so, the ephors summoned him before them and declared: "Even if you have no foresight for yourself, yet we cannot stand by and let the stock of Eurysthenes become extinct. Since this wife of yours does not produce children, send her away and take another; by so doing, you will please the people of Sparta." The king answered and said that he would do neither thing and that they did wrong to counsel him so and urge him to send away the wife he had, who had committed no offense against him, and marry another; he would not, he said, consent.

40. Then the ephors and the elders-in-council took thought together and approached Anaxandrides thus: "Since we see that you so cling to the wife that you have, will you do this? Do not oppose us in

the matter, lest the Spartiates [11] may take some unpleasant decision about yourself. We do not now ask you for the dismissal of the wife that you have. No; continue to give her all that now you are giving her, but, besides her, take another wife, one who can bear you children." To some such proposition as this Anaxandrides consented, and thereafter he had two wives and managed two households, in this acting quite differently from Spartan custom.

41. Some little time later this second wife had a child—this Cleomenes. So his mother gave to the Spartiates an heir to the kingship. The first wife, who had formerly been childless, now conceived at this very juncture. She was really pregnant; but the friends of the second wife, when they learned of it, took to harassing her, saying that hers was a vain boast and that she intended to substitute a child. They were very troublesome; and, as the time grew shorter, the ephors, in their doubtfulness, sat round to watch her in childbirth and keep guard over her. She gave birth first to Dorieus, then Leonidas, and then, straightway, Cleombrotus. (There are some who say that Cleombrotus and Leonidas were twins.) The wife who had borne Cleomenes—that is, the second wife, who was the daughter of Prinetadas, son of Demarmenus—had no child after Cleomenes.

42. Cleomenes, it is said, was not quite right in his head and was, indeed, a little mad; but Dorieus was the first of all the young men of his age, and he was certain that, in point of manly quality, he would be made king. So convinced was he of this that when Anaxandrides died and the Lacedaemonians, following their custom, made the eldest son, Cleomenes, king, Dorieus was very angry indeed and refused to be ruled by Cleomenes when he succeeded to the throne. So he asked the Spartiates for a body of people and led them away to found a colony. He did not consult the oracle at Delphi as to what land he should plant his colony in and did none of the customary things. In a bad temper he directed his ships to Libya, and some men of Thera were his guides. When he came to Libya, he colonized the fairest bit of Libya, by the river Cinyps. Two years later

11. "Spartiates" is the term for all Spartans in full possession of citizenship rights, whch were easily lost through failure to pay regimental dues, which were obligatory and payable out of family estates. If they were not forthcoming, the Spartan involved lost his citizenship—temporarily at least; if the financial condition continued adverse, he might be permanently degraded.

he was driven out of there by the Macae, Libyans, and Carthaginians and returned to the Peloponnesus.

43. Then Antichares, a man of Eleon, gave his advice, to the effect that Dorieus should put his colony at Heraclea in Sicily. This, he said, was in accordance with the oracles of Laius; for all the land of Eryx was the property of the children of Heracles, inasmuch as Heracles had won it. As soon as Dorieus heard this, he went off to Delphi to consult the oracle as to whether he would capture the land toward which he was sailing. Yes, said the Pythia, he would. So Dorieus took with him the force that he had led to Libya, and he made for Italy.

44. At this time,[12] as the people of Sybaris say, they themselves and their king, Telys, were making ready to campaign against Croton; and the Crotoniates, in great terror, requested Dorieus to be their defender and won his consent. Thereafter Dorieus joined in the attack on Sybaris and helped to take it. That is what the Sybarites say Dorieus and his men did. But the Crotoniates declare that they took no foreigner to help them in the war against the Sybarites save only Callias, an Elean seer, who was one of the Iamidae. And him they took with them in the following way. He had run away from Telys, the king of the Sybarites, and come to shelter with them when he could get no favorable omens in his sacrifices for the campaign against Croton.

45. That is the Crotoniate story. Each side produces evidence: the Sybarites show a sanctuary and shrine by the dry bed of the river Crathis, which, they say, Dorieus instituted in honor of Athena of Crathis and called it after her, when he had helped capture Sybaris. Besides, they furnish their greatest evidence in the manner of Dorieus' death—evidence that he was killed when he was acting against the oracles. For if he had not contravened his orders and had done what he set out to do, he would have taken the land of Eryx and held it, and he himself and his army would not have been destroyed. But the Crotoniates, in turn, show that there are many allotments of land that were given, in Croton country, to Callias of Elis (and these were in my time still settled by descendants of Callias) but for Dorieus and his descendants not a one. Yet if Dorieus

12. About 510 B.C.

had joined in the war against Sybaris, surely he would have been given far more than Callias—so the Crotoniates say. That is the evidence that each side musters. Whichever anyone finds convincing should be given preference.

46. There sailed along with Dorieus other Spartiates to join in the colonizing party: Thessalus, Paraebates, Celees, and Euryleon. When they came with their whole fleet to Sicily, they were beaten in a battle by Phoenicians and Egestans and died. The only one of the colonizers to survive this disaster was Euryleon. He gathered the remnants of the expedition and took possession of Minoa, a colony of Selinus, and he helped to free the Selinuntines from their despot, Pithagoras. After putting down this man, Euryleon himself made an attempt on the princedom of Selinus and became its ruler for some short time. The people of Selinus rose against him and killed him, though he had taken refuge at the altar of Zeus of the Marketplace.

47. There followed with Dorieus, and died with him, Philippus, the son of Butacides, a Crotoniate who had contracted to marry the daughter of Telys of Sybaris and was banished from Croton. Being disappointed of his marriage, he went sailing to Cyrene, and from there he joined the expedition of Dorieus, but with his own trireme and bearing the expense of his men himself. He was an Olympic victor and the handsomest Greek of his day. It was because of his beauty that he won from the Egestans what no one else had: on his tomb they set up a hero's shrine and propitiated him with sacrifices.

48. So died Dorieus. If he had endured to be ruled by Cleomenes and lived on in Sparta, he would have been king of Lacedaemon. For Cleomenes did not reign long[13] and died childless, leaving only a daughter, whose name was Gorgo.

49. But Aristagoras, the prince of Miletus, came to Sparta while Cleomenes held the power. And Aristagoras came to speech with him (according to the Lacedaemonian account) having in his hand a bronze tablet with the whole map of the world engraved upon it,

13. This is a curious remark, for, as How and Wells point out, Cleomenes had clearly been on the throne for a considerable time before he took part in the expulsion of Hippias from Athens in 510 B.C. (below, chapters 64–65) and before Dorieus left Sparta (the latter's campaign against Sybaris can also be dated to 510). Yet Cleomenes was still king in 490. How and Wells offer various explanations of the error.

and all the sea, and all the rivers. So Aristagoras came to speech with the king and said: "Cleomenes, be not amazed at the eagerness of my coming here. The circumstances are these: that the children of the Ionians should be slaves instead of free men is the greatest of reproaches to ourselves, and, of all the rest of men, especially to you, inasmuch as you are the leaders of Greece. Now, by the Greek gods, rescue from slavery the Ionians, for they are of your blood. It is easy for you to compass the matter. The foreigners are not men of valor, and you, in war, are in the foremost ranks of mankind for bravery. Their fighting is with bows and short spears. They wear trousers when they go to battle and peaked caps on their heads. So easy are they for the beating. What is more, these men that live on that continent have an abundance of good things such as not all other men together have—beginning with gold, and then silver, and bronze, and dyed raiment, and beasts of burden, and slaves. You may have of these all your heart's desire. They live, too, next to one another, as I can show you: here are the Lydians, right next to the Ionians, living in a fertile land, and they have much silver among them." As he spoke, he pointed to these places on the map of the earth that he carried around, engraved on his tablet. "And here, next to the Lydians," said Aristagoras, "are the Phrygians, to the east, with more flocks than any people on earth that I know and with greater crops. Next to the Phrygians are the Cappadocians, whom we call Syrians. On their borders are the Cilicians, whose land comes down to the sea right here, where the island of Cyprus lies. Fifty talents are what they contribute to the Great King yearly. Next the Cilicians are the Armenians, here—they, too, are rich in herds—and next the Armenians are the Matieni, who live in *this* country. Next them is the Cissian land, and in it, by this river, the Choaspes, is Susa, where the Great King has his lodging and where his treasure houses are. Capture that city and you may well boast that you rival Zeus in wealth. But here[14] you are fighting for land that is neither large nor fertile but of small bounds. Ought you to risk such a fight? It is against the Messenians, who are as good men as you, and Arcadians and Argives, who have no possessions of gold or silver, the lust for which has led many a man to fight and die. You

14. Pointing, on the map, to the Peloponnese.

have the chance of an easy empire over all Asia; will you choose something else?" That was what Aristagoras said, and Cleomenes answered him, "My friend from Miletus, I postpone my answer until the day after tomorrow."

50. That was as far as they went, then. When the day appointed for the answer came and they met at the place arranged, Cleomenes asked Aristagoras how many days' journey it was from the Ionian sea to where the Great King was. In everything else Aristagoras was very clever and had tricked Cleomenes successfully, but here he tripped up. He ought not to have told the truth if he wanted to bring the Spartans into Asia. However, he did tell it, saying that the journey from the sea up to Susa was a matter of three months. Cleomenes cut off all the rest of the story that Aristagoras was set to give him about the journey and said, "My friend from Miletus, away with you from Sparta before the sun sets! There is no argument of such eloquence that you can use on the Lacedaemonians if you want to bring them three months' journey from the sea."

51. With these words Cleomenes went to his house; but Aristagoras, taking on himself the signs of a suppliant,[15] went to Cleomenes' house and entered and sat down there as a suppliant, begging Cleomenes to hear him. He asked the king to send away his daughter (whose name was Gorgo), for the girl was standing beside her father. She was his only child and was perhaps eight or nine years old. Cleomenes bade him say whatever he liked and not to hold back because of the child. Then Aristagoras began with an opening promise of ten talents if the king would do what he asked. As Cleomenes refused, Aristagoras raised his bids, little by little, till he made an offer of fifty talents. At this the child cried out and said, "Father, this stranger will corrupt you if you do not take yourself away." Cleomenes was delighted by his daughter's advice and went into another room, and Aristagoras left Sparta altogether and never got another chance to give any more information about the journey from Ionia inland to the dwelling of the Great King.

52. For this, indeed, is what that road is like. All along it are Royal Stages and excellent places to put up; and, as it is all through inhabited country, the whole road is safe. Through Lydia and Phrygia

15. An olive branch, wreathed with wool.

there is a stretch of twenty stages, to the extent of ninety-four and a
half parasangs.[16] After Phrygia comes the river Halys. There are
gates to this, which must needs be passed before you can cross the
river; and at the river there is a great guard station. After crossing
into Cappadocia and going through it to the borders of Cilicia, the
journey is twenty-eight stages—in all, one hundred and four parasangs. On this border there are two gates that you must pass and
get by two guard stations. Once you are through these, you have
three stages of a journey through Cilicia—that is, fifteen and a half
parasangs. The border between Cilicia and Armenia is the river
Euphrates, which is navigable. In Armenia there are fifteen stages,
with places to put up—all together, fifty-six parasangs and a half.
There is a guard station in these.[17] From Armenia you cross into the
land of the Matieni, where there are thirty-four stages and one hundred and thirty-seven parasangs. There are four navigable rivers
flowing through this territory, all of which you must ferry over. The
first is the Tigris. The second and third bear the same name but
are not the same river nor flow from the same source; for the first-
mentioned of them flows from Armenia and the second from the
Matieni. The fourth river is the Gyndes, which Cyrus divided into
the three hundred and sixty channels.[18] When you pass the Gyndes
into the Cissian land, there are eleven stages and forty-two and a
half parasangs to the river Choaspes—this, too, being a navigable
river. It is on this river that the city of Susa stands.

53. In all, then, there are one hundred and eleven stages, and
there are places to put up at in number the same as the stages as one
goes up from Sardis to Susa. If the Royal Road has been measured
correctly in parasangs, and the parasang is taken as thirty furlongs—
and indeed it is so equivalent—there is a distance of thirteen thousand five hundred furlongs from Sardis to the so-called Memnonian

16. A parasang is between three and four miles long. It appears likely that
this Royal Road was not an invention of the Persian empire but an inheritance
from the much earlier Hittite empire. How and Wells think that the road was
built not so much to facilitate communication but for military defense. Hence
the forts, etc.

17. It is not clear whether he means that each stage has a guard station or
that there is a single guard station in this stretch of the journey.

18. That story is in 1.189.

palace; this amounts to four hundred and fifty parasangs; and if one hundred and fifty furlongs is reckoned as a day's journey for those who pass on the road, the journey will be exactly ninety days.

54. So when Aristagoras of Miletus told Cleomenes of Lacedaemon that the journey up-country to the Great King's palace was three months long, he spoke the truth. If you want an even more exact account of the distance, I will give you that, too; for the trip from Ephesus to Sardis must be reckoned in, additional to the previous account.[19] So I must say that the whole number of furlongs from the sea of the Greeks to Susa—for that is what is called the Memnonian city—is fourteen thousand and forty. For from Ephesus to Sardis is five hundred and forty furlongs; so our journey of three months has an additional three days in it.

55. So Aristagoras, being driven out of Sparta, came to Athens, which at that time had been freed of its tyrants—an event that happened like this: Hipparchus, the son of Pisistratus, had been killed by Harmodius and Aristogiton, who were distantly of the race of the Gephyraeans. This Hipparchus was the brother of the reigning prince, Hippias. Hipparchus had indeed seen a vision in his dream that very clearly foretold what would befall him. After the murder, for the following four years, Athens was ruled even more despotically than before.[20]

56. The dream vision that Hipparchus had seen was this: it was the night before the Panathenaea,[21] and Hipparchus dreamed that a great, handsome man stood above him and spoke to him the following mysterious lines:

19. Ephesus, on the seacoast, was at this time the ordinary place to begin a trip up-country into Asia Minor. However, the Royal Road began at Sardis, and so, in the "more exact" account that Herodotus offers us, we have to reckon in the piece of road from Ephesus to Sardis.

20. By Hippias. Hippias had succeeded his father, Pisistratus, as autocratic ruler of Athens when Pisistratus died in 528. Hipparchus was slain in 514, and Hippias himself was exiled in 510.

21. The Panathanaea was a festival held every year in Athens (and every fourth year with especial pomp) to celebrate the birthday of its patron goddess. A great procession, in which all of Athens joined, carried a new robe to Athena's statue in the Parthenon. (This procession is depicted on the Parthenon frieze—now in the British Museum.)

Lion, with heart enduring, suffer the unendurable:
None of mankind that does wrong shall fail of his deeds of
   requital.

As soon as day dawned, Hipparchus openly entrusted the matter to
the dream interpreters; but after that he would have none of it and
went on to conduct the procession and, in the course of it, met his
death.

57. The Gephyraeans—from whom came the murderers of Hipparchus—according to their own account had sprung originally from
Eretria. But as I find out from my own researches, they were Phoenicians—indeed, of those Phoenicians who came with Cadmus to the
land now called Boeotia; [22] and they got as their share, and lived in,
the country of Tanagra. After the Cadmeans were expelled from
there by the Argives, these Gephyraeans were, in their turn, expelled by the Boeotians, and then they made for Athens. The
Athenians admitted them to be citizens of their own, bating only
certain not very memorable privileges.

58. These Phoenicians who came with Cadmus, and from whom
the Gephyraeans were, brought to Greece, when they settled in it,
various matters of learning and, very notably, the alphabet, which
in my opinion had not been known to the Greeks before. At first the
Phoenicians used the same letters as all the other Phoenicians; but,
as time went on, as they changed their language, they also changed
the shape of the letters. [23] The Greeks who lived round about the
Phoenicians at this time were mostly Ionians. They learned the alphabet from the Phoenicians, and, making a few changes in the
form of the letters, they used them and, in using them, they called
the letters "Phoenicians." This was but just, inasmuch as it was the

22. According to Thucydides (1.12), sixty years after the fall of Troy, the
traditional date of which is 1220 B.C.
23. I.e., these Phoenicians (the ancestors of the Gephyreans), who had now
settled in Greece, began to speak Greek and, in order to *write* in Greek, they
had to make some changes in the Phoenician alphabet to accommodate certain
Greek sounds that were absent in Phoenician (e.g., as in Hebrew, there were no
vowels in Phoenician). The passage is a vexed one, but Herodotus' attribution of
the Greek alphabet to the Phoenicians was a traditional Greek belief from very
early times, the word for letters being simply *phoinikeia,* "Phoenician things."

Phoenicians who had brought the letters to Greece. The Ionians also from ancient times called books[24] "skins" because, from lack of papyrus, they used goat- and sheepskins. Still in my time many of the barbarians write on skins in this fashion.

59. I myself have seen Cadmean letters in the shrine of Ismenian Apollo in Thebes in Boeotia. These are engraved on certain tripods and in many respects are akin to Ionic letters. One of the tripods has an inscription saying, "Out of Teleboan spoils has Amphitryon dedicated me." This inscription would come from the age of Laius, son of Labdacus, son of Polydorus, son of Cadmus.

60. Another tripod has an inscription in hexameters:

Scaeus has dedicated to you, Far-Darter Apollo,
Me, the all-beautiful statue, boxer victorious he.

Scaeus would be the son of Hippocoon—if, indeed, he *is* the dedicator and not someone else with the same name as the son of Hippocoön—and he would be about the time of Oedipus, the son of Laius.

61. The third tripod says (this too in hexameters):

Laodamas himself dedicated me to Apollo,
King, to you, keen-eyed Apollo, me, the all-beautiful statue.

It was when this Laodamas, the son of Eteocles, was king that the Cadmeans, being moved out by the Argives, made for the Encheleis. The Gephyraeans were left behind but were afterwards forced by the Boeotians to retreat to Athens. They have sacred rites established in Athens wherein none of the rest of the Athenians may share; these are different from other rites, and this is especially the case with the ceremony and mysteries of the Achaean Demeter.

62. This, then, was the vision that Hipparchus had in his dream, and this the origin of the Gephyraeans, from which breed the murderers of Hipparchus came. I have told of both these matters and now, besides these, must recover the story I had started to tell at the beginning: how Athens was freed of her princes. Hippias held the absolute sovereignty and grew embittered against the Athenians because of the death of Hipparchus. The Alcmaeonidae were Athenians who were banished by the Pisistratids; and though they tried with might and main, along with others who were exiled by the Pisistra-

24. *Bybloi*, which means "papyrus."

tids, they could not manage to come home again. Their attempts to return and to free Athens resulted in great reverses (they had fortified Lipsydrium, which is above Paeonia). Then, using every contrivance against the Pisistratids, they took a contract from the Amphictyons to build at Delphi the temple that is now there but then did not exist. Inasmuch as they were men of wealth and of great distinction from of old, they finished the temple much more handsomely than the model given them, and especially, where the agreement was to make the temple of tufa stone, they made the front of it of Parian marble.[25]

63. As the Athenians tell it, these men sat as suppliants in Delphi and bribed the Pythia, whenever Spartiates, either privately or as part of a public delegation, came to consult the oracle, to urge on them the freeing of Athens. The Lacedaemonians, in the face of this injunction, constantly given, sent out Anchimolius, the son of Aster, a famous man among their citizenry, with an army to drive out the Pisistratids from Athens, although the Pisistratids were close friends of theirs; for in their dealings they, the Lacedaemonians, thought God rated higher than men. This army of theirs they sent by sea on transports. Anchimolius put in at Phalerum and disembarked his army; but the Pisistratids, who had advance knowledge of this, summoned assistance from Thessaly—for they had already made an alliance with the Thessalians. The Thessalians passed a public vote and sent them, at their request, a thousand cavalry and their own king, Cineas of Conium. As the Pisistratids had got these as their allies, they contrived the following: they cleared the plain of Phalerum and made this country into something suitable for cavalry action, and then they launched the horse on their enemy's army. Their attack killed many of the Lacedaemonians, including Anchimolius. The remnants of the Lacedaemonians they drove to their ships. This was the first of the Spartan expeditions, and this is how it ended.[26] The burial place of Anchimolius is at Alopecae in Attica, near to the Heracleum in Cynosarges.

25. In their note to this passage, How and Wells say that the Alcmaeonidae began this work in 514, after their defeat at Lipsydrium, but probably did not complete it until after their return to Athens in 510.

26. Herodotus is referring to their later, and finally successful, efforts to remove the Pisistratids (see chapter 65, below) and probably also to their still later, and unsuccessful, military intervention against Cleisthenes, when the

64. Afterwards the Lacedaemonians put together and sent another expedition against Athens, greater than the first, and appointed as commander of the army King Cleomenes, son of Anaxandrides; this time they did not send it by sea but by land. As they invaded Attica, the Thessalian horse was the first to join battle with them. It was, in a short time, routed, and there fell of its number some forty. The survivors took themselves off, straight back for Thessaly. Cleomenes came to the city, accompanied by such Athenians as stood on the side of freedom, and besieged the princes, who were shut up within the Pelasgic wall.[27]

65. Yet the Lacedaemonians certainly would never have driven out the Pisistratids at all, for they had no plans for a continued siege, and the Pisistratids were well supplied with food and drink. The Lacedaemonians would have besieged them for a few days and then gone back to Sparta. But now a chance befell that was as disastrous to the one side as it was a help for the others. The children of the Pisistratids, who were being secretly conveyed out of the country, were captured. When this took place, everything on the Pisistratid side was brought to confusion, and they were reduced to making any terms the Athenians wanted in return for the children; the terms were that the Pisistratids should get out of Attica in five days. So they departed for Sigeum on the Scamander, having ruled Athens for thirty-six years.[28] They were themselves, in distant origin, Pylians, descendants of Neleus, being sprung of the very same families as those of Codrus and Melanthus, who had been foreigners before they became kings of Athens. It was with this connection in mind, and recalling the same name, that Hippocrates called his son Pisistratus, after Pisistratus, the son of Nestor.[29]

So Athens was rid of her princes. But what the Athenians did or what was done to them, worthy of record, after they were freed and before Ionia revolted from Darius and Aristagoras of Miletus came to Athens to ask for their help, I must first narrate.

66. Athens had already been a large city, and now that it had rid

---

latter established the democracy. For a summary of Spartan-Athenian relations in matters of political interest, see chapter 75, below.

27. A fortification on the Acropolis.

28. From around 546 to 510.

29. The Homeric king of Pylos, famed as the oldest and wisest of the Greek warriors at Troy.

itself of its princes it became bigger yet. But in it there were two men who held the power. These were Cleisthenes, the Alcmaeonid who was reputed to have bribed the Pythia, and Isagoras, the son of Tisandrus, who was, it is true, of a distinguished family, but I cannot declare what their antecedents were. (His kinsfolk sacrifice to the Carian Zeus.) These two men fought it out for the supreme place, and when Cleisthenes was being beaten, he made friends with the popular party. The Athenians had been a four-tribe people, and he made them ten. The four had had the names of the sons of Ion— Geleon, Aegicores, Argades, and Hoples—and these Cleisthenes abolished and discovered in their stead the names of other local heroes—all local, except that of Ajax. He, indeed, was a stranger, but, as a neighbor and ally, Cleisthenes added him too to the list.

67. In all of this Cleisthenes imitated (in my opinion) his own grandfather on his mother's side, Cleisthenes, prince of Sicyon.[30] For this Cleisthenes made war upon the Argives and afterwards stopped the rhapsodic contests in Sicyon because they sang the verses of Homer, and far the most of these celebrated Argos and the Argives. Besides this matter of the contests, there was something else. There was, and still is, a shrine in the marketplace of the Sicyonians belonging to the hero Adrastus, son of Talaus. This hero Cleisthenes wished to banish from the land because *he* was an Argive. So he went to Delphi and asked the oracle if he might cast Adrastus out.[31] The Pythia in her answer said: "Adrastus was king of Sicyon; you are only a fellow who stones others to death." As the god refused to give him what he wanted, Cleisthenes went back and considered by what means he could get rid of Adrastus. He thought he found such a means and sent to Thebes in Boeotia, saying that he wanted to invite to his country Melanippus, the son of Astacus. The Thebans gave him this hero. Cleisthenes, in bringing in Melanippus, assigned him a shrine in the prytaneum[32] and set him there in the very

30. He ruled at Sicyon from 600 to 570.
31. The method of "casting out" a hero is to remove his bones, and to "bring in" a hero is often a matter of carrying his bones to your homeland. See 1.68 on the bones of Orestes. For a further and more mysterious link between a hero and his burial place, see *Oedipus at Colonus*, where, according to Sophocles' account, whichever nation got possession of the last place on earth where Oedipus was seen would have his ghost as its fighting ally.
32. The town hall.

strongest place. Now I must tell you something else: the reason Cleisthenes brought Melanippus to Sicyon was because he was Adrastus' bitterest enemy, for Adrastus had killed his brother, Mecisteus, and his son-in-law, Tydeus. Having assigned him the shrine, Cleisthenes then took away the sacrifices and festivals that belonged to Adrastus and gave them to Melanippus. The people of Sicyon had been used to give Adrastus very great honor, for this country of theirs had belonged to Polybus, and Adrastus was the son of Polybus' daughter, and, when Polybus was dying without a son, he gave his government over to Adrastus. Among other ways of honoring Adrastus, the people of Sicyon had celebrated the events of his life with tragic choruses, in which they specially honored Adrastus and not Dionysus. Cleisthenes gave the choruses back to Dionysus and the rest of the sacrificial rites to Melanippus.

68. All these things Cleisthenes did against Adrastus; but also, to prevent the Sicyonians and Argives from having the same tribes, which were the Dorian tribes, he gave them quite other names. Here he bitterly mocked the Sicyonians. For he replaced the heroic names by the words for pig and ass, adding to these the normal ending of the title—all except for his own tribe. For on it was placed the name drawn from his own lordship. They were called the Archelaioi;[33] but the others were called Hogites, others still Assites, and yet others Porkites. And these were the names of the tribes that the Sicyonians used during the government of Cleisthenes and after his death for a period of sixty years. Thereafter they bethought themselves and changed the names to Hylleis, Pamphyli, and Dymanatae, and to these three they added a fourth, Aegialeis, named after the son of Adrastus, Aegialeus.[34]

69. These, then, were the things done by the Sicyonian Cleis-

33. "Rulers of the People."
34. A few comments may make the politics of these chapters clearer. In many states, notably Corinth and Sicyon, there was a submerged non-Dorian population, the Dorians having invaded and taken over power some time in the ninth to eighth century B.C. The tyrants, such as Cleisthenes of Sicyon, were anti-Dorian and of non-Dorian stock. Cleisthenes also opposed the Homeric usage of "Argive" as a general term for all Greeks. The eponymous heroes of the tribes linked the tribes with a very definite ethnic past. So Cleisthenes wished to destroy the sense of dignity of people who called themselves after their Dorian

thenes. Now the Athenian Cleisthenes, who was the maternal grandson of the Sicyonian one and had his name from him, too, seems to
me to have had the same contempt for the Ionians and so imitated
his grandfather Cleisthenes in disrupting the sharing of the same
tribes between his people and the Ionians.[35] The main body of the
Athenian people had formerly been deprived of all rights, but now
he drew them into his own party, changing the names of the tribes
and making them more in number than they had been. He set up
ten leaders-of-the-tribes instead of four, and he assigned the demes
in ten parts to the tribes. And so, having won over the people to his
side, he was far stronger than his opponents.

70. Then Isagoras, in his turn being worsted, took *his* counter-
measures. He called in Cleomenes of Lacedaemon, who had become
his guest-friend from the siege of the Pisistratids (and there was an ill
rumor that Cleomenes was the lover of Isagoras' wife). Cleomenes at
first sent in a herald to Athens, demanding that the Athenians banish Cleisthenes and many other Athenians with him, for, he said,
"They were under a curse." What he said in this message was by the
instruction of Isagoras; for the Alcmaeonidae and those who were of

---

ancestors. Hence the animal names. The later replacements for the derogatory
names were once more taken from the Dorian tradition, except for Aegialeis
(which may well be from *aigialos*, "shore," "men of the shore," though Herodotus
has discovered an eponymous hero for this name, too).

35. This is a shortened and confusing statement, and it is not quite clear
what it means. The elder Cleisthenes broke up the *Dorian* tribes, not the Ionian,
and it looks as if Herodotus is saying that the later Cleisthenes did to the Ionian
tribes in Athens what his grandfather had done to the Dorian tribes in Sicyon.
But Herodotus also tells us that the elder Cleisthenes disliked Argives and banished the Homeric rhapsodes because they were forever telling of Argive actions.
Of course, in historical times both the tribes that the elder Cleisthenes remodeled and the Argives (the *name* of which in Homer Cleisthenes resented in
the rhapsodes' recitations) would have been Dorian. Hence the whole thing appears to mean this: the elder Cleisthenes hated Dorians—see what he did to the
rhapsodes, the hero Adrastus, and the remodeling of the Dorian tribes; the
younger Cleisthenes "*also* despised Ionians," i.e., as his grandfather had despised
Dorians, and he too remodeled the structure of tribes—this time Ionian tribes,
not Dorian—though the spirit of contempt is common to both statesmen. We
do not know any reason why Cleisthenes should have "despised" the Ionians as
the anti-Dorian Cleisthenes of Sicyon was bound to despise the Dorians.

their faction were indeed accused of the murder (of which I shall tell), but Isagoras had no share in it, nor his friends.

71. Here is how "the Accursed" came by their name. There was a man among the Athenians whose name was Cylon, an Olympic victor. He had high thoughts of becoming a prince in Athens, and he won to himself an association of young men of his own age and tried to seize the citadel. He failed; then he sat as a suppliant before the statue of the goddess. The presiding committee of the naval boards, who then had power in Athens, made him and his companions rise from their suppliant position as men who were liable to any penalty except death. But they were killed, and rumor had it that it was the Alcmaeonidae who killed them. This happened before the time of Pisistratus.

72. When Cleomenes sent his herald, demanding the expulsion of Cleisthenes and the "Accursed," Cleisthenes himself departed; but Cleomenes, even so, came to Athens, with no great military power, and on his arrival banished—to undo the curse—seven hundred Athenian families, all suggested by Isagoras. Having done that, he next tried to do away with the Council and entrusted the government to three hundred partisans of Isagoras. The Council resisted and refused to obey, and then Cleomenes and Isagoras and his party took possession of the Acropolis. The rest of the Athenians united and besieged them for two days, and on the third day all who were Lacedaemonians among them accepted a treaty and marched out of the country. So the prophecy was fulfilled for Cleomenes; for when he went up to the Acropolis—for he of course intended to seize it— he came up to the shrine of the goddess to address her. Whereupon the priestess rose from her seat, before he had crossed the doors into the room, and said, "Stranger from Lacedaemon, go back and enter not into the shrine. It is not lawful for Dorians to enter here." He said, "Woman, I am no Dorian, but an Achaean." So he heeded not at all the utterance of the priestess but tried out his purposes and so was again driven out with his Lacedaemonians. For the rest of those captured, the Athenians bound them to face their death, among them Timesitheus the Delphian, whose greatest deeds, both of hand and spirit, I could tell you of.

73. These men were, then, bound and executed. After that the

Athenians, having brought back Cleisthenes and the seven hundred households that had been banished by Cleomenes, sent off messengers to Sardis, since they wished to make an alliance with the Persians, for they knew well that the Lacedaemonians and Cleomenes had been provoked to war against them. The messengers came to Sardis and said what they had been told to say. Then Artaphrenes, son of Hystaspes, the viceroy of Sardis, asked his question: "Who are these people and where in the world do they live that they ask the Persians to become their allies?" When he got his answer from the messengers, he said, rather pithily, "If the Athenians are willing to give King Darius earth and water, he offers an alliance to them; if not, away from here with them!" The messengers took the risk on their own heads and said they were willing to make the alliance. They then went home to their own country and were very severely blamed for what they had done.

74. Cleomenes recognized that he had been extremely insulted both in word and deed by the Athenians and gathered an army from all the Peloponnese, without declaring for what purpose he was gathering them—which was to punish the popular party in Athens and to set up Isagoras as prince there; for Isagoras had come out from the Acropolis along with himself. With his great army Cleomenes invaded Eleusis, and, by agreement, the Boeotians seized Oenoe and Hysiae, which were the furthest demes in Attica, and the Chalcidians, on the other side, overran other parts of Attica and did them mischief. The Athenians, although caught between two fires, as it were, determined to think about the Boeotians and Chalcidians at a later date and for now confronted the Lacedaemonians in Eleusis.

75. As they were about to engage, the Corinthians, first of all, took to reflecting among themselves that what they were doing was unjust; so they wheeled about and went home. Then Demaratus, the son of Ariston, who was at this time the other king of Sparta and had joined in Cleomenes' leadership in bringing the Spartans from Lacedaemon and had in the previous time not been at difference with Cleomenes, similarly deserted. It was as a result of this break between the two kings that the rule was established in Sparta that, when the army went on campaign, both kings were not allowed to go with it at the same time. Up till now, both had gone with the

army. As one of the two kings was now released from this service, one of the two Tyndaridae could also be left behind.[36] For before this, these two heroes both went on campaign, being so summoned to give their assistance to the army.

76. Then, at Eleusis, the rest of the Spartan allies, seeing the two kings at variance and the Corinthians deserting, took themselves off and went home. This was the fourth time Dorians came to Attica. They came twice as invaders, to make war, and twice for the good of the commonalty of Athens. The first warlike invasion took place when the Dorians established Megara as theirs; this expedition may rightly be attributed to the time when Codrus was king of Athens. The second and the third times were when the Spartan army moved from Sparta to try to banish the Pisistratids, and then this fourth, when Cleomenes brought the Peloponnesians in their invasion to Eleusis. This, then, was the fourth Dorian invasion of Athens.

77. So this expedition broke up ingloriously, and the Athenians, bent on revenge, made a campaign, first, against the Chalcidians. The Boeotians came as far as the Euripus to help the Chalcidians, and the Athenians, as soon as they saw them, decided to attack the Boeotians before the Chalcidians. So they engaged the Boeotians and won a great victory, killing very many and capturing seven hundred. On that same day, the Athenians crossed to Euboea and engaged the Chalcidians, and, after beating these also, they left four thousand colonizing settlers on the land of the Horse Farmers (that is the name given to rich men among the Chalcidians). The prisoners they made among these they kept under ward, along with the Boeotian prisoners of war, and put them all in chains. Eventually they released them for a ransom of two minas apiece. The chains with which they bound them they hung up in the Acropolis, and these survived till my time, still hanging from the walls, though the walls themselves had been all scorched by the fires of the Persians; they hang right opposite the cella that faces west. The Athenians also took a tenth of the ransoms and with it built a four-horse chariot of

36. This refers to the *images* of the Dioscuri, the twin heros Castor and Pollux, only one of which need now accompany the army.

bronze. It stands on your left as you first enter the Propylaea on the Acropolis. The inscription on it runs:

> Boeotians and Chalcidians, both nations, have been conquered
> By sons of the Athenians, in deeds of warlike valor.
> In murk and iron bondage they quenched the flame of their insolence
> And from the tenth of their ransom gave these horses to Pallas.

78. So Athens had increased in greatness. It is not only in respect of one thing but of everything that equality and free speech are clearly a good; take the case of Athens, which under the rule of princes proved no better in war than any of her neighbors but, once rid of those princes, was far the first of all. What this makes clear is that when held in subjection they would not do their best, for they were working for a taskmaster, but, when freed, they sought to win, because each was trying to achieve for his very self.

79. That, then, is what the Athenians did. But afterwards the Thebans sent to the god, for they wished to take vengeance on the Athenians. The Pythia told them that there was no vengeance at their disposal from themselves alone. "Submit it to the Many-Voiced," said the oracle, "and beg those who are nearest to you." So the oracular consultants went away and called a popular assembly, to which they presented the oracle. When the assembly heard the messengers saying they should consult "those nearest to you," they said, "Are not our nearest neighbors the men of Tanagra, Coronea, and Thespiae? But these are with us already and are always our staunch partners in war. Why should we beg them? No, surely, the oracle must not mean this."

80. That was how they thought it over, and then someone understood and said, "I think I understand what the oracle wants to say to us. The story is that Asopus had two daughters, Thebe and Aegina. Those were sisters, and I think that the god is telling us to beg the Aeginetans to help us take vengeance." There did not seem to be any better opinion than this put forward, and so they at once made their request of the Aeginetans, begging them to help them accord-

ing to the terms of the oracle, since "they were our nearest." In response to this request, the Aeginetans said they were sending the
Aeacidae[37] to help them.

81. So the Thebans made their attack now, relying on their alliance with the Aeacidae, but they were roughly handled by the
Athenians. So they sent again to Aegina, gave back the Aeacidae,
and begged the Aeginetans for men. The Aeginetans were at this
time uplifted by great prosperity, and they also remembered their ancient enmity with the Athenians; and so, at the Theban request,
they waged unofficial[38] war on the Athenians. While the Athenians
were attacking the Boeotians, the Aeginetans set upon Attica with
warships and plundered Phalerum and many districts along the seacoast, and in so doing they hit the Athenians hard.

82. The old debt of enmity that the Aeginetans owed to the
Athenians came about from the following beginning. The land of
the Epidaurians would yield no crop. The Epidaurians consulted
Delphi about this misfortune of theirs, and the Pythia told them to
set up images of Damia and Auxesia[39] and things would go better for
them. The Epidaurians further asked whether they should make the
images of bronze or stone, and the Pythia would have neither of
these but instead wood from cultivated olive trees. The Epidaurians
asked the Athenians for permission to cut certain trees of this kind,
assuming that the Athenian olive trees would be the holiest. (Indeed, it is said that at this time there were no cultivated olive trees
anywhere else than in Athens.) The Athenians granted their request on condition that each year the Epidaurians should make offerings to Athena Polias and to Erechtheus. The Epidaurians agreed to
the terms, got what they asked for, made the images of the olive
wood, and set them up. Then their land bore crops, and they discharged all their obligations to the Athenians.

83. Still at this time, and before it, the Aeginetans were subject

37. The images of the sons of Aeacus and of Aeacus himself. These had
close connections with Aegina and also with Salamis, where we will hear of
them again at the time of Xerxes' invasion.

38. "War without herald," i.e., with no formal declaration and without the
conventional restraints involved in the international respect for the herald as a
white-flag officer.

39. Apparently, Earth and Increase, i.e., spirits associated with fertility.

to the Epidaurians; in especial, they used to cross over to Epidaurus and settle there their suits of law against one another. But after this the Aeginetans took to building ships and became very stiff-necked and gave up their subject relation to Epidaurus. The two were now enemies, and the Aeginetans injured the Epidaurians, having got the mastery of the sea, and they also stole away the images of Damia and Auxesia. These they brought and set up in their own land, inland, in a place called Oea, some twenty furlongs from their city. At the place they set them up, they propitiated the images with sacrifices and with choruses of mocking women, ten men being assigned as choregi for each goddess.[40] The choruses abused no man but the local women only. The same rites obtain among the Epidaurians, and the Epidaurians have also some secret rites.[41]

84. Once the images were stolen, the Epidaurians no longer made their contract payments to the Athenians. The Athenians sent them an angry message, but the Epidaurians made it clear that they, the Epidaurians, were doing nothing unjust. They said that as long as they had the images in their country, they fulfilled their contract; when they lost the images, it could not be fair that they should continue to pay; the Athenians should surely exact their dues from the Aeginetans, who had the images. Whereupon the Athenians sent to Aegina and demanded back the images. But the Aeginetans declared that they had nothing to do with the Athenians at all.

85. The Athenians say that, after they had demanded back the images, they sent off certain of their citizens in a single trireme. These men, who were emissaries of the commonalty of Athens, came to Aegina, where they tried to wrench the images from their pediments, claiming that they were made of their own wood, in order to take them home with them. They were unable to take the images this way, and so they tied ropes round them and pulled, and, as they pulled them, there came upon them a thunderstorm and, with the thunderstorm, an earthquake. The men from the trireme, who were pulling, were driven out of their wits by the storm and the

40. This means that twenty men assumed, as part of their tax obligation to their state, the provision of these choruses.

41. Both Epidaurians and Aeginetans were Dorians, and the Aeginetans were a colony of the mother city Epidaurus, with which they shared various religious ties.

quake and in this condition took to killing one another, as though they were enemies, until there was only one of them left that got back to Phalerum.

86. That is the Athenian story. But the Aeginetans say that it was not with one ship that the Athenians came; for if it had been one, or even a few more than one, and even if they had not had a fleet of their own, they would easily have driven off the Athenians. No, say they, the Athenians attacked our country with many ships, and we yielded and did not fight at sea. (They cannot show clearly whether they gave in because they felt their inferiority in numbers in the sea fight, or whether they did what they did deliberately.) They say that the Athenians, finding no opposition, landed and made for the images, and being unable to tear them from their pediments did indeed throw ropes round them and dragged them until, as they were being dragged, both images did the same thing. What this was is not credible to me, but perhaps someone else might find it so. They say that the images fell to their knees and since then have continued so. That is what the Athenians did, say the Aeginetans. But they also say that, in their own case, when they learned that the Athenians were about to make war on them, they got the Argives ready to help. The Athenians landed in the territory of Aegina, but the Argives, coming to give aid, crossed unperceived from Epidaurus to the island and fell upon the Athenians, who had no advance knowledge of their presence. They attacked them and cut them off from their ships, and it was during this attack that the thunder and the earthquake happened.

87. Now these are the stories of Argives and Aeginetans both, but there is common agreement—and, moreover, this is shared by the Athenians—that one alone of their men escaped and came back to Attica. The difference is that the Argives say that it was themselves who destroyed the Attic army of which only one survived, while the Athenians say that the force of destruction was the divine power. Even the one man, say the Athenians, did not survive finally but ended in the following way. He came back to Athens and told what had happened, and the womenfolk of the Athenian men who had fought against Aegina, furious that he alone of all should have escaped, encircled the man and stabbed him with the brooch-pins with which they fastened their robes, each one asking him, "Where is my man?"

88. So he too died; and to the Athenians this deed of the women seemed even worse than the defeat itself. They could think of no way to punish the women but to change their dress to the Ionian mode; for before this the Athenian women wore clothes of the Dorian fashion, which is very like that of Corinth. The Athenians now changed this into a linen tunic, that the women might use no pins. In truth, this women's clothing was not originally Ionian but Carian, for in Greece all the older sort of women's dress was what we now call Dorian. As a result of this, the Argives and Aeginetans have laid down a law for each of their peoples that their brooch-pins should be longer again by half than the usual measure and that, in especial, the women should dedicate the pins in the shrine of these goddesses and to it should be brought nothing Attic, not even earthenware, but that it be the rule henceforth to drink there from pots made in their own country.

89. From so long ago, then, the women of Argives and Aeginetans wear longer pins than before, because of this quarrel with the Athenians; they did so still, even to my own time, and the beginning of the hatred on the part of the Athenians against the Aeginetans had its origin in the events I have described. And now, when the Thebans asked their help, the Aeginetans, warmly remembering what had happened about the images, came to the help of the Boeotians. The Aeginetans were ravaging the parts of Attica by the seacoast, and when the Athenians were setting out to attack them there came to them an oracle from Delphi, which declared that if they kept their hands from punishing the wrongdoing of the Aeginetans for thirty years and, in the thirty-first, they consecrated a sanctuary to Aeacus, they might then begin the war against the Aeginetans and all would go as they wanted it. But if they attacked the Aeginetans right away, they would, within this period of thirty years, both do and suffer much, though even so in the end they would be the victors. When the Athenians heard this, they dedicated the sanctuary to Aeacus, the one that is established now in the marketplace; but when they heard about the thirty years, they would not put up with the necessity of waiting, since what they had endured from the Aeginetans was so vile.

90. They were preparing, then, to take vengeance on the Aeginetans, but the awakening of another matter in Lacedaemon hindered them. The Lacedaemonians had heard of what the Alcmaeonidae

had contrived with the Pythia and of her plot against themselves and the Pisistratids,[42] and they were doubly sorry; for they had driven out of Athens men who were Spartan guest-friends, and, for doing so, they had had no visible gratitude from the Athenians. In addition, there were oracles predicting the many dreadful deeds that would be done upon them by the Athenians—oracles of which they were before quite ignorant but of which they now had information, for Cleomenes had brought them back to Sparta. Cleomenes had got these oracles from the Acropolis in Athens; the Pisistratids had owned them before, and, when they were expelled, they left them in the temple, and Cleomenes recovered them when they were so abandoned.

91. When the Lacedaemonians got these oracles and saw that the Athenians were gaining in power and not at all ready to be their subordinates, and when they took cognizance that the Attic race, in its freedom, would be the equal of themselves but, if controlled by a despotism, would be weak and disposed to subjection—when they understood all this, they sent for Hippias, the son of Pisistratus, from Sigeum on the Hellespont, where the Pisistratids had taken refuge. As soon as Hippias came on their summons, the Spartiates sent for envoys from the rest of the allies, and this is what they said to them: "You allies of ours: we now realize that we have not acted rightly. Those oracles were false that incited us to drive out from their native land men who were staunch guest-friends of ours and who undertook to make Athens our subject; and after we had driven them out, we handed the city over to a thankless commonalty. These commons, freed by us, lifted their heads up and insulted and drove out both ourselves and our king. They grew a great pride among them and increased in power in a fashion that has taught a thorough lesson to their neighbors, the Boeotians and Chalcidians; soon there will be many another who will find out he has been mistaken. Since we have been wrong to do all these things, now, with the help of you who have come here, we shall try to punish these people. It is for that very reason that we have sent for Hippias here and have summoned you from the cities, that by common decision and with common forces we may restore him to Athens and give back to him what we have taken away."

42. Cf. 5.63.

92. That was what they said. But the majority of the allies did not accept their proposals. Though the rest of them kept silent, the Corinthian, Socles, spoke up: "Truly shall the heaven be beneath the earth, truly, earth above the sky! Truly shall men have their living in the sea, and fish have what men had formerly, when you, the Lacedaemonians, abolishing the rule of equality in the cities, make ready to return to them their absolute princes! Than such princes there is among mankind nothing that is unjuster or bloodier. However, if you, the Lacedaemonians, think it good that the cities should submit to princely power, do you first set up such power, a prince, among yourselves, and then seek to set up such among the rest of us. As things stand, you know nothing of princes; you take most heedful care that none such grow to be in Sparta; and so what you do to your allies is an abuse of our rights. If you knew the institution as we do, you would offer better judgments about it than you now do.

"This is the story of Corinth's condition. There was an oligarchy, and those who were called the Bacchiadae administered the state and married and gave in marriage among themselves. Among these men there was one Amphion who had a lame daughter, whose name was Labda. None of the Bacchiadae would marry this girl, and she was finally taken by Eëtion, son of Echecrates, of the township of Petra. His remoter ancestors were of the Lapithae and Caenids. Eëtion had no children either by this wife or any other woman. So he went to Delphi about the matter of his issue. As he came in, the Pythia addressed him at once in these lines:

Eëtion, you are rich in honor, yet none does you honor.
Labda will still conceive, and a rolling rock shall she bear
    you,
Such as shall fall upon princes and deal out justice in
    Corinth.

This oracle that was given to Eëtion was somehow reported to the Bacchiadae, who had not understood an earlier oracle about Corinth, which had the same purport as Eëtion's, and it ran thus:

An eagle shall breed in the rocks and bring as offspring
    a lion,
A savage eater of raw meat; he shall loosen the knees
    of many.

Heed these things well, men of Corinth, you who around fair
     Pirene
Dwell, and also about the crag-crested city of Corinth.

This oracle had earlier been given to the Bacchiadae, but they had
no clue to its meaning. When they heard of the new one for Eëtion,
they immediately understood the former as in harmony with the
latter.

"Although they understood this, they held their peace about it,
because they wanted to make away with whatever child should be
born to Eëtion. As soon as the woman gave birth, they sent ten of
their own number to the district where Eëtion lived to kill the child.
These men came to Petra and, entering the courtyard of Eëtion's
house, asked for the child. Labda had no idea of why they had come
there and thought that they asked for the child only out of good will
toward the father. So she brought the baby and handed it to one of
the ten. Now, when they had been on the way there, they had laid
their plans that whoever of them first got his hands on the child
would dash it to the ground. When Labda brought the baby and
gave it over, it happened, by some stroke of providence, that the
child smiled at the man who had taken it. The man noticed it, and a
moment of pity held him back from the killing; he pitied it and
handed it to a second man, and he to a third. So it was passed from
hand to hand of the ten, and no one wanted to make away with
it. So they gave it back to the mother and went out. But they
then stood in front of the door and attacked one another with reproaches—especially the one who had got the child first, because he
had not acted as they had determined, before, they would do. Eventually, as time went on, they resolved to go in again and all take a
share in the murder. But fate had determined that evil should grow
richly for Corinth from this child of Eëtion. For Labda, as she stood
by the doors, heard everything. She was afraid that they would
change their minds and the second time get hold of the child and
kill it; and so she took and hid it in what seemed to her the most
unlikely place to look, in a chest. For she knew that if they turned
back to search, they would look everywhere. That indeed is what
happened. They came and searched, but there was no sign of the
child; and so they resolved to go away and to tell those who had sent

them that they had done all they had been instructed to do. That was their tale when they came home.

"Thereafter, Eëtion's child grew up; and because he had avoided the danger by means of the chest, he got the nickname of Cypselus.[43] When Cypselus grew to manhood, he consulted Delphi and got there an oracle of ambiguous meaning; but through confidence in it he assaulted and captured Corinth. Here is the oracle:

> Happy indeed is this man who comes down into my palace,
> Cypselus Eëtides,[44] king of renowned Corinth,
> Happy himself and his sons, but no longer the sons of his
> children.

This was the oracle, and Cypselus held absolute power and became the kind of man I will tell you. Many of the Corinthians he drove into exile, and many he mulcted of their money, and, of even greater numbers of them, he took their lives. When he had reigned thirty years and in good fortune had woven up the skein of his life, his son Periander succeeded him in the sovereignty.[45]

"At the beginning Periander was gentler than his father had been. But afterwards, when he had dealt, by messengers, with Thrasybulus, prince of Miletus, he became yet bloodier than Cypselus. For he sent a herald to Thrasybulus inquiring about the safest political establishment for administering the city best. Thrasybulus led out Periander's messenger, outside the city, and with him entered a sown field; then he walked through the corn, questioning, and again questioning, the herald about his coming from Corinth. And ever and again as he saw one of the ears of corn growing above the rest he would strike it down, and what he struck down he threw away, until by this means he had destroyed all the fairest and strongest of the corn. So he passed through the whole place and, having added no suggestion, sent the herald away.

"When the herald came back to Corinth, Periander was anxious to know what suggestion Thrasybulus had made. But the man said that Thrasybulus had made no suggestion at all, and indeed he wondered what sort of a man this was he had been sent to, a madman

43. The word Cypselus means "chest."
44. A patronymic, "son of Eëtion."
45. In 625 B.C.

and a destroyer of his own property; for he recounted all that he had seen Thrasybulus do. But Periander understood the act of Thrasybulus and grasped in his mind that what he was telling him was that he should murder the most eminent of the citizens. And so from this time forth he displayed every form of wickedness toward his fellow countrymen. Whatever Cypselus had spared of death and banishment, Periander completed. One day he had all the women of Corinth stripped naked because of his wife Melissa.[46] Periander had sent to the Thesprotians, to the river Acheron, to the Oracle of the Dead there, to consult about a treasure that had been confided to his keeping by a guest-friend. Melissa had appeared to the messenger but refused to tell him in what place the treasure lay, for, she said, she was cold and naked, inasmuch as she had no profit of the clothes in which Periander had buried her, since they were not burned with her. The proof that she spoke the truth (she said) was that 'Periander put his loaves in an oven that was cold.'

"When this was reported back to Periander, he straightway made a proclamation that all the women of Corinth should come out to the temple of Hera. (You see, the token sign that Melissa had made to him convinced him; for he had lain with her when she was already a corpse.) So the women came out in their finest clothes, assuming they were going to a festival. Periander stationed his guards there and stripped them all naked, ladies and servants alike; heaping all the clothes into a pit, he made a dedicatory prayer to Melissa and burned them. After he had done that, he sent the second time to the Oracle of the Dead, and this time the shade of Melissa told him in what place she had stowed the deposit of his guest-friend.

"Such is absolute princely power, my friends from Lacedaemon, and such are its deeds. We, the Corinthians, were possessed by great wonder the moment we knew that you were sending for Hippias. Now we wonder even more at what you say. We call upon the Greek gods as our witnesses when we beg you not to set up princedoms within the cities. But let us assume that you will not give over this policy; let us assume that, against all justice, you will make your attempt and bring Hippias back. Well, know then that you will never win the assent of the Corinthians to it."

46. In 3.50 there is an account of how he came to kill his wife. She is at this time already dead.

93. That is what Socles said, the delegate from Corinth. Hippias answered him, invoking the very same gods against him: "Verily," he said, "the Corinthians more than any other people will yet long for the Pisistratids when the appointed days are accomplished and they are sorely vexed by the Athenians." That was the answer of Hippias, for he knew the oracles more accurately than any other man. The other allies till now had held themselves in silence; but when they heard Socles speaking so fearlessly, each one burst into speech and chose the position of the Corinthians and adjured the Lacedaemonians not to do such a revolutionary thing to a Greek city.

94. So the plan for Hippias was checked. When Hippias was thus driven away, Amyntas, king of Macedon, offered him Anthemon, and the Thessalians would have given him Iolcus. But he would have neither of them but went back to Sigeum, which Pisistratus had captured by force from the Mytilenaeans and, when he was master of it, had set up as its prince his own bastard son (by an Argive woman), Hegesistratus; but this ruler did not keep what he had got from Pisistratus without a fight. For the Mytilenaeans, making their base in Achilleum,[47] and the Athenians at Sigeum fought for a long time, the Mityleneans claiming back Sigeum and the Athenians not acknowledging their claim but declaring that Aeolians had no more share in the land of Ilium than themselves or any others among the Greeks who had taken part with Menelaus in avenging the rape of Helen.

95. All sorts of events took place during this war, and among them the case of the poet Alcaeus. During an encounter that the Athenians were winning, he took to his heels and escaped; but the Athenians got his arms and hung them up in the temple of Athena in Sigeum. Alcaeus made a poem about this, which he sent to Mytilene, in which he reports his misfortune to his friend Melanippus. It was Periander, son of Cypselus, who reconciled the Mytilenaeans and the Athenians, for they had entrusted the matter to him as arbiter. The terms of his reconciliation were that each party should keep what it had.

96. So Sigeum fell to the control of Athens. But when Hippias now came from Lacedaemon to Asia, he stirred everything up, slan-

47. The place where Achilles was buried.

dering the Athenians to Artaphrenes and trying to manage it that the Athenians would become subjects of himself and Darius. Such were the acts of Hippias; and the Athenians, when they learned of them, sent messengers to Sardis to urge the Persians not to listen to those who were banished from Athens. But Artaphrenes said to them that, if they would keep their skins safe, they should take back Hippias. The Athenians rejected this message when they got it, and, as they did so reject it, they resolved to be openly at enmity with the Persians.

97. It was just at this moment, when they were thinking like this and were at odds with the Persians, that Aristagoras of Miletus came to Athens, being driven out of Sparta by King Cleomenes; for Athens was far the most powerful of the remaining cities.[48] Aristagoras came before the popular assembly. He said all the same things that he had said in Sparta, about the riches of Asia and the Persian style of warfare and how these people were not used to spears or shields and would be right easy to conquer. He said this, and also said that Miletus was a colony of Athens and that, given the greatness of Athenian power, they should certainly protect the Milesians. He promised them anything and everything, for he was very eager indeed, and in the end he persuaded them. It seems that it is easier to fool many men than one; Cleomenes the Lacedaemonian was only one, but Aristagoras could not fool him, though he managed to do so to thirty thousand Athenians. The Athenians were convinced and voted to send twenty ships to help the Ionians, and they appointed as commander of the fleet Melanthius, one of their citizens who was very notable in all respects. These were the ships that were the beginning of evils for both Greeks and barbarians.

98. Aristagoras sailed on ahead and came to Miletus, having invented a plan that could not be at all useful to the Ionians; nor, indeed, was it for the sake of usefulness that he made the plan, but only to vex King Darius. He sent a man into Phrygia, to the Paeonian prisoners of war captured at the river Strymon by Megabazus. These people were now settled in a part of Phrygia in a village of their own. When the messenger came to these Paeonians, he said: "Paeonians, Aristagoras, prince of Miletus, has sent me to you to give you a

48. I.e., after Sparta, Athens was the greatest power.

counsel of rescue, if so be you will listen to him. Now all of Ionia has revolted from the King, and you have a chance to escape back to your own land. As far as the sea the matter lies in your own hands, but after that we will take care of you." The Paeonians were very pleased at what they heard and, taking their womenfolk and children, ran away to the sea. (Some of them, too, did stay where they were because they dreaded the danger.) When they got to the sea, they crossed over to Chios. When they were already in Chios, a large body of Persian horse came on their track, pursuing them. Failing to overtake them, the Persians sent word to Chios, commanding the Paeonians to return. But the Paeonians refused the proposition, and the Chians shipped them out of Chios to Lesbos, and the Lesbians conveyed them to Doriscus, and from there they went on foot and eventually came to Paeonia.

99. To return to Aristagoras: the Athenians then came with twenty ships, and they brought with them five triremes of Eretrians, who did not serve for good will toward the Athenians but for the sake of the Milesians themselves. They were paying back a debt, for the Milesians had borne a share in the Eretrians' war against Chalcis in the old days, when the Samians came to help the Chalcidians against both Eretrians and Milesians. These, then, came, and some other allies; and Aristagoras made an attack on Sardis. He did not serve on campaign himself but remained in Miletus and appointed other generals for the Milesians—his own brother, Charopinus, and another Milesian, Hermophantus.

100. Arriving, then, at Ephesus with this expedition, the Ionians left their transports at Coresus, in the territory of Ephesus, and themselves marched inland in great force, taking Ephesians to guide their line of march. They marched along the river Caicus and then, crossing over Mount Tmolus, they reached and captured Sardis with no opposition. They captured it all—all, that is, except the acropolis. But the acropolis was defended by Artaphrenes himself with a large force.

101. Here is the reason why, having captured the town, they failed to plunder it. Most of the houses in Sardis were made of rushes, and others of them that were made of brick had roofs of rushes. As soon as a soldier fired one of these, the fire went from house to house and ranged over the entire city. As the town burned,

the Lydians and those of the Persians who were in Sardis were cut off on every side, for the fire consumed the outer parts of the town; and, having no way of getting out, they ran together toward the marketplace and the river Pactolus (this is the river that carries down gold dust from Tmolus, flows through the center of the marketplace, and issues into the river Hermus, and the Hermus issues into the sea); and the Lydians and Persians, crowding together at this Pactolus, were forced to defend themselves. The Ionians, seeing some of their enemies putting up this defense and others in great numbers bearing down upon them, took fright and retreated to the mountain called Tmolus and from there, under cover of night, retreated to their ships.

102. So Sardis burned,[49] and, in it, the temple of the native goddess Cybebe, and it was this that the Persians took as their excuse later when they, in their turn, burned the temples of the Greeks. Then the Persians who inhabited the provinces west of the Halys, having information of what had happened, collected and rallied to the help of the Lydians. They found that the Ionians were no longer in Sardis; but following in their tracks they came up with them at Ephesus. The Ionians took up their position there against them, and there was a battle in which the Ionians were severely defeated. The Persians killed many of them, including, among distinguished men, the general of the Eretrians, Eualcides, one who had won crowns in the games and had had lavish praise from the poet Simonides of Ceos. The rest of the Ionians fled from the battle and scattered to their respective cities.

103. That was what the fight proved to be, then. But after it, the Athenians gave up the Ionians altogether; and although Aristagoras kept sending messages, urging them to help, they entirely refused to do so. But the Ionians, although they were bereft of their Athenian allies, nonetheless prepared war against the King. (They had, you see, already done so much against Darius.) They now sailed to the Hellespont and reduced Byzantium and all the other cities there, and, sailing beyond the Hellespont, they took over the greater part of Caria as their allies. For even Caunus, which had before been unwilling to join their alliance, now of itself came over to them, when Sardis had been burned.

49. 498 B.C.

104. All the Cypriots came over, too, of their own will, except for the Amathusians; for the revolt of the Cypriots from the Medes came about in the following way. There was one Onesilus, the younger brother of Gorgus, king of the Salaminians.[50] He was the son of Chersis, the son of Siromus, the son of Euelthon. This man had often already urged Gorgus to revolt from the King, and now, when he learned of the Ionians' revolt, he pressed his case vehemently. As he failed to convince Gorgus, Onesilus watched until the king had gone out of the city of Salamis, and then, with his fellow conspirators, he closed the gates against him. Gorgus, having lost his city, took refuge with the Medes, and Onesilus ruled over Salamis and persuaded all the Cypriots to join the revolt. He convinced all the rest, but not the Amathusians; and as these refused to listen to him, he set to and besieged them.

105. Onesilus was busy with the siege of Amathus. When King Darius was informed that Sardis had been captured and burned by the Athenians and the Ionians and that the leader of this alliance, who had woven the whole thing together, was Aristagoras of Miletus, he first (so the story goes), when he heard the news, made no account of the Ionians—for he knew well that they would surely not get off scot-free for their rebellion—but he put the question, "Who are the Athenians?" and, having his answer, asked for a bow. He took it, fitted an arrow to it, and shot it into the sky, and as he sent it up he prayed, "Zeus, grant me the chance of punishing the Athenians." Having said that, he ordered one of the servants that, as often as a meal was set before him, the man should thrice, on each occasion, say, "Master, remember the Athenians."

106. These were his instructions; and then he summoned to his presence Histiaeus of Miletus, whom Darius had kept so long with himself. "I learn, Histiaeus," he said, "that it is your deputy, to whom you entrusted Miletus, that has led this revolution against me. He has brought in men from the other continent, and the Ionians with them—who will surely pay me penalty for what they have done—and, having persuaded the Ionians and the others to follow him, he has robbed me of Sardis. Now, can any of this seem to you well done? And how could any of it be done without plans of yours being involved? Take heed lest afterwards you find yourself to

50. This Salamis is a city on Cyprus, not the island near Athens.

blame." Histiaeus answered him: "My lord, what a word is this you have spoken! That any plan of mine should be to your hurt, small or great! What would be my object in so doing? What do I lack that I should do it? All that is at your disposal is at my disposal; I am thought worthy to hear all your counsels. If indeed my deputy has done anything such as you say he has, you may be sure that what he has done was done by himself, at his own risk. I, for one, utterly reject the story that the Milesians or my deputy are in revolt against you. But if they *are* doing such a thing, and what you have heard *is* the truth, then, my lord, you may understand what you have done in dragging me hither, away from the seacoast. For it looks likely that the Ionians may have done what they have long desired—once I was removed from their sight. So long as I was in Ionia, not a city of them stirred. Now therefore send me quickly into Ionia, that I may bring all matters there into their former order and place in your own hands this deputy of mine in Miletus who has contrived all this. When I have done this according to your pleasure, I swear by your Royal Gods that I will not take off this tunic of mine, wearing which I will descend upon Ionia, until I make Sardo,[51] that greatest of islands, subject to your tribute."

107. In this story of his, Histiaeus was cheating, but Darius was convinced by him and sent him off, bidding him, when he had accomplished all that he had promised, to appear before himself again at Susa.

108. While, then, the message about Sardis came to the King, and Darius, having launched the arrow from his bow, had spoken with Histiaeus, and Histiaeus had been released by Darius to go to the coast—while all these things were happening, there were also the following events: Onesilus of Salamis was besieging Amathus when he was informed that Artybius, a Persian, was expected to arrive in Cyprus with a large Persian army. Onesilus, on this news, sent round heralds to Ionia to summon the Ionians to his help; and the Ionians, having taken no long time to debate the matter, arrived with a large force. So the Ionians were in Cyprus; and the Persians, having crossed over with their ships from Cilicia, came to Salamis by land, while the Phoenicians, with their fleet, rounded the cape that is called the Keys of Cyprus.

51. Sardo is Sardinia.

109. At this moment the princes of Cyprus called the generals of the Ionians together and said: "Ionians, we Cypriots give you the choice of which you will fight: the Persians or the Phoenicians. If you wish to draw up your army on land and try your strength against the Persians, now is the time for you to leave your ships and make your formations on land and for us to embark on your ships and fight the Phoenicians. If you would rather try your strength against the Phoenicians, then you must act so that, whichever of the two you choose, both Ionia and Cyprus will be free, as far as you can make it so." To this the Ionians said: "The commonalty of the Ionians sent us to guard the sea, but not so that we might turn over our ships to the Cypriots and ourselves confront the Persians on land. In this, our appointed place, then, we will try to be good men and true. As for you, it behooves you to remember all that you have suffered when you were enslaved to the Medes, and so prove yourselves brave men."

110. Such was the answer of the Ionians. Afterwards, the Persians came to the plain of Salamis, and the kings of Cyprus ranged their troops, placing other Cypriots in positions against the rest of the enemy, but, reserving the best of the men of Salamis and Soli, they ranged these against the Persians. The Persian general Artybius was confronted by Onesilus as his opponent; it was Onesilus' own choice.

111. Now, Artybius had a horse trained to rear against his foeman. Onesilus heard of this and spoke to his special man-at-arms, who was by race a Carian and a very famous soldier, of great courage. "I understand," said Onesilus, "that Artybius has a horse that rears and, kicking and biting, does away with anyone whom he engages. Take thought now, and tell me at once, which of the two you will watch and strike, Artybius or the horse." His squire said, "My lord, I am ready to do both or either, just as you bid me. But let me say what I think is more useful for your interests. I think a king and a general should engage a king and a general. For if you do away with a general, it will be a great thing; and again, if he should do the like to you—God forbid that it should be so!—death at the hands of a worthy enemy is only a half-misfortune. But for us, your underlings, we should fight with underlings and with the horse. You need not fear the horse's tricks. I will undertake that he will never rear again against another foeman."

112. So he spoke, and the battle was joined, both on land and on sea. The Ionians proved themselves very skillful with their ships that

day and beat the Phoenicians, and, among the Ionians, the Samians showed especial bravery. On land the two armies joined, charged, and fought. This is what happened the generals on both sides: as Artybius rode up to attack Onesilus, the latter, according to the agreement he had made with his squire, struck at Artybius himself, who was assailing him. The horse drove his front feet down upon Onesilus' shield, and then the Carian with his scimitar struck and shore the horse's legs away.

113. So the Persian general Artybius fell where he was, horse and all. The others fought on, but Stesenor, prince of Curium, with a fairly large body of men who were with him, deserted. (The Curians are said to be a colony sent out by Argos.) When the Curians gave in, immediately the war chariots of the Salaminians did the same, and then the Persians came to have the best of the Cypriots. The army was routed and many fell, among them Onesilus, the son of Chersis, who had brought about the revolt of the Cypriots, and the king of Soli, Aristocyprus, son of Philocyprus. This Philocyprus was the most praised of any of the princes in a poem written by Solon the Athenian when he came to Cyprus.

114. Because Onesilus had besieged them, the Amathusians cut off his head and carried it to Amathus, where they hung it over the gates. As the head hung there and became hollow, a swarm of bees entered it and filled it with honeycombs. The Amathusians consulted an oracle about this thing that had happened, and the answer was that they should take the head down and bury it and should each year make sacrifice to Onesilus as hero, and, if they did that, things would be the better for them.

115. The Amathusians did this and still do so in my time. Now the Ionians who had fought off Cyprus learned what had happened to Onesilus—that he had been defeated and that the other cities were besieged except for Salamis, which the Salaminians had surrendered to their former king, Gorgus. The Ionians, in the face of all this news, sailed right away to Ionia. Of the cities of Cyprus, Soli stood out the longest under siege; the Persians, by digging under its defending walls, captured it in the fifth month.

116. So for a year the Cypriots were free and then relapsed into slavery.[52] Daurises, who had married a daughter of Darius, and

52. In 497.

Hymaees and Otanes, who were also Persian generals (and these two also married daughters of Darius), pursued those Ionians who had made the campaign against Sardis and, after defeating them in battle, swept them to their ships; after that the generals divided up the cities among themselves and plundered them.

117. Daurises turned to the cities on the Hellespont and captured Dardanus, Abydos, Percote, Lampsacus, and Paesus. These he captured each on its own day. As he drove on from Paesus to the city of Parium, he got word that the Carians had made common cause with the Ionians and revolted from Persia. So he turned away from the Hellespont and invaded Caria.

118. The Carians somehow got news of this before Daurises arrived among them. So they collected to the place called the White Pillars and the river Marsyas, which flows from the Idrian country and empties into the Maeander. As the Carians collected in strength, various plans were put forward. The best seems to me to have been that of Pixodarus, son of Mausolus, a man of Cindye. He was married to the daughter of the king of Cilicia, Syennesis. This man's advice was that the Carians should cross the river Maeander and, keeping the river behind them, engage the Persians. Thus the Carians would have no line of escape but would have to stand their ground there and prove better than their natural inclinations. However, this plan did not win out, but another: that the Persians, not the Carians, should have the Maeander behind them and so, if they were worsted in the fight and tried to fly, they would have nowhere to escape to but would fall into the river.

119. When the Persians had come and crossed the Maeander, the Carians engaged them just by the river Marsyas; they fought a stout fight and a long one, but at last the numbers told against them and they were beaten. On the Persian side there fell two thousand and, of the Carians, ten thousand. So the Carians fled to Labraunda, to the shrine of Zeus, God of Battles, there; this is a great and holy grove of plane trees. (The Carians are the only people of whom we know who sacrifice to Zeus, God of Battles.) When they were penned up in this place, they discussed their chance of safety: would it be better for them to surrender to the Persians or leave Asia altogether?

120. As they debated this, there came to their aid Milesians and their allies, and the Carians gave over their former debate and made

themselves ready again for war. The Persians came upon them, and they engaged, and after the fight they had been defeated more disastrously than the first time. Of all the many that fell, the Milesians' losses were the greatest.

121. But after this disaster the Carians still rallied and renewed the fight. Learning that the Persians were setting out against their cities, they ambushed them on the road at Pedasus. The Persians fell into the ambush at night and were destroyed, including their generals Daurises, Amorges, and Sisimaces. With them died also Myrsus, the son of Gyges. The leader of the ambush was Heraclides of Mylasas, son of Ibanollis.

122. So these Persians were killed. But Hymaees, who had himself been one of those who pursued the Ionians who had marched on Sardis, turned toward the Propontis and captured Cius in Mysia. Having taken this place, he learned that Daurises had left the Hellespont and was marching on Caria. So he left the Propontis and drew off his army toward the Hellespont and captured all the Aeolians around the territory of Ilium and also the Gergithae, who are what is left of the old Teucrians; but Hymaees himself, while he was taking all these nations, caught a sickness and died in the Troad.

123. So Hymaees died. But Artaphrenes, the viceroy of Sardis, and Otanes, the third of the three Persian generals, were instructed to march against Ionia and the neighboring Aeolian territory. They captured Clazomenae in the Ionian part and Cyme in the Aeolian.

124. As these cities were being captured, Aristagoras of Miletus showed clearly that his courage was not of the high sort. He had set Ionia in tumult, he had made a vast muddle of everything, and now, when he saw the result, he contemplated running away. It seemed also to him that it was quite impossible to beat Darius. So he summoned together all those who were of his party and took counsel with them, saying that they had better have some sort of refuge at their disposal if they were driven out of Miletus. Perhaps he should lead them to settle Sardinia or Myrcinus in Edonia, which Histiaeus had received as a gift from Darius and had fortified? These were the questions Aristagoras put to his friends.

125. The judgment of Hecataeus, the chronicler, son of Hegesander, tended toward going to neither of these places but to building a fortification on the island of Leros and remaining quiet, if he were

driven out of Miletus. If he made this his base, thought Hecataeus, Aristagoras might later get back to Miletus.

126. This was the counsel of Hecataeus. But for Aristagoras the best plan seemed to draw off to Myrcinus. He entrusted Miletus to Pythagoras, a very distinguished fellow countryman of his own. He himself took everyone who would go with him and sailed away to Thrace, where he took possession of the place to which he had set out. He made this his headquarters and met his death at the hands of the Thracians there, himself and his army, while he was beleaguering a town, even though the Thracians were willing to leave it under treaty terms.

Book Six

1. That was the end, then, of Aristagoras, who had caused the Ionian revolt. But Histiaeus, prince of Miletus, who had been released by Darius to go to Sardis, duly arrived there. When he came from Susa, Artaphrenes, the viceroy of Sardis, asked him why he thought the Ionians had revolted. Histiaeus answered that he had no idea why they had done so and was very surprised, as though in fact he knew nothing of what had happened. Artaphrenes saw him at this trick and said to him—for he knew the very truth of the revolt—"Histiaeus, the business is this: it was you who stitched the shoe and Aristagoras who put it on."

2. That was what Artaphrenes said about the revolt. Histiaeus, being afraid that Artaphrenes understood, ran away to the coast at the first nightfall after that, having deceived King Darius; for he had promised to subdue to him Sardo, that greatest of the islands, but secretly he would have wormed himself into the leadership of the Ionians in the war against Darius. He crossed to Chios and there was cast into bonds by the Chians, being suspected by them of contriving mischief against them by orders of Darius. When the Chians learned the whole story—that he was an enemy of Darius—they released him.

3. But Histiaeus was then questioned by the Ionians as to what truly was in his head when he had sent to Aristagoras to revolt from the King and had caused such a vast deal of evil for the Ionians. Histiaeus did not give them the real reason but instead told them that King Darius had a design to move the Phoenicians and settle them in Ionia and put the Ionians in Phoenicia and that that was the reason for his sending to Aristagoras. Not a word of this had been planned by Darius, but Histiaeus used it to scare the Ionians.

4. Afterwards, Histiaeus, through a man of Atarneus, named Hermippus, as his messenger, sent letters to some Persians in Sardis; indeed, he had had previous parleys with them about revolt. How-

ever, Hermippus did not give the letters to the people to whom they were sent but took and put them in the hands of Artaphrenes. As soon as Artaphrenes learned everything that was happening, he instructed Hermippus to deliver the letters to their destination but to take the return letters that the Persians would write to Histiaeus and give them to himself. Artaphrenes killed a great number of the Persians when they were thus revealed to him.

5. That, then, was the trouble in Sardis. After Histiaeus had been disappointed in this hope, the Chians sought to restore him to Miletus at the entreaty of Histiaeus himself. But the people of Miletus, who had but now been glad to see the last of Aristagoras, were by no means eager to welcome back a prince into their country, for they had had their taste of freedom. It was nighttime when Histiaeus tried to come back, and it was a military attempt. He was wounded in the thigh by some Milesian or other, was thus driven out of his own country, and went back to Chios. He failed to persuade the Chians to give him ships but succeeded with the Lesbians, when he got across to Mytilene. These latter manned eight war vessels and with these made for Byzantium, along with Histiaeus. They made this their base, and all the ships sailing from the Pontus[1] were cut off by them, except such as consented to serve under Histiaeus.

6. So much for Histiaeus and the Mytilenaeans. But against Miletus itself a great army and navy were looked for. For the Persian generals had gathered all their forces and made one host of it and were driving on Miletus, thinking all the other cities of lesser account. The Phoenicians were the keenest of their sailors, and there served with them the Cypriots, who had been lately conquered, and the Cilicians and the Egyptians.

7. This force, then, moved against Miletus and the rest of Ionia. The Ionians, learning of it, sent representatives to act as counsel for them in the Panionium.[2] When they came there and joined in consultation, a resolution was passed that no land force be raised to oppose the Persians but that the Milesians themselves should defend their own fortifications and that the Ionians as a whole should man every ship they had, without reserve, and collect them with all

1. The Black Sea.
2. Cf. 1.148.

speed at Lade, to fight a sea battle in defense of Miletus. Now, Lade is a tiny island that lies off the city of Miletus.

8. Thereafter, with their ships all manned, came the Ionians and, with them, such Aeolians as live in Lesbos. The order of battle was as follows: the Milesians themselves held the eastern wing, bringing eighty ships; next them were the men of Priene, with twelve ships, and the men of Myus, with three. Next them were the men of Teos, with seventeen, and next them were the Chians, with one hundred. Next these were ranged the Erythraeans and the Phocaeans, the Erythraeans with eight ships and the Phocaeans with three; and next the Phocaeans were the Lesbians, with seventy. Finally, the Samians held the western wing with sixty ships. The total number of the whole was three hundred and fifty-three triremes.

9. These were on the Ionian side, but the number of the barbarian ships was six hundred. When they too came up to the territory of Miletus, and all the land army came up, the Persian generals, learning the number of the Ionian ships, were afraid that they would not be able to beat them, and so, if they failed to command the sea, they would not be able to destroy Miletus; and, after that, they would risk being punished by Darius. These were their considerations, and they brought together the Ionian princes who had been deprived of their powers by Aristagoras of Miletus and had then taken refuge with the Persians and were at this time serving with the army against Miletus. They called together such of these men as were there and said to them: "You men of Ionia: now let some one of you show himself forth as benefactor of the King's house. Let each of you approach his own fellow citizens and try to detach them from the Ionian alliance. Make them proposals and promises to the effect that they will not suffer for their revolt, neither in person nor will their temples or private property be burned, and the rule over them will be no more forceful than before. If they reject our offers and stake everything on a battle, you may menace them with what will certainly happen then: when conquered, they will be enslaved; we will castrate their male children and carry off the girls to Bactria, and their country we will turn over to the hands of others."

10. That was the Persian proposition to the princes. So throughout the night the princes sent messengers, each one to his own people. The Ionians to whom the messengers came persisted in

being stubborn; they refused to turn traitors; but each group of people thought that the Persian offer had been made to them alone.

11. These things happened directly after the Persians came against Miletus; but when the Ionians gathered into Lade, they held assemblies there, and, among other speakers, Dionysius in especial, being the general of the Phocaeans, spoke among them: "Men of Ionia, our fortunes are on the very razor edge of decision: whether we will be freemen or slaves—nay, runaway slaves at that. If you people are willing, for now, to endure hardships, you will have, for the immediate moment, a hard time, but you will be able to beat your enemies and be free. If you settle into sloth and disorder, I have no hope that any one of you shall avoid the punishment of the Great King for your revolt. Listen to me and entrust yourselves to me. If the gods give us equal treatment with our foes, I promise you that our enemy will either not engage us at all or will engage and be seriously defeated."

12. The Ionians listened and put themselves at the disposal of Dionysius. He would lead the fleet out each morning in column, and using the oarsmen he would make the maneuver of "breaking the line."[3] He also armed the marines on board, and for the rest of the day he kept the ships at anchor. So all day long he made the Ionians work. For seven days the Ionians obeyed him and did what he bade them; but on the next day they began to talk among themselves. They were entirely unaccustomed to work like this, and they were worn out with hardship and the heat of the sun. "What god can we have sinned against that we pay a penalty like this? We must have been entirely mad and sailed out of our minds' bearings to trust ourselves to this Phocaean braggart. Three ships are all he brings with him! He takes us over and afflicts us with sufferings from which we will never recover. Many of us are already sick and many more like to become sick. Rather than horrors like these it would be better for us to endure anything at all, including this future slavery—whatever that may be—rather than what now oppresses us. Enough of this; let's not listen to his orders any more." That is what they said, and after that not a man would obey him. They pitched tents, like a kind

3. This maneuver "consisted in breaking through the enemy's line and then turning rapidly to ram one of his ships on its defenceless side or stern. It demanded great skill in the coxswain and efficiency in the oarsmen" (How and Wells).

of army there on the island, and took shelter from the sun. They refused to go aboard their ships or do any further exercises in them.[4]

13. The generals of the Samians now learned of what the Ionians were doing. There had been those propositions earlier, which they had received through Aeaces, the son of Syloson, at the instruction of the Persians, urging them to quit the Ionian alliance, and the Samians now, seeing the great want of discipline on the Ionian side, accepted the Persian offers. They were urged to this also because it seemed to them entirely impossible to defeat the Great King; they knew well that, even if they got the better of the present force of Darius, there would be another straightway in front of them, five times as big. So as soon as they saw that the Ionians were not willing to live up to their duty, they laid hold of this as their excuse; they felt that the survival, intact, of their own temples and their own private property was an additional profit in yielding to the Persians. Aeaces, from whom they had received the offers, was the son of Syloson, the son of Aeaces; he had been prince of Samos and was put down by Aristagoras of Miletus, like all the rest of the Ionian princes.

14. When the Phoenicians sailed against them, the Ionians put to sea, they too—with their ships in column. They then neared one another and engaged. What happened after that I cannot say with real exactitude—as to which of the Ionians proved cowards or which good men—for they keep accusing one another. But it is said that the Samians, immediately, in accordance with their agreement with Aeaces, raised sail, deserted their place in the line, and made for home—all except eleven ships, whose trierachs stood fast and fought it out in disregard of the orders of their superiors. The commonalty of Samos afterwards gave them for their action the privilege of a record on a pillar, with their fathers' names as well, as good men and true. That pillar now stands in the marketplace. But the Lesbians, when they saw their nearest neighbors in the ranks fleeing, did the same as the Samians. So, indeed, did the most of the Ionians.

4. There is little doubt that this is an accurate account. Greek sailors were accustomed to having regular time off for meals, for which they went ashore. The battle of Aegospotami in 404 B.C. was lost for this very reason. For some remarks about the amateurishness of Greek warfare and—a closely related topic—the democratic nature of the relationship between a general and the citizen soldiers/sailors under his command, see the end note to this passage.

15. Of those who stood firm in the sea fight, those who suffered worst were the Chians. Their action was very brilliant, and they never shirked what they had to do. They had, as I said before, one hundred ships, and on each one of them were forty men, whom they had hand-picked from their own citizens, serving aboard as marines. They saw the most of the allies giving up but refused to be the equals of these cowards among them. Isolated except for a very few allies, they did the "break-the-line" maneuver repeatedly and continued the fight, until, having captured a great many of the enemy's ships, they had lost the most of their own.

16. Then the Chians, with what was left of their ships, made for home. Those whose ships had been disabled fled to Mycale, beached their ships right there, and abandoned them. They themselves marched overland through the country. When in the course of their journey the Chians came to Ephesus, it was dark when they came into it, and the Thesmophoria was being celebrated by the women there. The Ephesians, having no knowledge of what had happened the Chians, saw a land army invading their territory. Sure that these were thieves who had come after their women, they came out in force and killed the Chians.

17. Such were the chance deaths these encountered. Dionysius of Phocaea, when he realized that the Ionian venture was ruined, captured three ships of the enemy and sailed away—not to Phocaea, however, for he knew well that it would be enslaved with the rest of Ionia; so he sailed without more ado straight for Phoenicia, and after sinking merchant shipping there and collecting a lot of money, he made off for Sicily. He made this his base and set up for a pirate and plundered Carthaginians and Etruscans but never Greeks.

18. The Persians, after their victory at sea over the Ionians, besieged Miletus by sea and land. By digging under its fortifications and bringing up every kind of siege machinery against it, they captured the city in its entirety in the sixth year after Aristagoras' revolt.[5] So they enslaved the city, and what happened it fell in with the oracle that had been given concerning it.

19. For when the Argives were consulting Delphi about the safety of their city, an oracle was given them with a double reference, one part with bearing on the Argives themselves, and an-

5. Miletus fell in 494.

other, which the god added to it, about the Milesians. The part that concerns the Argives I will give at that point of my narrative; [6] but what the god said of the Milesians (who were not present) goes like this:

> On that very day, Miletus, deviser of deeds that are evil,
> You shall yourself be a feast to many, a glorious gift.
> Then shall your wives wash the feet of many a long-haired
>   warrior,
> And to the care of others shall fall our Didyman temple. [7]

Now, this fate overtook Miletus when so many of its men were killed by the Persians (who wore their hair long), and their women and children fell into the class of war captives, and the holy place at Didyma—both temple and oracle—was plundered and burned. I have made mention frequently, at other points in my story, of the treasures that were in this holy place.

20. After that, those of the Milesians who had been made prisoners of war were brought up to Susa. King Darius did them no further harm but settled them on what is called the Red Sea at the city of Ampe, by which the river Tigris flows and issues into the sea. Of the country of Miletus itself, the Persians took the parts around the city and the plain for themselves but turned over the higher land to the Pedasian Carians.

21. The debt of grief that the Sybarites should have felt for the Milesians in their suffering at the hands of the Persians was not paid by them in kind. For when the Sybarites had lost *their* city and were living in Laus and Scidrus—after Sybaris had been captured by the men of Croton—all the people of Miletus (from the young people upwards) had shaved their heads and taken great public lamentation on themselves. (These two cities had been more closely associated in guest-friendship than any others we know of.) The Athenians behaved toward the Milesians at this time very differently from the way the Sybarites did. For the Athenians showed how bitterly they felt for the capture of Miletus in many other ways and, in particular, when Phrynicus produced his play *The Capture of Miletus*, the whole audience at the theater burst into tears and fined Phrynicus a thou-

6. Chapter 77, below.
7. Apollo's temple at Didyma, a city near Miletus. Herodotus has earlier called this city Branchidae. Cf. 1.46.

sand drachmas for reminding them of a calamity that was their very own; they also forbade any future production of the play.

22. So Miletus was left empty of Milesians. But, of the Samians, there were among them men of wealth who did not at all like what their own generals had done with respect to the Persians.[8] They held a debate right after the sea fight and resolved to sail off to a colony before ever Prince Aeaces should come to their land; they would not remain to be the slaves of the Persians and Aeaces. For about this same time the people of Zancle in Sicily sent messengers to the Ionians, summoning them to Fair Coast, since they, the Zanclaeans, wished to found a colony of Ionians there. This place called Fair Coast belonged to the Sicels and is in Sicily, in the part facing toward Etruria. Alone, then, of those Ionians who were so invited, the Samians set out and, with them, those fugitives from among the Milesians. During their journey to their new home, the following thing befell them.

23. The Samians were traveling along to Sicily and came to Epizephyrian Locris[9] when the people of Zancle and their king, who was called Scythes, were beleaguering a city of the Sicels that they wanted to take. The prince of Rhegium, Anaxilaus, learned about this. He was himself at this time at difference with the people of Zancle, and he put himself into communication with the Samians. His argument was that they ought to give up Fair Coast, toward which they were sailing, and take possession of Zancle, which was at that moment undefended by its men. The Samians were persuaded and took Zancle. Then the people of Zancle, realizing that their city was now in the control of others, came to rescue it. They summoned to their help Hippocrates, prince of Gela; he was their ally. But when Hippocrates arrived with his army to help them, he, Hippocrates, put the Zanclaean king, Scythes, in chains (for losing his city). He did likewise with Scythes' brother, Pythogenes, and sent the two of them away to the city of Inyx. The rest of the Zanclaeans he turned over to the Samians, having made a public agreement with them and given and exchanged oaths. The Samians agreed to give him a price, which was that he should take half of the movable goods and

8. See chapter 13, above.
9. I.e., Western Locris, to distinguish it from Locris in Greece, its mother country.

slaves that were in the city and all that were in the countryside. He himself took and kept in bondage most of the Zanclaeans, as actual slaves, but he turned over three hundred of the chief men to the Samians, to cut their throats. However, the Samians did not do so.

24. Scythes, king of Zancle, succeeded in running away from Inyx to Himera and from there made his way to Asia and up to King Darius. Darius thought him, of all the men who had come up to him from Greece, the justest. For after persuading the Great King, he was allowed to return to Sicily but came back to him again after his stay there. He died full of years and wealth among the Persians. So cheaply did the Samians, having escaped the Medes, take possession of the beautiful city of Zancle.

25. After the sea fight for Miletus, the Phoenicians, under orders from Persia, restored to Samos Aeaces, son of Syloson, as a man, the Persians said, of great worth to the Persians and one who had done them great service. Also, the Samians were the only people who revolted from Darius who had neither their city nor temples burned. This was their reward for their desertion of the Ionians during the sea fight. After the capture of Miletus, the Persians immediately seized Caria. Some of the Carian cities submitted voluntarily; others were reduced by military force.

26. That, then, is how matters happened. But Histiaeus of Miletus, who was at Byzantium, arresting all of the Ionian merchant vessels that were sailing out of the Pontus, got news of what had happened at Miletus. He entrusted his concerns in the Hellespont to Bisaltes, son of Apollophanes, a man of Abydos, and himself, with a command of Lesbians, sailed for Chios. He attacked a Chian garrison, which would not let him through, at a place in their territory called the Hollows. Histiaeus killed many of those who fought him there and with his Lesbian troops got the best of the rest of the Chians, for they had been very badly mauled in the sea fight. During his campaign in Chios he made his base at Polichne.

27. There is, somehow, some warning given in advance when great evils are about to fall on either city-state or nation.[10] For in-

___

10. Herodotus tends to use a twofold political classification—"city" or "nation." By the former he means what is designated by us as "city-state"; by the latter, a people not significantly united politically by the common sharing of a city but rather by a common racial origin.

stance, in the case of the Chians, there were great signs given before their present disasters. There was a band of one hundred youths they had sent to Delphi, and only two of them returned; ninety-eight of them were seized by a sickness and took ill and died. Again, in the city at this time, a while before the sea fight, there were children learning their letters in a school, and the roof fell in on top of them, and, of the hundred and twenty children, one only escaped. These were the signs that the god showed in advance; thereafter, the sea fight brought the city to its knees, and, after the sea fight, Histiaeus and his force of Lesbians; for the Chians were so mauled that Histiaeus very easily made a total conquest of them.

28. From there Histiaeus, with a strong army of Ionians and Aeolians, made war upon Thasos. But while he was besieging Thasos, there came word to him that the Phoenicians were sailing out of Miletus against the rest of Ionia. On this information Histiaeus left Thasos unsacked and himself hurried toward Lesbos with his whole host. From Lesbos, because his army was in straits of hunger, he crossed over to reap the harvest in Atarneus and in the level land about the Caïcus river in the territory of the Mysians. There was at the time, in that part of the country, the Persian Harpagus with a large army. The Persians attacked Histiaeus' army after their landing there, captured Histiaeus alive, and killed the most of his troops.

29. This is how Histiaeus came to be taken alive: when the Greeks and the Persians fought at Malene, in the country of Atarneus, there was a close-locked battle for a long time. At last the Persian horse charged and fell upon the Greeks. It was this action of the horse that was decisive, and the Greeks were routed. Because Histiaeus still believed that the Great King would not doom him for his present peccadillo, he let himself mightily love his life, as this following act showed. In his flight he was captured by a Persian and was about to be stabbed by the man. At which he spoke in Persian and made himself known as Histiaeus of Miletus.

30. Even so, if he had been brought straight to Darius after being made prisoner, he would not, in my judgment at least, have suffered any ill. The King would have let him off. As it was, and exactly because there was this probability—that he might again, if he escaped, become a great man with the King—Artaphrenes, viceroy of Sardis, and Harpagus, who had taken him, dealt with him when he was

brought to Sardis. They impaled him then and there and cut off and embalmed his head and sent it to King Darius in Susa. Darius, as soon as he learned this, severely blamed those who had not brought the man alive into his presence. He ordered them to wash the head of Histiaeus and bury it with all due care, as that of a man who had been of great service to himself, the King, and to the Persians.

31. That, then, is the end of Histiaeus. The Persian fleet, after wintering around Miletus, sailed out the next year and easily captured the islands that lie off the mainland: Chios, Lesbos, and Tenedos. As they captured each of these islands, the barbarians "netted" the inhabitants. This is how they do this. Each man links, hand to hand, with another and they make a line stretching from the north sea to the southern; then they march through the whole island, hunting down the people in it. They also captured Ionian cities on the mainland in the same fashion—though here they did no "netting," since that was impossible.[11]

32. Then the Persian generals proved as good as the threats they had made against the Ionians when the two armies were encamped against one another. As they gained control of the cities, they chose out the best-looking boys and castrated them, making them eunuchs instead of men, and they sent off the best-looking girls to the King. This they did and then burned the cities, temples and all. So for the third time the Ionians were enslaved, once by the Lydians and twice, in order, by the Persians.

33. From Ionia the fleet departed and captured all the places on the left of the entrance of the Hellespont. What was on the right had already been subjected by the Persians themselves, attacking by land. These are the regions in Europe that belong to the Hellespont: the Chersonese (with many cities in it); Perinthus and the many forts toward Thrace; and Selymbria and Byzantium. The people of Byzantium and the Chalcedonians, beyond them, did not wait for the Phoenicians to sail against them but left their country and retired within the area of the Euxine Sea[12] and there settled in the city of Mesembria. The Phoenicians burned all these countries I have

11. Presumably because, on the mainland, there was no impenetrable barrier, like the sea, to assist the invaders; i.e., on the islands, the sea kept the fleeing inhabitants from escaping the net.
12. Another name for the Black Sea.

mentioned and made for Proconnesus and Artace, and, committing these too to the fire, they went back again to the Chersonese, to clear out what remained of those cities there that they had not thoroughly destroyed on their former landings. Against Cyzicus they did not sail at all. For the people of Cyzicus were, even before the Phoenicians' invasion, subjects of the King, having made an agreement with Oebares, son of Megabazus, who was the viceroy at Dascyleium.

34. The Phoenicians subdued all the cities except Cardia in the Chersonese. These cities until then were governed by Miltiades, son of Cimon, who was the son of Stesagoras. It was Miltiades, son of Cypselus, who had set up this sovereignty in former times; and this is how he came to do it. A Thracian tribe, the Dolonci, held the Chersonese, and they were sorely pressed in war by the Apsinthians. They sent their kings to Delphi to consult the oracle about the war, and the Pythia told them to bring home to their country as "founder" whoever it was who first offered them hospitality after they left the temple. The Dolonci marched off along the Sacred Road through Phocis and Boeotia, and not a one invited them in; so they turned off the road toward Athens.

35. At that time the supreme power in Athens was held by Pisistratus; but there was also a man of great influence, one Miltiades, son of Cypselus, a man who came from a house that raced four-horse chariots and was by ancient descent sprung from Aeacus and Aegina but was more recently of Athenian lineage—Philaeus, the son of Ajax, being the first of his house to become an Athenian. This Miltiades was sitting on his own porch when he saw the Dolonci passing along the road. Their clothes were not those of his country, and they carried spears. So Miltiades shouted to them, and, as they approached him, he offered them the shelter of his roof and hospitality. They accepted, and after their entertainment they made clear to him the whole matter of the oracle and therewith asked him to obey the god. As soon as he heard their story, Miltiades was persuaded by it because he was aggrieved by the government of Pisistratus and wished to be out of the way. So he set off for Delphi to ask the oracle whether he should do what the Dolonci asked him to do.

36. The Pythia said yes; and so Miltiades, son of Cypselus, who

had before this won an Olympic prize with the four-horse chariot, gathered together every Athenian who was willing to make part of his expedition and sailed away with the Dolonci. He took possession of the country, and those who invited him in made him their prince. First of all he walled off the isthmus of the Chersonese, from the city of Cardia to Pactya, so that the Apsinthians might not be able to do the people of the Chersonese a mischief by invading their country. The isthmus is four and a half miles wide; beyond the isthmus the length of the Chersonese is fifty and a quarter miles.

37. Having walled off the neck of the Chersonese and thus thrust back the Apsinthians, the first of the rest of the peoples there against whom Miltiades made war were the Lampsacenes. But the Lampsacenes laid an ambush for him and took him alive. Now Miltiades was well known to Croesus of Lydia, and, when Croesus heard of his capture, he sent word to the Lampsacenes to let Miltiades go. If they did not do so, he threatened that he would destroy them "even like a pine tree." The people of Lampsacus were at a loss, in this message, as to what the expression "like a pine tree" meant until, with some trouble, one of their older men hit on the truth of it, which was that the pine is the only tree that, once cut down, never puts out shoot more but perishes utterly. The Lampsacenes were thoroughly afraid of Croesus and struck the bonds from Miltiades and let him go.

38. So Miltiades escaped, thanks to Croesus, but he died child-less, leaving his kingdom and his property to Stesagoras, who was the son of Cimon, Miltiades' half-brother on his mother's side. The people of the Chersonese sacrifice to the dead Miltiades, as of cus-tom, as their founder, and they have instituted games with both horse and athletic contests, and at them no Lampsacene is allowed to compete. But during the war against the Lampsacenes death also overtook Stesagoras, and he, too, was childless. He was struck on the head in the town hall by a man with an axe, who claimed to be a deserter to his side but was indeed Stesagoras' enemy and rather a bitter one at that.

39. This was the end of Stesagoras, and then came Miltiades, son of Cimon and brother of the dead Stesagoras. This man was sent by the Pisistratids to the Chersonese in a warship, to take over affairs there. The Pisistratids had treated him well in Athens, as though

indeed they had no knowledge about the death of Miltiades' own father, Cimon.[13] (How that came about I will tell at a later point in my history.) Miltiades, when he came to the Chersonese, kept within doors, seeming to mourn for his brother, Stesagoras. The people of the Chersonese learned of this, and their chief men from all the cities gathered together and came in a public deputation to share in his grief, whereupon he put them all in bondage. So Miltiades took possession of the Chersonese and maintained a guard of five hundred mercenaries and married the daughter of the Thracian King Olorus, whose name was Hegesipyle.

40. But this Miltiades—son of Cimon—who had newly come to the Chersonese, was overtaken by something worse than what had happened before. For, in the third year before the events I have told of, he had been hunted out of the country by the Scythians. These were nomads who had been provoked by King Darius and had collected their forces and driven as far as the Chersonese. Miltiades did not await their attack but fled from the Chersonese altogether until the Scythians went home again and the Dolonci brought him back. All this had happened two years before the matters that now overtook him.

41. But now he learned that the Phoenicians were in Tenedos. So he loaded up five warships with the possessions he had and sailed away for Athens. Starting from the city of Cardia, he sailed through the Black Gulf, and, as he was coasting along the Chersonese, the Phoenicians fell upon him with their fleet. Miltiades himself, with four of his ships, took refuge in Imbros, but the Phoenicians, in pursuit, captured the fifth ship. It was, as it happened, commanded by the eldest son of Miltiades, one Metiochus—a son not by the daughter of the Thracian king, Olorus, but by some other woman. The Phoenicians took him prisoner, ship and all, and, learning that he was Miltiades' son, they sent him up to the King, thinking they would win great favor by so doing, inasmuch as it was Miltiades who had given his advice among the Ionians, urging them to listen to the Scythians when those Scythians had asked the Ionians to break the raft-bridge and sail off home. But Darius, when the Phoenicians sent Metiochus, son of Miltiades, up to Susa, did Metiochus no harm

13. They were in fact his murderers. See below, chapter 103.

at all—indeed, much good. For he gave the boy a house and possessions and a Persian wife, by whom he had children, and they
were reckoned as Persians.[14] Miltiades himself came from Imbros to
Athens.

42. For that year[15] nothing further was done by the Persians
to the Ionians that tended to enmity, but indeed some very useful
things. Artaphrenes, the viceroy of Sardis, sending for some from
the cities to be his messengers, forced on the Ionians certain com-
pacts: that they should submit their quarrels with one another to law
instead of plundering and harrying one another. This new course of
action he forced upon them, and he measured out their territory in
parasangs (which is the Persian name for a distance of thirty stades),
and, using this as his measure of land, he fixed the tribute that each
area should pay. They have continued to pay, district by district, according to the assessment of Artaphrenes, from then until my time.
The amount of the assessment was much the same as it had been
earlier.[16] These measures made for peace among the Ionians.

43. At the beginning of spring,[17] Mardonius, son of Gobryas,
came down to the coast; the King had dismissed from their command his other generals. Mardonius brought with him a very large
land force and a large fleet. He was a young man and lately married
to Darius' daughter Artozostre. Mardonius led the army himself until
he came to Cilicia; there he went on board ship and traveled with

14. It is tempting to translate this as "naturalized as Persians." The truth is,
however, that it is best to leave Herodotus' vague statement as it is because he
has not used a more definite phrase, as he does in 6.35, when he says that one of
Miltiades' ancestors was "the first of his house to become an Athenian." In the
present passage, the Greek words about the descendants of this Miltiades mean,
literally, "they were glorified into Persians," which probably indicates that at the
imperial court the favor of the Great King in regarding these men as Persians was
all that mattered to their status.

15. 493 B.C.

16. I.e., before the revolt. As for the phrase "until my time," in the preced-
ing sentence, there is clearly some difficulty. In Herodotus' time, certainly after
450 B.C. and perhaps as early as 465, these districts paid tribute to the Delian
Confederacy, run by Athens. Probably Herodotus' phrase is to be construed
loosely: "They were still paying according to this assessment when I was young"—
the traditional date of Herodotus' birth being 484 B.C.

17. 492 B.C.

the rest of the fleet, while other leaders brought the land force to the Hellespont. When Mardonius, coasting along Asia, came to Ionia, I will tell you of the most wonderful thing that happened—most wonderful, that is, for those Greeks who do not believe that among the Seven Persians Otanes *did* give his judgment that Persia should be ruled by democracy.[18] For here in Ionia Mardonius put down all the princes and set up democracies in the cities. Having done so, he hastened off to the Hellespont. Having collected this huge force of army and fleet there, the Persians crossed the Hellespont with the ships and marched by land through Europe, making for Eretria and Athens.

44. This, at any rate, was what they claimed for their expedition. But what they had in mind was to subdue as many Greek cities as possible; so first, with their fleet, they conquered the Thasians, who did not lift a hand against them, and then with their army they added the Macedonians to their already existing slaves; for all the peoples on their side of Macedonia had already been subjected to them. From Thasos they crossed over and traveled along, close to the land, as far as Acanthus; and setting out from Acanthus they tried to round Athos. But a great north wind, past coping with, fell on them as they would have rounded Athos and handled them very roughly indeed, wrecking a great number of their ships on Athos. It is said that the number of wrecks was three hundred and that more than twenty thousand men were killed. For as the sea there around Athos is infested with sharks, some were seized and destroyed by these creatures, and others of the men were battered to death on the rocks. Others of them drowned because they did not know how to swim, and others still died of the cold.

45. That is how the fleet fared; and by land, when Mardonius and his army were encamped in Macedonia, the Thracian Brygi attacked them by night. The Brygi killed very many and wounded Mardonius himself. Not that these people themselves escaped slavery at the hands of the Persians, for Mardonius refused to move a foot from the place until he had conquered them. After this conquest, however, he led the army homeward, having suffered some

18. See 3.80.

loss in his army from the Brygi and a very severe one in the fleet at Athos. So this expedition of his returned to Asia, having fought very ingloriously.

46. In the year after this,[19] Darius dealt first with the Thasians. They had been slandered by their neighbors, who said that they were planning to revolt. Darius sent them a message that they should pull down their defending walls and bring their ships to Abdera. For the Thasians, who had known what it was to be besieged by Histiaeus of Miletus, and who had, moreover, great revenues, used their money to build warships and to build themselves a stronger circle of defending walls. Their revenue came from the mainland and from the mines. From the gold mines of Scaptesyle there was, in general, a revenue of eighty talents and, from the mines in Thasos itself, less than that but so much that, in general, the Thasians (who paid no taxes on their crops) had an income, from both mainland and mines, of two hundred talents a year; when the revenue was greatest, it came to three hundred.

47. I myself saw these mines; far the most astonishing were those the Phoenicians discovered, who with Thasus colonized this island (it is because of this that the island has its name from Thasus, the Phoenician). These Phoenician mines are between the places called Aenyra and Coenyra, in Thasos and opposite Samothrace; there was a great hill there that was all dug up in the search for gold. That, then, is what I have to say about the mines. On the King's bidding, the Thasians pulled down their walls and brought all their ships to Abdera.

48. After this, Darius tried to find out what the Greeks had in mind. Would they fight him or surrender? He sent heralds here and there throughout Greece, under instructions, and bade them ask for earth and water for the King. These he sent to Greece itself; others he sent to his own tributary cities that lay along the coast, and these heralds were to demand the construction of warships and horse transports.

49. The tributary cities made these preparations; and when the heralds came to Greece, many of the mainlanders gave what the Persians asked for, and so did all the islanders to whom they came with

19. 491 B.C.

The woman had twins, say the Spartans, and Aristodemus only lived to see them born before he fell sick and died. The Lacedaemonians of that day resolved to follow custom and make the elder of the twins king, but they could not choose which of the two to take, since the children were alike and equal. When they were unable to come to any judgment—and perhaps before they even tried—they asked the mother. She said that she could not tell between them as to the elder birth, though she knew right well; she wanted both of them somehow to become kings. The Lacedaemonians were at a loss, and in their perplexity they sent to Delphi to ask what they should do in the matter. The Pythia answered them that they should "make both children kings but honor more the elder." That was the Pythia's answer; but it relieved the Lacedaemonians' anxiety not a jot, since they were no less unable to find out the elder of the two children. At this point a Messenian, whose name was Panites, made a suggestion: they should watch the mother for which of the two she washed and fed first. If she were discovered to do these acts always in the same order, then the Spartans would have everything they were seeking and wanted to find out; but if she wavered in her order, doing now one of the children first and now the other, then it would be clear to the watchers that she really did not know any more than they; in that case they had better find some other road of discovery. So the Spartiates, in accordance with the suggestion of the man of Messenia, watched the mother of Aristodemus' children and found that indeed she preferred one, always in the same order—the elder-born—in feeding and washing; for she had no knowledge why she was watched. So they took the child that was so preferred in honor by his mother as being indeed elder and brought it up at public expense. The name given to this one was Eurysthenes; to the other, Procles. These children, grown to manhood, brothers though they were, were, they say, continually at variance with one another all their lives, and so it has continued with all their descendants.

53. That is the story the Lacedaemonians tell—being alone among the Greeks to do so. Now I am going to write what is said by the other Greeks. This is that the kings of the Dorians back to Perseus, the son of Danaë—leaving out the god[21]—are correctly

21. That is, neglecting the story that Zeus fathered Perseus on Danaë.

reckoned up by the Greeks and shown to be Greeks; for by Perseus' time they were counted as Greeks. I said "as far back as Perseus" because I am taking things no further back then him; for no name of a mortal father is given for Perseus, as, for instance, Amphitryon is for Heracles. So I reasoned rightly and spoke correctly when I said "as far back as Perseus." For if one counts the ancestors of Danaë, daughter of Acrisius, straight back in each generation, then the leaders of the Dorians will come out as being native-born Egyptians.

54. That is the story of the generations as the Greeks tell it, but the Persian account is that Perseus himself was an Assyrian who turned Greek but that this was not the case with Perseus' ancestors. As to the forefathers of Acrisius, the Persians do not admit that there is any kinship at all between them and Perseus; they say that they were, as the Greeks claim, Egyptians.

55. That is enough about that. But why (being Egyptians) and for what great deeds these men gained the kingship of the Dorians— those matters have been declared by others, and I will let be that tale. But I will make mention of things that others have not laid hold of.

56. The following privileges have been granted by the Spartiates to their kings: two priesthoods, that of Zeus of Lacedaemon and that of Heavenly Zeus; the waging of war against any country they may choose—and, in this, no Spartiate may stand in their way or he will involve himself in a curse; in war service the kings must be the first in the march and the last to retreat; one hundred picked men apiece shall be their guard on campaign; at the setting-forth of the expeditions the kings shall have the right to as many animal victims as they will, and, of those sacrificed, they may take the skins and the backs.

57. These are what belong to them in war. In peace they are granted the following: whenever there is a public sacrifice, the kings must sit down first to the banquet, and from them the servants must begin, assigning a double share of everything to each of the kings over what is given to the other guests; to the kings also belong the right of first libation and the skins of all the sacrificed beasts. At every new moon and on the seventh day of each month there is granted to each king a perfect victim, paid for by the public treasury, for the temple of Apollo; also a medimnus of grain and a Laconian quart of wine; and seats in the front row are reserved for them at the

athletic contests. To them is also granted the appointment of whomsoever they please among the citizens as Spartan consuls for the protection of foreigners, and each of them also chooses two Pythians.[22] These Pythians are the messengers sent to inquire of the oracle at Delphi, and they eat with the kings at the public expense. If the kings do not come to the public dinner, there must be sent to them, to their homes, two choenixes apiece of grain and a cotyle of wine; if they are present at the dinner, they receive a double share of everything, and they are honored in this same way when they are invited to the dinners of private persons. The kings have the keeping of oracles that are given, though the Pythians also have knowledge of them. The kings are the sole judges in the following suits: the disposition in marriage of a maiden who is her father's only heir and has not been betrothed by him to anyone; matters of the public highways; and, if anyone wishes to adopt a child, he must do so in the presence of the kings.[23] When the twenty-eight members of the Gerousia[24] sit, the kings sit along with them. If the kings are not in attendance, those of the elders who are nearest in kinship to the kings have the prerogative of the kings, casting their two votes and a third for themselves.[25]

22. The provisions with regard to the "consuls" (*proxenoi*) are not entirely clear, and, if clear, we are not sure that Herodotus is right about them. He is referring to the appointment of Spartans to protect citizens of another state who were in Sparta, temporarily or permanently, and to expedite their business. In instances of which we know anything, however, notable citizens of, say, Athens, seem to have acted as proxenoi—consuls of a sort—for aliens on the basis of their own personal friendship, and the consulship seems to have passed hereditarily. However, it is possible that there is an official side to all this and that Herodotus is right about it. As for the "Pythians": Sparta's connections with Delphi and its management were very close—so close that it was often held that the oracle spoke with the voice of the Spartan "Foreign Office." Sparta's Pythians were members of the delegations that went constantly to consult the oracle on matters of Spartan policy. Clearly, the nomination of "suitable" candidates gave the king a considerable influence on the questions posed and the answers given by Delphi.

23. Clan property rights were at stake in adoptions of males and in the marriage of an unbetrothed girl who was her father's sole heir.

24. The Council of Elders.

25. A famously ambiguous passage because Thucydides, obviously referring to Herodotus, challenges the accuracy of "someone's" statement that the Spartan kings had two votes each. The Herodotean passage is a little confused, but it

58. These are the honors granted to the kings by the commonalty in life, and in death these: horsemen carry around the news of the death throughout Laconia, and, through the city, women go around beating on a cauldron. When this takes place, there must be, from each household, two free persons who defile themselves as a show of mourning—a man and a woman. If they do not do so, there are heavy fines imposed. The following custom of the Lacedaemonians on the deaths of their kings is the same as that among the barbarians in Asia—indeed, the most of the barbarians do practice the same usage at the deaths of their kings; for when a king of Lacedaemon dies, from all of Lacedaemon, besides those who are Spartiates, a certain number of those who are the subject people must attend the funeral.[26] When many thousands of all these, *perioeci* and helots and the Spartiates themselves and the women, are gathered in one place, they very earnestly beat their foreheads and make loud lament, proclaiming in each case that this last king that is dead was the best there had ever been. When the king has died in war, they make an image of him and set it on a well-dressed bier. When they bury him, there is no market for ten days nor any meeting for choosing magistrates; for all these days they hold mourning.

59. There is another respect in which the Lacedaemonians resemble the Persians. When a new king comes to reign on the death of the old, the incoming king frees of his debt any Spartiate who owes anything to king or commonalty. Among the Persians, the newly made king forgives all of the cities any tribute still owing.

60. In the following matter the Lacedaemonians resemble the Egyptians. Their heralds, flute-players, and cooks follow their trades from father to son; the flute-player takes over from his flute-playing father, the cook from the cook, the herald from the herald. Nor do others bar the hereditary family on the grounds of clarity of voice, in

---

seems to mean not what Thucydides says it does but simply that the two nearest-related members of the Gerousia each cast one proxy vote and then his own vote as well.

26. The Spartiates are the full citizens. The "subject people" are the descendants of the original inhabitants of the country, who were conquered by the Spartans and formally degraded to the status of *perioeci* (literally, "those who live around") and helots (tied tenants or serfs on the land).

the case of heralds, but they follow their trade as their fathers did before them.

61. So much for these matters. But when Cleomenes was in Aegina and was working for the common good of Greece, Demaratus was spreading slander about him, not because he cared about the Aeginetans but because he was led thereto by envy and hatred. Cleomenes, when he came back from Aegina, considered how he might remove Demaratus from the kingship; he made his attack upon him by means of the following event. When Ariston[27] was king in Sparta and had married two wives, he had children by neither of them. Inasmuch as he knew the fault was not in himself, he set about marrying a third wife, and this is how he did it. He had a friend among the Spartiates to whom, of all the Spartiates, he was most attached. Now this man had far the most beautiful wife of all the women in Sparta; moreover, she was the most beautiful after having been the ugliest. She had been very mean of appearance, and her nurse, seeing her a rich man's daughter and so ill-favored and, moreover, seeing that the parents took very hard the ugliness of the child, made her observation of all these matters and did as follows: she took the child every day to the shrine of Helen that is in the place called Therapne, above the temple of Phoebus. As often as the nurse brought her here, she would set the child close to Helen's image and pray the goddess to deliver her from her ugliness.[28] One day, it is said, as the nurse was leaving the temple, a woman appeared to her and asked her what she was carrying in her arms. The nurse said that she was carrying a child, and the woman bade her show it to her. But the nurse refused, saying that the parents had forbade her to show the child to anyone. The woman looked at her and was very urgent that she should show the child to her—which, finally, the nurse did. Then the woman touched the child on the head and said, "You shall be the most beautiful of all the women in Sparta." From

27. Demaratus' father.
28. It is worth noting that on this site, which is traditionally associated with the burial place of Helen and Menelaus (and where there are still the remains of a Mycenaean temple), Herodotus seems to see Helen worshiped as a goddess of beauty and love like Aphrodite rather than as, with her husband, a hero and heroine in what we think of as the usual Greek style of worshiping the great legendary figures.

that day forth her ugliness fell away from her, and when she came to her full womanhood she married with Agetus, the son of Alcidas; this was the friend of Ariston.

62. Now, love for this woman itched Ariston, and he took these measures. He promised his friend, whose wife she was, that he would give him any of his possessions that he himself would choose, and bade his friend do the like by him. The friend had no fear for his wife, seeing that Ariston was himself married. So Agetus agreed, and they sealed the compact with oaths. So Ariston gave his friend whatever it was that Agetus chose out of all his treasures; then, when it was his turn to seek the like from Agetus, he tried to take away his friend's wife. Agetus said that, apart from this one thing, he consented to anything else; but finally, under the constraint of his oath and the cunning of the treachery, he gave the woman up to Ariston.

63. This, then, was the third wife that Ariston married, after divorcing the second. But in a period less than the coming of the tenth month[29] she had a child, and the child was Demaratus. The king was sitting in council with the ephors when a servant came and told him that he had a son. He knew the time at which he had married the woman, and he reckoned up the months on his fingers and said with an oath, "That is no son of mine." The ephors heard him, but they paid no attention to the matter for the time being. The son grew up, and Ariston was sorry for what he had said, for he had come to think that Demaratus was really his own. Indeed, he gave him the name Demaratus because of the following: before this, the Spartan people had prayed that Ariston, because he was the most glorious king they had ever had, would have a son.[30]

64. That was how Demaratus got his name. As time went on and Ariston died, Demaratus succeeded to the throne. But it seems that all was destined to come out and deprive him of his kingship. Already Cleomenes and Demaratus had been bitterly at odds because Demaratus had drawn off the army from Eleusis.[31] And now there

29. The Greeks always figured in lunar months.
30. The name Demaratus may be translated as "answer to the people's prayer" (*demos* = people; *aratos* = prayed for).
31. Cf. 5.75.

was this affair in which Cleomenes had crossed over into Aegina to punish the Medizers there.[32]

65. Cleomenes was set on revenge, and so he made a compact with Leotychides, son of Menares, son of Agis, who was of the same house as Demaratus, that, on condition that Cleomenes should make him king instead of Demaratus, Leotychides would come with Cleomenes against the Aeginetans. Leotychides was a bitter foe of Demaratus because of the following matter: Leotychides had arranged to marry Percalus, the daughter of Chilon, the son of Demarmenus, but Demaratus laid a plot against him and robbed him of his marriage by seizing the lady first and making her his wife. In this was rooted the enmity of Leotychides against Demaratus; and now, with the connivance of Cleomenes, Leotychides swore a complaint against Demaratus to the effect that it was not fitting that he should be king of Sparta, inasmuch as he was no son of Ariston. After the sworn complaint Leotychides prosecuted Demaratus in court, reviving the remark that Ariston had made when the servant told him of the birth of the child and he had calculated the months and swore it was not his own. This was the utterance on which Leotychides based his case and tried to demonstrate that Demaratus was not the son of Ariston and was therefore unfit to reign in Sparta. He cited the ephors as witnesses—the ephors who had been sitting in council with the king and had heard him say what he did.

66. Finally, when there was so much quarreling about the matter, the Spartiates resolved to submit the question to the oracle at Delphi as to whether Demaratus was the son of Ariston. The question was referred to the Pythia at the instance of Cleomenes, who then won to his side Cobon, son of Aristophantus, who was a man with great influence at Delphi. Cobon persuaded Perialla, the prophetess, to say what Cleomenes wanted said. So when the sacred messengers put their questions, the Pythia gave her answer that Demaratus was no son of Ariston. But later everything came out, and Cobon was banished from Delphi, and Perialla was deprived of her office.

32. To "Medize" was to take the Persian side. Although the Medes had been conquered by the Persians, outsiders like the Greeks thought of them as joint holders of the empire; hence "to Medize." It is worth noticing that later, when Athens was turning her Delian Confederacy into an empire, the other Greeks bitterly formed the word "Atticize" to characterize those who voluntarily helped the Athenian cause.

67. This was how Demaratus lost his kingship; but his flight to Persia was because of the following insult. Though Demaratus was no longer king, there was an office he held by election. At the Festival of the Naked Boys he was among the spectators, and Leotychides, who had become king in his stead, sent his servant in mockery and insult to inquire of Demaratus how he relished elective office after kingship.[33] Demaratus was stung by the question and said truly he had now tasted both, and his inquirer had not, but that the question that was put might be the occasion of either ten thousand calamities to Lacedaemon or ten thousand blessings. With these words he covered his head and left the theater and went to his own house, where he made instant preparation and sacrificed an ox to Zeus and, having so done, sent for his mother.

68. When his mother came, he put into her hands a part of the entrails and made his supplication to her in these words: "Mother, I beseech you now by the other gods, but especially by Zeus of the House—our house—to tell the truth: Who in all honesty was my father? Leotychides said during the quarrel that you were pregnant by your former husband when you came to Ariston. There are even those who tell more of a gossipy tale, that you had a lover among the servants—the muleteer—and that I am his son. In the name of God, tell me the truth! If you have done any of the things you are said to have done, you are not alone to have done so; you have plenty of company. And there is a strong rumor in Sparta that Ariston had no seed in him for the getting of children; for otherwise his other wives would have conceived."

69. Those were his words, and she answered him: "My son, since you have so besought me to tell you the truth, the whole truth is what you will have of me. When Ariston brought me home, on the third night after that first, there came to me a phantom in the likeness of Ariston and lay with me and put upon me the garlands which he had when he came. The phantom vanished, and then came Ariston. When he saw the garlands, he asked me who had given them to me. I told him that he had given them himeslf, and he would not believe me. Then I swore to it and said that he did not

---

33. In chapter 57, above, one of the honors accorded the kings was front-row seats at the festivals. Leotychides was now occupying one of these, while Demaratus sat among the ordinary spectators.

well to deny what he had done, for 'A little while ago,' I said, 'you came here, lay with me, and gave me the garlands.' When Ariston saw that I swore to him the truth of this, he perceived that the matter had the hand of God in it. Besides, it turned out that the garlands came from the hero's shrine by the door of the palace, and this hero was called Astrabacus; and, moreover, the prophets said that it was the hero himself who had fathered the child. So, my son, you have everything you wish to know. For either you are the son of that hero and your father is Astrabacus, or it is Ariston; for it was in that night that I became pregnant with you. But as to the matter on which your enemies have fastened, saying that Ariston himself, when he heard of your birth, in the hearing of many declared you were none of his, for the ten months were not fully out—Ariston hurled that slander through ignorance of such matters. Women give birth at nine months and seven months; not all of them complete the full ten; I bore you, my son, at seven months. And Ariston himself came to recognize, a short while after, that it was in ignorance that he had thrown out such a taunt. Do not lend a word of belief to any other tales of your birth. I have given you the whole and absolute truth. For Leotychides and all who tell the stories like his: may their wives all bear them sons by their muleteers."

70. So she spoke, and Demaratus had learned all he wanted and took provisions with him and made for Elis, giving out that he was going to Delphi to consult the oracle. But the Lacedaemonians, suspecting that Demaratus was trying to run away, raised the pursuit after him. He crossed over to Zacynthus from Elis ahead of them; but they crossed over too and were trying to arrest him, and they did take away his servants. But the people of Zacynthus refused to give him up, and afterwards Demaratus went from there over into Asia and to the court of King Darius. Darius received him in the most honorable way and gave him land and cities.[34] That is how Demaratus came to Asia, and that is the story of how chance dealt with him. Among the Lacedaemonians he had had great distinction for his many deeds and his advice, and besides he conferred on them the honor of his Olympic victory with his four-horse team—something that no other of the Spartan kings has ever done.

34. Demaratus will play a considerable part in advising Xerxes during the assault on Greece. See 7.3, 101 f., 209, 234 f.

71. Leotychides, the son of Menares, succeeded to the kingship when Demaratus was deposed, and a son was born to him, named Zeuxidemus, whom some of the Spartiates called Cyniscus.[35] This Zeuxidemus did not become king of Sparta, for he died before his father, Leotychides; but he left behind a son, Archidemus. Having lost Zeuxidemus, Leotychides married a second wife, Eurydame, sister of Menius and daughter of Diactorides, by whom he had no male issue but a daughter, Lampito. Archidemus, son of Zeuxidemus, married this girl, his grandfather giving her to him.

72. But neither did Leotychides himself grow old in Sparta, and he paid in the following way his retribution to Demaratus: he led the Lacedaemonians into Thessaly, and when he might have had the whole country subject to him, he took a great bribe. He was caught in the act in the camp itself, sitting on his sleeve, which was full of silver. He was brought before a court and banished from Sparta, and his house was razed to the ground. He fled to Tegea, and there he died.

73. That was all later. At this time, when the road he had taken against Demaratus had carried him to success, Cleomenes took Leotychides with him in his expedition against the Aeginetans, for he had a bitter resentment against them for the insult they had given him. Now that both kings had come together against them, the Aeginetans did not think they dared fight them any more. The kings picked out from among the Aeginetans the ten men who were of most consequence for money and birth, including, especially, Crius, the son of Polycritus, and Casambus, the son of Aristocrates, who were the most powerful people in the island. The kings brought these people and gave them for safekeeping to the bitterest foes the Aeginetans had, the Athenians.

74. But, after this, it all came out about Cleomenes' evil dealings against Demaratus, and he was frightened of what the Spartiates would do to him and stole away into Thessaly. From there he went to Arcadia and began to stir up trouble, uniting the Arcadians against Sparta. He swore them in—that well and truly would they follow wherever he should lead—and, in especial, he brought the leading men in Arcadia to the town of Nonacris and was zealous

35. "Puppy Dog."

there to impose on them the oath by the river Styx. For in this town, say the Arcadians, is the water of the Styx; it is a small stream, trickling from a rock into a pool, and the pool is surrounded by a dry-wall. Nonacris, in which this spring exists, is a town in Arcadia near Pheneus.

75. When the Lacedaemonians found out what Cleomenes was doing, they became afraid and brought him home again to rule in Sparta on the same terms as before. But when he came home, he was immediately seized by some frenzy of madness (even earlier he had been somewhat disturbed in his mind). When he met any of the Spartiates, he would strike at them in the face with his stick. For so doing, and because of his distraction, his relatives confined him in a pillory. But being so a prisoner, as soon as he saw his guard alone from the rest, he asked him for a knife. At first the guard refused to give him one, but the king kept threatening him with what he would do to him afterwards, until the guard, who was just one of the helots, finally gave him a knife. Cleomenes took the knife and started mutilating himself from the shins up. He cut the flesh lengthwise and went up from shins to thighs and from the thighs to the hip and the flanks, until he got to the belly. And he made mincemeat of the belly too and so died. Most Greeks say this was because he corrupted the Pythia to say what she did about Demaratus. The Athenians are the only people to say that it was because, when he invaded Eleusis, he ravaged the precinct of the goddesses; the Argives say it was because he gathered those of the Argives out of their own sanctuary of Argus, where they had fled after the battle, and cut them all down and, in his contempt, burned down the sacred grove itself.[36]

76. For Cleomenes had consulted the oracle at Delphi and had been told that he would capture Argos. After this he led the Spartiates to the river Erasinus, which is said to issue from the Stymphalian lake. (They say the lake issues into a chasm, out of sight, and reappears in Argos, and that from Argos onward the waters of it are called by the Argives Erasinus.) When Cleomenes came to this river, he cut victims' throats into it but could not obtain favorable omens for the crossing. Then the king said, "I admire the river Erasinus for not playing false to his own countrymen; but

36. The story of this is in chapter 80, below.

all the same, the Argives will not come off scatheless." After that he withdrew his army into Thryeae, and having there, in the sea, cut the throat of a bull, he brought his men in ships to the territory of Tiryns and to Nauplia.

77. When the Argives heard of this, they came down in force to the sea; and when they were near Tiryns, at the place called Hesipaea, they encamped opposite the Lacedaemonians, leaving only a narrow no-man's-land between the two armies. At this point the Argives were not afraid of an open battle but only that they would be destroyed by some stratagem. For there was a prophecy, given in common to them and the Milesians, that bore on the matter. It ran as follows: [37]

> On that day when the female shall conquer the male in the
>   battle,
> Driving him off the field and winning glory from Argos,
> Many an Argive woman shall tear both cheeks in her
>   mourning.
> So shall it be; and someone, of men of another day also,
> Shall say, "The dread serpent, thrice coiled, died by the
>   spear of the victor."

All these things coming together made the Argives afraid. To counter them, they resolved to make a certain use of their enemy's herald. This is how they carried out their plan: whenever the Spartan herald gave a signal to the Lacedaemonians, the Argives did the same thing that the Spartan had ordered.

78. But when Cleomenes understood that the Argives were following exactly whatever the Spartan herald was ordering, he sent word that when his herald signaled the Spartans to make breakfast, they should instead pick up their arms and attack the Argives. This is exactly what the Lacedaemonians did. The Argives were making breakfast, as the Spartan signal had made them think they should do, when the Spartans fell upon them and killed many. The most of the Argives, however, took refuge in the grove of Argus, which the Spartans now surrounded and watched.

79. Now Cleomenes did this: he had some deserters with him,

---

37. Sparta is a feminine noun, Argos a masculine. The serpent is the national emblem of Argos. For the Milesians' "common share" in the prophecy, see chapter 19, above.

and getting information from them he sent a herald to summon out by name some of those who were shut up inside the grove. He called these men out, saying that he had in hand their ransom. (There is a regular ransom agreed among the Peloponnesians of two minas for each prisoner-of-war ransomed.) About fifty of the Argives were so called out, one by one, and Cleomenes killed them all. The others within the sacred precinct did not know what was happening; for the grove was so dense that those who were inside could not see what was being done to those who were outside until one of them climbed a tree and saw it. After that, those who were called out did not come.

80. At this, Cleomenes ordered all the helots to pile firewood around the grove, and, when they did so, he burned it down. As it was burning, the king asked one of the deserters to which of the gods the grove belonged. "To Argus," said the man. Cleomenes heard and uttered a heavy groan. "Apollo of Prophecy," he said, "how grossly you have deceived me when you said I would capture Argos! For my guess is that this is the Argos in which your prophecy is fulfilled."[38]

81. After that, Cleomenes sent most of his army home to Sparta, but he took a thousand of the best of them and went to the shrine of Hera to sacrifice. But when he wished to sacrifice on the altar, the priest forbade him, since, he said, it was unholy for a foreigner to sacrifice there. Cleomenes bade his helots take the priest away from the alter and flog him, and he then did the sacrifice himself. After so doing, he returned to Sparta.

82. On his homecoming, his enemies brought him before the ephors. They declared that he had accepted a bribe not to take Argos when he very easily could have taken it. His answer was— and whether he was speaking truth or falsehood I cannot exactly say—but he said that, once he had captured the shrine of Argus, he thought the oracle the god had given him had been fulfilled; and therefore he had held it unfit that he should try for the city of Argos until, by sacrifices, he could learn whether the god was giving him

38. There are many other examples in Herodotus in which a double significance of proper names constitutes the deception by the god, as in the case of Cambyses, who in book 2 confused the two cities named Ecbatana, one in Egypt, the other in Persia. Other instances in literature include King Henry IV's misunderstanding of "Jerusalem" in Shakespeare's 2 Henry IV.

the city or stood in his way. When he sought his omens in the shrine of Hera, he said that a flame had sprung from the breasts of the image, and thus he knew the truth: that he would not capture Argos. For if it had come from the head, then he would have been the city's captor from head to foot. As it came from the goddess' breast, it meant that he had done everything that the god wanted to happen. This defense of his appeared to the Spartans credible and probable, and he was easily acquitted of his enemies' challenge.

83. Argos, then, was so widowed of its stock of men that the slaves took over everything in government and all management until the sons of the dead grew to young manhood. They then won back Argos for themselves and drove out the slaves. The expelled slaves then took and held Tiryns. For a while the two communities lived in harmony, but then there came among the slaves a prophet, Cleander, from Phigalea in Arcadia by origin. He incited the slaves to attack their masters, and from that moment on there was war between them for a long time, until, with difficulty, the Argives at last won the upper hand.

84. That is the Argive account of why Cleomenes went mad and died so miserably. The Spartiates themselves say that the gods had nothing to do with the origin of his madness but that, through association with the Scythians, he had fallen into the habit of heavy drinking and that it was that that brought on his madness. For the Scythian nomads, at the time that Darius invaded their country, were bent on punishing him and sent to Sparta to form an alliance and an arrangement such that the Scythians themselves were to try to invade Media along the river Phasis, while the Spartiates were to start out from Ephesus and march inland and meet at the same place with the Scythians. They say that Cleomenes, when the Scythians came to Sparta to discuss this, had more than ordinarily to do with them and, in the process, learned from them the habit of very heavy drinking. The Spartiates think that this it was that drove Cleomenes mad. Ever since, when they want to drink more strongly than usual, they call for a "Scythian cup." [39] That is the story the Spartiates tell

39. The reference seems to be to drinking wine with no mixture of water rather than drinking something stronger than wine itself. The Greeks always drank their wine with liberal shares of water.

of King Cleomenes; but I still believe that Cleomenes was paying
what he owed to Demaratus.

85. When Cleomenes was dead and the Aeginetans heard of it,
they sent messengers to Sparta to denounce Leotychides for having
the hostages held in Athens. The Lacedaemonians assembled a
court and passed judgment that the Aeginetans had been extremely
wronged by Leotychides; the decision was that Leotychides should
be handed over to the Aeginetans in requital for the hostages. But as
the Aeginetans were about to remove Leotychides, there was this
said to them by one Theasides, the son of Leoprepes, a man of distinction in Sparta: "What is this that you would do, men of Aegina?
Here is the king of Sparta being surrendered by his own fellow
countrymen to you to carry away! Even if at this moment, in their
fury, the Spartiates have so decided, take heed lest another day shall
come, if you do as you are now doing, and they shall launch an all-
destroying plague against your land." At these words the Aeginetans
gave over the carrying-off of Leotychides but made an agreement
that he would go with them to Athens and get back their men
for them.

86. So Leotychides came to Athens and demanded the men who
had been formerly entrusted to the Athenians for safe-keeping; but
the Athenians refused to give them back, on various excuses. They
said that it was two kings who had placed the hostages with them,
and they could not justify themselves in giving them back to one
king without the other. On their refusal, Leotychides spoke to them
and said: "Men of Athens, do whichever of two things you want.
Give these men back, and you will be acting rightly; do not give
them back, and you will be doing the opposite. But there is a matter
that once happened in Sparta about safe-keeping which I would like
to tell you. We Spartiates have a story that there was in Lacedaemon,
three generations before my time, one Glaucus, son of Epicydes.
This man, according to our story, was preeminent in every sort of
excellence, and, in particular, he had the greatest reputation for justice of any man then living in Lacedaemon. But once upon a time
something happened to him—as we tell it. A Milesian came to
Sparta and wanted to speak with Glaucus, making the following
proposition: 'I am from Miletus, and I come here, Glaucus, because I
want to profit by your justice. Throughout all of Greece, and even in
Ionia, there is great talk of your justice. I have reflected on this; I

have reflected that Ionia is always a chancy country, where you
never see the same people continuing to hold the same possessions,
while the Peloponnese is a land of firmness and safety. I thought this
over, and it seemed to me that the best thing I could do was to con-
vert one half of all my property into silver and bank it with you,
knowing full well that when it was deposited with you it would be
safe. So, receive the money now, and also take and keep these symbols of receipt. Whoever comes to you with the tallies of these, give
him the money.' These were the words of the stranger from Miletus,
and Glaucus received the deposit on the terms stated. After a long
time, there came to Sparta the sons of the man who had made the
deposit; they spoke with Glaucus, showed the tallies, and asked for
the return of the money. He put them aside with this answer: 'I have
no recollection of the affair, nor does anything you have said bring
me back to any knowledge of it. But I will try to remember and do
everything that's fair. If I took the money, I will certainly render it
duly to you; and if I never had it at all, I will deal with you according
to Greek custom. In this matter, I must ask you to give me a postponement till the fourth month from now for the final settlement of
this matter.' The Milesians were very indignant and went away,
being sure that they had lost their money, and Glaucus went to
Delphi to consult the oracle. When he asked the oracle if he might
steal the money by means of an oath, the Pythia went after him with
the following verses:

> For now, Epicydes' son, you have an immediate profit
> By winning your case with an oath and taking the money in
>   plunder.
> Swear, then; for death too awaits even him who keeps fast
>   his oath-bond;
> But Oath has a child with no name, nor hands nor feet hath
>   he either.
> But swift in pursuit is this child until in his grasp he has all
> A man's breed, which he utterly slays, and all his household
>   to boot.
> But the breed of the oath-keeping man shall hereinafter be
>   better.

When Glaucus heard that, he asked pardon of the god for what
he had suggested. But the Pythia said that to tempt the god and to
commit the sin were exactly the same thing. Glaucus sent after the

Milesians and gave them back their money. But the reason why, men of Athens, I was inclined to tell you this story is this: at this moment there is no single descendant of Glaucus, nor is there a household that bears Glaucus' name. All is utterly uprooted from Sparta. So good a thing it is not even to form a thought about a deposit, save only the giving of it back when people ask for it."

87. Despite these words of his, Leotycides failed to convince the Athenians, and so he went off home. But the Aeginetans, before they paid penalty for the former outrageous wrongs they had done to the Athenians to pleasure the Thebans,[40] did the following thing. They had a grudge against the Athenians and claimed to have been wronged by them and so made their preparations to punish them. The Athenians had a five-yearly festival going on in Sunium, and the Aeginetans laid an ambush for the theoric ship[41] and captured it, full of the chief men of Athens. They took the men an put them in chains.

88. Because of what the Aeginetans had done to them, the Athenians no longer postponed contriving the utmost vengeance against Aegina. There was a man called Nicodromus, son of Cnoethus, who was a person of distinction in Aegina but who had a grudge against the Aeginetans, who once, in the past, had banished him. This man learned that the Athenians were bent on injuring Aegina, and so he arranged with the Athenians to turn over the island to them, telling them the day on which he would make the attempt and when they must come to his help.

89. After that, Nicodromus captured what is called the Old City, as he had arranged with the Athenians; but the Athenians failed to appear at the proper time. They didn't have enough warships with which to engage the Aeginetans. The time that it took them to ask the Corinthians to lend them ships was enough to ruin the affair. The Corinthians, who were at the time their closest friends, did give the Athenians on their demand twenty ships, at a price of five drachmas apiece (the law forbade them to make a clear gift of them). The Athenians took them and their own and put crews in them—in all, up to the number of seventy ships—and sailed against Aegina. They arrived just one day beyond the agreed time.

40. See 5.81.
41. The Athenian state ship, carrying the official delegation.

90. Nicodromus, when the Athenians didn't come on time, got into a boat and ran away from Aegina. With him went others of the Aeginetans, and the Athenians gave all these people Sunium to be their home. They made this their base, and from it they ravaged and plundered the Aeginetans on the island.

91. This all happened afterwards.[42] But the rich men of Aegina had gained victory over the popular party when it rose against them under the leadership of Nicodromus, and, having captured them, they led them out to execution. As a result of this, a curse fell on them; and they could not expiate it by sacrifice, despite all their attempts to do so, but were driven out of the island before they could propitiate the goddess. For they had taken prisoner seven hundred of the popular party and led them out to kill them; but one of the prisoners broke loose of his chains and fled to the temple gates of Demeter the Lawgiver, where he clasped the door handles and hung on to them. His enemies were not able to drag him off, for all their pulling, and so they chopped off his hands and took him so; the hands remained clinging to the door handles.

92. This is what one set of Aeginetans did to another. When the Athenians arrived with their seventy ships, the Aeginetans fought them at sea and, being defeated, called on the same friends they had appealed to before, the Argives. But these now refused to help them, being angry because Aeginetan ships, having been taken by force by King Cleomenes, had put in on the Argive coast, and their crews had landed to attack them, along with the Lacedaemonians; in this same attack there were also some men from ships of Sicyon. The Argives imposed a fine of a thousand talents on them, five hundred on each people. The Sicyonians acknowledged their fault and agreed to pay a hundred talents in return for being cleared. But the Aeginetans were more stiff-necked and would make no such acknowledgment. So to those who now came with the request of the Aeginetan state for help, not an Argive would answer the call on behalf of the state itself; but volunteers came, to the number of a thousand. The general commanding them was called Eurybates, a

42. The attempt to separate out the relations of Aegina and Athens from the main trend of events leading up to the battle of Marathon in 490 B.C. makes the narrative somewhat confusing. Herodotus' account of the Athenian dealings with Nicodromus, concluded in chapter 91, covers events between 490 and 480 B.C.—that is, in the ten years *after* Marathon.

man who had practiced the pentathlon. Most of these men never came home again but were killed in Aegina by the Athenians. The general, Eurybates himself, fought in single combat three times, killing his man each time; but he was then killed by his fourth opponent, Sophanes, a man from Decelea.

93. The Athenians having become disordered, the Aeginetans closed with their fleet and defeated it, and they captured, crews and all, four of the Athenian ships.

94. Thus was war joined between the Athenians and the Aeginetans. But the Persian was always going about his own thing: the slave was continually reminding him, "Remember the Athenians," [43] the Pisistratids were always at his elbow, making mischief against the Athenians, and there was Darius' own wish to have this excuse to subjugate those of the Greeks who would not give him earth and water. Mardonius, since he had had such ill success with the expedition already, he dismissed from the command and appointed other generals, whom he sent against Eretria and Athens. These generals were Datis, a Mede, and his own nephew, Artaphrenes, the son of Artaphrenes. He sent them off with instructions to enslave Athens and Eretria and to bring the slaves before him.

95. These generals who were appointed left the King's presence and came to the Aleian plain in Cilicia, bringing with them a vast and well-equipped army. When they were camped there, there came as an accession to them the whole fleet assigned to each of the generals, and there came also the horse transports that, in the year before, Darius had ordered his tributary subjects to make ready. They loaded the horses into these, embarked the army, and sailed away, with six hundred ships of war, for Ionia. From there on, they did not sail their ships along the land, heading straight for the Hellespont and Thrace, but, setting out from Samos, they made their voyage through the Icarian Sea and through the islands. I think this was because they were mostly afraid of the sailing round Athos, where, in the year before, their passage had brought such terrible disaster. Besides, Naxos, not yet being in their power, added further pressure on them.

96. When they turned from the Icarian Sea, they put to shore at Naxos; for they made this their first point of attack. The Naxians

43. Cf. 5.105.

remembered what had happened before this and took flight to the hills and never stood their ground. The Persians made slaves of all of them they caught, and they burned, besides, their temples and their city. Having done that, they set off for the other islands.

97. While they were doing this, the Delians too quit Delos and fled to Tenos. As the fleet was coming toward it, Datis sailed ahead and would not allow his ships to anchor off Delos itself but across, off Rhenaea. He himself, learning where the Delians were, sent a herald to them and said: "Holy men, why do you flee away, having put a misconstruction on my intentions, far from the truth? For my own thoughts go with the King's command to me, in addition, that in this land the two gods were born,[44] and this land must therefore suffer no mischief whatever, neither the land itself nor those who live in it. Now, then, come back to your own places and dwell again in your island." Such was his proclamation to the Delians, and afterwards he heaped up three hundred talents' weight of frankincense on the altar and burned it there.

98. Having done so, Datis sailed with his army to Eretria first, bringing with him Ionians and Aeolians. But Delos, after he had put out to sea from there, was shaken by an earthquake, and the Delians say that this was the first and last time it was shaken before my time. This was perhaps manifested by the god as a portent of the troubles that were to come. For in the days of Darius, son of Hystaspes, and of Xerxes, the son of Darius, and of Artaxerxes, the son of Xerxes— these three successive generations—more ills befell Greece than in all twenty generations before Darius. Some of these came about through the Persians, and some by the acts of the chief peoples of Greece warring against one another.[45] Thus it is not at all out of the way that Delos should have been shaken by an earthquake though never before shaken. Also, there was an oracle written, which said,

44. Artemis and Apollo, twin offspring of Leto and Zeus.

45. This is unmistakable evidence of Herodotus' linking-together of the Persian and Peloponnesian wars, but we are not so certain about which of the two Peloponnesian wars he is referring to. For Artaxerxes reigned from 465 to 424, and it is therefore not clear whether Herodotus is thinking, in the last phrase, of the First Peloponnesian War, which occurred before 445, or of the Second, which started in 432. If it was the latter, this clearly *may* mean that Herodotus was alive in the middle 420s, if it is implied that he is looking at the three Persian reigns as completed.

"Delos too will I shake, although 'twas unshaken aforetime." In Greek, the name Darius means the Doer, Xerxes means the Warrior, and Artaxerxes means the Great Warrior. And that is what the Greeks would correctly call these kings in their own tongue.

99. The barbarians sailed off from Delos and put in at the islands, and from them they generated an army and also hostages—the sons of the islanders. As they sailed round, they also put in at Carystus. The people of Carystus gave them no hostages, nor, said they, would they serve against cities that were their neighbors—by which they meant Eretria and Athens. So the Persians besieged them and ravaged their country until the people of Carystus too came over to the Persian persuasion.

100. The Eretrians, on understanding that the Persian host was sailing against themselves, begged the Athenians to give them help. The Athenians did not refuse help, but what they gave was the four thousand settled colonists who had taken over the land of the horse-breeding Chalcidians.[46] But the plans of the Eretrians, on their side, were not sound either; for though they sent for the Athenians, they had divided notions of what to do. Some of them were for quitting the city and taking to the heights of Euboea, but the rest, who looked to the private gains they would make from the Persians, were ready for treachery. Aeschines, the son of Nothon, who was one of the chief men of Eretria, knowing how each of the parties stood, told the Athenians who had come exactly how things were and urged them to take themselves off to their own country, that they might not add their destruction to that of the Eretrians. When Aeschines gave that advice to the Athenians, they took it.

101. So they crossed over to Oropus and saved themselves. The Persians, in their course, put their ships into the parts around Temenos and Choereae and Aegilea in the land of Eretria, and, having secured these places, they disembarked their horses and prepared to attack their enemy. The Eretrians had no intention of sallying out and fighting, for what they chiefly cared for was to preserve the walls of the city if they could, inasmuch as they had resolved not to quit their city. The attack on the walls was strong, and many fell on both sides for six days. On the seventh, Euphorbus, son of Alcimachus,

46. See 5.77.

and Philagrus, son of Cyneas, two men of distinction among the Eretrians, betrayed the town to the Persians. So the Persians entered and plundered and burned the temples, in retaliation for the temples that were burned in Sardis, and they enslaved the inhabitants, according to the orders of Darius.

102. So they conquered Eretria and stayed a few days there and then sailed for Attica, pressing the Athenians hard and thinking that they would do to them the very same as they had done to the Eretrians. And because Marathon was the most suitable spot in Attica for cavalry action and the nearest to Eretria, it was to Marathon that Hippias, son of Pisistratus, guided them.

103. On information of this, the Athenians too marched out to Marathon. They were led by ten generals, the tenth of whom was Miltiades. It was *his* father, Cimon, son of Stesagoras, whom it had befallen to be banished from Athens by Pisistratus, son of Hippocrates, and while he was in exile, he chanced to win an Olympic victory with his four-horse team, in this victory scoring just the same win as his brother on his mother's side, another Miltiades. At the next Olympics he won again, with the same team, but this time allowed Pisistratus to be proclaimed the victor. By yielding victory to Pisistratus, he made terms to gain a return to his homeland. But when he won yet another Olympic victory (still with the same mares), it was his lot to be killed by the sons of Pisistratus, Pisistratus being no longer alive. These men suborned fellows to lie in wait for him by night in the prytaneum and kill him. Cimon is buried outside the city, beyond the road called Through-the-Hollow. Right opposite him is buried his team of mares that won the three Olympic prizes. Other horses that have made the same win are those of Euagoras, the Laconian, but otherwise none. Stesagoras, who was the elder of the sons of Cimon, was at that time being raised by his uncle Miltiades in the Chersonese, but the younger one was with Cimon himself in Athens. This younger one was called Miltiades after the original Miltiades, who colonized the Chersonese.

104. This Miltiades, then, who had twice escaped death and had now come from the Chersonese, was a general of the Athenians.[47]

47. Here Herodotus refers to Miltiades as one member of the Board of Ten Generals. After Cleisthenes' reforms, one general was elected from each of the

Twice he escaped death; for the Phoenicians had chased him as far as Imbros and set much store on capturing him and bringing him to the court of King Darius, and when he had escaped them[48] and come to his own country and thought he was at last in safety, his enemies brought him before the courts and prosecuted him on the charge of his despotism, exercised in the Chersonese. But he was also acquitted before the courts and was appointed a general of the Athenians, being elected by the people.

105. First of all, when the generals were still within the city, they sent to Sparta a herald, one Phidippides, an Athenian, who was a day-long runner and a professional. According to the story of Phidippides himself, and what he told the Athenians, Pan met him on Mount Parthenium, above Tegea. Pan shouted his name, "Phidippides," and bade him say this to the Athenians: "Why do you pay no heed to Pan, who is a good friend to the people of Athens, has been many times serviceable to you, and will be so again?" This story the Athenians were convinced was true, and when the Athenian fortunes had again settled for the good, they set up a shrine of Pan under the Acropolis and propitiated the god himself with sacrifices and torch races, in accord with the message he had sent them.

106. This Phidippides, being sent by the generals, and after, as he said, Pan had appeared to him, arrived in the city of Sparta the day after he had left Athens.[49] He came before the rulers and said: "Men of Lacedaemon, the Athenians beg you to help them; do not suffer a most ancient city in Greece to meet with slavery at the hands of the barbarians. Even now Eretria has been enslaved, and Greece is the weaker by one distinguished city." So he discharged his orders. The Spartans wanted to help the Athenians; but, they said, it was impossible to do so at once, inasmuch as they were unwilling

---

ten new tribes, to serve for one year. To translate "Miltiades was general of the Athenians" gives the wrong impression to our ears, as the ensuing passage proves. He had nine colleagues, with equal votes. (The power of the Board of Ten Generals was considerable in domestic as well as military affairs. Pericles, for example, was a *stratēgos*, or general. However, their power, unlike that of the Pisistratid autocrats, was limited; they were accountable to the people, and they could be removed from office.)

48. See chapter 41, above.

49. According to some authorities, the distance was one hundred fifty miles.

to break their law. It was now the ninth day of the first phase of the month, [50] and on the ninth day, they said, they would not go out of Spartan territory until the full moon.

107. So they waited for the full moon. Now, the man who guided the barbarians was Hippias, son of Pisistratus, and he guided them to Marathon. In the previous night he had had a dream, and the dream was this: he thought that he was lying with his own mother. His reading of the dream's meaning was that he would return to Athens and, having reestablished his rule there, would die in his own country, an old man. That was how he read the dream. And now, being the Persians' guide, he took the slaves from Eretria and disembarked them on the island of the Styreans, which is called Aeglea; and when the ships put in at Marathon, he made them anchor there, and, when the barbarians had disembarked, it was he who put them in order of battle. While he was busy about all this, there came upon him a fit of coughing and sneezing greater than he was wont. As he was an old man, most of his teeth were shaky, and with the violence of the cough, one of the teeth fell out. It fell in the sand, and he tried exceedingly hard to find it again. When the tooth did not appear, he groaned heavily and said to the onlookers, "This land is not ours, nor shall we subjugate it; for the share of it that was mine—the tooth has it."

108. Thus Hippias saw the dream as being fulfilled. When the Athenians were ranged in fighting order in the sanctuary of Heracles, there came to their help, in full force as a people, the Plataeans; for the Plataeans had given themselves into the hands of the Athenians, and the Athenians had undertaken many labors on their behalf. The manner of their giving themselves to Athens was this: when the Plataeans were hard pressed by the Thebans, they had first given themselves to Cleomenes, the son of Anaxandrides, and to the Lacedaemonians, who happened to be in their country. But the Lacedaemonians would not accept them, saying, "We live too far away, and so our help would be cold comfort for you. You could be

50. The month was divided into three equal periods: the waxing moon, the "middle" moon, and the waning moon. The point of all this is that the Spartans were celebrating the Carnea, an important festival of Apollo, which lasted from the 7th to the 15th of the month (i.e., before the full moon). No Dorian engaged in warfare during the period of this festival.

many times enslaved before we heard a word of it. We advise you to give yourselves into the hands of the Athenians, who are your near neighbors and no bad people to bring help." This counsel the Lacedaemonians gave not out of good will to the Plataeans but because they wished the Athenians to have trouble by joining issue with the Boeotians. This was the advice of the Lacedaemonians to the Plataeans. The Plataeans took this advice, and, when the Athenians were celebrating the Feast of the Twelve Gods,[51] they sat as suppliants at the altar and formally rendered themselves to the Athenians. When the Thebans learned of this, they launched a campaign against the Plataeans, and the Athenians came to the help of the Plataeans. When the two sides were about to engage, the Corinthians took a hand in the game, as they chanced to be there, and they managed to reconcile the parties, both of whom were willing to accept their arbitration. They set a boundary between the territories, making it a condition that the Thebans should not force such of the Boeotians to be Thebans as did not want to be such. Having given this as their decision, the Corinthians marched away, but the Boeotians set upon the Athenians as they were departing; however, in their attack, they were defeated in the battle. Then the Athenians set up new boundaries for the Plataeans, beyond those the Corinthians had made. They set the river Asopus as a boundary for Hysiae and Plataea against the Thebans. So this, as I have told you, is how the Plataeans had given themselves into the hands of the Athenians, and thus it was that now they came to Marathon to help them.

109. The opinions of the Athenian generals were split in two. The one party did not want a battle, for they held that their army was too small in numbers to encounter the Persians; but the others, including Miltiades, were for fighting. Now, as the split was even and it was the worse opinion that was gaining, Miltiades approached Callimachus of Aphidna, who was then polemarch. This man was the eleventh to have a vote, being chosen by lot to the office of polemarch; for in ancient times the Athenians made the polemarch to

51. The twelve gods were Zeus, Hera, Poseidon, Demeter, Apollo, Artemis, Athena, Ares, Aphrodite, Hermes, and Hestia. Theirs was the central altar in the agora, and all distances were measured from it.

have a vote the equal of the board of generals.[52] Miltiades spoke to Callimachus as follows: "It lies in your hands, Callimachus, whether to enslave Athens or keep her free and thereby leave a memorial for all the life of mankind, such as not even Harmodius and Aristogiton left behind them.[53] For now the Athenians are in their greatest danger ever since they were Athenian at all; and if they bend their necks to the Mede, it has already been decided what they will suffer when they will have been handed over to Hippias; but if the city shall win, she may well become first among Hellenic cities.[54] How then all this can be, and how it hangs upon you to make the decision in the matter, I am going to tell you. The opinions of the ten generals—ourselves—are split in two. Some of us are for the fight, some against. Now, if we do not fight, I am confident that a great division will fall upon the minds of the Athenians and shake them so that they will Medize.[55] But if we fight before this rottenness infect some of the Athenians, we may well win the fight if the gods give us equal treatment with our foes. That is the whole matter that concerns you; that is what hangs on you. If you incline to my opinion, there is your city, free and the first in Greece. If you choose those who are for turning away from the fight, the exact opposite of the good things that I have described will be yours."

52. There was a board of archons—"rulers"—in Athens, chosen by lot, with titles such as "king archon," "warlord archon," etc. These titles were what was left of an older aristocratic order, which had been superseded by Cleisthenes' democracy; as an executive branch they had been supplanted by the Board of Ten Generals. The archons, however, retained ceremonial duties, such as the ordering of festivals. Herodotus is describing some slightly transitional state in which the polemarch still retained his voting privilege in matters of war; hence "in ancient times." It seems possible that in some details Herodotus is somewhat anachronistic in his rendering of the period. How and Wells, on the evidence of Aristotle's *Constitution of Athens* (chapter 22), say that the polemarch was not chosen by lot until several years after Marathon.

53. The two men who murdered Hipparchus, brother of the Pisistratid tyrant Hippias (cf. 5.55), and, for so doing, were popularly regarded as the deliverers of Athens from absolute power. The fact that Harmodius and Aristogiton were Callimachus' fellow demesmen, being also of Aphidna, must have made the appeal to their names all the more effective.

54. Certainly a glance forward at the Athens that headed the Delian Confederacy or, as others saw it, the Athenian empire.

55. Join the Persian side.

110. By these words Miltiades won over Callimachus, and with the addition of the polemarch's decision it was resolved that they would fight. Afterwards, on any day that the command fell to one of the generals who were of Miltiades' opinion, he turned over his right of command to Miltiades. He accepted the command but did not make the attack until the day of his own command came round.[56]

111. When it so came round to him, then the Athenians formed their ranks for battle. The right wing was commanded by the polemarch, Callimachus, for the law at that time demanded that the right wing should be led by the polemarch. Under his leadership the tribes followed in succession, according to the order of their numbers.[57] Finally, the last in order were the Plataeans, holding the left wing. (From the time of this fight on, when the Athenians hold their sacrifices at the grand festivals of the four-year cycle,[58] the Athenian herald prays: "May all good things come to the Athenians—and to the Plataeans.") This was the order of battle at Marathon, and it fell out that, as the line was equal in length to the Persian formation, the middle of the Greek side was only a few ranks deep, and at this place the army was weakest; but each of the two wings was very strong.

112. The lines were drawn up, and the sacrifices were favorable; so the Athenians were permitted to charge, and they advanced on the Persians at a run. There was not less than eight stades in the no-man's-land between the two armies. The Persians, seeing them coming at a run, made ready to receive them; but they believed that the Athenians were possessed by some very desperate madness, seeing their small numbers and their running to meet their enemies without support of cavalry or archers. That was what the barbarians thought; but the Athenians, when they came to hand-to-hand fighting, fought right worthily. They were the first Greeks we know of

56. What is meant is that each of the ten commanders had the leadership for a day. The Greek word I have translated as "leadership" actually denotes the revolving leadership of the new Council of Five Hundred. Each tribe's fifty Councillors acted in succession as the executive branch of the Council for a limited period (a little over a month). Here Herodotus indicates that the same principle applied to the generals.

57. "The fixed official order instituted by Cleisthenes" (How and Wells).

58. There were five of these quadrennial festivals at Athens. The greatest of them was the Panathenaea (lesser versions of which were held annually).

to charge their enemy at a run and the first to face the sight of the Median dress and the men who wore it. For till then the Greeks were terrified even to hear the names of the Medes.

113. The fight at Marathon went on for a long time, and in the center the barbarians won, where the Persians themselves and the Sacae were stationed. At this point they won, and broke the Greeks, and pursued them inland. But on each wing the Athenians and the Plataeans were victorious, and, as they conquered, they let flee the part of the barbarian army they had routed, and, joining their two wings together, they fought the Persians who had broken their center; and then the Athenians won the day. As the Persians fled, the Greeks followed them, hacking at them, until they came to the sea. Then the Greeks called for fire and laid hold of the ships.

114. At this point of the struggle the polemarch was killed, having proved himself a good man and true, and, of the generals, there died Stesilaus, son of Thrasylaus. And Cynegirus, the son of Euphorion, gripped with his hand the poop of one of the ships and had his hand chopped off with an axe and so died, and many renowned Athenians also.[59]

115. In this fashion the Athenians captured seven of the ships. With the rest of the fleet, the barbarians, backing water, and taking from the island where they had left them the slaves from Eretria, rounded Cape Sunium, because they wished to get to Athens before the Athenians could reach it. There was a slander prevalent in Athens that they got this idea from a contrivance of the Alcmaeonidae. It was said that the Alcmaeonidae, in accord with a covenant they had made with the Persians, showed a signal, the holding-up of a shield, for those barbarians who were on shipboard.

116. They rounded Sunium, all right; but the Athenians, rushing with all speed to defend their city, reached it first, before the barbarians came, and encamped, moving from one sanctuary of Heracles—the one at Marathon—to another, the one at Cynosarges. The barbarians anchored off Phalerum—for in those days that was the harbor of Athens—and, after riding at anchor there for a while, they sailed off, back to Asia.

59. Cynegirus was the brother of the poet Aeschylus, who also fought at Marathon.

117. In this battle of Marathon there died, of the barbarians, about six thousand four hundred men, and, of the Athenians, one hundred and ninety-two. Those were the numbers of the fallen on both sides. A strange thing happened there, also: an Athenian, Epizelus, son of Cuphagoras, who was in the thick of the fighting, and fighting bravely himself, lost the sight of his eyes. He was not struck on any part of his body or hit by a missile, but he continued blind from that day, all the rest of his life. But I heard that he told the story of the matter thus: that he saw confronting him a huge man-at-arms whose beard covered all his shield. This ghostly spirit passed by Epizelus himself but killed his comrade beside him. That is what I understood Epizelus to have said.

118. Datis was making his way back to Asia with his army when he arrived at Myconos, and there he saw in his sleep a vision. What the vision was is not said, but at dawn he made a search of the ships and found in a Phoenician ship a gilt image of Apollo. He inquired where this had been stolen from, and, after learning the shrine from which it came, he sailed with his own ship to Delos. (The Delians had come back to their island.) He placed the image in the shrine and bade the Delians to take the image to the Theban Delium, which is on the seacoast opposite Chalcis. After giving these instructions, Datis sailed away; but the Delians did not bring the image where he bade them. However, twenty years later, the Thebans themselves, on the urging of a prophecy, brought it to Delium.

119. When their ships reached Asia, Datis and Artaphrenes took the enslaved Eretrians up to Susa. King Darius had bitter wrath against the Eretrians before they became his prisoners of war, inasmuch as they, the Eretrians, had started the wrongs that had been done him. But when he saw them brought before him and entirely at his mercy, he did them no further harm but settled them in the land of Cissia, in an estate of his own, called Ardericca, about two hundred and ten stades from Susa and forty from a well that has three sorts of products: men draw from it asphalt, salt, and oil, and this is how they draw them. They draw up the liquid by means of a sweep, which has attached to it half of a skin for a bucket. A man dips with this, draws it up, and pours it out into a container. From this it travels into another container, which spreads it three ways. The as-

phalt and the salt solidify at once. But the oil[60] is what the Persians call "rhadinace." It is black and has a heavy smell. In this place, then, Darius settled the Eretrians, and they were there in that country still in my time, still speaking their ancient language. That is the story of the Eretrians.

120. *After* the full moon there came to Athens two thousand of the Lacedaemonians, who had shown such zeal to reach the city that they arrived in Attica on the third day out of Sparta. Though they had come too late for the battle, they were nonetheless anxious to see the Medes; and so they went to Marathon and saw. Thereafter, praising the Athenians and their action, they went home again.

121. It is a wonder to me—indeed, I do not accept the story— that the Alcmaeonidae ever showed that shield by arrangement with the Persians or that they were willing to subject the Athenians to the barbarians and Hippias, inasmuch as they can be clearly seen to be at least as much haters of despots as Callias or even more. Callias was the son of Phaenippus and father of Hipponicus, and he was the only one of all the Athenians who dared to buy at public auction the goods of the despot Pisistratus when he was expelled from Athens, and in other ways he showed the bitterest enmity to the despot.

122. Everyone should remember Callias on many grounds. First, as I said before, he was a man who had a chief share in freeing his country; and second for his wins at Olympia, where he won the horse race, ridden, and was second with the four-horse chariot, and for his earlier victories at the Pythian games. He made a great show before all the Greeks for his immense spending. And then again, what a man he proved himself to be in the matter of his three daughters! For when they were all ripe for marriage, he gave them the most magnificent present: their free-will choice of any man in Athens that each of them wanted![61]

123. The Alcmaeonidae were certainly no less against despots

60. Petroleum.

61. Many editors believe that this chapter is one of the very few passages in Herodotus that is an interpolation. It may be that some editor or copyist wrote a note on Callias that subsequently became added to the text. Certainly, several of the words or forms used are not fifth-century Greek.

than this man. As I said, it is a wonder to me, and I do not admit the charge, that they showed that shield as a signal. Why, they were banished all the time of the despots' government, and it was by their contrivance that the Pisistratidae were driven out of power, and so it is they who freed Athens far more than Harmodius and Aristogiton, in my judgment! For those latter only exasperated the rest of the Pisistratidae when they killed Hipparchus, and they had no effect on ending the rule of the rest of the Pisistratidae. But the Alcmaeonidae manifestly freed Athens, if it was truly they who persuaded the Pythia to signify to the Lacedaemonians that they should free her, as my account has earlier indicated.[62]

124. Someone might say that perhaps they betrayed their country in disgust at the democracy in it. But there were no other men who were of greater repute among the Athenians than the Alcmaeonidae, nor any who were more honored. So, reason will not have it that they signaled with the shield on such grounds as these. True, a shield *was* so displayed; that cannot be disputed, for it undoubtedly happened; but who it was that was the agent I cannot say, further than what I have declared already.

125. The Alcmaeonidae were, from of old, brilliant in the history of Athens, but from the time of Alcmaeon and then Megacles they became truly brilliant. For Alcmaeon, the son of Megacles, was aider and zealous abettor of those Lydians who came from Croesus in Sardis to the oracle at Delphi; indeed, when Croesus learned from those Lydians who had gone to the oracle of the good services done to himself by Alcmaeon, he sent for him to Sardis, and, when he came there, made him a present of all the gold he could carry away on his person. Faced with such a gift, Alcmaeon laid a cunning plan, which he put into practice. He put on a large tunic, leaving a deep fold in it, and he wore the broadest buskins he could find, and away he went to the treasure house to which they conducted him. Plunging into the heap of gold dust there, he first packed as much gold as his buskins would hold alongside of his legs; next, he filled all the fold of his tunic with gold and scattered gold dust all over his hair; more of it he took into his mouth and came out of the treasure house barely able to drag his buskins with him and looking like any-

62. This is in 5.62–63.

thing rather than a human being, his mouth being so stuffed and his whole person swollen. Croesus was overcome with laughter when he saw him and gave him everything he had taken and as much more. It was thus that the house of the Alcmaeonidae grew greatly rich and thus that this Alcmaeon kept four-horse teams and won at Olympia.

126. In the next generation, Cleisthenes, the prince of Sicyon, raised this house even higher, so that it grew to be among the Greeks more famous than before. For Cleisthenes, the son of Aristonymus, the son of Myron, the son of Andreas, had a daughter, whose name was Agariste. Now, Cleisthenes wanted to find out the best man in all Greece and give her to this man for his wife. Since the Olympic games were then in progress and Cleisthenes was the winner at them with his four-horse chariot, he had a proclamation made to the effect that whoever of the Greeks thought himself worthy to be son-in-law of Cleisthenes should come to Sicyon within sixty days or earlier, for Cleisthenese would decide the issue of the marriage within a year, beginning from the sixtieth day after the time of the proclamation. There and then all those Greeks who were uplifted with pride in themselves and their country came as the girl's suitors; and for them Cleisthenes furnished a place for running and wrestling, which he had made for this very purpose.

127. From Italy came Smindyrides, the son of Hippocrates, from Sybaris, who was the chief of all men in the practice of luxury—and Sybaris was at the time at the height of its luxury; and Damasus of Siris, the son of Amyris, who was called The Wise. These came from Italy; and from the Ionian Gulf, Amphimnestus, son of Epistrophus, from Epidamnus; this man was from the Ionian Gulf. From Aetolia came Males, brother of Titormus, who excelled all Greeks in strength and fled from all society of man to the limits of the Aetolian country. From the Peloponnesus came Leocedes, son of Phidon, prince of Argos. This was the Phidon who established weights and measures for the Peloponnesians and who displayed the greatest act of insolence of any Greek, in that he drove out the Elean marshals of the games and set the contests at Olympia himself. The son of this man came; and Amiantus, an Arcadian, the son of Lycurgus, came from Trapezus; and an Azenian came from the town of Paeus, one Laphanes, the son of Euphorion—that Euphorion who, according to the story that is told in Arcadia, received the Dioscuri into his

house and, after that, entertained all men; and, from Elis, came
Onomastus, son of Agaeus. These came from the Peloponnese itself.
And from Athens came Megacles, son of that Alcmaeon who had
been the guest of Croesus, and one other, Hippoclides, son of
Tisander, who in wealth and handsomeness excelled all the other
Athenians. From Eretria, which was flourishing at that time, came
Lysanias; he was the only one from Euboea. From Thessaly came one
of the Scopads, Diactorides of Crannon; and, from the Molossians,
Alcon.

128. In such numbers were the suitors. When they came on the
appointed day, Cleisthenes first inquired of them their countries and
the descent of each man, and then he kept them there for a year,
making trial of their manliness and their temper and their education
and disposition; he associated with them man to man and also in
company, and the younger men among them he gathered into the
gymnasium, and, most important of all, he made trial of them at the
common meals. For the whole time that he kept them with him he
did all these things and, at the same time, entertained them in magnificent style. Now, those he liked most were the suitors from
Athens and, of these two, he preferred Hippoclides, son of Tisander.
He made this judgment on the basis of Hippoclides' manliness and
because, further back in his ancestry, he was akin to the Cypselids of
Corinth.

129. When the appointed day came round for the marriage feast
and for Cleisthenes' declaration of his choice from among them all,
he slaughtered one hundred cattle and feasted the suitors and all the
people of Sicyon. After the dinner, the suitors engaged in competitions in music and speeches presented to the whole assembly. As the
drinking went on, Hippoclides, who was far excelling the others,
ordered the flute-player to strike up a tune for him, and, when the
musician complied, he started to dance. Indeed, he pleased himself
very much with his dancing, but Cleisthenes, as he looked on, became very sour about the whole business. In a while, Hippoclides
bade them bring in a table, and, when the table came, he danced on
it, first of all Laconian dance figures, but later Attic as well; and finally he stood on his head on the table and rendered the dance figures with his feet in the air. Cleisthenes, during the first and second
phase of this dancing, restrained himself—though he loathed that

Hippoclides should become his son-in-law, thanks to his dancing and lewdness—because he did not wish to make a public outburst against Hippoclides. But when he saw the feet in the air, rendering the dance figures, he could stand it no more and said, "Son of Ti-sander, you have danced—danced away your marriage!" Then Hip-poclides retorted, "Not a jot cares Hippoclides." From this happen-ing the byword has arisen.[63]

130. Then Cleisthenes called for silence and spoke before them all, as follows: "Suitors of my daughter, I give my praises to you all, and, if it were possible, I would gratify you all, making no exception in favor of one, nor rejecting the others. But it is not possible to pleasure you all when my plans concern this one daughter of mine only. So to those of you who are rejected in this marriage I give the gift of a talent of silver for your graciousness in wishing to wed with one of my house and also in compensation for your long absence from home. To Megacles, son of Alcmaeon, I betroth my daughter Agariste, according to the laws of the Athenians." Then Megacles said that he stood betrothed, and so the marriage was formally ratified by Cleisthenes.

131. So much for the decision concerning the suitors, and so it was that the Alcmaeonidae were much cried up in Greece. From the marriage of this couple was born the Cleisthenes who established the tribes and the democracy in Athens, the Cleisthenes who had his name from his maternal grandfather, the prince of Sicyon. He was born to Megacles, and so was another son, Hippocrates. From Hip-pocrates was born another Megacles and another Agariste, who had her name from the Agariste who was Cleisthenes' daughter. This woman married Xanthippus, the son of Ariphron, and in her preg-nancy saw a dream in which she brought forth a lion. A few days later she brought forth Pericles,[64] a son to Xanthippus.

132. After the Persian defeat at Marathon, Miltiades' former great fame in Athens grew still greater. He asked the Athenians for seventy ships and an army and money, without saying against what

63. Hippoclides' cheerful recklessness in the face of the disapproval of his prospective father-in-law gives rise to the "byword": "Not a jot cares Hippocli-des!" Actually, we do not know of any occurrence of the phrase outside of this passage.

64. This is, of course, the great Pericles.

country these would be used—only that they would grow rich if they followed him. For he would lead them to a country where they might easily win an abundance of gold. With these claims he asked for the ships. The Athenians were excited by his words and gave them to him.

133. Miltiades took the army and sailed against Paros. His excuse was that the Parians had provoked the aggression because they had served with their ships with the Persian at Marathon. This was but a pretext; for Miltiades had a grudge against the Parians because of Lysagoras, son of Tisias, a Parian, who had slandered him, Miltiades, to the Persian Hydarnes. When Miltiades came to Paros, to which he sailed, he penned the Parians within their walls and besieged them; he sent in a herald and demanded one hundred talents, saying that, if they would not give the money, he would never go home with his army till he had entirely destroyed them. The Parians had no intention of giving Miltiades any money, and among other plans for preserving their city they contrived that, where the walls were most vulnerable, at each several place they built them up under cover of night to twice their former height.

134. Up to this point in the story all the Greeks agree, but from here on the Parians say that it happened like this: when Miltiades was at a loss what to do, a woman who was a prisoner of war came to speak with him. She was a Parian, and her name was Timo, and she was an assistant priestess of the goddesses of the underworld. When she got to see Miltiades, she advised him to do as she suggested—if he really set such store on capturing Paros. After this he carried out her suggestion and passed through to the hill that was in front of the city, jumped over the fence around the temple of Demeter the Law-giver (for he was unable to open the doors), and, after so jumping over the fence, he went into the court of the shrine to do something or other there—either to steal one of the sacred objects or do something else.[65] When he was at the doors, a shudder of fear suddenly stole over him, and he went back on the road he had come; but when he jumped down from the dry-stone wall, he wrenched his thigh. Others say that he struck his knee violently on something.

135. So Miltiades sailed home in a very sad case, bringing no

65. How and Wells: "Probably Miltiades was to steal a sacred image, like the Palladium, on which the safety of the state depended."

money with him for the Athenians, nor having won Paros for them as an additional property, though he had besieged it for twenty-six days and had devastated the island. When the Parians learned that this underpriestess of the goddesses, Timo, had guided Miltiades, they wanted to punish her for what she had done, and, as soon as they had a moment of quiet from the siege, sent messengers to Delphi to know if they might make away with the underpriestess, since she had led their enemies to the capture of her fatherland and had made Miltiades free of mysteries that were prohibited for males.. But the Pythia refused her permission, saying that Timo was not the cause of what had happened but that Miltiades was destined to end ill and that his guide in his evil doings was a phantom.

136. That was the oracle the Pythia gave to the Parians. But when Miltiades came back from Paros, the Athenians had much to say against him, and, in especial, Xanthippus, son of Ariphron, brought him before the people on a death charge—the charge being fraud perpetrated on the people of Athens. Miltiades was present but did not plead himself. He could not, for the gangrening of his thigh. But as he lay there on a litter, his friends made his defense for him. They spoke much of the battle of Marathon and of his capture of Lemnos—how he had captured Lemnos, punished the Pelasgians, and turned the island over to Athens. The people came out on his side to the extent of freeing him from the death penalty, but for his offense they fined him fifty talents. After that, Miltiades' thigh mortified and rotted and he died, and his son Cimon paid the fifty talents.

137. Now this is the story of how Miltiades took Lemnos. The Pelasgians had been driven out of Attica by the Athenians— whether justly or otherwise I cannot say, only that Hecataeus, son of Hegisander, mentions it in his account and says that it was unjustly; for, he says, the Athenians had given the Pelasgians a piece of land to live in, under Hymettus, in payment for the wall that was at one time drawn round the Acropolis; and when the Athenians saw this place, which had before been very poor and worthless, now well tilled, they were seized with envy and longing to possess it and drove the Pelasgians out, urging no other pretext against them.[66] But the Athenians themselves say that their act was just; for, according to

66. The expulsion of the Pelasgians presumably occurred around 1000 B.C.

their story, the Pelasgians, when they were settled under Hymettus, made unjustified attacks on the Athenians in the following way. The Athenian young men and maidens were continually going to draw water at the Nine Springs—for in those days neither the Athenians nor any other Greeks had servants—and, when the girls came, the Pelasgians, out of lewdness and contempt for them, did them violence. They were not satisfied even with this but were finally caught in the act of planning an attack on Athens. The Athenians claim that they themselves were so much better men than the Pelasgians in that, when they might have killed them—since they had discovered their plot—they refused to do so but only warned them to leave the country. So they moved out, and, among other territories, they took over Lemnos. The one account is that of Hecataeus; this other, that of the Athenians.

138. So these Pelasgians, occupying Lemnos, and wishing to punish the Athenians, and being perfectly acquainted with the Athenian festivals, laid an ambush with their penteconters for the Athenian women when they were celebrating the feast of Artemis at Brauron. They snatched many women from this and sailed off with them and, bringing them to Lemnos, had them as their concubines. These women had children in great numbers, and they taught the children the Attic speech and Athenian ways. Their children would have nothing to do with the children born of the Pelasgian women, and, if one of them was struck by a Pelasgian child, all the others came to his assistance and so succored one another. And the Athenian-born children absolutely claimed to rule the others and were far more authoritative. The Pelasgians took note of this and considered. In their consideration, a strange and terrible thought overcame them: if these Attic-born children even now were making a distinction, by coming to the help of their fellows against the more lawfully born, and were trying outright to rule them, what would they do when they grew up? So they determined to kill the children of the Attic women. They did that and then killed the mothers into the bargain. From this act and from that other, when the women killed their own husbands, along with Thoas, it has grown to be a custom throughout Greece to call atrocious deeds "Lemnian."[67]

67. In another version of this story, Thoas, the king of Lemnos, was saved from death by his daughter, Hypsipyle. According to this account, the women of

139. When the Pelasgians had killed their own children and the women, their land would bear no fruit, nor were their women and their flocks and herds as fertile as they had been before. Being oppressed by hunger and childlessness, they sent to Delphi to beg some means of curing their present troubles. The Pythia bade them give such satisfaction to the Athenians as the Athenians themselves would desire. The Pelasgians came to Athens and offered to make reparation for all and every offense. The Athenians set out in their town hall a couch, beautifully arrayed, and a table laden with every manner of good thing, and they bade the Pelasgians give up their country in a similar condition. The Pelasgians answered and said, "When a ship shall in the very same day make the voyage from your land to ours, with the north wind to aid her, we shall then render you our country." For they knew well that this was impossible, since Attica lies far to the south of Lemnos.

140. That, then, was the story. But many years after, when the Athenians had conquered the Hellespontine Chersonese, Miltiades, son of Cimon, made the journey from Elaeus, in the Chersonese, to Lemnos when the Etesian winds were blowing and bade the Pelasgians get out of the island, reminding them of the oracle, which the Pelasgians never believed would be accomplished. The people of Hephaestia agreed to move, but the people of Myrina refused. These latter would not agree that the Chersonese was Attica. But the Athenians besieged them until they too capitulated. Thus it was that the Athenians and Miltiades came to possess Lemnos.

Lemnos refused to lie with their husbands, and, to punish them for this, Aphrodite, the goddess of love and marriage, plagued them with a foul odor. In disgust, their husbands brought in concubines from Thrace. The women then decided to kill all the males on the island and did so—*except* for Thoas.

Book Seven

1. When the message about the battle of Marathon came to King Darius, son of Hystaspes, greatly enraged as he already was against the Athenians because of their attack on Sardis, he was now even more full of wrath and more resolved to march upon Greece. So he sent forthwith, throughout the cities, messengers, bidding them provide a much greater force than before, and ships, horses, corn, and vessels.[1] With these demands Asia was all of a flutter for three years,[2] the best men being enrolled for service against Greece and getting ready. In the fourth year the Egyptians, who had been enslaved by Cambyses, revolted from Persia. So then Darius was even more set on making war, on both them and the Athenians.

2. But as Darius was making his preparations against Athens and Egypt, there arose among his sons a dispute concerning the primacy among them, inasmuch as, according to Persian law, the King must appoint his successor before leading an expedition. Before Darius had become King, he had already had three sons by his former wife, the daughter of Gobryas; after he had become King, he had four more by Atossa, the daughter of Cyrus. The eldest of the first three was Artobazanes, and, of the second family, Xerxes. As they were not of the same mother, they were at odds with one another, Artobazanes claiming that he was the eldest of all the children and that it was among all mankind the custom for the eldest to take over the rule, but Xerxes claiming that he was the son of the daughter of Cyrus and that it was Cyrus who had won their independence for the Persians.

3. Darius had not yet declared his opinion when it happened that, at this very time, there came up to Susa Demaratus, son of Ariston, who had been deprived of his kingship in Sparta and had imposed banishment from Lacedaemon upon himself. As soon as

1. "Vessels" are presumably transports, as distinct from warships.
2. 489–487 B.C.

tures and because he wanted to be viceroy of Greece. And in time he wrought upon Xerxes and persuaded him to do as he suggested. He had also other aids in persuading the King. In the first place, there were messengers come from the Aleuadae, the kings of Thessaly, proffering eager support; then there were those of the Pisistratids who had come up to Susa, who clung to the same arguments as the Aleuadae—and indeed offered Xerxes more than they. They had with them Onomacritus, an Athenian, who was an oracle-monger and editor of the oracles of Musaeus; he and the Pisistratids had made up their former quarrel. For Onomacritus had been banned from Athens by Hipparchus, son of Pisistratus, having been caught red-handed (by Lasus of Hermione) interpolating an oracle into the collection of Musaeus, an oracle that declared that the islands lying off Lemnos would vanish into the sea. Hipparchus banished him for this, though he had been very close to him before. Onomacritus now came up to Susa with the Pisistratids, and, whenever he came into the King's presence, they would make very solemn reports of him, and he would give readings of some of his oracles. If there was among these any one that bore on some defeat of the barbarian, nothing was said of that; he picked out the most fortunate, spoke of the bridging of the Hellespont (to be done by a Persian), and sketched the course of the invasion. This man, with his oracle-mongering, made great assaults on Xerxes, and so did the Pisistratids and the Aleuadae, with their proffered judgments on what to do.

7. Once Xerxes had been persuaded to march on Greece, he first, in the year after Darius' death, made an assault on the rebels. Having subdued these and made the slavery of all Egypt much harsher than it had been in Darius' time, he entrusted it to Achaemenes as viceroy, his own brother, Darius' son. This Achaemenes, viceroy of Egypt, was later murdered by Inaros, son of Psammetichus, a Libyan.

8. After the subjugation of Egypt, Xerxes was about to take in hand the expedition against Athens, and so he summoned a special council, composed of the greatest nobles of Persia, to learn their opinions and himself to declare his pleasure among them all. When they were assembled, Xerxes spoke: "Men of Persia, it is no new law that I initiate among you; it has come to me from the tradition. For as I learn from older men, we have never been at peace since we took over the supremacy from the Medes, when Cyrus deposed As-

tyages. It is the god that leads us on, and so, when we of ourselves set about our many enterprises, we prosper. What Cyrus and Cambyses and my father Darius won, how many additional nations they subdued, you all know, and one need not tell you of that. When I assumed the throne, I considered how I might not fall short of those before me in this place of honor and how I might win no less power for Persia than they did. In my thought of this I find that there is at once honor for me to win and land that is no less in size and not less fertile but far more productive than what we now own; and, besides this, vengeance and requital. That is why I have now summoned you together, that I may impart to you what I mean to do. I will bridge the Hellespont and drive my army through Europe to Greece, that I may punish the Athenians for what they have done to the Persians and to my father. You saw Darius, my father, making ready to campaign against these men. But he is dead and therefore failed to exact punishment of them. But I, on his behalf and that of the rest of the Persians, will never stop till I have destroyed and burned Athens, since it was the people of Athens who of themselves began the wrongdoing against me and my father, first when they came against Sardis, in company with Aristagoras of Miletus, our slave, and burned the groves and holy places there. What, secondly, they did to us when we landed in *their* country, when Datis and Artaphrenes were our generals, you all know. For these reasons I am determined to war upon them, and, as I turn it over, I find these many advantages: if we subdue them and their neighbors who live in the land of the son of Pelops, the Phrygian, we shall show to all a Persian empire that has the same limit as Zeus's sky. For the sun will look down upon no country that has a border with ours, but I shall make them all *one* country, once I have passed in my progress through all Europe. For I learn the case is so, that then there will be no city of men nor nation among mankind left that shall be able to come to battle against us, once these people I have mentioned are destroyed. So those who are innocent in our sight and those who are guilty will alike bear the yoke of slavery. The following are the acts in which you will pleasure me. As soon as I tell you the time at which you should come, it shall behoove each and every one of you most zealously to come. To the one who has his contingent best equipped I will give gifts—gifts that among us are regarded as the most honorable. This indeed is how it *must* be done. But, that I do not appear in your eyes as one who takes counsel only with himself, I put the whole matter before you. I tell you now, whoever wishes to declare his opinion, let him do so." With that he ceased talking.

9. After him Mardonius spoke: "Master, not only are you the one greatest among the Persians that have been but also of those that shall be, seeing how your words have hit the pith and very truth of the matter, and how you will not suffer these Ionians who live in Europe[4] to mock at us—something they are surely not worthy to do. For it would certainly be a terrible thing if, for no injury done to Persia but simply to increase our power, we should have subdued and taken for our slaves the Sacae, the Indians, the Ethiopians, the Assyrians, and many other great nations, and then did not punish Greeks, who on their side *began* the wrongdoing. What should we fear? What gathering of vast numbers of their people? What power of their wealth? We know these peoples' fighting; we know their power is mere weakness. We have subjugated their children who live in our territory, those who are called Ionians and Aeolians and Dorians. I myself have served against these men, under your father's orders; I have driven as far as Macedonia and within an ace of Athens herself, and no one ventured to come against me to fight. Yet, as I learn of it, the Greeks *do* fight, in the most ill-advised way—out of mere ignorance and stupidity. When they declare war on one another, they find the fairest and most level piece of ground and go down into it and fight, so that the conquerors come off with great losses—I say nothing at all of the defeated, for they are entirely blotted out. Yet surely they ought—being people who have the same tongue and use heralds and messengers—surely they ought to settle their differences by any means save fighting; and if, no matter what, they *must* fight against one another, then they should find out the spot where each is most difficult to subdue and try the fight there. The Greeks have an altogether bad way of dealing with this; and when I invaded as far as Macedonia, they never came even to the thought of fighting. Indeed, my lord, who will confront you

4. Here Mardonius is using "Ionians" as a generic term for all Greeks (not just those living on the Aegean coast of Asia Minor and the nearby islands). Possibly also, as Herodotus represents him, he may remember that the Athenians are Ionians or, in the distant past, were colonists of the Ionians of Asia Minor.

with warlike offers, seeing the host you bring with you from Asia and all your ships? Certainly, as I see it, the power of the Greeks does not come to any such degree of boldness. If I should prove false in my judgment and, uplifted by their foolishness, they should engage us in battle, they would soon learn that we are the best of men in war. But let us leave nothing untried. Nothing happens entirely of its own, but it is from trying that mankind gains everything."

10. So spoke Mardonius and stopped, having put a smooth coating on Xerxes' opinion. All the rest of the Persians held their tongues and did not venture to declare a judgment opposite to that which was in discussion. But then Artabanus, the son of Hystaspes and Xerxes' uncle—and who trusted in his kinship—spoke up: "My lord, when no opposing opinions are presented, it is impossible to choose the better, but one must accept what is proposed. When such opposites are stated, it is as it is with gold, the purity of which one cannot judge in itself, but only if you rub it alongside other gold on the touchstone and see the difference.[5] I told your father, my brother Darius, not to wage war against the Scythians; they are a people who have in their land no city anywhere. He thought that he could subdue these nomads and did not listen to me. He made his campaign and returned, having lost many good men from his army. My lord: you are planning a campaign against men who are far better than the Scythians, men who have a reputation of being very brave, both on sea and on land. There is danger in all this, and it is but just that I should declare it to you. You say that after you have bridged the Hellespont you will drive with your army through Europe to Greece. Suppose you meet with a reverse on either land or sea—or even both. These people are said to be good fighters; we can make measurement of that, inasmuch as the Athenians alone destroyed so large an army as came with Datis and Artaphrenes into Attica. Or let us suppose that they are not successful on both elements but that they engage our fleet and win the fight and head for the Hellespont and then break down the bridge. The danger for you, my lord, is there. I am not speaking out of some private wisdom of my own; it is something that very nearly happened us when your father spanned with rafts the Thracian Bosporus and, bridging the river Ister,

5. Pure gold would leave a dark stain on the touchstone.

crossed over it to attack the Scythians. The Scythians did everything in the world to induce the Ionians to destroy his passage
home—those Ionians who had been entrusted with the guarding of
the raft-bridges over the Ister.[6] On that day, if Histiaeus, the prince
of Miletus, had followed the judgment of the other princes instead of
opposing them, the empire of Persia would have been over. It is a
terrible thing, even to hear, that all the power of the King should lie
at the disposal of one man. Do not plan to let yourself come into any
such danger when there is no need to do so; instead, listen to me.
Let us break up this council meeting now. Another time, whenever
it pleases you, when you have considered the whole matter on your
own, inform us of what you think best. I think that to have a good
plan laid is the best of all things. If there proves to be some adverse
circumstance, still the plan was well laid, and the plan was defeated
by chance. But he that has planned ill, if fortune attend him, has
only had a stroke of luck; but nonetheless his plan was bad. Do you
see how it is the living things that exceed others in size that the god
strikes with lightning and will not let them show their grandeur,
while the little ones do not itch the god to action? Do you see how it
is always the greatest houses and the tallest trees that the god hurls
his bolts upon? For the god loves to thwart whatever is greater than
the rest. It is in this way that a great army may be destroyed by a
small one; for once the god has conceived jealousy against the great
army, he may hurl fear upon it or his thunder, and it will perish in a
way unworthy of itself. The god does not suffer pride in anyone but
himself. Speed in everything begets failure, and from failure the
penalties are wont to be severe. There is good in hesitation, though
one may not see it at the time; later, one will find it good. That is my
advice to you, my lord. But do you, Mardonius, son of Gobryas, stop
saying your foolish things about the Greeks, who are not worthy to
be so described. You are slandering the Greeks in order to incite the
King to fight. It is for this reason that all your eagerness is shown. Do
not do this. Slander is the most terrible thing. In it there are two
that do the wrong and one that suffers it: the man who slanders does
the wrong he does against someone who is not there; the other does
the wrong he does by being persuaded before he truly understands

6. Cf. 4.136 ff.

the issue. And the one who is absent from the discussion suffers his wrong in being slandered by the one and thought a villain by the other. But if war must be made upon these people, no matter what, here is what I say. Let the King himself remain in the land of Persia, and let the two of us stake our children on the outcome: do you yourself lead the campaign, choosing what men you please and as large a force as you choose. If the outcome for the King is what you say it will be, let my children be killed and myself to boot; but if it goes as I say it will, let it be yours who suffer the same, and yourself with them—if so be that you come home safe. But if you will not enter any such contest, and you are utterly determined to lead the host to Greece, I tell you that the Persians who are left here will hear of Mardonius as a man who has done the Persians great evil and himself has been torn asunder by birds and dogs somewhere in the land of the Athenians or in Lacedaemon, if not even earlier, on the road thither; then you will have found out what sort of people are those you are inciting the King to attack."

11. So spoke Artabanus; but Xerxes was mightily angry and answered: "Artabanus, you are my father's brother; that shall save you from a punishment adequate for your empty words. But for that you are a coward and spiritless, I shall attach to you this dishonor: that you shall not go with me, along with the army, to Greece, but remain here with the women. For I shall do to perfection all that I have spoken, without any aid from you. May I be no son of Darius, son of Hystaspes, son of Arsames, son of Ariaramnes, son of Teïspes, son of Cyrus, son of Cambyses, son of Teïspes, son of Achaemenes, if I do not punish the Athenians, knowing full well that, if we leave all in peace, *they* will not do so; nay, they will make war upon our land, if we may judge of their actions already, when they burned Sardis and invaded Asia. So we cannot either of us retreat, but the struggle is on, for doing and suffering, that either everything here shall fall to the domination of the Greeks or everything there to the Persians.[7] There is no middle ground for this enmity. It is but honorable that, at this moment, we, who have been the first to suffer,

7. At the moment at which Xerxes speaks, it must have seemed utter nonsense to imagine the Greeks invading and conquering Asia Minor. Strangely, it is a preview of what will happen one hundred and fifty years later, under Alexander the Great.

should punish them, that I may learn about that 'terror' I shall suffer when I invade these people, whom even Pelops the Phrygian,
who was one of my ancestor's slaves, so subjugated that right until
now both the people and the land are called by the name of him that
conquered them."

12. Thus ended the speeches. But afterwards it was night, and
Artabanus' judgment irked Xerxes. He took counsel of the night and
found that it was not at all to his good that he should invade Greece.
So he made up his mind for the second time and fell asleep; and in
the night he saw a vision, and it was this, according to what the
Persians tell: Xerxes thought that there was a great and handsome
man that stood over him and said, "Are you changing your mind,
Persian, and will not lead your army against Greece after you have
bidden the Persians to gather their host? You will not do well, so to
alter your counsel, nor will he who stands before you prove forgiv-
ing. As you have resolved by day to do, that is the road for you to
tread."

13. As the figure said these words, Xerxes thought it vanished;
and when the day dawned, he made nothing of the dream but assembled those Persians whom he had before assembled and said to
them: "Men of Persia, I ask your pardon for the change in plans. I
have not yet come to the height of my understanding, and those
who urge me on this course of fighting give me no rest. When I
heard the counsel of Artabanus, straightway the hot zest of youth
surged up in me, so that I hurled at an older man words very unsuitable and wrong. Now, however, I confess my error, and I will follow
his advice. I have now changed my judgment and will not make the
war against Greece. So be at peace."

14. When the Persians heard that, they were very pleased and
did obeisance. But when night came, the same vision stood over
Xerxes in his sleep and said to him, "Son of Darius, you have appeared before the Persians and revoked your war and set my sayings
aside, treating them as of no account and coming from a nobody. Be,
then, very sure of this: if you do not launch your war at once, this
shall be the outcome: just as a short while raised you to be great and
mighty, so with speed again shall you become humble."

15. Xerxes was terrified by the vision and jumped up from his bed
and sent a messenger to summon Artabanus. When he came, he said

to him, "Artabanus, for a moment I acted very indiscreetly when I spoke vain words against you for the good counsel you gave me. But it was not long before I changed my mind and knew that I must do as you had suggested. But now, though I wish to do this, I cannot; for since I have changed and turned from my other purpose, there is a vision keeps haunting me in sleep and will not suffer me to do what I would; even now he has threatened me and vanished. If it is a god that sends it, and it is entirely his pleasure that this expedition against Greece should take place, then this same dream will hover about you too and will lay the same charge on you as on me. And I think this would be most likely to happen if you would take all this raiment of mine and put it on and sit upon my throne and then go to sleep in my bed."[8]

16. That is what Xerxes said to him. But Artabanus would not obey his first bidding, for he did not think he was worthy to sit on the royal throne; but finally he was forced to do as the King said. But he himself said to the King first: "To me it seems of the same value whether a man is wise himself or is willing to fall in with the advice of someone who tells him right. You have both qualities yourself, but it is bad company that trips you up, even as they say of that element that is most useful to man, the sea, that it is the winds that blow upon it that will not suffer it to follow its own good nature. When you found fault with me, it was not the pain of this that bit deepest but that when two propositions were before the Persians, the one increasing violent insolence, the other directed to its abatement (for the latter showed how evil it is to teach the soul always to seek to have more than it has at the moment)—when, I say, there were these two propositions before the Persians, you chose the one that was more dangerous both for yourself and the Persians. Now, when you have turned toward the better course and would give up this expedition against the Greeks, you say that there is a dream that keeps

8. How and Wells have an interesting note on Xerxes' raiment: "The king wore a special upright tiara and saffron-colored shoes. His mantle and trousers were purple, his robe too was purple, and on it were embroidered white hawks or falcons, the sacred birds of Ormuzd. The robe was girt in by a golden girdle (cf. 8.120), from which hung his sword, adorned with precious stones." They also add, "It was a capital offence to sit on the king's throne . . . ; hence Artabanus might suspect a trap and hesitate."

haunting you, sent by some god or other, that will not suffer you to abandon your warlike preparation. But these things have nothing of the god in them, my son. The dreams that wander about among men are such as I shall tell you now, and I am a man a great deal older than you. Mostly the visions that are wont to flit about us in dreams are the things that we have had to do with by day; and in the days before the dream we have had this matter of the expedition very much in our hands. But if indeed this is not as I judge it to be, and there is something of the divine in it, in your speech to me you have summed it up altogether. Let the vision appear to me with the same orders. But there is no necessity that it should rather appear to me because I am wearing your clothes rather than my own or sleep in your bed rather than my own—that is, if it is minded to appear at all. The vision that appears to you in your sleep, whatever it is, has hardly attained such a degree of simplicity that it will think me to be you when it sees me, drawing its evidence solely from your clothes. If it shall disdain me altogether and shall not choose to appear, whether I wear your clothes or my own—that is what we now have to find out. For if it is persistent in its haunting, I would myself say that this is something of a divine kind. But if you are determined to do the matter thus and cannot be persuaded otherwise, and I must sleep in your bed, let me do it that way, and let the vision come to me too. Till then I cling to the opinion I have given you."

17. So spoke Artabanus, and, hoping to prove that Xerxes had been deluded, he did as the King bade him. He put on Xerxes' raiment and sat upon the royal throne and afterwards went to bed, and in his sleep the same dream vision came to him as it had to Xerxes, and standing above Artabanus it said, "You are the man who turns Xerxes from making war upon Greece, because you are so concerned for him! But neither hereafter nor for the present will you escape scot free for trying to reverse fate. What Xerxes shall suffer if he disobeys has already been told him."

18. It seemed to Artabanus that with these words the apparition threatened him and made as if to burn out his eyes with hot irons. He gave a great cry and jumped out of bed, and sitting by Xerxes he narrated all that he had seen in his dream and the vision in it, and then he said, "My lord, as a man who had seen many great fall under the assault of lesser ones, I would not have had you yield altogether

to the impulse of youth; I knew how bad it was to desire many things; I remembered Cyrus' expedition against the Massagetae and how it fared; I remembered Cambyses' attack on the Ethiopians; and I myself served with your father, Darius, against the Scythians. I knew all this, and so I formed the opinion that, if you could remain inactive, in the eyes of all mankind you would be happiest. But since there is some divine impulse afoot here, and, as it seems, there is some divine destruction that seizes on the Greeks, I of myself change and retract my judgment. Do you convey to the Persians what the god has sent to you as a message, and bid them follow out your first instructions—to make preparations; and so act that, with the god handing all over to you, nothing shall be lacking on your side." That was what was said; and then, uplifted by the vision, when day dawned, Xerxes entrusted the matter to the Persians; and Artabanus, who had before been the sole voice openly dissuading, was now manifestly urging on the war.

19. Xerxes was now set on making war; and in his sleep there came yet a third vision, which the Magi heard and pronounced upon: that it referred to all the earth and that all mankind should be slaves to Xerxes. The vision was this: Xerxes thought that he was crowned with an olive branch, and from the olive there were shoots that overshadowed all the earth, but that afterwards the crown, which was set upon his head, vanished. When the Magi had made their interpretation, at once every man of the assembled Persians went off to his seat of rule and showed the greatest zeal in carrying out his instructions, because everyone sought to win the offered gifts of the King; so Xerxes collected his army, searching every part of the continent.

20. After the subduing of Egypt, for four full years[9] he made ready his host and all that they must have, and at the beginning of the fifth year he started his campaign with a huge force of men. This was far the greatest host of any we have heard of; Darius' expedition against the Scythians was as nothing in comparison, nor that of the Scythians when, in pursuit of the Cimmerians, they invaded the land of Media[10] and subdued and occupied nearly all the upper lands

9. 484–481 B.C.
10. Cf. 1.103; 4.1.

of Asia—for which acts Darius organized *his* punishing campaign against them—nor as great was the expedition of the Atreidae against Troy, in the account given, nor yet that of the Teucrians and Mysians (which happened before the Trojan War) when they crossed over into Europe by way of the Bosporus and subjugated all the Thracians and came down to the Ionian Sea[11] and as far to the south as the river Peneus.

21. All these forces, and whatsoever others might be added to them, could not together equal this single one. For what nation did Xerxes not bring out of Asia against the Greeks? What water did not fail their drinking—save for the great rivers only? These peoples furnished ships of war; those marched with the army; to others still the provision of horsemen was assigned, and to others that of horse transports, though they themselves were marching with the rest; others, still, must furnish warships for the bridges, and others corn and boats.

22. In the first place, since the first expedition had come to grief as they sailed around Athos, for about the last three years early preparations had been made to deal with Athos. Triremes were anchored off Elaeus in the Chersonese; and men from these, composed of all nations in the army, were set to work digging a channel, which they did under the lash, and they went to the task in relays. Those who lived around Athos also dug. The overseers of the task were Bubares, the son of Megabazus, and Artachaees, son of Artaeus, both Persians. Athos is a great and renowned mountain that runs down to the sea and is inhabited. Where it ends on the mainland, it is in the shape of a peninsula, and there is an isthmus there some twelve furlongs wide. This part is level, or with only small hills, from the sea of the Acanthians to the one opposite Torone. On this isthmus, in which Athos ends, is the settled Greek city of Sane; other cities, seaward of Sane but still within Athos, the Persian was determined to turn from mainland into island cities. These were Dium, Olophyxus, Acrothoi, Thyssus, and Cleonae.

23. These, then, are the cities of Athos, and this is how the barbarians dug the place, dividing the ground among their nations. They drew a straight line near the city of Sane; and, when the chan-

11. The sea we call the Adriatic.

nel grew deep, some of the men stood at the bottom and dug, and others handed over the spoil, as it was dug out, to others, who stood higher, on steps, and they, receiving it, to others higher still, until they came to those at the top. And these men carried it out and cast it away. Now all the other peoples, except for the Phoenicians, found that the steep sides of their trench broke and so made double work for them; this was bound to happen, because they made it as wide at the top as at the bottom. But the Phoenicians showed their usual cunning in this too. Taking the portion of the task assigned to them, they dug the top part of the trench twice as wide as the channel itself needed to be, and, as the work went on, they contracted the width continually. At the bottom, their channel was the same width as that made by the rest of the workmen. There is a meadow near there where they held a market to buy and sell in. A great deal of their corn was brought them from Asia ready-ground.

24. As far as my guess goes, it was out of mere arrogance that Xerxes made them dig the channel, because he wanted to show his power and leave a memorial behind him. For with no trouble at all it was possible to draw the ships across the isthmus; but instead he bade his men dig a channel for the sea of a width for two triremes to sail together through it under oars. The same men as had their instructions for the digging of the channel were also ordered to build a bridge of ships over the river Strymon.

25. So he did all this and prepared, also, gear for the bridges: ropes of papyrus and of white flax, the provision of which he assigned to the Phoenicians and Egyptians and, also to these, the storage of corn for the army, that neither the men should starve nor the pack animals on their drive to Greece. Making inquiry about the regions, he ordered them to deposit the stores where it was most suitable, carrying them here and there in merchantmen and transports from everywhere in Asia. The most of it they gathered to a place in Thrace that is called the White Shore, though there were others who brought the goods to Tyrodiza in the Perinthian land, and others to Doriscus, and others to Eïon on the Strymon, and others to Macedonia.

26. While these people were working at their appointed tasks, the whole land army was marching, along with Xerxes, to Sardis, having started from Critalla in Cappadocia. For to this place had

been ordered to assemble all the army that was to march with Xerxes himself by land. Now which of the viceroys brought the most splendidly equipped army to win the rewards of the King, I cannot say. For I do not even know whether this came to decision. But when they crossed the Halys, they went into Phrygia, and marching through this country they came to Celaenae, where the springs of the river Maeander issue forth and also those of another river, no less than the Maeander, the name of which is Cataractes, which rises in the very marketplace of Celaenae and empties into the Maeander. In this marketplace also hangs the skin of the Silenus Marsyas, which the Phrygian story would have as being flayed off him by Apollo and hung up there.

27. In this city there lay, awaiting the King, one Pythius, the son of Atys, a Lydian, who entertained the entire army of the King with every sort of hospitality, and Xerxes as well. This man also declared that he wished to contribute money to the war. When Pythius made this offer, Xerxes asked the Persians who were near him who on earth was this fellow Pythius and what money he possessed that he should make such an offer. They told him: "My lord, this is the man who gave your father Darius the golden plane tree and vine, and he is now the first of men for his wealth—after yourself—of any we know."

28. Xerxes was surprised at this final comment, and so he in turn asked Pythius how much he possessed. He said, "My lord, I will not conceal anything from you, nor will I pretend not to know exactly my possessions. I know them and will tell you exactly; for as soon as I heard you were coming down to the coast, to the Greek sea, I made my inquiries because I wanted to give you money for the war; and on my reckoning I find that I have two thousand talents of silver, and, of Daric staters in gold, I have four million, lacking some seven thousand. All of these now I give you; for me the livelihood from my slaves and my estates will suffice."

29. Thus he spoke. Xerxes was delighted with his words and in answer to them said, "My Lydian host, since coming from the land of Persia I have till this day never met with a man who would offer hospitality to my army, nor one who stood before me and of his own will was willing to contribute money to my war except yourself. You have entertained my army magnificently, and magnificent is the

offer of money you have made me. So I will give you rewards to answer your gifts. I will make you my friend, and I will fill up your four million staters, giving you the seven thousand from my purse, that your four millions may not be lacking those seven thousands but that, thanks to me, you will have the full tale made up. Possess, then, that of which you stand possessed; know how to be ever such a one as now you are; for, if you do so, you shall neither now nor for all time to come repent it."

30. That is what he said, and made the four million complete, and on he went, forward always. He passed by the city of the Phrygians called Anaua and the lake from which salt comes and came to a great city in Phrygia called Colossae. In it the river Lycus descends into a pit in the ground and vanishes, and afterwards, reappearing some five stades further on, it issues, too, into the Maeander. From Colossae the army set out toward the bounds of Phrygia and Lydia and came to the city of Cydrara, where there stands a pillar set up by Croesus, declaring, in its inscription, the boundary.

31. From Phrygia he passed on into Lydia. Here the road splits, the left hand going toward Caria and the right to Sardis, by the latter of which the traveler must cross the river Maeander and must needs also go by the city of Callatebus, where men who are craftsmen at the task make honey of tamarisk and wheat. By this road went Xerxes and found a plane tree which, for its beauty, he adorned with gold and then entrusted it to a steward who was one of the Immortals; the day after, he came to the chief city of the Lydians.

32. When he came to Sardis, he first of all sent off heralds to Greece to demand earth and water and to give orders in advance for the preparation of meals for the King. Only to Athens and Sparta he sent no messengers for the demand of earth; everywhere else he sent them. The reason he sent for earth and water this second time was that he was very sure that those who had not given them before, on the sending of Darius, would certainly do so now, out of fear. So, because he wished to be accurately informed of this, he sent.

33. After that he made ready to march to Abydos. Meanwhile, his men were building the bridge over the Hellespont, connecting Asia and Europe. Now, there is in the Hellespontine Chersonese, midway between the cities of Sestos and Madytus, a broad headland running out into the sea opposite Abydos. There, not so long afterwards, the

Athenians, commanded by Xanthippus, son of Ariphron, took Artaÿctes, a Persian, viceroy of Sestos, and crucified him alive. This man had been collecting women even into the temple of Protesilaus at Elaeus and had perpetrated deeds of lawlessness upon them.

34. To this headland, then, starting from Abydos, they built the bridge, those who were instructed so to do, the Phoenicians making the one bridge of white flax, the Egyptians the other, of papyrus. It is seven stades from Abydos to the land opposite. But when the strait had been bridged, there came a great storm upon it and smashed it and broke it all to pieces.

35. On learning this, Xerxes was furious and bade his men lay three hundred lashes on the Hellespont and lower into the sea a yoke of fetters. Indeed, I have heard that he sent also branders to brand the Hellespont. He told those who laid on the lashes to say these words, of violent arrogance, worthy of a barbarian: "You bitter water, our master lays this punishment upon you because you have wronged him, though he never did you any wrong. King Xerxes will cross you, whether you will or not; it is with justice that no one sacrifices to you, who are a muddy and a briny river." So he commanded that the sea be punished, and he ordered the beheading of the supervisors of the building of the bridge.

36. They did that, those who were set over that thankless office; and other builders constructed the bridge anew. This is how they built the bridge: they set together both penteconters and triremes, three hundred and sixty to bear the bridge on the side nearest the Euxine and three hundred and fourteen for the other bridge,[12] all at an oblique angle to the Pontus but parallel with the current of the Hellespont. This was done to lighten the strain on the cables. Having so laid the boats together, they let down great anchors, both at the end of the ship that faced toward the Pontus, against the winds blowing from inside that sea, and at the other end, toward the west and the Aegean, to deal with the winds from the west and south. They left a narrow opening among the penteconters and triremes to permit to sail through anyone with small boats who wanted to sail into the Pontus or out again. Having done that, they stretched cables from the land, which they twisted with wooden windlasses;

12. The one nearest to the Aegean.

these cables were no longer used separately; instead, for each bridge there were now two cables of white flax and four of papyrus. There was the same thickness and beauty in these, but the flaxen ones were heavier in proportion, a cubit weighing a talent. When the strait was bridged, they sawed logs of wood, making them equal to the width of the floating raft, and set these logs on the stretched cables, and then, having laid them together alongside, they fastened them together again on top.[13] Having done this, they strewed brushwood over it, and, having laid the brushwood in order, they carried earth on the top of that; they stamped down the earth and then put up a barrier on either side so that the baggage animals and horses might not see the sea beneath them and take fright.

37. When the bridges had been seen to, and also the digging in Athos, and the moles at the mouth of the channel, which were made there as a breakwater, that the mouths of the channel might not be filled up, and when the channel itself was reported as entirely finished, the army wintered there; and in spring,[14] with their preparations made, they marched out of Sardis for Abydos. But as they went off, the sun left his place in the heaven and was no more seen, even though there were no clouds and the sky was particularly clear; and it became night instead of day. Xerxes saw and noted this and was troubled; he asked the Magi what such an appearance could mean. The Magi told him that the god was declaring to the Greeks the eclipse of their cities; for, they said, the sun was the prophet of the Greeks, whereas their own was the moon. When Xerxes heard that, he was very pleased and marched on.

38. As Xerxes marched away, Pythius the Lydian, because he had been terrified by the appearance of the heavens and had been encouraged by the gifts the King had given him, came before Xerxes and said, "Master, I have a request for you, which I would greatly wish you could grant me; it is easy for you to do me this kindness, but for me it is a great matter." Xerxes thought that he would ask for anything rather than what he did, and said, yes, he would do him the kindness, and only bade him tell him what it was that he needed. When Pythius heard that, he took heart and said, "Master,

---

13. Presumably he means with cross-pieces.
14. Probably in April, 480 B.C.

I have five sons, and it behooves them all to go with you to Greece. My lord, do you take pity on me, at the age to which I have come, and release one of my sons—the eldest—from your army, that he may be the caretaker of me and of my possessions. Take the other four with you, and may you come home again, having accomplished all that you intend."

39. Xerxes was violently angry and answered, "Vile creature, I am myself marching to Greece, and with me are my children, my brothers, my household, and my friends, and you dare to speak of your son—you who are my slave, who ought, with all who live in your house, and your wife herself, to follow in my train? I would have you know that a man's spirit dwells in his ears. When he hears what is good, it fills his body with delight; when he hears the opposite, it swells with anger. When you did good to me and offered more such, you will never boast that you surpassed your King in deeds of kindness. But now that you have turned to this shameless course, you shall not receive the full value of your deeds—no, it will be less than the full value. You and four of your sons will be protected by the hospitality you showed to me, but for this one son of yours, for whom you care so mightily—your request will cost him his life." Such was his answer; and immediately he ordered those who were charged with such matters to find the eldest of the sons of Pythius and cut him in two and to set the two halves of the body on each side of the road, to the left and to the right, and the army should march between them.

40. When that had been done, the army filed through. In the van came the baggage train and its pack animals and, after them, a mingled host of every nation, with no divisions. When over half these had gone by, there was a break, and none of these came near the King. Ahead of the King came a thousand horsemen, the elect of all the Persians. After them, a thousand spearmen, these also the elect from all, carrying their spears with the points reversed to the ground. After them came the ten sacred horses called Nesaean, splendidly arrayed. (They are called Nesaean after the great plain in Media that produces these big horses.) Behind these ten horses came the sacred chariot of Zeus,[15] drawn by eight white horses, and be-

15. I.e., Ormuzd.

hind the horses their charioteer followed on foot, holding the reins; for no human being may mount into that seat. Behind this came Xerxes himself in a chariot drawn by Nesaean horses. Standing beside him was his charioteer, whose name was Patiramphes, son of Otanes, a Persian.

41. So Xerxes marched out of Sardis; and he would ever and anon, as the notion struck him, shift from his chariot to a small covered carriage. Behind him came spear-bearers, a thousand of the best and the noblest of the Persians, carrying their spears in the ordinary position,[16] and, behind, another thousand horse, also chosen out of all the Persians; and behind the horse were men chosen from the rest of the Persians, in this case to the number of ten thousand. These were infantry. One thousand of them had on their spears, instead of points, golden pomegranates, and these thousand men encircled the rest, which nine thousand men, inside the circle, had silver pomegranates on their spears. Those who turned their spears to the ground also had golden pomegranates, and those who followed Xerxes most closely had apples. After the ten thousand infantry followed an ordered body of ten thousand horse. After the horse was a break of two furlongs and then the rest of the army, not in divisions.

42. The army made the march from Lydia to the river Caïcus and the land of Mysia; after the Caïcus, they kept the mountain of Cane to the left and marched through Atarneus to the city of Carene. From it they marched through the plain of Thebe, passing by the city of Adramytteum and the Pelasgian city of Antandrus. Then the army kept Mount Ida on its left and marched into the country round Ilium; and when it halted for the night under Ida, it befell them for the first time to be assailed by thunder and lightning, which destroyed many of the men right there.

43. When the army came to the river Scamander—which was the first river after they had taken the road from Sardis that had its stream dry up and fail by the drinking of the men and the cattle—I say, when Xerxes came to this river, he climbed up to Priam's Pergamus,[17] which he was eager to see. Having observed it and inquired about it all, he sacrificed one thousand cattle to Athena of Ilium,

16. As distinct from those ahead of the King, who carried them with the points down, as a sign of respect.

17. The citadel of Troy.

and the Magi offered libations to the heroes. After their doing so, the host was seized with panic fear by night; but with dawn they marched away, keeping the city of Rhoetium on the left and also Ophryneum and Dardanus, which borders Abydos. On the right were the Teucrian Gergithae.

44. When he got to the middle of Abydos, Xerxes had the wish to see the whole of his army. A platform of white stone had been set up for him expressly on a hill, in advance. This had been made beforehand, by command of the King, by the people of Abydos. Xerxes sat there and looked down over the shore on his land army and his fleet; and, as he viewed it, he longed to see a race in actual progress between the ships. So it took place, and the Sidonian Phoenicians won, and Xerxes was pleased with the race and with his army.

45. When he saw all the Hellespont covered with ships and all the shores and plains of Abydos full of men, then Xerxes declared himself a happy man; but after that he burst into tears.

46. Artabanus, his uncle—the man who at the first gave his judgment freely against Xerxes' invasion of Greece—noticed the tears and said, "My lord, how different is what you are doing now compared with a little while since! For then you congratulated yourself, but now you are in tears." Xerxes answered, "Yes, for pity stole over me as I made my meditation on the shortness of the life of man; here are all these thousands, and not a one of them will be alive a hundred years from now." Artabanus answered, "Life gives us greater occasion for pity than this. Short as his life is, no man is so happy— either of these or all the rest—that it shall not be his lot, not only once but many times, to wish himself dead rather than alive. For there are calamities that meet him and diseases that derange him, so that they make this life, for all its shortness, seem long. So death comes to be for man a most desirable escape from a life of wretchedness. And therein is the god discovered to be envious; for he gives us but a taste of the sweetness of life."

47. Xerxes answered, "Artabanus, human life is indeed as you define it; but let us give all this over and no more remember its ills, since what we have in our hands is good. Tell me, then: if that dream vision had not been so clear, would you have still held to your old opinion in not suffering me to make war on Greece? Would you not have altered? Tell me the very truth." Then said Artabanus,

"My lord, may the vision that appeared in sleep have final issue as we both would wish! Yet I am still full, nay, overfull, of fear—indeed, I can scarcely contain myself—when among the many other matters that occur to me I see that the two greatest things in the world are your bitterest enemies."

48. Xerxes answered him, "You are a strange fellow! What can you mean by my two 'bitterest enemies'? Is it in respect of numbers that our land army seems to you at fault? Do you think that the Greek army will prove more numerous than ours? Or that our fleet falls behind theirs? Or even that both are inferior? If you think that our power is less at any point, let us with all speed make another muster of more men."

49. He answered him, "My lord, no one in his senses would find fault with this army of yours or with the number of your ships. If you were to assemble more men, the two things of which I speak would be but the more your enemies. These two are land and sea. At sea there is no harbor anywhere (as I see it) big enough to be a trustworthy haven for your ships at the moment of the rising of a storm. Yet there should be not merely one such, but you need them all along the land where you are coasting. Since there are no harbors for you, you must understand that it is the event that will be master of men rather than the other way round. There is one of the two elements of which I spoke; here is the other: the land is your enemy in this way: for if there should be never a hint of an opposing enemy, yet the land grows to be more of an enemy the further you go on; it cheats you always of your advance. But no man has ever a satiety of success. I am assuming that there is no opposition at all; still, I tell you that more land becoming yours, and more time spent in getting it, will breed famine. He is the best of men who, when he is laying his plans, dreads and reflects on everything that can happen him but is bold when he is in the thick of the action."

50. Xerxes answered him, "Artabanus, you are altogether reasonable in the way you lay this out, piece by piece. But do not fear everything; do not always take account of everything. As each opportunity arises, if you were to take account of everything that is involved, you would never do anything. It is better to have a brave heart and endure one half of the terrors we dread than to make forecalculation of all the terrors and suffer nothing at all. If you quarrel

with everything that is said and cannot show where security lies, then you ought to fail in these debates no less than the man who urges the opposite view. The score is even between you. Anyway, how can a human being know what security is? I think he cannot. It is those, then, who are willing to act who for the most part win the prizes; for those who are forever calculating everything over and hesitating, this is not often so. You see how far the Persian power has advanced. If those who were kings before me had followed the same counsels as yours, or even if they did not hold such counsels themselves but had employed such counselors as you, you would never have seen our power advance so far. No, it was by risking dangers that they brought that power to where it is. Big things are won by big dangers. We, likening ourselves to my ancestors, will march on, at this the fairest season of the year, and, after subduing all Europe, come back home again, having encountered no famine anywhere or anything untoward. We carry large amounts of food with us on the march, and, as well, through whatever land and nation's territory we march, we shall have their food. For we are marching against men who cultivate the earth, not against nomads."

51. Artabanus said, "My lord, you will not let us be afraid of anything, but take this counsel of me; for when there are many matters involved, one must talk a lot about them. Cyrus, son of Cambyses, subdued all Ionia, except the Athenians, to pay tribute to Persia. I would advise you by no means to lead these Ionians against their ancestors. We are surely able to conquer our enemies without their help. For if they follow you, they must either be utter scoundrels to enslave their motherland or else prove themselves the justest of men in helping her to freedom. If they prove scoundrels, they will bring no great gain to us; but if they prove just, they are able greatly to injure this army of yours. Lay up in your mind also how well said is that ancient saw, 'Every end doth not appear in the hour of its beginning.'"

52. Xerxes answered Artabanus, "Artabanus, you are especially wrong in this judgment of yours, in that you are afraid that the Ionians will change sides. We have the surest token of them, which you yourself witnessed—you and all those who fought by the side of Darius against the Scythians; for the whole Persian army lay at their disposal, for either its destruction or survival, and what they gave us

was fairness and loyalty and not a hint of what was evil. Besides this, they have left behind, in our territory, their children, their wives, and their property, and so they cannot even dream of treason. So do not have any such fears; have a stout heart, and keep safe for me my household and my empire. For to you in sole charge I entrust my sovereign scepter."

53. With that, Xerxes sent Artabanus back to Susa, and once more he summoned the most renowned of the Persians, and, when they came, he spoke to them as follows: "Men of Persia, I have brought you together to ask this of you: be good men, and do not shame the former great deeds of the Persians, which are indeed very great and worthy; let us each and every one show zeal, for it is our common good that is our cause of endeavor. For these reasons I bid you lay hold of the war with eagerness. As I learn it, these men we go to fight are good men. If we conquer them, there shall be no other army in the world to stand against us. So now let us first pray to those gods who have charge of the Persians and then cross over."

54. So for that day they prepared for the crossing, and on the next day they waited, for they wanted to see the sun rising. They burned all sorts of incense on the bridges and strewed the road with myrtle branches. When the sun rose, Xerxes poured the libation from a golden cup into the sea and prayed to the sun that no chance should befall him such that it should check his conquest of Europe until he had come to the furthest limits of that continent. When he had finished his prayer, he threw the cup into the Hellespont and also a golden mixing bowl and a Persian sword, which they call an "acinaces." I cannot exactly determine whether he launched these things into the sea as a dedication to the sun or whether he had repented of having lashed the Hellespont and so gave the sea these gifts as recompense.

55. When all this was done, they crossed over, all the horse and foot by the bridge nearest to the Pontus, while the baggage animals and the service train went by the bridge next the Aegean. In the vanguard were the Ten Thousand Persians, all of them wearing garlands, and behind them a mixed host of all nations. These were the troops that crossed that day, and, on the next, first came the cavalry and those that carried their spears reversed; these, too, wore garlands. After that came the sacred horses and the sacred chariot

and, behind them, Xerxes himself and his bodyguard and his thousand horsemen, and, behind these, all the rest of the host. At this time also, the fleet put to sea and crossed to the opposite shore. (It is true that I have heard, too, that the King crossed last of all.)

56. When Xerxes had crossed into Europe, he watched his army crossing under the lash. Seven days and seven nights did his army cross, and never a moment's break. Then it is said that, when Xerxes himself had crossed the Hellespont, a man of that country of the Hellespont said, "O Zeus, why did you liken yourself to a man of Persia and take the name of Xerxes instead of Zeus because you wish to destroy Greece, bringing all the people of the world with you? You could have done that without them."

57. When they had all crossed and were hastening on their road, there appeared to them a great portent, which Xerxes made of no account, though it was easy enough to construe: it was a mare that brought forth a hare. For the obvious construction of it is thus: that Xerxes was to drive his army against Greece in the most glorious and magnificent way but that he would come back to his own land running for his very life. There was another portent that happened to him when he was in Sardis: a mule gave birth to a mule with two genitals, one male, one female, and the male was above the female. But Xerxes made of no account both of these portents; and on he went, and with him all his land army.

58. The fleet sailed out of the Hellespont and went along the coast, doing the opposite of the land army. For the fleet sailed west, making their descent on the cape of Sarpedon, where they had instructions to wait for his coming. But the land army traveled east toward the rising sun, through the Chersonese, with the tomb of Helle, daughter of Athamas, on their right and, on the left, the city of Cardia; and they marched straight through the middle of a town called Marketplace.[18] Then they rounded what is called the Black Gulf and crossed the Black River, the stream of which failed for the drinking of the army, and, crossing this river, which gives its name to the gulf too, the army marched west, passing by the city of Aenus, an Aeolian city, and the marsh of Stentor, until they came to Doriscus.

18. Agora.

59. Doriscus is a beach and a great flat place in Thrace, and through it runs a big river, the Hebrus. In this country had been built the royal fort called Doriscus, and a Persian guard station was set up there by Darius from the time when he campaigned against the Scythians. So Xerxes judged that this place was suitable for the ordering and numbering of his army, and this is what he did there. All of the ships having arrived at Doriscus, the captains brought them to the beach near Doriscus by command of Xerxes; at this place there is the Samothracian town of Sale and also Zone, and at the end of it is the famous cape of Serreum. This land in ancient times belonged to the Cicones. To this beach the commanders brought in their ships and hauled them up to dry. Then, at this time, he made the numbering of the army in Doriscus.

60. How much mass of number each arm contributed to the total I cannot say for sure, for no one has any record of that. But the multitude of the whole land army came out at one million seven hundred thousand. This is how they counted them: they drew together into one place ten thousand men; and packing them in as tightly as they could, they drew a circle round the outside. Having drawn this and let out their ten thousand, they built a dry-wall on the circumference of the circle, in height reaching to a man's navel. They then pushed others into the walled space until in this fashion they had counted them all. After the counting, they arranged them by nations.[19]

61. This, then, is the roll of those that marched with the army.

19. Though it is unfortunately somewhat wearying to the general reader, the document that follows is of first-rate historical importance, for it is without parallel as an account of the peoples of Asia Minor and those of the islands and Ionia in the fifth century. It is certainly based on an official military list that Herodotus was permitted to see and to have explained to him by someone—presumably someone of importance. That Xerxes, who had the numbers of his troops tested by the system of numbering "cages," as stated by Herodotus, would have a full listing of all national contingents in his army, with their commanders, is very likely indeed. It is somewhat mysterious as to how Herodotus got access to this roster, but perhaps no more so than his acquaintance with the posts on the Royal Road or his knowledge of the tax districts under Darius. However, along with the basic information of the military document, there are surely pieces added by Herodotus himself. For some remarks about these, see the end note to this passage.

First the Persians. For their equipment, they wore on their heads loose caps called tiaras and, on their bodies, sleeved tunics of blended colors [and corselets][20] with iron plates, something like fish scales; on their legs, trousers; and instead of shields they had wicker bucklers—their quivers hung underneath these. They had short spears, great bows, and arrows made of reed, and they carried, as well, daggers, which hung by the right thigh, from their belts. As commander they had Otanes, father-in-law of Xerxes and son of Amestris. In olden times the Greeks called these people (the Persians) Cephenes, but by themselves and their neighbors they were known as Artaei. But when Perseus, son of Danaë and Zeus, came to Cepheus, son of Belus, and took to wife his daughter, Andromeda, there was born to him a son to whom he gave the name Perses. He left him there in his grandfather's kingdom, for Cepheus had no male issue; it is from this Perses that the Persians took their name.[21]

62. The Medes served with the same equipment; indeed, the style of it is Median and not Persian. The commander of the Medes was Tigranes, an Achaemenid. The Medes were in the old time called by everybody Arians, but when Medea, the Colchian, came from Athens to the country of the Arians, they too changed their name.[22] That is the story the Medes tell of themselves. The Cissians in the army were habited in general like the Persians, but instead of loose caps they wore turbans. The commander of the Cissians was Anaphes, son of Otanes. The Hyrcanians' gear was the same as the Persians', and their commander was Megapanus, who was afterwards governor of Babylon.

63. The Assyrians who served with the army had bronze helmets on their heads. These helmets were twisted in a barbarian fashion not easy to describe, and they had shields, spears, and daggers like

20. With How and Wells and others, I am assuming that the Greek word for "corselets," now missing in the text, was once present, since it is necessary to the meaning.

21. This and the following item about the Medes represent the inveterate Greek habit of connecting the name of a nation with some entirely mythical eponymous ancestor. Apart from other improbabilities, all the eponymous ancestors of these Asian peoples here become eponymous in virtue of Greek names—which is more than a little odd.

22. To Medes. (Medea was Jason's jealous wife, the tragic heroine of Euripides' Medea.)

those of the Egyptians but had, besides, clubs made of wood, studded with iron, and linen breastplates. The Greeks call these people Syrians, but the barbarians call them Assyrians. With them were the Chaldaeans. Their commander was Otaspes, son of Artachaees.

64. The Bactrians wore headgear likest to the Medes', and their native bows were made of reeds, and their spears were short. The Sacae, who are Scythians, have high caps tapering to a point and stiffly upright, which they wear on their heads. They wore trousers and carried native bows and daggers and, in addition, axes, which they called "sagaris." These were Amyrgian Scythians but were called Sacae, for the Persians call all Scythians Sacae. The commander of the Bactrians and Sacae was Hystaspes, son of Darius, and of Atossa, daughter of Cyrus.

65. The Indians wore garments of cotton[23] and had reed bows and arrows likewise, but with an iron tip. Such was the equipment of the Indians, and in their service they were assigned to the commander Pharnazathres, son of Artabates.

66. The Arians had bows like those of the Medes, but otherwise their equipment was like the Bactrians'. Their commander was Sisamnes, son of Hydarnes. The Parthians, Chorasmians, Sogdians, Gandarians, and Dadicae had the same gear as the Bactrians. They had the following commanders: of the Parthians and Chorasmians, Artabazus, son of Pharnaces; of the Sogdians, Azanes, son of Artaeus; of the Gandarians and the Dadicae, Artyphius, son of Artabanus.

67. The Caspians wore cloaks and had native bows, made of reeds, and short swords. This is how they were habited, and their commander was Ariomardus, brother of Artyphius. The Sarangae wore brilliant dyed garments and boots up to the knee and carried bows and Median spears. Their commander was Pherendates, the son of Megabazus. The Pactyes wore cloaks and carried native bows and daggers. Their commander was Artaÿntes, son of Ithamitres.

68. The Utians, Mycians, and Paricanians were equipped like the Pactyes. The commanders were the following: of the Utians and Mycians, Arsamenes, son of Darius, and, of the Paricanians, Siromitres, son of Oeobazus.

23. Literally, clothes made "from trees."

69. The Arabians wore girded mantles and carried, on their right side, long bows, bent backwards. The Ethiopians wore leopard and lion skins; their bows were made of palm-wood strips—very long bows, not less than four cubits—and their little arrows had points not of iron but of sharpened stone—the same stone they use for signet rings. They had spears as well, with gazelle's horn on the tip, sharpened, like a lance. They also carried studded clubs. One half of their bodies they smeared with gypsum when they went into battle; the other half, with vermilion. The commander of the Arabians and of the Ethiopians who live above Egypt was Arsames, son of Darius and of Artystone, daughter of Cyrus, whom Darius loved most of all his wives and had an image made of her of hammered gold.

70. The commander of the Arabians and of the Ethiopians who live above Egypt was indeed Arsames; but the Ethiopians of the east (the Ethiopians served in two divisions) were assigned to the Indian contingent, though they differed not at all in appearance from the other Ethiopians, except in their speech and hair. For the Ethiopians of the east are straight of hair, but those of Libya are those of mankind that are woolliest. These Ethiopians of Asia were for the most part equipped like the Indians, but they wore on their heads the skins of horses' foreheads, flayed off along with the ears and the mane. The mane was used by them for a crest, and they wore the horses' ears stiffly upright; and instead of shields they carried targes made of the skin of cranes.

71. The Libyans came wearing clothes made of leather, and they used as weapons stakes of charred wood. Their commander was Massages, son of Oarizus.

72. The Paphlagonians served with woven helmets on their heads and little shields and rather small spears, but with the addition of javelins and daggers; and on their legs they wore native boots that reached halfway up their shanks. The Ligyans, Matieni, Mariandyni, and Syrians served with the same equipment as the Paphlagonians. These Syrians are called by the Persians Cappadocians. The commander of the Paphlagonians and Matieni was Dotus, son of Megasidrus, and, of the Mariandyni and Ligyans and Syrians, Gobryas, son of Darius and Artystone.

73. The Phrygians were equipped closest to the Paphlagonians in style—indeed, the differences are slight. The Phrygians, as the Mace-

donians say, were called Briges as long as they were Europeans and lived as neighbors of the Macedonians; but when they moved over into Asia, they changed their name to Phrygians at the same time as they changed their place of residence. The Armenians were equipped like the Phrygians, being indeed colonists of the Phrygians. The commander of both of these together was Artochmes, who was married to a daughter of Darius.

74. The Lydians had arms nearest to those of the Greek style. The Lydians in the old days were called Maeonians and changed their national name in favor of their eponymous hero, Lydus, son of Atys. The Mysians had on their heads native helmets; they carried small spears, and they used javelins made of charred stakes. They are colonists of the Lydians and are called Olympieni, from the mountain Olympus. The commander of the Lydians and Mysians was Artaphrenes, son of Artaphrenes, the man who made the Marathon invasion, sharing the command with Datis.

75. The Thracians served with foxskins on their heads and tunics on their bodies and were all wrapped round with cloaks of different colors, and on their feet and shins they wore doeskin boots; they carried javelins and targes and small daggers. When these people crossed over into Asia, they were called Bithynians, but in the old days, according to their own account, they were called Strymonians, as living by the river Strymon. They say that they were driven out of their customary country by Teucrians and Mysians. The commander of the Thracians of Asia was Bassaces, son of Artabanus.

76. The . . .[24] had shields made of raw oxhide—rather small; each of them carried two wolf-hunter's spears and on their heads wore helmets of bronze. On these helmets were the ears and horns of an ox, made in bronze, and crests as well. They wrapped their shins around with strips of scarlet cloth. There is in the country of these people an oracle of Ares.

77. The Cabalees, who are Maeonians and are called Lasonii, had the same equipment as the Cilicians, which I will indicate when, in my discussion, I come to the ordering of the Cilicians. The Milyae had short spears, and their garments were fastened with

24. Some tribal name is omitted here.

brooches. Some of them had Lycian bows and on their heads wore caps made of leather. The commander of all of these was Badres, son of Hystanes.

78. The Moschi had on their heads wooden helmets and carried shields and little spears, but with very long lance-points. The Tibareni and the Macrones and Mossynoeci served with the same equipment as the Moschi. These are the officers who jointly were responsible for the ordering of these troops: for the Moschi and Tibareni, Ariomardus, son of Darius and of Parmys, the daughter of Smerdis, son of Cyrus; for the Macrones and Mossynoeci, Artaÿctes, son of Cherasmis, who was governor of Sestos on the Hellespont.

79. The Mares had on their heads helmets woven after the fashion of their country and carried shields—small and made of hides—and javelins. The Colchians had on their heads wooden helmets and carried rawhide shields, small short spears, and swords. The commander of the Mares and the Colchians was Pharandates, the son of Teaspis. The Alarodians and Saspires served with arms like those of the Colchians. They were commanded by Masistius, son of Siromitres.

80. The island nations that came from the Red Sea, and the people of the islands where the Great King settles those called Exiles, wore clothes and carried arms most like those of the Medes. The commander of these islanders was Mardontes, son of Bagaeus, who died in battle at Mycale the year after this, when he was general on the Persian side.

81. These were the peoples who served and marched by the mainland in the land army. The commanders of the host were those I have already mentioned; these were the men who established the military formations and did the counting of the numbers and appointed the commanders of thousands and the commanders of ten thousands; the commanders of hundreds and those of tens were appointed by the commanders of ten thousands. There were other leaders, too, of squadrons and tribes.[25]

25. The Greek word I have translated as "leaders" means, in a military context, persons who issue the commands to charge, to retreat, etc. Since Herodotus makes it clear in chapter 96, below, that the commanding officers of the native (non-Persian) contingents were all Persians and that the native leaders in the army were "as much slaves as the soldiers were," it seems reasonable to sup-

82. The commanders were, then, as I have listed them. But the supreme generals over them and over the whole land army were Mardonius, son of Gobryas, and Tritantaechmes, son of the Artabanus who gave as his counsel not to invade Greece, and Smerdomenes, the son of Otanes (both of these latter were children of brothers of Darius and therefore Xerxes' cousins), and Masistes, son of Darius and Atossa, and Gergis, son of Ariazus, and Megabyzus, son of Zopyrus.

83. These were the commanders-in-chief of the whole land army, except for the Ten Thousand. These ten thousand picked Persians were under the generalship of Hydarnes, son of Hydarnes, and they were called the Immortals because as soon as their number was depleted by death or disease, another man was chosen, and so they were never fewer or more than exactly ten thousand. Throughout the army it was Persians who showed the most brilliant equipment, and they themselves were the best in the army. They had the gear I have described, and, besides, they made a lavish display of gold, and they brought with them their light carriages,[26] and in these were their concubines and many servants, who were also well provided with everything. Corn was carried for them, as distinct from the rest of the soldiers, by camels and pack animals.

84. These peoples were all horsemen, yet not all of them furnished horses, but only those in the list I give below. The Persian cavalry was equipped like their infantry, save that, on their heads, some of them wore helmets of hammered bronze and iron.

85. There are some nomads called Sagartians, who are in race and language Persians but in equipment are in between that of the Persian and the Pactyan. They furnished eight thousand horse. It is not their custom to have any weapons of iron or bronze except for their daggers, but they use ropes of twisted leather.[27] It is these they rely on in battle. The way these men fight is that when they come into contact with the enemy they throw their ropes, which have a

---

pose that the men being mentioned here served as interpreters; that is, each would receive his Persian commander's orders in Persian and then relay them, in their own tongue, to the troops under him.

26. Like that in which Xerxes rode "at whim," leaving his heavy ceremonial chariot (7.41).

27. Clearly, a sort of lasso.

noose at the end. Whatever the rope captures, be it horse or man, the fighter draws to himself, and the enemy entangled in the coils is killed.

86. That is their method of fighting, and they were placed in the Persian contingent. The Median and the Cissian cavalry were equipped like their infantry. The Indian cavalry likewise had the same equipment as their infantry, but they rode swift horses and also drove chariots, to which they harnessed both horses and wild asses. The Bactrian and Caspian cavalry were equipped like their foot. The Libyans were also furnished like their foot, and all of them, too, drove chariots. The Caspians and Paricanians, in their cavalry, were equipped as in the infantry. The Arabians had the same gear as their foot, but they all rode on camels, which in speed were as quick as horses.

87. These were the only peoples who served as cavalry. The number of the cavalry was eighty thousand, apart from the camels and the chariots. The rest of the horse was arranged by regiments, but the Arabians always served in the rear. They held this post because the horses could not endure the presence of the camels, and the Arabians thus avoided frightening the horses.

88. The commanders of the cavalry were Harmamithres and Tithaeus, both sons of Datis. The third, who was joint commander with them, was Pharnuches, but he was left behind in Sardis, ill; as they set out from Sardis, an unlooked-for accident befell him. As he was riding out, a dog ran under his horse's feet, and the horse, in sudden fear, reared and threw Pharnuches. He fell vomiting blood, and the sickness turned into a consumption. His men immediately, under their commander's orders, took out the horse to where he had thrown his master and sawed off his legs at the knees. So Pharnuches in this way lost his share in the command.

89. The number of triremes was twelve hundred and seven. The peoples who furnished them were as follows. The Phoenicians and Palestinian Syrians furnished three hundred. These men wore on their heads helmets made almost in the Greek fashion and wore linen breastplates and carried rimless shields and javelins. The Phoenicians lived of old, so they say, about the Red Sea, but they then came out of there and settled in that part of Syria that is next the sea. That piece of Syria, and all as far as Egypt, is called Pal-

estine. The Egyptians furnished two hundred ships. They wore on their heads plaited helmets and carried hollow shields, with great rims, and spears for fighting at sea, and great poleaxes. The most of them wore breastplates and had big daggers.

90. So were these equipped. The Cyprians furnished one hundred and fifty ships, and their dress was, for their kings, turbans on their heads; the rest wore tunics and otherwise wore clothes like the Greeks. The nations of Cyprus are these: some are from Athens and Salamis,[28] some from Arcadia, some from Cythnus, some from Phoenicia, some from Ethiopia, all according to the account of the Cypriots themselves.

91. The Cilicians furnished one hundred ships. They had on their heads the helmets of their country, carried bucklers of raw oxhide instead of shields, and wore woolly tunics. Each had two javelins and a sword, made much in the fashion of the Egyptian sword. These people were in the old days called Hypachaei but took their name from Cilix, son of Agenor, who was a Phoenician. The Pamphylians furnished thirty ships; they themselves were armed with Greek arms. These Pamphylians are descended from those Greeks who scattered from Troy with Amphilochus and Calchas.

92. The Lycians furnished fifty ships. They wore breastplates and shin-protectors and had bows of cornel wood and unfeathered arrows, made of reeds, and javelins; and they had a goatskin hung around the shoulders and feathered caps on their heads. They had daggers and scimitars. The Lycians came originally from Crete and were called Termilae, but they have their name from Lycus, son of Pandion, a man of Athens.

93. The Dorians of Asia furnished thirty ships and had Greek arms, as they were themselves originally from the Peloponnese. The Carians furnished seventy ships and were equipped like Greeks, except that they had scimitars and daggers. Of what they were called originally I have told in the first part of my history.[29]

28. Much of this is quite doubtful. There *was* a Salamis in Cyprus, but whether there was any real connection with the Salamis near Athens is uncertain. The Greeks thought there was and therefore tagged the Cyprian Salamis as Attic. There were, of course, all sorts of racial elements in Cyprus, as there are still, though the mix of peoples now is quite different.

29. In 1.171.

94. The Ionians furnished one hundred ships; their equipment was like the Greeks'. The Ionians were called Aegialian Pelasgians (say the Greeks) for all the time they lived in the Peloponnese, in what is now called Achaea, and before Danaus and Xuthus came to the Peloponnese. Afterwards they were called Ionians, from Ion, the son of Xuthus.

95. The islanders furnished seventeen ships and were armed like Greeks; they were also of Pelasgian origin but afterwards came to be called Ionian in the same way as were the Ionians of the Twelve Cities, who came from Athens. The Aeolians furnished sixty ships; their equipment was like that of the Greeks, and they were in the old time called Pelasgians, according to the Greek account. The people of the Hellespont (all except those of Abydos, for these had been ordered to stay at home by the King, to guard the bridges) furnished one hundred ships; their equipment was like the Greeks'. These were colonists of both the Ionians and the Dorians.

96. On board all these ships there served fighting men of the Persians, Medes, and Sacae. The Phoenicians, and, among the Phoenicians, the Sidonians, furnished the fastest-sailing ships. Over all these, as over those who served in the infantry, there were native commanders in each unit. I do not record the names of these because it is not necessary for the purpose of my *History*. For these native leaders of each people are not worthy of mention. There were, for each people, as many leaders as there were cities, and these native officers did not serve as generals but were as much slaves as the soldiers were. But the Persian generals, who had supreme power and commanded each of the nations—these I have already recorded.

97. The admirals in charge of the navy were Ariabignes, son of Darius; Prexaspes, son of Aspathines; Megabyzus, son of Megabates; and Achaemenes, son of Darius. Of the Ionian and Carian navies, the admiral was Ariabignes, son of Darius and of Gobryas' daughter. The commander of the Egyptians was Achaemenes, full brother of Xerxes himself. The two other admirals commanded all the rest. The triaconters, penteconters,[30] light vessels, and horse transports were, all together, three thousand in number.

98. Of those who sailed on board, the most notable, after the

30. Boats of thirty and fifty oars.

admirals, were Tetramnestus of Sidon, son of Anysus; Matten, son of Siromus, a Tyrian; an Aradian, Merbalus, son of Agbalus; Syennesis of Cilicia, son of Oromedon; a Lycian, Cyberniscus, son of Sicas; two Cyprians, Gorgus, son of Chersis, and Timonax, son of Timagoras; three Carians, Histiaeus, son of Tymnes, Pigres, son of Hysseldomus, and Damasithymus, son of Candaules.

99. I do not mention the other captains, as being not so obliged; but I do find occasion for admiration in Artemisia, that she, a woman, served in the expedition against the Greeks. Her husband had died, and she took over the power (and must also deal with her young son), and yet served out of pure spirit and manliness, with no compulsion on her so to do. Her name was Artemisia, daughter of Lygdamis, by race on her father's side from Halicarnassus, on her mother's side, a Cretan. She was leader of the men of Halicarnassus and of the Coans and Nisyrians and Calydnians. She furnished five ships, and of all the host her ships were in the most repute, after those of the Sidonians. And of all the allies it was Artemisia who gave the King the best counsels. The cities of which I have spoken as being under her direction were, I declare, all Dorian, the Halicarnassians being in origin from Troezen, the others from Epidaurus. This is the end of what I have to say about the fleet.

100. Xerxes, when the host had been numbered and ranged in formation, was set on driving through them in person and seeing them all. So he did just that; and driving through in his chariot, nation by nation, he inquired about each one, and his secretaries wrote down the information until he had gone from one end to the other, both of horse and of foot. When that was done and his ships were drawn down and launched in the sea, Xerxes, transferring from his chariot to a Sidonian ship, sat there under a golden canopy and sailed past the prows of the ships, putting his questions to them just as he had done with the army and recording it all. Then the captains put their ships to sea, perhaps four plethra from the shore,[31] and stood out at anchor, with the prows turned toward the shore, all in a closed line, and with all the fighting men aboard them armed, ready for battle. Xerxes sailed between their prows and the shore and watched.

31. About four hundred feet.

101. When he had sailed past them all and had disembarked, he sent for Demaratus,[32] the son of Ariston, who was part of his expedition against Greece; and having summoned him, he said "Demaratus, it is my pleasure to ask of you a question on something I wish to know. You are a Greek, and, as I learn from yourself and from the other Greeks who have come into speech with me, yours is not the least or the weakest of Greek cities. Now, then, tell me: will these Greeks stand their ground and take issue with me? For, as I see it, even if all the Greeks, and moreover all the other men who live in the western countries, were assembled together, they would not be able to fight me—to abide my onslaught—if they were not at harmony with one another. But I would like to know from you, too, what you have to say about them." That was his question, and Demaratus' answer was this: "My lord, shall I follow truth in my answer to you, or your pleasure?" The King bade him speak the very truth, saying he would be no worse friend to him thereafter.

102. At which Demaratus said: "My lord, since you have bidden me speak the truth utterly, so that I should hereafter be not convicted by you of speaking anything less than truth: poverty has always been native in Greece, but the courage they have comes imported, and it is achieved by a compound of wisdom and the strength of their laws. By virtue of this, Greece fights off poverty and despotism. My praise applies to all those Greeks who live in Dorian countries, but I am prepared to make my speech not about all of these but about the Lacedaemonians alone; and the first thing I say is that in no way will they accept your proposals bearing slavery to Greece, and the second is that they will challenge you to battle, even though all the other Greeks were on your side. For their numbers, ask me not how many they are who are able to do this. If there are a thousand of them ranged to fight you, they will fight you—or less or more than a thousand."

103. At this, Xerxes laughed and said, "Demaratus, what a word is this—that a thousand men will fight so great an army as this! Tell me. You say that you yourself were the king of these people. Would *you* be willing to fight with ten men? Yet, if the political arrange-

32. The exiled king of Sparta. See chapter 3, above.

ments be as you say they are,[33] it befits you as king, in accordance with your ordinances, to fight twice that number ranged against you. If each individual Greek is worth ten men in my army, I ask you, would you be worth twenty? Yet this is how the story should come out, according to your telling of it. But if they are such men, and of such stature, as you and the other Greeks who have talked with me boast yourselves to be, take heed that this be not an utterly vain boast. Now, I would like to see this in plain reason: how could a thousand or ten thousand or even fifty thousand confront so great an army as mine if they were all alike free and not subject to one command? We would be more than a thousand to one if they were five thousand strong. If they were commanded by one, as our men are, for fear of him and reaching beyond the courage that is natural to them, they might go forward, though few against many, under compulsion of the lash. But being suffered to be free, they would do neither of these things. I myself believe that even if they were equal in numbers, the Greeks would find it hard to fight against the Persians alone. The quality you speak of resides in us and no others, and, even with us, in few, not many. There are those of my Persian bodyguard who would each fight with three Greeks at once. But you don't know of these things, and what you say is great nonsense."

104. Demaratus answered: "My lord, I knew at the beginning that if I spoke the truth you would not like it. But since you compelled me to speak the veriest truth, I spoke, and what I spoke concerned the Spartans. Yet how much I am disposed to love them you know yourself: they stripped me of my office and the privileges that were my fathers'; they made me a cityless exile; it was your father who took me in and gave me a livelihood and a house. A man of natural feeling does not reject good will when it is shown to him but requites it with love. I do not undertake to be able to fight with ten men or with two; of my own free will I would not fight with one. But if I had to, or if there were some great contest to spur me on, I would like best to fight with one of those men who in his person claims to be a match for three Greeks. So it is with the Lacedaemonians;

33. He refers to the fact that the Spartan kings had two votes instead of one, double portions at the feasts, etc., which Herodotus has earlier recorded (6.57).

fighting singly, they are no worse than any other people; together, they are the most gallant men on earth. For they are free—but not altogether so. They have as the despot over them Law, and they fear him much more than your men fear you. At least they do whatever he bids them do; and he bids them always the same thing: not to flee from the fight before any multitude of men whatever but to stand firm in their ranks and either conquer or die. If you think that in talking like this I am talking nonsense, I am willing in the future to hold my tongue. As it is, I have spoken when forced by yourself. I hope that everything goes as you would have it, my lord."

105. That was his answer. But Xerxes turned the whole thing into a joke and showed no anger at all, dismissing Demaratus with all kindness. After he had talked with Demaratus, Xerxes put in, as viceroy in Doriscus, Mascames, son of Megadostes, displacing the man whom Darius had installed. And so he marched off with his army for Greece, going through Thrace.

106. This man Mascames, whom he left in Doriscus, was one of such quality that to him alone Xerxes sent gifts continuously, regarding him as the bravest of all the viceroys that either he himself or Darius had appointed. He sent these gifts yearly, and in the same fashion Artaxerxes, son of Xerxes, sent them to the descendants of Mascames. Such viceroys had been appointed even before the invasion, throughout Thrace and the Hellespont. After the invasion was over, the Greeks put out all these Persians, except for Mascames in Doriscus. Nobody succeeded in expelling him, though many tried. That is why the gifts keep coming to him from whoever is the reigning King of Persia.

107. Of those who were expelled by the Greeks, Xerxes thought none had proved a good man and true except only Boges in Eïon. Him he was forever praising, and those of his children who survived in Persia he greatly honored; for Boges had deserved great praise. He was besieged by the Athenians and Cimon, son of Miltiades, and, when he might have marched out under treaty and come home safe to Asia, he refused to do so lest the King should judge his survival an act of cowardice; instead, he endured to the end. When there was no longer any provender within the fortress, he built a great fire and, having cut the throats of his children, his wife, his concubines, and his servants, he threw the bodies into the fire. Then he gathered all

the gold and silver that were in the city and scattered it from the walls into the river Strymon, and, having done all this, he threw himself into the fire. So he earned the praise of the Persians and does so still to this day.

108. Xerxes marched from Doriscus toward Greece and forced all the peoples that lay in his route to serve with him. For, as I have said before, all the country as far as Thessaly had been enslaved and made tributary to the King when conquered by Megabazus and, later, by Mardonius. As he marched from Doriscus, he passed by the forts in Samothrace, the last of which, to the west, was a city by the name of Mesembria. Nearby it is a city of the Thasians called Stryme, and between the two cities there is the river Lisus, whose waters failed, not sufficing for the drinking of the army of Xerxes. This country used to be called Gallaïce, but now Briantice; but, strictly, it belongs to the Cicones.

109. Crossing the river Lisus, the stream of which had been so dried up with drinking, he passed by the Greek cities of Maronea, Dicaea, and Abdera. These he passed and also some famous lakes near them—the Ismarid lake, between Maronea and Stryme, and the Bistonian, near Dicaea, into which two rivers empty. These rivers are the Trauos and the Compsantus. By way of Abdera, Xerxes passed no famous lake, but he crossed the river Nestus where it flows into the sea. After these places he went on his march and passed by mainland cities, in one of which there is a lake of thirty stades round; it is full of fish and very briny. Here only the baggage animals drank, and then it was dry. The name of the city is Pistyrus.

110. These cities, which are Greek and situated on the coast, Xerxes passed by, keeping them on the left hand. The Thracian peoples through which he made his march are the Paeti, Cicones, Bistonians, Sapaei, Dersaei, Edoni, and Satrae. Of these, the ones who lived by the seaboard joined his host with their ships; of those who lived inland, who have already been mentioned by me, all except the Satrae went with Xerxes' land army, under compulsion.

111. The Satrae have never been subject to anyone, as far as we know, but right down to my time have continued as the only free Thracians. They live in high mountains, covered with woods of all kinds and with snow, and they are very keen soldiers. These people have the well-known oracle of Dionysus. It is in the very highest

mountains; those who are the prophets of the shrine are the people of the Satrae called Bessi. The person who utters the prophecy is, as at Delphi, a priestess, and the procedure is no more complicated in the one place than the other.

112. Through this territory Xerxes passed, and, after this, he passed the forts of the Pierians, one of them called Phagres, the other Pergamus. In this direction he marched right under the walls, keeping Mount Pangaeus on his right, a great and high mountain in which there are gold and silver mines worked by the Pierians and Odomanti, and especially by the Satrae.

113. The people—Paeonians, Doberes, and Paeoplae—who live above Pangaeus to the north he passed by as he marched westward, till he came to the river Strymon and the city of Eïon; this was the city of which Boges was governor, of whom I spoke a while ago; at this time Boges was still alive. The country round Pangaeus is called Phyllis; it stretches westward to the river Angites, which empties into the Strymon, and, in the south, it stretches as far as the Strymon itself. Into this river the Magi cut the throats of white horses, seeking a favorable omen.

114. After such rites practiced at the river and many more besides, they crossed it at the Nine Roads (a place among the Edonians), over the bridge they found spanning the Strymon. Learning that the name of the place was Nine Roads, they buried alive nine boys and girls of the local people. It is a Persian custom, this burying-alive; for I learn that Amestris, wife of Xerxes, when she had grown old, had fourteen children of noble Persians buried alive as a gift on her behalf to the so-called god of the underworld.

115. As the army marched away from the Strymon, it passed, toward the west, a stretch of seacoast in which there is the Greek city Argilus. This area and the country above it are called Bisaltia. From there Xerxes kept on his left hand the gulf off Posidium and passed through the plain of Syleus, so called, and, passing by the Greek city of Stagirus, he came to Acanthus. Xerxes brought with him every one of those peoples and those who live around Pangaeus, and, as in the case of those I mentioned before, taking to serve with the fleet those from the coastal country and, with the army, those from further inland. This road by which King Xerxes led his army the Thra-

cians do not plough or sow but hold it in great reverence, right till my own time.

116. When he came to Acanthus, Xerxes proclaimed the Acanthians to be his guest-friends. He awarded them the Median Garment and praised them highly, seeing them as people of great zeal for the war and hearing of their digging the canal.

117. When Xerxes was in Acanthus, it happened that there died of disease the chief architect of the canal, one Artachaees, a man of repute with Xerxes, by birth an Achaemenid and the tallest man in Persia, for he lacked only four fingers of five royal cubits in stature,[34] and he had the loudest voice in the world. Xerxes was bitterly sorry for his loss and gave him a splendid funeral and burial. The whole army poured libations on his grave. To this Artachaees the Acanthians sacrifice as a hero, in accord with an oracle, and they call on his name.

118. So Xerxes sorrowed for the dead Artachaees. But those of the Greeks who received the army and entertained Xerxes were brought to the utmost pitch of misery, so that they were driven out of the homes they had. For example, when the Thasians received and feasted Xerxes' army on behalf of their cities on the mainland, and Antipater, son of Orgeus, a citizen as renowned as any among them and chosen for the task, turned in his books, he showed that four hundred silver talents had been spent on the dinner.

119. In the other cities, too, those in charge turned in accounts very similar to this. For the dinner was something ordered long before and was treated as as very serious matter. As soon as they heard the proclamations being carried around by the King's heralds, the citizens in the cities divided up corn and for many months ground it to flour and meal. Also, as to cattle, they chose the best they could find for money and fattened them; and they kept landfowl and waterfowl in cages and ponds for the entertainment of the army and made drinking cups and bowls of gold and silver and also all the tableware. This latter was done only for the King and those who ate with him. For the rest of the army they provided food only. When the army would arrive, a pavilion was erected for Xerxes to stay in;

34. About eight feet tall.

the rest of the army remained outside, under the sky. When the dinner hour came, the hosts had trouble enough; but their guests, when full fed, passed the night there, and, next day, tearing up the pavilion and taking everything that was movable, they marched off, carrying everything with them and leaving nothing.

120. At this time there was a very witty comment made by Megacreon, a man of Abdera. He bade the people of Abdera, men and women, as a public act, go to their shrines and there, as suppliants, beseech the gods also in time to come to turn aside one-half of evils that were to be, and, for those past, they should acknowledge great gratitude, inasmuch as King Xerxes was not accustomed to eat *twice* a day. For had the people of Abdera been ordered to furnish a breakfast on the scale of the dinner, they must either have fled before the King's approach or, if they had stayed for his coming, they must have been ground to the dust, worse than any people on earth had ever been.

121. So, for all their oppression, the local people nevertheless completed the tasks commanded them. After Acanthus, Xerxes, laying commands on the generals that the fleet should await him in Therme, sent his ships from him on their course (Therme is the town on the Thermaic Gulf from which the gulf gets its name). He had learned that this was the shortest way. From Doriscus to Acanthus, this is the order in which the army had marched: Xerxes had divided up his whole land army into three parts. One of them he ordered to march along the sea, beside the fleet. Of this part, the generals were Mardonius and Masistes. Another third of the army marched inland, commanded by Tritanaechmes and Gergis. The final third, with which Xerxes himself marched, went between the two others, and its generals were Smerdomenes and Megabyzus.

122. The fleet, when dispatched by Xerxes, sailed through the canal in Athos, the canal that reached through to the gulf on which are the cities of Assa and Pilorus and Singus and Sarte; after that, when it had taken on troops from these cities too, it sailed straight for the Thermaic Gulf, and, rounding Ampelus, the cape of Torone, it passed the Greek cities of Torone, Galepsus, Sermyle, Mecyberna, and Olynthus, from all of which it took on ships and troops.

123. This country is called Sithonia. Xerxes' fleet, cutting across from Cape Ampelus to Cape Canastra, which is the jaw of Pallene,

which projects there furthest into the sea, there took on ships and additional forces from Potidaea and Aphytis and Neapolis and Aege and Therambos and Scione and Mende and Sane. For these are the cities of the country now called Pallene but formerly called Phlegra. Sailing along this coast, the fleet made for the place of their destination and took on troops from those cities adjacent to Pallene and bordering the Thermaic Gulf, the names of which are Lipaxus, Combrea, Aesa, Gigonus, Campsa, Smila, and Aenea. Their territory is called Crossaea to this very day. From Aenea, which is the last name on my list of cities, into the Thermaic Gulf itself the course of the fleet lay, and to the Mygdonian land; and, as they sailed, they came to Therme, which is where they were appointed to go, and to the cities of Sindus and Chalestra on the river Axius, which is the boundary between the Mygdonian land and the Bottiaean, in the latter of which the cities of Ichnae and Pella occupy a narrow strip of seacoast.

124. The fleet here lay off the river Axius and the city of Therme and the cities between them, waiting for the King; and Xerxes and the land army marched from Acanthus, taking the short cut across the land, since he wanted to get to Therme. He marched through Paeonia and Crestonia to the river Cheidorus, which starts in the Crestonian land and flows through Mygdonia and empties into the marshes of the river Axius.

125. As Xerxes marched along, lions set upon his camels, which were carrying the corn. The lions would come constantly at night and, leaving their usual haunts, would touch nothing else, baggage animal or human; they ravaged the camels only. I wonder what the cause can be that forced the lions to leave the other creatures alone and attack the camels, since this was an animal they had never seen before or had any experience of.

126. There are in these parts many lions and wild oxen, the enormous horns of which are brought to Greece. The boundary of the lions is the river Nestus, which flows through Abdera, and the Achelous, which flows through Acarnania. To the east of the Nestus, in all of the nearer part of Europe, you will never see a lion, nor west of the Achelous in the rest of the mainland; but they are found in the land between these rivers.

127. When Xerxes came to Therme, he quartered his army there.

His army in its encampment occupied all the country by the sea from the city of Therme and the land of Mygdonia as far as the rivers Lydias and Haliacmon, which, mingling their waters into the same stream, draw the boundary between the Bottiaean country and that of Macedonia. The barbarians camped in that territory, and, of the rivers I have mentioned, only the Cheidorus, which flows from Crestonia, failed to suffice for the army's drinking; *it* failed.

128. Xerxes looked from Therme on the Thessalian mountains—Olympus and Ossa in all their hugeness—and learned that between them there was a narrow pass through which the Peneus flows; and hearing that here there was a road leading into Thessaly, he was anxious to sail and see the mouth of the Peneus, because he planned to drive by the upper road, through the Macedonians of the upper territory, to the Perrhaebi and the city of Gonnus. For he learned that here was the safest way. Acting on his wish, he boarded a Sidonian ship, which he used as often as he was minded to do anything like this, and gave his signal also to the rest of the fleet to put to sea, leaving his land army where it was. When Xerxes came and saw the mouth of the Peneus, he was in great amazement, and, summoning his guides, he asked them whether it was possible to turn the river aside from its course and lead it into the sea somewhere else.

129. There is a story that in ancient times Thessaly was a lake, being shut in on all sides by huge mountains. For the parts of it to the east are shut in by Pelion and Ossa, which here join their lower spurs; to the north, Olympus shuts it in, and, to the west, Pindus, and, to the south and the south wind, Othrys. In the midst of these aforementioned mountains lies the vale of Thessaly. Many other streams flow into it, but the five most notable ones are the Peneus, the Apidanus, the Onochonus, the Enipeus, and the Pamisus. These flow from the mountains surrounding Thessaly and then, joining into one stream, they issue into the sea through a single passage (and that a narrow one). As soon as they all mingle their waters into the same channel, the Peneus masters the others with its name and renders them nameless. In the old times, it is said, this channel and passage to the sea did not yet exist, and so these rivers and, besides the rivers, the Boebean lake, which were not even named then but flowed with no less volume than now, by the course of their waters made the whole of Thessaly one vast sea. The Thessalians

themselves say that Poseidon made the channel through which the Peneus flows. Their suggestion is very natural; for anyone who thinks that Poseidon shakes the earth and that the earthquake's splits in the earth's surface are the god's work—anyone, looking at this, will say that Poseidon did it. It *is* the action of an earthquake, as it seems to me—this split between the mountains.

130. Xerxes asked the guides whether there was any other way out to the sea for the Peneus, and of their sure knowledge they answered him: "My lord, there is no other way for this river to get out to the sea save this one alone; for all Thessaly is ringed round with mountains." At this Xerxes, according to the story, said, "They are clever men, the Thessalians. This is why they took their precautions long ago and conceded victory to me; it was especially because they have a country that is easy and quick to capture. It would only be a matter of letting the river in upon their country by shifting it out of that channel and turning it from the course in which it travels with a dam, and all of Thessaly, except the mountains, would be beneath the waves." What he spoke had reference to the sons of Aleues, because they were the first of the Greeks to surrender to the King. Xerxes supposed that they were offering friendship from all the people there.[35] Having said that and looked at what was there, he sailed back to Therme.

131. Xerxes spent many days around Pieria, for one-third part of his army was chopping at the Macedonian mountains, that through them the whole army might move down to the Perrhaebian country. The heralds he had sent to Greece to demand earth came back, some empty-handed but some bearing earth and water.

132. Of those who gave such, there were the Thessalians, Dolopians, Enienes, Perrhaebians, Locrians, Magnetes, Melians, Achaeans of Phthiotis, Thebans, and the rest of the Boeotians except the Thespians and the Plataeans. Against these who surrendered, the Greeks who undertook war against the barbarians took a solemn oath. The oath was this: that as many as were Greeks and

35. The sons of Aleues were the Aleuadae, princes of Thessaly. Apparently, what Herodotus means one to understand is that the princes did not in fact speak for all the nations of Thessaly or even perhaps for all of their own people. Actually, even the Aleuadae had only very recently—not "long ago"—made up their minds to Medize.

surrendered to the Persians without compulsion so to do should be mulcted of one-tenth of their possessions for the benefit of the god at Delphi when the good times should come again. Such was the oath taken by the Greeks.[36]

133. But Xerxes sent no heralds for the demand of earth to Sparta and Athens, and this is why: before this, Darius had sent such for this purpose, and the one of the two cities, casting those who made the demand into the Pit,[37] and the other, casting them into a well, bade them fetch earth and water from there to bear to the King. For these reasons, Xerxes sent none to ask of these two cities. What bad things happened to the Athenians for what they did to the heralds I cannot say, save that their land and city were devastated; but I believe that this murder of the heralds was not truly the reason why the devastation happened.[38]

134. But on the Lacedaemonians there fell like a lightning bolt the anger of Talthybius, the herald of Agamemnon. There is in Sparta a shrine of Talthybius, and his descendants are called the Talthybiadae, and to them at Sparta all matters concerning the functioning of heralds pertain. After this, as often as the Spartans tried to obtain favorable omens from their sacrifices, they failed to get any, and this lasted for a long time. The Lacedaemonians were very distressed and disturbed at this, and they held the assembly many times and issued a proclamation to the effect that some Lacedaemonian should offer his life for Sparta. At this, Sperthias, the son of Aneristus, and Bulis, the son of Nicolaus, Spartiates of high birth and great property, volunteered to pay the penalty to Xerxes for Darius' heralds that were murdered in Sparta. These men the Spartiates then sent to Media to meet their deaths.

135. Their courage was admirable and also their words. When they were on their journey to Susa, they came before Hydarnes. Hydarnes was the Persian who was general over the peoples of the

36. It is not quite clear whether this is the meaning or whether it refers to a much more terrible punishment, in which, after killing the inhabitants or selling them into slavery and confiscating their property, one-tenth of the proceeds would be offered to the god at Delphi.

37. The place in Athens into which criminals were thrown.

38. Herodotus evidently thought that the principal motive was revenge for the burning of Sardis (5.101–2, 105).

seacoast in Asia. He entertained the Spartans hospitably and, in his place as host, asked them, "You men of Lacedaemon, why do you avoid friendship with the King? You see how the King knows how to honor good men; you can take as your standards myself and my fortunes. So, too, if you put yourself in the King's hands, you will be judged by him as good men, and each of you might hold office in Greece under the King's mandate." They then answered the Persian: "Hydarnes, your advice with relation to us comes from something less than an equality of position. You counsel us as one who has tried one condition but knows nothing of the other. You know what it is to be a slave, but you have no experience of freedom, to know whether it is sweet or not. If you had had such experience, you would bid us fight for it, not with spears only, but with axes as well."

136. Such was their answer to Hydarnes. Thereafter they left him and went to Susa and came into the presence of the King. At first the bodyguards were for ordering them, and indeed forcing them, to fall down and do obeisance to the King, but they declared that, even if thrown headlong, they would not do these things; for, said they, it was not the custom among their people to do obeisance to a human creature, and it was not for this purpose that they had come. Having fought off this demand, they then spoke as follows: "King of the Medes, the Lacedaemonians have sent us to pay the penalty for those heralds who were murdered in Sparta." As they said that, Xerxes with magnanimity said that he would not be like the Lacedaemonians, "for they," he said, "have broken what is customary usage among all mankind by killing the heralds; but I will not myself do what I rebuke them for, nor by counterkilling will I release the Lacedaemonians from their guilt."

137. So it was that the wrath of Talthybius rested for the moment, because the Spartiates had done as they had, even though the men, Sperthias and Bulis, came back home to Sparta. But long afterwards it woke into life, at the time of the war between the Athenians and Peloponnesians, according to the story the Lacedaemonians tell. It is indeed in this aspect that the thing seems to me to be most clearly the work of gods. For that the wrath of Talthybius fell upon envoys, and never ceased until it had found its fulfillment, is the course of justice. But that it should fall upon the children of those men who had gone up to Susa to the King's presence—upon

Nicolas, the son of Bulis, and on Aneristus, the son of Sperthias (this is the Aneristus who captured Halieis, a settlement from Tiryns, when he landed there with a merchantman manned with a crew)— that is what makes it clear to me that it was a matter of divine contrivance because of Talthybius' wrath. For these two men were sent by the Lacedaemonians as envoys into Asia, were betrayed by Sitalces, son of Tereus, king of Thrace, and by Nymphodorus, son of Pytheas of Abdera, were taken prisoner at Bisanthe on the Hellespont, and, being shipped to Attica, were executed by the Athenians and, along with them, Aristeas, son of Adimantus, a Corinthian. This happened many years after the King's expedition.[39] I now resume the track of my former story.

138. The King's expedition was in name directed against Athens, but it was sent against all Greece. Though the Greeks knew this far in advance, they did not all take it in the same way. Some of them gave earth and water to the Persian and were confident that they would suffer nothing unpleasant at the hand of the barbarian; but others, who had not given these symbols, were reduced to great fear, inasmuch as there were not enough ships in Greece to meet the invader, nor were many of these people willing to prosecute the war seriously but were turning eagerly to the Persian interest.

139. At this point I am forced to declare an opinion that most people will find offensive; yet, because I think it true, I will not hold back. If the Athenians had taken fright at the approaching danger and had left their own country, or even if they had not left it but had remained and surrendered to Xerxes, no one would have tried to oppose the King at sea. If there had been no opposition to Xerxes at sea, what happened on land would have been this: even if the Peloponnesians had drawn many walls across the Isthmus for their defense, the Lacedaemonians would have been betrayed by their allies, not because the allies chose so to do but out of necessity as they were taken, city by city, by the fleet of the barbarian; thus the Lacedaemonians would have been isolated and, though isolated, would have done deeds of the greatest valor and died nobly. That would have been what happened; or else they would, before this end, have seen that all the other Greeks had Medized and so themselves would have

39. It occurred in 430 (it is the latest event reported by Herodotus).

come to an agreement with Xerxes. In both these cases, all of Greece would have been subdued by the Persians. For I cannot see what value those walls drawn across the Isthmus would be, once the King was master by sea. So, as it stands now, a man who declares that the Athenians were the saviors of Greece would hit the very truth. For to whichever side they inclined, that was where the scale would come down. They chose that Greece should survive free, and it was they who awakened all the part of Greece that had not Med-ized, and it was they who, under Heaven, routed the King. Not even the dreadful oracles that came from Delphi, terrifying though they were, persuaded them to desert Greece; they stood their ground and withstood the invader when he came against their own country.

140. For the Athenians had sent envoys to Delphi and stood ready to consult the god; and when they had performed the usual rites about the shrine and had entered the inner hall and sat down there, the Pythia, whose name was Aristonice, gave utterance as follows:

Wretched ones, why sit you here? Flee and begone to remotest
Ends of earth, leaving your homes, high places in circular city;
For neither the head abides sound, no more than the feet or the body;
Fire pulls all down, and sharp Ares, driving his Syrian-bred horses.
Many a fortress besides, and not yours alone shall he ruin.
Many the temples of God to devouring flames he shall give them.
There they stand now, the sweat of terror streaming down from them.
They shake with fear; from the rooftops black blood in deluging torrents.
They have seen the forthcoming destruction, and evil sheerly constraining.
Get you gone out of the shrine! Blanket your soul with your sorrows.

141. When the Athenian envoys heard this, they were in ex-treme distress. They were prostrated by their calamity, foretold by

the oracle; but Timon, son of Androbulus, who was as notable a Delphian as any, counseled them to take suppliant boughs and con-sult the oracle a second time, as suppliants. The Athenians followed his advice and said to the god: "My Lord, give us a better oracle about our fatherland; be moved to pity the suppliant boughs with which we come before you, or we will never go away from your shrine but remain right here till we die." When they said this, the priestess gave them this second answer:

No: Athena cannot appease great Zeus of Olympus
With many eloquent words and all her cunning counsel.
To you I declare again this word, and make it as iron:
All shall be taken by foemen, whatever within his border
Cecrops contains, and whatever the glades of sacred
    Cithaeron.
Yet to Tritogeneia shall Zeus, loud-voiced, give a present,
A wall of wood, which alone shall abide unsacked by the
    foemen;
Well shall it serve yourselves and your children in days that
    shall be.
Do not abide the charge of horse and foot that come on you,
A mighty host from the landward side, but withdraw before
    it.
Turn your back in retreat; on another day you shall face
    them.
Salamis, isle divine, you shall slay many children of women,
Either when seed is sown or again when the harvest is
    gathered.

142. This oracle seemed to be kinder than the earlier, and indeed it was so. So the envoys wrote it down and went home to Athens. When they had left Delphi and made their report to the people at home, there were many judgments on the part of those who sought what the meaning of the oracle might be, but there were two that clashed more than all the others. Some of the elder men said that they thought that the god predicted that the Acropolis would be saved. For in the old days the Acropolis of Athens had been fenced in with a thorn hedge. Some, therefore, construed this thorn hedge to be the wooden wall. But there were others who said that the god signified the ships, and they urged the abandonment of all else and

the preparation of the fleet. But these who claimed that the wooden wall was the ships were baffled by the last two verses of the Pythia's oracle, "Salamis, isle divine, you shall slay many children of women, Either when seed is sown or again when the harvest is gathered." In respect of these lines of verse, the opinion of those who construed the ships as the wooden wall was confounded. For the interpreters of the oracles took the verses in this sense: that the Athenians must prepare themselves for a sea battle at Salamis, which they would certainly lose.

143. Now there was a man among the Athenians who at this moment was but lately come into their front ranks. His name was Themistocles, and he was called the son of Neocles. This man said that the oracle-interpreters construed the whole matter wrongly. For if the verses had been really directed against the Athenians, then the oracle would have been given much less mildly; it would have run "O cruel Salamis" instead of "Salamis, isle divine," if its inhabitants were going to die there. No, he said, to anyone who interpreted the oracle of the god rightly, it was given against the enemy and not the Athenians. So he counseled them to prepare for a fight at sea, since the ships were their wooden wall. This was Themistocles' explanation, and the Athenians decided that it was preferable to that of the oracle-interpreters; for the latter would not have them prepare for a sea fight or indeed, to tell the truth, put up a hand's-worth of resistance at all; they should just leave Attica and settle in some other country.

144. Before this, Themistocles' judgment had proved the best at an important moment; it was when the commonalty of Athens had received great sums that came to them from the mines at Laurium, and they were disposed to share them out, with each citizen getting ten drachmas apiece. It was then that Themistocles persuaded the Athenians to abandon this distribution and make instead, with this money, two hundred ships "for the war," he said, naming the war against the Aeginetans.[40] It was indeed their engagement in this war, just then, that saved Greece, for it compelled the Athenians to become men of the sea. These ships were not used for the purpose for

40. The probable dates of Athens' war with Aegina are 488–486 B.C. According to How and Wells, Themistocles' proposal came later than the war with Aegina but was inspired by Athens' shortage of ships at that time (see 6.89).

which they were built, but they were there for Greece at the moment of her need. They were at the disposal of the Athenians, already made, and then it behooved the Athenians to make more of them to boot. For in the debate following the discussion of the oracle they determined to resist the onset of the barbarians as they invaded Greece, to receive them with their fleet as a whole nation, feeling confident in the god, and with the aid of such Greeks as were willing to help.

145. This, then, was the story of the oracles given to the Athenians. When all the Greeks who were of the better persuasion assembled together and exchanged their judgments and their pledges with one another, their first resolution was that they would utterly do away with all enmities and wars with one another. There were certain such in existence, and the greatest was that between the Athenians and the Aeginetans. Next, when they learned that Xerxes was with his army in Sardis, they determined to send spies into Asia, to learn of the King's power, and messengers to Argos, to form an alliance against the Persian, and other messengers, again, to Sicily, to Gelon, son of Dinomenes, and to Corcyra, and others, still, to Crete, all asking for help for Greece. The thought behind all this sending was that the entire Greek people might somehow unite and take common action, since the invaders threatened all Greeks alike. The power of Gelon was said to be very great—far greater than anything else that was Greek.

146. When they came to this resolution and had reconciled their mutual enmities, they started by sending three men into Asia as spies. These men came to Sardis and took note of the King's host. They were discovered, and after being tortured by the commanders of the land army, they were led away for execution. Their sentence of death was determined; but Xerxes, on hearing of it, faulted the judgment of the commanders and sent to them certain of his bodyguards with orders, if they should find the men still alive, to bring them before himself. They found them still alive and brought them into the presence of the King. He inquired of them for what purpose they had come and then ordered his bodyguards to take them about and show them everything—all the infantry and cavalry—and, when they were satisfied with such sightseeing, to send them away unharmed to whatever country they wished.

147. He gave these orders and added this explanation: he said that, if these spies had been killed, neither would the Greeks have had any advance information as to the unspeakable greatness of his power, nor would he have injured his enemies to any important extent by killing three of their men; if the men went back to Greece, he said, the Greeks, when they learned of the power that was his— now, before the expedition—would themselves surrender their peculiar freedom, and so there would be no need to go to the trouble of campaigning against them. This judgment of his is much like another he gave on another occasion. When he was in Abydos, Xerxes saw corn-carrying ships sailing from the Pontus on their way through the Hellespont, conveying corn to Aegina and the Peloponnese. Xerxes' fellow generals, once they understood that these were enemy vessels, were ready to capture them and glanced at the King for him to give the order. Xerxes asked them where the ships were sailing to; they said, "My lord, they are bringing corn to your enemies." But he answered them and said, "Are we not ourselves sailing to where they are, and, among the other things we carry, is there not also corn? What wrong are they doing us by carrying corn thither for us?"

148. So the spies, having seen everything, as I have said, and having been released, went home to Europe. Next after sending the spies, those of the Greeks who had sworn an alliance against the Persians sent messengers to Argos. The Argives tell their own story of what happened, as follows: they had information, they said, from the very beginning, of the stirring of the Persian preparation against Greece, and with this information they came to know that the Greeks would try to enlist them against the Persian. So they sent messengers to Delphi to ask the god what would be the best thing for them to do. They had, they said, just had six thousand of their best fellow countrymen killed by the Lacedaemonians[41] and Cleomenes, son of Anaxandrides—that, indeed, was why they were now sending to Delphi. In answer to their question, the Pythia declared:

Hated you are of your neighbors, but dear to the gods immortal.
Keep still your spear at rest, and stay in your seat well guarded.

41. In 494 B.C. Cf. 6.77 ff.

And guarded, too, keep your head; and your head shall save
your body.

This prophecy the Pythia had made to them earlier. Afterwards,
when the messengers came to Argos and entered the council chamber and said what they had been told to say, the Argives say that
they made this answer to what was told them: they were ready to do
what was requested of them provided that the Lacedaemonians first
made a peace treaty with them for thirty years and provided that
they, the Argives, were given the leadership of one half of the confederacy. In justice, the whole leadership should be theirs, but they
would be contented with the half of it.

149. They say that this was the answer their council gave, even
though the oracle had forbidden them to make any alliance with the
Greeks. They said that they were very anxious for a thirty years'
peace, in spite of their fear of the oracle, so that their children might
grow up into men in those years. If there were not such a treaty, they
added, and if, in addition to the trouble that had already befallen
them, there was another disaster, this time inflicted by the Persians,
they might be, forever after, subjects of the Lacedaemonians. But
(said they) those of the messengers who were from Sparta made answer in the following terms to what the Argive council had put forward: in the matter of the thirty years' treaty, they must refer that to
a larger body at Sparta, but in regard to the leadership they had been
instructed to answer. They did so, to the effect that the Spartans had
two kings and the Argives only one; it would be impossible to force
from the leadership either of the Spartan kings, but there was no
objection to having the Argive as one with an equal right to vote
with the Spartan kings. At this, the Argives say, they found the
Spartan greed intolerable; they preferred to be ruled by the barbarians than to yield in anything to the Lacedaemonians. So they bade
the messengers get out of Argos before the sun should set; otherwise
they would be treated as enemies.

150. That is what the Argives themselves say about this. But
there is another story current through Greece, that Xerxes sent a
herald to Argos before he set out to march on Greece. This herald
came and said (so the story goes), "You men of Argos, this is the
word of King Xerxes to you. We believe that the ancestor from
whom we are descended is Perses, the child of Perseus, son of Danaë.

His mother was Andromeda, daughter of Cepheus. So we would be descendants of your stock. It is not right that we should make war on those who are of our own ancestry or that you should be our opponents, as you are when you take up the cause of others against us; you should remain by yourselves at peace. If all goes as I would have it, you shall be rated by me as high as any nation can be." It is said that the Argives, when they heard this, thought much of it; and for the moment they offered nothing and demanded no share in the command; but when the Greeks tried to enlist them on their side, because they knew very well that the Lacedaemonians would never give them a share in the leadership, they made the request for the share, so that, on this pretext, they might remain at peace.

151. There is some confirmation of this story in what some Greeks say took place many years afterwards. There happened to be in Memnonian Susa a delegation of Athenians about some other matter; this was headed by Callias, son of Hipponicus. At this same time the Argives had sent messengers to Susa to ask Artaxerxes, son of Xerxes, whether the friendship they had compounded with Xerxes still held, as they wished it should, or if they were considered as enemies by the present King. Whereat King Artaxerxes said the treaty certainly stood and that, for his part, he thought no city more his friend than Argos.

152. Now, whether Xerxes sent a herald to Argos with these proposals, and whether the messengers of the Argives went up to Susa and asked Artaxerxes about the matter of the friendship, I cannot exactly say, nor do I declare any other judgment in regard to this other than what the Argives themselves say. But this much I know: that if all of mankind should assemble, for market, their own vicious deeds, wanting to barter them for those of their neighbors, on close inspection of those neighbors' ill acts they would be glad enough to take back home again their own, which they had brought with them. So, in this, it is not the Argives who did the most shameful things. I must tell what is said, but I am not at all bound to believe it, and this comment of mine holds about my whole History. For there is another tale, too, to the effect that it was the Argives who summoned the Persian into Greece because, after the failure of their conflict with the Lacedaemonians, they wanted to have anything rather than a continuation of the trouble in which they lived.

153. That, then, is the story as far as the Argives are concerned.

But there were the other messengers, who went from the allies to Sicily to make contact with Gelon; and among them was Syagrus of Lacedaemon. The ancestor of this Gelon, the man who settled in Gela, was from the island of Telos, which lies off Triopium. When Gela was settled by Lindians from Rhodes and by Antiphemus, this ancestor of Gelon was not left behind. As time went on, his descendants became hierophants of the underworld goddesses[42] and held this post continuously. One of their ancestors, Telines, had got the priesthood in the following way. There were some men who were banished after a factional fight among the Geloans, and they took refuge in the city of Mactorium, which lies inland of Gela. These men Telines restored to Gela without any force of men to help him but only the sacred things belonging to the underworld goddesses. Where he got these from, or whether he owned them of himself, I cannot say. But with them as his resource he restored the exiles, on condition that his descendants should be hierophants of the goddesses. In face of this story, I am amazed that Telines achieved such an action. For such acts I have always thought were those of no ordinary man but of a resolute soul and masculine strength. But according to the inhabitants of Sicily, Telines was exactly the opposite, being naturally a soft fellow and of a womanish disposition.

154. Anyhow, he got the hereditary priesthood. And when Cleandrus, son of Pantares, died, who had been monarch of Gela for seven years (he was killed by a Geloan named Sabyllus), Hippocrates, brother of Cleandrus, took the throne. During the reign of Hippocrates, Gelon, who was a descendant of Telines the hierophant— along with many others, including Aenesidemus, the son of Pataecus—was one of Hippocrates' bodyguards. Before long, because of his merit, he was appointed to command all the cavalry. For when Hippocrates besieged the people of Callipolis and the Naxians and the Zanclaeans and the people of Leontini, and faced the Syracusans, too, and many of the barbarians, in all these wars Gelon shone the brightest. Of these cities I have mentioned, not one escaped slavery by Hippocrates except for Syracuse. The Syracusans were saved by the Corinthians and Corcyraeans after they were worsted in a battle by the river Elorus, and their rescuers won them peace by making

42. Demeter and Persephone.

the Syracusans surrender to Hippocrates Camarina, which had from of old been the property of the Syracusans.

155. When Hippocrates had ruled as many years as his brother Cleandrus, he died near the city of Hybla, where he had been campaigning against the Sicels. Thereupon Gelon in name fought for the cause of the sons of Hippocrates, Euclides and Cleandrus; for indeed, the citizens did not want any more to be governed by despots.[43] But in fact, as soon as he had beaten the Geloans in battle, he robbed the sons of Hippocrates and took the rule himself. After this lucky hit, when those of the Syracusans who are called "gamoroi"[44] were expelled by the democracy and by their own slaves (who are called Cyllyrians), Gelon restored these gamoroi from the city of Casmenae to Syracuse and took over that city also. For the popular party in Syracuse surrendered both the democracy and the city to Gelon when he approached it.

156. Once he had got Syracuse, Gelon troubled himself the less about Gela and turned its government over to his brother, Hiero. But Syracuse he strengthened, and Syracuse was everything to him. And Syracuse flourished and increased right away. First of all, Gelon brought all the Camarinaeans to Syracuse and made them citizens of it and demolished the city of Camarina itself; and then he did the same thing to more than half of the citizenry of Gela. In the case of the Megarians in Sicily, after they had been besieged and had come to terms with him, he selected out the rich among them, who had begun the war against him and expected to be killed on that account, and brought them to Syracuse and made them citizens of it. However, the democratic party in Megara, who were quite without complicity in making war on him and never looked to have any evil overtake them from him, them too he brought to Syracuse but sold them for export from Sicily itself. He did the same to the Euboeans in Sicily, with the same discrimination. He did so because in both cases he thought that democracy was a thankless fellow to share a house with himself.

157. So in this way Gelon had become a great prince. And now, when the messengers of the Greeks came to Syracuse, it was with

43. That is, he fought against the Geloan people, who had risen in revolt against the ruling family.
44. Landowners.

him that they held their converse: "The Lacedaemonians and their allies have sent us to enlist your aid against the barbarian. We make no doubt but that you have heard of his coming against Greece— this man of Persia, who is about to bridge the Hellespont, and, leading all the host of the East from Asia, make war on Greece, in pretext that he is attacking Athens, but it is in his head to bring all of Greece under him. You have gained greatly in power, and a great portion of Greece is yours, as you are master of Sicily; so help us now, who are the saviors of Greece for freedom; indeed, join in that freeing of Greece. All of Greece, if she is united, draws together, is a mighty hand, and we are fighters of consideration for any invader. But if some of us are traitors and others are unwilling to help, and if what is left as the sound portion of Greece is slight, then there is the very present danger that all Greece will fall. Do not think that if the Persian defeats us in battle and subdues us, he will not go on to you; take your measures against him before that happens, for in helping us you are helping yourself. It is the well-planned act that most often has the prosperous outcome."

158. That is what they said, but Gelon attacked them vehemently, in these words: "You men of Greece, it is with a selfish argument for yourselves that you have ventured to come and summon me to be your ally against the barbarian. When I begged you to bear a hand with me in the fight against a barbarian enemy—when my quarrel was joined with the Carthaginians—and when I kept urging you to avenge the murder of Dorieus,[45] the son of Anaxandrides, at the hands of the Egestans, and when I offered to join in freeing the trading ports—from which you have derived all sorts of advantage and profit—*you* did not come to help, either for my sake or to avenge the murder of Dorieus; and, as far as you are concerned, all of our territory is now the province of the barbarian. It does not matter; things have turned out well for me. But now, when the war has come round to yourselves, has arrived among *you*, now you remember Gelon! But though I have met with dishonor from you, I will not be like you. I am ready to help you with two hundred ships of war, and twenty thousand soldiers, and two thousand cavalry, and two thousand archers, and two thousand slingers, and two thousand light-

45. See 5.42–46.

armed to run alongside of the cavalry. I make my offer, besides, to
furnish food for the whole Greek army till we fight to the finish. But
I make this offer with one condition: that I shall be the Captain and
leader of the Greeks against the barbarian. On no other condition
will I go myself or send any others."

159. When he heard that, Syagrus could bear it no longer and
said, "Loud would be the lamentation of Agamemnon, son of Pelops, if he heard that the leadership had been taken from the Spartans by Gelon and the Syracusans![46] Make no further talk about your
condition—that we shall surrender the leadership to you. If you are
minded to help Greece, know that you will do so under the orders of
the men of Lacedaemon. If you do not think it fit to obey our orders,
do not come to our help."

160. To this speech, Gelon, seeing how hostile the words of Syagrus were, made his last definitive speech: "My friend from Sparta,
when insults get to the inside of a man, they are wont to rouse his
fury. But you, for all the insults your speech has contained, will not
persuade me to show the same ugliness in my answer. Since you
cling so to the leadership, it is natural that I should cling to it even
more, inasmuch as I am leader of an army many times as large as
yours and of many more ships. Since my proposal has been repug-
nant to you, I will abate my first condition to some degree. Suppose
you lead the land army and I the fleet. Or if it is your pleasure to
command the fleet, I am willing to take the land army. And you
must either rest satisfied with these conditions or go away bereft of
such allies as we are."

161. Such was Gelon's offer; but the messenger from Athens answered before he of Lacedaemon could do so: "King of Syracuse,
Greece did not send us to you as in need of a leader but of an army.
You are clearly not minded to send an army unless you are to be the
leader of Greece, so greedy are you for that military command. As
long as you were demanding the command of all the Greek host, we
of Athens were content to keep silent, knowing well that the Laconian was able to make an answer for both of us. But since now, when
you are turned aside from the project of commanding the whole, you
are demanding the command of the fleet, here is this for you: even if

46. The first part of this sentence is based on *Iliad* 7.125.

the Laconian were ready to surrender this to you, we are not. This command is ours, providing the Lacedaemonians do not want it. If they want to have the command, we will stand down for them, but we will not yield the command at sea to anyone else. For it would then be in vain that we had acquired the greatest force of sea-shoremen in Greece,[47] if, being Athenians, we should concede the leadership to the Syracusans—we who are the oldest race in Greece, we who are the only ones who have not changed our country, and Homer, the epic writer, has declared that the best man at Ilium to arrange and order the host was ours.[48] So there is no reproach due to us for speaking as we do."

162. Gelon answered: "My friend from Athens, you seem to have officers, but there will be no men. Since you will yield nothing and wish to have all, be off with you home, with all speed, and tell Greece that her spring has been taken out of the year." The point of this comment was this: it is clear that the spring is the most regarded part of the year, and so his own army was of the Greek host. So Greece deprived of his alliance he likened to the spring being taken out of the year.

163. This was the business that the Greek envoys transacted with Gelon, and so they sailed away. But Gelon feared for the Greeks, that they would be unable to beat the barbarians; yet he also treated his going to the Peloponnese under orders of the Lacedaemonians as a thing terrible and insupportable, inasmuch as he was monarch of Sicily; so he disregarded the road he had traveled before and took to a new one. As soon as he learned that the Persian had crossed the Hellespont, he sent, with three penteconters, Cadmus, the son of Scythes, a Coan, to Delphi with much money and propositions of friendship, to watch which way the battle would go; if the barbarian should win, he was to give him the money and earth and water for Gelon's territories; if the Greeks won, he was to bring it back home.

164. This man Cadmus, who had before this taken over from his father a princedom over the Coans that was well established, quite

---

47. This seems to be a reference to the large new fleet that Themistocles, not long before, had induced the Athenians to build (above, chapter 144).

48. Menestheus, in *Iliad* 2.552.

voluntarily and with no impending danger to force him, but out of sheer justice, turned over the power to the commonalty of the Coans and went off to Sicily. There the Samians gave him the city of Zancle, which he took over and settled, its name being changed to Messene. Now, as I said, this man Cadmus, who came to Messene in such a way as I have described, was sent on this mission by Gelon because of the justice he had known to be in him from other proofs. Indeed, Cadmus, to crown the other just acts he did, left the following as by no means the least: he became master of the great deal of money with which Gelon entrusted him, and, though he could have taken possession of it, he refused; for when the Greeks won the sea fight and Xerxes was gone off home, Cadmus returned to Sicily with all the money.

165. But this is also said by those who live in Sicily: that Gelon, even though he was to be under orders of the Lacedaemonians, would have come to the help of the Greeks had it not been for Terillus, son of Crinippus, prince of Himera. Terillus was driven out of Himera by Theron, son of Aenesidemus, prince of Acragas. And at about this time Terillus came with an army of Phoenicians and Libyans and Iberians and Ligurians and Elisyces and Sardinians and Corsicans—some thirty thousand men—with Hamilcar, the son of Hanno, as their general. Hamilcar was king of the Carthaginians, and it was through guest-friendship with Terillus that Terillus persuaded him to help him, and particularly through the ardent support of Anaxilaus, son of Cretines, the prince of Rhegium, who gave his own children as hostages to Hamilcar and brought him into Sicily to help his father-in-law. For Anaxilaus had married the daughter of Terillus. Her name was Cydippe. So, according to this story, it was thus that Gelon was not able to help the Greeks and so sent the money to Delphi.

166. The Sicilians also say this: that Gelon and Theron defeated Hamilcar, the Carthaginian, in Sicily on the very same day that the Greeks beat the Persian at Salamis. Hamilcar was a Carthaginian on his father's side and a Syracusan on his mother's, and he had gained the monarchy among the Carthaginians because of his bravery in action. Yet when the battle was engaged and he was being routed, he disappeared, I understand. Neither alive nor dead was he ever discovered anywhere, although Gelon went to all lengths to find him.

167. The Carthaginians themselves say—and the story is likely enough—that the barbarians fought the Greeks in Sicily from dawn till late evening (so long was the fight protracted), and that all that time Hamilcar remained in camp, sacrificing and offering for favorable results whole bodies of victims on a great pyre. But when he saw the rout of his troops happening and he was at that moment pouring the libations on the victims, he threw himself headlong into the pyre and so, being completely consumed by the fire, vanished. Whether Hamilcar vanished as the Phoenicians say or in some other way, as the Carthaginians and Syracusans say, the people sacrifice to him and have made memorials to him in all the cities of the colonists, the greatest monument of all being in Carthage itself.

168. That is what happened in Sicily. But the people of Corcyra made answer to the envoys and took such action as I shall now show. The same envoys had tried to enlist their help as had come to Sicily, and the arguments they used were the same as they had used with Gelon. The Corcyraeans promised them that they would send help at once, saying that it was certainly not for them to stand idly by and see Greece in her death throes. If Greece went under, there was nothing for them, the Corcyraeans, the very next day, but to become slaves; hence they must at all costs help her. This answer had a very fair appearance; but when they had to send help, their thoughts were quite otherwise. They manned sixty ships and made a great to-do about putting to sea, and touched on the coast of the Peloponnese; but there they kept the ships at anchor off Pylos and Taenarum in the Lacedaemonians' country. They, too, were craning their necks to see which way the war would go; for they had no hope that the Greeks would win but thought that the Persians would win a big victory and would come to rule all Greece. Their action was expressly what it was so that they would be able to say to the Persians: "King, the Greeks would have enlisted us for this war; and the power we possess was none of the least, nor our ships the least numerous, for of these we could have furnished the most—after the Athenians themselves; but we would not oppose you or contrary you in any way." By arguments like these they hoped to win more than any other of the Greeks, a thing which, in my opinion, would have actually happened. But for the Greeks they also made up an excuse, which in fact they used; for when the Greeks blamed them for the help they did not send, they declared that indeed they had manned sixty ships

of war but had been foiled by the Etesian winds in their attempt to round Cape Malea. That was why they did not make it to Salamis; it was no cowardice that made them fail to take part in the battle.

169. So they tried to fool the Greeks. But the Cretans, when the appointed envoys of the Greeks tried to get them on their side, did as follows. They sent envoys to Delphi to ask the god whether it would be for their benefit to go to the aid of the Greeks. The Pythia answered, "You fools, are you not satisfied with the tears that Minos sent you in his wrath for the help you gave Menelaüs, because the others [49] would not help avenge *his* death in Camicus, but you helped *them* take vengeance for a woman stolen away by a barbarian from Sparta?" When the Cretans heard that, they gave over any project of helping the Greeks.

170. The story goes that Minos, when he sought for Daedalus, went to Sicania (which is now called Sicily) and there met a violent death. After a time, the Cretans, all except for the people of Polichne and Praesus, were bidden by the god to go with a great host to Sicania; and for five years they besieged the city of Camicus, which in my day the Agrigentines occupied. At last they could neither take it nor stay there any longer to starve, and so they left the siege and went away. As they sailed, they were near Iapygia when a great storm overtook them and forced them on land. Their vessels were shattered, and they had no way of conveyance back to Crete. So they founded there the city of Hyria and remained there and, instead of Cretans, became Messapian Iapygians and, instead of islanders, mainlanders. From this city of Hyria they founded others, from which, long afterwards, the Tarentines tried to drive them and, in so doing, endured a terrible defeat. This indeed was the greatest slaughter of Greeks of all that we know, both of the Tarentines themselves and the people of Rhegium. These latter had been forced by Micythus, son of Choerus, to come to the help of the Tarentines, and they died to the number of three thousand. There was no counting how many of the Tarentines died. Micythus was a servant of Anaxilaus and was left behind as the governor of Rhegium. It was this man who was banished from Rhegium and settled in Tegea, in Arcadia, and dedicated all those statues at Olympia.

171. This account of the people of Rhegium and Tarentum is an

49. I.e., the Greeks, who did not help the Cretans.

addition, a side issue, to my *History*. But into Crete, left thus desolate, there came and settled, according to the story of the Praesians,
another population, chiefly Greeks, and then, in the third generation after the death of Minos, came the Trojan War. In it the Cretans played a brilliant part in helping Menelaus. But when they
came home again from Troy, there befell them and their livestock a
famine and a sickness, and so for the second time Crete was emptied
of her people. Those who dwell there now are the third nation of
Cretans, along with the remnants of the second. It was by reminding
them of these things that the Pythia prevented the Cretans when
they would have gone to the help of the Greeks.

172. The Thessalians at first Medized only under stress of necessity, as they clearly showed that they did not like the contrivances of
the Aleuadae. For as soon as they learned that the Persian was about
to cross into Europe, they sent envoys to the Isthmus. In the Isthmus
were gathered the counsellors chosen from the cities of Greece—
from the cities, that is, that had the better thoughts for Greece herself. These envoys of the Thessalians came to them and said, "Men
of Greece, the Olympian pass must be guarded in order that Thessaly
and all of Greece may be sheltered from the war. We are ready to
help you guard it, but you must also send a large army; if you do not
do so, we would have you know that we will make terms with the
Persian. We have no obligation, because we are in the advanced
position in Greece, to be the only ones to die for the rest of you. If
you do not want to assist us, there is no compulsion that you can
apply to us; for there is no compulsion that is stronger than sheer
want of power. For ourselves we will certainly try to contrive some
form of safety."

173. That is what the Thessalians said. In the face of this, the
Greeks determined to send a land army, by sea, to guard the pass.
When the army had assembled, it sailed through the Euripus, and
when it came to Alus, in Achaea, it disembarked and marched to
Thessaly, leaving the ships where they were, and came to Tempe, to
the pass that goes from lower Macedonia into Thessaly along the
course of the river Peneus, between the mountains Olympus and
Ossa. There the assembled Greek army encamped, to the number of
ten thousand men-at-arms, and they had, besides, the Thessalian
horse. The general of the Lacedaemonians was Euaenetus, son of

Carenus, who had been chosen from the polemarchs to command, although he was not of the royal stock. Of the Athenians, the commander was Themistocles, son of Neocles. But they remained in this position for only a few days; for messengers came from the Macedonian, Alexander, son of Amyntas, urging them to go off home and not stand in the pass "to be trampled underfoot by the invading army"—and he referred to the multitude of the enemy's army and his ships. That is what the messengers said, and the Greeks thought it good advice and that Alexander was their friend, and they took the advice. Myself, I think that fear was the persuasive force, once they learned that there was another pass into Thessaly, by upper Macedonia, through the country of the Perrhaebi, near the city of Gonnus (it was indeed the invasion road that Xerxes took). So the Greeks reembarked in their ships and went back to the Isthmus.

174. That was the expedition to Thessaly when the King was about to cross into Europe and was still in Asia—indeed, at Abydos. So the Thessalians, being abandoned by their allies, Medized, but now with enthusiasm and being no longer of two minds at all, so that they proved themselves very valuable men to the King.

175. The Greeks, as soon as they came to the Isthmus, debated, in view of Alexander's words, as to how and in what country to make their stand to fight the war. The winning opinion was for guarding the pass of Thermopylae. It was manifestly narrower than the pass into Thessaly and was, moreover, nearer their own land. (The mountain track, through which those of the Greeks who were destroyed at Thermopylae *were* destroyed, was not yet known of by them until they came to Thermopylae and heard about it from the Trachinians.) They decided that, if they guarded this pass, they would stay the entry of the barbarian into Greece, while their fleet should sail around to Artemisium, in the territory of Histiaea. The two forces would then be near enough to one another to communicate as how things were going with each; the lie of the land is as follows.

176. Artemisium first. The Thracian sea contracts to a narrow channel between the island of Sciathus and the mainland of Magnesia. After this strait comes Artemisium, a beach on the coast of Euboea and, on it, a temple of Artemis. The entrance through Trachis into Greece is, at its narrowest, fifty feet wide. But actually this is

not the narrowest stretch of the whole country, which is right in front of Thermopylae and behind it; behind, at Alpeni, it is only a wagon-track wide, and in front, at the river Phoenix, near the city of Anthela, it is again a mere wagon-track. To the west of Thermopylae is a mountain, trackless, high, and sheer, stretching to Mount Oeta. To the east of the road there are only the sea and marshes. In the pass itself there are warm springs, which the natives call Chutri,[50] and there is an altar of Heracles there at them. A wall had been built across this pass, and in the old days there was a gate in it. The Phocians built this wall in fear when the Thessalians came from Thesprotia to settle the land of Aeolia, which they now possess. Inasmuch as the Thessalians were trying to subjugate them, the Phocians took this advance measure, and they turned the hot water into the pass so that the place became a mass of gullies; all their contrivances were designed to prevent the Thessalians getting access to their country. This old wall had indeed been built a great while before, and most of it had, through time, fallen to the ground. The Greeks decided to raise these walls again, to keep the barbarian out of Greece. The village nearest to the road is called Alpeni, and the Greeks figured that they would be able to provision themselves from there.

177. This region, then, seemed to the Greeks most suitable. For they examined all in advance and came to the conclusion that the barbarians would not be able here to use their numbers or their cavalry, and so it was here they resolved to withstand the invader. As soon as they learned that the Persian was in Pieria, they broke up their assembly at the Isthmus and advanced, some by land to Thermopylae and others by sea to Artemisium.

178. The Greeks, then, went with speed to their several stations. But at that time the Delphians were consulting the god, in terror for themselves and for Greece; they were directed to pray to the winds, for these would be great allies for Greece. The Delphians received this oracle and first declared the terms of the oracle to such Greeks as wished to be free; by this announcement they earned the everlasting gratitude of these Greeks, who were in horrible fear of the barbarian. After that, the Delphians made an altar to the winds in Thyia, where is now the sanctuary of Thyia, the daughter of

50. "The Pots."

Cephisus, after whom the place takes its name, and there they approached the winds with sacrifice.

179. So the Delphians propitiated the winds according to the prophecy, and they still do, to this day. But the fleet of Xerxes started from the city of Therme; their ten fastest-sailing ships laid their course straight for Sciathus, where were three Greek ships on advance guard, one from Troezen, one from Aegina, and one from Attica. These, when they sighted the Persian ships, took to flight.

180. The ship of Troezen, with Prexinus in command, was immediately captured by the pursuing barbarians; they then took out the handsomest man that served aboard her to the prow of the ship and cut his throat. They regarded it as a right good omen that the first Greek they had taken prisoner was the handsomest. The man's name was Leon, so perhaps he had also his name to thank for his fate.[51]

181. The Aeginetan ship, whose commander was Asonides, even gave the Persians some trouble. For Pytheas, son of Ischenous, was serving on board, the man who proved himself the best man that day. When his ship was captured, he stayed fighting until he was fairly butcher's meat. He then fell, but not dead, and there was breath in him still. The Persians who manned the ships took elaborate care for his survival because of his valor; they treated his wounds with myrrh and bound them round with strips of fine linen, and when they brought him back to their own camp, they displayed him to the whole army and, in their admiration for him, treated him really well. But the others they captured aboard that very ship they treated just as slaves.

182. Thus two of the ships were captured. The third, whose commander was Phormus, an Athenian, took to flight, and he ran her aground at the mouth of the Peneus; the barbarians got the shell of the boat but not its crew; for as soon as the Athenians had beached the ship, they jumped off her and made their way through Thessaly till they came safe to Athens.

183. Of all these things, the Greeks who were stationed at Artemisium were informed by beacon fires from Sciathus; when they

51. The meaning here is obscure. Apparently it means that the unlucky sailor's name being Leon ("Lion") gave a particular pleasure to his killers, as denoting the king of beasts.

did learn of them, they took fright and changed their anchorage from Artemisium to Chalcis, to keep guard over the Euripus, while they left day-watchmen on the heights of Euboea. Of the ten barbarian ships, three were wrecked on the reef between Sciathus and Magnesia, which is called the Ant. Then the barbarians brought out a white pillar and set it on the reef;[52] and, since the way was now clear, their whole fleet sailed out from Therme, eleven days after the King himself had marched from there. It was Pammon of Scyros who was mainly their guide to the reef in their passage. The barbarians sailed all day long and made Sepias, in the land of Magnesia, and the beach that lies between the city of Casthanaea and the cape of Sepias.

184. Until they reached this place and Thermopylae, the forces of the barbarian sustained no losses at all, and their numbers, as I find by calculation, were still: in ships that came over from Asia, 1,207, and the whole sum of the nations that were aboard was 241,400 men, reckoning 200 men to a ship.[53] On board each of these ships there were, apart from the natives who were fighting aboard, 30 men each who were Persians, Medes, and Sacae; the sum of this additional contingent therefore comes to 36,210. I shall add to this, and to the original number, the crews of the penteconters, treating 80 men, more or less, as the number on each penteconter. There were gathered, as I said before, some 3,000 of these transports.[54]

52. The white pillar served as a danger signal, to warn the rest of the fleet of the sunken reef.

53. We here enter into the vexed question of the size of Xerxes' invading force. It is worth noting that Herodotus makes it perfectly clear that these numbers are based on what he himself regards only as reasoned guesses of his own. The extreme example of this is the addition of camp followers as being as many again as the fighting men. There is hardly any doubt that the final Herodotean figure is greatly exaggerated. Perhaps it is as well to remember the extraordinary discrepancy between the thousands of the French slaughtered at Agincourt and the negligible British losses in the account given in Shakespeare's Henry V. Surely the Greeks wanted to believe that immense numbers of Persians invaded Europe and that the defending forces were tiny. All the same, one may disregard Herodotus' figure of five million and, making all sensible deductions, still see that the odds were overwhelmingly against the Greeks.

54. The word penteconter means "a boat with fifty oars." However, the transports mentioned clearly include the penteconters, and there are, all together, three thousand of such boats.

There would be in these, then, 240,000 men. This would be the sea force as it came out of Asia, to the number of 517,610 men. The infantry came to 700,100, and the horsemen to 80,000. I will add to these the Arabian camel-drivers and the Libyan charioteers, making 20,000 men. So you see, if both navy and army are added together, the total comes to 2,317,610. So far I have mentioned only the host of fighting men that were brought over from Asia, without the service train and corn-bearing vessels and those who sailed on them.[55]

185. I must still add to all that I have listed in the numbers those armed forces that Xerxes brought from Europe. Here I must simply state my own belief. The ships that the Greeks from Thrace and the islands off Thrace furnished were 120. The men involved in the manning of these ships come to 24,000. The land forces were furnished by the Thracians, Paeonians, Eordi, Bottiaei, Chalcidians, Brygi, Pierians, Macedonians, Perrhaebi, Enienes, Dolopians, Magnesians, Achaeans, and those who lived along the seaboard of Thrace. I *think* that there were from these nations 300,000. These must be added to the forces from Asia, and so the full list of the fighting men comes out at 2,641,610.

186. This is simply the fighting force. But the service train that went with them and the crews of the small corn-carrying boats and

55. There is something very curious here. Herodotus is clearly meticulous in his calculations; all the other numbers but one come out right (the exception is the number of bushels of grain consumed daily by Xerxes' forces [chapter 187], where his arithmetic is off). But even the preliminary study of the number of fighting men here looks quite impossible, simply in terms of provisioning and movement. Aeschylus, a source contemporaneous with the actual battle of Salamis, more or less confirms Herodotus' number of the *ships* in the fleet. In any case, the proportion of Persian to Greek ships works out at six to one, which is perhaps a conceivable balance between the Great King and his Greek opponents. The numbers of *men* involved, both on land and shipboard, cannot be right. One is left with the paradoxical conclusion that Herodotus qua historian failed to see the importance of a major error in the numbers tabulated or, rather, a major error in the human possibility that there could have been this number of people there. As I mentioned before, the figures for Agincourt are equally ludicrous but are produced in *Henry V* with all the solemn emphasis of fact. Anyway, what is startling in Herodotus is the *combination* of extreme accuracy in compilation and no natural incredulity when the figures reckoned produce an impossibility.

the carriers that were also larger transports that came with the army—the men in these must, I think, be at least as many as the fighting men, if not more. But I am willing to take these as just as many, and neither more nor fewer. If they are equal in numbers with the fighting forces, there will be as many tens of thousands of them as of the others.[56] Thus 5,283,220 was the number of men whom Xerxes, son of Darius, led as far as the Sepiad headland and Thermopylae.[57]

187. This is the number of the whole of Xerxes' fighting force; but no one could give the exact number of the women who baked the bread, or of the concubines, or the eunuchs, or the transport animals and baggage-carrying cattle and Indian dogs that came with the army—of all these creatures no one could count the numbers, they were so large. So I do not wonder that the streams of some rivers gave out; no, rather I wonder that there was food enough for so many tens of thousands of people. For I find in my calculations that if each man got one choenix of wheat a day, and not more, there would every day be used up 1,100,340 bushels, and I am not figuring into my calculations the food for the women, eunuchs, baggage animals, and dogs. And of those many tens of thousands of men, for handsomeness and size there was none worthier than Xerxes to hold that power.

188. So the fleet set out and sailed and finally put in at a place in the Magnesian country midway between the city of Casthanaea and the Sepiad headland. Then the first ships to arrive lay close by the land, and the others, beyond them, lay at anchor. For inasmuch as the beach is not a large one, the ships lay eight deep, with their prows pointing toward the sea. That is how it was that night; but with the dawn, the sky being cloudless and windless, the sea started to boil up, and a great storm and hurricane of wind fell upon them— that wind, a northeaster, that is called by the local people the

56. This is not just as silly as it sounds. The army lists on which Herodotus apparently drew were based on a system of decads and their multiples—tens, hundred, thousands, etc. Thus he is saying here: "Further scores of thousands and tens of thousands are involved."

57. Note the rhetorical flourish of Xerxes' patronymic at the conclusion, and note also that Herodotus' grounds for making the enumeration at this point are that this was *before* the disastrous storm that destroyed so much of the Persian armament.

"Hellespontian." Those who marked how the wind was rising, and those whose anchorage made it possible, pulled their ships on shore before the storm got them, and so they themselves and their ships survived; but of such of the ships as the storm caught afloat, some were driven on the rocks of Pelion called the Ovens, and some on the beach. Others, still, came to grief on the Sepiad headland itself, and others were wrecked at the city of Meliboea, and others at Casthanaea. There was no resisting this storm at all.

189. It is said that the Athenians had summoned Boreas, the North Wind, to help them, being so bidden to do by a prophecy, there having been another oracle given them to "call in their son-in-law to help them." Now, according to the Greek story, Boreas married an Attic wife, Orithyia, daughter of Erechtheus. The Athenians construed this in terms of a marriage connection with themselves, so the tale goes, and saw Boreas as their son-in-law. They were at their station in Chalcis in Euboea when they saw that the storm was rising, and then, or even before then, they sacrificed to Boreas and Orithyia and called on them to come to their help and to destroy the ships of the barbarians, even as before, at Athos.[58] Now, whether this was why Boreas fell upon the barbarians as they anchored there, I cannot say. But the Athenians say that Boreas came to their help before and now again, and that this action[59] was his; and so, when they went home, they built a shrine to Boreas by the river Ilissus.

190. In this disaster they say that, at the least, there were no fewer than four hundred ships lost, and of men the loss was beyond counting, and a vast amount of property. So that Aminocles, son of Cretines, a Magnesian, who was an estate-owner about the Sepiad headland, was immensely benefited by the shipwreck. Afterwards he picked up many gold cups that had been dashed ashore, and many of silver, and found treasures of the Persians besides. Altogether he gathered an unspeakable amount of property. He grew great in his wealth, thanks to these finds; but his luck did not hold otherwise,

58. This refers to the wreck of the Persian fleet that Mardonius had earlier led against Greece. See 6.44.

59. The storm. In connection with this account, recall the oracle about the helping winds in chapter 178. (Recall also Artabanus' warning about inadequate harbors in chapter 49.)

for, in his case too, there was a dreadful disaster that overtook him, in the grievous killing of his son.

191. Of corn-carrying transports and other freighters, there was no numbering the losses; so that the commanders of the fleet, fearing that they were in such bad shape that the Thessalians might attack them, built a high wall round their ships, made of the wreckage of the others; for the storm raged for three days. Finally the Magi, using victims and also casting enchantments upon the wind (through their wizards), and, besides this, sacrificing to Thetis and the Nereids, contrived to stop the storm on the fourth day—unless it stopped of its own will. They sacrificed to Thetis because they heard from the Ionians the story that it was from this country that Thetis was snatched away by Peleus, and so the whole shore about Sepias would belong to her and the other Nereids.

192. Anyway, on the fourth day the storm ceased. The daywatchers on the Euboean heights ran down from their positions on the second day after the storm's commencement and told the Greeks of all that had happened in the shipwrecking. Then the Greeks, when they learned this, made prayers to Poseidon the Savior and, having poured libations, hastened back with all possible speed to Artemisium, having formed the expectation that there would be very few ships left to oppose them.

193. So for the second time they came to Artemisium and lay there; and from that day to this they use the title Poseidon the Savior. The barbarians, when the wind ceased and the waves died down, got their ships to sea and sailed along the mainland and, rounding the cape of Magnesia, sailed straight into the gulf that stretches toward Pagasae. There is a place on this gulf in Magnesia where it is said that Heracles was left behind by Jason and his comrades of the Argo when they sailed after the Golden Fleece to Aea in Colchis. Heracles had been sent to fetch water for the ship, since it was the purpose of the Greeks to draw water from there and so launch out to sea. Hence the name of the place is Aphetae.[60] It was here that Xerxes' men anchored.

194. Fifteen of these Persian ships were much later than the rest at putting to sea, and they glimpsed the ships of the Greeks at Ar-

60. "Launching Place."

temisium. The barbarians thought that these were their own ships and they sailed into the midst of their enemies. The Persian commander was Sandoces, son of Thamasius, a man from Cyme, who was viceroy of that part of Aeolia. Him King Darius had once taken on the following charge and crucified when he was one of the royal judges: Sandoces had settled a suit unjustly for a bribe. As the man hung on the cross, Darius, as he summed things up, found that the royal house had had more of good than of ill from all that Sandoces had done. Then Darius, realizing that he had acted with more speed than wisdom, had him taken down from the cross. So he escaped King Darius and survived; but now that he had sailed into the midst of the Greeks, he was not to escape the second time. For the Greeks saw the approaching Persian ships, realized their error, and, putting to sea against them, easily took them captive.

195. There sailed on one of these ships, and was captured in it, Aridolis, prince of Alabanda in Caria, and, in another, a Paphian general, Penthylus, son of Demonous, who had brought twelve ships from Paphos and had lost eleven of them in the storm that happened off Sepias; with his one remaining ship he sailed to Artemisium and was captured there. These men the Greeks questioned on all that they wanted to know about Xerxes' army and got the information; they then sent them in bonds to the Isthmus of Corinth.

196. The barbarian fleet, apart from the fifteen ships I have mentioned as being commanded by Sandoces, came to Aphetae. Xerxes and the land army journeyed through Thessaly and Achaea and came into Malis three days after the fleet arrived. In Thessaly he set up a contest, matching his own horses against those of the Thessalians, having learned that the Thessalian horses were the best in Greece. However, the Greek mares proved very much inferior. Of the Thessalian rivers, only the Onochonus failed for the drinking of the host. But in Achaea even the very largest of them, the Apidanus, gave out, save for a small driblet.

197. When Xerxes came to Alus in Achaea, his guides, who wished to tell him everything, informed him of a local story, which has to do with the rites of Laphystian Zeus. The story went that Athamas, son of Aeolus, contrived the death of Phrixus, having plotted it with Ino, and so, in accordance with an oracle, the Achaeans lay upon the descendants of Phrixus certain hard trials.

They forbid whoever is eldest of the family to enter their town hall, which they call the People's Assembly, and they themselves see to the guarding of this. If the eldest does enter, he may not come out again, save to be sacrificed. The guides said, further, that many who were going to be sacrificed took fright and went away to another country; but if they returned and were caught, they were sent into the town hall. The guides showed Xerxes how the man is sacrificed, all covered up with fillets and led out with a procession. That is the fate of the descendants of Cytissorus, son of Phrixus, because the Achaeans, on instruction of an oracle, had made Athamas, son of Aeolus, a scapegoat for their country and were about to sacrifice him when this Cytissorus came from Aea in Colchis and protected him and, by doing so, brought the wrath of the god upon his own descendants. Xerxes, when he heard all that had happened, when he came to the grove, kept away from it himself and bade his whole army do so, and treated with reverence both the house and the precinct of the descendants of Athamas.

198. That is what happened in Thessaly and Achaea. From there, Xerxes marched into Malis along the gulf of the sea, where there is ebb tide and flood tide every day; and around this gulf is level ground, sometimes wide and sometimes very narrow, and the mountains around it are high and trackless and shut in the whole Malian country. They are called the Rocks of Trachis. The first city on this gulf as one comes from Achaea is Anticyra, beside which the river Spercheus flows from the country of the Enienes into the sea. At a distance of nearly twenty stades from this river there is another, called the Dyras. This is the river of which the story tells that it appeared and came to the rescue of Heracles when he was burning. Another twenty stades from there, there is yet another river, called the Black River.

199. Trachis is a city five stades distant from this Black River. This is the part of all this land that is widest between the sea and the mountains, on which the city of Trachis is built. The plain is about five thousand acres in extent. South of Trachis there is a ravine in the mountains that shut in the land of Trachis, and through this ravine the river Asopus flows along the lower foothills of the mountains.

200. South of the Asopus there is another river, not a large one, the Phoenix, which flows from these mountains into the Asopus river, and near this river—the Phoenix—is the narrowest place.

Here there is built only a wagon-track. From the river Phoenix it is fifteen stades to Thermopylae. In the country in between the river Phoenix and Thermopylae there is a village, the name of which is Anthele, past which the Asopus flows as it empties into the sea, and there is a wide space near the village in which there is a shrine of Amphictyonid Demeter and seats within for the Amphictyons and a temple of Amphictyon himself.

201. King Xerxes camped in the part of Malis that belongs to Trachis, and the Greeks camped in the pass itself. This place is called Thermopylae,[61] though the local inhabitants and neighbors call it The Gates. So each camped in these places, Xerxes being master of all the country to the north of Trachis, and the Greeks in control of the south and west, toward this part of the mainland.

202. Those of the Greeks who awaited the Persian in this place were: three hundred men-of-war who were Spartiates, and one thousand from Tegea and Mantinea—five hundred from each; from Orchomenus in Arcadia, one hundred and twenty, and, from the rest of Arcadia, one thousand; besides these Arcadians, from Corinth, four hundred, and, from Phlius, two hundred, and, of the Mycenaeans, eighty. These all came from the Peloponnese, and, besides, there were, from Boeotia, seven hundred Thespians and four hundred from Thebes.

203. Besides these there were Opuntian Locrians, in full force, and a thousand Phocians; these had been expressly summoned, for the Greeks had so called them, alleging through messengers that they themselves were but an advance guard of the rest, that the other allies were every day expected, and that the sea was under the strong guard of the Athenians and Aeginetans and those who had been assigned to the naval duty, and so these people who were so summoned need fear no danger; for, said the messengers, this invader of Greece was no god but a human being, and everyone that is mortal and everyone that shall be so has evil blended in his lot at his birth, and the greatest evil for the greatest of mortals. So the invader too, since he was mortal, must surely fall from his high hopes. When they heard this message, the Locrians and Phocians marched into Trachis.

204. These all had commanders, each city its own, but the one

61. The name means Warm (thermo-) Gates (pylae).

who commanded the whole army and was the most admired was the
Lacedaemonian, Leonidas, he that was the son of Anaxandrides,
the son of Leon, the son of Eurycratides, the son of Anaxandrus, the
son of Eurycrates, the son of Polydorus, the son of Alcamenes, the
son of Teleclus, the son of Archelaus, the son of Hegesilaus, the son
of Doryssus, the son of Lebotes, the son of Echestratus, the son of
Agis, the son of Eurysthenes, the son of Aristodemus, the son of
Aristomachus, the son of Cleodaeus, the son of Hyllus, the son of
Heracles.[62] This man Leonidas became king of Sparta, though quite
unexpectedly.

205. For there were two elder brothers of his, Cleomenes and
Dorieus, and so Leonidas had been very far from any thought of the
kingship. But when Cleomenes had died childless of male issue, and
when Dorieus was already also gone, having met his end in Sicily,
the kingship devolved upon Leonidas, both because he was older
than Cleombrotus, who was the youngest son of Anaxandrides, and
because he had married Cleomenes' daughter.[63] He, then, it was
who came to Thermopylae, having picked the usual force of three
hundred, selecting those Spartans who had children;[64] he also came
bringing those Thebans whom I have already enumerated, whose
commander was Leontiades, son of Eurymachus. Leonidas made a
particular issue of bringing these with him, more than any other
Greeks, because they were very seriously accused of Medism. He

62. Here again the rolling list of patronymics marks the solemnity of the
occasion, just as the single patronymic of Xerxes did when he was cited as the
Persian leader in 7.186 (see also 7.11). I think one must also associate this tremendous list of names, connecting the existing Spartan king with Heracles, so
far in the past, with the euphonic effect that the reading would produce. And
here again one should notice that much of this writing is based on the idea of
"publication" through public readings.
63. Cleomenes was Leonidas' *half*-brother. For Anaxandrides' two wives and
two sets of children, see 5.39–48.
64. It is not clear whether "those who had children" are, in addition to the
regular three hundred, a special regiment of the Spartan king or whether the
three hundred themselves were selected on the criterion of having children. But
there is no mistaking the reason for the criterion. Thucydides, in Pericles' Funeral Speech, speaks of how those who were parents and had sons to lose could
not debate issues of war and peace on the same terms as those who had none.
These selected Spartiates were committed both by their social position and by
their parenthood to be those for whom the survival of Sparta would mean most.

urged them to the war to find out whether they would in fact send their men with him or would cry off from such a clear support of the Greek alliance. The Thebans sent them indeed, but their mind was not the same as the sending implied.

206. The Spartiates sent Leonidas and his men first, so that the other allies, seeing them there, would serve and not Medize, which they would do if they saw the Spartans hanging back. Afterwards— since the celebration of the Carnean month was presently a hindrance to them—the Spartans intended, after they had performed the ceremony and left guards in Sparta, to go to the war speedily and in full force. The rest of the allies had similar thoughts and were minded to do just the same themselves. For in their case there was the Olympic festival, which fell in at just the same time as this outbreak of war. They never dreamed that the war at Thermopylae would be decided so quickly, and so they sent off their advance guards.

207. That was what they intended to do. But the Greeks at Thermopylae, when the Persian came near the pass itself, were in sheer terror and debated whether to stay or go. The other Peloponnesians were for going to the Isthmus to guard it; but Leonidas, when the Phocians and Locrians buzzed angrily around him against this plan, gave his vote to remain where they were and to send messengers to the cities, bidding them come to their help, on the grounds that they that were there were too few to drive off the Medes.

208. While they were debating so, Xerxes sent off a mounted spy to discover how many the Greeks were and what were they doing. He had heard, when he was still in Thessaly, that there were small forces gathered here and that the leaders were Lacedaemonians and, among them, Leonidas, of the stock of Heracles. The horseman approached the camp and watched and surveyed—not, indeed, the whole camp, for it was impossible to see those of the Greeks who were stationed inside the wall, which they had restored and were now guarding. But he saw those who were outside, whose arms were stacked outside the wall, and it happened that at this time it was Lacedaemonians who were stationed outside. Some of these men he saw exercising and some combing their hair. When he saw that, he was amazed and noted their numbers; and having learned everything accurately, he rode back at his leisure, for no one pursued him; what

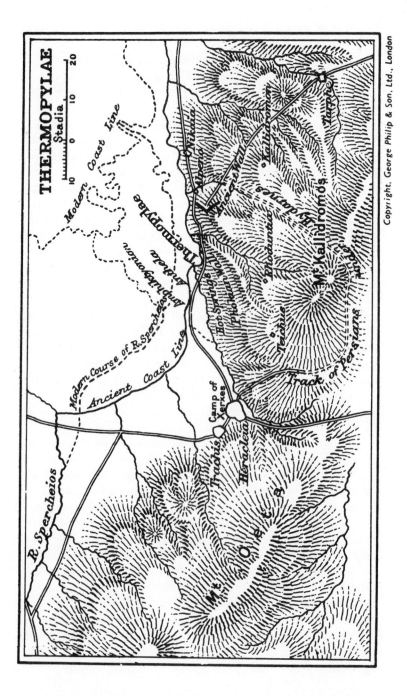

THERMOPYLAE

Stadia

10 0 10 20

Modern Coast Line

Modern Course of R.Spercheios

Ancient Coast Line

R. Spercheios

Lamia

Trachinian

Anthela

Thermopylae

Hot Springs

Phokian Wall

Asopos

Anopaia

Alpenos

Ancient Wall

Trachis

Camp of Xerxes

Heraclea

Teichius

Phoinix

Mt. Kallidromos

Track of Persians

Mt. Oeta

Copyright, George Philip & Son. Ltd., London

544

he encountered was indeed total indifference. So he went back to Xerxes and told him all he had seen.

209. When Xerxes heard his story, he could not conjecture from it the actual truth: that these men were making their preparations for being killed or killing others, so far as in them lay; he thought that what they were doing was something absurd, and so he sent for Demaratus, son of Ariston, who was in the camp. When he arrived, Xerxes asked him about all the details, for he wanted to know what it was that the Lacedaemonians were doing. Demaratus said: "You heard from me before about these men, when we were setting off for Greece; and when you heard what I had to say, you mocked me for telling you how I saw these matters would turn out; for my greatest endeavor, my lord, is, in your presence, to practice truth. So listen to me now: these men have come here to fight us for that pass; that is what they are making their preparations for. This is their custom: that when they are going to risk their lives, they make their heads beautiful. Know, then, that if you beat these, and those of them who are still in Sparta, there is no other nation in the world, my lord, that will withstand you and lift a hand against you. For now you are making your attack on the fairest kingship and fairest city among the Greeks, aye, and the bravest men." Xerxes thought what he said was past belief and asked him again how so few men as these would fight his, Xerxes', army. Demaratus said: "My lord, use me as a liar if things do not turn out as I say."

210. But his words did not convince Xerxes, who let four days go by, assuming that the men would run away. But on the fifth day, as they were not gone, and their standing there seemed to come of their shamelessness and folly, he sent against them Medes and Cissians; he was very angry and bade them capture the Greeks alive and bring them to his presence. The Medes charged the Greeks full tilt and had many of their own men killed. Others replaced them, and their attack did not cease, although they were very sorely mauled; but they made it quite clear to everyone, and especially to the King himself, that, though they had many men there, there were few *men*. The encounter lasted all day.

211. The Medes, after their rough handling, withdrew, and those Persians whom the King called the Immortals succeeded to the attack. Their commander was Hydarnes, and they assumed that they would do the task easily. But when they tangled with the Greeks,

they came off no whit better than the Medes had done but just the same. For they were fighting in a confined space and used spears shorter than those of the Greeks, and they could not avail of their superior numbers. The Lacedaemonians fought notably; all their performance was that of skilled soldiers against unskilled, and, in particular, they would at times turn their backs and give the impression of mass flight; but when the barbarians saw them fleeing and attacked them with war cries and all the din of battle, the Greeks turned round and destroyed tremendous numbers of the pursuing Persians; some few of the Spartans themselves were also killed at that time. As the Persians failed in their attempts to gain control of the pass, by their attacks in regiments or in all other ways, they finally withdrew.

212. During these encounters in the battle, the King, it is said, as he looked on, leaped thrice from his throne in fear for his army. This was the way the fight went that day, and on the next the barbarians had no better fortune. For the Greeks were so few that their enemies thought that they must all be wounded and so would be unable to lift their hands against them, and so they charged again. But the Greeks were ordered by regiments and nations, and each fought in turn, except for the Phocians. These were posted on the mountain, to guard the path. So when the Persians found the Greeks just the same as they had been the day before, they withdrew.

213. The King did not know what to do with this difficulty, and then Ephialtes, son of Eurydemus, a man of Malis, came to speak with him. Thinking that he would get a great reward from the King, he told him of the path that led over the mountain to Thermopylae, and so he destroyed the Greeks who stood firm there in the pass. Afterwards, this man, out of his fear of the Lacedaemonians, took refuge in Thessaly, and when he was in exile there, the Pylagori,[65] at the meeting of the Amphictyons at Thermopylae, proclaimed a price on his head. A long time later, he returned to Anticyra and there was killed by a Trachinian called Athenades. Athenades killed Ephialtes for some other reason (which I shall relate later on),[66] but he was no less honored by the Lacedaemonians for his deed on that account.

65. Representatives sent by the various states to the Amphictyonic council.
66. An unkept promise.

214. Ephialtes died, then, long after all these events; but there is another story told, that Onetes, son of Phanagoras, a Carystian, and Corydallus, from Anticyra, were the ones who spoke with the King and led the Persians around the mountain. I do not at all believe this. One must draw one's conclusions from the action of the Pylagori, on the Greek side, who put a price on the head of Ephialtes of Trachis and *not* on Onetes and Corydallus; surely they must have inquired out the truth of the matter; and we know that this was the reason why Ephialtes was banished. It *is* true, of course, that, even without being a Malian, Onetes might have known of that path if he had been very constantly in the locality; but no, it was Ephialtes who led the Persians round the mountain by the path! And that is the man I declare is the guilty one.

215. Xerxes, well satisfied with what Ephialtes promised to accomplish, was delighted and immediately sent Hydarnes and his men. They started out from the camp about the time the lamps were lit. This path had been found by the local Malians, and, when they found it, they had guided the Thessalians by it into Phocis at a time when, having barricaded the pass with a wall, the Phocians were safe from the war. From so long ahead, the deadliness of this path had been shown by the Malians.

216. This is how the path is: it begins from the river Asopus as it flows through the ravine, and the names of the mountain there and the path are the same: Anopaea. This Anopaea stretches along the ridge of the mountain and ends at the city of Alpenus, which is the Locrian town nearest to Malis, and at the rock that is called Blackbuttock and the place of the Cercopes,[67] where it is at its narrowest.

217. Along this path (which is as I have said) marched the Persians all that night, having crossed the river Asopus; they kept on their right the mountains of Oeta and, on their left, those of Trachis. The dawn was showing when they were on the summit of the pass. One thousand hoplites of the Phocians kept guard at this part of the mountain, as I said before, protecting their own country and guarding the path. For the lower pass was held by those I have spoken of, but the path over the mountain was guarded by volunteers of the Phocians, who had given their undertaking so to do to Leonidas.

67. Dwarfs with whom Heracles tried to deal.

218. This is how the Phocians realized that the enemy had climbed up the mountain: while the Persians were actually climbing, the Phocians had not noticed them at all, since the mountain was full of oak trees. But there was no wind, and finally, as was natural, the leaves under the feet of the Persians made a great sound, and so the Phocians jumped up and began to arm; immediately the barbarians were upon them. When the Persians saw men putting on their arms, they were amazed, for they thought that there was no one here to oppose them, and now they encountered an army. Hydarnes was afraid that the Phocians were Lacedaemonians and so asked Ephialtes what countrymen these were. When he was correctly informed, he drew up the Persians in battle order. But the Phocians, under the fire of many arrows that fell thick on them, fled to the top of the mountain, being convinced that the Persian attack had been mounted against themselves in the first place; and so they prepared to die. That was the feeling on the Phocian side; but the Persians with Ephialtes and Hydarnes paid no heed to the Phocians[68] but hurried down the mountain as speedily as they might.

219. For those of the Greeks who were in the pass at Thermopylae, it was the prophet Megistias who, as he looked at his holy offerings, first predicted that their death would come upon them with the dawn; after him, there were deserters, who came and told them that the Persians had made their way around them. This news came while it was still night; but the third informants were the day-watchers, who ran down from the peaks as the dawn was breaking. Thereupon the Greeks bethought them of what they ought to do, and their opinions were divided; for some were not in favor of leaving their post of battle, but there were also those of the contrary opinion. Afterwards, these split up, and some ran away and scattered, each to his own city; but there were others of them who made their preparations to stand where they were, with Leonidas.

220. It is said that Leonidas himself sent them away, out of care that they should not die there; but for himself and his Spartiates he thought it disgraceful to quit the post they had come to guard in the first place. I am myself strongly of this opinion: that when Leonidas saw that the allies were fainthearted and unwilling to run the risk in

68. Once Hydarnes knew that they were Phocians, not Lacedaemonians.

his company, he bade them be off home, but for himself it would be dishonorable to leave. If he stood his ground, he would leave a great name after him, and the prosperity of Sparta would not be blotted out. For there was a prophecy that had been given to the Spartiates by the Pythia when they consulted her about the war, just at its beginning. The prophecy said that either Sparta would be destroyed by the barbarians or the king of Sparta would be destroyed. This was the prophecy that the Pythia uttered in hexameters:

> For all of you people who dwell in Sparta, the city of broad
>   roads,
> your city is great and glorious, but by the manhood of Persia
> she shall be sacked—or she shall not, but then Lacedaemon's
>   watcher
> shall mourn for a king that shall die, from Heracles' race
>   descended.
> Neither the fury of bulls nor of lions shall stem the foeman,
> though force matches force; the power of Zeus in himself he
>   possesses;
> and none, I dare say, shall restrain him, until the one or the
>   other
> utterly shall be undone and utterly rent asunder.

I believe that Leonidas thought this over and wanted to store up the glory for the Spartiates alone; and so he sent off the allies rather than that those who went away should do so after a disorderly split in their counsels.

221. There is one more piece of evidence, and that a great one in my judgment of what happened; it is that the prophet who followed the army, this Megistias the Acarnanian (who is said to have been descended originally from Melampus), the man who predicted from his holy offerings the outcome of the event, was very openly ordered by Leonidas to go away, so that he might not share in the death of his comrades. But though so sent away, he would not go but sent home his only son, who was serving in the army.

222. So the allies who were sent away went off, and, in their going, obeyed the orders of Leonidas; but the Thespians and Thebans remained, the only ones to do so alongside of the Lacedaemonians. Of these, the Thebans did so unwillingly and against their own choice. For Leonidas kept them as a kind of hostages. But the Thespians were

right willing to remain; they said that going home was not for them, leaving Leonidas and his friends; they stayed and died with him. Their commander was Demophilus, the son of Diadromes.

223. At sunrise, Xerxes made his libations and, waiting till it was the time of the greatest crowd in the marketplace,[69] made his attack; this was how Ephialtes bade him do it. For the descent from the mountain was more direct and much shorter than the way round and the ascent. Now Xerxes' men attacked, and Leonidas' Greeks advanced far more than at the first to the broader part of the pass, making this outbreak as men who were going to their death. For it was the protection of the wall they had guarded, and on the previous days the Greeks had withdrawn into the narrow part and fought there. But now they joined battle outside of the narrows, and many of the barbarians fell; for behind their regiments their captains with whips in their hands flogged on every man of them, pressing them ever forward. Many of them, too, fell into the sea and were drowned, and even more were trampled to death by their comrades; for there was no heed of who it was that was dying. For the Greeks, knowing that their own death was coming to them from the men who had circled the mountain, put forth their very utmost strength against the barbarians; they fought in a frenzy, with no regard to their lives.

224. Most of them had already had their spears broken by now, and they were butchering Persians with their swords. And in this struggle fell Leonidas, having proved himself a right good man, and with him other famous Spartiates, of whom I know the names, as men worthy of the record; I have learned indeed the names of all the three hundred. On the Persian side, too, there fell, among many other distinguished men, two sons of Darius, Abrocomes and Hyperanthes, who were born to Darius by Phratagune, daughter of Artanes. Artanes was brother of King Darius and son of Hystaspes, son of Arsames. He it was who had married his daughter to Darius and gave her all the wealth of his house, since she was his only child.

225. So two brothers of Xerxes fell there, fighting; and over the dead body of Leonidas there was a fierce jostle of Persians and Lacedaemonians until the Greeks, by sheer bravery, dragged him away

69. This is simply a Greek expression for a certain hour of the morning. No reference is being made to an actual marketplace on the scene.

and four times routed their enemy. The battle was closely joined until the soldiers with Ephialtes arrived. But as soon as the Greeks realized that these had come, the fight changed its character; the Greeks retreated into the narrow part of the road, and, passing behind the wall, took up their position on the little hill, all massed together except the Thebans. This little hill is in the entrance of the pass, where now there is a stone lion in honor of Leonidas. In that spot the Greeks defended themselves with daggers—those who had any of them left—yes, and with their hands and their teeth, and the barbarians buried them in missiles, some attacking them from in front and throwing down their wall of defense, while those who had come round the mountain completed the circle of their attackers.

226. Of the Lacedaemonians and Thespians, for all that there were so many brave men among them, he that was said to be the bravest was a Spartiate, Dieneces. Of him there is a saying recorded, one that he uttered before the battle was joined: when he heard a Malian saying that, when the barbarians shot their arrows, the very sun was darkened by their multitude, so great was the number of them, Dieneces was not a whit abashed, but in his contempt for the numbers of the Medes said, "Why, my Trachinian friend brings us good news. For if the Medes hide the sun, we shall fight them in the shade and not in the sun."

227. This and other sayings of the same sort are recorded as having been the memorials of Dieneces the Lacedaemonian. After him, they say two Lacedaemonian brothers were the bravest, Alpheus and Maron, two sons of Orsiphantus. The most famous name among the Thespians was that of Dithyrambus, son of Harmatides.

228. They were buried there where they fell, and over them, as over those who had died earlier, before Leonidas had sent any troops home, was an inscription which said:

Here is the place that they fought, four thousand from
    Peloponnesus,
And here, on the other side, three hundred ten thousands
    against.

That was the inscription over them all; but over the Spartiates there was a particular one:

Go tell the Spartans, stranger passing by,
that here obedient to their words we lie.

This was for the Lacedaemonians; but for the seer there was this one:

Here lies Megistias; think on him, a brave man whom once
    the Persians
Killed when they crossed the Spercheus and came to the
    other side.
He was a prophet who knew, right clearly, the doom coming
    on him,
But he had not in his heart to desert the leader of Sparta.

It was the Amphictyons who set up these epitaphs and pillars in honor of the fallen, except for that for the prophet; this one, for the seer Megistias, was made for him, as a friend's tribute, by Simonides, son of Leoprepes.

229. There is a story about two of the Three Hundred, Eurytus and Aristodemus. They could both have used a shared excuse for going off safe to Sparta, having been released by Leonidas as they lay, severely in pain with their eyes, in Alpeni; or, if they had not wanted to go home, they could have died there with the others. But though they could have done either of these things, they could not agree between them, but they were minded to take different courses. Eurytus, when he heard of the Persians making their roundabout attack, asked for his arms and bade his helot take him into the thick of the fighting; when he did so, the helot who led him ran away, and Eurytus was killed in the crowd when he charged. Aristodemus was left behind, half-conscious. Now, if Aristodemus alone had been sick and so had come home to Sparta, or if they had made the return together, I do not think the Spartiates would have shown such anger. As it was, when one of them had died, who had the same excuse, but the other had refused to die, necessarily the Spartans were extremely angry with Aristodemus.

230. There are some who say that Aristodemus came safe to Sparta with the above excuse; but others say that he was sent as a messenger from the army and might have come back in time for the battle but would not do so; he dallied on the road and so saved his life, while his fellow messenger came in time for the battle and died.

231. When Aristodemus came home to Lacedaemon, he met

with insults and degradation. The form of the degradation was this, that no Spartiate would give him spark of fire or would speak to him, and his insult was that they called him "Aristodemus the Coward."

232. But at the battle of Plataea he set right all of the dishonor that had been laid upon him. It is said, too, that another of the Three Hundred was sent into Thessaly as a messenger and survived. His name was Pantites, and when he came back to Sparta he was so dishonored that he hanged himself.

233. The Thebans, whom Leontiades commanded, fought on as long as they were with the Greeks; but they fought under constraint against the King's army, and, when they saw that the Persians had the upper hand and that the Greeks who were with Leonidas were hurrying to the little hill, at that moment they broke off from them, and, stretching out their hands in surrender, they approached the barbarians, telling the absolute truth, which was that they were on the Persian side and had been among the first to offer earth and water to the King, but that under constraint they had come to Thermopylae and were innocent of any harm to the King. That was their plea, and they saved their lives; for they had the Thessalians as witnesses to the truth of what they said. They were not entirely successful, however, because, when the barbarians caught some of them approaching them, they killed them, and most of them, on Xerxes' orders, were branded with the royal brand, beginning with their general, Leontiades, whose son, Eurymachus, long afterwards was killed by the Plataeans when he led an army of four hundred Thebans and took possession of the city of Plataea.

234. Such was the fight of the Greeks at Thermopylae. Then Xerxes sent for Demaratus and asked him questions, saying, first of all: "Demaratus, you are a good man. It is the truth that has convinced me of that, for everything that you told me has come out your way. So now, tell me: How many are the Lacedaemonians that are left? And how many of them are soldiers like these men, or are they all so?" He answered: "My lord, the number of all the Lacedaemonians is great, and their cities are many; but what you want to know, you shall have knowledge of. There is in Lacedaemon a city, Sparta, with about eight thousand men in it, and these are all like the men who fought here. The rest of the Lacedaemonians are not the equals of these, but they are good men, all the same." Xerxes then said to him,

"Demaratus, what is the easiest way I can master these men? Tell me, you who know the ins and outs of their counsels, since you were their king."

235. He said, "My lord, if you are consulting me in all serious-ness, I must tell you the best way. Do you send to Laconia three hun-dred ships of your navy. There is an island off the Laconian coast called Cythera. Chilon, who was rated the wisest man among us, once said that it would be a greater profit to the Spartiates if it were drowned in the sea instead of floating on the top of it; for he always thought that some such danger as I am now suggesting to you might come of it. I do not mean that he had any advance knowledge of this invasion, but he dreaded alike all expeditions of men. Making this island as their base, let your fleet set about frightening the Lace-daemonians. When they have a war in their homeland, you need not fear that they will go to the help of the rest of Greece, though Greece should all be taken by your armies. Once all the rest of Greece is enslaved, there shall remain only Laconia, a weak rem-nant. But if you will not do this, here is what you must expect. There is in the Peloponnese a narrow isthmus. *At this place*, once all of the Peloponnesians have taken their oaths of support for one an-other, you may look to have battles tougher than this one was. But if you do as I say, this isthmus and the cities will yield without a fight."

236. After him there spoke Achaemenes, who was Xerxes' brother and admiral of the fleet; he happened to be present as they spoke, and he feared that Xerxes would be persuaded to do as Dem-aratus said. "My lord," he said, "I see that you are accepting the plans of a man who envies you your success and may even be betray-ing you. It is in just such conduct that the Greeks delight. For they are jealous of success and they hate what is bigger than themselves. If in the present contingency, in which we have lost four hundred ships in shipwreck, you send off another three hundred from your fleet to sail around the Peloponnese, your enemies will be on an equality with you for fighting. So long as the fleet holds together, it is too hard a handful for them to manage, and they will not fight on an equality with you at all; and the whole fleet will help the army, and the army, marching at the same time as the fleet moves, will help the fleet. If you split the two arms, you will not be able to help

them, nor they you. What I advise is that you reckon your own side of the business shrewdly and give no further thought to your opponents' side, as to where they will fight, what they will do, or how many they will be. They are well able to think for themselves, and so are we for *our*selves. If the Lacedaemonians come to confront the Persians in battle, they will surely not heal their present hurts."

237. Xerxes answered him: "Achaemenes, I think you speak well, and I will do as you say. But Demaratus says what he thinks is best for me, though he is worsted by you in this matter of judgment. I will certainly never believe of him that he is no friend to my cause; I judge from what he has told me before and from the very truth that one fellow countryman *does* have a grudge against another in the day of his prosperity and is his enemy by keeping silent; nor will such a fellow countryman give what he thinks is the best advice, even when he is asked for it, unless he be of extreme excellence—and there are few such. But a stranger-friend is the kindest thing of all to another stranger in the day of his success; and if the successful man asks for advice, the other will give him the best advice. So no more of this slander of Demaratus, who is a stranger and is *my* friend; I would have you all give it over for ever after."

238. That is what Xerxes said; and he went then through the bodies of the dead, and, in the case of Leonidas, when he learned that he was the king of the Lacedaemonians and their leader, he ordered his head to be cut off and put upon a pole. This makes me quite certain, in addition to other evidence, that King Xerxes was especially angry against Leonidas in life. For otherwise he would never have so outraged proper order against the dead man, since the Persians, more than any other people I know, honor men who are brave in war. Those whose duty it was to follow commands did as he bade them.

239. I return to the former point in my story. The Lacedaemonians were the first to learn that the King was launching an expedition against Greece, and so they sent away to the oracle at Delphi, where they were told what I mentioned a little while ago. But they had the information of the expedition in a remarkable way. For Demaratus, son of Ariston, this exile among the Medes, was, in my opinion (and reason is all on my side), no friend to the Lacedaemonians, but, still, one must guess that he did what he did either out of

Book Eight

1. The Greeks who received their orders for the fleet were these: the Athenians had a contingent of one hundred and twenty-seven ships. The Plataeans, by reason of their courage and enthusiasm, served jointly as crews with the Athenians, although they were quite inexperienced in seamanship. The Corinthians brought forty ships, the Megarians twenty. The Chalcidians manned twenty, though it was the Athenians who furnished the ships themselves; the Aeginetans eighteen, the Sicyonians twelve, the Lacedaemonians ten, the Epidaurians eight, the Eretrians seven, the Troezenians five, the Styrians two, and the Ceans two, and two penteconters. The Opuntian Locrians served with seven penteconters.

2. These were they who assembled in battle order at Artemisium,[1] and I have now declared the number of ships furnished by each people. The total number of the ships assembled at Artemisium was, apart from the penteconters, two hundred and seventy-one. The supreme commander was provided by the Spartiates—Eurybiades, son of Euryclides; for the allies refused to follow the Athenians as leaders; unless a Laconian was in the chief position, they declared that they would break up the projected force.

3. There had been talk at the beginning, before ever they sent to Sicily about the alliance, that one ought to trust the fleet to the Athenians. When the allies objected, the Athenians gave way; they thought what mattered most was the survival of Greece and knew very well that if there was a dispute about the leadership, Greece would perish—and that thought was correct, for strife within the nation is as much a greater evil than a united war effort as war itself is more evil than peace. So because the Athenians knew this, they put up no resistance, but yielded, but only so long as they had urgent

---

1. The sea fights at Artemisium, described in the first twenty-three chapters, were concurrent with the battle of Thermopylae, as Herodotus finally explains in chapter 15.

need of the others, as they later proved. For as soon as they had driven out the Persian and were fighting for *his* territory rather than their own, the Athenians stripped the Lacedaemonians of their primacy (though nominally this was because of the arrogance of Pausanias). But all this happened afterwards.[2]

4. As of now, the Greeks who had come to Artemisium, when they saw the large number of the barbarian ships launched at Aphetae and everywhere full of armaments—when, in fact, the fortunes of the barbarians had turned out altogether differently from what they had expected—were thoroughly afraid and thought of running away from Artemisium into the interior of Greece.[3] The Euboeans knew of these thoughts and begged Eurybiades to remain for a little while, until they could convey away their children and their household people. When they failed to convince him, they changed their tactics and gave the Athenian commander, Themistocles, a bribe of thirty talents, on condition that the fleet would remain and fight in defense of Euboea.

5. This is how Themistocles made the Greeks stop there. He gave a share—five talents—of the money to Eurybiades, as though the money came from himself. When Eurybiades had been persuaded, there remained only, among the rest, the Corinthian commander, Adimantus, the son of Ocytus, who put up any resistance. This man said that he would not hold the line but would sail away from Artemisium; but to him Themistocles said, and confirmed it with an oath, "You will not desert us, for I will give you more money than the king of the Medes would send you for deserting your allies."[4]

2. The reader should remember that Herodotus was certainly alive as late as 430 B.C. and very probably till 424. That is, he lived until the Second Peloponnesian War was well under way. There is no doubt that there existed many threads connecting the Greek national defeat of Persia with what happened afterwards, when Athens and Sparta split up and the League of Delos became the Athenian empire. What is very interesting but not so easy to determine is how much Herodotus saw the Greek-Persian struggle, especially in its later phases—during this campaign and the events detailed in book 9—as the preliminary, or as the shadow-anticipation, of the struggle within Greece for the hegemony, or primacy in power, between its two chief representatives, Athens and Sparta.

3. They had thought that only a small part of the Persian fleet had survived the storm. See 7.192.

4. There is a great deal of resistance on the part of the older and more respectable editors, like R. W. Macan and How and Wells, against this Herodo-

He had scarcely ended this statement before he sent three talents of silver to Adimantus' ship. So they were all made to change their convictions by gifts, the desires of the Euboeans were met, and Themistocles himself was the one who profited; for no one knew that he kept the rest of the money, but those who had the share in it believed that it had come from Athens for the actual purpose for which it was used.

6. So they remained in Euboea and fought their sea fights, and it turned out like this. When the barbarians came to Aphetae in the early part of the afternoon, they saw for themselves the few Greek ships lying off Artemisium, whose location they had already known; so they were eager to attack them in the hope of taking them. But they did not yet resolve to attack them head on, for fear that the Greeks, seeing them coming, might run away in flight and the darkness might cover their flight; they then (of course) would have fled away safely, whereas, by the barbarian account, there ought to be not so much as a fire-bearer to live as the survivor.[5]

7. This is how they dealt with the situation. They separated out two hundred ships from all the rest and sent these outside Sciathus, that they might not be observed by the enemy when they sailed around Euboea; they were to sail about Caphereus and around Geraestus into the Euripus.[6] Thus they would trap the Greeks, the one group going there and barring their retreat, while they themselves attacked frontally. With this in mind, they sent away the ships they had put under these orders, while they themselves never thought of attacking the Greeks on that self-same day or before they

tean account of bribery practiced by Themistocles on his colleagues. The same accounts, however, persist in Plutarch. It is quite true that we have no means of checking Herodotus' sources for such statements, but neither is there any evidence, of a solid kind, in either How and Wells or Macan, *against* the bribery. They just don't believe that Greeks of the fifty century B.C. would be guilty of conduct unsuitable to nineteenth- and twentieth-century English professional military men.

5. The fire-bearer carried the sacred fire that was kept alight for the sacrifices to the gods that were regularly made on behalf of the army.

6. Euboea is a large and very long island, separated from mainland Greece by a narrow stretch of water. The Greek ships lying at Artemisium were not far from the northern entrance of the strait. The Persian contingent was to sail around Euboea and up into the Euripus—the very narrowest part of the strait—to block the Greeks' southern escape route.

got their signal clear, from those who were sailing round, that they had arrived. So they sent off this party and set about numbering the rest of the ships that were at Aphetae.

8. At the time when they were numbering the ships, there was in the encampment one Scyllias of Scione, the best diver of his time, who on the occasion of the wrecking of the fleet off Pelion saved many of their belongings for the Persians and won much for himself, too. This man Scyllias had apparently, for some time before this, made up his mind to desert to the Greeks but had had no such good opportunity as now. How he managed to reach the Greeks from where he was I cannot say exactly, but I would be surprised if what is told about the matter is true. For it is said that he dived into the sea at Aphetae and never emerged until he came to Artemisium—that is, he traversed some eighty stades underwater.[7] There are other stories about this man that are very like lies, and some that are true. About this particular thing I would like to record my own opinion, which is that he came to Artemisium in a boat. When he came there, he brought news immediately to the commanders of how the shipwrecks had happened and about the sending of the ships round Euboea.

9. When the Greeks heard that, they held discussions with one another. Though much was said, the opinion prevailed that they should wait out that day where they were and bivouac and then, once midnight was about past, put to sea and meet the ships that were sailing round Euboea. But after this, as no one came sailing against them, they waited out the late afternoon of the day following and then attacked the barbarians, because they wanted to put to the proof his method of fighting and the tactic of breaking the line.[8]

10. Now, when Xerxes' soldiers and his generals saw the Greeks attacking them with such a small body of ships, they thought them surely mad and put their own ships to sea, for they were confident that they would easily win against them; indeed, their hopes were very reasonable, since they saw how few were the Greek ships and how they themselves had many times more and better ships to sail. So in their contempt for the enemy they maneuvered them into the

7. About ten miles!
8. See above, 6.12.

center of their own ships. Now, those of the Ionians who were well disposed toward the Greeks served there unwillingly and were bitterly sorry to see the Greeks encircled, for they were convinced that not a one of them would ever see home again, so feeble appeared the power that was theirs; but those who were glad at what was happening strove with one another for which would be the first to take an Athenian vessel and so win the King's awards, for among the Persians it was the Athenians who were most talked of.

11. But when the signal was given, the Greeks turned their prows toward the enemy and drew their sterns together, and at the second signal they went hotly to work, though hemmed in in a small space and fighting front to front. They took thirty ships of the barbarians and Philaon, son of Chersis, a man of great note on the Persian side; he was the brother of Gorgus, king of Salamis.[9] The first of the Greeks who captured an enemy ship was an Athenian, Lycomedes, son of Aeschraeus; and so he won the award of honor. They fought very evenly in the sea battle, and while they were at it in these terms the night came on them and parted them. The Greeks sailed back to Artemisium and the barbarians to Aphetae, having waged a fight very different from what they had expected. In this sea fight Antidorus, a Lemnian, alone among the Greeks on the King's side to do so, deserted to the Greeks. For that action the Athenians awarded him land in Salamis.

12. When night came on (it was midsummer), there fell, all night long, a violent rain, with violent thunder from Pelion; the dead men and the wrecks drifted in to Aphetae and fell foul of the prows of the vessels and became confused with the oars. And those of the enemy who were there and heard of this were greatly frightened, thinking that they would surely perish, in the evil plight in which they were. For before they could catch their breaths after the wrecking and the storm that had befallen them off Pelion, they were faced with a stiff sea fight and, after the sea fight, the violent rainstorm and mighty torrents that poured down upon the sea, and then this savage thunder.

9. Not the famous island near Athens but a city on Cyprus (for Gorgus of Cyprus, see 5.104 and 115). However, the Salamis mentioned at the end of this chapter *is* the Athenian Salamis.

13. Such was their night; but for those deputed to sail around Euboea, the same night was much wilder, inasmuch as it overtook them in the open sea, and a harsh end they had. For it was as they were sailing around the Hollows of Euboea that the storm and the rain assailed them, and they drifted before the wind and had no idea of where they were headed, and so came on the rocks. All this was done by the god, that the Persian armament might be made equal with that of the Greeks and not much greater.

14. So these last met their end at the Hollows of Euboea. But the barbarians at Aphetae, when to their great joy the day dawned, remained with their fleet inactive and were well content in their present evil case not to stir. But fifty-three Attic ships came to the help of the Greeks, and their arrival put great heart into them; and along with them came a message saying that the barbarian ships that were sailing round Euboea had all been destroyed by the storm that had happened. So the Greeks waited for the same hour as before and, putting to sea, attacked the Cilician ships, and, having destroyed these, they sailed back again to Artemisium at nightfall.

15. On the third day the commanders on the barbarian side, indignant that they should be so injured by so few vessels, and in fear of how Xerxes would take it, waited no longer for the Greek assault but issued battle orders and put their ships into action in the middle of the day. And it turned out that these same three days saw these sea fights and also the land battle at Thermopylae. All the struggle was the same for those at sea and those with Leonidas—and the struggle was to guard a pass.[10] On the Greek side, their cry was, "Let us not let the barbarians into Greece," and, on the Persian, "We must destroy the Greek host and gain mastery of the channel." So now it was the men of Xerxes who under orders sailed to the attack and the Greeks who stood steady, off Artemisium. The barbarians formed into crescent order and tried to encircle the Greeks and so trap them.

16. Then the Greeks sailed out and on, and the two sides clashed. In this battle they were on an equality with one another. For Xerxes' host, by reason of its size and numbers, was its own destroyer, for the ships fell foul of one another and became entangled; yet the Persians

10. The Euripus and Thermopylae, respectively.

held out and did not yield, for they thought it truly terrible that they should be routed by so few ships. And many Greek vessels were lost and many men too, but the ships and the men lost on the barbarian side were even more. And so they fought and parted.

17. In this sea fight the Egyptians proved themselves the best men on Xerxes' side; among their other great deeds they captured five Greek ships, crews and all. Of the Greeks on that day, the Athenians were the best and, among the Athenians, Clinias, son of Alcibiades, who served at his own expense with two hundred men and his own ship.

18. When they broke away from one another, both sides were glad to hasten to anchorage. The Greeks, when they broke off and retreated from the battle, were in possession of the dead and the wrecks; but they had been very roughly handled—and, not least, the Athenians, one half of whose vessels were disabled—and at length they resolved to retreat into the inner parts of Greece.[11]

19. But Themistocles had the thought that, if the Ionian and the Carian contingents could be split off from the Persians, the Greeks might be able to conquer the rest; so when the Euboeans were driving their flocks down to the sea beside him, he summoned a meeting of the generals and said that he thought he had the means of making the best of the King's allies desert him. Only so far did he disclose his design; under the circumstances, he said, what ought to be done was for them to take and sacrifice as many of the flocks of the Euboeans as they pleased. It would be better, he said, for the army to have them rather than the enemy. He advised each of the commanders to have his own men light a fire; as to the actual moment of leaving, he would himself take thought for that, so that they would reach Greece unscathed. They were pleased to do this, and so they lit fires at once and set about the flocks.

20. The Euboeans had indeed neglected the oracle of Bacis as mere nonsense and so had conveyed nothing out of the way, nor had they made any preliminary stowing-away of anything to meet the trouble, as they might have with war already in front of them; and so they were the cause of their own downfall. This is the oracle of Bacis that they had got:

11. I.e., to the seas nearer home.

Heed when a man, strangely speaking, shall cast on sea-
    waters his yoke,
Yoke of papyrus; then keep from Euboea's coasts bleating flocks.

They had made no use of these lines; but in their present troubles,
and those they must look for, they must needs now make use of their
calamity to the utmost degree.[12]

21. That was what the Greeks were doing when the scout came
in from Trachis. For there was a scout posted at Artemisium, one
Polyas, a man of Anticyra, whose assignment it was (and he had a
rowboat ready for his purposes) to communicate to those in Thermopylae if the fleet should be engaged. In the same way, Abronichus, the son of Lysicles, an Athenian, was with Leonidas, ready to
use a triaconter to bring the news to those at Artemisium if anything
new happened to the land army. This Abronichus came and gave
word of what had happened to Leonidas and his army; and when the
Greeks heard that, they delayed no longer about their departure but
retreated in the order in which each contingent was posted—first
the Corinthians and last the Athenians.

22. Themistocles, after picking out the quickest-sailing ships,
went around to the drinkable-water places and on the rocks cut messages that the Ionians read the next day, when they came to Artemisium. The inscriptions said: "You men of Ionia, you do not deal
justly in making war on us, who are your ancestors, and in enslaving
Greece. The best thing you can do is to join us; but if that is not in
your power, you should withdraw and be neutral between us and beg
the Carians to do the like; and if you cannot do either of these
things, but you are so under the yoke of necessity that you cannot
desert the Persian, do you, during the action, when we are engaged,
prove coward of your own will, remembering that you are born of
our stock and that it is from you that our quarrel with the barbarian
came in the first place." Themistocles wrote this, I think, with two
things in mind: either that the King might not notice the writing
and so the Ionians might be made to desert him and come over to
our side, or, when the matter was reported to Xerxes and fault found
with it, it might make him distrustful of the Ionians and make him
hold them back from the sea battles.

---

12. Having neglected to use the oracle to guide them, they must now use
their misfortune for the same purpose.

23. These were the inscriptions that Themistocles wrote. But directly after this there came to the barbarians in a small boat a man of Histiaea, who brought word that the Greeks had run away from Artemisium. The Persians, out of sheer disbelief, kept the messenger under guard and sent their fastest ships to spy out what had happened; and when these brought back word of the actual fact, then, just at sunrise, the whole armament sailed off to Artemisium. There they stopped until midday and then sailed to Histiaea. On their arrival they captured the city of the Histiaeans and overran all the seaboard towns of the Ellopian country of Histiaea.[13]

24. While they were there, Xerxes, having first taken some measures of readiness about the dead bodies, sent a herald to the fleet. The making-ready of the bodies had been as follows: those of his own army that were dead at Thermopylae—which were twenty thousand—of these he left only one thousand, and the rest he dug trenches for and buried, with leaves piled upon them and earth he had scraped up, so that the men from the fleet might not see them. When the herald crossed over to Histiaea, he assembled all the men in the encampment and said: "Allies of ours, King Xerxes gives, to any of you who will, permission to leave his post and come and see how he fights against those fools of mankind who thought that they could surpass the power of the King."

25. After that proclamation, there was nothing rarer to find than a boat, so many wished to see for themselves. They crossed over and went through the dead and saw. They were all sure that all who were lying there were Lacedaemonians and Thespians, though they were seeing helots as well. Not that those who crossed over were fooled by Xerxes' action about his own dead. For the thing was indeed absurd. There were the thousand dead men lying in plain view, but the others—the Greeks—had been conveyed to one place and lay all together, to the number of four thousand. They spent the day on their sightseeing, and on the morrow they sailed away to Histiaea and the ships, and Xerxes' army moved off on their march.

26. There came then to them a handful of deserters from Arcadia—needy men, who would be employed. The Persians brought them into the King's presence and inquired what the Greeks were doing. One of the Persians put the questions on behalf of them all.

13. The northern half of Euboea.

The Arcadians said that the Greeks were celebrating the Olympic festival and were watching gymnastic and horse contests. So the King asked them what was the prize for which they competed. They said it was the giving of an olive crown. At that, Tigranes, son of Artabanus, said something very fine, though the King thought him a coward for it. For Tigranes, when he heard that the prize was a wreath and not money, burst out with the words, "What, Mardonius! What sort of men have you led us to fight against, who contend, not for money, but purely for the sake of excelling?" This is what he said.

27. In the meantime, after the disaster of Thermopylae had happened, the Thessalians at once sent a herald to the Phocians. They had had a grudge against them for ever and ever, and now more than before, after this last disaster. For the Thessalians and their allies had invaded the Phocian country in full force, not many years before the King's expedition, and they had been worsted by the Phocians and very roughly handled. For when the Phocians had been hemmed in on Parnassus, they had with them the seer Tellias, an Elean, and at that time Tellias invented the following trick for them: he smeared some six hundred of the best of the Phocians with gypsum, both the men themselves and their arms, and attacked the Thessalians by night. He told his men to kill whomsoever they saw that was not whitened. The sentries of the Thessalians, who were the first to see the men, were terrified, thinking that this must be something unnatural, and fled, and after the sentries the rest of the army did likewise. And so the Phocians got possession of four thousand dead and their shields; one half of those they dedicated at Abae and the other half at Delphi. The tenth that was paid from this battle set up the great statues that stand around the tripod in front of the temple at Delphi, and there are others like them that are dedicated at Abae.

28. That is what the Phocians did to the Thessalian infantry when the Thessalians were besieging them; and when their cavalry invaded the Phocian country, they did them cureless damage. For in the pass near Hyampolis the Phocians dug a great trench and buried in it empty jars; they then carried the spoil back on to the top of the trench and made it like the rest of the land nearby, and stood their ground against the charge of the Thessalians. These charged, assuming that they would carry all before them, and fell straight into the jars, where their horses' legs were broken.

29. For both these things the Thessalians bore the Phocians a settled grudge, and now they sent them a herald and said: "You men of Phocis, now at last concede that you are less men to win a fight than we are. For in the old days we were always preferred above you by the Greeks, so long as we liked the Greek side best. But now we have such influence with the barbarian that it rests with us whether you shall lose your country and become slaves into the bargain. For all that we have complete power over you, we do not bear grudges; but in return for our restraint you must pay us fifty talents of silver, and then we will guarantee to turn aside the invasion from your country."

30. That was the Thessalian proposition. The Phocians were the only people in that country who did not turn to the Persian interest, for no other reason, if my guess is right, than the hatred they bore for the Thessalians. For if the Thessalians had helped the Greek cause, in my opinion the Phocians would indeed have Medized. When the Thessalians made their offer, the Phocians answered that they would give no money. They could Medize just as well as the Thessalians, if they so chose, but they would not, if they could help it, prove traitors to Greece.

31. When these words were returned to them, the Thessalians were so furious with the Phocians that they became guides to the barbarian on his journey. From Trachis into Doris they pushed on— for there stretches at this point a narrow tongue of Dorian land, a matter of thirty stades in width,[14] which lies between the countries of Malis and Phocis, which was anciently Driopis and is indeed the country that was motherland of the Dorians who live in the Peloponnese. This Dorian land the barbarians did not injure in their invasion, for the people had turned to the Persian interest, and the Thessalians would not suffer the Persians to injure them.

32. From Doris into Phocis they went, but they failed to catch the Phocians themselves. For some of them had ascended the heights of Parnassus; and the peak of Parnassus, called Tithorea, is big enough to accommodate a large number. This peak is near the city Neon and lies off to itself. To it the Phocians carried their goods and went up into it themselves. But the most of the Phocians made off to the Ozolian Locrians, to the city of Amphissa, above the Crisaean

14. Close to four miles.

plain. The barbarians overran all Phocis, for in this direction the Thessalians guided them; and whatever country they occupied, they set it ablaze and ravaged it, and they put fire to the cities and the 'holy places.

33. On they marched by the banks of the Cephisus and ravaged all, and they burned down the city of Drymus, and Charadra and Erochus and Tethronium and Amphicaea and Neon and Pediea, and Tritea and Elatea, and Hyampolis and Parapotamii, and Abae, where there was a rich shine of Apollo, with store of many treasuries and dedications, and there was and still is an oracle there. This holy place too they plundered and burned. And they pursued and caught some of the Phocians near the mountains, and some women, too, they murdered with the multitude of those that raped them.

34. The barbarians passed by Parapotamii and came to Panopea, and there their army split and parted asunder. The largest and strongest part of it marched with Xerxes himself in the direction of Athens and went into Boeotia, to the country of Orchomenus. The whole people of Boeotia Medized, and some Macedonians who were assigned the task, and had been sent by Alexander, saved the towns. They saved them by making it clear to Xerxes that the Boeotians were on the Median side.

35. These, then, were those of the barbarians who came on this road; but the others, with guides, marched on the shrine of Delphi, keeping Parnassus on their right. All the land of Phocis that they occupied they took, marauding and burning the cities of the Panopeans and those of the Daulians and Aeolidaeans. They split off from the other body of troops and came this way so as to plunder the shrine at Delphi and show its treasures to King Xerxes. But Xerxes knew about everything of consequence in the temple (as I learn) better than what he had left in his palace at home, through the numbers of those who told him of it; he was particularly aware of the dedications of Croesus, son of Alyattes.

36. The Delphians, learning of this, were reduced to every sort of terror, and in the greatness of their fear they consulted the oracle about the holy property—whether they should dig it into the ground or carry it away into some other country. But the god bade them to stir nothing; he was well able, he said, to protect his own. The Delphians, when they heard that, thought about themselves. They sent

their women and children across the water to Achaea, and the most of themselves went up to the peaks of Parnassus and carried their goods to the Corycian cave, while others stole off to Amphissa in Locris. All of the Delphians abandoned the city, except for sixty men and the prophet.[15]

37. When the barbarians drew near in their invasion and were looking at the temple from outside, the prophet, whose name was Aceratus, saw the sacred arms, which no human hand might touch without impiety, brought out from inside the shrine and laid in front of the temple. So he went to tell the Delphians of the miracle. But when the barbarians in their haste to invade were near the temple of Athena Pronaia, there befell them miracles greater than the first one. For it was indeed a wonder that arms of war should stir of themselves and come to lie outside the temple; but what happened after that was the most marvelous of anything miraculous yet seen. For when the barbarians were, in the rush of their attack, near the temple of Athena Pronaia, at that moment' there fell upon them bolts from heaven, and from Parnassus two chunks of cliff broke off and crashed upon them with a vast din and destroyed many of them, while from the temple of Athena there came a shout and a war cry.

38. With the conjunction of all this, the barbarians were seized by panic. The Delphians seeing them in flight, descended on them and killed a large number. Those who survived fled straight for Boeotia. Those of the foreigners who came home spoke, as I learn,

15. Of course, as everybody knows, the oracles at Delphi were given by the Pythia, who was a woman. But according to 7.111 and other sources, there was also a class of men attached to Delphi, "the prophets," from which the one "prophet" came. This man interpreted the medium (the Pythia), and what were incoherent cries and hysterical outbursts were turned by him into proper oracular responses. Thus runs the ordinary comment in How and Wells. The trouble is that those who have in more recent times made a study of the Delphic oracle (e.g., H. Parke and D. Wormell) are not sure that the procedure at the oracle was the same earlier and later, and most of the evidence we have is for centuries later than the fourth. There is also the difficulty that Herodotus himself several times says that the Pythia herself delivered the oracle "in hexametric verse." I think that the procedure described by How and Wells and the function of "the prophet" were as they say but that the times when the Pythia herself spoke "in hexametric verse" are regarded as special, almost miraculous, occurrences, as in the reference to the father of Pisistratus in book 1.

of seeing other miraculous things besides these. They said that two warriors of more than human stature pursued them hotly, killing men as they did so.

39. The Delphians say that these two were native heroes, Phylacus and Autonous, whose precincts are near the temple—that of Phylacus right by the road, above the shrine of Athena Pronaia; that of Autonous near the Castalian spring, above the peak Hyampaea. The rocks that fell from Parnassus were still there undisturbed in my time, lying in the sanctuary of Athena Pronaia, into which they rolled in their wild course, as they went through the barbarians. Such, then, was the departure of these men from the temple.

40. The Greek navy, leaving Artemisium, put in at Salamis at the request of the Athenians. The Athenians asked this so that they might themselves get their women and children safely out of Attica and, furthermore, make up their minds as to what to do. For as things were, they had to lay their plans as men who had been deceived in their judgment. For they had thought that they would find the Peloponnesians, in full force, awaiting the onset of the barbarians in Boeotia, but not a particle of this was true; instead, they learned that the Peloponnesians were fortifying the Isthmus, which showed that what they were really concerned with was the survival of the Peloponnese; this was what they were going to guard and let everything else go. That was the knowledge the Athenians had when they asked the Greeks to put the fleet into Salamis.

41. The rest of the Greeks made for Salamis, but the Athenians for their own country. After arriving there, they made a proclamation that every Athenian should save his children and household in any way he could. Then most sent them off to Troezen, and some to Aegina, and some to Salamis. They hurried to bring what belonged to them into safety, because they wished to comply with the oracle,[16] and also for this reason, particularly: the Athenians say that there is a large snake that inhabits the shrine, as a guard of the Acropolis. They say, besides, that they make him a monthly provision of "food," as for a real creature—the monthly food being a honey cake. This honey cake in all time past had been eaten up, but, now only, it was left untouched. When the priestess told them this, the Athenians

16. The reference is to the "wooden wall" in 7.141.

were even more bent on leaving the city, thinking that Athena herself had deserted the Acropolis. So when all was conveyed away, they themselves returned to the fleet.

42. When the Greeks who sailed from Artemisium had put in at Salamis, the rest of the fleet heard of it and came in from Troezen; for the arrangement had been that they would assemble at Pogon, the harbor of Troezen. There gathered at Salamis far more ships than had fought at Artemisium, and from more cities. The commander over them was the same as he had been at Artemisium, Eurybiades, son of Euryclides, a Spartiate, though not of the royal blood; but the Athenians supplied by far the most ships and those that had the greatest speed.[17]

43. Those who served in this campaign were: from the Peloponnese, the Lacedaemonians, with sixteen ships; the Corinthians, with the same complement of ships as at Artemisium; the men of Sicyon, with fifteen ships; the Epidaurians, with ten; the Troezenians, with five; the men of Hermione, with three. All of these, with the exception of the men of Hermione, were of Dorian and Macedonian stock and were the last to come from Erineus and Pindus and Dryopis. The people of Hermione are Dryopians and had been driven out by Heracles and the Malians from the country now called Doris.

44. These came with the armament as Peloponnesians. Of those who came from the mainland outside of the Peloponnese, the Athenians alone furnished more ships than all the rest, to the number of one hundred and eighty. For at Salamis the Plataeans did not serve along with the Athenians, and this is why: when the Greeks were retiring from Artemisium and were near Chalcis, the Plataeans disembarked to the part of Boeotia opposite to Chalcis and set about the conveyance of their household people to safety. So they were left behind in the process of saving these people. (The Athenians, at the time when the Pelasgians held all of what is now called Greece,

17. The Greek here means actually "the ships that *sailed best.*" I have rendered it as though this meant "fastest sailing," which I think is what is meant; but one must remember that these ships depended primarily on sails and, when wind was not available, on oarsmen; so their speed and maneuverability—their "best sailing"—depended on the skill and physical fitness of the crew as well as on the material aspects of the ship.

were themselves Pelasgians and were called Cranai; but in the time of their King Cecrops they acquired the name Cecropidae; and when Erechtheus took over the rule, they changed their name again, to Athenians; and when Ion, the son of Xuthus, became their commander-in-chief, they were called, after him, Ionians.)

45. The Megarians had the same complement of ships as at Artemisium, and the Ambraciots came with seven ships, and the Leucadians with three (these were of Dorian stock, from Corinth).

46. Of the islanders, the Aeginetans brought thirty ships. They had indeed other ships, ready manned, but with these they did guard duty on their own land and fought at Salamis with their thirty best sailing vessels. The Aeginetans are Dorians from Epidaurus; the name of their island was originally Oenone. After the Aeginetans there were the Chalcidians, who furnished the twenty ships that they had at Artemisium, and the Eretrians, with their seven. These are Ionians. After them were the Ceans, who furnished the same number;[18] they are of Ionian stock, from Athens. The Naxians furnished four; they, being sent to join the Medes by their fellow countrymen, as the other islanders were, disregarded these commands and came over to the Greek side at the urging of Democritus, a distinguished man among them and, at this time, their trierarch. The Naxians are Ionians, of Athenian stock. The Styrians sent the same number of ships as at Artemisium, the Cythians one and a penteconter; these people are, both, Dryopians. There also served on the Greek side the Seriphians, Siphnians, and Melians, these being the only ones of the islanders who did not give earth and water to the barbarian.

47. These were all that served who came from south of the Thesprotians and the river Acheron; for the Thesprotians live on the borders of the Ambraciots and Leucadians, who came from the farthest of the countries. Of those who live farther off than these, only the people of Croton brought help to the Greeks at their time of peril, with one ship, whose commander was Phaÿllus, a three-times victor in the Pythian games. The people of Croton are by race Achaeans.

48. Now, all the rest served with triremes, but the Melians,

18. As at Artemisium.

Siphnians, and Seriphians with penteconters. The Melians are, in stock, Lacedaemonians, and they furnished two penteconters; the Siphnians and Seriphians are of Athenian stock and furnished one penteconter apiece. The full number of the ships, aside from the penteconters, was three hundred and seventy-eight.

49. When the commanders from these aforementioned cities met at Salamis, they held a debate. Eurybiades presented the proposition that anyone who pleased should declare where, among the territories of which the Greeks were master, would be most suitable place to fight their sea battle; for Attica was at this point already given over for lost; it was about the rest that he inquired. The most of the opinions of those who spoke agreed that they should sail to the Isthmus and fight for the Peloponnese; the reason they produced for this was that, if they were beaten in the sea fight and were at Salamis, they would be beleaguered in an island where no help could show up for their rescue; but if they fought off the Isthmus, they could put into a coastline that was their own.

50. At the moment when the Peloponnesian commanders were arguing like this, there came a man of Athens with the news that the barbarian had arrived in Attica and was giving it to fire and sword. For the army that was with Xerxes had come through Boeotia and, having burned the city of the Thespians (the inhabitants of which had themselves gone away to the Peloponnese) and likewise the city of the Plataeans, had now come to Athens and there was ravaging everything entirely. They had burned Thespia and Plataea when they learned from the Thebans that these cities had not espoused the Persian cause.

51. From the crossing of the Hellespont, from which the barbarians began their march, they had spent one month in their passage into Europe, and then, in three more months, they were in Attica, during the archonship of Calliades at Athens. The city they captured was empty; in it there were only a few Athenians, whom they found in the temple; these were temple stewards and poor men, and they had barricaded the Acropolis with doors and planks to defend themselves from the attackers. These men had not gone away with the rest to Salamis because of lack of means and, besides, because they had their own conviction of having found out the mean-

ing of the oracle that the Pythia had given about the wooden wall that would be impregnable. This,[19] they decided, was that very refuge according to the prophecy, and not the ships.

52. The Persians established themselves on the hill opposite the Acropolis that is called by the Athenians the Areopagus, and they besieged the Acropolis in this way: they wrapped tow around their arrows and set them alight and shot them into the barrier. There the Athenians who were besieged still defended themselves, all the same, although they were reduced to the extremity of ill, and their barrier had betrayed them. They refused to receive any propositions of the Pisistratids about surrender, but they staunchly defended themselves by various means and especially by launching down great stones on the barbarians as they approached the gates, so that for a great time Xerxes was at a loss, being unable to beat them.

53. But at last the barbarians found a way out of their difficulties. For according to the prophecy, all of Attica on the mainland must be overcome by the Persians. In front of the Acropolis, but behind the gates and the road up, there was a place where no one was on guard, for no one had thought that any man could ascend there; it was near the shrine of Aglaurus, the daughter of Cecrops, and at it, though it was a very precipitous place, some men managed to climb up. When the Athenians saw that these had got to the top, to the Acropolis itself, some of them threw themselves down headlong from the wall and so found their deaths; but others fled to the inner chamber. Those of the Persians who had climbed up turned to the gates and opened these up and butchered the suppliants there. When these had all been laid low, the barbarians plundered the shrine and set the whole Acropolis afire.

54. Having taken Athens absolutely, Xerxes sent a horseman to Susa to tell Artabanus of his present good fortune. On the day after the sending of the messenger, he summoned such exiles of the Athenians as were in his train and bade them go up to the Acropolis and in their own fashion perform the sacrifices. He did this either because he had seen some vision in his sleep or because he began to have scruples about having burned the temple. The exiles did as he bade them.

19. The barricade of doors and planks.

55. I will tell you why I have mentioned this. There is on the Acropolis a temple that is called the shrine of Erechtheus Earthborn, and there is in the shrine an olive tree and a salt pool, about which the story goes among the Athenians that, when Poseidon and Athena had their contest for the possession of the land, the two gods made these two objects their witnesses. [20] Now it happened that the olive was burned, with all the rest of the shrine, by the barbarians; but on the day after the burning, when those Athenians by the King's instructions came up to the shrine to sacrifice, they saw the olive had put forth from its stump a shoot of about a cubit's length. They reported this.

56. The Greeks in Salamis, when they had word of what had happened to the Acropolis of Athens, were in such turmoil of mind that some of the generals did not even wait for the formal settlement of the proposition that they were debating but fell into their ships and hoisted the sails to run away. Those of them who were left decided formally to fight at sea for the Isthmus. So night came on, and the conference broke up and the people went to their ships.

57. At this moment, when Themistocles got to his ship, one Mnesiphilus, an Athenian, asked him what decision had been reached. This man was then told by Themistocles that it was resolved to draw off the ships to the Isthmus and fight for the Peloponnese. Mnesiphilus said, "If once they draw off the ships from Salamis, you will never again fight for any fatherland at all; everyone will run off, each one to his own city, and neither Eurybiades nor any other man will be able to keep the army from scattering. Greece will be lost, and all through sheer folly. If there is any means at all by which you can undo this decision, if by any means you can persuade Eurybiades to change his mind and stay here, do so."

58. What Mnesiphilus suggested pleased Themistocles extremely, but he made the man no answer and went off to Eurybiades' ship. When he came there, he said that he wanted to consult the commander on a matter of common interest. So Eurybiades told him to come aboard and talk, if he pleased. Then Themistocles sat down

20. "Witnesses," a literal rendering of the Greek, perhaps leaves something obscure in the English. Poseidon created the salt pool, Athena the olive, and Cecrops gave his judgment in favor of the goddess. These objects were made as *evidence* of the power of each god.

and spelled out all that he had heard from Mnesiphilus, but he recounted it as though it were his own idea, and he added much besides until, in his urgency, he persuaded the commander to disembark and to summon the generals to a conference.

59. When they had all collected, but before Eurybiades put before them the reason for which he had summoned them, Themistocles was most vehement in the words of entreaty that he used. While he was talking, the Corinthian general Adimantus, son of Ocytus, said, "Themistocles, in the games, those who get off the mark too soon are whipped." Themistocles, in his defense, said, "But those who get left behind never get crowned."

60. So he made a soft answer to the Corinthian; but to Eurybiades he said not a word of what had passed between them before—to the effect that, if they once left Salamis, they would break up and run away—for in the presence of the allies it would not have been suitable for him to make accusations against anyone. But he held to quite another tack in his argument and said to Eurybiades: "It is in your hands to save Greece if you will be persuaded by me and stand and fight at sea here rather than yield to the arguments of these others and draw away your ships to the Isthmus. Just listen and compare the two cases. If you engage off the Isthmus, you will be fighting in the open sea, which suits us least, since our ships are the heavier and fewer in number. Besides, you will lose Salamis, Megara, and Aegina, even if we win a general victory. And the enemy's land army will follow his fleet, and so you will bring them down into the Peloponnese and endanger the safety of all Greece. If you do what I say, you will find corresponding advantages: first, we will be engaging their many ships with our few in a confined space, and, if the probable chances of war occur, we shall win a great victory. For to fight in a confined space is to our advantage, as to fight in the open sea is to theirs. Again, there is the survival of Salamis, to which we have conveyed for safety our wives and children. Finally, there is this matter, too, in my plan, which is exactly what you set most store by: if you stay here and fight your sea battle here, you will be defending the Peloponnese exactly as though you were fighting near the Isthmus, and you will *not* be bringing the enemy down to the Peloponnese—if you are wise. If what I expect happens and we win with the fleet, the barbarians will never get to the Isthmus at all;

they will never move a foot beyond Attica, and they will depart in disorder. Besides, we will profit by the survival of Megara and Aegina and Salamis; about the last there is an oracle among us that at that place we shall have the upper hand of our enemies. It is when men make probable designs that success oftenest attends them; if their designs are improbable, not even the god is willing to lend his help to the plans of men."

61. While Themistocles spoke like this, the Corinthian, Adimantus, again inveighed against him: "Hold your tongue," said he; "you have no country." And he was for not letting Eurybiades put the question to the vote on the motion of a "cityless man"; Themistocles should contribute an opinion only when had a city behind him. The taunts of the Corinthian were directed at Themistocles because Athens had been captured and was now occupied by the enemy. At this moment Themistocles abused Adimantus and the Corinthians both; he made it clear to them in his speech that Athens had a city and land greater than theirs—the Corinthians'— so long as they had two hundred fully manned ships; "for," said he, "there are no Greeks able to withstand an attack by us."

62. Having made this point, he went on in his speech to Eurybiades, speaking ever more vehemently: "Eurybiades, if you stand your ground here, by such standing you will be a good man; if you go away, you will utterly destroy Greece; for the whole power of this war is carried in our ships. Do what I say. If you refuse, we will straightaway gather all our households and take them away to Siris in Italy. It is ours of old, and there are oracles that say that it is by us that it must be colonized. When you people are deprived of such allies as we are, you will remember my words."

63. At these words of Themistocles, Eurybiades was forced to change his mind. In my opinion, this change was because he especially dreaded that the Athenians would desert them if he drew off the fleet to the Isthmus; for if the Athenians quit, the rest of the alliance was not capable of sustaining the fight. So he chose the plan that they should stay where they were and fight the sea fight through.

64. So it was that there was at Salamis first a verbal skirmish; but once Eurybiades made up his mind, they prepared to fight there. The day dawned, and with the rising of the sun there was an earthquake by sea and land. The Greeks resolved to pray to the gods and sum-

mon to their help the sons of Aeacus. As they resolved, so they did; for they prayed to all the gods; called, from their residence on the spot in Salamis, Ajax and Telamon; and sent a ship to Aegina to fetch Aeacus and his sons.[21]

65. There was an Athenian, one Dicaeus, son of Theocydes, who was an exile and had at this time come to be someone of note among the Medes; he said that when Attica was being ravaged by Xerxes' army and there were no more Athenians left in it, he happened to be with Demaratus, the Lacedaemonian, on the Thriasian plain, and he saw a cloud of dust coming from Eleusis, as it were of some thirty thousand men; and as both he and Demaratus marveled at the dust cloud and what thousands of men could have occasioned it, they suddenly heard a great cry, and it seemed to him that it was the cry that is the Iacchus song, which belongs to the Mysteries. Demaratus was without knowledge of the rites that take place at Eleusis, and so he asked his companion what was this cry that the voices carried. Dicaeus said, "Demaratus, there shall surely be some dreadful mischief to the King's army; for it is quite clear—inasmuch as Attica is abandoned of her people—that this sound is a thing divine and indeed is coming from Eleusis to the aid of the Athenians and their allies. If this shall come down on the Peloponnese, there will be danger for the King himself and his land host that are there on the mainland; but if it turns toward the ships at Salamis, it will be the fleet that the King will risk losing. This festival the Athenians celebrate every year in honor of the Mother and her Daughter,[22] and whoever wishes, both of the Athenians themselves and of other Greeks, may be initiated; the cry that you hear is the Iacchus-cry, with which they celebrate this festival." Demaratus said to him: "Hold your peace, and tell this story to no one else; for if these words are carried back to the King, you will lose your head, and no one, neither I nor any living mortal, will be able to save you. Just hold your peace; and, as for that host of the Medes, the god will take care of that." Such was the counsel of Demaratus; and out of the dust and the cry a cloud was borne aloft, and it floated toward Salamis and the Greek host. So those two men came to know that the fleet of

---

21. The images of these heroes.
22. Demeter and Persephone, goddesses of the Eleusinian Mysteries.

Xerxes would surely perish. That is the story that Dicaeus told, and he claimed that Demaratus and others were witnesses to the truth of it.

66. Those who had their orders to join Xerxes' fleet, after they had come from Trachis, from viewing the Laconian disaster at Thermopylae, crossed over into the country round Histiaea, stayed three days, sailed through the Euripus, and three days later were at Phalerum.[23] To my thinking there were as many in number now, entering Athens, both on land and at sea, as when they came to Sepias and Thermopylae; for against those who died in the storm and those who died at Thermopylae and in the sea fights off Artemisium I set these, who had, until now, never joined the King's armament: the Melians, the Dorians, the Locrians, and the Boeotians, who were there now in full force, except for the Thespians and Plataeans; furthermore, there were the Carystians and the people of Andros and Tenos and all the rest of the islanders, except for the five states I have listed, with their names, before this.[24] For the farther into Greece the Persian went, the more peoples followed him.

67. So when all these came to Athens (all, that is, except the Parians, for they had been left behind in Cythnus and were craning their necks to see which way the war would go)—when all the rest came to Phalerum, Xerxes went down to his fleet in person, because he wished to make contact with those who had just sailed in, to learn their opinions. When he came there, he sat upon a raised throne; and on his summons the princes and taxiarchs of their several peoples assembled, disembarking from their ships and taking their places as the King assigned honor to each one: first the king of Sidon, then the Tyrian, and after that the others. When they had taken their places in due order, the King sent Mardonius to them and made trial of each by asking him whether he should fight the sea battle or not.

68. Mardonius went the rounds and asked his question, starting with the king of Sidon; he and the others gave their judgment to the same common tenor in bidding him fight. But Artemisia said as follows: "Mardonius, tell the King that I have this to say, I who have

23. In this period the main harbor serving Athens.
24. In chapter 46.

not been the most backward in his fights in Euboea, nor were my exploits the least. Master, it is but just that I should declare my true opinion, those thoughts that I find will serve your purposes best. And so I say to you: spare your ships and do not fight this sea battle. For these men, your adversaries, are, at sea, as much better than yours as men are than women. Why must you put all at risk in sea fights? Have you not Athens, which is why you set out to make the war? Have you not all the rest of Greece? No one stands against you; those who have done so have come off as befitted them. Let me tell you how I think the fortunes of your adversaries will turn out. If you are not so hasty as to fight at sea but keep your ships here, near the land, or even advance into the Peloponnese, you will easily compass, my master, all that you have come for. For the Greeks are not able to hold out against you for any length of time; you will scatter them, and they will fly to their several cities. For they have no food in this island of theirs, as I learn, and it is not likely, once you drive with your land army toward the Peloponnese, that those who came here from that Peloponnese should stand firm and care to fight at sea to save Athens. But if here and now you are in such haste to fight at sea, I fear lest the worsting of your fleet will bring mischief upon your army as well. Besides, King, lay this up in your heart: how good masters are wont to have bad slaves and bad masters good slaves. You are the best of men, and you have bad slaves who are reckoned as your allies—these Egyptians and Cypriots and Cilicians and Pamphylians; they are no good."

69. When she made this speech to Mardonius, those who were her well-wishers were regretful at her words, inasmuch as they believed she would suffer for them at the hands of the King, for dissuading him from fighting. But those who envied her and had malice toward her, because she was in the very forefront of those whom Xerxes honored, were delighted at what she said, for they thought it would be the end of her. But when the judgments were reported back to Xerxes, he was very pleased with Artemisia's opinion; he had before this thought her someone of serious worth, but now he praised her far more. Yet he gave his decision to follow the judgment of the majority. He thought that his men had not fought as well as they should off Euboea because, as he saw it, he had not been there, whereas now he was all prepared to watch them fighting.

70. When they passed along the word of command to sail, the men put their ships to sea for Salamis and at their leisure were drawn up in line of battle. At that moment the daylight did not suffice for fighting, for night came on; so they prepared for the morrow. The Greeks were possessed by dread and agony, especially the Peloponnesians, because, sitting there at Salamis, they were going to fight for the land of the Athenians, and, when beaten, they would be cut off in an island, leaving their own homeland unprotected. Meanwhile, under cover of that very night, the barbarian land forces started their march toward the Peloponnese.

71. Yet the Greeks had indeed done everything they could to prevent the barbarian invasion by land. For as soon as the Peloponnesians had word that Leonidas and his men were dead at Thermopylae, they rushed out from their cities and took up their position at the Isthmus; the general in command was Cleombrotus, son of Anaxandrides, the brother of Leonidas. They sat down at the Isthmus and destroyed the Scironian road,[25] and afterwards, by deliberative decision, they built a wall across the Isthmus. They had many thousands of men there, and every man working, and the task went ahead quickly. They carried in stones and bricks and logs and crates full of sand, and those who had come to help rested from their work neither night nor day.

72. Those who came forward to the Isthmus in full force on the Greek side were these: the Lacedaemonians and all the Arcadians, and the Eleans, Corinthians, Sicyonians, Epidaurians, Phliasians, Troezenians, and the men of Hermione. These are those who came actively to help in their dread for the danger of Greece. The rest of the Peloponnesians gave it never a care, and now their time for the Olympian and Carnean celebrations had passed by.[26]

73. There are seven peoples living in the Peloponnese, of which two are aboriginal and live now where they have always lived. These are the Arcadians and the Cynurians. There is also one nation, the Achaeans, that has never moved from the Peloponnese but has changed its habitation there. The other four out of the seven are im-

---

25. There is considerable controversy among the commentators about this road, but it appears that, in this period, it was the only road—itself barely passable—for wheeled traffic.

26. I.e., they no longer had this excuse for not coming.

migrants: the Dorians, Aetolians, Dryopians, and Lemnians. Among the Dorians there are many distinguished cities, and one among the Aetolians: Elis. The Dryopians have Hermione and Asine, which is near to Cardamyle in Laconia; and among the Lemnians, all the Paroreatae. Among the aboriginal inhabitants, only the Cynurians seem to be Ionians, and they have been completely Doricized by the rule of their Argive masters and by the passage of time; they are the people of Orneae and the places round it. Now, of these seven peoples, all of the cities, save for those I have listed, remained neutral. If one may speak frankly, their remaining neutral was taking the Persian side.

74. Those who were in the Isthmus were engaged in such labor because they were running the risk of losing their all, and they had no further hope of distinguishing themselves with the fleet. Those at Salamis, although they heard of the work,[27] were dreadfully afraid, not so much for themselves as for the safety of the Peloponnese. For a while they would stand close together, man with man, and whispering their bewilderment at the stupidity of Eurybiades. But at last it all burst into the open. There was a meeting, and much was said on the same matters as before, some saying that they ought to sail off to the Peloponnese and run the danger for that country rather than stay and fight for a land that was already a prisoner-of-war of the enemy; but the Athenians, Aeginetans, and Megarians were for staying there and fighting.

75. Themistocles, since he was losing out in the debates with the Peloponnesians, secretly left the council and went and sent a message to the camp of the Medes. His messenger was dispatched in a small boat with instructions as to what to say; his name was Sicinnus, and he was part of Themistocles' household and looked after his children. After all this, Themistocles made him a Thespian at a time when the Thespians were accepting men for citizenship, and he made him a very rich man besides.[28] He arrived in his boat and

27. The building of the wall across the Isthmus.
28. This man was probably a slave. After the middle forties of the fifth century, one could not acquire Athenian citizenship unless born of two citizens. So Themistocles used his interest to get this ex-slave into a state that was still, at given moments, open to immigrants.

spoke to the barbarian generals as follows: "The general of the Greeks has sent me, unknown to the other Greeks; for he is indeed an adherent of the King and wants his side to win rather than the Greeks. I am to tell you that the Greeks are plotting to run away, in their extreme fear, and now you have the chance of achieving the very finest of your actions—unless you stand by and watch them run away and escape. For they are divided among themselves, and they will not put up a resistance to you; you will see that they will fight one another, those who are on your side and those who are not."

76. Having made this communication, he stole away. They, believing in his message, disembarked many Persians on to the little island of Psyttaleia, which lies between Salamis and the mainland; then about midnight they advanced their western wing toward Salamis to encircle the Greeks; and those who were stationed about Ceos and Cynosura put to sea and occupied with their ships all the channel as far as Munychia. They put their ships to sea so that, you see, the Greeks might not have even anywhere to flee to but, cut off in Salamis, might pay the Persians for the victory they had won at Artemisium. And the reason they disembarked Persians onto the island called Psyttaleia was that, when the sea fight was under way, both crews and wrecks would be washed ashore on to it—for the island lay in the path of the fight that was to be—and so they might be able to save their friends and kill their foes. They did these things quite silently, that their enemies might not know of them; so they made these preparations at night, without even taking any sleep.

77. As for oracles, I cannot rebut their truth, for I do not want to attempt to set at nothing oracles that speak so clearly when I look at matters like these:

When with their ships they build bridges to the coast of the
    Golden-Sworded
Artemis and to the sea-line of the island Cynosura,
Mad indeed is their hope, having sacked the glory of Athens;
Then shall bright Justice quench their savage wrath, child of
    Hybris,
For all its fury so dreadful, thinking to drink off destruction;
For bronze shall encounter bronze, and with blood shall the
    sea be crimsoned

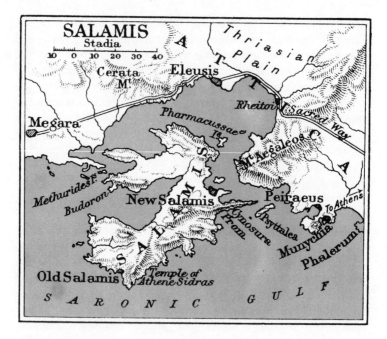

> By Ares, and Greece's free day shall the wide-heard voice of
> Cronides [29]
> Bring to fulfillment—yes—holy Victory shall bring it to pass.

When I look at matters like these and at how clearly Bacis has spoken, I do not dare myself to speak in denial of oracles, nor will I take that argument from another.

78. Many heated words were being spoken by the generals at Salamis. And they did not yet know that the barbarians had encircled them with their ships but thought that they were still in the spot where they had seen them stationed during the day.

79. While the generals were still debating, there crossed over from Aegina one Aristides, son of Lysimachus, a man of Athens but ostracized [30] by the democracy. I have information of this man's char-

---

29. Zeus, son of Cronus.
30. Sent into exile by vote of the citizens.

acter and am convinced that he was the best and the justest man in Athens. He went to the meeting and called Themistocles aside, out from it. Themistocles had been no friend of his—indeed, his chief enemy—but by reason of the greatness of their present troubles he forgot their enmity and summoned him out, for he wanted to have converse with him. He had heard in advance that those from the Peloponnese were bent on drawing off their ships to the Isthmus, so when Themistocles came out of the meeting, Aristides said to him, "The rivalry between us, both in time past and assuredly now, must be only which of us two can serve our country better. I tell you that it is all one whether the Peloponnesians talk much or little about sailing away from here; I have seen, myself, what I am saying, that now, even if the Corinthians and Eurybiades himself want to sail out, they cannot do so, for we are encircled by the enemy. Go you in and tell them that." But Themistocles answered him as follows.

80. "What you tell us to do is good, and your news is good, too. You come with the witness of your eyes of what I most wish should happen; for it is I who caused the Persians to do what they are doing. I had to; for since the Greeks were unwilling to stand and fight, I had to force them against their will. But since you have come with the good news, go tell it to them yourself. If I tell them of it, they will think I have made up a lie and will not believe me, because they will not believe that the barbarians are doing what they are doing. Go in yourself before them and tell them how matters really are. When you have told your story, they may be convinced, and that would be best. But if they do not believe, it is all one for us; for they will not be able to run away if, as you say, we are encircled."

81. Then Aristides went before the meeting and spoke to them. He said that he had come from Aegina and that it was only with great difficulty that he had made the passage out, slipping through the enemy's blockade. For the whole Greek force was surrounded by Xerxes' ships. He bade them therefore prepare to defend themselves. With these words he went away, and once again the controversy started up again in words, for the most of the commanders did not believe the news.

82. But when they were still full of disbelief there came a trireme of Tenians, deserting to the Greek side. Its commander was one Panaetius, the son of Sosimenes, who conveyed the whole truth to them. (This is why the Tenians had their names inscribed on the

omestor, son of Androdamas, and Phylacus, son of Histiaeus, both of them Samians. The reason I mention just these two is because, thanks to his action, Theomestor became prince of Samos by establishment of the Persians, and Phylacus had his name put on the roll of the King's Benefactors and got the award of a great deal of territory. The King's Benefactors are, in Persian, called "Orosangae."

86. That is the story of those men. But the majority of the ships at Salamis were crippled, some being destroyed by the Athenians and some by the Aeginetans. For since the Greeks fought with proper discipline and in ordered ranks, and the barbarians with no order and no longer doing anything with a sense of purpose, what was bound to happen to them was what happened. For all that, they were and proved themselves on that day far better than they had been off Euboea; for everyone fought with zest and in fear of Xerxes, and every man of them thought that the King was watching him.

87. As far as the generality of them went, I cannot exactly say how each of the barbarians or the Greeks fought. But in respect to Artemisia the following thing happened, as a result of which she gained even greater renown with the King. For when the King's fortunes had been reduced to utter confusion, at that very moment the ship of Artemisia was pursued by an Attic ship. And she, not being able to make her escape, inasmuch as there were other friendly ships in front of her and she herself happened to be nearest to the enemy, she resolved to do this, which turned greatly to her advantage when she had done it: being pursued by the Attic vessel, she charged and rammed a friendly ship, of men of Calyndus, with the king of the Calyndians himself on board, Damasithymus. Whether there had been some quarrel between her and him while they were both still at the Hellespont, I cannot say, nor whether she did what she did deliberately or whether it was pure accident that the ship of the Calyndians happened to fall in her way. But when she rammed him and sank him, by her good luck she gained doubly by what she had done. For the trierarch of the Attic ship, when he saw her ramming a ship manned by barbarians, believed that Artemisia's ship was either Greek itself or must be deserting from the barbarians to the Greek side and helping them, and so he turned his line of pursuit to other vessels.

88. That is the way her stroke of luck befell her, that she escaped

and did not meet destruction there. But there is the additional fact that, having done evil to Xerxes, as a result of that very evil she won particular renown with him. For it is said that, as the King watched, he noticed the vessel doing the ramming, and some one of his court-iers, standing by, said, "Master, do you see Artemisia, how well she fights? And lo, she has sunk a vessel of the enemy." He asked if the action was really that of Artemisia, and they said yes, for they could clearly read the ensign on her ship. The destroyed vessel they con-cluded was an enemy. As I said, everything happened to her good luck in this, and most of all that the ship of the Calyndians that was destroyed had not a single man escape alive to accuse her. So Xerxes, they say, in answer to what they had told him, observed, "My men have become women, and my women men." That is what they say Xerxes said.

89. In the stress of this action there died the general, Ariabignes, the son of Darius, who was the brother of Xerxes himself, and many other distinguished Persians and Medes and other allies. On the Greek side, very few; for inasmuch as they knew how to swim, those whose vessels were destroyed and who had not perished in the hand-to-hand fighting swam across to Salamis. But of the barbarians, the most died in the sea, because they could not swim. At the time their first vessels fled is when most of them were destroyed; for the men who were arrayed further back were trying to move forward with their vessels, past the others, in the hope that they too might show some action of mettle before the Great King, and so they fell foul of their own boats, which were in flight.

90. The following thing also happened at this moment of confu-sion. Certain Phoenicians whose ships had been destroyed came to the King and spoke evil of the Ionians. It was thanks to them, they said, that the fleet had been destroyed, for they were traitors. Yet the outcome was that the commanders of the Ionians did not meet their doom, and the Phoenicians who accused them received the follow-ing reward. While they were still talking, as I have said, a Samothra-cian ship rammed an Attic one. The Attic ship was sinking, but an Aeginetan vessel, bearing down, sank the ship of the people of Samothrace. Now, the Samothracians, who are javelin men, from the decks of their sunk vessel shot down the men who were on board the vessel that had sunk her, swept them off, boarded her, and took

possession of her. This saved the Ionians; for when Xerxes saw them achieve this great deed, he turned to the Phoenicians and in the bitterness of his heart blamed them all for everything and bade his servants take their heads off, that they might not, being cowards, slander men who were better than themselves. For as often as Xerxes saw any of his own men perform some great action in this sea fight, as he sat under the hill that is opposite Salamis and is called Aegaleos, he would inquire who it was had done it, and his clerks wrote down the trierarch, with his father's name and his city. It may also have contributed to the destruction of the Phoenicians that by Xerxes was a Persian named Ariaramnes, who was a friend of the Ionians. That is how the Persians dealt with the Phoenicians.

91. As the barbarians turned to flight and tried to sail out of Phalerum, the Aeginetans formed an ambush in the passage and did deeds of great note. For the Athenians, in the general confusion, demolished all vessels that resisted and those who fled as well, and the Aeginetans did the same with those that tried to make their passage out. And as often as some of them would escape the Athenians, in full tilt they ran into the hands of the Aeginetans.

92. Then there met together the ship of Themistocles, which was in pursuit of another, and that of Polycritus, the son of Crius, who was an Aeginetan. Polycritus had rammed a Sidonian vessel, the very one that had captured the Aeginetan ship that was guarding off Sciathus, on which sailed Pytheas, the son of Ischenous—that Pytheas whom the Persians, when he had been chopped almost to pieces, had for his valor's sake kept in their ship, out of admiration for him. This man was being carried among the Persians in this Sidonian ship, which was now captured, and so in this way Pytheas escaped safe into Aegina. When Polycritus saw the Attic ship, he read the admiral's sign and recognized it and called aloud to Themistocles, mocking him for his insults against the people of Aegina in the matter of their friendship with Persia.[32] These were the taunts that Polycritus threw at Themistocles as he rammed the Sidonian vessel. The barbarians whose ships had come through safe fled and arrived at Phalerum under cover of the land army.

32. See above, 6.49, 73, 85. Polycritus is saying something like "That's how we love the Persians."

93. In this sea fight, those who came through on the Greek side with the greatest reputation were the Aeginetans and, after them, the Athenians. And among individuals, Polycritus of Aegina, and, among Athenians, Eumenes of Anagyrus and Aminias of Pallene, who was the captain who had pursued Artemisia. If he had known that Artemisia was sailing on that ship, he would never have stopped until he had captured her or lost his own vessel. For the Athenian trierarchs had been given special instructions, and, besides, a prize of ten thousand drachmas had been added, for whoever should capture her alive; for they regarded it as a scandal that a woman should make war upon Athens. But she herself, as I said before, escaped safe, and there were others, too, whose ships remained undestroyed and who got into Phalerum.

94. The Athenians say that Adimantus, the Corinthian commander, right at the beginning of the engagement, when the ships were locked together, in terror and fear hoisted his sails and fled, and that the Corinthians, when they saw their admiral's ship in flight, followed his lead. And when in the course of their flight they came to the part of Salamis where the temple of Athena Sciras is, then there met them a boat; it must have been sent by some god, for there never appeared anybody who sent it, nor did those of the Corinthians who met with it know anything, before this, of what was happening with the fleet. And this is the way in which they came to feel that the thing had happened by the god's contrivance: as they came near to their ships, the men who were on the boat spoke and said, "Adimantus, you have turned your ships away and moved off in flight, and in so doing have betrayed the Greeks. Yet those same Greeks are conquering to the utmost extent of their prayers that they would vanquish their enemies." As they said that, Adimantus distrusted the truth of the matter, and so the men in the boat spoke again, saying that they themselves were prepared to be taken for hostages and die for it if the Greeks did not turn out to have been the victors. So Adimantus turned his ship back, and so did the others, and they came back to the fleet to find everything finished. Such is the story told about them by the Athenians; but the Corinthians themselves do not agree but think that they were the first in the engagement; and the rest of Greece bears them witness.

95. Now, Aristides, the son of Lysimachus, a man of Athens,

whom I mentioned a little while ago as being the best of men, in this general rout at Salamis did as follows. He took many of the men-at-arms who were ranged along the coast of Salamis (these were in stock Athenian) and brought them over to the island of Psyttaleia; and it was they who killed all the Persians who were on that little island.[33]

96. When the sea fight broke off, the Greeks towed to Salamis those of the wrecks that were still there and made themselves ready for another sea fight; for they were sure that the King would still use what ships were left him. But the west wind carried many of the wrecks to the beach in Attica that is called Colias, and thus it was that not only all the other prophecies were fulfilled—those made by Bacis and Musaeus about the sea fight—but also one about the wrecks cast ashore at this place—the prophecy given many years before by an oracle-monger named Lysistratus, an Athenian—which had gone unnoticed by all the Greeks. It ran:

Truly the women of Colias shall roast their barley with oar-
    blades.

But this was to happen after the King had left.

97. Now Xerxes, when he understood what had happened, being afraid lest one of the Ionians might suggest to the Greeks (or, indeed, they might think of it themselves) that they should sail to the Hellespont, to break down the bridges, and so he would be caught in Europe and in danger of total destruction, planned to run away. But because he did not want this to be obvious, either to the Greeks or to his own men, he tried to build a mole to Salamis; and to do so he bound together Phoenician merchantmen, so that they should be in the place of a bridge and a wall. And he made preparations for the war, as though he would fight another sea fight. And all the others who saw him doing these things were well convinced that in whole heart he was prepared to stand his ground and fight there. Only Mardonius was well aware of the meaning of all of these things; he was especially experienced in the way in which Xerxes thought.

98. At the same time that he was doing these things, Xerxes sent

33. Before the battle, these Persians had been stationed on Psyttaleia to kill any Greeks who tried to find refuge there and to help any friends who washed ashore. See chapter 76.

to Persia to tell of the present calamity. Than this system of messengers there is nothing of mortal origin that is quicker. This is how the Persians arranged it: they say that for as many days as the whole journey consists in, that many horses and men are stationed at intervals of a day's journey, one horse and one man assigned to each day. And him neither snow nor rain nor heat nor night holds back for the accomplishment of the course that has been assigned to him, as quickly as he may. The first that runs hands on what he has been given to the second, and the second to the third, and from there what is transmitted passes clean through, from hand to hand, to its end, even as among the Greeks there is the torch-race that they celebrate in honor of Hephaestus. This course of horse-posts the Persians call "angareion."

99. The first message that arrived in Susa, saying that Xerxes had possession of Athens, so delighted those of the Persians who were left there that they strewed all the roads with myrtle boughs, and burnt incense, and were themselves altogether given over to sacrificial feasts and jollity. But the second message, which followed after the first, so shattered them that they all tore their garments and cried and lamented endlessly, blaming Mardonius. But their grief was not so much for the ships that were lost as it was for their fear for Xerxes himself.

100. Thus it was for the Persians for the whole time intervening until Xerxes himself came and, in his coming, stopped their grief. But Mardonius saw that Xerxes was bitterly unhappy as a result of this sea fight; he suspected also that the King intended to fly from Athens and reflected, in regard to himself, that he would certainly have to pay for having urged the King to make war upon Greece and that it would be better for him to run the ultimate risk of either subduing Greece or himself dying honorably, at the end of his life, by playing for a great stake. (But his judgment actually inclined him to think that he would subdue Greece.) Reflecting on all of this, he advanced to Xerxes the following argument: "My master, do not grieve or distress yourself unduly for the thing that has happened you. For the contest that carries all and everything for us is not one of wood [34] but of men and of horses. Of all these people who now deem that they have already won a supreme victory there is not one

34. I.e., ships.

who will disembark from his ship and risk standing against you, nor one from this whole mainland. Those who have so stood against us have paid for it. If it now is your pleasure, let us immediately attack the Peloponnesus; if it is your decision to wait, we can do that too. Do not lose heart; for as far as the Greeks go, they have no escape from paying for the evils they have done us, now and before, and from becoming your slaves. This is the best thing for you to do; but if you have decided that you will yourself withdraw and lead your army off, I have in that eventuality also a plan for you. Do you, my lord, not make the Persians a laughingstock before the Greeks; for whatever mischief your fortunes have experienced, it is not because of the Persians. You cannot say that *we* have been cowards on any occasion. But if Phoenicians and Egyptians and Cyprians and Cilicians have been cowards, the catastrophe that resulted has nothing to do with us Persians. So now, since the Persians are not guilty, listen to me. If you have resolved not to stay here, take off the bulk of your army and lead it back home; and be it mine to hand over to you a Greece totally enslaved, if you will let me pick some three hundred thousand out of your army."

101. When Xerxes heard that, he was as pleased and delighted with it as a man might be in his misfortune, and he said to Mardonius that he would give him an answer as soon as he had consulted with others as to which of the two plans he should adopt. And when he was consulting with the Persians he had invited, he decided to summon Artemisia to the council too, because she had been the only one before who manifestly had known what ought to be done. When Artemisia came, he dismissed the others—the Persian councillors and his bodyguards—and spoke as follows: "Mardonius bids me remain here and attack the Peloponnese. He says that the Persians and my land army have been the cause of no misfortune and that they would very gladly show what they can do for me. He bids me either do this, or else he is willing himself, choosing three hundred thousand of my army, to hand over to me a Greece entirely enslaved, and me myself he bids withdraw, with the rest of my army, to my own land. Now, since you manifestly gave me the right counsel about the sea fight that has just happened, not wishing that I should fight it, give me counsel now as to which of these two ways I would be well advised to follow."

102. So he consulted her, and she said as follows: "My lord, it is

difficult for one who is giving you counsel to say the right thing. But in the present circumstances I think that you ought to withdraw home and that Mardonius, if he is willing and has undertaken to do as he said, should be left here with such troops as he chooses. For if he subdues these people as he claims he will do, and if his plans go as he hopes, it will, my lord, still be your act; for it will be your slaves who have done it. But if things go opposite to what Mardonius has planned, there is no great catastrophe as long as you survive and your power in your own house. For if you survive, and that house of yours, these Greeks will run many a risk of their own lives yet. As for Mardonius, if anything happens him, that is a matter of no consequence. Nor will the Greeks, in winning, win much, for they will have destroyed only a slave of yours; but you have done what you made the expedition for: you will march home having burned Athens."

103. Xerxes was delighted with her counsel, for she really said exactly what he thought himself. For if all the men and women in the world had counseled him to remain there, I personally believe that he would not have done so, he was so completely in the grip of fear. But he praised Artemisia and sent her off to take his children to Ephesus; for there were certain bastard children of his that followed the army.

104. He sent along with the children, to guard them, Hermotimus. This man was by race a Pedasian and of all the eunuchs in the King's court was the one whom the King regarded most highly. The Pedasians live above Halicarnassus, and among these Pedasians it happens that whenever, within a certain period, ill is threatened to all those who dwell around the city, the priestess of Athena there grows a great beard. This has already happened them twice.

105. From these Pedasians was Hermotimus, and he was a man who, being wronged, achieved, of all the people I have known, the greatest vengeance. He was captured by enemies, who sold him, and he was bought by a man of Chios called Panionius. This man made a living from the most infamous of actions. He would get boys of great beauty, castrate them, and then take them to Sardis and Ephesus and sell them for great sums; for among the barbarians eunuchs are held in higher value than whole men because of the entire trust they put in them. Panionius castrated many others in the course of making a livelihood from these practices, and among them castrated

Hermotimus. Yet Hermotimus was not utterly unlucky as a result of this; for he came from Sardis to the court of the King, along with other gifts given to the King, and as time went on he was honored more than all the other eunuchs by Xerxes.

106. Now when the King was launching the Persian armament against Athens and was, at that point, in Sardis, Hermotimus came down on some business to the Mysian land that the Chians live in, which is called Atarneus, and there he found Panionius. He recognized him and made him various friendly propositions. First of all, he said how many great benefits he had had, thanks to Panionius; and secondly he promised that, in return, he would do all the good he could for Panionius if the latter would bring his whole household and live there. Panionius accepted his offer very gladly and brought there his children and his wife. And when he had caught him with his entire household, Hermotimus spoke as follows: "You are of all mankind the one who has got a livelihood from the most infamous of actions. What harm did I, either in my own person or in any of my people, do to you or to any of your people, that instead of a man you made me into a nothing? You thought that the gods would not notice what you did then. You have acted vilely, and they in the justice of their law have brought you into my hands, so that you cannot complain of the vengeance that will come to you from me." After these taunts, he had the children brought into their father's sight, and Panionius was compelled there to cut off the testicles of his four children. He did this under compulsion, and then, when it was done, the children were forced to do the same to their father. So it was that vengeance and Hermotimus overtook Panionius.

107. After entrusting his children to Artemisia, to take them to Ephesus, Xerxes summoned Mardonius and bade him take whatever men he pleased out of his army and to try to match deeds to the things he had professed. That was as far as things went during that day; but that night, at the King's command, his admirals put out to sea from Phalerum, making for the Hellespont as quickly as each could, to guard the rafts for the King to cross over. When they came near Zoster,[35] as they sailed on their way, the barbarians, seeing certain little headlands that jutted out from the mainland, thought that

35. This promontory lies between Piraeus and Sunium on the coast of Attica.

these were ships, and they fled for a great distance. But at last, realizing that they were not ships but headlands, they gathered themselves together again and continued on their way.

108. When day dawned, the Greeks saw that the land army was still where it had been, and so they assumed that the fleet was also at Phalerum; they thought that the Persians would fight again at sea, and so they prepared to defend themselves. But when they found out that the ships were really gone, they immediately decided to pursue them. But though they pursued them as far as Andros, they never caught a glimpse of Xerxes' fleet; and when they came to Andros, they held a debate. Themistocles gave as his opinion that they should drive through the islands and, in pursuit of the ships, make straight for the Hellespont, to break the bridges there. Eurybiades declared the opposite opinion to this, saying that breaking the bridges would be to do the very greatest mischief to Greece; for if the Persian were compelled to remain in Europe, his efforts would all be toward action, for it would be impossible to have his cause prosper by inactivity, nor, that way, would there be any escape home for him possible, and his men would die of hunger; but if he tried hard and made great efforts, Europe, city by city, and nation by nation, might come over to him, either conquered or coming to terms before that; and the Persian army would live off the crops that the Greeks would grow yearly. He was convinced that, after the sea fight, the Persian would not remain in Europe, and so they, the Greeks, should let him flee till, in his flight, he reached his homeland. "Henceforth," said Eurybiades, "it will be his country and not ours that will be at risk in the war." To this opinion the other generals of the Peloponnesians stuck.

109. When Themistocles saw that he would not convince the majority to sail to the Hellespont, he changed his position and made his address to the Athenians; for it was they who were most vexed for the escape of the barbarians and were eager to sail to the Hellespont and take the risk of fighting on their own if the others would not. "I myself have been present on many occasions, and have heard about far more, where the same thing has happened—that men who were beaten and penned in a corner would fight again and redeem their former faintheartedness. We have found it to our great good luck and that of Greece that we have driven out such a veritable

cloud of invaders; let us not pursue men who are in hot flight. It is
not we who have done the deed but the gods and the heroes, who
grudged that there should be one man to lord it over both Asia and
Europe—a man, moreover, impious and reckless. Did he not treat
alike temples and private property, burning and overthrowing the
images of the gods? Did he not scourge the sea and lay his fetters on
it? All is well with us for now; and now let us abide here in Greece
and take thought for ourselves and our households; let each man repair his house and be diligent in sowing his land,[36] since he has
utterly driven out the barbarian; and with the spring let us sail for
the Hellespont and Ionia." So he spoke, but he intended that this
act should be as a reserve to his credit with the Persians, that he
might have a refuge if, one day, trouble overtook him at the hands of
the Athenians—which is indeed what took place.

110. With such words Themistocles deceived them, but the
Athenians were convinced. They had judged him before to be a
clever man, but now he came out as the cleverest and best counselor
possible, and they were ready to listen to anything he said. As soon
as they had believed him, Themistocles directly sent off men in a
small boat, men he could trust to keep silent under any form of torture about what he bade them say to the Great King when they came
to him. Again his household slave Sicinnus was one of them. When
they arrived in Attica, the rest stayed in the boat; but Sicinnus went
to the presence of Xerxes and said: "Themistocles, son of Neocles,
general of the Athenians and, of all the allies, the man who is the
best and the wisest, has sent me to tell you that Themistocles the
Athenian, because he wishes to serve you, has held back the Greek
fleet when they would have pursued your ships and destroyed your
bridges over the Hellespont. So now take your way back completely
at your ease." Having delivered this message, they sailed back again.

111. The Greeks, since they had decided against pursuing the
barbarians' ships further and also against sailing to break the bridges
over the Hellespont, beleaguered Andros with the purpose of taking
it. For the Andrians, the first of the islanders to be asked for money
by Themistocles, had refused him. Themistocles put his proposition
in these words: "We Athenians have come with two great gods to aid

36. The Greeks sowed their land in autumn.

us, Persuasion and Necessity, and so you should render up your money to us." But the Andrians answered this by saying, "It is indeed according to reason that the Athenians are great and prosperous, since they are so well off in useful gods; but for ourselves, the Andrians, we have a most plentiful poverty of land and two useless gods, who never quit our island but love to dwell in it without interruption, and these are Penury and Helplessness. These are the gods we Andrians possess, and so we will give no money. For never could there be a power of the Athenians that would be stronger than the powerlessness of the Andrians."

112. Such was the answer of the Andrians, and they gave no money and were now besieged. Themistocles, whose greed for money was insatiable, kept sending threatening messages to the other islands, asking for money through the same emissaries he had used with the King. He said that if they did not pay up he would lead the host of the Greeks upon them and destroy them by siege. By such arguments he collected great sums from the Carystians and the Parians when these people learned that Andros was besieged because it had taken the King's side and that Themistocles was the most highly regarded of the generals; and so they were afraid and sent money. Whether there were other islanders who paid I cannot exactly say, though I believe that there were others, and not these alone, although the Carystians got no respite from misfortune by the payment. But the Parians did escape the assault of the Greek army by propitiating Themistocles with money. So Themistocles, making Andros his base, got money from the rest of the islanders, unknown to the other generals.

113. Those who were with Xerxes waited a few days after the sea fight and then marched into Boeotia by the same road they had come. For Mardonius resolved to escort the King on his way, and it was now an unseasonable time of year for making war, and he thought it better to winter in Thessaly and with the spring have a try at the Peloponnese. Arrived in Thessaly, Mardonius selected his men: first the Persians, all of them that were called the Immortals, except for their general, Hydarnes, who refused to stay behind the King. After the Immortals he took, from the rest of the Persians, the cuirassiers and the Thousand Horse; also Medes, Sacae, Bactrians, and Indians, both infantry and the rest of their horse. These he picked as whole nations; but of the rest of the allies he chose only a

few here and there, picking some for their good appearance, others for some service he knew to have been good. The Persians were the most numerous people he took, men who wore torques and bracelets, and, after them, the Medes; these were in numbers not less than the Persians but lesser in strength. So that, in all, he had three hundred thousand, including the cavalry.

114. At this time, when Mardonius was choosing his troops and Xerxes was still in Thessaly, there came an oracle from Delphi for the Lacedaemonians, bidding them demand retribution of Xerxes for the murder of Leonidas and to take whatever retribution he should offer. At this the Spartiates sent on a herald at full speed, who overtook the whole army when it was still in Thessaly and came before Xerxes and said, "King of the Medes: the Lacedaemonians and the sons of Heracles from Sparta demand retribution of you because you killed their king as he defended Greece." Whereupon Xerxes burst into a laugh and, after a great while, as Mardonius stood by him, he pointed at him and said: "There is Mardonius for you; he will pay you such retribution as befits you."

115. So the herald received the word that was spoken and took himself home again, and Xerxes left Mardonius in Thessaly and himself marched off speedily toward the Hellespont and in forty-five days came to the ford for his crossing. He brought away with him what one might describe as none of his army at all, and wherever they came in their march and among whatever nations, they plundered their crops and ate them up. And where they found no crop, they ate the grass that grew from the earth and stripped the bark and leaves from the trees, making no difference between wild and cultivated but ate them all and left nothing behind them. All this they did out of sheer hunger. Besides, a plague set upon his army, and dysentery destroyed them on the march. Those of them who were sick he left to be cared for and fed in the cities he came to in his march, some in Thessaly, and some in Siris of Paeonia, and some in Macedonia. There he had left his chariot, which was sacred to Zeus, on his course into Greece, but he received it not again on his homeward journey; for the Paeonians had given it to the Thracians, and, when Xerxes demanded it again, they declared that the mares in their grazing had been carried off by the Thracians of the upper country, who live around the sources of the Strymon.

116. It was here that a Thracian, the king of the Bisaltians and of

the Crestonian country, did a truly monstrous thing. He himself declared that he would never willingly be a slave of Xerxes, and so he betook himself to the mountain called Rhodope and forbade his sons to march against Greece. But they made nothing of his words, or maybe their inclination was to see the war; and they went to serve with the Persian. And for this offense, when all six of them came back unscathed, their father gouged their eyes out.

117. This is the reward they earned. But when the Persians, in their march from Thrace, arrived at the Hellespont, they made haste to cross to Abydos in their ships; for they found that their bridges were no longer securely fastened but had been loosened by a storm. They stopped there some time and got more food than they had had on their march; but they observed no order in stuffing themselves with it, and, what with that and the change of water, many of the survivors in the army died. The rest came with Xerxes to Sardis.

118. There is another story told, that when Xerxes in his retreat from Athens came to Eïon on the Strymon, he marched no further by land but entrusted the rest of his army to Hydarnes, to bring it to the Hellespont, and himself embarked on a Phoenician ship and made for Asia. As he was sailing, a great tempestuous wind, called the Strymonian, overtook him, and great waves as well. The ship was weathering it even worse because so heavily laden, as there were many Persians on deck who were making the journey with Xerxes. The King was in such terror that he screamed to the helmsman, asking him, was there no hope for their safety? At this the helmsman said, "Master, none, save we can get rid of these many that are on board." The story goes that when Xerxes heard that, he said, "You men of Persia, now let each of you prove your care for your King; for in you, it seems, lies my safety." That is what he said, and the men did obeisance and jumped into the sea, and the ship was lightened and came safe to Asia. As soon as Xerxes landed, he did the following: because the helmsman had saved the life of the King, he awarded him a golden crown; but for causing the death of many Persians, he had his head cut off.

119. This is the other story of Xerxes' retreat, but, for myself, I do not believe it—not any of it, and particularly not what happened about the Persians. For if Xerxes was really told that by the helmsman, I do believe there would be not one dissenting opinion in ten

thousand that the King would instead have done this: he would have sent down into the hold of the ship those who were on deck—who were Persians and Persian grandees—and would have taken a number of Phoenician oarsmen equal to that of the Persians and thrown *them* overboard. No, as I said before, Xerxes certainly marched with the rest of his army homeward into Asia.

120. There is great proof of this. For it is clear that Xerxes in his homeward course came to Abdera, where he made a treaty of friendship with its people and gave them a golden scimitar and a turban of gold tissue. The people of Abdera themselves declare—though I do not believe a word of it—that Xerxes never loosed the girdle he wore in his flight from Athens till he came there, assuming that now he was in safety. (Moreover, Abdera is nearer to the Hellespont than the Strymon and Eïon, where they say he took ship.)

121. The Greeks, when they were not able to destroy Andros, turned to Carystus and, having devastated that country, went back to Salamis. First they drew out firstfruits for the gods and, chief among them, three Phoenician triremes. One was to be dedicated at the Isthmus, where it still was in my time, and one at Sunium, and one for Ajax at Salamis, where they were. After that they divided up the spoils and sent their firstfruits to Delphi, and from these latter was made a statue that has in its hand the figurehead of a ship, the statue itself being twelve cubits high. This stood where the gold statue of Alexander the Macedonian stands.

122. When the Greeks sent these firstfruits to Delphi, they asked the god in common whether the firstfruits he had received were enough and satisfactory. He said that from the rest of the Greeks he had had enough but not from the Aeginetans; from them he demanded the chief prize for the victory at Salamis.[37] The Aeginetans, on learning this, dedicated golden stars, which stand, three of them, on a mast of bronze in the corner nearest to the mixing bowl of Croesus.

123. After this division of the loot, the Greeks sailed away to the Isthmus to award the prize for that Greek who in the war had been most worthy of it. When the commanders came and gave their sev-

---

37. In chapter 93 we were told that the Aeginetans won first prize for valor in the battle of Salamis. So the gold stars on the mast are the firstfruits of that prize.

eral votes at the altar of Poseidon, deciding the first and second choice out of all the forces, everyone voted for himself, thinking that he indeed had been the bravest of all; but the most votes agreed in giving second place to Themistocles. So the votes for first place were all singles, but Themistocles was far ahead in the vote for second.

124. Since the Greeks were unwilling, out of jealousy, to give final judgment of the thing, each nation sailed home, leaving the matter unjudged. But Themistocles was cried up and thought to be far the cleverest of the Greeks through all the land. But when, for his victory, he was not honored by those who had fought at Salamis, he immediately went to Sparta in his wish to find his honor there; and indeed the Lacedaemonians welcomed him nobly and honored him mightily. They gave Eurybiades the victor's prize—the olive wreath;[38] but they also bestowed one on Themistocles for his cleverness and dexterity, and they gave him the finest chariot in Sparta. They made many addresses in his praise, and, when he was going away, three hundred chosen Spartiates (those who are called the Knights) escorted him to the boundaries of Tegea. He is the only man whom I know to have been so escorted by the Spartiates.

125. From Lacedaemon he came back to Athens, and there Timodemus, an Athenian of the deme Aphidna, who was an enemy of his but by no means one of the notable men, was mad with envy and taunted Themistocles. He threw Themistocles' reception at Sparta in his teeth and said that he had those honors from the Lacedaemonians because of Athens and not on his own account. As Timodemus kept on talking like this, Themistocles said, "The truth is this: I would not have been honored so by the Spartans had I come from Belbina,[39] but neither would you, sir, though you are a native of Athens." That was the end of that story.

126. Artabazus, son of Pharnaces, was already a person of distinction among the Persians and became even more so as a result of the Plataean affair. He now, with some sixty thousand of Mardonius'

38. One of the rare gaps occurs at this point in the Greek text. It is therefore not perfectly clear that the victor's wreath went to Eurybiades, but it seems very probable that it did. The passage indicates, however, that Themistocles received a prize that was almost equivalent.

39. A little place south of Sunium and a synonym for local insignificance.

picked troops, escorted the King as far as his passage out of Europe. Once the King was in Asia, Artabazus turned back, and when he was near Pallene and found the people of Potidaea in revolt, he did not think fit to spare them from slavery. (Mardonius was wintering in Thessaly and Macedonia, and Artabazus was in no hurry to join the rest of the army.) The people of Potidaea, once the King had passed them by and the Persian fleet had fled from Salamis, had openly thrown off their allegiance to the barbarian, and so too had the rest of the people of Pallene.

127. So Artabazus besieged Potidaea; and because he suspected that the Olynthians, too, were in revolt against the King, he besieged Olynthus as well. The Bottiaeans had taken possession of it when they were driven by the Macedonians from the Thermaic gulf. When Artabazus took it by siege, he led the inhabitants out to the lake and there cut their throats; the city he gave over to Critobulus of Torone, to be its governor, and to the Chalcidian people. That is how the Chalcidians got ownership of Olynthus.

128. Having taken Olynthus, Artabazus gave his attention to Potidaea right vehemently. When he was doing so, one Timoxenus, a general of the people of Scione, negotiated the betrayal of the town to him. I cannot say how the matter was arranged at the beginning, for there is no account of that, but finally it was managed like this: as often as Timoxenus would write a dispatch to Artabazus or Artabazus to Timoxenus, they would wrap it round the shaft of an arrow at the notches and, having covered the dispatch with feathers, they shot it into an agreed place. But Timoxenus' betrayal of Potidaea was discovered; for Artabazus, in shooting the arrow to the place agreed, missed the place and hit a man of Potidaea in the shoulder. A crowd surrounded the man who was hit, as often happens in war, and they straightway, taking the arrow, noticed the dispatch and went to their commanders with it. There were also the rest of the allies from Pallene present there. The generals read the dispatch and understood who was guilty of the treachery but, for the sake of the city of Scione, resolved not to overwhelm Timoxenus with his treachery lest for all time to come the people of that town should be looked on as traitors.

129. Such was the discovery of the traitor. Now, when Artabazus had been three months about the siege, there came a great ebbtide,

which lasted for a long time. The barbarians saw the place becoming
a marsh, and so they made to pass over it to Pallene. But when they
had gone through two-fifths of the way, and there remained three-
fifths still to pass before they would be in Pallene, there was a violent
floodtide; there had been many of these before, say the inhabitants,
but never one so big. Those of the barbarians who did not know how
to swim were drowned, and those who did know how were killed by
the people of Potidaea, who put out against them in small boats.
The Potidaeans say that the cause of the high tide and flood and
what happened the Persians was because the barbarians had behaved
sacrilegiously toward the temple and image of Poseidon in the outer
parts of the town; and so these men were destroyed by the sea. I
think they are right in the cause they give. Artabazus brought off the
survivors to Mardonius in Thessaly. That was what happened to
those who had escorted the King.

130. When the surviving navy of Xerxes touched Asia in its
flight from Salamis, it ferried over the King and the army from the
Chersonese to Abydos; it then passed the winter in Cyme. But right
early, at the first glow of spring, it gathered to Samos. (Some of the
fleet had also wintered there.) Most of the fighting men aboard were
Persians and Medes. There came to them, as commanders, Mardontes, son of Bagaeus, and Artaÿntes, son of Artachaees. By the
choice of Artaÿntes himself there was joined in the command, with
them, his own nephew, Ithamitres. They had had a very severe
blow[40] and so advanced no further toward the West, nor indeed was
anyone putting any compulsion on them to do so; but they sat down
in Samos and watched Ionia, lest it should revolt; the Persians had,
including the Ionian contingent, three hundred ships. It was not,
of course, that they expected the Greeks to come to Ionia; they
thought that they would be quite content to guard their own country; this guess was based on the fact that the Greeks had not pursued
them when they fled from Salamis but had been very glad to be rid of
them. The Persians themselves, as far as the sea went, were men
beaten in spirit, but they still thought that on land Mardonius would
be greatly superior. So they stayed in Samos and looked about for
what harm they could do their enemies, and they had their ears to
the ground for what way the fortunes of Mardonius would turn.

40. He means at the sea battle of Salamis.

131. But the coming of spring and the presence of Mardonius in Thessaly *did* stir the Greeks. The army had not yet collected, but the navy went to Aegina—in number, one hundred and ten vessels. The commander on land and sea was Leotychides, the son of Menares, the son of Hegesilaus, of Hippocratides, of Leotychides, of Anaxilaus, of Archidemus, of Anaxandrides, of Theopompus, of Nicandrus, of Charilaus, of Eunomus, of Polydectes, of Prytanis, of Euryphon, of Procles, of Aristodemus, of Aristomachus, of Cleodaeus, of Hyllus, who was the son of Heracles. This man was thus of the second of the two royal houses. All of these ancestors of his, except for the seven named first after Leotychides, were kings of Sparta. The commander of the Athenians was Xanthippus, son of Ariphron.

132. When all the ships had come to Aegina, there arrived in the Greek camp messengers of the Ionians; they had been in Sparta a little before this and urged the Lacedaemonians to free Ionia. (One of them was Herodotus, son of Basileïdes.)[41] These had been part of an association aimed at killing Strattis, the prince of Chios, and their number had originally been seven; but when their conspiracy was discovered through the revelation of one of those who took part in it, the remaining six stole away from Chios. They went to Sparta and, as I said now, to Aegina to ask the Greeks to sail to Ionia; but these envoys managed to bring the Greeks only as far as Delos, and that with difficulty. Further than that was all terror for the Greeks; they did not know those parts, and everywhere seemed to be full of the enemy's forces. From what they judged, they thought Samos was no nearer to them than the Pillars of Heracles.[42] And so it fell out that there was great terror among the barbarians to venture to sail further west than Samos, just as the Greeks, even at the urging of the Chians, would not venture to go further east than Delos. Thus did fear guard the space between the two sides.

41. Otherwise unknown.

42. Gibraltar, of course; though, curiously enough, although there are repeated references in the same terms—Heraclean Pillars—in Herodotus and other authors, we do not know why they were so called. There is a variety of conjecture: twin islands, twin temples, or even literally pillars in honor of Heracles. There is also some doubt as to whether Herodotus is slandering the Greek navigators or their timidity in his attribution of ignorance. But he is certainly following a personal source, probably Ionian.

133. So the Greeks sailed to Delos, and Mardonius spent the winter in Thessaly. From there he sent out a man of Europus, called Mys, to make the rounds of the oracles, charging him to consult whatever ones he could make trial of. What he wanted to learn from the oracles when he gave this instruction I cannot say (we have no record of that), but I am convinced that he was consulting them about his present business and nothing else.

134. It seems this fellow Mys came to Lebadea and bribed one of the local people to descend into the cave of Trophonius and that he also went to Abae, among the Phocians, to consult their oracle. He went first, too, to Thebes, where he consulted the oracle of Ismenian Apollo. (It is there the rule to make divination by sacrifice, as it is at Olympia.) It was certainly a stranger and no Theban whom he persuaded with his money to sleep in the cave of Amphiaraus. For no Theban may consult the oracle there, and this is why: Amphiaraus, speaking in oracles, gave the Thebans a choice, which of two courses they would take: to have him as a prophet or to have him as an ally. But they must choose one of the two. The Thebans chose to have him as an ally. Therefore, no Theban may lie down to sleep in that place.

135. Then a very extraordinary wonder happened, according to the Thebans. This Mys, man of Europus, having wandered up and down among all the oracles, came to the sanctuary of Ptoan Apollo. This is the sanctuary called Ptoum and is the possession of the Thebans. It lies above Lake Copaïs on a mountain, near to the town Acraephia. When the man called Mys came into this shrine, there followed him three men of the city, selected by the commonalty to write down what was prophesied; and suddenly the prophet[43] spoke in a foreign language. Those of the Thebans who followed Mys were in astonishment when they heard the foreign tongue instead of Greek, and they did not know how to handle their present difficulty. But Mys of Europus snatched from them the tablet they carried that he might write on it what the prophet said. He said that what was spoken was Carian, and he wrote it down and made off to Thessaly with it.

43. As in other instances, cited from Delphi, it is not quite clear whether this "prophet" was the official "spokesman" for the god, i.e., the interpreter who relayed in intelligible words what the god's medium had spoken in frenzy, or some other temple official, connected with the transmission of the text of the prophecy.

136. As soon as Mardonius had read over what the oracles said, he sent as his messenger to Athens Alexander, son of Amyntas, a Macedonian. He chose him because, in the first place, the Persians were akin to him; for Bubares, a Persian, had married the sister of Alexander, Gygaea, and by him she had Amyntas of Asia, who had the name of his maternal grandfather; and he had been given by the King the great city of Alabanda in Phrygia for his holding. Apart from this relationship, Mardonius sent him because he understood that Alexander was Consul and Well-Doer for the Athenians,[44] and he thought that thus he would best win them over. He had heard that they were a populous and valiant people, and he knew that the defeats that had been inflicted on the Persians at sea were the work of the Athenians chiefly. With them as allies, Mardonius thought that he would easily gain the mastery at sea—and indeed he would have in that case—and by land he believed he was much stronger anyway; and so he reckoned that he would surely have the upper hand of the Greeks. Perhaps that is what the oracles had told him—counseling him to make the Athenian his ally—and it was in obedience to their predictions that he sent to Athens as he did.

137. Now this Alexander was the seventh in descent from Perdiccas, who created the Macedonian monarchy, and this is how he won it. There were three brothers, of the line of Temenus, who went into banishment from Argos into Illyria. Their names were Gauanes, Aeropus, and Perdiccas. They crossed from Illyria into the mountainous part of Macedonia and came to the city of Lebaea. There they worked for hire in the service of the king, one tending horses, one cattle, and the youngest of them, Perdiccas, the flocks of lesser size.[45] The king's wife used to cook their food for them, for in the old days it was not only the common folk who were weak in money but the very princes' families themselves. Now, whenever she baked, the loaf of the young serf Perdiccas became twice its proper size. When

44. As noted before, important states had their nationals protected elsewhere than at home by foreign dignitaries, and this office tended to be hereditary. At one stage of the Peloponnesian War, Alcibiades thought he should have inherited his father's distinction of being "consul" (*proxenos*) for the Spartans. The Spartans thought differently and chose someone else. As a result, Alcibiades did everything he could to destroy sympathy for Sparta in the relevant circles in Athens.

45. As elsewhere, this seems to mean "lesser in physical size," i.e., sheep and goats.

the same thing happened again and again, the lady told her husband of it, and, when he heard it, it came over him right away that this was a portent and presaged some great thing. So he summoned the three serfs to his presence and bade them be gone out of his country. They said that they would go readily, but first it was but just that they receive their wages. Now, as the king heard them speak of wages, the sun was streaming down into the house through the smoke-hole, and he was so besotted that he pointed to the sunlight and said, "There are the wages I give you—and wages worthy of you, too." Gauanes and Aeropus, the two older ones, stood there dumbfounded when they heard that; but the boy had a knife and said, "My lord, we receive what you give us," and with his knife he drew a circle around the sunlight on the floor of the house, and, having so drawn it, he gathered into the fold of his garment that sunlight, thrice over, and went away with his brothers.

138. So they went on their way; but one of those who had sat by the king told him what it was that the boy had done and how cunningly this youngest of the brothers had accepted the gift. At this the king was very angry and sent horsemen after them to kill them. But there is a river in that country to which descendants of those men from Argos sacrifice as their deliverer. When the Temenidae crossed that, it flowed so strongly that the horsemen could not cross. So the Temenidae came to another part of Macedonia and dwelt there, near what are called the Gardens of Midas, son of Gordias. In these gardens there grow, without planting, roses, each bearing sixty blossoms and in scent exceeding every rose anywhere. In these gardens was Silenus captured, as the Macedonians tell the story; above them is the mountain called Bermius, which none can ascend because of the cold. When the boys had possession of this country, they went forth from it and subdued the rest of Macedonia, too.

139. From this Perdiccas was Alexander descended, and thus: Alexander was the son of Amyntas, and Amyntas of Alcetes; and the father of Alcetes was Aeropus; and of him the father was Philippus, and, of Philippus, Argaeus; and of him the father was Perdiccas, who established the monarchy.

140. Such was the descent of Alexander, son of Amyntas. Now, when he was sent by Mardonius and came to Athens, he spoke as follows: "You men of Athens, here are the words of Mardonius: 'A

message has come to me from the King, and it says: "For the Athenians, I remit freely to them all the offenses they have committed against me. Now, Mardonius, this you must do. Give them back their land, and let them take besides whatever other territory they choose, and let them live free and independent. All those temples of theirs that I burned do you now raise again, if they are willing to come to terms with me." Since this is the message that I, Mardonius, have received, I must necessarily execute what is said, unless you of yourself stand in my way. What *I* have to say to you is this: Why are you so mad as to undertake a war against the King? You cannot beat him, nor can you even withstand him for ever. For you have seen the multitude of the host of Xerxes and what they have done; you are informed also of the power I now have with me. So that, if you were to beat us—of which there is no hope for you whatever, if you are in your right minds—there will be another to take its place, many times as great. Do not try to set yourself to equal the King—to the loss of your country and to the perpetual risk of your own lives. Come to peace with him. You can come to peace with him most nobly, for the King is that way given. Be free, making your covenant with us, void of deceit and treachery.' These, men of Athens, are the things Mardonius has instructed me to declare to you. About my personal good will toward you I will not speak; it would not be the first time you have heard of that; but I beg of you to be persuaded by Mardonius. I see no possibility at all that you would be able forever to make war upon Xerxes. If I did see any such possibility, I would never have come to you with propositions like these. Truly, the power of the King is something beyond that of men, and his arm is long. If you do not come to terms at once, when they are willing to agree on such good terms, I am greatly afraid on your behalf, since, of all the allies, you live most in the very track of the war, and you alone will be destroyed, your country being a very chosen-out no-man's-land between two foes. Do what Mardonius says; for it is not of little worth, that to you alone of the Greeks the Great King is willing to remit your offenses and be your friend."

141. So spoke Alexander. Now, the Lacedaemonians had heard that Alexander had come to Athens to bring the Athenians into agreement with the barbarian. They remembered also the prophecies that they themselves, with all the rest of the Dorians, must be

expelled from the Peloponnese by a combination of Medes and Athenians, and they were mightily afraid that the Athenians would come to terms with the Persian. So they at once resolved to send messengers. It so fell out that the presentation of the envoys of the two parties happened at the same time. For the Athenians had delayed and waited, knowing full well that the Lacedaemonians would learn that an envoy had come from the barbarian about the possibilities of an agreement and, having so learned, would with all speed send envoys themselves. So the Athenians acted deliberately, in order to make the declaration of their position to the Lacedaemonians most publicly.

142. So when Alexander stopped speaking, the envoys of Sparta took his place: "The Lacedaemonians have sent us to beg of you to make no harmful change in your policy toward Greece nor receive propositions from the barbarian. For it is no way just or honorable for any Greek to do so, but least of all for yourselves, and that for many reasons. It was you who stirred up this war—it was no matter of our willing it—and it was about your land that in the beginning the struggle started. Now it has meaning for the whole of Greece; but apart from all that, it is intolerable that slavery should come on the Greeks because of the Athenians, who have always of old stood forth as the savior of the freedom of many men. But we have common feeling for your pressure under suffering; you have lost two harvests, and your household gear has been destroyed now for a long time. Therefore, the Lacedaemonians and their allies make you this offer: that we will take over your womenfolk and all of your household that is useless in the war and feed them for as long as the war lasts. Do not let Alexander of Macedon convince you with his smooth talk of Mardonius' offers. This is the way he has to act, for he is a despot and is hand-in-glove with a despot. But it is not the way for you to act—not, at least, if you are in your right minds; for you know that the barbarians cannot be trusted, nor do they tell the truth." That is what the envoys said.

143. The Athenians made their answer to Alexander: "We know of ourselves that the power of the Mede is many times greater than our own; therefore, you need not throw that in our face. Yet we have such a hunger for freedom that we will fight as long as we are able. Do not try to induce us to make terms with the barbarian, for we will not listen to you. Now tell Mardonius that this is the word of the

Athenians: So long as the sun keeps his wonted track where even now he is going, we will never make terms with Xerxes, but putting our trust in our gods and our heroes we will go out to fight him in our defense. He had scant regard for those gods and heroes when he burned their homes and their images. And for the future do not make your appearance before the men of Athens with propositions like these, nor, seeming to do us a service, advise us to do what is against all law for us; for we would not have anything untoward happen to you at the hands of the Athenians—you who are our consul and our friend."

144. That was their answer to Alexander; but to the Spartan envoys they said: "That the Lacedaemonians should be afraid that we would make an agreement with the barbarian is indeed very human; and yet we think that this fear of yours is a base one, knowing, as you do, the spirit of the Athenians—that there is not enough gold in the world anywhere, nor territory beautiful and fertile enough, that we should take it in return for turning to the Persian interest and enslaving Greece. There are many great things that stand in our way of so doing even if we wanted to; there are, first and greatest, the shrines of the gods and their images, burned and destroyed; it lies upon us of necessity to avenge these to the uttermost rather than make terms with him who did these things; and then there is our common Greekness: we are one in blood and one in language; those shrines of the gods belong to us all in common, and the sacrifices in common, and there are our habits, bred of a common upbringing. It would be indecent that the Athenians should prove traitors to all these. So you know now, if not before, that while a single Athenian survives we will not make terms with Xerxes. For your forethought on our behalf, in foreseeing the ruin of our households and your willingness to look after these people of ours, we admire you. The grace you have shown us is full to the brim of the cup, but we will endure our lot as best we can without troubling you. But now, since things are as they are, send an army as quickly as ever you may. For as we guess what shall be, the time is not distant when the enemy will invade our country; it will be in the very first moment, as soon as he receives our message that we will do nothing that he asks us to do. Before he comes to Attica is the time for us to have moved into Boeotia." After this response from Athens, the Spartan envoys went home.

Book Nine

1. Mardonius, when Alexander came back and told him what the Athenians had said to him, set out from Thessaly and with great eagerness led his army against Athens.[1] To whatever people he came, he drafted them. The chief men of Thessaly had no repentance for what they had already done—indeed, they urged on the Persian all the more—and Thorax of Larissa, who had escorted Xerxes on his flight, now manifestly opened a passage for Mardonius into Greece.

2. When in the course of its march the army was in Boeotia, the Thebans tried to hold Mardonius there; they gave him as their counsel that there was no place more suitable for him to make his encampment. They would have him go no further but sit down there and, they said, take measures such that he would conquer all Greece without a fight. To beat the Greeks by sheer force, if these Greeks were really united, as they had been before, was very difficult for all the people on earth. "But," said the Thebans, "if you do as we advise, you will overcome all their strong plans without trouble on your part. Send money to the leading men in the cities, and in so sending you will split Greece apart. From then on you will easily, with the aid of those of *your* party, master those who are of the other."

3. That was their advice, but he did not fall in with it. A terrible longing had seeped into his heart to take Athens a second time. It was partly arrogant pride and partly that he saw himself proving to the King (who was in Sardis), through beacon fires across the islands, that he had taken Athens. Yet, when he came to Attica, he again found no Athenians there. Most of them, he learned, were in Salamis with the fleet, and the city he took was empty of men. Between Xerxes' first capture of Athens and this later capture by Mardonius was just ten months' space.

1. In the summer of 479 B.C.

4. When Mardonius was in Athens, he sent to Salamis one Murychides, a Hellespontian, with the same offers that Alexander of Macedon had transmitted to the Athenians before. He sent this second time, although he knew that the Athenians had no friendly sentiments toward him, because he thought they would give up their stiff-neckedness to some extent, seeing that Attica was the captive of his spear and entirely subject to him.

5. For these reasons he sent Murychides to Salamis, and the man came and went before the Council and put to them the offers of Mardonius. One of the councillors, Lycidas, gave as his opinion that it seemed best, once they themselves had received the proposition that Murychides brought, to submit it to the people. This then was the judgment he openly declared, either because he was in receipt of money from Mardonius or perhaps out of his personal conviction. But the Athenians, both those of the Council and those outside, when they learned of this, raised a very storm about it. They surrounded Lycidas and stoned him to death, though they sent Murychides, the Hellespontian, away unscathed. There was a tumult in Salamis about this business of Lycidas; and when the Athenian women heard what was happening, one woman summoned another and came and took her along, and they went of their own prompting to the house of Lycidas, where they stoned to death his wife and his children.

6. This is how the Athenians had crossed over into Salamis: so long as they expected the army from the Peloponnese to come to their help, they waited in Attica; but when what the Peloponnesians did took ever longer and grew ever slower, and when now the invader was said already to be in Boeotia—faced with this, the Athenians conveyed away all their goods and themselves went across to Salamis. They also sent messengers to Lacedaemon, both to declare their anger against the Lacedaemonians for standing by and watching the barbarian invade Attica instead of, with the Athenians, meeting him in Boeotia, and to remind them of the offers the Persian had made them if they should change sides and to warn them that, unless they came to the help of the Athenians, they, the Athenians, would themselves find some sort of escape from their danger.

7. For the Lacedaemonians were at this time celebrating a festival; it was the Hyacinthia, and they made a great matter of giving

the god his due. Besides, the fortification they were building at the Isthmus was right now having the battlements put on it. When the messengers from the Athenians came to Lacedaemon, bringing with them messengers as well from the Megarians and the Plataeans, they came before the ephors and addressed them: "The Athenians have sent us to tell you that the King of the Medes is giving us back our country; that he is willing to make us his allies on fair and equal terms, without fraud or deceit; he is willing, moreover, to give us other territory in addition to our own—such territory as we shall choose. Out of shame before the God of the Hellenes and thinking it a dreadful thing to betray Greece, we did not consent, but refused, though we are being unjustly treated by the Greeks and left in the lurch, and though we know full well that it would be more to our profit to come to an agreement with the Persian than to make war. But indeed, we will not, insofar as our willingness goes, make terms with him. So, in our dealings with the Greeks, we have passed no false coin. But what of you? Some time ago, in utter terror you came to us to beg us not to make terms with the Persian; but after that you came to understand the Athenian mind thoroughly—that we would never betray Greece. Besides, that wall of yours that you are building across the Isthmus is now finished; and so now you make no account at all of the Athenians! You made a bargain with us to go into Boeotia to meet the Persian there, and you broke your word; you have stood by and watched the barbarian invade Attica. As of this moment, the Athenians are wroth against you, for you have acted contrary to all decency. But now they bid you with the utmost speed send out an army with us, that we may meet the barbarian in Attica. For, since we have lost Boeotia, the Thriasian plain, in our country, is the most suitable place for us to fight."

8. When the ephors heard that, they postponed making their answer until the day following, and on that next day to the next, and so on for ten days, always postponing the decision from one day to the next. During this time all the Peloponnesians were working with might and main, building their fortification of the Isthmus; they had the work almost done. I cannot myself say why it was that when Alexander of Macedon came to Athens they took such trouble to plead against the Athenians' taking the Persian side while now they did not care about that at all—except that the Isthmus was

now fortified and they thought they had no further need of the Athenians, but, when Alexander had come to Attica, the fortifications were not complete, and they were working on them, in great dread of the Persians.

9. But the final settlement of what answer was to be given, and the decision to send out the Spartan army, came about like this: on the day before what was to be the last meeting, a man of Tegea called Chileus, who had more influence in Sparta than any other foreigner, learned from the ephors all that the Athenians had said. When Chileus heard this, he said to the ephors, "Ephors, this is how the matter stands. If the Athenians are not going to be on our side but are to be allies of the barbarian, you may draw whatever strong walls you please across the Isthmus; there will still be huge gates wide open for the Persian into the Peloponnese. Listen, you, before the Athenians come to a different decision—one that will bring all Greece to the ground."

10. That was his counsel; and the ephors, when they had grasped what he had said, straightway, while it was still night, sent off five thousand Spartiates and assigned seven helots to each one, with Pausanias, son of Cleombrotus, entrusted with the command for leading them out for the expedition. (They told nothing whatever to the messengers who had come to them from the cities.) The leadership indeed belonged to Pleistarchus, son of Leonidas, but he was still a child, and Pausanias was his guardian and cousin. For Cleombrotus, the father of Pausanias and the son of Anaxandrides, was no longer living; he had brought the army out of the Isthmus— the army that had built the wall—and lived only a short space thereafter and then died. (The reason Cleombrotus drew off the army from the Isthmus is this: as he was sacrificing for triumph over the Persian, the sun failed in the heaven.) [2] Pausanias coopted, to join him in the command, Euryanax, the son of Dorieus, a man of his own house.

11. So this force with Pausanias had marched out of Sparta; and at daybreak the messengers, who knew nothing of the marching-out, came before the ephors, having in mind to go off home, each to his own country. And when they came, they said this: "You men of

2. There was an eclipse.

Lacedaemon, stay right here and celebrate your Hyacinthia in playful spirit, now that you have betrayed your allies. The Athenians, being wronged by you, and for lack of allies, will make their terms with the Persian as best they may. It is quite clear that we will become allies of the King, and, once we have made our terms with him, we will campaign against whatever land he may lead us to. From then on you will find out what will happen to you as a result of what you have now done." That was what the messengers said; but the ephors told them, upon oath, that as far as they knew the Spartans were even then in Orestheum, marching against "the foreigners." (They always called the barbarians "the foreigners.") The spokesmen for the allies, being unable to understand this, asked them again for the meaning of what they said, and in response to their questions they learned the whole truth. So, being much amazed, they set out in hot pursuit. And with them on the same tack went five thousand chosen hoplites of the Lacedaemonian "Dwellers Around."[3]

12. On they hastened to the Isthmus. But the Argives, as soon as they learned that Pausanias and this expedition had set out from Sparta, picked the best of the day-runners[4] they could find as their herald and sent him off to Attica; for they had earlier, and of their own will, promised Mardonius to prevent the Spartans from getting out of Sparta to the war. So this man came to Athens and said, "Mardonius, the Argives have sent me to inform you that the youth of Sparta has marched out of Lacedaemon and that the Argives are unable to stay them from going out. So lay your best plans in the face of this circumstance."

13. Having given his message, he went off home. But Mardonius, when he heard the news, was no longer anxious to remain in Attica. Now, before he knew this, he had hung back, wanting to know what the Athenians would do; and during this time he did no damage nor devastated the land of Attica, because he kept expecting that the Athenians would come to terms with him. But when he failed to persuade them, and learned everything, he withdrew before

---

3. This is the technical term (*perioikoi*) for the Lacedaemonians who lived in the territory around Sparta but were not possessed of full Spartan citizenship.
4. Long-distance runners.

of Orchomenus, one of the chief men of distinction in Orchomenus. Thersander said that he himself had been invited by Attiginus to the dinner and, along with him, fifty Thebans; the men of the two peoples were not kept separate, but on each couch for the dinner there were a Persian and a Theban. When the dinner was over and they were drinking to one another, the Persian who was the partner of Thersander on the couch asked him, in Greek, what countryman he was. Thersander answered that he was from Orchomenus. Then the other said: "Because we have eaten at the same table and have shared the libation too, I would like to leave with you a record of what I think, so that you may be forewarned and take proper measures for your own safety. You see these Persians feasting here and the army we left encamped on the river? Of all these many, within a very short time indeed, you will see but few survivors." That was what the Persian said, and he cried bitterly. At this Thersander was very surprised and said to him, "Should you not tell this to Mardonius and to those who are, with him, in great esteem among the Persians?" But the Persian answered, "Sir, what comes from God, no man can turn back. Even if what was said was credible, no one would believe it. Many of us Persians know all this, but we follow in the bondage of Necessity. This is the bitterest pain to human beings: to know much and control nothing." That was what I heard from Thersander of Orchomenus, and, in addition to this, that he himself had told it to others before the battle of Plataea took place.

17. So Mardonius was making his encampment in Boeotia, and all the Greeks who lived in that part of Greece and took the Persian side contributed troops and, except for the Phocians, they had all joined in the invasion of Athens. For the Phocians, though they too Medized, strongly, did so unwillingly and of necessity. So a few days after the Persians had arrived in Thebes there came a thousand Phocian hoplites to join them, their leader being Harmocydes, a very renowned Phocian. When these too arrived in Thebes, Mardonius sent some horsemen and told the Phocians to encamp by themselves on the plain. They did so, and immediately the entire Persian cavalry appeared. Thereafter the rumor ran through the Greek army that was with the Medes that the cavalry was going to shoot them down. (The very same rumor went through the ranks of the Phocians themselves.) Thereupon Harmocydes, their general, exhorted

them as follows: "Phocians," said he, "it is clear that these men are going to send us to our death—indeed, it stares us in the face; I suppose we were slandered to them by the Thessalians. So now it behooves each one of you to be a good man and true; for it is better to end your life in action and defense of yourselves than to offer yourselves to a death of the greatest dishonor. But let each one of our enemy know that they are barbarians and that those whose murder they have contrived are men of Greece."

18. Such was his exhortation. But the cavalry, after encircling them, charged, seemingly to cut them down. They stretched their bows to shoot the arrows, and some perhaps did shoot. The Phocians fronted them every way by drawing together in a solid mass, crowding together as closely as they could. Thereupon the cavalry wheeled about and rode away. I cannot exactly say whether they came there to destroy the Phocians on the urging of the Thessalians and then, when they saw them turning to their own defense, were afraid that there would be losses on their own side and so retired again (because Mardonius had so ordered them), or whether Mardonius had wanted to test the Phocians and see what courage was in them. But when the cavalry had retired, Mardonius sent a herald and said, "Be of good cheer, men of Phocis, for you have shown yourselves as good men and not such as I have been informed you were. Now carry on the war zealously, for you will not surpass either me or the King in the giving of good for good." That was how far this matter of the Phocians went.

19. The Lacedaemonians, when they came to the Isthmus, camped there. And the rest of the Peloponnesians—those who were for the better cause—seeing the Spartans gone out upon their expedition, did not think fit to be left behind them. And so, having sacrificed, and with favorable results, they all marched from the Isthmus and came to Eleusis. There they sacrificed again, and again successfully, and on they went and, with them, the Athenians, who had crossed over from Salamis and joined forces with them at Eleusis. When they advanced (it is said) into Boeotia as far as Erythrae, they learned that the barbarians were encamped at the Asopus, and, having taken note of the position, the Greeks ranged their ranks against them on the foothills of Cithaeron.

20. Now Mardonius, when the Greeks did not come down into

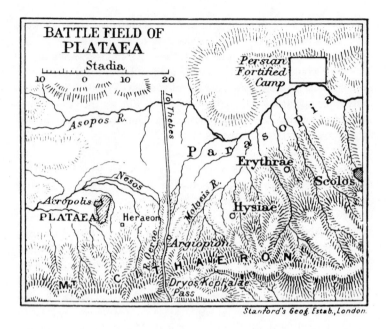

Stanford's Geog. Estab., London.

the plain, sent all his cavalry against them. Their commander was
Masistius, a man of renown among the Persians, whom the Greeks
call Macistius. He rode a Nesaean horse, with a golden bit and other
forms of special decoration. When the Persian cavalry charged the
Greeks, they made the attack by squadrons[6] and in the attack inflicted great damage and taunted the Greeks, calling them women.

21. It happened that the Megarians were stationed where the
whole position was most accessible to attack, and it was on them
that the onset of the cavalry fell most. The Megarians were sorely
pressed by the charge and sent a herald to the Greek generals with
the following message: "The Megarians say: We who are your allies
are not able alone to receive the attack of the Persian cavalry, in the

6. The Persian cavalry attack was made in successive waves. One squadron
would charge, attack, turn, and ride back. Then, on command, another would
do the same. And so on.

position in which we were placed at the beginning. So far we have held our ground, despite sore stress, with sheer courage and endurance. Now, however, unless you send troops to succeed us in this post, we would have you know that we will leave it." That was the message he brought, and Pausanias tried whether there were any others among the Greeks who would be willing to go as volunteers to this place and replace the Megarians. All the others refused, but the Athenians volunteered, some three hundred picked men, commanded by Olympiodorus, the son of Lampon.

22. These were the men who volunteered, and it was they who stationed themselves to defend all the rest of the Greeks who were present at Erythrae, and they also chose archers to aid them. So they fought for a long time, and this was the end of it: as the cavalry charged by squadrons, Masistius' horse, which was in front of the rest, was hit in the ribs by an arrow and, in his pain, reared and threw Masistius. As soon as he fell, the Athenians were upon him. They took the horse at once, and they killed Masistius, despite his defense, though they failed at first; for he had for his armor a golden breastplate with the metal laid on in scales, and over the breastplate he wore a scarlet tunic. So those whose blows upon him reached the breastplate did nothing at all to him, till someone noticed what was happening and struck him in the eye. So he fell and died.[7] The other cavalry, as it chanced, failed to notice all this. They neither saw his fall from his horse nor his dying; because the wheeling-round and retreat were taking place, they had not noticed what was happening.[8] But when they halted, they immediately missed him, because there was no one to give them orders. When they realized what had happened, they shouted to one another, and all drove their horses on to recover the dead body.

23. When the Athenians saw that the Persians were no longer charging by squadrons but in a mass, they called on the rest of the army to help. While the whole of their own infantry was rallying to their defense, there was a sharp fight over the dead man. While the

7. This is one of the rare accounts of what cavalry fighting was like among the Greeks.

8. As How and Wells remark, "Each squadron would advance, hurl its missiles, and then retire rapidly without special orders. In their hasty retreat the fall of their leader passed unnoticed."

three hundred were by themselves, they were very much worsted and were quitting the body; but when the main part of the army came to their aid, then the cavalry no longer withstood them, nor could they pick up the corpse; indeed, in addition to losing their leader's body, they lost many of their own men. So, drawing off a matter of two stades, they debated what they should do. In view of their position, being without a commander, they decided to ride away to Mardonius.

24. When they got back to their camp, Mardonius and the whole army bitterly mourned for Masistius, shaving their own heads and their horses' manes and those of their baggage animals as well and indulging in endless lamentation. The sound filled all of Boeotia, for the man who had been killed was, after Mardonius himself, of the most consideration with both the Persians and the King.

25. So the barbarians paid honor to the dead Masistius after their own fashion. But the Greeks took heart greatly for their withstanding of the charge of the cavalry and, after such withstanding of it, for having repulsed it. So, at the first, they laid the dead man on a wagon and conveyed him along the ranks of the soldiers. He was indeed worth seeing for his great stature and beauty, and that was exactly why they so showed him. The men left their ranks and came all the time to view Masistius. Then the Greeks decided to come down to Plataea. For the country there seemed far more suitable for their camping than that around Erythrae, in particular because it had more water. To this place, then, and to the spring Gargaphia, which is in that locality, they resolved to come and to encamp in their various divisions. Then taking up their arms,[9] they went through the foothills of Cithaeron to the country round Plataea, going past Hysiae, and formed their battle order nation by nation near the spring Gargaphia and the sanctuary of the hero Androcrates, among low hills and a flat piece of country.

26. Then, in the matter of the lineup of the army, there was a great altercation between the Tegeans and the Athenians. For each of them claimed the right to the *other* wing of the army,[10] and each of

9. This apparently means the heavy armor (shields, etc.), which was stacked overnight and taken up again in the morning.

10. One wing being conceded to the Spartans as of right, the dispute arose as to which of the Greek states had the right to the other wing.

them brought forward deeds new and old to justify their claims. Thus the Tegeans said, "We have always been adjudged fit for this place in the ranks, we out of all the allies,[11] as often as there have been common military expeditions involving all the Peloponnesians, both in old days and lately, from the time when the Heraclidae made their attempt to return to the Peloponnese after the death of Eurystheus. This privilege we have won as our own in the following way. When we took up our stand at the Isthmus, along with the Achaeans and Ionians who were then in the Peloponnese, and did so facing against the returning exiles, Hyllus,[12] as the story goes, gave it as his opinion that there should be no great risk taken of army encountering army but that, out of the Peloponnesian camp, whichever man they adjudged their best should fight in single combat against himself, Hyllus, on fixed conditions. The Peloponnesians agreed that this was what should be done and swore an oath that, in very truth, if Hyllus conquered the Peloponnesian champion, the Heraclidae should return to their native land; but if he was the one to be conquered, the Heraclidae should go away, leading off their army, and not for a hundred years should they seek to return to the Peloponnese. Now, out of all the allies, there was chosen a volunteer, Echemus, son of Eëropus, son of Phegeus; he was our general and king, and he fought that single combat and killed Hyllus. For that deed we have had from the Peloponnesians among other great privileges of honor (which we possess to this day) the right of leading the other of the two wings when there is a common expedition of the Peloponnesians forward. Of course, men of Lacedaemon, we will not oppose you in any way; we will concede to you whichever of the two wings you choose to command; but we claim that the command of the other wing comes to us as it always has in times past. And apart from what we have related, we are worthier than the Athenians to have this post. For we have had many glorious conflicts with yourselves,[13] you men of Sparta, and many with others also. So it is just that we have the other wing rather than the Athenians. They have no deeds either new or old to match ours."

27. That is what they said, and the Athenians answered like

11. I.e., all the Spartan allies.
12. The son of Heracles.
13. See 1.66 ff.

this: "We know that this is a gathering of us all together to fight the barbarian, not to talk; but since our friend from Tegea has put forward challenges about stout deeds in war, old and new, achieved by our two states in all the length of time, we must make clear to you[14] whence it comes about that we, rather than the Arcadians, have a right from our fathers to be the first among brave men. First, as concerns the Heraclidae, whose leader the Tegeans say they killed at the Isthmus: those Heraclidae—who had been driven out, before this, by all the Greeks to whom they had come when they were fleeing from slavery by the Mycenaeans—we alone received, and with them we abolished the insolence of Eurystheus and conquered all those who then held the Peloponnese. Secondly, there were those Argives who marched with Polynices against Thebes and died there and lay unburied: those Argives we claim to have picked up for burial and buried in our land in Eleusis, having fought against the Cadmeans to do so. We have also a good deed to our credit in fighting the Amazons, who came from the river Thermodon and invaded the land of Attica; and in the Trojan troubles we were as good as any. But it really does no good to remember all this. For men who were brave then might be of no account now, and those who were then slight men might now be better. Let that be enough about these deeds of old. If we had nothing else to show—though indeed we have more and better things to show than any other Greeks—it is from what we did at Marathon that we are worthy to have this honor and others on top of that; for we are the only ones of the Greeks who have singlehanded fought the Persian, and, having attempted so great a deed, we triumphed and conquered forty-six nations.[15] Is not this action alone an entitlement to this post in battle? But at such a crisis as this it is not fitting to wrangle about position in the ranks. We are ready to obey you, Lacedaemonians, wherever you think it proper to place us and against which of the enemy. Once we are placed there, we will try to prove to be brave men. Command us, then, as men who are ready to obey you." That is what they answered, and a vast cry went up from all the Lacedaemonian host that the Athenians were more worthy to have the wing than the Arca-

14. The Spartans.
15. This last exploit also refers to Marathon.

dians. So it was that the Athenians got the better of the men of Tegea.

28. After that, the Greek army took up its positions for battle, both the Greeks who had come at the beginning and those who kept joining them afterwards. The right wing was held by ten thousand Lacedaemonians. Of these, five thousand were Spartiates, and they were guarded by thirty-five thousand helots—light-armed troops—seven of them ranged in the ranks for each Spartiate. Next to themselves the Spartiates chose to station the men of Tegea, for the honoring of them and for their valor. Of these there were fifteen hundred men-at-arms.[16] Next to them stood five thousand Corinthians, and by them Pausanias allowed the Corinthians to have stand three hundred men of Potidaea, from Pallene, who were there present. Next to these stood the Arcadians from Orchomenus, six hundred strong, and, next these, three thousand men of Sicyon. Next these were eight hundred Epidaurians. By them were ranged one thousand men of Troezen, and, next these, two hundred men of Lepreum; next these, four hundred Mycenaeans and men of Tiryns. Next these, one thousand Phliasians. By them stood three hundred men of Hermione, and, next the men of Hermione, stood some six hundred Eretrians and Styreans, and next them four hundred Chalcidians, and next them five hundred Ambraciots. After these stood eight hundred Leucadians and Anactorians, and next these two hundred men from Pale in Cephallenia. After these were ranged five hundred of the Aeginetans, and, by these, three thousand Megarians, and, beside these, six hundred of the Plataeans. At the end of the line and at the head of it stood the Athenians, holding the left wing to the number of eight thousand, their commander being Aristides, son of Lysimachus.

29. These—except for the seven assigned to each Spartiate—were men-at-arms, in all to the number of thirty-eight thousand seven hundred. These were all the men-at-arms collected against the barbarian. The numbers of the light-armed were as follows: in the Spartiate ranks there were thirty-five thousand—that is, seven assigned to each Spartiate—and every one of these was equipped for war; the light-armed of the rest of the Lacedaemonians and the

16. Hoplites (infantry wearing heavy armor).

Greeks were in proportion of one to each man-at-arms, and so these came to thirty-four thousand five hundred.[17]

30. So the total numbers of all the light-armed men who were also fighters was sixty-nine thousand five hundred, and the number of the entire Greek army that came together at Plataea, men-at-arms and fighting light-armed, amounted to one hundred and ten thousand, with a shortfall of eighteen hundred. But the sum of one hundred and ten thousand was filled out by the attendance of the Thespians; these were the surviving Thespians[18] who were in the camp, to the number of eighteen hundred. All these, then, were formed in line and encamped by the Asopus.

31. The barbarians with Mardonius, when they had finished their mourning for Masistius, learning that the Greeks were at Plataea, came themselves to the part of the river Asopus that flowed there; and when they came there, Mardonius set them in line of battle against the Greeks in the following order. Against the Lacedaemonians he stationed the Persians. The Persians far exceeded the Lacedaemonians in numbers, and so they were arrayed in deeper ranks and also covered the men of Tegea. His arrangement was to select out the most able of the Persians and post them opposite the Lacedaemonians, and the weaker contingents he placed opposite the Tegeans. All these placings he made on the suggestion and under instruction of the Thebans. Next to the Persians he ranged the Medes. These covered, on the Greek side, the Corinthians, the Potidaeans, and the men of Orchomenus and Sicyon. Next to the Medes he posted the Bactrians, and these covered the Epidaurians, the Troezenians, the men of Lepreum and Tiryns, and the Mycenaeans and Phliasians. Next to the Bactrians he posted the Indians,

17. As in all his accounts of numbers, Herodotus is challenged by most if not all of the editors of the past fifty years. In this case the target of criticism is the seven light-armed attached to each Spartiate, for it is not clear whether these are servants or have some paramilitary function. It is remarkable that Herodotus repeats this information several times. In the light of this repetition, it can scarcely be a fault in the text, and one must either challenge some (unknown) source from which Herodotus drew his figure or challenge the military expertise of the editors. I think that we probably have no very clear ideas of how the Greek army was provided with service personnel. It is possible that this relatively large mob of attendants in the Spartan army served as such.

18. Survivors of Thermopylae.

and these covered the men of Hermione, Eretria, Styra, and Chalcis. Next the Indians were the Sacae, who covered the Ambraciots, Anactorians, Leucadians, Paleans, and Aeginetans. Next the Sacae he posted the Boeotians, Locrians, Malians, Thessalians, and the thousand Phocians—all these to confront the Athenians, Plataeans, and Megarians. I say "the thousand" Phocians; for not all the Phocians took the Persian side, but some of them strengthened the Greek cause. They had been penned in on Parnassus, and, using that as their base, they harried the army of Mardonius and those Greeks who were with him. Mardonius also posted against the Athenians the Macedonians and those who lived in Thessalian country.

32. These that I have named were the greatest of those posted in the ranks by Mardonius—those that were most distinguished and of most account. There was also a mixture of other peoples—Phrygians, Thracians, Mysians, Paeonians, and others, as well as Ethiopians and, from the Egyptians, the Hermotybies and those who are called the "sword-bearing Calasiries," who are the only fighting men in Egypt.[19] These Mardonius had put on land from their ships when he was still at Phalerum; they were properly marines, for the Egyptians were not posted to the land army that came with Xerxes to Athens. Of the barbarians there were, then, three hundred thousand, as I demonstrated before. Of the Greeks who were allies of Mardonius no one knows the number—they were indeed never counted. On a guess, I should say that there were up to fifty thousand of them gathered there. Such were the ranks of the infantry; the cavalry were ranked separately.

33. When all then were ranked according to their peoples and regiments, on the next day both sides made their sacrifices. For the Greeks, he that made the sacrifice was Tisamenus, son of Antiochus. He had followed their army as prophet. He was an Elean, of the stock of the Iamidae, and the Lacedaemonians had made him a full citizen of their own. For when Tisamenus was consulting the oracle of Delphi about having children, the Pythia predicted that he should win the "five greatest contests." He mistook the meaning of the oracle and cultivated gymnastics, assuming that it was athletic contests that were meant and that he should win; and he practiced

19. Cf. 2.164-66, 68.

the pentathlon and came within one wrestling fall of winning the Olympic prize in it when he competed against Hieronymus of Andros.[20] But the Lacedaemonians realized that the oracle given to Tisamenus concerned not athletic contests but those that were warlike, and so they tried to persuade Tisamenus by bribes to become their leader in war along with their kings, the sons of Heracles. He saw that the Spartiates thought it mattered greatly to make him their friend, and, having noticed that, he raised his price, signifying to them that he would indeed become such a friend, but only if they should make him their citizen and give him a share of everything, and on no other terms would he accede to what they wanted. When the Spartiates heard this, at first they thought it outrageous and retracted their request to Tisamenus altogether; but finally, with the great threat of the Persian army hanging over them, they changed their position again and granted what he asked. He saw that their minds were turned but said that he would not be content even with these favors alone but that his own brother Hegias must become a Spartiate on the same terms as himself.

34. In this proposition of his he copied what Melampus had done, if one may equate the request for kingship and a request for citizenship. For at the time the Argive women lost their senses and Melampus was being hired by the Argives to come from Pylos and cure them of their frenzy, he demanded as his wages the half of the kingship. The Argives would not put up with this and went away; but as more and more of their women went mad, they promised what Melampus demanded and came prepared to give it. Whereupon, seeing their change of mind, he raised his terms, saying that if they did not give his brother Bias one third of the kingship he would not do what they wanted. The Argives, who had a very tight position for maneuver, consented to this, too.

35. So the Spartiates, also, finally made the concession, so desperate was their need of Tisamenus. When the Spartiates agreed to the terms, then Tisamenus, a man of Elis, now turned Spartiate, by his prophesying helped them win five great contests. These men[21]

20. Note that the Eleans were the main source of supply of seers and prophets. Mardonius also used a Greek prophet who was an Elean. The passage also shows clearly how very important the great athletic contests were in the eyes of the Greeks.

21. Tisamenus and his brother.

were the only people who ever became Spartan citizens. And the five contests were these: one—and the first—was the win here at Plataea. Next, that at Tegea, a victory over the Tegeans and the Argives; then the victory at Dipaea over all the Arcadians except the people of Mantinea; then that over the Messenians at Ithome; and the last one at Tanagra, over the Athenians and Argives. This closed the series of the five contests.[22]

36. This, then, was the man Tisamenus, who had been brought there by the Spartans and prophesied at Plataea. The sacrifices showed fair for them if they stood on the defense but not if they crossed the Asopus and began the fight.

37. Mardonius wanted to begin the fight, but for this his sacrifices also were unfavorable; and for him, too, they were favorable only if he stood on the defense. For he also used the Greek style of sacrifice and had as his seer Hegesistratus, an Elean and the most notable of the Telliadae, whom, before the present occasion, the Spartans had caught and put into bonds with a mind to execute him for the many grievous wrongs he had done them. When he was in this plight, being indeed in mortal danger and likely to suffer much grisly torture before his death, he achieved a deed that is beyond all story-telling. He had been bound in iron-secured stocks, but somehow or other someone conveyed to him a knife. With this he managed the bravest act of anyone I know. He calculated that the rest of his foot could slip out of the stocks if he cut it off at the instep. Having done that, to avoid the watching of his guards, he dug a hole under a wall and fled to Tegea, walking by night and by day creeping into the forest, where he slept; so, though the Lacedaemonians sought him with all the forces of their state, on the third night he managed to get to Tegea. The Lacedaemonians were indeed greatly amazed to see the half of his foot lying there while they were unable to find the man himself. So, for that time, he escaped the Lace-

22. Here, as in several other places in books 8 and 9, one becomes aware of how the events of the great Greco-Persian war are the forerunner of the fights between the Greek states—the First and Second Peloponnesian wars. One of the most interesting points on which to speculate is how much Herodotus' view of the Persian wars lives under the shadow of the civil wars that followed and how he sees the defeat of the Persian empire at Plataea in 479 against the emergence of the Athenian empire out of the Delian League, which was organized in 478 B.C., ostensibly to continue the naval war against Persia.

daemonians and fled to Tegea, which was then not friendly to the
Lacedaemonians. His wound healed, and he had a wooden foot
made for himself and became openly the foe of Sparta. But in the
end this hatred of the Lacedaemonians, which had so much become
part of all that happened to him, did not turn out well for him; for
when he was prophesying in Zacynthus, he was captured by the
Spartans and put to death.

38. However, this death of Hegesistratus happened after the
Plataean affair, and at this time he was at the Asopus, hired by Mardonius for a great sum, and he performed the sacrifices and was a
very zealous man indeed, out of his hatred for the Lacedaemonians
and for the money he was making. But when the sacrifices would not
come out favorably for fighting, either for the Persians themselves or
for those Greeks who were on the Persian side—for they too had a
seer on their own behalf, one Hippomachus of Leucas—and when
more and more Greeks were arriving to join the Greek side, and
their army increased in size, Timagenides, son of Herpys, a Theban,
advised Mardonius to set a watch on the passes out of Cithaeron; he
said that the Greeks were streaming in every day and that he, Mardonius, would thus be able to cut many of them off.

39. For eight days the two armies had lain opposite to one another
when this man gave Mardonius this advice. Mardonius thought the
counsel good, and at nightfall he sent off his cavalry to those passes
of Cithaeron that lead toward Plataea, those that the Boeotians call
the Three Heads and the Athenians the Heads of Oak. There were
results from the coming of the cavalry so sent, for they seized some
five hundred pack animals just as these were coming into the plain,
bringing provisions from the Peloponnese to the camp, and also the
men with them, who tended to the animals. Having captured this
booty, the Persians killed without mercy, sparing neither animal nor
human. When they had had enough of slaughter, they surrounded
the remainder and drove them into Mardonius' camp.

40. After this action, they wasted another two days, neither side
being willing to start the fight. For the barbarians would advance up
to the Asopus, so making trial of the Greeks, but neither side would
cross the river. Mardonius' horse, however, was continually attacking and inflicting damage on the Greeks. For the Thebans, who were
strong in their support of Persia, were zealously pushing the war;

they would constantly conduct the horsemen up to the moment of encounter, but after that it was very much the Persians and Medes who took over from there and showed the deeds of valor.

41. For ten days nothing more happened; but on the eleventh day of their being ranged against each other at Plataea, the Greeks having grown far more numerous, and Mardonius chafing exceedingly at the inactivity, they came to talk with one another, did Mardonius, son of Gobryas, and Artabazus, son of Pharnaces—a man of very great repute with Xerxes. As they debated, these were the views put forward: that of Artabazus was that they should pack up the whole army and move off with all speed to within the walls of Thebes, where they had already stored a great deal of food, as well as fodder for the pack animals; they would sit there at their ease and do their business in the following way. They had much gold there, minted and otherwise, and much silver and silver drinking services. None of this should be spared but should be sent here and there among the Greeks, but particularly among those Greeks who were in high places in the cities and who, said Artabazus, would very soon deliver over their freedom. Certainly the Persians should not put everything to risk by a pitched battle. This view of his was the same as that of the Thebans, and again, in his case, it was based on more knowledge than other people had. But Mardonius' position was stronger—more reckless and totally uncompromising. He was convinced that his army was much better than that of the Greeks, and so he was for engaging at once rather than watching still more of his enemies collect than had already done so. As for the sacrifices of Hegesistratus, he was for dismissing them and not trying to force some favorable answer; let them follow the customs of Persia and give battle.

42. Against this argument of his, no one took a stand, and so his plan won out. For he and not Artabazus had the supreme power of command from Xerxes. So he sent for the regimental commanders and the generals of those Greeks who were on his side and asked them whether they knew of any oracle about the Persians meeting their destruction in Greece. Those he summoned kept silent, some because they did not know the prophecies, some because, though they knew them, they did not think that opening their mouths was a safe thing to do. At this Mardonius said, "Since you either know

none such or don't venture to tell them, I will speak for myself, for I know them well. There is an oracle that Persians shall come to Greece and despoil the temple at Delphi and, after that despoiling, must all perish. We know that very thing, and so we will not go to that temple nor try to spoil it, and that is why we shall *not* meet our destruction. So those of you who are loyal to the Persian cause may be pleased that, as far as this goes, there is nothing to hinder our conquest of the Greeks." After these words he gave another instruction for the readying of everything and getting it into good order for the engagement, which was to start at dawn on the following day.

43. Now this oracle, the one that Mardonius said had pertinence to the Persians, I myself know was designed for the Illyrians and the host of the Encheleës, and not for the Persians. But there is a prophecy of Bacis that *was* given for this battle:

> Yes, by Thermodon's stream and the bed of grass by Asopus,
> there shall be conflict between the Greeks and the screaming
>   barbarians;
> there indeed many shall fall beyond what need be and must
>   be
> of the Medes who carry the bow, when Fate's day has
>   overtaken them.

These verses and others, like them, from Musaeus I know bore on the Persians. The river Thermodon flows between Tanagra and Glisas.

44. After his inquiry about the oracles and the exhortation that Mardonius gave, the night came on, and the two armies posted their sentries. When the night was far advanced and there seemed to be quiet everywhere throughout the camps and the men deeply asleep, Alexander, son of Amyntas, general and king of the Macedonians, rode up to the Athenian sentries and sought to come to speech with the commanders. Most of the sentries remained where they were, but some ran to their generals and, on arrival, told them that there was a fellow who had come to them on a horse from the camp of the Medes who would disclose nothing of what he wanted save that he wanted to speak with the commanders, and he had given their names.

45. As soon as the commanders heard that, they at once fol-

lowed the men to the sentry posts. When they came there, Alexander said, "Men of Athens: here is a message that I want to make as a
kind of deposit with you; I must urge you to secrecy—that you tell
no one but Pausanias, lest you involve me as well in destruction.
Surely I would never speak but that I care so much for the whole of
Greece. I am myself a Greek of ancient stock, and I would not with
my good will see Greece enslaved rather than free. What I have to
tell you is this: Mardonius and his army cannot get sacrifices to come
out as he would have them. Otherwise you would have had a fight
on your hands long ago. But now he has resolved to let sacrificing
alone and, with day's dawning, to engage. For he is afraid that you
are continuing to gain in numbers; that, at least, is my guess. So
make your preparations in the face of that action of his. But if Mardonius postpones the attack and does not make it, still stand your
ground and be patient, for he has provisions left for only a few days.
If this war has an issue to suit you people, then it behooves you to
take thought for my freedom, too, since, for the sake of the Greeks,
I have staked my all on the toss, out of zeal; for I wanted to let you
know Mardonius' intention lest the barbarians fall on you suddenly,
when as yet you did not look for them. I am Alexander of Macedon." With these words he rode away to his own camp and his own
position.

46. The generals of the Athenians came to the right wing and
told Pausanias what Alexander had said. At the story they told,
Pausanias was in deadly fear of the Persians and said to the generals:
"Since the engagement is going to take place at dawn, it behooves
you, the Athenians, to stand facing the Persians, while we deal with
the Boeotians and the Greeks who are arrayed against you. My reason is this: you know the Medes and their fighting, for you fought
them at Marathon, while we have no experience of these men, of
whom we know nothing. No single Spartiate has encountered the
Medes in battle, but we have experience of the Boeotians and Thessalians. So you must pick up your arms and move over to this wing,
while we move over to the left." In return, the Athenians said,
"From the very beginning, when we saw the Persians mustering opposite you, we ourselves had exactly in mind what you have now
anticipated us in saying. We were, however, afraid that what we
would have said would be unpleasant to you. But since you your-

selves have spoken of the matter, we take great pleasure in your proposition and are ready to do as you say."

47. Since they were both satisfied in the matter, they exchanged their positions at the first peep of dawn. The Boeotians realized what was being done and informed Mardonius, and when he heard this from them he immediately also tried to change his own positions, bringing the Persians again opposite the Lacedaemonians. When Pausanias learned that this was so and realized that he could not act unperceived, he led his Spartiates back to the right wing, and Mardonius similarly acted with his left wing.

48. So they ranged themselves as they had been at the first, and Mardonius sent a herald to the Spartiates and said, "Lacedaemonians, you are said, by all the people of these parts, to be the bravest of men; they are all admiration for how you neither flee from battle nor leave your ranks but stand and kill or be killed. There is not a word of truth in all this; for before we ever joined battle or came to hand-to-hand fighting, lo! we have seen you fleeing and leaving your position, turning over to the Athenians the place of honor and ranging yourselves opposite people who are slaves of ours. In no way is that the action of brave men; we have been entirely deceived in you. What we looked for in the light of your reputation is that you would send a herald to us to challenge us, to express your will that you were ready to fight with the Persians alone; we were ready, too, for this, but we find that you do nothing of the sort but cower abjectly before us. Now, since you have made no such beginning, we will. Why should we not fight with equal numbers on both sides, you for the Greeks, since you are thought to be the bravest among them, and we for the barbarians? If the decision be that the rest shall fight too, let them do so after our conflict; or, if the decision be that we alone should fight, let our two sides fight it out to the finish, and, whichever of us wins, let that be counted a victory for the whole army."

49. That was what he said; and after waiting for a while, when no one answered, he went back again and told Mardonius what had chanced. Mardonius was delighted, and, elated by his empty victory, he launched his cavalry against the Greeks. The charge of the cavalry injured the whole Greek army greatly, inasmuch as they were mounted archers and very difficult to deal with; they shot their arrows and their javelins at the Greeks. And, choking it up with dirt,

they destroyed the spring of Gargaphia, from which the whole Greek camp drew its water. The Lacedaemonians were the only Greeks stationed right at the spring, and for the rest of the Greeks in their several posts this spring was far to go to and the Asopus was near. However, as they were kept away from the Asopus by the cavalry—for it was impossible to draw water from the river under the attack of the cavalry and their missiles—they had to make the journey constantly to the spring.

50. Such being their case—their army being deprived of water and in sore stress from the cavalry attacks—the generals of the Greeks gathered to talk about these and other matters, coming to Pausanias on the right wing to do so. This bad condition of affairs was made even worse for the Greeks by something else: they had no more provisions, and their own service train, which had been sent to the Peloponnese to bring in further supplies, had been cut off by the cavalry and could not reach the camp.

51. The generals held their council and resolved that if the Persians delayed their engagement for that day, the Greeks would go to the Island. This place lies at a distance of some mile and a quarter from the Asopus and the spring Gargaphia, where they were then encamped; it is in front of the city of Plataea and might be an island but that it is on dry land. That is, the river splits above, by Cithaeron, and flows down into the plain, its two streams separating from one another to a distance of three furlongs, then joining together again. The name of this river is the Oëroë, and the natives say that she was the daughter of Asopus. The generals, then, resolved to withdraw to this place, that they might profit by the abundance of water and freedom from injury by the cavalry, which at this point they found themselves facing in full confrontation. They decided, also, to make the move during the second watch of the night, that the Persians might not be aware that they had got into motion and so have the cavalry follow and harass them. It was further decided that when they got to this position, which is formed by Oëroë (daughter of Asopus) splitting as it flows from Cithaeron, they would send off one half of the army to Cithaeron during that night, to retrieve the baggage train, which had gone after provisions and had been hemmed in by the enemy on Cithaeron.

52. After their decision they endured severe hardship all that day

under the attacks of the cavalry; but when the day ended and the cavalry ceased its attacks, then, when night came and it was the hour when they had agreed to go off, the majority got into motion and withdrew—but with no intention of going to the place agreed upon. Once they were on the move, they fled gladly from the cavalry to the city of Plataea, and when they escaped thither they came to the temple of Hera. The temple is in front of the city of Plataea, two miles and a half from the spring Gargaphia; here they came and encamped and piled their arms.

53. So these encamped around the temple of Hera. But Pausanias, when he saw them leave their original position, sent word to the Lacedaemonians also to take up their arms and follow in the track of those who had gone ahead. He assumed that they were going to the position they had agreed on. The other regimental commanders were ready to obey Pausanias, but Amompharetus, son of Poliades, who was colonel of the Pitanate regiment, said that he would not retreat before the "foreigners"; he was not willing to disgrace Sparta. (He was at a loss, observing what was happening, for he had not been present at the recent council.) Pausanias and Euryanax made a great to-do about the colonel's refusing to obey their orders but an even greater one at the contingency that, if he continued to refuse, they would have to leave the Pitanate regiment behind if they marched off, doing what they had agreed with the rest of the Greeks to do. In that case, Amompharetus and his men, being abandoned, would perish. When they came to reflect on this, they halted the movement of the Laconian camp and tried to persuade Amompharetus that truly he must not act in this fashion.

54. So they argued with Amompharetus, he being the only one of the Lacedaemonians and Tegeans to remain behind; but the Athenians acted as follows. They did not move from where they were stationed, for they knew very well the spirit of the Lacedaemonians, that they would say one thing and think another; but when the camp started to move, they sent one of their own men on horseback to look at whether the Spartans were really trying to make a move or if, indeed, they had no intention at all of departing. This man was also to ask Pausanias what the Athenians were to do.

55. As soon as the herald came to the Lacedaemonians, he saw that they were ranged in their ranks in the same place and that their

chiefs were quarreling bitterly. Pausanias and Euryanax were arguing with Amompharetus that he should not endanger the Lacedaemonians, which he would do if they were left there alone. They failed to convince him, and finally, just as the herald of the Athenians came up and stood by them, they fell to open abuse of one another. As they quarreled, Amompharetus took up a rock with both his hands and hurled it down at Pausanias' feet. "There is my vote against fleeing before the 'foreigners,'" he said, meaning, by "foreigners," barbarians.[23] Pausanias said, "You are a madman! You are quite crazy," and he turned to the Athenian herald, who had asked the question he was to ask, and said, "Tell the Athenians the position I am in," and he requested them to join his troops and, as for the withdrawal, to do whatever he did.

56. So the herald went back to the Athenians; but when daybreak still found the Spartans hot in dispute with one another, Pausanias, who all this time had halted his army, now gave the signal and led all the rest through the hills, the Tegeans following; for he thought that if the rest of the Lacedaemonians departed, Amompharetus would not stay behind (and in the end this is indeed what happened). The Athenians set themselves in order and marched, but by a different route from the Lacedaemonians. For the latter held to the broken ground and the foothills for fear of the Persian horse, but the Athenians marched down to the plain.

57. At first, Amompharetus refused to believe that Pausanias would actually dare to leave him and his regiment, and so he insisted that they should stay where they were and not give up their position; but as Pausanias' men went forward, he came to the unpleasant conviction that they had indeed straightforwardly deserted him, and so he ordered his regiment to pick up their arms, and he led them forward at a footpace in the direction of the other column, which, after advancing for a mile and a half, was waiting for Amompharetus, halting at a place called Argiopium near the river Moloïs, where there is a shrine of Eleusinian Demeter. Pausanias' troops waited there so that if Amompharetus and his regiment should re-

23. A very funny passage. The Athenians voted by stone tallies called *psēphoi*. It is easy to see Pausanias watching the enraged colonel take up a huge rock (with both hands!) with apprehension of the "vote" that was being registered.

fuse to quit the position in which they had been stationed and insist on staying there, Pausanias might come back to his help. At the same time as Amompharetus' men came up with them, the entire cavalry of the barbarian attacked. For the cavalry did what they were always wont to do, and when they saw the position in which the Greeks had stood on the days before empty, they urged their horses ever forward, and, as soon as they came up with the enemy, they attacked them.

58. Mardonius, when he learned that the Greeks had gone away under cover of night and saw the position vacated, summoned Thorax of Larissa and his brothers, Eurypylus and Thrasydeius, and said, "You sons of Aleuas: *now* what will you say, when you see this vacated position? You are neighbors of these people, and you kept telling me that the Lacedaemonians do not fly from battle but are the very first of men in warfare. Earlier you saw the way they kept changing their station in the battle line, and now you and all the rest of us can see that last night they ran clean away! At the moment when they had to find the decision in conflict with men who are beyond any falsehood the best of warriors, these Lacedaemonians have proved themselves the most complete nobodies in a nation of Greek nobodies. You, of course, have had no experience of the Persians, and so I have a great deal of pardon for *you* for praising them, whom you do know to some extent. But I am much more amazed at Artabazus, both for his fear of the Lacedaemonians and, because of that fear, for his declaring that cowardly opinion of his, that we should pack up the camp and go to the shelter of Thebes, there to be besieged! The King shall certainly hear from me about *that*, and we shall have occasion to talk of it, but at other times. At present we must not suffer the enemy to do as they are doing; we must, instead, pursue them until we catch them and make them pay us for all the things they have done to the Persians."

59. With these words he led the Persians at a run across the Asopus and on the track of the Greeks, assuming that the latter were fleeing. He aimed solely for the Lacedaemonians and Tegeans; for the Athenians had turned toward the plain, and he could not see them because of the ridges between him and them. When the rest of the commanders of the barbarian regiments saw the Persians rushing on to pursue the Greeks, they at once hung out their standards, and

their troops went as fast as their feet would carry them after the Persians, with no ordering or positioning in the ranks.

60. So they charged on, in their masses, shouting, thinking they would destroy the Greeks. Pausanias, when the horses made their attacks on him, sent to the Athenians a mounted messenger and said: "You men of Athens; the greatest of our trials is upon us, and the stake whether Greece will be free or enslaved! At such a moment, we the Lacedaemonians and you the Athenians have been betrayed by our allies: they have run away during the past night. So now we have made up our minds what to do; to the limits of what we can, we must make a defense by protecting one another. If the horse had attacked you first, it would have been the duty of us and such Greeks as are on our side—the Tegeans, who are no traitors to Greece—to succor you. As it is, since the whole force of the enemy has come upon us, it is fair that you should come to the defense of this part of our armies that is hardest pressed. If circumstances are such that it is impossible for you to succor us, send us your archers, and we will be thankful; for we are fully aware that in this war you have been the most zealous of all. And so you will listen to us now in this, too."

61. When the Athenians heard this, they were eager to help and to defend them to their very utmost; but when they were already on their way, they were set upon by the Greeks ranged opposite them, who were on the side of the King, and so they were no longer able to come to the help of Pausanias. For the attacks on themselves were distressing them powerfully. So the Lacedaemonians and the Tegeans were isolated, there being fifty thousand of the Lacedaemonians, counting in the light-armed, and the three thousand men of Tegea, who never separated from the Lacedaemonians. They now offered sacrifice, as they were on the point of engaging Mardonius and that army of his that was there. But their sacrifices did not turn out favorably, and meanwhile many of their men were being killed and many more were wounded. For the Persians made a barrier of their wicker shields and shot their missiles at the Greeks without stint, so that, hard pressed as the Spartans were, and the sacrifices not turning out well, Pausanias, with his eyes fixed on the temple of Hera in Plataea, invoked the goddess, begging her that the Greeks should not be cheated of their hopes.

62. While he was still uttering his prayer, the men of Tegea took the lead in attacking the barbarians, and, right after Pausanias' prayer, the sacrifices proved favorable for the Lacedaemonians. As this had at last turned out right, they too attacked the Persians, and the Persians confronted them, throwing away their bows. First there was a fight around the barricade of wicker shields, and when this was thrown to the ground, the fight grew really fierce around the temple of Demeter, and it lasted a long time, until it came to hand-to-hand struggling. The barbarians seized their spears and broke them off. In spirit and strength, the Persians were the equals of the Greeks, but they had no armor, and they were unskilled besides and no match for their enemies in cunning. They made their charges singly or in tens, in close-packed groups of greater or lesser numbers, hurling themselves on the Spartans; and so they were destroyed.

63. At the place where Mardonius himself was, fighting on horseback (with a white charger) and surrounded by the picked force of the thousand bravest Persians, there the Persians pressed the enemy very hard. For as long as Mardonius survived, they kept on resisting and defending themselves and killed many Lacedaemonians. But when Mardonius fell, and the ranks that were around him—the strongest part of the army—were also destroyed, the others yielded to the pressure of the Spartans and were put to flight. What ruined them mostly was that they wore their clothes without armor, and so the fight they waged was that of light-armed men against fully equipped soldiers.

64. So was retribution rendered upon Mardonius and given to the Spartans for the death of Leonidas, even as the oracle had said;[24] and Pausanias, son of Cleombrotus, son of Anaxandrides, won the fairest of victories of any we have known. (The names of Pausanias' ancestors beyond Anaxandrides I have already given in reference to Leonidas; Leonidas and Pausanias at that point have the same lineage.)[25] Mardonius was killed by Aeimnestus, a notable man of

24. The reference is to the account in 8.114, where the Spartan herald, in accordance with Delphi's instructions, asked for "retribution" from Xerxes for the killing of Leonidas ("fighting in defense of his country") and was referred by the King to Mardonius, "who will give you such retribution as befits you."

25. In 7.204, the solemnity of the moment was marked by Herodotus by citing the full lineage of the Spartan king who defended Greece at Thermopylae.

Sparta, who long after the Persian war, with three hundred men at his side, fought all the Messenians in the battle of Stenyclerus. He died there himself, and his Three Hundred.[26]

65. When at Plataea the Persians were routed by the Lacedaemonians, they fled utterly disordered to their own camp and to the wooden fort they had made in the Theban country. I find it wonderful that though they fought alongside the grove of Demeter, not a single Persian seems to have entered the sanctuary or died in it, and the most of the barbarians fell near the temple in ground unsanctified. If one may judge of such things as belong to the Divine, I think that the goddess did not give a welcome to those who had burned her temple, the shrine at Eleusis.

66. This, then, was as far as that battle went. But Artabazus, the son of Pharnaces, had from the very beginning been dissatisfied with the King's leaving Mardonius behind, and, on the present occasion, he had been able to effect nothing with his constant advice to Mardonius, begging him not to fight. He then took certain measures, which I will show, out of his discontent with the actions of Mardonius. He had under him a considerable body of men—to the extent of some forty thousand; of these he was in complete command, and, as soon as the engagement took place, as he was very certain how it would turn out, he led them in regular order, having given instructions that they should follow exactly where he led, according to what they observed of his sense of urgency. With these orders he led them, presumably to battle. But as he went forward on the road and saw the Persians fleeing, he no longer led them in the same formation but at a quick run fled, and not to the wooden fort nor yet to the stronghold of Thebes but to the territory of the Phocians, because he wanted to make all speed in getting to the Hellespont.

67. That was the direction in which Artabazus and his troops moved. Though the rest of the Greeks who were on the King's side were cowards by intent, the Boeotians fought for a long time against the Athenians. For those of the Thebans who took the King's side had real zeal in the matter and in their fighting did not willfully play

26. This is one more of the references connecting particular people or events in the Persian war with the later wars between Sparta and Athens and with alliances and struggles in the Greece actually contemporary with Herodotus; similarly, the great national fight between Persia and Greece was replaced by the wars of the Greek states against Athens and her empire.

the coward, with the result that three hundred of them, the chief men and the bravest, died by the hands of the Athenians. But when these too were routed, they fled to Thebes, though not by the same route as the Persians and the main body of the rest of the Persian allies, who had fled after no determined fighting at all with anyone and without achieving anything in the way of notable action.

68. It is quite clear to me that everything on the barbarian side depended on the Persians, since these allies fled as they did that day before ever they grappled with the enemy—just because they saw the Persians run. So they all fled except the cavalry, especially the Boeotian cavalry. But the cavalry did indeed help those who fled by staying close to the enemy and so shielding their friends from the pursuing Greeks.

69. The Greeks pursued victorious, following and slaughtering Xerxes' men. In the terror that was on them there came word to the rest of the Greeks, who were standing in their ranks about the temple of Hera and had kept out of the fighting, that there had been a battle and that Pausanias' men had won. As soon as they heard that, they got into motion, in no ordered ranks at all, those with the Corinthians going along the spurs of the mountain and the hills, on the road that made straight for the temple of Demeter, others with the Megarians and the Phliasians through the level land, which was the smoothest road of all. But when the Megarians and Phliasians came near the enemy, the Theban cavalry, spying them coming along in a hurry and disordered (the Theban commander of cavalry was Asopodorus, son of Timander), fell upon them and laid on the ground some six hundred of them, and they pursued the rest and swept them to Cithaeron.

70. So, ingloriously, these perished. But the Persians and the rest of the army, having fled to their wooden stronghold, managed to mount up to the towers of it before the Lacedaemonians came upon them; and mounting up, they strengthened the wall as best they could. When the Lacedaemonians attacked, there was a very stiff fight indeed; for as long as the Athenians were out of it, the Persians defended themselves and had much the best of the Lacedaemonians, because the latter had no skill in sieges. But when the Athenians came up, the fighting grew very strong and lasted a long time. Finally, by their courage and endurance, the Athenians climbed the

wall and tore it down, and through the breach the Greeks poured in. First to enter the fortification were the men of Tegea, and they it was who rifled the tent of Mardonius, taking from it in especial the manger of his horses, which was all of bronze and quite admirable. This horse manger for Mardonius the men of Tegea dedicated in the temple of Athena Alea, but the rest of the plunder that they took they put into the common Greek store. Once the wall was down, the barbarians did not again regroup, nor did any of them think of his valor, but they were crazed with fear, as befits terrified fugitives pent in a small space, and many tens of thousands of them there. So great was the Greek opportunity for butchery that of the three hundred thousand of the barbarians (that is, lacking the forty thousand that Artabazus took with him when he fled) there were hardly three thousand that escaped alive. Of the Lacedaemonians from Sparta there died in the engagement ninety-one in all, and of the men of Tegea sixteen, and of the Athenians fifty-two.

71. Of the forces on the barbarian side, the best of infantry were the Persians and, of cavalry, the Sacae. Of particular men, Mardonius. On the Greek side, though both the Tegeans and Athenians were brave soldiers, the Lacedaemonians excelled all in courage. I have no proof of this other than that the Lacedaemonians attacked the strongest part of the enemy forces—the Persians—and overcame it; I say this is the only proof, because all did conquer those who were opposed to them; but the Persians were the strongest. Far the best of the Lacedaemonians was Aristodemus, in my judgment, who, because he alone of the Three Hundred survived Thermopylae, had been shamed and dishonored.[27] After him the bravest were Posidonius and Philocyon and Amompharetus, the Spartiate. When there was some dispute about who was actually the bravest, those Spartiates who were present gave as their judgment that Aristodemus was but that he had openly wanted to die to redress the dishonor that lay on him, and that the great deeds he did that day were those of a man crazy and leaving his rank, but that Posidonius was not seeking death in his bravery and so he was that much the better man of the two. They may have urged this out of mere jealousy. All those I have mentioned were killed in the fight and were decorated

27. Cf. 7.229–31.

for honor, except Aristodemus. But Aristodemus, because he wanted
to die, for the reason just stated, was not honored.

72. These were the men who at Plataea were the most renowned.
Callicrates might be another but that he died outside the battle it-
self; when he came to the army, he was the most handsome of the
Greeks of that day, not only of the Lacedaemonians but of the
Greeks all together. When Pausanias was making the sacrifices,
Callicrates was sitting in his position in the ranks and an arrow
struck through his ribs. So there were his countrymen fighting, but
he was carried out. He took his death very ill and said to Arim-
nestus, a Plataean, that he did not mind dying, since it was for
Greece; what he minded was that he had done no actual fighting
and had done no deed worthy of himself, for all his longing to do so.

73. They say that, among the Athenians, Sophanes earned
glory. Sophanes was the son of Eutychides and of the deme Decelea,
and the people of Decelea had once done a deed of value for all
time, as the Athenians themselves declare. It was in the old days,
and the Tyndaridae had invaded Attica with a great army to take
back Helen; they were ransacking the demes,[28] for they did not
know where Helen lay hidden. Some say that it was the people of
Decelea, others that it was Decelus himself (because he was vexed at
Theseus' insolence and feared for the entire country of Attica),[29]
who at this point instructed the Tyndaridae in the truth of the
matter and led them to Aphidna, which Titacus, who was natively
of that place, then betrayed to the Tyndaridae. Because of that deed
there was conferred in Sparta, on the people of Decelea, freedom
from all dues and also privileged places at the festivals, and so it has
continued for ever, right until this later war, so many years later
(that between the Athenians and the Peloponnesians), when the

28. Here the word means villages, townships, in general. Technically, in
Attic Greek, demes are the electoral units that constituted the local base for
the subdivisions of the tribes. The Tyndaridae—sons of Tyndareus—were the
Dioscuri, Helen's twin brothers. She had been stolen away from Sparta by Theseus and Perithous.

29. According to How and Wells, the "insolence" of Theseus consisted in
his deposing the local princes and unifying Attica under one ruler.

Lacedaemonians, though they ravaged all of Attica, left Decelea alone.[30]

74. From this township came Sophanes, and he proved himself the best of the Athenians on that day. There are two stories told about him. One was that he carried an iron anchor fastened to the girdle of his cuirass with a bronze chain. Now as often as he drew near to the enemy he would throw his anchor down, that the enemy, as they moved upon him out of their fixed position in their ranks, might not avail to stir him from his place but that, when his enemies fled, he might pick up his anchor again and pursue them. That is that story. But there is another that is told, and at variance with the first, according to which he bore the device of an anchor on his shield, which he ceaselessly whirled round, never leaving it at rest; there is in this story no iron anchor fastened to his cuirass.

75. Sophanes achieved another notable action when at the Athenians' siege of Aegina he challenged Eurybates of Argos and killed him; Eurybates was a winner of the pentathlon. Death overtook Sophanes himself, many years later, when, as a gallant soldier and general of the Athenians, along with Leagrus, son of Glaucon, he was killed by the Edoni at Datus, fighting for the gold mines there.

76. After the barbarians had been slaughtered by the Greeks at Plataea, there came to the Greek side a woman deserter. She had learned that the Persians were destroyed and the Greeks victorious. She was the concubine of Pharandates, son of Teaspis, a Persian; and having decked herself with many gold ornaments (her attendants did likewise) and with the fairest dress she had, descended from her carriage and approached the Lacedaemonians, who were still in the blood of the battlefield. She saw Pausanias directing everything there, and having before this learned his name and his country (as she was hearing them so often), she recognized him, clasped his

30. This *must* refer to the invasion of Attica by the Spartans between the years 431 and 425 B.C. We therefore have absolute proof that Herodotus' life extended so far. Also that he did *not* live until 413, when the Spartan King Agis captured and plundered Decelea—a loss to the Athenians that many think was decisive in the last phase of the Second Peloponnesian War.

knees, and said: "King of Sparta, I am your suppliant. Save me from the slavery of being a prisoner of war. Till now you have been my benefactor in that you have destroyed these people, who regarded not the wrath of god or hero. I am a Coan by race, the daughter of Hegetorides, son of Antagoras. The Persian took me prisoner in Cos and has kept me ever since." At this Pausanias answered, "Lady, be of good cheer, both as my suppliant and also if you are really telling the truth and are a daughter of Hegetorides the Coan; truly, he is my chiefest guest-friend of all that live thereabouts." With that, he entrusted her to the ephors who were in attendance and sent her afterwards to Aegina, where she herself wanted to go.

77. After the arrival of this lady, there came immediately Mantineans, to find everything in the war finished, and, learning that they had arrived late for the engagement, they lamented greatly and declared that it was only fit that they should punish themselves for the offense. But hearing of those Medes who had fled with Artabazus, they were for pursuing them to Thessaly; but the Lacedaemonians were against their pursuit of the fugitives. When the Mantineans came back to their own country, they banished their leaders of the army from the land. After the Mantineans came the Eleans, who lamented in the same fashion as the Mantineans and went off home again. When they departed, they too banished their leaders. That is the Mantinean and Elean part of the events.

78. There was in the Aeginetan army at Plataea one Lampon, son of Pytheas; he was one of the chief men of Aegina. He approached Pausanias with a most infamous proposition, for he came with all eagerness and said, "Son of Cleombrotus, you have achieved a deed of superhuman greatness and fair fame, and God has given you, for your defense of Greece, a store of glory more than any Greek we have ever known. Now, besides this, do you do the rest on top thereof, that still greater renown may be yours and that, for time to come, no barbarian may take it on himself to be the first to commit against Greeks deeds of unholy violence. Leonidas died at Thermopylae, and Mardonius and Xerxes cut off his head and impaled it. Now you give as good again, and you will have praises from all Spartans and from the other Greeks besides; by impaling Mardonius, you will take vengeance for your own uncle, Leonidas."

79. He said this because he thought it would please Pausanias,

but the other answered him thus: "Stranger from Aegina, my acknowledgments for the good will you show me and your forethought for me! But you have missed the mark of good judgment. You set me on high, and my country and my action, and then you would abase me to nothingness by urging me to do despite to a dead man's body, and you say that if I did so I would have even more repute than now! Such actions are more fit for barbarians than Greeks, and even in them we find it a matter of offense. For conduct such as this, God forbid that I should find favor with Aeginetans—or with any who approve such acts! It is enough for me to please the men of Sparta by decent action and decent words. For Leonidas, whom you bid me avenge, I tell you he has been greatly avenged; he has found great honor in these countless souls here—both he himself and the others who died at Thermopylae. Do not approach me with any such proposition again, nor give me such counsel; you should be grateful that you go unscathed for this one."

80. With that answer, Lampon went away. Pausanias made a proclamation that no one should lay a finger on the booty, and he ordered the helots to collect it all together. They scattered throughout the camp and found tents fitted with gold and silver, and couches both gilded and overlaid with silver, and gold mixing bowls and cups and various drinking vessels. They found on wagons sacks in which were discovered gold and silver cauldrons. They stripped from the corpses armlets and twisted ornaments and scimitars made of gold; and of curiously wrought raiment no account at all was taken. On that field the helots stole and sold a great deal to the Aeginetans (the helots also declared a great deal, when it was too much to conceal), so that from this source came the great fortunes among the Aeginetans, who were continually buying from the helots what purported to be bronze but was actually gold.

81. So they brought all the booty together and drew out a tenth, which they assigned to the god at Delphi. It was from this source that the gold tripod was made and dedicated that sits on the bronze three-headed serpent[31] and is nearest the altar; for the god of Olym-

---

31. The bronze serpent column was removed by Constantine and taken to Constantinople, where it can still be seen in the Hippodrome (Atmeidan). The names of thirty-one Greek cities whose men fought at Plataea are inscribed on the serpents' coils.

pia, also, they took out another tenth and from this dedicated the ten-cubit Zeus made of bronze; and another tenth for the god of the Isthmus, from which was made the seven-cubit bronze Poseidon. Having withdrawn these tenths, the rest they divided, and each received his due share of the concubines of the Persians and all their gold and silver and other gear and their pack animals. What portion of the booty was drawn out for those who were supreme in bravery at Plataea and was given to them is not recorded by anyone, but I myself am sure that something was given to them too. But tenfold of everything was drawn out and given to Pausanias—women, horses, talents, camels, and all the other booty.

82. It is said that the following also happened. When Xerxes fled from Greece, he left Mardonius all his gear. Pausanias looked at Mardonius' tent and its furnishings of gold and silver and richly colored curtains, and he ordered the bakers and the cooks to serve up a meal exactly as they had done for Mardonius. They did so, on his orders; and when Pausanias looked at the couches of gold and silver, so richly covered, and the tables of gold and silver and the magnificent preparation of the dinner, he stood amazed at all the good things so set out. Then, for the laughter of it, he told his own servants to prepare a Laconian meal. When this meal was ready (and the difference was great), Pausanias broke out laughing and sent for the Greek generals. When they assembled, Pausanias pointed to the two meals and said, "Men of Greece, the reason I have summoned you together is because I want to show you the stupidity of the leader of the Medes. He had daily meals like this,[32] and came upon us to take from us the miserable fare we have here."[33] That, as the story goes, is what Pausanias said to the Greek generals.

83. Long after all this happened, many of the Plataeans found chests of gold and silver and other things. There were sights to see also when the dead were bared of their flesh, for the Plataeans had gathered their bones into one place. There was found a skull without suture, but all of one bone; there was also a jaw that on its upper part grew the teeth, both front teeth and grinders, as a single bone; there were also the bones of a man seven and a half feet tall.

32. Pointing to the Persian dinner.
33. Pointing to the Spartan dinner.

84. The body of Mardonius vanished the day after the battle of Plataea; who it was that stole it I cannot exactly say, though I have heard of many men of all nations who buried Mardonius, and I know of many who obtained great rewards from Artontes, son of Mardonius, for having so done. But who it was that filched away the body and gave it burial I have been unable to learn with certainty, though there is a rumor that it was a man of Ephesus, Dionysophanes, who did it. Anyhow, in some such fashion he was buried.

85. The Greeks at Plataea, when they had divided up the spoil, buried their own dead, each people separately. The Lacedaemonians made three burial places. In one they buried the irens,[34] and among them Posidonius and Amompharetus and Philocyon and Callicrates. So the irens were in one grave, and in another the rest of the Spartiates, and in a third the helots. That is how the Spartans buried; but the Tegeans buried all their dead in one grave, apart, and the Athenians likewise with their own, and the Megarians and Phliasians did likewise with their dead, who fell before the cavalry. The graves of all these peoples were full of dead; but in the case of the other peoples whose graves are seen at Plataea, these, as I learn, are merely empty barrows they built for the sake of coming generations, because they were ashamed that they had not been in the fight. Indeed, there is there the so-called tomb of the Aeginetans, which was put up even ten years after the battle at the request of the Aeginetans; this was done by Cleades, son of Autodicus, a Plataean, who was the Aeginetans' consul.[35]

86. So the Greeks buried their dead at Plataea, and then, after a debate in council, they resolved to march on Thebes and demand the surrender of those who had promoted the Persian interest, and especially Timagenidas and Attaginus, who were the leaders among the chief men of the country. If the Thebans would not give these men up, the Greeks resolved not to raise the siege before totally destroying the town. With this determination they advanced on Thebes ten days after the battle and besieged and bade the Thebans

34. Young Spartan soldiers between the ages of twenty and thirty.
35. See previous notes on the functions of the *proxenos*, a title that can best be rendered by the modern term "consul" for a native citizen who handles the affairs of a foreign nation.

turn over the men. When the Thebans refused, the Greeks ravaged the country and assailed the walls.

87. As the Greeks persisted in their ravaging, after nineteen days Timagenidas addressed the Thebans: "Men of Thebes, since the Greeks are determined not to raise the siege until they destroy the town or you surrender us, let not the land of Boeotia have more of its fill of punishment for our sake. If it is money that the Greeks want and their demand for our surrender is but a pretext for that, let us give them money from the communal chest—after all, our espousing of the Persian cause was also a communal act, and we were not the only people to be on the Persian side. But if their siege is really because they want *us*, we will surrender ourselves to stand an open trial before them." The Thebans thought this well and timely said, and so they immediately sent a herald to Pausanias, expressing their willingness to surrender the men.

88. On these terms, then, they made an agreement. But Attaginus escaped from the city, and when his sons were seized and brought to Pausanias, Pausanias set them free of any charge; for, he said, the children were in no sense guilty of the association with Persia. As for the rest of the men whom the Thebans surrendered, they thought they would have a hearing in law and of course were confident that they could put aside the charges by using bribery. But Pausanias, as soon as he got them into his hands, had the very same suspicion, and so he discharged the whole allied army and took the men to Corinth, where he had them executed. That is the story of what happened at Plataea and Thebes.

89. Artabazus, son of Pharnaces, who fled from Plataea, was by now far on the road. When he arrived in their country, the Thessalians gave him a banquet and asked him about the rest of the army; they had no knowledge of what had happened at Plataea. Artabazus knew that, if he told the whole truth of the fight, he would probably be cut down, himself and all his army with him; for he thought that every single one of the Thessalians, once they heard what had happened, would set upon him. Taking this into account, he said to the Thessalians (just as, earlier, he had revealed nothing at all to the Phocians), "As you see, men of Thessaly, I am in haste to push with all speed into Thrace; I am very anxious about this, since I am sent on a certain matter by the army, and these with me likewise. Mardonius and *his* army are driving right on my heels, and you may look

so to see him. Entertain him and show your good will, and, if you do so, you will not hereafter repent it." With these words he marched hurriedly through Thessaly and Macedonia straight for Thrace, being genuinely in haste and cutting inland by the very shortest road. He came to Byzantium, leaving many of his men hacked to pieces by the Thracians on the road or overcome by hunger and weariness; from Byzantium he crossed over by boats. That was how *he* came home to Asia.

90. On the same day that the Persians met their disaster at Plataea, there fell upon them a coincident defeat at Mycale in Ionia. For when the Greeks who had come in their ships with Leotychides, the Lacedaemonian, had established themselves at Delos, there came to them messengers from Samos—Lampon, son of Thrasycles, and Athenagoras, son of Archestratides, and Hegesistratus, son of Aristagoras—who had been sent by the Samians, unknown to the Persians and unknown, too, to the prince Theomestor, the son of Androdamas, whom the Persians had set up as absolute ruler of Samos. These messengers came before the generals, and Hegesistratus made a long speech, using all sorts of arguments to the effect that, "If the Ionians only get a glimpse of you, they will desert the Persian side; the barbarians will not stand their ground against you, and, even if they do, you will have such a quarry for your hunting as will never come your way again." He invoked the gods they had in common and urged them to free men of Greece from slavery and repel the barbarian; it would be easy (so he said) for them to bring about all these things, for the enemies' ships were bad sailers and no match in fighting for their own. "If you suspect us of leading you on craftily, we are ready to be carried in your ships as hostages."

91. As the Samian stranger was so strong in his urging, Leotychides asked him (perhaps hoping for an omen or perhaps it was by God's contrivance of a coincidence): [36] "What is your name, stranger

36. The Greek is literally "by coincidence of chance, God doing it." I think this literal meaning should be taken very seriously in the implications of the statement. There is a happening that at first seems the result of pure coincidence; on closer inspection, it is part of God's stage management of the whole piece. For example, in Sophocles' *Oedipus the King,* the messenger from Corinth happens to have been originally a shepherd who knew the other shepherd to whose keeping the infant Oedipus had been entrusted, and so the discovery of the tragedy results.

from Samos?" He answered, "Hegesistratus." Leotychides cut off
whatever else Hegesistratus started to say and said, "I accept the
omen of your name,[37] stranger from Samos. Now, before you sail, do
you and your men give us your pledges that truly the Samians will be
our loyal allies."

92. This is what he said, and he took the appropriate action; for
the Samians gave their pledges and took the oaths of alliance with
the Greeks and, having done so, sailed away; but Leotychides had
Hegesistratus sail with his own men for the omen's sake that lay in
the name.

93. The Greeks remained for that day, but on the next they sacrificed and with favorable results, their prophet being Deïphonus,
son of Euenius, a man of Apollonia—I mean the Apollonia that is
on the Ionic Gulf. This prophet's father, Euenius, had the following
happen to him: there is in *that* Apollonia a certain flock that is sacred to the sun. By day it grazes along the river Chon, which flows
from the mountain Lacmon through the territory of Apollonia to
the sea by the harbor of Oricum; by night certain chosen men, who
are of the highest repute among the citizenry for their wealth and
birth, guard it, each one for one year's space; for the people of Apollonia reverence this flock highly because of a prophecy. The flock
passes the night in a cave far from the city. There, then, this Euenius
of whom I speak, being so chosen, kept guard over it. But one night
he fell asleep on his watch, and some wolves slipped by him into the
cave and killed about sixty of the flock. When he realized what had
happened, he kept quiet about it and told no one, intending to replace them by others he would buy. But the people of Apollonia
came to know of the matter, and, when they knew, they cited him
before a court and found him guilty; and for sleeping on his watch
they condemned him to lose his eyes. So they then blinded Euenius;
but from that day on, their flocks had no young, nor their land any

37. The word *hēgesistratus* means "leader of the army." Greek names tend to
have a direct meaning like this one, though of course such names recur as family
names, and therefore an individual so called may never have been named for the
quality that the word means. For purposes of identification, Herodotus and other
Greek writers nearly always include the patronymic. Sometimes what was originally a patronymic becomes incorporated into the personal name; for example,
"Callicratides" means "Son of him whose strength is in beauty." Names as omens
are very common in Greek literature.

crop, as it had before. Declarations were made to them at both Dodona and Delphi when they asked the prophets the reason for the calamity that oppressed them, and the prophets told them that it was because they had unjustly blinded the guardian of the sacred flock, Euenius. They themselves, said the gods, had set on the wolves, and they would not cease from avenging Euenius until the people of Apollonia gave reparation for what they had done to Euenius—such reparation as he personally chose and found just. After that had been done (said the gods), they themselves would give Euenius such a gift as all mankind would congratulate him on possessing.

94. Those were the oracles that were given, and the people of Apollonia, keeping them a dead secret, entrusted management of the matter to certain of their citizens. These latter then managed as follows: as Euenius sat on his official seat, they approached him and, sitting beside him talked of this and that until they finally spoke of their sympathy for what had happened him. They gradually led the conversation on until they asked him what retribution he would choose if the people of Apollonia were of a mind to promise him requital for what they had done to him. Now, he had not heard of the oracle, and he said that he would settle for the offer of the two finest estates in Apollonia, naming the citizens to whom he knew they belonged, and, in addition, the finest house he knew of in the city. "If I get those," he said, "my anger will be laid to rest for all time to come, and this justice rendered to me will be enough." As soon as he said that, those who sat beside him lost no time in saying, "Euenius, that is the justice that the people of Apollonia will pay you for your blinding—in accordance with the prophecy given." At that he was very angry, feeling, when he heard the whole story, that he had been tricked. But they bought the farms from their possessors and gave them to him—the farms he had selected. And from that day forth he had a natural gift of prophecy and became very famous for it.

95. This is the Euenius whose son Deïphonus was brought by the Corinthians and prophesied for the Greek fleet. However, it is true that I have heard that this Deïphonus was really not a son of Euenius at all but one who, on the strength of his name, practiced prophecy as a trade throughout Greece.

96. When they had sacrificed with favorable results, the Greeks

put to sea from Delos, making for Samos. When they came to that part of the Samian land that is near Calamisa, they anchored there by the temple of Hera that is in those parts and prepared for a sea fight. The Persians, learning of their approach, themselves put to sea in the direction of the mainland with their other ships—all but the Phoenicians', which they sent home. In their council they had decided not to give fight, for they did not think they were a match for the Greeks. They sailed away toward the mainland that they might be under the shelter of their own army, which was at Mycale. This was the force that had been left behind, at Xerxes' orders, to guard Ionia. In number they were sixty thousand; their general, Tigranes, supreme among the Persians for his stature and beauty. It was the plan of these commanders of the fleet to flee to the shelter of the army and to draw up their ships on shore and build around them a stockade, both as a protection for the ships and as a refuge for themselves.

97. That was their plan when they put to sea. Passing the temple of the Holy Ones[38] at Mycale, they came to Gaeson and Scolopoïs, where there is a temple of Eleusinian Demeter, built by Philistus, son of Pasicles, when he went with Nileus, son of Codrus, to the founding of Miletus, and there they drew up their ships on shore and built their stockade of stones and wood, cutting down cultivated trees round about; and they also fixed stakes around the fence. So they prepared for a siege or for victory, making their plans with a deliberate choice for either result.

98. When the Greeks learned that the barbarians were gone toward the mainland, they were vexed that they should have made good their escape and were in some perplexity what to do—whether to go back home or to sail to the Hellespont. Finally, they decided to do neither of these things but to sail on to the mainland themselves. So they made their preparations for a sea fight in the matter of boarding bridges and all the rest needed for the fight. They then set sail for Mycale. When they got near to the camp and no one put to sea against them, but they saw ships drawn up inside the stockade and a great army ranged along the shore, Leotychides first sailed past

38. Demeter and Kore, the Mother and her daughter, the Maiden. The term (in Greek, Potniai) is otherwise used only of the Eumenides.

in his own ship and, keeping as close to the shore as possible, made this proclamation by his herald to the Ionians: "Men of Ionia who are there and may hear me, mark what I say to you. The Persians will certainly not understand the instructions I am giving you. When we join battle, let each one of you remember first of all your freedom and secondly the watchword 'Hera,' and let those of you who do not hear this message learn of it from those who did." The intention of this action was the same as that of Themistocles at Artemisium.[39] Either the words would elude the barbarians and persuade the Ionians, or, if reported to the barbarians, would make them mistrustful of the Greeks on their own side.

99. When Leotychides had made his proposal, afterwards the Greeks brought their ships to land and themselves disembarked on the beach. They formed in ranks; and the Persians, seeing the Greeks making ready for the fight and urging the Ionians, first of all deprived the Samians of their arms—for they suspected that they were really, in their minds, on the Greek side. For the Samians had indeed released certain Athenian prisoners of war who had been brought over in the barbarians' ships. (These were Athenians who had been stranded in Attica and captured by Xerxes' army.) They sent the prisoners on their way to Athens and gave them provisions for the road. This was the chief ground for the suspicion of the Persians against the Samians: "They had released five hundred heads of Xerxes' enemies."[40] The second thing the Persians did was to give orders to the people of Miletus to guard the passes that give on the mountains of Mycale; they said, of course, that this was because the Milesians best knew the country there, but it was really to get them away from the army. These measures of caution the Persians took against those of the Ionians they suspected would revolt if they got

39. Cf. 8.22.
40. "Heads" is a literal translation of the Greek *kephalas*. Its oddity consists in its being an echo of the Homeric line containing the same word in the same significance. I have therefore ventured to enclose the phrase in quotes, as I think the Homeric phrase corresponds with something people felt at the time linked their words, in recollection, with the old poetic formulation. "Souls" will not do, because we have had *psyche*, literally "soul," in exactly that significance in 9.79; and if that is what Herodotus felt was the appropriate literary tag, he would have used it. He used another, and I have therefore given another English version. They are both conscious echoes of Homer.

the chance; for themselves, they set their shields close together to make a barricade.

100. When the Greeks had made their preparations, they advanced against the barbarians. During the advance a rumor ran through the whole camp, and a herald's baton[41] was seen lying at the edge of the waves on the shore. The rumor ran through the men to the effect that the Greeks had beaten Mardonius' army in the fight in Boeotia. There are many indications of the divine ordering of events and in particular this one, that when the Persian disaster at Plataea fell on the same day as what was to prove their disaster at Mycale, this rumor should come to the Greeks here, so that their army was thereby greatly encouraged and more willing to take its risks with a good heart.[42]

101. Here is something else that links the two battles: there was a shrine of Eleusinian Demeter near both battlefields. For the fight at Plataea took place right by the temple of Demeter itself, as I said before, and it was to be the very same at Mycale. The coming of the rumor of the victory at Plataea also is right in time with the other event; for the battle of Plataea took place early in the day, and that at Mycale in the afternoon; that both of them happened on the same day of the same month was noticed not long after, when people came to think of it again. Before the coming of the rumor there was deep fear on the Greek side, not for themselves so much as for the Greeks,[43] lest Mardonius be the rock on which Greece would split. When the rumor winged its way to them, the Greek assault became stronger and quicker. So the two sides, Greeks and barbarians, went eagerly into battle, with the islands and the Hellespont for the stakes of the game.

102. For the Athenians and their neighbors in the battle order—about half of the line—the way ahead lay along the shore and level ground; but for the Lacedaemonians and those next to them it lay

41. This staff was the mark of the herald's right to inviolability in dealing with the enemy—rather like our white flag or the Red Cross on hospital vehicles.

42. This is much in the spirit of chapter 91, above (see footnote 36), where a coincidence turns out on closer examination to be an indication of a general divine plan of events.

43. This is, they feared for the Greeks as a whole, as a nation.

through a ravine and hills. While the Lacedaemonians were making their way round, the men on the other wing were already fighting. So long as the Persians kept straight upright their shield-barricade, they defended themselves and did not have the worst of the fighting; but when the Athenians and their neighbors in the line, wanting the victory to be theirs and not the Lacedaemonians', shouted encouragement to one another and went very heartily to work, then the tide of the battle immediately turned. For they dashed aside the wicker shields and broke in with a massed charge, all together, upon the Persians. The latter stood their charge and, for a long time, fought back, but at last they fled to within the wall. The Athenians, Corinthians, Sicyonians, and Troezenians (these were all alongside of one another in the ranks there) made a joint assault upon the wall. When the Greeks won that, the barbarians no longer had any fighting spirit left but took to flight—all except the Persians themselves, who in small groups fought on against the successive waves of Greeks that poured into the fort. Of the Persian commanders, two fled and two were killed. Artaÿntes and Ithamitres, who were the fleet's admirals, fled, but Mardontes and Tigranes, the general of the army, were killed fighting.

103. While the Persians were still fighting, the Lacedaemonians and those with them came up, and they bore a share in what was left of the fight. There fell there also many of the Greeks and, in especial, the Sicyonians and their general, Perilaus. Those Samians who were in the Persian army and had been disarmed, seeing right at the beginning that the battle might go one way or the other, did all they could in their anxiety to help the Greeks. The other Ionians, seeing the Samians starting the business, in the same spirit themselves deserted the Persians and attacked them.

104. The Milesians had had their orders from the Persians to guard the mountain passes to secure the Persian retreat, so that, if a catastrophe such as actually happened should overtake them, they would have guides to take them safely to the peaks of Mycale. That is why the Milesians were stationed there, and also that they might not stay in the camp and cause an insurrection. But what the Milesians did was entirely the opposite of what had been commanded them, for they led the barbarians to flee along quite other roads, which brought them straight among their enemies, and at last

they themselves became the greatest enemies the barbarians had in their killing of them. So, for the second time, Ionia revolted from the Persians.

105. In this battle, the best on the Greek side were the Athenians and, among the Athenians, Hermolycus, son of Euthoenus, a man who had practiced the pancration.[44] Later than the date of which I am speaking, in the war between the Athenians and the people of Carystus, this man fell at Cyrnus, in the territory of Carystus, and lies buried on Geraestus. After the Athenians, the bravest Greeks were the Corinthians, the Troezenians, and the Sicyonians.

106. When the Greeks had killed the most of the barbarians, some fighting and some fleeing, they burned the ships and all the wall; before this they had brought the spoil down to the seashore and had found several stores of treasure. They then burned the ships and sailed off. When they came to Samos, the Greeks held a debate about dispeopling Ionia and where within the territory of which they were masters they could resettle them, while they abandoned Ionia to the barbarians. For it seemed to them impossible to stand guard in defense of Ionia for all time to come, and, if they did not give such protection, they had no hope that the Persians would allow the Ionians to get off scot free. So those who were in authority in the Peloponnese resolved to remove all the marts[45] from the land of those Greek peoples who had chosen the Persian cause and give that land to the Ionians to settle in. But the Athenians would not stand for any dispeopling of Ionia or that the Peloponnesians should settle matters in council about *their* colonists; and when the Athenians put up this strong opposition, the Peloponnesians yielded. So they brought into the alliance the Samians, the Chians, the Lesbians, and the other islanders who had fought with the Greeks, binding them with pledges and oaths to abide in it and not desert. Having thus sworn them in, they sailed off to break down the bridges,[46] for they thought they would find these still securely fastened. So off they sailed to the Hellespont!

107. Those barbarians—they were not many—who had fled to

44. A mixture of boxing and wrestling.
45. Apparently including their population.
46. Xerxes' bridges over the Hellespont.

the heights of Mycale and had been penned up there got away to Sardis. As they were marching on their way, Masistes, the son of Darius, who had been present at the defeat, spoke eloquently and abusively of the general, Artaÿntes. He said, among other taunts, that such generalship as his was worse than a woman's and that no ill-treatment was too bad for someone who had done such harm to the King's house. (Among the Persians it is the worst of insults to be reputed worse than a woman.) When Artaÿntes had listened to much of this, he was furious and drew his scimitar on Masistes with intent to kill him.[47] But Xenagoras, son of Praxilaus, a Halicarnassian, was standing behind Artaÿntes, and, when he saw him running at Masistes, he seized him from behind and, grasping him by the middle and lifting him up, threw him to the ground. Meanwhile, Masistes' guards stood in front of him, to protect him. Xenagoras, by so doing, won the gratitude of Masistes himself and Xerxes for saving the King's brother, and because of this service Xenagoras was given by grant of the King the rulership of all Cilicia. They then continued on their way and nothing more came of it, and they arrived in Sardis.

108. Now the King had been in Sardis ever since his flight from Athens, after his defeat at sea there. While he was in Sardis, he fell in love with Masistes' wife, who was also in the place. He sent to her many times but failed to win her over, and he tried no violence because he had concern for his brother, Masistes. The woman was in the same case, for she knew that no force would be applied to her. Finally, as Xerxes failed every other way, he arranged a marriage for his own son, Darius, with the daughter of the woman he courted and Masistes. He thought that, if he did this, he would be more likely to get Masistes' wife. When he had betrothed them with the usual procedures, he went off to Susa; and when he came there and took into his own house Darius' bride, he gave up altogether the idea of Masistes' wife but changed round and fell in love with Darius' wife (who was Masistes' daughter) and gained her. The name of the girl was Artaÿnte.

109. As time went on, it all came out, and this is how. Amestris,

47. The point of Artaÿntes' hesitation up to this point is presumably because his reviler is Darius' son and therefore a half-brother of King Xerxes.

the wife of Xerxes, had woven a great, subtly colored cloak, beautiful to look at, and she gave it to Xerxes. He was delighted with it, put it on, and paraded with it in front of Artaÿnte. He was delighted with her, too, and bade her ask him for whatever she wanted, in return for the favors she had granted him. She could have, he said, whatever she asked for. It was destined that she and all her house would come to a bad end, and so she said, in answer to Xerxes, "Will you give me whatever I ask for?" He, thinking that she would ask for anything but what she actually did, promised and swore to do so. When he had sworn, she coolly asked for the cloak. Xerxes was at his wits' end, for he did not want to give it, for no other reason than that he was in dread of Amestris, lest he should be found out clearly doing what she already guessed at. He offered the girl cities and all the gold in the world and an army, which no one should command but herself. (The army is a real Persian gift.) But when he could not persuade her, he gave the cloak. She, charmed with the gift, wore it, exulting.

110. Amestris learned that she had the cloak; but having learned of what was done, she held no grudge against the girl but thought the guilty party was the girl's mother and that she had managed the whole thing; and so she plotted the destruction of Masistes' wife. She waited for the moment when Xerxes, her husband, should be giving the feast that is held once a year on the King's birthday. (The name of this feast is in Persian *tukta*, which means, in Greek, "perfection.") Then and at no other time the King anoints his head, and he distributes gifts among the Persians. Amestris waited for that day and then asked Xerxes to give her Masistes' wife. He thought it a terrible and abominable thing to do to turn over his brother's wife to her and, in addition, someone entirely innocent of the whole matter; for he had a notion of what she wanted her for.

111. Finally, in the face of her importunity and also under the constraint of the law that no one could fail of a request preferred during the King's banquet, he consented, very much against his will. He bade his wife do with the woman what she willed, but he also sent for his brother and said, "Masistes, you are Darius' son and my brother, and, besides, you are a good man. Please live with your present wife no longer; I will give you in her stead a daughter of my own. Live with her, and do not keep as your wife your present one; I

do not wish it so." Masistes was utterly amazed at what he said and answered, "Master, what an improper word is this you speak, in bidding me put aside my wife and marry your daughter! From my present wife I have young sons and daughters, one of whom you have married to a son of your own; besides, the woman is exceedingly to my mind. My lord, of course I esteem very highly being thought worthy to marry a daughter of yours. But I will do neither of these things you bid me. Please do not put pressure on me by insisting on this business. Some other man will appear for your daughter as good as myself, but suffer me to continue to live with my own wife." That was his answer. Xerxes was furious and answered, "Masistes, this is how it has turned out: I will *not* give you my daughter for your wedded wife, nor will you live any longer with the other that you have, so that you may learn how to accept what is offered you." When Masistes heard that, he walked out of the presence, saying, "Master, you have not yet quite destroyed me!"

112. In the meantime, while Xerxes was talking to his brother, Amestris sent for Xerxes' bodyguard and savagely mutilated Masistes' wife. She had her breasts cut off and threw them and her nose, ears, and lips to the dogs and had her tongue cut out and so sent her home mutilated.

113. Masistes had heard not a word of this but foreboded something of evil and came into his house at a run. He saw his ruined wife and at once took counsel with his children and set off for Bactria with his sons and certain other people, where he intended to raise the province in revolt and do the King the greatest mischief he could. In my opinion, this indeed would have happened if he had got to the Bactrians and Sacae first; for they loved him, and he was viceroy of Bactria. But Xerxes had knowledge of his doings and sent an army against him when he was yet on his road and killed him, his sons, and his supporters. Such is the story of Xerxes' love and Masistes' death.

114. The Greeks who had started out from Mycale toward the Hellespont first came to anchor at Lectum, being held up by the winds, and from there they came to Abydos and found the bridges broken down, which they thought they would still find securely fastened, and this was one of the chief reasons why they had come to the Hellespont. So the Peloponnesians who were with Leotychides

resolved to sail away to Greece; but the Athenians and their general, Xanthippus, were for staying where they were and for attacking the Chersonese. So the Peloponnesians sailed off, and the Athenians crossed over from Abydos into the Chersonese and besieged Sestos.

115. To this town of Sestos, as being the strongest place in that neighborhood, there came together people from the towns around and, in especial, one Oeobazus, a Persian from the city of Cardia, where he had stored the gear of the bridges; all this happened as soon as they heard that the Greeks were making for the Hellespont. The Aeolians of that country held Sestos, but with them were Persians and a large number of other allies.

116. The supreme governor of the province was a satrap of Xerxes, Artaÿctes, a Persian, a man clever and abominable, who had cheated the King, as he drove toward Athens, by his theft of the goods of Protesilaus, son of Iphiclus, from Elaeus. For in Elaeus in the Chersonese there is a tomb of Protesilaus[48] and a sanctuary round it, where there was much property—gold and silver drinking bowls and bronze and raiment and other dedicatory offerings—which Artaÿctes plundered—by the gift of the King. Artaÿctes deceived Xerxes by saying this: "Master, there is the house of some Greek fellow here who made war upon your land and met his deserts and was killed. Give me his house that hereafter all men may learn not to make war on land of yours." With that sort of talk he would easily persuade Xerxes to give him the man's house, the King not understanding at all what Artaÿctes' words really meant. Artaÿctes had said "made war on the King's land" designedly, because the Persians consider all of Asia their own and the property of whoever is the reigning King of Persia. When Artaÿctes was given the goods, he had them carried away from Elaeus to Sestos; and he sowed the sanctuary with corn and farmed it, and whenever he himself came to Elaeus he used to lie with women in the holy place. At this time, then, he was besieged by the Athenians, and a siege is what he had not looked for; nor did he expect the Greeks there at all, and, when they attacked, he could not get away.

48. Protesilaus was a Greek hero killed in the Trojan War. Afterwards he enjoyed the status of a local hero or even of some sort of god.

117. When the autumn came upon them still at the siege, the Athenians were vexed, being away from their own land and not able to capture the fortification; so they asked their generals to lead them off home. But the generals refused until they had either captured the fort or the commonalty of Athens recalled them. So the men endured their present lot.

118. But the people inside the fort were at the extremest edge of misery; they even boiled down the leather strings of their beds to eat. When they had not even these any more, the Persians and Artaÿctes and Oeobazus ran away under cover of night, descending at the back of the fortress, where the enemy were least. At daybreak the Chersonesians signaled from their towers to the Athenians what had happened and opened their gates. Most of the Athenians set off in pursuit of the fugitives, but some held the city.

119. Oeobazus fled into Thrace, where the Thracian Apsinthians caught him and sacrificed him, after their own fashion, to a local god, Plistorus. They killed those who were with him in another way. But the rest, with Artaÿctes, had begun their flight later; and when they were overtaken, a little above Aegospotami, they put up a defense for a long time, and some died and some were captured alive. The Greeks put these in chains and brought them to Sestos and, with them, Artaÿctes himself and his son, also in chains.

120. One of the men guarding him had a wonderful thing happen to him, according to the story told by the people of the Chersonese. He was frying sprats, and the sprats, as they lay on the coals, jumped and gasped like fishes newly caught. The men who were crowding around wondered at it, but Artaÿctes, when he saw the marvel, summoned the man who was cooking the fish and said, "Stranger from Athens, do not fear this marvel, for its appearance is not directed at you, but it is to me that Protesilaus of Elaeus signifies that, dead and dry as he is, he yet has power with the god to take vengeance on the one who wronged him. Now I am willing to impose the following penalty on myself: to offer the god one hundred talents for the property I took from his shrine; and I will give two hundred talents to the Athenians for my life and that of my son." But these promises did not move Xanthippus, the general. For the people of Elaeus were begging for the man's destruction as a revenge due to Protesilaus, and the general's own inclinations were that way

anyhow. So they brought him down to the shore where Xerxes had bridged the strait (but others say that it was to the little hill above the city of Madytus), and they nailed him to boards and hanged him up; and his son they stoned to death before his eyes.

121. Having so done, they sailed away to Greece, bringing with them the rest of the stuff and, in especial, the gear of the bridges, intending to dedicate it at their shrines. And in that year nothing further was done.

122. This Artaÿctes who was so hanged up was the grandson of Artembares, who put forward a proposal that the Persians took from him and offered to Cyrus, and it was this: "Since Zeus has given leadership to the Persians and, among men, to you, Cyrus, now that you have destroyed Astyages, let us move from this land of ours—for it is little and rocky, too—and take something better than it. There are many lands next to us and many further off, and if we take one of these we shall be more admired for more things. It is natural for those who hold rule to do so. When shall we have a fairer opportunity than now, when we are rulers of many subjects and of all Asia?" When Cyrus heard that, he was not amazed at their argument but said that they should do as they said; but in that case they should prepare to be no longer those who rule but those who would be ruled. "From soft countries come soft men. It is not possible that from the same land stems a growth of wondrous fruit and men who are good soldiers." So the Persians took this to heart and went away; their judgment had been overcome by that of Cyrus, and they chose to rule, living in a wretched land, rather than to sow the level plains and be slaves to others.

End Notes

NOTE TO 1.14
The weight of the bowls raises a problem that must often be faced in an English Herodotus: how to render his weights, measures, and money in terms the reader of today will understand. Some matters are easy enough to solve. For instance, the authorities tell us that the Attic talent weighed 58 pounds, the Aeginetan talent, 82. We know, too, that the stade is roughly equal to a furlong, and anyone who knows racecourses knows that there are eight furlongs in a mile. So a stade, or furlong, is one-eighth of a mile, or 660 feet. A plethrum (pl. plethra) was slightly over 100 feet. We also know that a "palm" was 4 inches, that the common cubit was 18¼ inches, and that the "royal" cubit was 20½ inches.

At the other end of the scale, it is impossible to convey accurately to a modern reader the value of monetary sums mentioned by Herodotus. We know from Thucydides that the standard soldier's pay was one drachma per day. How would you translate that into contemporary terms? Frequently, moreover, Herodotus is dealing with kings' revenues, and these are in talents, which may, I suppose, be mentally translated into something imprecise and enormous, like $50,000 to a talent.

As for long distances, it is perhaps interesting to note that, according to Herodotus, the average day's walk for a "well girt-up man," i.e., one who is reasonably energetic, was about twenty miles; a horse's journey (see Darius' Imperial Post, 5.52–53) was about the same (carrying a man); and the day's journey for a ship, when it sailed before the wind and did little time by oar-power, was between a hundred and a hundred and twenty miles.

NOTE TO 1.32
Throughout this story Herodotus keeps altering the nouns and adjectives with which he describes the desired object of human life—roughly, what we would call happiness. It is perhaps a feature of his reading style and his delivery that he exploits many of the conversational values of the words he uses and explains them. He is not a philosopher, using his terms to fix a definition, but a conversationalist, employing subtle differences in common usage. For instance, the word he starts with—*olbios*—is what I have rendered "blessed." In Greek it is used of the gods and, generally, of any supreme happiness; it is also used colloquially of the very rich. He next uses *eudaimonia*, the ordinary Greek word for happiness (e.g., "Solon assigned his second prize in *happiness*"), which means the condition in which you have all the means of happiness that are the result of your own exertions

and, in addition, everything that is more than human smiles on you: the daimons are in your favor. Hence the stress on the envy and trouble-making of the divine powers: the daimons may alter their graciousness from one day to the next. But in the last part of Solon's statement Herodotus uses *olbios* ("blessed") with a slightly different submeaning. A man may be rich but be strictly *unblessed;* i.e., the gods positively frown on him. In that case his condition is much worse than that of the man who is moderately rich but "lucky." Here the word is *eutychia*, which is simple "good luck." The lucky man *may* have the signal favor of the gods, or he may, just by accident, be fortunate. (Every fifth-century Greek who has written, including Herodotus, believes that there is a certain amount of pure chance in any event.) If all goes well with him till the end, then he is what Croesus wanted to know about: the blessed man; till he is dead, you should describe him only by the sensibly limited term "lucky."

NOTE TO 2.3
This is one of the sentences hardest to interpret in Herodotus. The first difficulty is: does he mean "equally much" or "equally little"? The Greek is rendered in my translation exactly; the sentence is just as ambiguous in Greek as in English. I think he means "equally much." I think so because of my view of the second difficulty, which is how to interpret this sentence in the context in which it is embedded. Herodotus is asserting the importance of the statements made by the priests at Memphis. He has checked them against the other Egyptian sources, at Thebes and Heliopolis, and what he then gives is a statement on which they all agree. (Apparently he first decided to check these sources against one another in the matter of the "first language" and the experiment with the children. Thus his inquiries seem to have been slanted toward origins in time and matters of dating.) In the course of his conversations with the priests he got a lot of information about "divine stories"—stories in which the divine plays a part. These he is *not* anxious to pass on, except for "their names," i.e., the gods' names. His disowning of any wish to deal directly with the divine is echoed elsewhere in several different contexts. Perhaps the most striking for our purpose, because in tone it is so close to the present passage, is in 2.65; "If I were to say why it is that the animals are dedicated as sacred, my argument would drive me into talking of matters divine [*ta theia prēgmata*], and the declaration of these is what I would particularly shun. To the degree that I have spoken of them, it was with but a touch [*epipsausas*] and under stress of necessity, that I have spoken." In 2.4, the following chapter, Herodotus goes on more happily to what the priests told him about *human* things, and later he states that Min is the first king of Egypt, "that is, human king." It certainly looks as though Herodotus is asserting that the divine lies in the background of many practices and perhaps of all history (if you go far enough back). He does not want to discuss such matters but rather the human parts. It is here that the discussible and *not* equally shared knowledge exists. The divine is equally

shared by all. For example, in 3.38, we learn that certain Greeks and Indians were horrified by each other's burial customs, which involved, respectively, burning their dead and eating them. These burial practices were the province of *nomos* (custom), and they varied. But the basic sense of awe before the dead they all felt. This they would all "know equally." Herodotus, neither in the remote past of history, which trenched on the stories of the gods, nor in the various religious practices of the present, wishes to deal with the divine, unambiguously and universally felt, but on its transmission and interpretation, which vary and which belong to the historian's task. In addition, Herodotus is disinclined to approach the divine directly because, in its various manifestations, you may get into trouble with divine power itself if you probe beneath the surface of differing human accounts. At 2.45 he discusses at length the separate identities of an old god, Heracles, and a quasi-divine figure of the same name, i.e., a hero. The chapter concludes: "That is what I have to say about the matter; as I do so, may both gods and heroes view me kindly!"

NOTE TO 2.47
The enigmatic quality of Herodotus' reticences is definable within certain limits. He does not seem to exhibit any signs of refusing to be explicit about ordinary or extraordinary sexual behavior on the part of human beings toward one another, including cruelty or horror connected with sexual punishment. The castration of a father and his sons in 8.106 is, I think, one of the most awful that can be described so exactly, and the same is true of the deliberate physical and mental torments that Xerxes' wife visits on her sister-in-law in 9.110–12. But Herodotus often refrains from a complete description of men's religious observances, especially when these involve conduct toward animals in the worship of the gods. I do not know why, in 2.46, he says he does not wish to say why Pan is depicted as part goat or what lies behind his squeamishness, in 2.47, about telling why pigs are not used in a particular sacrifice. But it is certainly the interaction of animal and man in ritual scenes that is troubling him.

In chapter 64 of this book Herodotus speaks of those who show no scruples about sexual license inside the precincts of temples and then justify their behavior by saying, "If the gods do not object to the animals' so doing, neither should we; for man is like any other animal." Herodotus disassociates himself entirely from this. In this connection we should note his report, in 9.120, of the terrible punishment visited on Artaÿctes, the Persian satrap who got possession of the shrine of the Greek hero Protesilaus and who, by stealing its rich possessions and having intercourse with women within the shrine (9.116), called down on himself the hero's wrath.

It would seem that Herodotus insists on a difference between men and animals in regard to their conduct in shrines, because man is capable of willfulness, or self-consciousness, in dealing with the gods. Such "wrong acts" are in the nature of something like a Black Mass, as could be said of the sins of

Artaÿctes. And even the first instances, i.e., those involving the *traditional* rites of worship, like some of the mimed sexual scenes of a man-god relationship, though not identical with the conscious offense of Artaÿctes, are still likely to provoke the anger of the god—if reported. Clearly, Herodotus thought that man, either consciously or unconsciously, is capable of insulting or injuring the divine.

That these various matters are mentioned at all is due to Herodotus' sense of duty as narrator. They are all of the type "There is a story, but I do not find it proper to tell it." He evidently thought that the impiety of the act carried a risk to the historian who described it.

NOTE TO 4.42
The very circumstance that Herodotus disbelieved, while faithfully mentioning, the Phoenicians' report that they had had the sun on their right is excellent evidence of what they did. "The sun," say How and Wells, "in the southern hemisphere would actually be 'on the right,' so long as they sailed west, and from the Equator to the Cape of Good Hope the course would be south-west and then west, while on the return journey it would be slightly north-west" (How and Wells, vol. 1, p. 318). Herodotus for some reason makes no mention of the discoveries of the Carthaginians, at the beginning of chapter 43, but moves straight on to the abortive journey round Libya undertaken by Sataspes.

The Zopyrus mentioned in this story is almost certainly a relative of the Zopyrus of book 3, chapters 153–60. It may even be the same man, serving now in the reign of the son instead of the father. The Zopyrus of book 3 had a grandson who deserted to the Athenians, and Herodotus may well have heard the story of the attempted circumnavigation from him.

NOTE TO 6.12
The story of Dionysius' failed attempt to discipline the Ionian fleet at Lade lifts the veil from the extreme amateurishness of Greek warfare, at least on the Athenian side—all the more so, since the navy was certainly the more professional of the two services. For when one turns from fleet to army and looks not only at Herodotus but Thucydides, the amateurishness or, let us say, the dual personality of the citizen soldier/sailor becomes even more apparent. This dual personality explains the many speeches given by generals to their soldiers, even in Thucydides—speeches in which new maneuvers are explained or, in some cases, the general ruefully begs his men not to vote against him when they come home at the end of the campaign. This was undoubtedly a very democratic military body but one hard to persuade to victory when what was needed was sheer brute endurance. On the other side, there is Pericles' Funeral Speech, in which he claims that Athenians need no special training for warfare. He says that, when war comes, they do just about as well as anyone else. Clearly, Herodotus sees it differently.

NOTE TO 7.60

The elaborate account of the clothes and arms worn by the various people seems a probable Herodotean addition to the official record, for I think it unlikely that Xerxes or his commanders-in-chief demanded this; and one must wonder, too, from what source Herodotus derived the information as to the troops' equipment. Lastly, and certainly of Herodotean authorship, are the accounts of each contingent's earlier and later local habitations and their changes of name, almost always in terms of eponymous ancestors bearing *Greek* names. The Greek notion that almost all peoples were named after eponymous ancestors is, in itself, very doubtful.

Tenedos

Ida Mt.
Antandrus
Assus
Adramyttium

Methymna
Antissa
Arisbe
LESBOS
Eresus
Mytilene
Pyrrha
Pitane
Gryneum
Cyme
Myrina
Neontichos
Phocaea
Larisa
Aegiroessa
Smyrna
Erythrae
Clazomenae
Teos
Lebedos
Colophon
Notium
EPHESUS
Magnesia

Atarneus
Cilla
Aegae
Pergamum

L Y D I A
SARDIS
Hermus R.

Meander R.

CHIOS
Chios

I O N I A

Anaea
Priene
MYCALE
MILETUS
Myus
Lade
Branchidae

SAMOS

ICARIA

C A R I A
Mylasa

Leros

Amorgos

Calymna
Cos

Cnidus

Halicarnassus

Syme

Ialysus
Camirus
Rhodus
Rhodus

MAP OF
IONIA AND
WESTERN ASIA MINOR

RHODUS
Lindus

Scale
0   100   200   300   400 Stadia
0   10   20   30   40   50 Miles

Edward Stanford Ltd., London

671

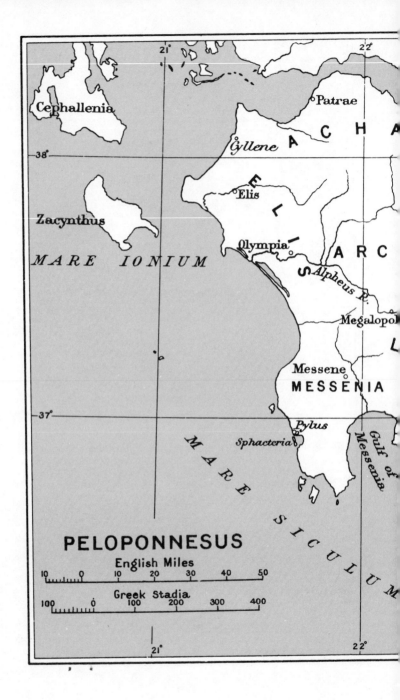

PELOPONNESUS

English Miles

Greek Stadia

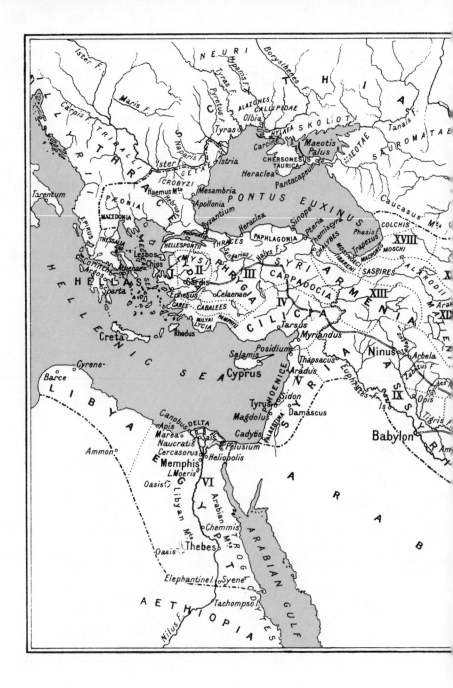

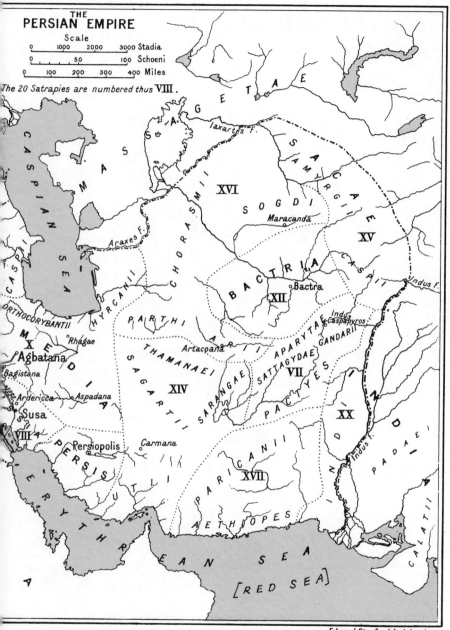

THE
PERSIAN EMPIRE

Scale

0	1000	2000	3000 Stadia
0		50	100 Schoeni
0	100	200	300	400 Miles

The 20 Satrapies are numbered thus **VIII**.

M A S S A G E T A E

Iaxartes F.

CASPIAN SEA

XVI

CHORASMII

S A R A N G A E

SOGDI

Maracanda

S · A · M · A · R · G · I · A · E

XV

Araxes F.

ORTHOCORYBANTII

HYRCANII

PARTHI

BACTRIA

Bactra

XII

ARII

CASPII

Indus F.

Indus

Caspapyros

APARYTAE

GANDARII

MEDIA

Rhagae

Agbatana

Bagistana

Ardericca

Aspadana

Susa

VIII

PERSIS

Persiopolis

THAMANAEI

SAGARTII

XIV

Carmana

SARANGAE

SATTAGYDAE

VII

PACTYES

XX

UTII

PARICANII

XVII

I N D I

Indus F.

PADAEI

AETHIOPES

GALATII

E R Y T H R E A N   S E A

[RED SEA]

A

Edward Stanford Ltd., London.
DS 2100

THE ROUTE OF XERXES

Greek Stadia
100 0 100 200 300 400

English Miles
10 0 10 20 30 40 50

MACEDONIA

Edessa
Cyrtiae R.
Bermius Mt.
Pella
Bottiaeis
Chalestra
Sindus
R. Haliacmon

Ichnae
Echeidorus R.
MYGDONIA
Crestonaei
Axius R.
Crestonaea

Therma
Aenea
Crossaea
Smila
Campsa
Lisae
Combrea
Gigonus
Olynthus
Potidaea
Lipaxus
Sane

Thermaic Gulf

Pieria Mt.
Mt. Olympus
Gonnus
Tempe Pass
Perrhaebi
Peneius R.
THESSALY
MAGNESIA
Mt. Ossa

Pindus Mt.
Papineus R.
Onochonus R.
Apidanus R.
Enipeus R.
Boebeis L.
Pagasae
PHTHIOTIS
Othrys Mt.
Dolopes
Enienes
Anticyra
Anthela
Alpeni
Thermopylae
Mt. Oeta
AETOLIA
R. Achelous

Boebeis
Mt. Pelion
Casthanaea
Sepias
Aphetae
Myrmex Pr.
Artemisium
Histiaeotis
Scyros
Sciathus

Argilus
Bisaltae
Syleos
Stagirus
Acanthus
Sana
Assa
Megybena
Olophyxus
Dion
Piloros
Singus
Stolus
Sithonia
Cleonae
Mt. Athos
Acrothoon
Aphytis
Neapolis
Mendi Pr.
Theramba
Sane
Canastraean Pr.
Sarte
Torone
Ampelus Pr.
THRACE

Nestus R.
Paeonians
ODOMANTI
Odomanti
Doberus
EDONI
Mt. Pangaeus
Pergamus
Pistyrus
Phagres
Eion
SAPAEI
Sapaei
MARE
THR

Delphi
LOCRIS
BOEOTIA
Thespiae
Plataeae
Thebae
Euripus
Chalcis
Eretria
Marathon
EUBOEA

Gulf of Corinth
Patrae
ACHAIA
Sicyon
Isthmus
Elis
ARCADIA
Orchomenus
Corinth
Mycenae
Salamis
Aegina
Athens

24°
23°
24°
40°
39°
39°
30°

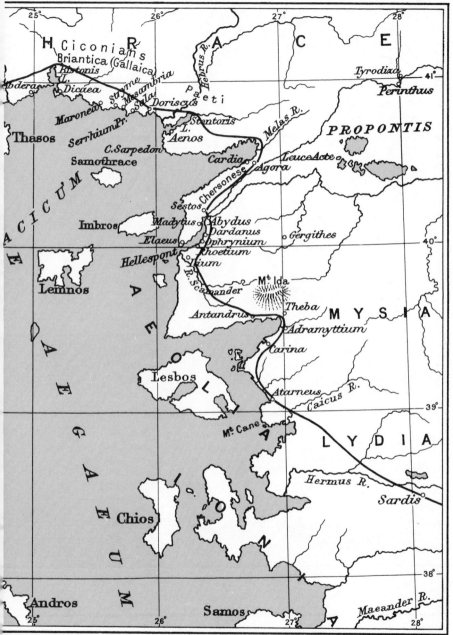

Index